THE BEST 173 LAW SCHOOLS

2016 EDITION

**Eric Owens, Esq., John Owens, Esq.,
Jennifer Adams, Andrea Kornstein,
and The Staff
of The Princeton Review**

Penguin
Random
House

The Princeton Review
24 Prime Parkway, Suite 201
Natick, MA 01760
E-mail: editorialsupport@review.com

Published in the United States by Penguin
Random House LLC, New York, and in Canada
by Random House of Canada, a division of
Penguin Random House Ltd., Toronto.

ISBN: 978-1-101-88195-8
ISSN: 2161-5764

Production: Best Content Solutions, LLC
Production Editor: Melissa Duclos-Yourdon

Printed in the United States of America on partially
recycled paper.

9 8 7 6 5 4 3 2 1

2016 Edition

The Princeton Review is not affiliated with
Princeton University.

Editorial

Rob Franek, Senior VP—Publisher
David Soto, Director of Content Development
Kristen O'Toole, Editorial Director
Steven Koch, Student Survey Manager
Pia Aliperti, Editor

Random House Publishing Team

Tom Russell, Publisher
Alison Stoltzfus, Publishing Manager
Ellen L. Reed, Production Manager
Melinda Ackell, Managing Editor
Kristin Lindner, Production Supervisor
Andrea Lau, Designer

5008

ACKNOWLEDGMENTS

Thanks to Laura Braswell and Kristen O'Toole for their support and guidance on this book and to Bob Spruill for his LSAT expertise.

In addition, many thanks should go to David Soto and Stephen Koch for spearheading the law school data collection efforts. Their survey allowed for the completion of a totally cohesive stat-packed guide.

A special thanks must go to our production team: Scott Harris and Melissa Duclos-Yourdon. Your commitment, flexibility, and attention to detail are always appreciated in both perfect and crunch times.

—Eric Owens

I'd like to send my thanks:

To Eric Owens, my quasi-cousin, who kept me in mind for this project.

To my editors at The Princeton Review, who trusted me (and the other Owens) enough to give me the chance.

To my family and friends, who support me in the things I do.

To the law students who took the time to complete the law student survey.

—John Owens

ABOUT THE AUTHORS

Eric Owens, Esq., attended Cornell College for his undergraduate degree and Loyola University—Chicago for law school. He is now an American diplomat.

John Owens, Esq., earned his undergraduate degree in accountancy at the University of Illinois, Urbana-Champaign. He then matriculated at Loyola University—Chicago School of Law, where he earned his JD. John works in the tax department of a Chicago law firm. He is currently working on a book, which he hopes to finish up this year. In his spare time, John likes to rock.

CONTENTS

PREFACE

Welcome to *The Best 173 Law Schools*, The Princeton Review's truly indispensable guide for anyone thinking about entering the law school fray. This is not simply a reprint of the garden-variety fluff in each law school's admissions booklet. We have attempted to provide a significant amount of essential information from a vast array of sources to give you a complete, accurate, and easily digestible snapshot of the best law schools in the country. Here you'll find a wealth of practical advice on admissions, taking and acing the Law School Admission Test (LSAT), choosing the right school, and doing well once you're there. You'll also find all the information you need on schools' bar exam pass rates, ethnic group and gender breakdown percentages, tuition, average starting salaries of graduates, and much more. For 173 ABA-approved law schools, you'll find descriptive profiles of the student experience based on the opinions of the only true law school experts: current law school students. Indeed, with this handy reference, you should be able to narrow your choices from the few hundred law schools in North America to a handful in no time at all.

Never trust any single source of information too much, though—not even us. Take advantage of all the resources available to you, including friends, family members, the Internet, and your local library. Obviously, the more you explore all the options available to you, the better decision you'll be able to make. We hope you will be happy wherever you end up and that this guide will be helpful in your search for the best law school for you.

Best of luck!

ALL ABOUT LAW SCHOOL

CHAPTER 1
SO YOU WANT TO GO TO LAW SCHOOL

Congrats! Law school is a tremendous intellectual challenge and an amazing experience. It can be confusing and occasionally traumatic—especially during the crucial first year—but the cryptic ritual of legal education will make you a significantly better thinker, a consummate reader, and a far more mature person over the course of three years.

The application process is rigorous, but it's not impossible. Here's our advice.

WHAT MAKES A COMPETITIVE APPLICANT?

It depends. One of the great things about law schools in the United States is that there are a lot of them, and standards for admission run the gamut from appallingly difficult to not very hard at all.

Let's just say, for example, you have your heart set on Yale Law School, arguably the finest law school in all the land. Let's also say you have stellar academic credentials: a 3.45 GPA and an LSAT score in the 99th percentile. With these heady numbers, you've got a whopping 2 percent chance of getting into Yale, at best. However, with the same 3.45 GPA and LSAT score in the 99th percentile, you are pretty much a lock at legal powerhouses like Duke University School of Law and Boston College Law School. With significantly lower numbers—say, a 3.02 GPA and an LSAT score in the 81st percentile—you stand a mediocre chance of getting into top-flight law schools like Case Western or Indiana. With a little bit of luck, these numbers might land you a spot at George Washington or UCLA.

> ### Essential Acronyms
>
> **LSAC:** Law School Admission Council, headquartered in beautiful Newtown, PA
> **LSAT:** Law School Admission Test
> **CAS:** Credential Assembly Service
> **ABA:** American Bar Association

This is good news. The even better news is that there are several totally respectable law schools out there that will let you in with a 2.5 GPA and an LSAT of 148 (which is about the 37th percentile). If you end up in the top 10 percent of your class at one of these schools and have even a shred of interviewing skill, you'll get a job that is just as prestigious and pays just as much money as the jobs garnered by Yale grads. Notice the important catch here, however: You *must* graduate in the top 10 percent of your class at so-called "lesser" schools, while almost every Yale Law grad who wants a high-paying job can land one.

Ultimately, there's a law school out there for you. If you want to get into a "top-flight" or "pretty good" school, you're in for some fairly stiff competition. Unfortunately, it doesn't help that the law school admissions process is somewhat formulaic; your LSAT score and your GPA are vastly more important to the process than anything else about you. If your application ends up in the "maybe" pile, your recommendations, your major, the reputation of your college alma mater, a well-written and nongeneric essay, and various other factors will play a larger role in determining your fate.

THE ADMISSIONS INDEX

The first thing most law schools will look at when evaluating your application is your "index." It's a number (which varies from school to school) made up of a weighted combination of your undergraduate GPA and LSAT score. In virtually every case, the LSAT is weighted more heavily than the GPA.

While the process differs from school to school, it is generally the case that your index will put you into one of three piles.

(Probably) Accepted. A select few applicants with high LSAT scores and stellar GPAs are admitted pretty much automatically. If your index is very, very strong compared with the school's median or target number, you're as good as in, unless you are a convicted felon or you wrote your personal statement in crayon.

(Probably) Rejected. If your index is very weak compared with the school's median or target number, you are probably going to be rejected without much ado. When Admissions Officers read weaker applications (yes, at almost every school every application is read) they will be looking for something so outstanding or unique that it makes them willing to take a chance. Factors that can help include ethnic background, where you are from, or very impressive work or life experience. That said, don't hold your breath because not many people in this category are going to make the cut.

Well... Maybe. The majority of applicants fall in the middle; their index number is right around the median or target index number. People in this category have decent enough LSAT scores and GPAs for the school, but not high enough for automatic admission. Why do most people fall into this category? For the most part, people apply to schools they think they have at least a shot of getting into based on their grades and LSAT scores; Yale doesn't see very many applicants who got a 140 on the LSAT. What will determine the fate of those whose applications hang in the balance? One thing law schools often look at is the competitiveness of your undergraduate program. On the one hand, someone with a 3.3 GPA in an easy major from a school where everybody graduates with a 3.3 or higher will face an uphill battle. On the other hand, someone with the same GPA in a difficult major from a school that has a reputation for being stingy with A's is in better shape. Admissions Officers will also pore over the rest of your application—personal statement, letters of recommendation, résumé, etc.—for reasons to admit you, reject you, or put you on their waiting lists.

ARE YOU MORE THAN YOUR LSAT SCORE?

Aside from LSAT scores and GPAs, what do law schools consider when deciding who's in and who's out? It's the eternal question. On the one hand, we should relieve you hidebound cynics of the notion that they care about nothing else. On the other hand, if you harbor fantasies that a stunning application can overcome truly substandard scores and grades, you should realize that such hopes are unrealistic.

Nonquantitative factors are particularly important at law schools that receive applications from thousands of numerically qualified applicants. A "top ten law school" that receives ten or fifteen applications for every spot in its first-year class has no choice but to "look beyond the numbers," as admissions folks are fond of saying. Such a school will almost surely have to turn away hundreds of applicants with near-perfect LSAT scores and college grades, and those applicants who get past the initial cut will be subjected to real scrutiny.

Less competitive schools are just as concerned, in their own way, with "human criteria" as are the Harvards and Stanfords of the world. They are on the lookout for capable people who have relatively unimpressive GPAs and LSAT scores. The importance of the application is greatly magnified for these students, who must demonstrate their probable success in law school in other ways.

CAN PHYSICS MAJORS GO TO LAW SCHOOL?

"What about my major?" is one of the more popular questions we hear when it comes to law school admissions. The conventional answer to this question goes something like, "There is no prescribed, pre-law curriculum, but you should seek a broad and challenging liberal arts education, etc."

Translation: It really doesn't matter what you major in. Obviously, a major in aviation or hotel and restaurant management is not exactly ideal, but please—we beg you!—don't feel restricted to a few majors simply because you want to attend law school. This is especially true if those particular majors do not interest you. Comparative literature? Fine. American studies? Go to town. Physics? No problem whatsoever. You get the idea.

Think about it. Because most would-be law students end up majoring in the *same* few fields (e.g., political science and philosophy), their applications all look the *same* to the folks in law school Admissions Offices. You want to stand out, which is why it is a good idea to major in something *different*. Ultimately, you should major in whatever appeals to you. Of course, if you want to major in political science or philosophy (or you already have), well, that's fine too.

DOES GRAD SCHOOL COUNT?

Your grades in graduate school will not be included in the calculation of your GPA (only the UGPA, the undergraduate grade point average, is reported to the schools) but will be taken into account separately by an Admissions Committee if you make them available. Reporting grad school grades would be to your advantage, particularly if they are better than your college grades. Admissions Committees are likely to take this as a sign of maturation.

ADVICE FOR THE "NONTRADITIONAL" APPLICANT

The term "nontraditional" is, of course, used to describe applicants who are a few years or many years older than run-of-the-mill law school applicants.

In a nutshell, there's no time like the present to start law school. While it's true that most law students are in their early to mid-twenties, if you aren't, don't think for a minute that your age will keep you from getting in and having a great experience. Applicants for full-time and part-time slots at U.S. law schools range in ages from twenty-one to seventy-one and include every age in between. Some of these older applicants always intended to go to law school and simply postponed it to work, travel, or start a family. Other older applicants never seriously considered law school until after they were immersed in other occupations.

Part-time attendance is especially worth checking into if you've been out of college for a few years. Also, dozens of law schools offer evening programs—particularly in urban centers.

YOUR CHANCE OF ACCEPTANCE

Who knows how law schools end up with their reputations? Everything else being equal, you really do want to go a to a well-respected school. It will enhance your employment opportunities tremendously. Remember, whoever you are and whatever your background, your best bet is to select a couple of "reach" schools, a couple of schools at which you've got a good shot at being accepted, and a couple of "safety" schools where you are virtually assured acceptance. Remember also that being realistic about your chances will save you from unnecessary emotional letdowns. Getting in mostly boils down to numbers. Look at the acceptance rates and the average LSATs and GPAs of incoming classes at various schools to assess how you stack up.

Waiting Lists

If a law school puts you on its waiting list, it means you may be admitted depending on how many of the applicants they've already admitted decide to go to another school. Most schools rank students on their waiting list; they'll probably tell you where you stand if you give them a call. Also, note that schools routinely admit students from their waiting lists in late August. If you are on a school's waiting list and you really, really want to go there, keep your options at least partially open. You just might be admitted in the middle of first-year orientation.

Engineering and Math Majors Make Great Law Students

A disproportionate number of law students with backgrounds in the so-called "hard sciences" (math, physics, engineering, etc.) earn very high grades in law school, probably because they are trained to think methodically and efficiently about isolated problems (as law students are supposed to do on exams).

CHAPTER 2
CHOOSING A LAW SCHOOL

There are some key things you should consider before randomly selecting schools from around the country or just submitting your application to somebody else's list of the Top 10 law schools.

LOCATION

It's a big deal. If you were born and raised in the state of New Mexico, care deeply about the "Land of Enchantment," wish to practice law there, and want to be the governor someday, then your best bet is to go to the University of New Mexico. A school's reputation is usually greater on its home turf than anywhere else (except for some of the larger-than-life schools, like Harvard and Yale). Also, most law schools tend to teach law that is specific to the statutes of the states in which they are located. Knowledge of the eccentricities of state law will help you immensely three years down the road when it comes time to pass the bar exam. Even further, the Career Services Office at your school will be strongly connected to the local legal industry. As a purely practical matter, it will be much easier to find a job and get to interviews in Boston, for example, if you live there. Still another reason to consider geographical location is the simple fact that you'll put down professional and social roots and get to know many really great people throughout your law school career. Leaving them won't be any fun. Finally, starting with geographic limitations is the easiest way to reduce your number of potential schools dramatically.

SPECIALIZATION

Word has it that specialization is the trend of the future. General practitioners in law are becoming less common, so it makes sense to let future lawyers begin to specialize in school. At certain schools, you may receive your JD with an official emphasis in, say, taxation. Specialization is a particularly big deal at smaller or newer schools whose graduates cannot simply get by on their school's reputation. Just between us, it's kind of hard to specialize in anything at most law schools because every graduate has to take this huge exam—the bar—that tests about a dozen topics. Most of your course selections will (and should) be geared toward passing the bar, which leaves precious few hours for specialization. You'll almost certainly specialize, but it's not something to worry about until you actually look for a job. All of that said, if you already know what kind of law you want to specialize in, you're in good shape. Many schools offer certain specialties because of their locations. If you are very interested in environmental law, you'd be better off going to Vermont Law School or Lewis and Clark's Northwestern School of Law than to Brooklyn Law School. Similarly, if you want to work with children as an attorney, check out Loyola University Chicago's Child Law Center. So look at what you want to do in addition to where you want to do it.

> **Dean's List**
>
> According to a letter signed by just about every dean of every ABA-approved law school in the country, you should consider the following factors when choosing a law school:
>
> - Breadth and support of alumni network
> - Breadth of curriculum
> - Clinical programs
> - Collaborative research opportunities with faculty
> - Commitment to innovative technology
> - Cost
> - Externship options
> - Faculty accessibility
> - Intensity of writing instruction
> - Interdisciplinary programs
> - International programming
> - Law library strengths and services
> - Loan repayment assistance for low-income lawyers
> - Location
> - Part-time enrollment options
> - Public interest programs
> - Quality of teaching
> - Racial and gender diversity within the faculty and student body
> - Religious affiliation
> - Size of first-year classes
> - Skills instruction
> - Specialized areas of faculty expertise

JOINT-DEGREE PROGRAMS

In addition to offering specialized areas of study, many law schools have instituted formal dual-degree programs. These schools, nearly all of which are directly affiliated with a parent institution, offer students the opportunity to pursue a JD while also working toward some other degree. Although the JD/MBA combination is the most popular joint-degree sought, many universities offer a JD program combined with degrees in everything from public policy to public administration to social work. In today's perpetually competitive legal market, dual degrees may make some students more marketable for certain positions. However, don't sign up for a dual-degree program on a whim—they require a serious amount of work and often a serious amount of tuition.

YOUR CHANCE OF ACCEPTANCE

Who knows how law schools end up with their reputations? Everything else being equal, you really do want to go a to a well-respected school. It will enhance your employment opportunities tremendously. Remember, whoever you are and whatever your background, your best bet is to select a couple of "reach" schools, a couple of schools at which you've got a good shot at being accepted, and a couple of "safety" schools where you are virtually assured acceptance. Remember also that being realistic about your chances will save you from unnecessary emotional letdowns. Getting in mostly boils down to numbers. Look at the acceptance rates and the average LSATs and GPAs of incoming classes at various schools to assess how you stack up.

The Dreaded Bar Exam

Once you graduate, most states require you to take a bar exam before you can practice law. Some state bar exams are really, really hard, like New York's and California's. If you don't want to take a bar exam, consider a law school in beautiful Wisconsin. Anyone who graduates from a state-certified Wisconsin law school does not need to take the state bar exam to practice law in the Badger State, as long as they are approved by the Board of Bar Examiners.

PERSONAL APPEAL

A student at a prominent law school in the Pacific Northwest once described his law school to us as "a combination wood-grain bomb shelter and Ewok village." Another student at a Northeastern law school told us her law school was fine except for its "ski-slope classrooms" and "East German Functionalist" architecture. While the curricula at various law schools are pretty much the same, the weather, the surrounding neighborhoods, the nightlife, and the character of the student populations are startlingly different. An important part of any graduate program is enjoying those moments in life when you're not studying. If you aren't comfortable in the environment you choose, it's likely to be reflected in the quality of work you do and your attitude. Before you make a $10,000 to $130,000 investment in any law school, you really ought to check it out in person. While you are there, talk to students and faculty. Walk around. Kick the tires. *Then* make a decision.

EMPLOYMENT PROSPECTS

Where do alumni work? How much money do they make? What percentage of graduates is employed within nine months of graduation? How many major law firms interview on campus? These are massively important questions, and you owe it to yourself to look into the answers before choosing a school.

YOUR VALUES

It is important that you be honest about defining your criteria for judging law schools. What do you want out of a law school? Clout? A high salary? A hopping social life? To live in a certain city? To avoid being in debt up to your eyeballs? A non-competitive atmosphere? Think about it.

MAKE A LIST

Using these criteria (and others you find relevant), develop a list of prospective schools. Ideally, you'll find this book useful in creating the list. Assign a level to each new school you add (something like *reach*, *good shot*, and *safety*).

At your *reach* schools, the average LSAT scores and GPAs of incoming students should be higher than yours. These are law schools that will probably not accept you based on your numbers alone. In order to get in, you'll need to wow them with everything else (e.g., personal statement, stellar recommendations, work experience).

Did You Know?

According to the people who take the LSAT, the average applicant applies to four or more law schools.

Your *good shot* schools should be the schools you like that accept students with about the same LSAT scores and GPA as yours. Combined with a strong and *cohesive* application, you've got a decent shot at getting into these schools.

At your *safety* schools, the average LSAT scores and GPAs of current students should be below yours. These schools should accept you pretty painlessly if there are no major blemishes on your application (e.g., a serious run-in with the law).

CHAPTER 3

APPLYING TO LAW SCHOOL

Our advice: Start early. The LSAT alone can easily consume eighty or more hours of prep time, and completing a single application form might take as many as thirty hours if you take great care with the essay questions. Don't sabotage your efforts through last-minute sloppiness or by allowing this already-annoying process to become a gigantic burden.

WHEN TO APPLY

Yale Law School's most recent final due date was February 28, but Loyola University Chicago's School of Law was accepting your application materials up to April 1. There is no regular pattern. However, the longer you wait to apply to a school, regardless of its deadline, the worse your chances of getting into that school may be. No efficient admissions staff is going to wait to receive all the applications before starting to make their selections.

If you're reading this in December and hope to get into a law school for next fall but haven't done anything about it, you're in big trouble. If you've got an LSAT score you are happy with, you're in less trouble. However, your applications will get to the law schools after the optimum time and, let's face it, they may appear a little rushed. The best time to think about applying is early in the year. Methodically take care of one thing at a time, and *finish by December*.

Early Admissions Options. A few schools have Early Admissions options (for instance, New York University's Early Decision deadline is November 15), so you may know by late December if you've been accepted. Early Admission is a good idea for a few reasons. It can give you an indication of what your chances are at other schools. It can relieve the stress of waiting until April to see where you'll be spending the next three years of your life. Also, it's better to get wait listed in December than in April (or whenever you would be notified for regular admission); if there is a "tie" among applicants on the waiting list, they'll probably admit whoever applied first. Of course, not every school's Early Admission option is the same (and many schools don't even have one), so do your research. Keep in mind that some Early Admission offers (such as NYU's) are binding. If the decision is binding, you should only apply early if you are certain you want to attend a particular school.

Rolling Admissions. Many law schools evaluate applications and notify applicants of admission decisions continuously over the course of several months (ordinarily from late fall to midsummer). Obviously, if you apply to one of these schools, it is vital that you apply as early as possible because there will be more spots available at the beginning of the process.

Applying Online. Almost all law schools allow applicants to submit applications online. The LSAC online service (LSAC.org) has a searchable database and applications to ABA-approved schools.

LAW SCHOOL ADMISSION COUNCIL: THE LAW SCHOOL APPLICATION SOURCE

In addition to single-handedly creating and administering the LSAT, an organization called the Law School Admissions Council (LSAC) maintains the communication between you and virtually every law school in the United States. It runs the Credential Assembly Service (CAS), which provides information (in a standard format) on applicants to the law schools. They—not you—send your grades, your LSAT score, and plenty of other information about you to the schools. You'll send only your actual applications directly to the law schools themselves. Oh, by the way, the fee for this service is $170 of your hard-earned money plus $30 every time you want CAS to send a report about you to an additional law school.

THE BIG HURDLES IN THE APPLICATION PROCESS: A BRIEF OVERVIEW

Take the LSAT. The Law School Admission Test is a roughly three-and-a-half-hour multiple-choice test used by law schools to help them select candidates. The LSAT is given in February, June, October (or, occasionally, late September), and December of each year. It's divided into five multiple-choice sections and one writing sample. All ABA-approved and most non-ABA-approved law schools in the United States and Canada require an LSAT score from each and every applicant.

Register for CAS. You can register for the Credential Assembly Service at the same time you register to take the LSAT. Both can be done online at lsac.org.

Get applications from six or seven schools. Why so many? Because it's better to be safe than sorry. As early as July, select a couple of *reach* schools, a couple of schools to which you've got a good shot at being accepted, and a couple of *safety* schools to which you are virtually assured of acceptance. Your safety school—if you were being realistic—will probably accept you pretty quickly. It may take a while to get a final decision from the other schools, but you won't be totally panicked because you'll know your safety school is there for you. If, for whatever reason, your grades or LSAT score is extremely low, you should apply to several safety schools. Most schools won't post online applications until mid-September at the earliest. Still, it is a good idea to familiarize yourself with the previous year's applications as soon as possible, as law schools tend not to radically alter components of their applications from one year to the next.

Write your personal statement. With any luck, you'll only have to write one personal statement. Many, many schools will simply ask you the same basic question: "Why do you want to obtain a law degree?" However, just in case you need to write several personal statements and essays, you need to select your schools fairly early.

Obtain two or three recommendations. Some schools will ask for two recommendations, both of which must be academic. Others want more than two recommendations and want at least one to be from someone who knows you outside traditional academic circles. As part of your CAS file, the LSAC will accept up to three letters of recommendation on your behalf, and they will send them to all the schools to which you apply. This is one of the few redeeming qualities of the LSAC. The last thing the writers of your recommendations are going to want to do is sign, package, and send copies of their letters all over the continent.

Update/create your résumé. Most law school applicants ask that you submit a résumé. Make sure yours is up to date and suitable for submission to an academic institution. Put your academic credentials and experience first—no matter what they are. This is just a supplement to the rest of the material; it's probably the simplest part of the application process.

Get your academic transcripts sent to CAS. When you subscribe to CAS, you must request that the Registrar at every undergraduate, graduate, and professional school you ever attended send an official transcript to Law Services. Don't even think about sending your own transcripts anywhere; these people don't trust you any farther than they can throw you. *Make these requests in August.* If you're applying Early Decision, start requesting transcripts as early as May. Law schools require complete files before making their decisions, and CAS won't send your information to the law schools without your transcripts. Undergraduate institutions can and will screw up and delay the transcript process—even when you go there personally and pay them to provide your records. Give yourself some time to fix problems should they arise.

Write any necessary addenda. An addendum is a brief explanatory letter written to explain or support a "deficient" portion of your application. If your personal and academic life has been fairly smooth, you won't need to include any addenda with your application. If, however, you were ever on academic probation, arrested, or if you have a low GPA, you may need to write one. Other legitimate addenda topics are a low/discrepant LSAT score, DUI/DWI suspensions, or any time gap in your academic or professional career.

An addendum is absolutely not the place to go off on a rant about the fundamental unfairness of the LSAT or how that evil campus security officer was only out to get you when you got arrested. If, for example, you have taken the LSAT two or three times and simply did not do very well, even after spending time and money preparing with a test prep company or a private tutor, simply tell the Admissions Committee that you worked diligently to achieve a high score. Say you explored all possibilities to help you achieve that goal. Whatever the case, lay out the facts, but let them draw their own conclusions. Be brief and balanced. Be fair. Do not go into unneccessary detail. Explain the problem and state what you did about it. This is no time to whine.

Send in your seat deposit. Once you are accepted at a particular school, that school will ask you to put at least some money down to hold your place in that year's class. A typical fee runs $200 or more. This amount will be credited to your first-term tuition once you actually register for classes.

Do anything else. You may find that there are other steps you must take during the law school application process. You may request a fee waiver, for example. Also make sure you thoroughly peruse the LSAC website. It has the forms you'll need, a sample LSAT, admissions information, the current Law Forum schedule, and sample application schedules.

LAW SCHOOL APPLICATION CHECKLIST (suitable for framing)	
January	• **Take a practice LSAT.** Do it at a library or wherever you won't be interrupted. Also, take it all at once.
February	• **Investigate LSAT prep courses.** If you don't take one with The Princeton Review, do *something* to devise a preparatory schedule. Just as with any test, you'll get a higher score on this one if you prepare for it first.
March	• Create an account with the Law School Admission Council at lsac.org.
April	• **Register for the June LSAT.** • **Begin an LSAT prep course.** At the very, very least, use some books or software.
May	• **Continue your LSAT prep.**
June	• **Take the LSAT.** If you take the test twice, many schools will average them. Your best bet is to take it once, do exceedingly well, and get it out of your hair forever.
July	• **Register for CAS.** • **Research law schools.**
August	• **Obtain law school applications.** You can call or write, but the easiest and cheapest way to get applicationa is via the Internet. This is, of course, only necessary if you plan to send in paper applications. Go to lsac.org to access and submit online applications. • **Get your undergraduate transcripts sent to CAS.** Make sure to contact the registrar at each undergraduate institution you attended.
September	• **Write your personal statements.** Proofread them. Edit them. Edit them again. Have someone else look them over for all the mistakes you missed. • **Update your résumé,** or create a résumé if you don't already have one. • **Get your recommendations in order.** You want your professors to submit recommendations exactly when you send your applications (in October and November).
October	• **Complete and send early decision applications.**
November	• **Complete and send all regular applications.**
December	• **Chill.** • **Buy holiday gifts.** • **Make plans for New Year's.**

CHAPTER 4
THE LSAT

As you may know, we at The Princeton Review are pretty skeptical of most of the standardized tests out there. They make us a lot of money, of course, and we like that, but they are hideously poor indicators of anything besides how well you do on that particular standardized test. They are certainly not intelligence tests. The LSAT is no exception. It is designed to keep you out of law school, not facilitate your entrance into it. For no good reason we can think of, this 125-question test is *the single most important factor in all of law school admissions*, and, at least for the foreseeable future, we're all stuck with it.

Unfortunately, with the possible exception of the MCAT (for medical school), the LSAT is the toughest of all the standardized tests. Only 24 to 26 of the 125 questions have a "correct" answer (Logic Games), as opposed to Arguments and Reading Comprehension, for which you must choose the elusive "best" answer. As ridiculous as they are, the GMAT, GRE, SAT, MCAT, and ACT at least have large chunks of math or science on them. There are verifiably correct answers on these tests, and occasionally you even have to know something to get the right answers. *Only the LSAT requires almost no specific knowledge of anything whatsoever, which is precisely what makes it so difficult.* The only infallible way to study for the LSAT is to study the LSAT itself. The good news is that *anybody* can get significantly better at the LSAT by working diligently at it. In fact, your score will increase exponentially directly in proportion to the amount of time and work you put into preparing for it.

HOW IMPORTANT IS THE LSAT?

The LSAT figures very prominently in your law school application, especially if you've been out of school for a few years. Some law schools won't even look at your application unless you achieve a certain score on your LSAT. Most top law schools average multiple LSAT scores, so you should aim to take it only once. By the way, each score you receive is valid for five years after you take the test.

LSAT STRUCTURE

Section Type	Sections	Questions Per Section	Time Per Section
Logical Reasoning (Arguments)	2	2 sections, about 25 questions each	35 minute sections
Analytical Reasoning (Games)	1	25	35 minutes
Reading Comprehension	1	27	35 minutes
Experimental	1	22–28	35 minutes
Writing Sample	1	1	35 minutes

Each test has approximately 99 to 102 questions. Neither the Experimental section nor the Writing Sample counts toward your score. The multiple-choice sections may be given in any order, but the Writing Sample is always administered last. The Experimental section can be any of the three types of multiple-choice sections and is used by the test writers to test out new questions on your time and at your expense.

The Writing Sample is not scored, and unlikely to be read by anyone other than you. However, the law schools to which you apply will receive a copy of your writing sample, so you should definitely do it. A blank page would stand out like a sore thumb, and you wouldn't want the Admissions Office to think you were some kind of revolutionary.

WHAT'S ON THE LSAT, EXACTLY?

We asked the experts in the LSAT Course Division of The Princeton Review for the lowdown on the various sections of the LSAT. Here's what they had to say.

Registering for the LSAT

You can register for the LSAT by mail, over the phone, or online. To register by mail, you will need a copy of the Registration and Information Bulletin, which you may request from Law Services or pick up from your pre-law advisor. You may also register for the LSAT online at Lsac.org. The LSAT fee is currently a whopping $175; if you're late, it's an extra $90. To avoid late fees, mail your registration form at least six weeks—six weeks—before the test. Also, by registering early, you are more likely to be assigned your first choice of test center.

You can reach the Law School Admissions Council at

Phone: 215-968-1001

www.lsac.org

lsacinfo@lsac.org

Analytical Reasoning: If you've ever worked logic problems in puzzle books, then you're already somewhat familiar with the Analytical Reasoning section of the LSAT. The situations behind these problems—often called "games" or "logic games"—are common ones: deciding in what order to interview candidates, or assigning employees to teams, or arranging dinner guests around a table. The arrangement of "players" in these games is governed by a set of rules you must follow in answering the questions. Each Analytical Reasoning section is made up of four games, with five to seven questions each. Questions may ask you to find out what *must* be true under the rules or what *could* be true under the rules; they may add a new condition that applies to just that question; or they may ask you to count the number of possible arrangements under the stated conditions. These questions are difficult mostly because of the time constraints under which they must be worked; very few test-takers find themselves able to complete twenty-four questions on this section in the time allotted.

Logical Reasoning: Because there are two scored sections of them, Logical Reasoning questions on the LSAT are the most important to your score. Each Logical Reasoning—sometimes called "arguments"—question is made up of a short paragraph, often written to make a persuasive point. These small arguments are usually written to contain a flaw—some error of reasoning or unwarranted assumption that you must identify to answer the question successfully. Questions may ask you to draw conclusions from the stated information, to weaken or strengthen the argument, to identify its underlying assumptions, or to identify its logical structure or method. There are most often a total of fifty or fifty-one argument questions between the two sections—roughly half of the scored questions on the LSAT.

As of June 2007 a modification, called Comparative Reading, appears as one of the four sets in the LSAT Reading Comprehension section. In general, Comparative Reading questions are similar to traditional Reading Comprehension questions, except that Comparative Reading questions are based on two shorter passages that together are roughly the same length as one Reading Comprehension passage. A few of the questions that follow a Comparative Reading passage pair might concern only one of the two passages, but most questions will be about both passages and how they relate to each other. Also, since June 2007, test-takers no longer are randomly assigned one of two different kinds of writing prompt—decision or argument—for the writing sample. All test-takers will be assigned a decision prompt. The Writing Sample will continue to be unscored.

We strongly recommend that you prep for this test. Although we provide the best prep for the LSAT, you certainly don't have to take The Princeton Review's course (or buy our book, *Cracking the LSAT*, or sign up for our awesome online course), as much as we would obviously like it. There are plenty of books, software products, courses, and tutors out there. The people who make the LSAT will gleefully sell you plenty of practice tests as well. The key is to find the best program for you. Your first step should be taking a free full-length practice LSAT given under realistic testing conditions (we offer them across the country), so you can gauge where you stand and how much you need to improve your LSAT score. Whatever your course of action, however, make sure you remain committed to it, so you can be as prepared as possible when you take the actual test.

WHEN SHOULD YOU TAKE THE LSAT?

Here is a quick summary of test dates along with some factors to consider for each.

JUNE

The June administration is the only time the test is given on a Monday afternoon. If you have trouble functioning at the ordinary 8:00 A.M. start time, June may be a good option. Furthermore, taking the LSAT in June frees up your summer and fall to research schools and complete applications. However, if you are still in college, you'll have to balance LSAT preparation with academic course work and, in some cases, final exams. Check your exam schedules before deciding on a June LSAT test date.

OCTOBER/SEPTEMBER

The October test date (which is sometimes in late September) will allow you to prepare for the LSAT during the summer. This is an attractive option if you are a college student with some free time on your hands. Once you've taken the LSAT, you can spend the remainder of the fall completing your applications.

DECEMBER

December is the last LSAT administration that most competitive law schools will accept. If disaster strikes and you get a flat tire on test day, you may end up waiting another year to begin law school. December test-takers also must balance their time between preparing for the LSAT and completing law school applications. Doing so can make for a hectic fall, especially if you're still in college. You should also remember that, while a law school may accept December LSAT scores, taking the test in December could affect your chances of admission. Many law schools use a rolling admissions system, which means that they begin making admissions decisions as early as mid-October and continue to do so until the application deadline. Applying late in this cycle could mean that fewer spots are available. Check with your potential law schools to find out their specific policies.

FEBRUARY

If you want to begin law school in the following fall, the February LSAT will be too late for most law schools. However, if you don't plan to begin law school until the next academic year, you can give yourself a head start on the entire admissions process by taking the LSAT in February, spending your summer researching schools, and devoting your fall to completing applications. As you chart your own timeline, keep in mind that the LSAT is administered four times a year—in February, June, October, and December. Visit www.lsac.org for specifics about dates, deadlines, and local testing centers.

HOW IS THE LSAT SCORED?

LSAT scores currently range from 120 to 180. Why that range? We have no idea. The table on page 16 indicates the percentile rating of the corresponding LSAT scores between 141 and 180. This varies slightly from test to test.

Your raw score (the number of questions you answer correctly) doesn't always produce the same scaled score as previous LSATs. What actually happens is that your raw score is compared with that of everyone else who took the test on the same date you did. The LSAC looks at the scales from every other LSAT given in the past three years and "normalizes" the current scale so that it doesn't deviate widely from those scaled scores in the past.

LSAT Score	Percent Below	LSAT Score	Percent Below
180	99.9	160	80.2
179	99.9	159	77.1
178	99.9	158	73.5
177	99.8	157	70.6
176	99.7	156	66.9
175	99.5	155	63.0
174	99.3	154	60.1
173	98.9	153	56.1
172	98.6	152	51.8
171	98.1	151	48.0
170	97.4	150	44.2
169	96.5	149	40.5
168	95.7	148	37.0
167	94.3	147	33.7
166	93.0	146	30.3
165	91.4	145	26.8
164	89.6	144	24.1
163	87.6	143	20.9
162	85.1	142	18.5
161	82.5	141	16.1

A GOOD LSAT SCORE

A good score on the LSAT is the score that gets you into the law school you want to attend. Remember that a large part of the admissions game is the formula of your UGPA (undergraduate grade point average) multiplied by your LSAT score. Chances are, you are at a point in life where your UGPA is pretty much fixed (if you're reading this early in your college career, start getting very good grades pronto), so the only piece of the formula you can have an impact on is your LSAT score. We cannot emphasize enough the notion that you must prepare for this test.

A LITTLE IMPROVEMENT GOES A LONG WAY

A student who scores a 154 is in the 60th percentile of all LSAT-takers. If that student's score was 161, however, that same student would jump to the 82nd percentile. Depending upon your score, a seven-point improvement can increase your ranking by more than twenty-five percentile points.

COMPETITIVE LSAT SCORES AROUND THE UNITED STATES

The range of LSAT scores from the 25th to 75th percentile of incoming full-time students at U.S. law schools is pretty broad. Here is a sampling.

Law School	Score 25 to 75 percentile
Widener University, School of Law, Delaware	148–151
Gonzaga University, School of Law	151–155
Rutgers University—Newark, School of Law	153–159
University of Pittsburgh, School of Law	152–160
University of Arizona, College of Law	155–163
Temple University, James E. Beasley School of Law	156–162
University of Florida, Levin College of Law	155–161
University of Tennessee, College of Law	154–160
Case Western Reserve University, School of Law	157–162
University of Alabama, School of Law	157–166
Southern Methodist University, School of Law	155–163
Loyola University Chicago, School of Law	155–159
University of San Diego, School of Law	155–161
Emory University, School of Law	157–166
The College of William & Mary, Law School	157–165
George Washington University, Law School	162–168
University of California—Berkeley, School of Law	164–169
Georgetown University, Law Center	163–168
Stanford University, School of Law	169–174
University of Chicago, Law School	166–172
Yale University, Yale Law School	170–176

PREPARING FOR THE LSAT

No matter who you are—whether you graduated *magna cum laude* from Cornell University or you're on academic probation at Cornell College—the first thing you need to do is order a recent LSAT. You can download one for free at lsac.org. Once you get the test, take it, but not casually over the course of two weeks. Bribe someone to be your proctor. Have them administer the test to you under strict time conditions. Follow the test booklet instructions exactly, and do it right. Your goal is to simulate an actual testing experience as much as possible. When you finish, score the test honestly. Don't give yourself a few extra points because "you'll do better on test day." The score on this practice test will provide a baseline for mapping your test preparation strategy.

If your practice LSAT score is already at a point where you've got a very high-percentage shot of getting accepted to the law school of your choice, chances are you don't need much preparation. Order a half dozen or so of the most recent LSATs from LSAC and work through them over the course of a few months, making sure you understand why you are making specific mistakes. If your college or university offers a free or very cheap prep course, consider taking it to get more tips on the test. Many of these courses are taught by pre-law advisors who will speak very intelligently about the test and are committed to helping you get the best score you can.

If, after you take a practice LSAT, your score is not what you want or need it to be, you are definitely not alone. Many academically strong candidates go into the LSAT cold because they assume that the LSAT is no more difficult than or about the same as their college courses. Frankly, many students are surprised at how poorly they do the first time they take a dry run. Think about it this way: It's better to be surprised sitting at home with a practice test than while taking the test for real.

If you've taken a practice LSAT under exam conditions and it's, say, ten or fifteen points below where you want it to be, you should probably consult an expert. Ask around. Assess your financial situation. Talk to other people who have improved their LSAT scores and duplicate their strategies.

Whatever you decide to do, make sure you are practicing with real LSAT questions and you take full-length practice tests under realistic testing conditions—again and again and again.

SOME ESSENTIAL, DOWN-AND-DIRTY LSAT TIPS

Slow down. Way down. The slower you go, the better you'll do. It's that simple. Any function you perform, from basic motor skills to complex intellectual problems, will be affected by the rate at which you perform that function. This goes for everything from cleaning fish to taking the LSAT. You can get twenty-five questions wrong and still get a scaled score of 160, which is a very good score (it's in the 84th percentile). You can get at least six questions wrong per section or, even better, you can ignore the two or three most convoluted questions per section, *still* get a few more questions wrong, and you'll get an excellent overall score. Your best strategy is to find the particular working speed at which you will get the most questions correct.

There is no penalty for guessing. If you don't have time to finish the exam, it's imperative that you leave yourself at least thirty seconds at the end of each section in which to grab free points by bubbling in some answer to every question before time is called. Pick a letter of the day—like B—don't bubble in randomly. If you guess totally randomly, you might get every single guess right. Of course, you may also get struck by lightning in the middle of the test. The odds are about the same. *You are far more likely to miss every question if you guess without a plan.* However, if you stick with the same letter each time you guess, you will definitely be right once in a while. It's a conservative approach, but it is also your best bet for guaranteed points, which is what you want. By guessing the same letter pretty much every time as time runs out, you can pick up anywhere from two to four raw points per section. Be careful about waiting until the very last second to start filling in randomly, though, because proctors occasionally cheat students out of the last few seconds of a section.

Use process of elimination all the time. This is absolutely huge. On 75 percent of the LSAT (all the Logical Reasoning and Reading Comprehension questions), you are *not* looking for the *right* answer, only the *best* answer. It says so right there in the instructions. Eliminating even one answer choice increases your chances of getting the question right by 20 to 25 percent. If you can cross off two or three answer choices, you are really in business. Also, very rarely will you find an answer choice that is flawless on the LSAT. Instead, you'll find four answer choices that are definitely wrong and one that is the least of five evils. You should constantly look for reasons to get rid of answer choices so you can eliminate them. This strategy will increase your odds of getting the question right, and you'll be a happier and more successful standardized test-taker. We swear.

Attack! Attack! Attack! Read the test with an antagonistic, critical eye; look for holes and gaps in the reasoning of arguments and in the answer choices. Many LSAT questions revolve around what is wrong with a particular line of reasoning. The more adept you become at identifying what is wrong with a problem before going to the answer choices, the more successful you'll be.

Write all over your test booklet. Actively engage the exam, and put your thoughts on paper. Circle words. *Physically cross out wrong answer choices you have eliminated.* Draw complete and exact diagrams for the logic games. Use the diagrams you draw.

Do the questions in whatever order you wish. Just because a logic game question is first doesn't mean you should do it first. There is *no order of difficulty* on the LSAT—unlike some other standardized tests—so you should hunt down and destroy those questions at which you are personally best. If you are doing a Reading Comprehension question, for example, or tackling an argument, and you don't know what the hell is going on, then cross off whatever you can, guess, and move on. If you have no idea how to solve a particular logic game, don't focus your energy there. Find a game you can do and milk it for points. Your mission is to gain points wherever you can. By the way, if a particular section is really throwing you, it's probably because it is the dastardly Experimental section (which is often kind of sloppy and, thankfully, does not count toward your score).

CHAPTER 5
WRITING A GREAT PERSONAL STATEMENT

There is no way to avoid writing the dreaded personal statement. You'll probably need to write only one personal statement, and it will probably address the most commonly asked question: "Why do you want to obtain a law degree?" This question, in one form or another, appears on virtually every law school application and often represents your only opportunity to string more than two sentences together. Besides your grades and your LSAT score, it is the most important part of your law school application. Your answer should be about two pages long, and it should amount to something significantly more profound than "A six-figure salary really appeals to me," or "I watch *Law & Order* every night."

Unlike your application to undergraduate programs, the personal statement on a law school application is not the time to discuss what your trip to Europe meant to you, describe your wacky chemistry teacher, or try your hand at verse. It's a fine line. While you want to stand out, you definitely don't want to be *overly* creative here. You want to be unique, but you don't want to come across as a weirdo or a loose cannon. You want to present yourself as intelligent, professional, mature, persuasive, and concise because these are the qualities law schools seek in applicants.

THE BASICS
Here are the essentials of writing essays and personal statements.

Find your own unique angle. The admissions people read tons of really boring essays about "how great I am" and how "I think there should be justice for everyone." If you must explain why you want to obtain a law degree, strive to find an angle that is interesting and unique to you. If what you write *isn't* interesting to you, we promise that it won't be remotely interesting to an Admissions Officer. Also, in addition to being more effective, an interesting essay will be far more enjoyable to write.

In general, avoid generalities. Again, Admissions Officers have to read an unbelievable number of boring essays. You will find it harder to be boring if you write about particulars. It's the details that stick in a reader's mind.

Good writing is easily understood. You want to get your point across, not bury it in words. Don't talk in circles. Your prose should be clear and direct. If an Admissions Officer has to struggle to figure out what you are trying to say, you'll be in trouble. Also, legal writing courses make up a significant part of most law school curricula; if you can show that you have good writing skills, you have a serious edge.

Buy and read *The Elements of Style* by William Strunk Jr. and E. B. White. We can't recommend it enough. In fact, we're surprised you don't have it already. This little book is a required investment for any writer (and, believe us, you'll be doing plenty of writing as a law student and a practicing attorney). You will refer to it forever, and if you do what it says, your writing will definitely improve.

Have three or four people read your personal statement and critique it. If your personal statement contains misspellings and grammatical errors, Admissions Officers will conclude not only that you don't know how to write but also that you aren't shrewd enough to get help. What's worse, the more time you spend with a piece of your own writing, the less likely you are to spot any errors. You get tunnel vision. Ask friends, boyfriends, girlfriends, professors, brothers, sisters—somebody—to read your essay and comment on it. Use a computer with a spellchecker. *Be especially careful about punctuation!* Another tip: Read your personal statement aloud to yourself or someone else. You will catch mistakes and awkward phrases that would have gotten past you otherwise because they sounded correct in your head.

Don't repeat information from other parts of your application. It's a waste of time and space.

Stick to the length that is requested. It's only common courtesy.

Maintain the proper tone. Your essay should be memorable, without being outrageous, and easy to read, without being too formal or sloppy. When in doubt, err on the formal side.

Being funny is much harder than you think. An applicant who can make an Admissions Officer laugh never gets lost in the shuffle. The clever part of the personal statement is passed around and read aloud. Everyone smiles and the Admissions Staff can't bear to toss your application into the "reject" pile. But beware! Most people think they're funny, but only a few are able to pull it off in this context. Obviously, stay away from one-liners, limericks, and anything remotely off-color.

WHY DO YOU WANT TO GO TO LAW SCHOOL?

Writing about yourself often proves to be surprisingly difficult. It's certainly no cakewalk explaining who you are and why you want to go to law school, and presenting your lifetime of experiences in a mere two pages. On the bright side, the personal statement is the only element of your application over which you have total control. It's a tremendous opportunity to make a great first impression as long as you avoid the urge to communicate your entire genetic blueprint. Your goal should be much more modest.

A Great Resource

Visit us at PrincetonReview.com to access tons of information about the LSAT and the law school admissions process.

DON'T GET CARRIED AWAY

Although some law schools set no limit on the length of the personal statement, you shouldn't take their bait. You can be certain that your statement will be at least glanced at in its entirety, but Admissions Officers are human, and their massive workload at admissions time has an understandable impact on their attention spans. You should limit yourself to two or three typed, double-spaced pages. Does this make your job any easier? Not at all. In fact, practical constraints on the length of your essay demand a higher degree of efficiency and precision. A two-page limit allows for absolutely no fluff.

MAKE YOURSELF STAND OUT

We know you know this, but you will be competing against thousands of well-qualified applicants for admission to just about any law school. Consequently, your primary task in writing your application is to separate yourself from the crowd. Particularly if you are applying directly from college or if you have been out of school for a very short time, you must do your best to ensure that the Admissions Committee cannot categorize you too broadly. Admissions Committees will see innumerable applications from bright twenty-two-year-olds with good grades. Your essay presents an opportunity to put those grades in context—to define and differentiate yourself.

WHAT MAKES A GOOD PERSONAL STATEMENT?

Like any good writing, your law school application should be clear, concise, and candid. The first two of these attributes, clarity and conciseness, are usually the result of a lot of reading, rereading, and rewriting. Without question, repeated critical revision by yourself and others is the surest way to trim and tune your prose. The third quality, candor, is the product of proper motivation. Honesty cannot be superimposed after the fact; your writing must be candid from the outset.

In writing your personal statement for law school applications, pay particularly close attention to the way your essay is structured and the fundamental message it communicates. Admissions Committees will read your essay two ways: as a product of your handiwork and as a product of your mind. Don't underestimate the importance of either perspective. A well-crafted essay will impress any Admissions Officer, but if it does not illuminate, you will not be remembered. You will not stand out. Conversely, a thoughtful essay that offers true insight will stand out unmistakably, but if it is not readable, it will not receive serious consideration.

THINGS TO AVOID IN YOUR PERSONAL STATEMENT

"MY LSAT SCORE ISN'T GREAT, BUT I'M JUST NOT A GOOD TEST-TAKER."

If you have a low LSAT score, avoid directly discussing it like the plague in your personal statement. Law school is a test-rich environment. In fact, grades in most law-school courses are determined by a single exam at the semester's end, and as a law student, you'll spend your Novembers and Aprils in a study carrel, completely removed from society. Saying that you are not good at tests will do little to convince an Admissions Committee that you've got the ability to succeed in law school once accepted.

Consider also that a low LSAT score speaks for itself—all too eloquently. It doesn't need you to speak for it too. The LSAT may be a flawed test, but don't go arguing the merits of the test to Admissions Officers, because ordinarily it is the primary factor they use to make admissions decisions. We feel for you, but you'd be barking up the wrong tree. The attitude of most law school Admissions Departments is that while the LSAT may be imperfect, it is equally imperfect for all applicants. Apart from extraordinary claims of serious illness on test day, few explanations for poor performance on the LSAT will mean much to the people who read your application.

About the only situation in which a discussion of your LSAT score is necessary is if you have two (or more) LSAT scores and one is significantly better than another. If you did much better in your second sitting than in your first, or vice versa, a brief explanation couldn't hurt. However, your explanation may mean little to the committee, which may have its own hard-and-fast rules for interpreting multiple LSAT scores. Even in this scenario, however, you should avoid bringing up the LSAT in the personal statement. *Save it for an addendum.*

The obvious and preferable alternative to an explicit discussion of a weak LSAT score would be to focus on what you *are* good at. If you really are bad at standardized tests, you must be better at something else, or you wouldn't have gotten as far as you have. If you think you are a marvelous researcher, say so. If you are a wonderful writer, show it. Let your essay implicitly draw attention away from your weak points by focusing on your strengths. There is no way to convince an Admissions Committee that they should overlook your LSAT score. You may, however, present compelling reasons for them to look beyond it.

"MY COLLEGE GRADES WEREN'T THAT HIGH, BUT..."

This issue is a bit more complicated than the low LSAT score. Law school Admissions Committees will be more willing to listen to your interpretation of your college performance but only within limits. Keep in mind that law schools require official transcripts for a reason. Members of the Admissions Committee will be aware of your academic credentials before ever getting to your essay. As with low LSAT scores, your safest course of action is to *explain low grades in addendum.*

If your grades are unimpressive, you should offer the Admissions Committee something else by which to judge your abilities. Again, the best argument for looking past your college grades is evidence of achievement in another area, whether in your LSAT score, your extracurricular activities, your overcoming economic hardship as an undergraduate, or your career accomplishments.

"I'VE ALWAYS WANTED TO BE A LAWYER."

Sure you have. Many applicants seem to feel the need to point out that they really, really want to become attorneys. You will do yourself a great service by avoiding such throwaway lines. They'll do nothing for your essay but water it down. Do not convince yourself in a moment of desperation that claiming to have known that the law was your calling since age six (when—let's be honest—you really wanted to be a firefighter) will somehow move your application to the top of the pile. The Admissions Committee is not interested in how much you want to practice law. They want to know *why.*

"I WANT TO BECOME A LAWYER TO FIGHT INJUSTICE."

No matter how deeply you feel about battling social inequity, between us, writing it down makes you sound like a superhero on a soapbox. Moreover, though some people really do want to fight injustice, way down in the cockles of their hearts, most applicants are motivated to attend law school by less altruistic desires. Among the nearly one million practicing lawyers in the United States, there are relatively few who actually earn a living defending the indigent or protecting civil rights. Tremendously dedicated attorneys who work for peanuts and take charity cases are few and far between. We're not saying you don't want to be one of them; we're merely saying that people in law school admissions won't *believe* you want to be one of them. They'll take your professed altruistic ambitions (and those of the hundreds of other personal statements identical to yours) with a (huge) grain of salt.

If you can, in good conscience, say that you are committed to a career in the public interest, show the committee something tangible on your application and in your essay that will allow them to see your statements as more than mere assertions. If however, you cannot show that you are already a veteran in the good fight, don't claim to be. Law school Admissions Committees certainly do not regard the legal profession as a saints versus sinners proposition, and neither should you. Do not be afraid of appearing morally moderate. If the truth is that you want the guarantee of the relatively good jobs a law degree practically ensures, be forthright. Nothing is as impressive to the reader of a personal statement as the ring of truth, and what's wrong with wanting a good job, anyway?

CHAPTER 6

RECOMMENDATIONS

The law schools to which you apply will require two or three letters of recommendation in support of your application. Some schools will allow you to submit as many letters as you like. Others make it clear that any more than the minimum number of letters of recommendation is unwelcome. If you've ever applied to a private school (or perhaps a small public school) then you know the drill.

Unlike the evaluation forms for some colleges and graduate programs, however, law school recommendation forms tend toward absolute minimalism. All but a few recommendation forms for law school applications ask a single, open-ended question. It usually goes something like, "What information about this applicant is relevant that is not to be found in other sources?" The generic quality of the forms from various law schools may be both a blessing and a curse. On the one hand, it makes it possible for those writing your recommendations to write a single letter that will suffice for all the applications you submit. This convenience will make everybody much happier. On the other hand, if a free-form recommendation is to make a positive impression on an Admissions Committee, it must convey real knowledge about you.

WHOM TO ASK

Your letters of recommendation should come from people who know you well enough to offer a truly informed assessment of your abilities. Think carefully before choosing them to do this favor for you, but, as a general rule, pick respectable people whom you've known for a long time. If the writers of your recommendations know you well and understand the broader experience that has brought you to your decision to attend law school, they will be able to write a letter that is specific enough to do you some good. You also want people who can and are willing to contribute to an integrated, cohesive application.

The application materials from most law schools suggest that your letters should come, whenever possible, from people in academic settings. Some schools want at least two recommendations, both of which must be academic. Others explicitly request that the letters come from someone who has known you in a professional setting, especially if you've been out of school for a while.

HELP YOUR RECOMMENDATION WRITERS HELP YOU

Here, in essence, is the simple secret to great recommendations: Make sure the writers of your recommendations know you, your academic and professional goals, and the overall message you are trying to convey in your application. The best recommendations will fit neatly with the picture you present of yourself in your own essay, even when they make no specific reference to the issues your essay addresses. An effective law school application will present to the Admissions Committee a cohesive picture, not a montage. A great way to point your recommendation writers in the right direction and maximize their abilities to contribute to your overall cause is to provide them with copies of your personal statement. Don't be bashful about amiably communicating a few "talking points" that don't appear in your personal statement, as well.

ACADEMIC REFERENCES

Most applicants will (and should) seek recommendations from current or former professors. The academic environment in law school is extremely rigorous. Admissions Committees will be looking for assurance that you will be able not just to survive but to excel. A strong recommendation from a college professor is a valuable corroboration of your ability to succeed in law school.

You want nothing less than stellar academic recommendations. While a perfunctory, lukewarm recommendation is unlikely to damage your overall application, it will obviously do nothing to bolster it. Your best bet is to choose at least one professor from your major field. An enthusiastic endorsement from such a professor will be taken as a sign that you are an excellent student. Second—and we hope that this goes without saying—you should choose professors who do not immediately associate your name with the letter C.

Helpful Websites

findlaw.com

This site is the mother lode of free information about law, law schools, and legal careers.

ilrg.com

An index of websites concerning law or the legal profession.

hg.org/students.html

Legal resources geared toward students.

jurist.law.pitt.edu

The University of Pittsburgh School of Law's splendid "Legal News and Research" website offers a wealth of useful information.

Specifics are of particular interest to Admissions Officers when they evaluate your recommendations. If a professor can make *specific* reference to a particular project you completed, or at least make substantive reference to your work in a particular course, the recommendation will be strengthened considerably. Make it your responsibility to enable your professors to provide specifics. Drop hints, or just lay it out for them. You might, for example, make available a paper you wrote for them of which you are particularly proud. Or you might just chat with the professor for a while to jog those dormant memories. You might feel uncomfortable tooting your own horn, but it's for the best. Unless your professors are well-acquainted enough with you to be able to offer a very personal assessment of your potential, they will greatly appreciate a tangible reminder of your abilities on which to base their recommendation.

ESCAPING THE WOODWORK

If you managed to get through college without any professors noticing you, it's not the end of the world. Professors are quite talented at writing recommendations for students they barely know. Most consider it part of their job. Even seemingly unapproachable academic titans will usually be happy to dash off a quick letter for a mere student. However, these same obliging professors are masters of a sort of opaque prose style that screams to an Admissions Officer, "I really have no idea what to say about this kid who is, in fact, a near-total stranger to me!" Although an Admissions Committee will not outrightly dismiss such a recommendation, it's really not going to help you much.

REELING IN THE YEARS

Obviously, the longer it has been since you graduated, the tougher it is to obtain academic recommendations. However, if you've held on to your old papers, you may still be able to rekindle an old professor's memory of your genius by sending a decent paper or two along with your request for a recommendation (and, of course, a copy of your personal statement). You want to provide specifics in any way you can.

NON-ACADEMIC REFERENCES

Getting the mayor, a senator, or the CEO of your company to write a recommendation helps only if you have a personal and professional connection with that person. Remember, you want the writers of your recommendations to provide specifics about your actual accomplishments. If you're having trouble finding academic recommendations, choose people from your workplace, from the community, or from any other area of your life that is important to you. If at all possible, talk to your boss or a supervisor from a previous job who knows you well (and, of course, likes you).

SEND A THANK-YOU NOTE

Always a good idea. It should be short and handwritten. Use a blue pen so the recipient knows for sure that your note is no cheap copy. As with any good thank-you note and any good recommendation, mention something specific. (Send a thank-you note if you have an interview at a law school, too.)

CHAPTER 7
REAL-LIFE WORK EXPERIENCE
AND COMMUNITY SERVICE

WORK EXPERIENCE IN COLLEGE

Most law school applications will ask you to list any part-time jobs you held while you were in college and how many hours per week you worked. If you had to (or chose to) work your way through your undergraduate years, this should come as good news. A great number of law schools make it clear that they take your work commitments as a college student into consideration when evaluating your undergraduate GPA.

WORK EXPERIENCE IN REAL LIFE

All law school applications will ask you about your work experience beyond college. They will give you three or four lines on which to list such experience. Some schools will invite you to submit a résumé. If you have a very good one, you should really milk this opportunity for all it's worth. Even if you don't have a marvelous résumé, these few lines on the application and your résumé are the only opportunities you'll have to discuss your post-college experience meaningfully—unless you choose to discuss professional experience in your personal statement as well.

The kind of job you've had is not as important as you might think. What interests the Admissions Committee is what you've made of that job and what it has made of you. Whatever your job was or is, you want to offer credible evidence of your competence. For example, mention in your personal statement your job advancement or any increase in your responsibility. Most important, though, remember your overriding goal of cohesive presentation—you want to show off your professional experience within the context of your decision to attend law school. This does not mean that you need to offer geometric proof of how your experience in the workplace has led you inexorably to a career in law. You need only explain truthfully how this experience influenced you and how it fits nicely into your thinking about law school.

COMMUNITY SERVICE

An overwhelming majority of law schools single out community involvement as one of several influential factors in their admissions decisions. Law schools would like to admit applicants who show a long-standing commitment to something other than their own advancement.

It is certainly understandable that law schools would wish to determine the level of such commitment before admitting an applicant, particularly since so few law students go on to practice public interest law. Be forewarned, however, that nothing—*nothing*—is so obviously bogus as an insincere statement of a commitment to public interest issues. It just reeks. Admissions committees are well aware that very few people take the time out of their lives to become involved significantly in their communities. If you aren't one of them, trying to fake it can only hurt you.

CHAPTER 8

INTERVIEWS

The odds are very good that you will never have to sit through an interview in the law school admissions process. Admissions Offices just aren't very keen on them. They do happen occasionally, however, and if you are faced with one, here are a few tips.

BE PREPARED

Interviews do make impressions. Some students are admitted simply because they had great interviews; less often, students are rejected because they bombed. Being prepared is the smartest thing you can do.

Don't ask questions that are answered in the brochures you got in the mail. You have to read those brochures—at breakfast before the interview would be an ideal time.

If there is a popular conception of the school (e.g., Harvard is overly competitive), don't ask about it. Your interviewer will have been through the same song and dance too many times. While you don't want to seem off the wall by asking bizarre questions, you don't want to sound exactly like every other boring applicant before you.

LOOK GOOD, FEEL GOOD

Wear nice clothes. If you aren't sure what to wear, *ask the Admissions Staff*. Get a respectable haircut. Don't chew gum. Clean your fingernails. Brush your teeth. Wash behind your ears. You can go back to being a slob as soon as they admit you.

DON'T WORRY ABOUT TIME

Students sometimes are told that the sign of a good interview is that it lasts longer than the time allowed for it. Forget about this. Don't worry if your interview lasts exactly as long as the assistant said it would. Don't try to stretch out the end of your interview by suddenly becoming long-winded or asking questions you don't care about.

CHAPTER 9
MONEY MATTERS

Law school is a cash cow for colleges and universities everywhere and, especially at a private school, you are going to be gouged for a pretty obscene wad of cash over the next three years. Take American University Washington College of Law, where tuition is about $50,000 a year. If you are planning to eat, live somewhere, buy books, and (maybe) have health insurance, you are looking at about $68,500 per year. Multiply that by three years of law school and you get about $205,600. Now faint. Correct for inflation (AU certainly will), add things like computers and other miscellany, and you can easily spend $225,000 to earn a degree. Assume that you have to borrow every penny of that $225,000. Multiply it by 8 percent through ten years (a common assumption of law school applicants is that they will be able to pay all their debt back in ten years or less). Your monthly payments will be about $2,730.

On the bright side, while law school is certainly an expensive proposition, the financial rewards of practicing can be immensely lucrative. You won't be forced into bankruptcy if you finance it properly. There are tried-and-true ways to reduce your initial costs, finance the costs on the horizon, and manage the debt with which you'll leave school—all without ever having to ask, "Have you been in a serious accident recently?" in a television commercial.

LAW SCHOOL ON THE CHEAP

Private schools aren't the only law schools, and you don't have to come out of law school saddled with tens of thousands of dollars of debt. Many state schools have reputations that equal or surpass some of the top private ones. It might be worth your while to spend a year establishing residency in a state with one or more good public law schools. Here's an idea: Pack up your belongings and move to a cool place like Minneapolis, Seattle, Berkeley, Austin, or Boulder. Spend a year living there. Wait tables, hang out, listen to music, walk the Earth, write the great American novel, and *then* study law.

COMPARISON SHOPPING

The table on page 30 lists the full-time tuition costs at law schools around the country. The two schools listed for each state are randomly paired schools in the same region (one public and one private) and are provided to help you get a feel of what law school costs are going to run you. Those schools that have the same tuition in both columns are private law schools.

Law School	In-State	Out-of-State
Florida State University, College of Law (tuition + fees)	$20,653	$40,706
University of Miami, School of Law	$45,200	$45,200
Indiana University—Bloomington, Maurer School of Law	$29,820	$48,626
University of Notre Dame, Law School	$50,040	$50,040
University of Tennessee, College of Law	$16,078	$34,522
Vanderbilt University, Law School	$49,300	$49,300
The University of Iowa, College of Law	$21,964	$39,500
Drake University, Law School	$38,754	$38,754
Southern University, Law Center	$12,054	$21,614
Tulane University, Law School	$41,500	$41,500
University of California—Los Angeles, School of Law	$45,226	$51,720
University of San Francisco, School of Law	$46,780	$46,780
The University of Texas at Austin, School of Law	$33,162	$49,244
Baylor University, School of Law	$50,106	$50,106
University of Illinois, College of Law	$38,250	$46,000
Northwestern University, School of Law	$56,134	$56,134
University of Oregon, School of Law	$30,586	$38,056
Lewis & Clark College, Law School	$40,114	$40,114

LOAN REPAYMENT ASSISTANCE PROGRAMS

If you are burdened with loans, we've got more bad news. The National Association of Law Placement (NALP) shows that while salaries for law school graduates who land jobs at the big, glamorous firms have skyrocketed in the past few years, salaries of less than $85,000 are more common than salaries of $100,000 to $130,000 for the general run of law school grads. There are, however, a growing number of law schools and other sources willing to pay your loans for you through loan forgiveness programs in return for your commitment to work in public interest law.

While doing a tour of duty in public service law will put off dreams of working at a big firm or becoming the next Mark Geragos, the benefits of these programs are undeniable. Here's how just about all of them work. You commit to working for a qualified public service or public interest job. As long as your gross income does not exceed the prevailing public service salary, the programs will pay off a good percentage of your debt. Eligible loans are typically any educational debt financed through your law school, which really excludes only loan sharks and credit-card debts.

The Skinny on Loan Repayment Assistance Programs
For a comprehensive listing of assistance programs and for other loan-forgiveness information, call Equal Justice Works at 202-466-3686, or look them up online at equaljusticeworks.org.

MAXIMIZE YOUR AID

A simple but oft-forgotten piece of wisdom: If you don't ask, you usually don't get. Be firm when trying to get merit money from your school. Some schools have reserves of cash that go unused. Try simply asking for more financial aid. The better your grades, of course, the more likely schools are to crack open their safe of financial goodies for you. Unfortunately, grants aren't as prevalent for law students as for undergrads. Scholarships are not nearly as widely available either. To get a general idea of availability of aid at a law school, contact the Financial Aid Office.

PARENTAL CONTRIBUTION?!

If you are operating under the assumption that, as a tax-paying grownup who has been out of school for a number of years, you will be recognized as the self-supporting adult you are, you could be in for a surprise. Veterans of financial aid battles will not be surprised to hear that even law school Financial Aid Offices have a difficult time recognizing when apron strings have legitimately been cut. Schools may try to take into account your parents' income in determining your eligibility for financial aid, regardless of your age or tax status. Policies vary widely. Be sure to ask the schools you are considering exactly what their policies are regarding financial independence for the purposes of financial aid.

BORROWING MONEY

It's an amusingly simple process, and several companies are in the business of lending large chunks of cash specifically to law students. Your law school Financial Aid Office can tell you how to reach them. You should explore more than one option and shop around for the lowest fees and rates.

WHO'S ELIGIBLE?

Anyone with reasonably good credit, regardless of financial need, can borrow enough money to finance law school. If you have financial need, you will probably be eligible for some types of financial aid if you meet the following basic qualifications:

- You are a United States citizen or a permanent U.S. resident.

- You are registered for Selective Service if you are a male, or you have the documentation to prove that you are exempt.

- You are not in default on student loans already.

- You don't have a horrendous credit history.

- You haven't been busted for certain drug-related crimes, including possession.

> **Let the Law School Pick Up the Tab for Phone Calls Whenever Possible**
> Many schools have free telephone numbers that they don't like to publish in books like this one. If the number we have listed for a particular law school is not an 800 number, it doesn't necessarily mean that you have to pay every time you call the school. Check out the school's website, or ask for the 800 number the first time you call.

WHAT TYPES OF LOANS ARE AVAILABLE?

There are three basic types of loans: federal, private, and institutional.

Federal

The federal government funds federal loan programs. Federal loans, particularly Federal Direct Loans, are usually the first resort for borrowers. Most federal loans are need-based, but some higher-interest loans are available regardless of financial circumstances. Visit studentaid.ed.org for the most comprehensive, up-to-date information.

Private

Private loans are funded by banks, foundations, corporations, and other associations. A number of private loans are targeted to aid particular segments of the population. You may have to do some investigating to identify private loans for which you might qualify. As always, contact your law school's Financial Aid Office to learn more.

Institutional

The amount of loan money available and the method by which it is disbursed vary greatly from one school to another. Private schools, especially those that are older and more established, tend to have larger endowments and can offer more assistance. To find out about the resources available at a particular school, refer to its catalog or contact—you guessed it—the financial aid office.

TABLE OF LOANS

NAME OF LOAN	SOURCE	ELIGIBILITY	MAXIMUM ALLOCATION
Federal Direct Unsubsidized Loans https://studentaid.ed.gov/sa/types/loans/subsidized-unsubsidized	Federal, administered by school.	Not need-based.	The total unsubsidized loan limit is $20,500. The maximum aggregate total of subsidized and unsubsidized loans is $138,500, including undergraduate loans.
Federal PLUS Loans	Federal, administered by school.	Not need-based.	The maximum allocation is the cost of attendance (including tuition, educational expenses, and reasonable living expenses as determined by the school minus any other financial aid received.).
Perkins Loan Contact school for more information.	Federal, administered by school.	Exceptional financial need.	$8,000/year, with aggregate of $60,000. Aggregate amount includes undergraduate loans.

TABLE OF LOANS (Continued)			
REPAYMENT AND DEFFERAL OPTIONS	**INTEREST RATE**	**PROS**	**CONS**
10–25 years to repay. Interest begins to accrue from day loan is disbursed; you can pay the interest or have it capitalized (added to principal). Begin repayment 6 months after graduation.	Fixed, 6.21%.	Fixed, relatively low interest rate.	Interest is not paid by the government while you're in school.
10 years to repay. Begins 6 months after graduation. Deferrable during residency and under special circumstances.	Fixed, 7.21%.	Fixed, relatively low interest rate.	Very limited availability.
10 years to repay. Begin repayment 9 months after graduation.	Fixed, 5%	Fixed, relatively low interest rate.	Low maximum allocation.

CHAPTER 10
LAW SCHOOL 101

IS IT REALLY THAT BAD?

The first semester of law school has the well-deserved reputation of being among the greatest challenges to your intellect and stamina that you'll ever face. It requires tons and tons of work and, in many ways, it's an exercise in intellectual survival. Just as the gung-ho army recruit must survive boot camp, so, too, must the bright-eyed law student endure the humbling effects of the first year.

Though complex and difficult, the subject matter in first-year law school courses is probably no more inherently difficult than what is taught in other graduate or professional schools. The particular, private terror that is shared by roughly 40,000 1Ls every year stems more from law school's peculiar *style*. The method of instruction unapologetically punishes students who would prefer to learn passively.

THE FIRST-YEAR CURRICULUM
The first-year curriculum in the law school you attend will almost certainly be composed of a combination of the following courses:

TORTS
The word comes from the Middle French for *injury*. The Latin root of the word means *twisted*. Torts are wrongful acts, excluding breaches of contract, over which you can sue people. They include battery, assault, false imprisonment, and intentional infliction of emotional distress. Torts can range from the predictable to the bizarre, from "Dog Bites Man" to "Man Bites Dog" and everything in between. The study of torts mostly involves reading cases to discern the legal rationale behind decisions pertaining to the extent of, and limits on, the civil liability of one party for harm done to another.

CONTRACTS
They may seem fairly self-explanatory, but contractual relationships are varied and complicated, as two semesters of contracts will teach you. Again, through the study of past court cases, you will follow the largely unwritten law governing the system of conditions and obligations a contract represents, as well as the legal remedies available when contracts are breached.

CIVIL PROCEDURE
Civil procedure is the study of how you get things done in civil (as opposed to criminal) court. "Civ Pro" is the study of the often dizzyingly complex rules that govern not only who can sue whom, but also how, when, and where they can do it. This is not merely a study of legal protocol, for issues of process have a significant indirect effect on the substance of the law. Rules of civil procedure govern the conduct of both the courtroom trial and the steps that might precede it: obtaining information (discovery), making your case (pleading), pre-trial motions, and so on.

PROPERTY
You may never own a piece of land, but your life will inevitably and constantly be affected by property laws. Anyone interested in achieving an understanding of broader policy issues will appreciate the significance of this material. Many property courses will emphasize the transfer of property and, to varying degrees, economic analysis of property law.

CRIMINAL LAW
Even if you become a criminal prosecutor or defender, you will probably never run into most of the crimes to which you will be exposed in this course. Can someone who shoots the dead body of a person he believes to be alive be charged with attempted murder? What if they were both on drugs or had really rough childhoods? Also, you'll love the convoluted exam questions in which someone will invariably go on a nutty crime spree.

CONSTITUTIONAL LAW

"Con Law" is the closest thing to a normal class you will take in your first year. It emphasizes issues of government structure (e.g., federal power versus state power) and individual rights (e.g., personal liberties, freedom of expression, property protection). You'll spend a great deal of time studying the limits on the lawmaking power of Congress as well.

LEGAL METHODS

One of the few twentieth-century improvements on the traditional first-year curriculum that has taken hold nearly everywhere, this course travels under various aliases, such as Legal Research and Writing or Elements of the Law. In recent years, increased recognition of the importance of legal writing skills has led more than half of the U.S. law schools to require or offer a writing course after the first year. This class will be your smallest, and possibly your only, refuge from the Socratic Method. Methods courses are often taught by junior faculty and attorneys in need of extra cash and are designed to help you acquire fundamental skills in legal research, analysis, and writing. The methods course may be the least frightening you face, but it can easily consume an enormous amount of time. This is a common lament, particularly at schools where very few credits are awarded for it.

In addition to these course requirements, many law schools require 1Ls to participate in a moot-court exercise. As part of this exercise, students—sometimes working in pairs or even small groups—must prepare briefs and oral arguments for a mock trial (usually appellate). This requirement is often tied in with the methods course so that those briefs and oral arguments will be well researched—and graded.

THE CASE METHOD

In the majority of your law school courses, and probably in all of your first-year courses, your only texts will be things called casebooks. The case method eschews explanation and encourages exploration. In a course that relies entirely on the casebook, you will never come across a printed list of "laws." Instead, you will learn that in many areas of law there is no such thing as a static set of rules, but only a constantly evolving system of principles. You are expected to understand the principles of law—in all of its layers and ambiguities—through a critical examination of a series of cases that were decided according to such principles. You will often feel utterly lost, groping for answers to unarticulated questions. This is not only normal but also intended.

In practical terms, the case method works like this: For every class meeting, you will be assigned a number of cases to read from your casebook, which is a collection of (extremely edited) written judicial decisions in actual court cases. The names won't even have been changed to protect the innocent. The cases are the written judicial opinions rendered in court cases that were decided at the appeals or Supreme Court level. (Written opinions are not generally rendered in lower courts.)

Your casebook will contain no instructions and little to no explanation. Your assignments will be to simply read the cases and be in a position to answer questions based on them. There will be no written homework assignments, just cases, cases, and more cases.

You will write, for your own benefit, summaries—or briefs—of these cases. Briefs are your attempts to summarize the issues and laws around which a particular case revolves. *By writing briefs, you figure out what the law is.* The idea is that, over the course of a semester, you will try to integrate the content of your case briefs and your notes from in-class lectures, discussions, or dialogues into some kind of cohesive whole.

Tips for Classroom Success

- Be alert. Review material immediately before class so that it is fresh in your memory. Then review your notes from class later the same day and the week's worth of notes at the end of each week.

- Remember that there are few correct answers. The goal of a law school class is generally to analyze, understand, and attempt to resolve issues or problems.

- Learn to state and explain legal rules and principles with accuracy.

- Don't focus on minutiae from cases or class discussions; always try to figure out what the law is.

- Accept the ambiguity in legal analysis and class discussion; classes are intended to be thought-provoking, perplexing, and difficult.

- No one class session will make or break you. Keep in mind how each class fits within the course overall.

- Write down the law. Don't write down what other students say. Concentrate your notes on the professor's hypotheticals and emphases in class.

- Review the table of contents in the casebook. This is a simple but effective way of keeping yourself in touch with where the class is at any given time.

- If you don't use a laptop, don't sit next to someone who does. The constant tapping on the keys will drive you crazy, and you may get a sense that they are writing down more than you (which is probably not true).

- Don't record classes. There are better uses of your time than to spend hours listening to the comments of students who were just as confused as you were when you first dealt with the material in class.

THE SOCRATIC METHOD

As unfamiliar as the case method will be to most 1Ls, the real source of anxiety is the way in which the professors present it. Socratic instruction entails directed questioning and limited lecturing. Generally, the Socratic professor invites a student to attempt a cogent summary of a case assigned for that day's class. Hopefully, it won't be you (but someday it will be). Regardless of the accuracy and thoroughness of your initial response, the professor then grills you on details overlooked or issues unresolved. Then, the professor will change the facts of the actual case at hand into a hypothetical case that may or may not have demanded a different decision by the court.

The overall goal of the Socratic Method is to forcibly improve your critical reasoning skills. If you are reasonably well prepared, thinking about all these questions will force you beyond the immediately apparent issues in a given case to consider its broader implications. The dialogue between the effective Socratic instructor and the victim of the moment will also force nonparticipating students to question their underlying assumptions of the case under discussion.

WHAT IS CLINICAL LEGAL EDUCATION?

The latest so-called innovation in legal education is ironic in that it's a return to the old emphasis on practical experience. Hands-on training in the practical skills of lawyering now travels under the name "Clinical Legal Education."

HOW IT WORKS

Generally, a clinical course focuses on developing practical lawyering skills. "Clinic" means exactly what you would expect: a working law office where second- and third-year law students counsel clients and serve human beings. (A very limited number of law schools allow first-year students to participate in legal clinics.)

In states that grant upper-level law students a limited right to represent clients in court, students in a law school's clinic might actually follow cases through to their resolution. Some schools have a single on-site clinic that operates something like a general law practice, dealing with cases ranging from petty crime to landlord-tenant disputes. At schools that have dedicated the most resources to their clinical programs, numerous specialized clinics deal with narrowly defined areas of law, such as employment discrimination. The opportunities to participate in such live-action programs, however, are limited.

> *Watch* **The Paper Chase.** *Twice.*
> This movie is the only one ever produced about law school that comes close to depicting the real thing. Watch it before you go to orientation. Watch it again on Thanksgiving break — and laugh when you can identify prototypes of your classmates.

OTHER OPTIONS

Clinical legal education is much more expensive than traditional instruction, which means that few law schools can accommodate more than a small percentage of their students in clinical programs. If that's the case, check out external clinical placements and simulated clinical courses. In a clinical externship, you might work with a real firm or public agency several hours a week and meet with a faculty advisor only occasionally. Though students who participate in these programs are unpaid, they will ordinarily receive academic credit. Also, placements are chosen quite carefully to ensure that you don't become a gopher.

There are also simulated clinical courses. In one of these, you'll perform all of the duties that a student in a live-action clinic would, but your clients are imaginary.

CHAPTER 11
HOW TO EXCEL AT ANY LAW SCHOOL

Preparation for law school is something you should take very seriously. Law school will be one of the most interesting and rewarding experiences of your life, but it's also an important and costly investment. Your academic performance in law school will influence your career for years to come. Consider the following facts when thinking about how important it is to prepare for law school:

- In the academic year 2012-2013, the average amount borrowed by law students was $32,289 for those enrolled in public institutions and $44,094 for those enrolled in private institutions. (Source: American Bar Association)

- The median starting salary for 2013 law school graduates was $62,467. (Source: National Association for Legal Career Professionals)

> B-pluses put you in the top quarter at most schools and in the top fifth at many.

As you can see, most law students cannot afford to be mediocre. Money isn't everything, but when you're strapped with close to six figures of debt, money concerns will weigh heavily on your career choices. Even if money is not a concern for you, your academic performance in law school will profoundly affect your employment options after graduation and, ultimately, your legal career. Consider these additional facts:

- Students who excel in law school may have opportunities to earn up to $135,000 plus bonuses right out of law school.

- Only law students who excel academically have opportunities to obtain prestigious judicial clerkships, teaching positions, and distinguished government jobs.

As you can see, law students who achieve academic success enjoy better career options and have a greater ability to escape the crushing debt of law school. The point is obvious: Your chances of achieving your goals—no matter what you want to do with your career—are far better if you succeed academically.

Now comes the hard part: How do you achieve academic success? You are going to get plenty of advice about how to excel in law school—much of it unsolicited. You certainly don't need any from us. We strongly advise, however, that you pay close attention to what Don Macaulay, the former president of Law Preview (now BARBRI Law Preview), has to say about surviving and thriving as a law student. Macaulay, like all the founders of Law Preview, graduated at the top of his law school class and worked at a top law firm before he began developing and administering Law Preview's law school prep course in 1998.

> *Contact Law Preview*
> *Law Preview is an intensive week-long seminar designed to help you conquer law school. To learn more, visit www.lawpreview.barbri.com.*

While there are many resources that claim to provide a recipe for success in law school, Law Preview is the best of the lot. They have retained some of the most talented legal scholars in the country to lecture during their week-long sessions, and they deliver what they promise—a methodology for attacking and conquering the law school experience.

We asked Macaulay a few questions to which we thought prospective law students might like to know the answers:

It is often said that the first year of law school is the most important year. Is this true, and, if so, why?

It is true. Academic success during the first year of law school can advance a successful legal career unlike success in any other year because many of the top legal employers start recruiting so early that your first-year grades are all they will see. Most prestigious law firms hire their permanent attorneys from among the ranks of the firm's "summer associates"—usually second-year law students who work for the firm during the summer between the second and third years of law school. Summer associates are generally hired during the fall semester of the second year, a time when only the first year grades are available. A student who does well during the first year, lands a desirable summer associate position, and then impresses his or her employer, is well on his or her way to a secure legal job regardless of his or her academic performance after the first year.

In addition, first-year grades often bear heavily upon a student's eligibility for law review and other prestigious scholastic activities, including other law journals and moot court. These credentials are considered the most significant signs of law school achievement, often even more than a high grade point average. Many of the top legal employers in the private and the public sectors seek out young lawyers with these credentials, and some employers will not even interview candidates who lack these honors, even after a few years of experience. As a result, a solid performance during the first year of law school can have a serious impact upon your professional opportunities available after graduation.

Save on Books

LawBooksForLess.com is the best place to purchase case-books and legal study aids, cheap!

How does law school differ from what students experienced as undergraduates?

Many students, especially those who enjoyed academic success in college, presume that law school will be a mere continuation of their undergraduate experience, and that, by implementing those skills that brought them success in college, they will enjoy similar success in law school. This couldn't be further from the truth. Once law school begins, students often find themselves thrown into deep water. They are handed an anchor in the form of a casebook (they are told it's a life preserver), and they are expected to sink or swim. While almost nobody sinks in law school anymore, most spend all of their first year just trying to keep their heads above water. In reality, virtually every student who is admitted into law school possesses the intelligence and work ethic needed to graduate. But in spite of having the tools needed to survive the experience, very few possess the know-how to truly excel and make Law Review at their schools.

What makes the law school experience unique is its method of instruction and its system of grading. Most professors rely on the case method as a means for illustrating legal rules and doctrines encountered in a particular area of the law. With the case method, students are asked to read a particular case or, in some instances, several cases, that the professor will use to lead a classroom discussion illustrating a particular rule of law. The assigned readings come from casebooks, which are compilations of cases for each area of law. The cases are usually edited to illustrate distinct legal rules, often with very little commentary or enlightenment by the casebook editor. The casebooks often lack anything more than a general structure, and law professors often contribute little to the limited structure. Students are asked to read and analyze hundreds of cases in a vacuum. Since each assigned case typically builds upon a legal rule illustrated in a previous case, it isn't until the end of the semester or, for some classes, the end of the year, that students begin to form an understanding of how these rules interrelate.

One of the objectives of Law Preview's law school prep course is to help students to understand the big picture before they begin their classes. We hire some of the most talented law professors from around the country to provide previews of the core first-year law school courses: Civil Procedure, Constitutional Law, Contracts, Criminal Law, Property, and Torts. During their lectures, our professors provide students with a roadmap for each subject by discussing the law's development, legal doctrines, and recurring themes and policies that students will encounter throughout the course. By providing entering law students with a conceptual framework for the material they will study, Law Preview eliminates the frustration that most of them will encounter when reading and analyzing case law in a vacuum.

What is the best way to prepare for law school, and when should you start?

When preparing for law school, students should focus on two interrelated tasks: (1) developing a strategy for academic success, and (2) preparing mentally for the awesome task ahead. The primary objective for most law students is to achieve the highest grades possible, and a well-defined strategy for success will help you direct your efforts most efficiently and effectively toward that goal. You must not begin law school equipped solely with some vague notion of hard work. Success requires a concrete plan that includes developing a reliable routine for classroom preparation, a proficient method of outlining, and a calculated strategy for test-taking. The further you progress in law school without such a plan, the more time and energy you will waste struggling through your immense workload without moving discernibly closer to achieving academic success.

You must also become mentally prepared to handle the rigors of law school. Law school can be extremely discouraging because students receive very little feedback during the school year. Classes are usually graded solely based on final exam scores. Midterm exams and graded papers are uncommon, and classroom participation is often the only way for students to ascertain if they understand the material and are employing effective study methods. As a result, a winning attitude is critical to success in law school. Faith in yourself will help you continue to make the personal sacrifices during the first year that you need to make to succeed in law school, even when the rewards are not immediately apparent.

Incoming law students should begin preparing for law school during the summer prior to first year, and preparation exercises should be aimed at gaining a general understanding of what law school is all about. A solid understanding of what you are expected to learn during the first year will give you the information you need to develop both your strategy for success and the confidence you need to succeed. There are several books on the market that can help in this regard, but those students who are best prepared often attend Law Preview's one-week intensive preparatory course specifically designed to teach beginning law students the strategies for academic success.

What factors contribute to academic success in law school?

Academic success means one thing in law school—exam success. The grades that you receive, particularly during the first year, will be determined almost exclusively by the scores you receive on your final exams. Occasionally, a professor may add a few points for class participation, but that is rare. In most classes, your final exam will consist of a three- or four-hour written examination at the end of the semester or—if the course is two semesters long—at the end of the year. The amount of material you must master for each final exam will simply dwarf that of any undergraduate exam you have ever taken. The hope that you can "cram" a semester's worth of information into a one-week reading period is pure fantasy and one that will surely lead to disappointing grades. The focus of your efforts from day one should be success on your final exams. Don't get bogged down in class preparation or in perfecting a course outline if it will not result in some discernible improvement in your exam performance. All of your efforts should be directed at improving your exam performance in some way. It's as simple as that.

What skills are typically tested on law school exams?

Law school exams usually test three different skills: (1) the ability to accurately identify legal issues, (2) the ability to recall the relevant law with speed, and (3) the ability to apply the law to the facts efficiently and skillfully. The proper approach for developing these skills differs, depending on the substantive area of law in question and whether your exam is open book or closed book.

Identifying legal issues is commonly known as issue spotting. On most of your exams, you will be given complex, hypothetical fact patterns. From the facts you are given, you must identify the particular legal issues that need to be addressed. This is a difficult skill to perfect and can only be developed through practice. The best way to develop issue-spotting skills is by taking practice exams. For each of your classes, during the first half of the semester, you should collect all of the available exams that were given by your professor in the past. Take all of these exams under simulated exam conditions—find an open classroom, get some blue books, time yourself, and take the exams with friends so that you can review them afterward. It is also helpful for you to practice any legal problems you were given during the semester. Spotting issues is an important skill for all lawyers to develop. Lawyers utilize this skill on a daily basis when they listen to their clients' stories and are asked to point out places where legal issues might arise.

The ability to recall the law with speed is also very important and frequently tested. On all of your exams, you will be given a series of legal problems, and for each problem you will usually be required to provide the relevant substantive law and apply it to the facts of the problem. Your ability to recall the law with speed is critical because, in most classes, you will be under time constraints to answer all of the problems. The faster you recall the law, the more problems you will complete and the more time you will have to spend on demonstrating your analytical skills. For courses with closed-book exams, this means straight memorization or the use of memory recall devices, such as mnemonics. Do not be passive about learning the law— repeatedly reviewing your outline is not enough. You must actively learn the law by studying definitions and using memory-assistance devices like flash cards. When you have become exceedingly familiar with your flash cards, rewrite them so as to test your memory of different words. This is particularly critical for courses such as torts and criminal law where you must learn a series of definitions with multiple elements. For courses with open-book exams, this means developing an index for your outline that will enable you to locate the relevant law quickly. Create a cover page for your outline that lists the page number for each substantive subtopic. This will help you get there without any undue delay.

The final skill you need to develop is the ability to apply the law to the facts efficiently and skillfully. On your exams, once you have correctly identified the relevant issue and stated the relevant law, you must engage in a discussion of how the law applies to the facts that have been given. The ability to engage in such a discussion is best developed by taking practice exams. When you are practicing this skill, you should focus on efficiency. Try to focus on the essential facts, and do not engage in irrelevant discussions that will waste your energy and your professor's time.

Books About Doing Well in Law School

Getting to Maybe: How to Excel on Law School Exams, Professors Jeremy Paul and Michael Fischl

This book is excellent! While many books and professors may preach "IRAC"—Issue, Rule, Application, Conclusion—as a way of structuring exam answers, *Getting to Maybe* rightly points out that such advice does not help students correctly identify legal issues or master the intricacies of legal analysis.

Law School Confidential: A Complete Guide to the Law School Experience (Second Edition), Robert H. Miller, Esq.

Robert H. Miller, a former federal judicial clerk, Law Review editor, and graduate of University of Pennsylvania Law School, covers every aspect of the law school experience in thoughtful detail. Whether you are a college student just starting to think about law school, a student in the midst of law school applications, or someone who has already been admitted, Law School Confidential is a book you should not be without. An extensive new chapter is devoted to an exclusive one-on-one interview with Dean of Admissions Richard Geiger of the Cornell Law School, wherein closely guarded secrets of the increasingly competitive admissions process are discussed openly for the first time anywhere. In another chapter, Miller goes one-on-one with the hiring partners of two prestigious U.S. law firms about how to succeed in the hiring process, and what it takes to make it to partnership.

Any final comments for our audience of aspiring law students?

The study of law is a wonderful and noble pursuit, one that I thoroughly enjoyed. Law school is not easy, however, and proper preparation can give you a firm foundation for success. I invite you to visit our website (lawpreview.barbri.com) and contact us with any questions (888-PREP-YOU).

CHAPTER 12
CAREER MATTERS

Okay, it's a long time away, but you really ought to be thinking about your professional career beyond law school from day one, especially if your goal is to practice with a major law firm. What stands between you and a job as an associate, the entry-level position at one of these firms, is a three-stage evaluation: first, a review of your résumé, including your grades and work experience; second, an on-campus interview; and last, one or more call-back interviews at the firm's offices. It's a fairly intimidating ordeal, but there are a few ways to reduce the anxiety and enhance your chances of landing a great job.

YOUR RÉSUMÉ

The first thing recruiters tend to notice after your name is the name of the law school you attend. Tacky, but true. Perhaps the greatest misconception among law students, however, is that hiring decisions are based largely upon your school's prestige. All those rankings perpetuate this myth. To be sure, there are a handful of schools with reputations above all others, and students who excel at these schools are in great demand. But you are equally well situated, if not better off, applying from the top of your class at a strong, less prestigious law school class than from the bottom half of a Top Ten law school class.

FIRST-YEAR GRADES ARE THE WHOLE ENCHILADA

Fair or not, the first year of law school will unduly influence your legal future. It's vital that you hit the ground running because law school grades are *the* critical factor in recruitment. An even harsher reality is that *first-year grades are by far the most critical in the hiring process.* Decisions about who gets which plum summer jobs are generally handed down before students take a single second-year exam. Consequently, you're left with exactly *no* time to adjust to law school life and little chance to improve your transcript if you don't come out on top as a first-year student.

WORK EXPERIENCE

If you're applying to law school right out of college, chances are your most significant work experience has been a summer job. Recruiters don't expect you to have spent these months writing Supreme Court decisions. They are generally satisfied if you show that you have worked diligently and seriously at each opportunity. Students who took a year or more off after college obviously have more opportunities to impress but also more of a burden to demonstrate diligence and seriousness.

Work experience in the legal industry—clerkships and paralegal jobs for instance—can be excellent sources of professional development. They are fairly common positions among job applicants, though, so don't feel you have to pursue one of these routes just to show your commitment to the law. You'll make a better impression by working in an industry in which you would like to specialize (e.g., a prospective securities lawyer summering with an investment bank).

Making Law Review

Every law school has an academic periodical called Law Review, produced and edited by law students. It contains articles about various aspects of law—mostly written by professors. While some schools sponsor more than one Law Review, there is generally one that is more prestigious than all the others. In order to "make" Law Review, you will have to finish the all-important first year at (or very, very near) the top of your class or write an article that will be judged by the existing members of the Law Review. You might have to do both. Making Law Review is probably the easiest way to guarantee yourself a job at a blue-chip firm, working for a judge, or in academia. In all honesty, it is a credential you will proudly carry for the rest of your life.

A Couple Good Books

If you are thinking about law school, here are a few books you might find interesting:

The Princeton Review's Law School Essays That Made a Difference

Check out successful essays written for an assortment of selective schools.

Jeff Deaver, The Complete Law School Companion: How to Excel at America's Most Demanding Post-Graduate Curriculum

This straightforward law school survival guide gives excellent advice on how to brief cases, sample briefs, survive class, and plenty more.

THE INTERVIEWS

There are as many right approaches to an interview as there are interviewers. That observation provides little comfort, of course, especially if you're counting on a good interview to make up for whatever deficiencies there are on your résumé. Think about the purpose of the initial 30-minute interview you are likely to have: it provides a rough sketch of not only your future office personality but also your demeanor under stress. The characteristics you demonstrate and the *impression* you give are more important than anything you say. Composure, confidence, maturity, articulation, and an ability to develop rapport are characteristics recruiters are looking for. Give them what they want.

CHAPTER 13
How to Use This Book

It's pretty simple.

The first part of this book provides a wealth of indispensable information covering everything you need to know about selecting and getting into the law school of your choice. There is also a great deal about what to expect from law school and how to do well. You name it—taking the LSAT, choosing the best school for you, writing a great personal statement, interviewing, paying for it—and it's all in the first part.

The second part is the real meat and potatoes of *The Best 173 Law Schools*. It contains portraits of 173 law schools across the United States and Canada. Each school has one of two possible types of entries. The first type of entry is a two-page descriptive profile. It contains data The Princeton Review has collected directly from law school administrators and textual descriptions of the school we have written based on our surveys of current law students. The second type of entry is a data listing, which includes all the same data that appears in the sidebars of the descriptive profiles but does not have the student survey-driven descriptive paragraphs. For an explanation of why all schools do not appear with descriptive profiles, turn to page 59. As is customary with school guidebooks, all data, with the exception of tuition (which should be for the current year if the school reported it by our deadline), reflects figures for the academic year prior to publication unless otherwise noted on the pages. Since law school demographics vary significantly from one institution to another and some schools report data more thoroughly than others, some entries will not include all the individual data described below.

The third part of the book hosts the "School Says..." profiles. The "School Says..." profiles give extended descriptions of admissions processes, curricula, internship opportunities, and much more. This is your chance to get even more in-depth information on programs that interest you. These schools have paid us a small fee for the chance to tell you more about themselves, and the editorial responsibility is solely that of the law school. We think you'll find these profiles add tremendously to your picture of a school.

WHAT'S IN THE PROFILES: DATA
The Heading: The first thing you will see for each profile is (obviously) the school's name. On the facing page, you'll find the school's snail mail address, telephone number, fax number, E-mail address, and website. You can find the name of the Admissions Office contact person in the heading, too.

INSTITUTIONAL INFORMATION
Public/Private: Indicates whether a school is state-supported or funded by private means.

Affiliation: If the school is affiliated with a particular religion, you'll find that information here.

Student/Faculty Ratio: The ratio of law students to full-time faculty.

% Faculty Part-Time: The percentage of faculty who are part-time.

% Faculty Female: The percentage of faculty who are women.

% Faculty Minority: The percentage of people who teach at the law school who are also members of minority groups.

Total Faculty: The total number of faculty members at the law school.

Yet Another Good Book

Scott Turow, *One L: The Turbulent True Story of a First Year at Harvard Law School*

This law school primer is equal parts illuminating and harrowing.

SURVEY SAYS

The Survey Says list appears in the sidebar of each law school's two-page descriptive profile, and up to three Survey Says items will appear on each list. As the name suggests, these items communicate results of our law student surveys. There are nine possible Survey Says items, each explained below. Of these nine, the items that appear are those about which student respondents demonstrated the greatest degree of consensus. Survey Says items represent the agreement among students only at *that particular law school* and are not relative to how students at other law schools feel about that particular Survey Says item.

Liberal students: Students report that their fellow law students lean to the left politically.

Conservative students: Students report that their fellow law students lean to the right politically.

Students love Hometown, State: Students are pleased with the location of their law school.

Good social life: Students report a lively social life at the law school.

Strong sense of community: Students report that their community is close-knit.

Law school well run: Students are pleased with how smoothly their law school runs overall.

Great research resources: Students report that the library, computer databases, and other research tools are good.

Great judicial externship/internship/clerkship opportunities: Students rate these opportunities as excellent.

Diverse opinions in classrooms: Students agree that differing points of view are tolerated in the classroom.

STUDENTS

Enrollment of Law School: The total number of students enrolled in the law school.

% Male/Female: The percentage of full-time students with an X and a Y chromosome and the percentage of students with two X chromosomes, respectively.

% Out-of-state: The percentage of full-time students who are out-of-state.

% Part-time: The percentage of students who attend the school on a part-time basis.

% Underrepresented Minority: The percentage of full-time students who represent underrepresented minority groups.

% International: The percentage of students who hail from foreign soil.

# of Countries Represented: The number of different foreign countries from which the current student body hails.

Average Age of Entering Class: On the whole, how old the 1Ls are.

ACADEMICS

Academic Experience Rating: The quality of the learning environment, on a scale of 60 to 99. The rating incorporates the Admissions Selectivity Rating and the average responses of law students at the school to several questions on our law student survey. In addition to the Admissions Selectivity Rating, factors considered include how students rate the quality of teaching and the accessibility of their professors, the school's research resources, the range of available courses, the balance of legal theory and practical lawyering skills stressed in the curriculum, the tolerance for diverse opinions in the classroom, and how intellectually challenging the course work is. This individual rating places each law school on a continuum for purposes of comparing all law schools within this edition only. If a law school receives a "low" Academic Experience Rating, it doesn't mean that the school provides a bad academic experience for its students. It simply means that the school scored lower than other schools in our computations based on the criteria outlined above. Because this rating incorporates law student opinion data, only those law schools that appear in the section with the descriptive profiles based on student surveys receive an Academic Experience Rating.

> *Law School Fun Fact*
>
> The least litigated amendment in the Bill of Rights is the Third Amendment, which prohibits the quartering of soldiers in private homes without consent of the owner.

Professors Interesting Rating: Based on law student opinion. We asked law students to rate the quality of teaching at their law schools on a scale from 60 to 99. Because this rating incorporates law student opinion data, only those law schools that appear in the section with the descriptive profiles receive a Professors Interesting Rating.

Professors Accessible Rating: Based on law student opinion. We asked law students to rate how accessible the law faculty members at their schools are on a scale from 60 to 99. Because this rating incorporates law student opinion data, only those law schools that appear in the section with the descriptive profiles receive a Professors Accessible Rating.

Hours of Study Per Day: From our student survey. The average number of hours students at the school report studying each day.

Academic Specialties: Different areas of law and academic programs on which the school prides itself.

Advanced Degrees Offered: Degrees available through the law school and the length of the program.

Combined Degrees Offered: Programs at this school involving the law school and some other college or degree program within the larger university, and how long it will take you to complete the joint program.

Grading System: Scoring system used by the law school. (Appears in the data listings section only.)

Academic Requirements: Most law schools require their students to complete some courses and/or programs that go beyond traditional legal theory, whether to broaden their understanding of and experience with the law or to develop important practical lawyering skills.

Clinical Program Required? Indicates whether clinical programs are required to complete the core curriculum.

Clinical Program Description: Programs designed to give students hands-on training and experience in the practice of some area of law. (Appears in the data listings section only.)

Legal Writing Course Requirement? Tells you whether there is a required course in legal writing.

Legal Writing Description: A description of any course work, required or optional, designed specifically to develop legal writing skills vital to the practice of law. (Appears in the data listings section only.)

Legal Methods Course Requirements? Indicates whether there is a mandatory curriculum component to cover legal methods.

Legal Methods Description: A description of any course work, required or optional, designed specifically to develop the skills vital to legal analysis. (Appears in the data listings section only.)

Legal Research Course Requirements? If a school requires course work specifically to develop legal research skills, this field will tell you.

Legal Research Description: A description of any course work, required or optional, designed specifically to develop legal research skills vital to the practice of law. (Appears in the data listings section only.)

Moot Court Requirement? Indicates whether participation in a moot court program is mandatory.

Moot Court Description: This will describe any moot court program, mandatory or optional, designed to develop skills in legal research, writing, and oral argument. (Appears in the data listings section only.)

Public Interest Law Requirement? If a school requires participation on a public interest law project, we'll let you know here.

Public Interest Law Description: Programs designed to expose students to the public interest law field through clinical work, volunteer opportunities, or specialized course work. (Appears in the data listings section only.)

ADMISSIONS INFORMATION

Admissions Selectivity Rating: How competitive admission is at the law school, on a scale of 60 to 99. Several factors determine this rating, including LSAT scores and the average undergraduate GPA of entering 1L students, the percentage of applicants accepted, and the percentage of accepted applicants who enrolled in the law school. We collect this information through a survey that law school administrators completed for the Fall 2014 entering class. This individual rating places each law school on a continuum for purposes of comparing all law schools within this edition only. All law schools that appear in this edition of the guide, whether in the section with the descriptive profiles based on student surveys or in the section with school-reported statistics only, receive an Admissions Selectivity Rating. If a law school has a relatively low Admissions Selectivity Rating, it doesn't necessarily mean that it's easy to gain admission to the law school. (It's not easy to get into any ABA-approved law schools, really.) It simply means that the school scored lower relative to other schools in our computations based on the criteria outlined in the previous page.

# of Applications Received: The number of people who applied to the law school's full-time JD program.

% of Applicants Accepted: The percentage of people who were admitted to the school's full-time class.

% of Acceptees Attending: The percentage of those admitted who chose to attend the school full-time.

Average LSAT/LSAT Range: Indicates the average LSAT score of incoming 1Ls, as reported by the school. The range is the 25th to 75th percentiles of 1Ls.

Average Undergrad GPA: It's usually on a 4.0 scale.

Application Fee: How much it costs to apply to the school.

Regular Application Deadline and "Rolling": Many law schools evaluate applications and notify applicants of admission decisions on a continuous, rolling basis over the course of several months (ordinarily from late fall to mid-summer). Obviously, if you apply to one of these schools, you want to apply early because there will be more spots available at the beginning of the process.

Regular Notification? The official date by or on which a law school will release a decision for an applicant who applied using the regular admission route.

Early Application Program? Whether the law school has an early application program. If you are accepted to an early decision program, you are obligated to attend that law school. If you are accepted under an early action program, you have no obligation to attend. You just get to know earlier whether you got in.

Early Application Deadline: The official date by which the law school must receive your application if you want to be considered for its early application program.

Early Application Notification: The official date on which a law school will release a decision for an applicant who applied using the early application route.

Transfer Students Accepted? Whether transfer students from other schools are considered for admission.

Evening Division Offered? Whether the school offers an evening program in addition to its full-time regular program. Evening division programs are almost always part-time and require four years of study (instead of three) to complete.

Part-time Accepted? Whether part-time students may enroll in the JD program on a basis other than the standard full-time.

CAS Accepted? "Yes" indicates that the school utilizes the Credential Assembly Service. *Please note—the organization formerly known as Law School Data Assembly Service is now Credential Assembly Service (CAS).

Applicants Also Look At: The law schools to which applicants to this school also apply. It's important. It's a reliable indicator of the overall academic quality of the applicant pool.

INTERNATIONAL STUDENTS

TOEFL Required/Recommended of International Students? Indicates whether or not international students must take the TOEFL, or Test of English as a Foreign Language, to be admitted to the school.

Minimum TOEFL: Minimum score (paper and web) an international student must earn on the TOEFL to be admitted.

FINANCIAL FACTS

Annual Tuition (Residents/Nonresidents): What it costs to go to school for an academic year. For state schools, both in-state and out-of-state tuition is listed.

Books and Supplies: Indicates how much students can expect to shell out for textbooks and other assorted supplies during the academic year.

Fees: Any additional costs students most pay beyond tuition in order to attend the school.

Room and Board (On-/Off-campus): This is the school's estimate of what it costs to buy meals and to pay for decent living quarters for the academic year. Where available, on- and off-campus rates are listed.

Financial Aid Application Deadline: The last day on which students can turn in their applications for monetary assistance.

% First-Year Students Receiving Some Sort of Aid: The percentage of new JD students who receive monetary assistance.

% All Students Receiving Some Sort of Aid: The percentage of all the students at the school presently accumulating a staggering debt.

% of Aid That Is Merit-Based: The percentage of aid not based on financial need.

% Receiving Scholarships: The percentage of students at the school who received some sort of "free money" award. This figure can include grants as well.

Average Grant: Average financial aid amount awarded to students that does not have to be paid back. This figure can include scholarships as well.

Average Loan: Average amount of loan dollars accrued by students for the year.

Average Total Aid Package: How much aid each student at the school receives on average for the year.

Average Debt: The amount of debt—or, in legal lingo, arrears—you'll likely be saddled with by the time you graduate.

EMPLOYMENT INFORMATION

Career Rating: How well the law school prepares its students for a successful career in law, on a scale of 60 to 99. The rating incorporates school-reported data and the average responses of law students at the school to a few questions on our law student survey. We ask law schools for the median starting salaries of graduating students, the percentage of graduating students who find employment after graduation, and the percentage of students who pass the bar exam the first time they take it. We ask students about how much the law program encourages practical experience; the opportunities for externships, internships, and clerkships; and how prepared to practice law they will feel after graduating. If a school receives a "low" Career Rating, it doesn't necessarily mean that the career prospects for graduates are bad; it simply means that the school scored lower relative to how other schools scored based on the criteria outlined above. Because this rating incorporates law student opinion data, only those law schools that appear in the section with the descriptive profiles receive a Career Rating.

Total 2014 JD Grads: The number of students who graduated with JD degrees in 2014.

% Grads Employed Ten Months Out: Percent of graduates who secured employment within ten months of graduating from law school.

Median Starting Salary: The average amount of money graduates of this law school make the first year out of school.

Employment Status: A snapshot of what graduates reported they were up to including the number of grads who were holding down full-time and part-time jobs, who were pursuing advanced degrees, who were unemployed, or who weren't looking for employment.

State for Bar Exam: The state for which most students from the school will take the bar exam.

Pass Rate for First-Time Bar: After three years, the percentage of students who passed the bar exam the first time they took it. It's a crucial statistic. You *don't* want to fail your state's bar.

Prominent Alumni: Those who made it... *big*.

Grads Employed by Field: The percentage of students in the most recent graduating class who have obtained jobs in a particular field.

Academia: The percentage of graduates who got jobs at law schools, universities, and think tanks.

Business/Industry: The percentage of graduates who got jobs working in business, corporations, consulting, and so on. These jobs are sometimes law-related and sometimes not.

Government: Uncle Sam needs lawyers like you wouldn't even believe.

Judicial Clerkships: The percentage of graduates who got jobs doing research for judges.

Private Practice: The percentage of graduates who got jobs in traditional law firms of various sizes or "put out a shingle" for themselves as sole practitioners.

Public Interest: The percentage of (mostly) altruistic graduates who got jobs providing legal assistance to people who couldn't afford it otherwise.

NOTA BENE

If a 60* appears for any of a law school's ratings, it means that the school's administrators did not report by our deadline all of the statistics that rating incorporates.

Please note that we target each law school for resurveying at least every other year, which means we rewrite each law school's descriptive profile at least every other year, too. Student surveys captured via our online survey (http://survey.review.com) are considered current for the purposes of our own rating, rankings, and Survey Says items for two years.

WHAT'S IN THE PROFILES: DESCRIPTIVE TEXT

Academics, Life, and Getting In Sections: The text of the descriptive profiles is broken out into three sections: Academics, Life, and Getting In. The Academics and Life sections of each descriptive profile are driven by the student survey responses collected from current law students at the school, and the quotations sprinkled throughout each of these sections come directly from the written comments students provided us with on their surveys. In the Academics section, we often discuss professors and their teaching methods, the workload, special clinical programs, the efficiency of the administration, and the helpfulness of the library staff. In the Life section, we often discuss how academically competitive the student body is, how (and if) students separate into cliques, clubs, or organizations students often join, and the amenities of the town in which the school is located. We don't follow a cookie-cutter formula when writing these profiles. Instead we rely on students' responses to the open-ended questions on our student survey and analysis of their aggregate responses to our multiple choice questions to determine each profile's major "theme." The information in the Getting In section is based on the data we collect from law school administrators and our own additional research.

DECODING DEGREES

Many law schools offer joint- or combined-degree programs with other departments (or sometimes even with other schools) that you can earn along with your Juris Doctor. You'll find the abbreviations for these degrees in the individual school profiles, but we thought we would give you a little help in figuring out exactly what they are.

AMBA	Accounting Master of Business		MEERM	Master of Earth and Environmental Resource Management
BCL	Bachelor of Civil Law		MELP	Master of Energy Regulation and Law
DJUR	Doctor of Jurisprudence		MEM	Master of Environmental Management
DL	Doctor of Law		MFA	Master of Fine Arts
EdD	Doctor of Education		MHA	Master of Health Administration
HRIR	Human Resources and Industrial Relations		MHSA	Master of Health Services Administration
IMBA	International Master of Business Administration		MIA	Master of International Affairs
JD	Juris Doctor		MIB	Master of International Business
JSD	Doctor of Juridical Science		MIP	Master of Intellectual Property
JSM	Master of the Science of Law		MIR	Master of Industrial Relations
LLB	Bachelor of Law		MILR	Master of Industrial and Labor Relations
LLCM	Master of Comparative Law (for international students)		MJ	Master of Jurisprudence
LLM	Master of Law		MJS	Master of Juridical Study (not a JD)
MA	Master of Arts		MLIR	Master of Labor and Industrial Relations
MAcc	Master of Accounting		MLIS	Master of Library and Information Sciences
MALD	Master of Arts in Law and Diplomacy		MLS	Master of Library Science
MAM	Master of Arts Management		MMA	Master of Marine Affairs
MM	Master of Management		MOB	Master of Organizational Behavior
MANM	Master of Nonprofit Management		MPA	Master of Public Administration
MAPA	Master of Public Administration		MPAFF	Master of Public Affairs
MAUA	Master of Arts in Urban Affairs		MPH	Master of Public Health
MBA	Master of Business Administration		MPIA	Master of Public and International Affairs
MCJ	Master of Criminal Justice		MPP	Master of Public Planning or Master of Public Policy
MCL	Master of Comparative Law		MPPA	Master of Public Policy
MCP	Master of Community Planning		MPPS	Master of Public Policy Sciences
MCRP	Master of City and Regional Planning		MPS	Master of Professional Studies in Law
MDiv	Master of Divinity		MRP	Master of Regional Planning
ME	Master of Engineering or Master of Education		MS	Master of Science
MEd	Master of Education		MSEL	Master of Studies in Environmental Law
MED	Master of Environmental Design		MSES	Master of Science in Environmental Science

MSF	Master of Science in Finance
MSFS	Master of Science in Foreign Service
MSI	Master of Science in Information
MSIA	Master of Science in Industrial Administration
MSIE	Master of Science in International Economics
MSJ	Master of Science in Journalism
MSPH	Master of Science in Public Health
MSW	Master of Social Welfare or Master of Social Work
MT	Master of Taxation
MTS	Master of Theological Studies
MUP	Master of Urban Planning
MUPD	Master of Urban Planning and Development
MURP	Master of Urban and Regional Planning
PharmD	Doctor of Pharmacy
PhD	Doctor of Philosophy
REES	Russian and Eastern European Studies Certificate
SJD	Doctor of Juridical Science
DVM	Doctor of Veterinary Medicine
MALIR	Master of Arts in Labor and Industrial Relations

Law Schools Ranked By Category

ABOUT OUR LAW SCHOOL RANKINGS

On the following few pages, you will find eleven top ten lists of ABA-approved law schools ranked according to various metrics. It must be noted, however, that none of these lists purports to rank the law schools by their overall quality. Nor should any combination of the categories we've chosen be construed as representing the raw ingredients for such a ranking. We have made no attempt to gauge the *prestige* of these schools, and we wonder whether we could accurately do so even if we tried. What we have done, however, is presented a number of lists using information from two very large databases—one of statistical information collected from law schools and another of subjective data gathered via our survey of more than 19,700 law students at 173 ABA-approved law schools. We target each law school's student body for resurveying at least every other year. This means that schools' student opinion data is considered current for the book's rankings and descriptive profiles for two years.

Ten of the ranking lists are based partly or wholly on opinions collected through our law student survey. The only schools that may appear in these lists are the 173 ABA-approved law schools from which we were able to collect a sufficient number of student surveys to accurately represent the student experience in our various ratings and descriptive profiles.

One of the rankings, Toughest to Get Into, incorporates *only* admissions statistics reported to us by the law schools. Therefore, any ABA-approved law school appearing in this edition of the guide, whether we collected student surveys from it or not, may appear on this list.

In the 2010 edition of this book, we introduced the Best Classroom Experience list, based on student assessment of professors' teaching abilities, balance of theory and practical skills in the curricula, and tolerance for differing opinions in class discussion.

Under the title of each list is an explanation of the criteria on which the ranking is based. For explanations of many of the individual rankings components, go back to page 46–49.

It's worth repeating: There is no one best law school in America, but there is a best law school for you. By using these rankings in conjunction with the descriptive profiles and data listings of the schools in this book, we hope that you will begin to identify the attributes of a law school that are important to you, as well as the law schools that can best help you to achieve your personal and professional goals.

The schools in each category appear in descending order.

TOUGHEST TO GET INTO
BASED ON THE ADMISSIONS SELECTIVITY RATING (SEE PAGE 47 FOR EXPLANATION)

1. Yale University
2. Harvard Law School
3. Stanford University
4. The University of Chicago
5. Columbia University
6. University of Pennsylvania
7. University of California—Berkeley
8. University of Virginia
9. Duke University
10. New York University

BEST PROFESSORS
BASED ON STUDENT ASSESSMENT OF PROFESSORS' TEACHING ABILITIES AND ACCESSIBILITY OUTSIDE CLASS

1. Duke University
2. Boston University
3. University of Virginia
4. Washington and Lee University
5. The University of Chicago
6. Pepperdine University
7. University of St.Thomas
8. Stanford University
9. Samford University
10. Charleston School of Law

MOST COMPETITIVE STUDENTS
BASED ON LAW STUDENT ASSESSMENTS OF: THE NUMBER OF HOURS THEY SPEND STUDYING OUTSIDE OF CLASS EACH DAY, THE NUMBER OF HOURS THEY THINK THEIR FELLOW LAW STUDENTS SPEND STUDYING OUTSIDE OF CLASS EACH DAY, THE DEGREE OF COMPETITIVENESS AMONG LAW STUDENTS AT THEIR SCHOOL, AND THE AVERAGE NUMBER OF HOURS THEY SLEEP EACH NIGHT

1. Baylor University
2. Case Western Reserve University
3. Nova Southeastern University
4. Campbell University
5. Faulkner University
6. Brigham Young University
7. Widener University (PA)
8. University of California—Hastings
9. Oklahoma City University
10. Widener University (DE)

BEST CAREER PROSPECTS
BASED ON THE CAREER RATING (SEE PAGE 49 FOR EXPLANATION)

1. University of Pennsylvania
2. New York University
3. The University of Chicago
4. Stanford University
5. Columbia University
6. Harvard Law School
7. University of California—Berkeley
8. Northwestern University
9. University of Virginia
10. Georgetown University

BEST CLASSROOM EXPERIENCE

BASED ON STUDENT ASSESSMENT OF PROFESSORS' TEACHING ABILITIES, BALANCE OF THEORY AND PRACTICAL SKILLS IN THE CURRICULA, AND TOLERANCE FOR DIFFERING OPINIONS IN CLASS DISCUSSION

1. Stanford University
2. University of Virginia
3. The University of Chicago
4. Northwestern University
5. Duke University
6. University of Michigan
7. New York University
8. University of Pennsylvania
9. Georgetown University
10. Columbia University

MOST CONSERVATIVE STUDENTS

BASED ON STUDENT ASSESSMENT OF THE POLITICAL BENT OF THE STUDENT BODY AT LARGE

1. Ave Maria School of Law
2. Regent University
3. Brigham Young University
4. Samford University
5. George Mason University
6. Faulkner University
7. University of Notre Dame
8. Texas Tech University
9. University of Alabama
10. Louisiana State University

MOST LIBERAL STUDENTS

BASED ON STUDENT ASSESSMENT OF THE POLITICAL BENT OF THE STUDENT BODY AT LARGE

1. Northeastern University
2. American University
3. University of Oregon
4. New York University
5. University of San Francisco
6. University of California—Hastings
7. University of California—Davis
8. Seattle University
9. University of California—Berkeley
10. Lewis & Clark College

BEST ENVIRONMENT FOR MINORITY STUDENTS

BASED ON THE PERCENTAGE OF THE STUDENT BODY THAT IS FROM UNDERREPRESENTED MINORITIES AND STUDENT ASSESSMENT OF WHETHER ALL STUDENTS RECEIVE EQUAL TREATMENT BY FELLOW STUDENTS AND THE FACULTY, REGARDLESS OF ETHNICITY

1. University of Hawaii at Manoa
2. University of the District of Columbia
3. Southern University
4. Faulkner University
5. University of California—Davis
6. University of New Mexico
7. University of the Pacific
8. St. Thomas University
9. St. Mary's University
10. University of San Francisco

MOST DIVERSE FACULTY

BASED ON THE PERCENTAGE OF THE LAW SCHOOL FACULTY THAT IS FROM A MINORITY GROUP AND STUDENT ASSESSMENT OF WHETHER THE FACULTY MAKES UP A BROADLY DIVERSE GROUP OF INDIVIDUALS

1. Southern University
2. University of the District of Columbia
3. University of Hawaii at Manoa
4. Florida International University
5. University of California—Davis
6. Arizona Summit Law School
7. City University of New York
8. St. Thomas University
9. Seattle University
10. University of New Mexico

BEST QUALITY OF LIFE

BASED ON STUDENT ASSESSMENT OF: WHETHER THERE IS A STRONG SENSE OF COMMUNITY AT THE SCHOOL, THE LOCATION OF THE LAW SCHOOL, THE QUALITY OF THE SOCIAL LIFE

1. University of Virginia
2. Vanderbilt University
3. University of St.Thomas
4. New York University
5. Florida State University
6. Chapman University
7. Duke University
8. Northwestern University
9. Samford University
10. University of Georgia

MOST CHOSEN BY OLDER STUDENTS

BASED ON THE AVERAGE AGE OF ENTRY OF LAW SCHOOL STUDENTS AND STUDENT REPORTS OF HOW MANY YEARS THEY SPENT OUT OF COLLEGE BEFORE ENROLLING IN LAW SCHOOL

1. Arizona Summit Law School
2. University of the District of Columbia
3. City University of New York
4. University of Hawaii at Manoa
5. St. Mary's University
6. University of New Mexico
7. University of Maine
8. Southern University
9. William Mitchell College of Law
10. Touro Law Center

LAW SCHOOL DESCRIPTIVE PROFILES

In this section you will find the two page descriptive profile of each of the 173 ABA-approved law schools. As there are currently a total of 205 ABA-approved law schools in the country, there are obviously law schools not appearing in this section; those schools appear in the following section, Law School Data Listings.

In order for a law school to appear in this section, we had to collect the opinions of a sufficient number of current law students at that school to fairly and responsibly represent the general law student experience there. Our descriptive profiles are driven primarily by (1) comments law students provide in response to open-ended questions on our student survey, and (2) our own statistical analysis of student responses to the many multiple-choice questions on the survey. While many law students complete a survey unsolicited by us at http://survey. review.com, in the vast majority of cases we rely on law school administrators to get the word out about our survey to their students. In an ideal scenario, the law school administration e-mails a Princeton Review-authored e-mail to all law students with an embedded link to our survey website (again, http://survey.review.com). If for some reason there are restrictions that prevent the administration from contacting the entire law student body on behalf of an outside party, they often help us find other ways to notify students that we are seeking their opinions, like advertising in law student publications or posting on law student community websites or electronic mailing lists. In almost all cases, when the administration is cooperative, we are able to collect opinions from a sufficient number of students to produce an accurate descriptive profile and ratings of its law school.

There is a group of law school administrators, however, that doesn't agree that the opinions of current law students presented in descriptive profile and rankings formats are useful to prospective law school students who are trying to choose the right schools to apply to and attend. Administrators at the 32 ABA-approved law schools not appearing in this section are a part of this group. They either ignored our multiple attempts to contact them to request their assistance in notifying their students about our survey, or they simply refused to work with us at all. While we would like to be able to write a descriptive profile on each of these 32 schools anyway, we won't do so with minimal law student opinion. So if you are a prospective law school student and would like to read the opinions of current law students about your dream school(s), contact the missing school(s) and communicate this desire to them. (We include contact information in each of the data listings.) If you are a current law student at one of the 32 ABA-approved law schools not profiled in this section, please don't send us angry letters; instead, go to http://survey.review.com, complete a survey about your school, and tell all of your fellow students to do the same. If we collect enough current student opinion on your school in the coming year, we'll include a descriptive profile in the next edition of the guide.

SPECIAL NOTE ON THE TEXT OF EACH DESCRIPTIVE PROFILE

The Academics and Life sections of each descriptive profile are driven by the student opinions collected from current law students at the school, and the quotations sprinkled throughout each of these sections comes directly from the written comments with which students provided us on their surveys. The Getting In section is based on the data we collect from law school administrators and our own additional research. Every law school with a descriptive profile has its students resurveyed and its profile rewritten at least every other year.

SPECIAL NOTE ON THE SIDEBAR STATISTICS

Explanations of what each field of data signifies may be found in the How to Use This Book section, which begins on page 45.

ALBANY LAW SCHOOL

INSTITUTIONAL INFORMATION

Public/private	Private
Affiliation	No Affiliation
Student-faculty ratio	14:1
% faculty part-time	21
% faculty female	34
% faculty underrepresented minority	10
Total faculty	54

SURVEY SAYS...

Students love Albany, NY, Abundant externship/internship/clerkship opportunities

STUDENTS

Enrollment of law school	475
% male/female	50/50
Average age of entering class	23

ACADEMICS

Academic Experience Rating	**74**
Profs interesting rating	74
Profs accessible rating	77
Hours of study per day	4.01

Academic Specialties

Civil Procedure, Constitutional, Criminal, Environmental, Government Services, International, Labor, Taxation, Intellectual Property

Advanced Degrees Offered

LLM - must be continuously enrolled and complete 24 credits within 3 yrs. LLM for International Law Graduates - must be continuously enrolled and complete 24 credits within 3 yrs. For those on an F1 visa - full time, 1 yr. MS in Legal Studies

Combined Degrees Offered

JD, 3 yrs; JD/MBA 3.5–4 yrs; JD/MPA 3.5–4 yrs; JD/MSW 3.5–4 yrs; JD/MRP 3.5–4 yrs; JD/MPP 3.5–4 yrs; LLM 1–3 yrs; LLM for International Law Graduates 1 yr.

Academics

Students come to Albany Law School for a variety of reasons, and in particular they praise the potential for great "internship opportunities," "recreational opportunities," and the "availability of joint degree programs." In addition to access to "clinical experience and pro bono work," a lot of students chose to attend Albany because of the scholarships, "merit-based aid" and the opportunity to attend part-time. Law students can expect a "great experience, and pretty good facilities," staffed with "faculty and administration [who] want people to succeed." Being in Albany is also huge asset: "As a small private school in New York, its biggest advantage is prepar[ing] students to become New York lawyers and pass the New York State bar." Another student echoes that Albany is "an ideal location for a legal education." Albany emphasizes a "small-school feel" with "excellent," "knowledgeable professors." Students can rely on the breadth of "practical experience, [and the] availability of local alumni and employers. Students have a range of mentorship and internship opportunities at "various federal and state courts, as well as various state agencies, attorney generals' offices, and [the] legislature."

In response to restructuring in faculty and administration, the school has been rather receptive to student comments: "The administration is undergoing some changes, and it is reflected in the response to student concerns such as bar passage, availability of courses, and job searching." The change has only been for the better, as the students remark, "leadership seems much better equipped to run the school" and the "accessibility of professors has dramatically increased." The students also praise the new Dean, who "is very involved, committed and energetic, and I look forward to seeing the changes with her in charge."

Albany Law students are also proud of their professors, "who are ready to offer all kinds of outside help and assistance to students in writing, job interviews and opportunities, help in course work, independent studies. . . . [They are] a very personable bunch, and generally helpful and enthusiastic."

Life

Proximity to the main legislative buildings and a center of the judicial process is a big part in Albany's success in finding great applicants, or as students will attest: "Location, location, location." The program is mostly made up of New York residents, who account for 82 percent of the study body. There's a huge benefit to being "in the center of the state government of one of the most influential and progressive state governments in the country."

Students take classes in two buildings. One student laments the lack of "central area" for all the students to congregate, but others point out that Albany Law is in a rigorous environment in a thriving city filled with other schools and activities. One student pointed out that "areas around the capital are really beautiful, clean and fun."

NADIA CASTRIOTA, ASSISTANT DEAN AND DIRECTOR OF ADMISSIONS
80 NEW SCOTLAND AVENUE, ALBANY, NY 12208
TEL: 518-445-2361 • FAX: 518-445-2369
E-MAIL: ADMISSIONS@ALBANYLAW.EDU • WEBSITE: WWW.ALBANYLAW.EDU

New students will find that if they live downtown, near campus, "there is always something going on." Even so, another student cautions future applicants: "If coming from New York City, this may seem like a small city. . . . There are multiple graduate schools in the area, creating an atmosphere where there are a lot of social young adults." Students bond in an "environment . . . that is it competitive, but not cutthroat. Students are interested to help others out, but at the same time work to be the best they can be."

As for experiences after graduation, students point out, "if you come to this school and do really well, the opportunities are endless, the alumni network is expansive, and you will not have to worry about getting a job." The professors and administrators go out of their way to remain open and available to students: "Their doors are always open and they are quick to respond to phone calls." The school has taken a lot of student comments to heart and has made a huge effort to refocus on helping their students prepare for the future, with a "big concentration on training students to enter the job market."

Another student is grateful for the real-life experience, as they would "draft court memos, interview witnesses, and represent multiple clients in family court and administrative proceedings through the school's clinic program." "For practical experience," they said, "It doesn't get much better than that."

Getting In

Albany Law School accepts a range of qualified applications with strong academic backgrounds. The Admissions office reviews LSAT scores and undergraduate GPAs. The median GPA for recently accepted students is 3.51. Student recently admitted at the 25th percentile have LSAT scores of 148, and those admitted at the 75th percentile have LSAT scores of 154.

Clinical program required	No
Legal writing course requirement	Yes
Legal methods course requirement	Yes
Legal research course requirement	Yes
Moot court requirement	No
Public interest law requirement	No

ADMISSIONS

Selectivity Rating	76
# applications received	964
% acceptees attending	12
Median LSAT	151
LSAT Range (25th to 75th percentile)	148–154
Median undergrad GPA	3.51
Application fee	$70
Regular application deadline	3/1
Transfer students accepted	Yes
Evening division offered	No
Part-time accepted	No
CAS accepted	Yes

International Students

TOEFL required of international students.	Yes

FINANCIAL FACTS

Annual tuition (in-state/ out-of-state)	$43,248
Books and supplies	$1,050
Fees	$150
% first-year students receiving some sort of aid	98
% all students receiving some sort of aid	90
% of aid that is merit based	100
% receiving scholarships	67
Average grant	$20,629
Average loan	$35,918
Average total aid package	$47,737
Average debt	$125,048

EMPLOYMENT INFORMATION

Career Rating	86	**Prominent Alumni**
Total 2014 JD Grads	204	Thomas Vilsack, Secretary US Agriculture;
% for whom you have useable information	34	former Governor of Iowa; Richard D. Parsons, Former Chairman Citibank; for-
# employed full-time	163	mer CEO AOL Time Warner; Andrew
# employed part-time	5	Cuomo, Governor of New York State;
# employed bar required	129	David Beier, VP of Global Government
# employed JD preferred	32	Affairs of Amgen; Victoria Graffeo, Former
# employed professional/other	3	Assoc. Justice, New York State Court of
# employed non-professional	3	Appeals
# pursuing advanced degree	2	**Grads Employed by Field (%)**
# unemployed and seeking employment	21	Academic (0)
		Business/Industry (22)
# not seeking employment	1	Government (27)
% grads employed by school	0	Judicial Clerkship (2)
State for bar exam	NY	Private Practice (48)
Pass rate for first-time bar	81.5	Public Interest (7)

AMERICAN UNIVERSITY
WASHINGTON COLLEGE OF LAW

INSTITUTIONAL INFORMATION

Public/private	Private
Student-faculty ratio	11:1
% faculty part-time	66
% faculty female	39
% faculty underrepresented minority	13
Total faculty	282

SURVEY SAYS...
Abundant externship/internship/clerkship opportunities, Liberal students

STUDENTS

Enrollment of law school	1,367
% male/female	41/59
% part-time	18
% underrepresented minority	36
% international	4
Average age of entering class	24

ACADEMICS

Academic Experience Rating	85
Profs interesting rating	84
Profs accessible rating	83
Hours of study per day	4.33

Academic Specialties
Commercial, Constitutional, Corporation Securities, Criminal, Environmental, Government Services, Human Rights, International, Labor, Legal History, Property, Taxation, Intellectual Property

Advanced Degrees Offered
LLM, International Legal Studies; LLM, Law and Government; LLM, Advocacy 12–18 months; LLM, International Human Rights Law and Humanitarian Law and LLM, Intellectual Property; SJD

Combined Degrees Offered
JD/MA International Affairs, JD/MBA JD/MS Justice, Law & Criminology, JD/MPA, JD/MPP: all 3.5–4 yr programs. LLM/MBA, LLM/MPA, LLM/MPP 2–3 yrs

Academics

Boasting some of the country's top international law programs, American University's Washington College of Law takes a student-centered approach in which students internalize material and gain working knowledge of the law. Professors are "less interested in embarrassing students and cold-calling on them, and more interested in helping students work through nuance in legal theory and practice," and there is an "abundance of opportunities for practical, experiential programs." The centers and offices (such as the War Crimes Research Office and the Center for Human Rights and Humanitarian Law) at WCL "provide students with practical experience all without leaving the school."

The atmosphere at WCL is "encouraging and developmentally oriented, while simultaneously being highly rigorous and constantly challenging." The professors are "experts in their fields," "easily accessible," and "do everything they can to help their students find internships and jobs." Every professor has "a true open door policy" and "is willing to provide assistance with class materials and general advice concerning choosing law as a career." The school offers "a broad array of classes" taught by a list of well-respected legal experts, and there is a great breadth of international exchange and dual-degree programs, including "a rich curriculum of courses" in private and public international law.

A prime location in the nation's capital creates fertile career ground—D.C. is where "basically every heavy-hitting law firm has an office"—and "the adjunct faculty is essentially composed of partners at these firms." For example, the higher-level electives are taught by "former ambassadors and government employees, all [of whom] teach wonderful courses." "I cannot imagine wanting to be an international lawyer and attending school anywhere else," says a student.

WCL also makes "excellent use" of the resources that K Street and the federal government provide in regard to hiring faculty and providing internship/externship/clinical opportunities. The "great legal writing program" helps to imbue the American law degree with a good deal of cache when starting out, but many say that "the Office of Career and Professional Development could be more accessible and energetic," particularly to those students who are interested in niche areas of the law. The school also has a "growing" business law program, and the American University Business Law Review is the first business-focused journal in D.C..

Life

The diversity of the school is second to none; WCL is "packed" with students and staff that "come from all over the world and bring various and insightful points of view," and "you can hear three or four languages easily at any time." The renowned international law and human rights focus means the school is "an excellent venue for important events," and there are "so many activities and incredible speakers every day that it is positively overwhelming." "In less than one year, I have attended lectures by the Swiss Ambassador to the U.S., was seated next to the Cypriot Ambassador to the U.S. while listening to the Lichtenstein Foreign Minister discuss the ICC, [and] attended a panel discussion with three OAS Ambassadors on the current state of OAS," says a 1L.

AKIRA SHIROMA, ASSISTANT DEAN OF ADMISSIONS AND FINANCIAL AID
4801 MASSACHUSETTS AVENUE, NW, WASHINGTON, D.C. 20016
TEL: 202-274-4101 • FAX: 202-274-4107
E-MAIL: WCLADMIT@WCL.AMERICAN.EDU • WEBSITE: WWW.WCL.AMERICAN.EDU

While it's true that "the facilities are not the prettiest," the planned new building (opening in January 2016) "will be a tremendous and welcomed change," particularly since the current law school "is not within walking distance of the nearest Metro station." Students are "generally not competitive with each other," this "definitely very liberal school" as a whole "is very cooperative," with the sharing of outlines and notes a commonplace practice. "The academic environment is nurturing and does not feel nearly as competitive as I thought it would be," says a 1L.

Getting In

Admitted students at the 25th percentile have LSAT scores of 152 and GPAs of about 3.15. Admitted students at the 75th percentile have LSAT scores of 159 and GPAs of 3.54. WCL says that it generally considers your highest score if you take the LSAT more than once.

Clinical program required	No
Legal writing course requirement	Yes
Legal methods course requirement	No
Legal research course requirement	Yes
Moot court requirement	No
Public interest law requirement	No

ADMISSIONS

Selectivity Rating	83
# applications received	4,723
% applicants accepted	50
% acceptees attending	15
Median LSAT	156
LSAT Range (25th to 75th percentile)	152–159
Median undergrad GPA	3.37
Application fee	$70
Regular application deadline	3/1
Transfer students accepted	Yes
Evening division offered	Yes
Part-time accepted	Yes
CAS accepted	Yes

International Students

TOEFL required of international students.	Yes

FINANCIAL FACTS

Annual tuition (in-state/ out-of-state)	$48,662/$48,662
Books and supplies	$7,983
Fees	$880
Room & Board	$15,477
Financial aid application deadline	3/1
% first-year students receiving some sort of aid	74
% all students receiving some sort of aid	77
% of aid that is merit based	50
% receiving scholarships	39
Average grant	$14,231
Average loan	$57,657
Average total aid package	$61,450
Average debt	$145,722

EMPLOYMENT INFORMATION

Career Rating	84
Total 2014 JD Grads	460
% for whom you have useable information	99
% grads employed ten months out	84
Median starting salary	$62,000
# employed full-time	348
# employed part-time	22
# employed bar required	263
# employed JD preferred	85
# employed professional/other	14
# employed non-professional	8
# pursuing advanced degree	14
# unemployed and seeking employment	63
# not seeking employment	4
% grads employed by school	10
State for bar exam	NY, MD, VA
Pass rate for first-time bar	79.0

Prominent Alumni
Hon. Gerald B. Lee, US Dist Court Judge for the Eastern District of Virginia; Kenneth G. Lore, Partner, Katten Muchin Rosenman LLP

Grads Employed by Field (%)
Academic (3)
Business/Industry (10)
Government (22)
Judicial Clerkship (10)
  Federal: (4)
  State or local: (6)
Private Practice (21)
  2-10: (5)
  11-25: (4)
  26-50: (2)
  51-100: (2)
  101-250: (2)
  251-500: (2)
  251-500: (6)
Public Interest (13)

APPALACHIAN SCHOOL OF LAW

INSTITUTIONAL INFORMATION

Public/private	Private
Student-faculty ratio	20:1
% faculty female	45
% faculty underrepresented minority	20
Total faculty	20

SURVEY SAYS...
Diverse opinions accepted in classrooms

STUDENTS

Enrollment of law school	364
% male/female	62/38
% part-time	2
% underrepresented minority	9
% international	0

ACADEMICS

Academic Experience Rating	**69**
Profs interesting rating	67
Profs accessible rating	69
Hours of study per day	NR

Advanced Degrees Offered
JD 3 yrs

Academics

The Appalachian School of Law is a young, private institution, organized in 1994 and given full accreditation from the American Bar Association in 2006. The traditional-looking campus is very beautiful and the library is "new." Wireless Internet access is available and, in recent years, "The technology aspect of the Law School has shown a significant improvement."

Students report that "trial advocacy training," "moot court programs," and other "practical courses" are "first rate" at ASL. The mock trial team "has trounced big names" in national competitions. "the law school's emphasis on practical legal skills has thoroughly prepared me for everyday situations in the general practice of law," says a 3L. "I will graduate and know what to do in a courtroom besides espouse constitutional theory with opposing counsel at lunch." Appalachian also "distinguishes itself from the majority of other law schools by requiring 150 hours of community service." A summer externship is also "required of all first-year students." "The community-service requirement promotes student involvement in law school organizations, benefits the community, and strengthens the reputations of both ASL and the legal profession in general," explains one student. "The summer externship program provides all rising 2Ls with the opportunity to apply the knowledge they gained from first-year classes to real-life situations." There is also a "mandatory alternative dispute resolution requirement," though the school seems keener on this than the students.

The "knowledgeable" and "very approachable" professors here are "down-to-earth people who have a wide variety of legal experience" and "extensive practical and theoretical knowledge of the subjects they teach." Their dedication means that "they are exceptionally concerned with bar passage" and always "available outside of the classroom." "My experience at the Appalachian School of Law has been nothing short of exceptional," confides one student. "The teachers love interacting with the students and are our greatest cheerleaders, mentors, and leaders." "Faculty turnover" has been a problem, though. The "remote location" is "not the most appealing place" for academics to "hang their hats for the long term." However, "the town and area are progressing."

Students tell us that "the greatest strength" of their law school is its "concern and respect for students as individuals." "The administration, faculty, staff, and students have created a community where you can receive an excellent legal education in the midst of the natural beauty of the Appalachian Mountains," explains one student. However, there is a "communication gap between students and administration," meaning that "it often takes days to cut through whatever hidden red tape or underlying ineptness or unwillingness exists." "The administration is very unpredictable" as well. "I realize every new school needs to work out its quirks, but ASL especially needs to do so," gripes one student. Career Services could stand to be "more active," and there seems to be a revolving door regarding deans. "The school appears to promote diversity among our deans with the tenure running about a dean a year," observes a wry 2L.

NANCY PRUITT, ADMISSIONS COUNSELORS
P.O. BOX 2825, GRUNDY, VA 24614
TEL: 276-935-4349 • FAX: 276-935-8261
E-MAIL: ASLINFO@ASL.EDU • WEBSITE: WWW.ASL.EDU

Life

Grundy is a "small community" located near the convergence of Virginia, Kentucky, and West Virginia. "You can't go to the grocery store without seeing another law student." "The remote location of the school" helps to make "studying [the] number-one priority." One student explains, "There's nothing to do but study in Grundy, so I went from a below-average college student to above average," adds a proud 3L. "I will probably graduate with honors. I'm not so sure that's [because] of the law school itself…[or] the general area."

Town-gown relations are strained. "There is some resentment from locals toward law students and vice versa," most agree. "The rugged, desolate terrain" and "isolation" lead students to say that "Appalachian could benefit from more things to do in Grundy outside of law school activities." Students lament that "there isn't a bar or club in the town" where they could "relieve stress and get a drink." (In fact, there is "no liquor by the drink in the county.") "The three-screen movie theater is the most diversion many will get," says one student. That said, people here take a DIY approach to entertainment and "typically find or make [their] own fun to blow off the steam and stress of law school." "A culture of frugal bacchanalia persists in the form of student-hosted house parties." When cabin fever sets in, students take "sojourns" to the nearest bigger cities, "both of which are over the mountains and about forty-five minutes away."

Not surprisingly, "you definitely develop a sense of family with the law school students and faculty." "The law students are a very tight-knit group," though beware as "gossip flourishes" and "everyone's life is an open book." "With scant few exceptions, the student body is Caucasian." Most students would like to see "diversity promoted" at ALS, feeling that "out in town" "underlying discrimination" exists "based on race, sexual orientation, socioeconomic status, and even geographic origin."

Getting In

Appalachian Law School's admitted students at the 25th percentile have LSAT scores of 146 and GPAs of 2.60. Admitted students at the 75th percentile have LSAT scores of 152 and GPAs of 3.30.

Clinical program required	Yes
Legal writing course requirement	Yes
Legal methods course requirement	Yes
Legal research course requirement	Yes
Moot court requirement	Yes

ADMISSIONS

Selectivity Rating	75
# applications received	990
% applicants accepted	46
% acceptees attending	32
Average LSAT	148
LSAT Range (25th to 75th percentile)	146–152
Average undergrad GPA	2.80
Application fee	$50
Regular application deadline	4/1
Transfer students accepted	Yes
Evening division offered	No
Part-time accepted	No
CAS accepted	Yes

FINANCIAL FACTS

Annual tuition	$19,900
Books and supplies	$2,500
Fees	$250
Room & Board	$12,295
% all students receiving some sort of aid	64
Average grant	$6,468
Average loan	$21,372

EMPLOYMENT INFORMATION	
Career Rating	68
Median starting salary	$45,000
State for bar exam	VA, TN, KY, NC, WV
Pass rate for first-time bar	52.0

ARIZONA STATE UNIVERSITY
SANDRA DAY O'CONNOR COLLEGE OF LAW

INSTITUTIONAL INFORMATION

Public/private	Public
Affiliation	No Affiliation
% faculty part-time	53
% faculty female	32
% faculty underrepresented minority	12
Total faculty	126

SURVEY SAYS...

Diverse opinions accepted in classrooms, Great research resources, Abundant externship/internship/ clerkship opportunities

STUDENTS

Enrollment of law school	576
% male/female	60/40
% from out-of-state	27
% part-time	0
% underrepresented minority	26
% international	3
# of countries represented	
13 Average age of entering class	25

ACADEMICS

Academic Experience Rating	**91**
Profs interesting rating	86
Profs accessible rating	84
Hours of study per day	3.61

Academic Specialties
Constitutional, Environmental, International, Legal Philosophy, Intellectual Property

Advanced Degrees Offered
LLM; LLMin Biotechnology/ Genomics; LLM in Tribal Policy, Law and Government; MLS Master of Legal Studies.

Combined Degrees Offered
JD/MBA; JD/MSW; JD/PhD Psychology; JD/PhD Justice & Social Inquiry; JD/MD with Mayo Clinic; Master of Legal Studies/ Master of Accountancy; Master of Legal Studies/MBA; Master of Legal Studies/Master of Real Estate Development; Master of Legal Studies/Master of Taxation; Master

Academics

Despite the Sandra Day O'Connor College of Law at Arizona State University's smaller size—around 550 students—these future lawyers praise its variety of courses, noting that particularly with "the certificate program through the Center for Law, Science and Innovation, it is easy to formally specialize." The broad spectrum of courses "allow students to focus on what they are interested in and develop a unique, individualized curriculum," says one law student, with focus areas in health law, law and sustainability, and international law. Preparation for life after law school comes into play in the classroom as well as with the school's extensive externship opportunities. Praising the "perfect balance of theory and practicality" at ASU Law, one student noted a particularly helpful course that combined the two: "I took a class on Mergers & Acquisitions... with a Wall Street attorney (public M&A) and Main Street attorney (private M&A) where we learned the statutory law and case law while performing actual M&A negotiations with other classmates and writing a disclosure checklist (things only done in practice)."

ASU Law offers two centers and several programs for law students looking to specialize, as well as a clinical program that provides practical, hands-on experience in a variety of settings. In addition to its standard JD program, ASU Law also offers degree programs such as the LLM (Master of Laws), for those attorneys who already hold JDs but want to specialize, the MLS (Master of Legal Services), for students looking to learn about the law but who don't want to become attorneys, and the Master of Sports Law and Business.

Established in 1988, ASU Law's Indian Legal Program, which aims to provide legal education in the area of Indian law and provide public service to tribal governments, is a key draw for law students. One student, noting general strength of ASU professors, says that the ASU Law has "some of the best Professors in their fields, especially in Indian Law." Students can earn an Indian Law Certificate in addition to their JD from ASU Law; the Indian Legal Program helps train students to "effectively engage the representation of Native peoples" as well as educating students in the differences between the legal systems of Indian Nations and state and federal governments.

On the whole, the faculty generally earns high marks—"Most of the professors are wonderful [and a] lot of attorneys and judges from the area teach courses"—but the administration gets mixed review. While some students "have nothing but great things to say about the administration" and say that "members [of] the administration are not only approachable and friendly, they are receptive to questions of all types," others note that "for a small school...the administration feels oddly distant and inaccessible at times" and say students should "expect to get shuffled around from person to person with the administration before you get a straight answer on anything." But students agree on the school's "monopoly on Phoenix job market."

BarbaraKaye Miller, Dean of Admissions
1100 S. McAllister Ave., P.O. Box 877906, Tempe, AZ 85287-7906
Tel: 480-965-1474 • Fax: 480-727-7930
E-Mail: law.admissions@asu.edu • Website: www.law.asu.edu

Life

The consensus on ASU Law's facilities is decidedly negative—"really old," "sub-par," "dated"—but when the school opens the doors to its new location in downtown Phoenix in Fall 2016, students agree that the new digs will be "excellent." One graduating student even says that "I only wish I could stay one more year to experience what this amazing building will have to offer. It's going to be a huge step up from our current law school building in Tempe." Even with the less-than-desirable building in Tempe, "the library is a great place to work and study," with one student praising the "excellent librarians who helped me with many research projects, including locating international legal resources." Students praise ASU Law's "sense of community" and the lack of a "cutthroat environment." Instead, "we are a community here and encourage each other to excel collectively." In fact, in addition to service through externships and clinics, there are student-led pro bono groups that serve children, the homeless, veterans, victims of domestic violence, artists, the elderly, animals, disenfranchised populations, and more, Diversity, both within the student body and on the faculty, is an issue that splits students' opinions. Some say that "minorities still seem underrepresented in both the student body and faculty," while another student notes that "I think the greatest strength of the law school here is that ASU has an incredibly diverse student body . . . I have met different individuals with many different religious, cultural, and economic backgrounds."

Getting In

ASU Law receives approximately 1,500 applications per year and has a roughly 44 percent acceptance rate. Enrolled students at the 25th percentile have an LSAT score of 157 while enrolled students at the 75th percentile have an LSAT score of 163. The average undergraduate GPA is 3.55. If your scores fall in that range, your chances of admission aren't bad.

EMPLOYMENT INFORMATION

Career Rating	**92**	
Total 2014 JD Grads	198	
% for whom you have useable information	99	
% grads employed ten months out	96	
Median starting salary	$60,000	
# employed full-time	188	
# employed part-time	2	
# employed bar required	146	
# employed JD preferred	36	
# employed professional/other	8	
# pursuing advanced degree	4	
# unemployed and seeking employment	2	
# not seeking employment	1	
% grads employed by school	4	
State for bar exam	AZ	
Pass rate for first-time bar	89.5	

Prominent Alumni
Dan Burk, Founding faculty member at Univ of California Irvine School of Law; Rebecca Berch, Former Chief Justice, Arizona State Supreme Court

Grads Employed by Field (%)
Academic (2)
Business/Industry (17)
Government (19)
Judicial Clerkship (9)
Federal: (2)
State or local: (7)
Private Practice (44)
Solo: (3)
2-10: (19)
11-25: (5)
26-50: (5)
51-100: (2)
101-250: (4)
251-500: (6)
501+: (3)
Public Interest (56)

of Legal Studies/Master of Science in Information Management; Master of Legal Studies/Master of Science in Management; Master of Legal Studies/Master of Mass Communication.

Clinical program required	No
Legal writing course requirement	Yes
Legal methods course requirement	Yes
Legal research course requirement	Yes
Moot court requirement	Yes
Public interest law requirement	No

ADMISSIONS

Selectivity Rating	**90**
# applications received	1,410
% applicants accepted	44
% acceptees attending	23
Average LSAT	160
Median LSAT	162
LSAT Range (25th to 75th percentile)	157–163
Average undergrad GPA	3.55
Median undergrad GPA	3.61
Application fee	$65
Regular application deadline	2/1
Early application deadline	11/15
Transfer students accepted	Yes
Evening division offered	No
Part-time accepted	No
CAS accepted	Yes

International Students

TOEFL required of international students.	Yes

FINANCIAL FACTS

Annual tuition (in-state/ out-of-state)	$26,060/$41,058
Books and supplies	$1,888
Fees	$693
Room & Board	$12,366
Financial aid application deadline	3/1
% first-year students receiving some sort of aid	90
% all students receiving some sort of aid	93
% of aid that is merit based	77
% receiving scholarships	39
Average grant	$17,029
Average loan	$38,152
Average total aid package	$42,700
Average debt	$97,431

ARIZONA SUMMIT LAW SCHOOL
PHOENIX LAW

INSTITUTIONAL INFORMATION

Public/private	Private
Affiliation	No Affiliation
Student-faculty ratio	20:1
% faculty part-time	46
% faculty female	47
% faculty underrepresented minority	24
Total faculty	45

SURVEY SAYS...

Diverse opinions accepted in classrooms, Great research resources, Abundant externship/internship/clerkship opportunities

STUDENTS

Enrollment of law school	662
% male/female	47/53
% from out-of-state	48
% part-time	26
% underrepresented minority	48
% international	1
# of countries represented	2
Average age of entering class	30

ACADEMICS

Academic Experience Rating	**73**
Profs interesting rating	89
Profs accessible rating	97
Hours of study per day	4.24

Academic Specialties

Civil Procedure, Criminal, International

Advanced Degrees Offered

JD

Combined Degrees Offered

JD, part-time, 4 yrs; JD, full-time, 3 yrs

Academics

Arizona Summit Law School received provisional accreditation from the ABA in 2007, and received full ABA approval in June 2010, the shortest possible under ABA accreditation requirements. Arizona Summit is the only private law school in Arizona with both full- and part-time programs. Though this lack of tradition means that many areas of the school can still be considered "reactive," students claim Arizona Summit is "on the cusp," and its eventual reputation rests on its performance in the next few years. As of now, the rapidly growing (and somewhat expensive) school seems to be aiming to become a "unique, niche law school targeting nontraditional students with practice ready skills." Indeed, "practice readiness" is something the school not only proclaims it focuses on, but also "genuinely centers most of its activities toward."

"Phenomenal" professors are very devoted to their students and "will work with you on any issues and really encourage excellence." The mix of adjunct and full-time teachers "are very accessible, treat us as colleagues, and devote hours to practical, hands-on applications of the law." Arizona Summit has "great teachers and very high expectations" (including a strict attendance policy and a C curve), making the achievement of the elusive A difficult, but there's ample help available from the "knowledgeable, intelligent" professors, and the school even offers intersession classes, which provides even more class availability. "There are many options for class times, if you are willing to take a night class." "The school's administration could not do more to try to help and encourage students to succeed. Every school activity and function is centered toward student success," says a student.

Though the name of the school could certainly use some rooftop screaming, its strong practical focus on experience is highly employable, which bolsters its reputation among those firms that are familiar with Arizona Summit. The externship programs and Center for Professional Development are well-lauded, leading one student to claim that "more than any other school I researched, it really bridges the gap between law school and a law career." The school has also recently begun small-sized review classes, "which are very informative because they discuss how to approach bar questions."

GLEN FOGERTY, DIRECTOR OF ADMISSIONS
ONE NORTH CENTRAL AVENUE, PHOENIX, AZ 85004
TEL: (602) 682-6800 • FAX: (602) 682-6999
EMAIL: ADMISSIONS@AZSUMMITLAW.EDU • WEBSITE: WWW.AZSUMMITLAW.EDU/

Life

There's a lack of competition at Arizona Summit, due to the friendly, Southwestern nature of the students. "When someone wants notes because they missed class, notes are provided. When someone needs help understanding something, there's always student help nearby. I think the cooperative nature of the student body is a huge asset of this school," says a 3L. Most students are from Phoenix and the sprawling suburbs, and many have come here to embrace a career change. The increased attempt by the administration to gain student opinions is reflected in their recent strides of reaching out to night students to help them to participate in school functions.

Though the school itself doesn't have much of a campus, "it feels like a law school" in its aesthetics. Classes are held in one building located in downtown Phoenix; outfitted with high tech classrooms and common areas designed to facilitate student collaboration. The library is "clean and organized, and the staff is incredibly helpful." Most students have some form of transportation at their disposal but "there is also a light rail and bus system with which people can get anywhere in the city." Social events do exist but typically occur in the city itself. The older average age of students means that many must attend to full-time jobs and families instead of socializing with their fellow classmates.

Getting In

Class sizes have only grown since the school's formation, as has the applicant pool. For Fall 2014, admitted students had average undergraduate GPAs of 2.98. Admitted students at the 25th percentile had LSAT scores of 140 and admitted students at the 75th percentile had LSAT scores of 149.

Clinical program required	No
Legal writing course requirement	Yes
Legal methods course requirement	No
Legal research course requirement	Yes
Moot court requirement	No
Public interest law requirement	Yes

ADMISSIONS

Selectivity Rating	70
# applications received	1,323
% applicants accepted	69
% acceptees attending	29
Average LSAT	144
Median LSAT	144
LSAT Range (25th to 75th percentile)	140–149
Average undergrad GPA	2.92
Median undergrad GPA	2.94
Application fee	$0
Transfer students accepted	Yes
Evening division offered	Yes
Part-time accepted	Yes
CAS accepted	Yes

International Students
TOEFL required of international students.

FINANCIAL FACTS

Annual tuition	$40,822
Books and supplies	$1,500
Fees	$1,934
Room & Board	$11,000
% first-year students receiving some sort of aid	98
% all students receiving some sort of aid	98
% of aid that is merit based	54
% receiving scholarships	54
Average grant	$15,318
Average loan	$62,597
Average total aid package	$77,915
Average debt	$187,992

EMPLOYMENT INFORMATION

Career Rating	82	
Total 2014 JD Grads	326	
% grads employed ten months out	91	
Median starting salary	$60,000	
% job accepting grads providing useable salary information	25	
# employed full-time	269	
# employed part-time	28	
# employed bar required	145	
# employed JD preferred	110	
# employed professional/other	40	
# employed non-professional	2	
# pursuing advanced degree	8	
# unemployed and seeking employment	18	
# not seeking employment	3	
% grads employed by school	10	
State for bar exam	AZ	
Pass rate for first-time bar	54.7	

Prominent Alumni

Mark Boesen (JD 2013), Quarles & Brady, LLP; Melissa Lopez (JD 2013), Greenburg Traurig; Kimberly Suciu (JD 2013), Jones, Skelton and Hochuli; Jessie Tasselmyer (JD 2013), Roig, Tutan, Rosenberg, Martin, & Stoller, P.A.; Julia Guinane (JD 2008), Kercsmar & Feltus, PLLC; Selected 2013 Southwest Rising Satr Super Lawyer

Grads Employed by Field (%)

Academic (4)
Business/Industry (20)
Government (10)
Judicial Clerkship (1)
Public Interest (6)

AVE MARIA SCHOOL OF LAW

INSTITUTIONAL INFORMATION

Public/private	Private
Affiliation	Roman Catholic
% faculty part-time	34
% faculty female	45
% faculty underrepresented minority	3
Total faculty	38

SURVEY SAYS...

Students love Naples, FL,
Conservative students

STUDENTS

Enrollment of law school	269
% male/female	48 / 52
% part-time	1
% underrepresented minority	36
% international	1

ACADEMICS

Academic Experience Rating	**72**
Profs interesting rating	82
Profs accessible rating	87
Hours of study per day	4.75

Advanced Degrees Offered
JD Program: 3 yrs, full-time

Academics

As a Catholic school with a strong commitment to its "mission" and "religious foundation," Ave Maria "incorporates the Catholic faith into classes." Many students choose the school for its "conservative" ideology, and some feel that "Ave Maria may be the only school in America where God and American Values are paramount." This Catholic foundation engenders "a very strong community at our school," and also attracts like-minded faculty, who "all come from the tops of their respective fields:" "Because the school is mission-oriented, some very high quality professors have chosen to teach here instead of a more prestigious school." Many students love that Ave Maria has "built an environment conducive to learning how my Catholic faith informs my understanding of the law, without sacrificing the quality study of the black-letter law." Others point out what they miss in the Catholic curriculum; one student wishes the school would directly confront discussions on "morally repugnant" issues.

Students also appreciate Ave Maria's "small size," which "encourages personal accountability, facilitates smooth registration, and increases access to faculty and resources." "There are few enough students that the instructors actually care if I succeed." With an eye on the future, the school offers "courses that prepare the students for real life lawyering," "which focus on practical skills and focuses on students' success on practicing law and not just on theory." Of course, it's "the superb professors with amazing career experience" who foster this academic environment, and students say the "unparalleled" faculty "are extremely approachable and accommodating," "genuinely want you to succeed," and "are interested in your development as a person and a lawyer."

Notably, Ave Maria moved from Michigan to its present location in Naples, Florida in 2009, and students say the move has resulted in some "disarray" in promoting the school as nationally recognized: "this school needs its faculty and students to push its name on a national scale." There are ways in which the new location works in the school's favor, though; for one, Ave Maria is "the only law school within ninety-plus miles," so "the opportunities for internships are definitely there." The school "is striving to improve the bar passage rate and is making significant progress" after the relocation, partially due to a newly added "bar prep" class; some students believe that more "state specific classes" might also be helpful. Overall, students choose Ave Maria for its "unique educational philosophy that emphasizes the moral foundations of the law, presents insights from the Catholic intellectual tradition, and encourages a broader perspective of the law and its role in society."

Claire T. O'Keefe, Director of Admissions
1025 Commons Circle, Naples, FL 34119
Tel: 239-687-5300 • Fax: 239-352-2890
E-Mail: info@avemarialaw.edu • Website: www.avemarialaw.edu

Life

"The Naples, Florida area is a beautiful place to study," students agree, and the "classroom and campus [are] beautiful" as well. Even though breaks in law school can be few and far between, students love that "the beach is always there for a nice relaxing break". However, some students claim that Naples isn't much more than a pretty face: "Naples is small and the law school is small so if you want a life away from law school, it's not easy to do…there aren't a lot of twenty-somethings." That said, students bond together on campus: "Ave Maria School of Law is a small institution, which foster[s] a true sense of community and purpose." The "rigorous" second semester is notoriously devoid of fun, as students go from "six classes to seven classes." As noted above in terms of the school's improving bar passage rates, student reviews of Ave Maria's locational integration are mixed. Students praise its "close proximity to a federal courthouse, creating many internship opportunities." Career Services was previously described as "in shambles" but during the 13-14 school year, the office increased recruitment activities and participation by over 50 percent. Perhaps, as one student diagnoses, "The school simply needs time to adjust to a new location," and "the bar passage rate will improve as the faculty and students adjust."

Getting In

Ave Maria seems to be settling into its new location, as reflected in its reports that this year about three-quarters of its students passed the bar on their first try. The median LSAT score for its entering class is 143, meaning that if you haven't got the grades or scores for a better-known school, especially if a Catholic education is high priority for you, Ave Maria may be a very solid choice.

EMPLOYMENT INFORMATION

Career Rating	70	Grads Employed by Field (%)
Total 2014 JD Grads	110	Academic (1)
% for whom you have useable information	100	Business/Industry (12)
% grads employed ten months out	60	Government (18)
# employed full-time	60	Judicial Clerkship (4)
# employed part-time	6	Private Practice (30)
# employed bar required	43	Public Interest (0)
# employed JD preferred	12	
# employed professional/other	10	
# employed non-professional	1	
# pursuing advanced degree	5	
# unemployed and seeking employment	35	
# not seeking employment	0	
% grads employed by school	2	
State for bar exam	FL, NY, IL, MI, TX	
Pass rate for first-time bar	63.0	

Clinical program required	No
Legal writing course requirement	Yes
Legal methods course requirement	Yes
Legal research course requirement	Yes
Moot court requirement	Yes
Public interest law requirement	No

ADMISSIONS

Selectivity Rating	72
# applications received	603
% applicants accepted	75
% acceptees attending	19
Average LSAT	143
Median LSAT	143
LSAT Range (25th to 75th percentile)	139–148
Average undergrad GPA	3.06
Median undergrad GPA	3.06
Application fee	$0
Regular application deadline	7/1
Transfer students accepted	Yes
Evening division offered	No
Part-time accepted	No
CAS accepted	Yes

International Students

TOEFL required of international students.	Yes

FINANCIAL FACTS

Annual tuition	$37,950
Books and supplies	$1,500
Fees	$2,186
Room & Board	$13,131
Financial aid application deadline	6/1
% first-year students receiving some sort of aid	100
% all students receiving some sort of aid	97
% of aid that is merit based	27
% receiving scholarships	88
Average grant	$17,707
Average loan	$46,315
Average total aid package	$61,935
Average debt	$132,760

BAYLOR UNIVERSITY
SCHOOL OF LAW

INSTITUTIONAL INFORMATION

Public/private	Private
Affiliation	Baptist
Student-faculty ratio	14:1
% faculty part-time	35
% faculty female	28
% faculty underrepresented minority	10
Total faculty	40

SURVEY SAYS...
Conservative students

STUDENTS

Enrollment of law school	382
% male/female	59/41
% from out-of-state	22
% part-time	<1
% underrepresented minority	23
% international	<1
# of countries represented	3
Average age of entering class	25

ACADEMICS

Academic Experience Rating	**88**
Profs interesting rating	81
Profs accessible rating	82
Hours of study per day	5.80

Academic Specialties
Civil Procedure, Criminal, Property, Intellectual Property

Combined Degrees Offered
JD/MBA, JD/M Taxation, JD/MPPA, JD/MDiv all are 3.5–4 year programs. JD/MD program is 6+ yrs.

Academics

Baylor University School of Law was founded in 1857, making it the oldest law school in the state of Texas. Since that time, Baylor has "developed a justifiable reputation as the best school in Texas," and a program where students "are fully prepared to argue cases the moment they graduate and pass the bar." "In terms of practical legal education, Baylor is second to none," a 3L student says. "There is a heavy emphasis on litigation" and students rave about "the training students receive here in procedure, evidence, and oral and written advocacy." One of the most celebrated parts of Baylor's education is "the required course Practice Court." Practice Court "really teaches you how to perform under stress" and students leave feeling that they "could try a case right out of law school." If there is any downside to the school's great trial practice emphasis, it is that "other areas of law, especially on the transactional side, tend to fall to the wayside." Still, Baylor's reputation is sterling in Texas and around the country. "I had one employer from a large national law firm say 'Baylor students are the only law students I have no hesitation about hiring,'" one happy student says.

Baylor has a reputation as a "Marine Corps" "where fun goes to die." Some students say that reputation is "not true anymore," and others suggest that the "no mercy" atmosphere is "created by the faculty." "However, as a trade-off for the misery, humiliation, anxiety, and relentless exhaustion, I'm ready to file a lawsuit, take any deposition, and walk in to any courtroom and know how to handle myself," one student explains. "While the professors are tough in class, they are very knowledgeable and helpful outside of class" and keep an "open door" policy "when it comes to helping students." "Even the adjuncts are dedicated professors," and "really get to know every student." "However, most of our professors (including adjuncts) are Baylor Law graduates," which leads to "little diversity in perspective." Students do wish for more diversity among professors, including "more women" as professors. "The administration is always easy to contact" and "the staff (cafeteria, janitors, maintenance people) are like family to us." Students rave about the "beautiful" school. "The law library takes nearly half of the building" and "classrooms are very nice with comfortable chairs and very well lit and air conditioned." "I really doubt there is a nicer facility in the country," one student boasts. All in all, Baylor is a school where "the campus is beautiful, the professors are tough but supportive, and the curriculum is challenging."

NICOLE NEELEY, ASSISTANT DEAN OF ADMISSIONS
ONE BEAR PLACE #97288, WACO, TX 76798
TEL: 254-710-1911 • FAX: 254-710-2316
E-MAIL: NICOLE_NEELEY@BAYLOR.EDU • WEBSITE: WWW.BAYLOR.EDU/LAW

Life

At a little under 400 students, Baylor "is a very small school," which makes it "easy to get around the whole school." "The building and campus [are] lovely," and "Baylor Law School has a great social scene." Everyone knows each other here and "no one gets lost. You find your group of friends almost immediately." With the amount of work expected from Baylor Law students, some say that "the social life truly is minimal." Another student says that "even without a great nightlife, Baylor Law students still know how to party...and do." "Waco nightlife has actually improved significantly" in the last few years thanks to "an all-around gentrification of the area" making the town "increasingly more hip." "More and more young professionals" stick around, which gives rise to "new businesses, restaurants, and bars." "I love Waco!" a happy 1L shouts. "Coming from a city with huge congestion and traffic problems, everything [in Waco] is in easy reach."

Baylor Law could be "more diverse" as "the ethnic and socioeconomic backgrounds for most students are very similar." Despite Baylor's "cut throat culture" reputation, most students say that students get along with each other. "There are certainly individual students that carry that cut throat attitude, but those are the exceptions, not the rule," a 2L says. "From what I heard before coming to Baylor I would have expected peer subterfuge to be commonplace," another student explains. "Rather, I have always found that the student body works cooperatively."

Getting In

The Fall 2014 entering class had LSAT scores between 158 and 163 in the 25th to 75th percentiles, with a 160 median score. The 25th and 75th percentile GPA scores were 3.38 and 3.70, respectively. Baylor encourages minority candidates to apply and considers minority status to be a "plus factor" in application review. Baylor operates on a quarter system, meaning you can apply for the Fall, Spring, or Summer class.

Clinical program required	Yes
Legal writing course requirement	Yes
Legal methods course requirement	Yes
Legal research course requirement	Yes
Moot court requirement	Yes
Public interest law requirement	No

ADMISSIONS

Selectivity Rating	89
# applications received	1,816
% applicants accepted	39
% acceptees attending	12
Average LSAT	160
Median LSAT	160
LSAT Range (25th to 75th percentile)	158–163
Average undergrad GPA	3.49
Median undergrad GPA	3.55
Regular application deadline	3/15
Early application deadline	11/15
Early application notification	1/1
Transfer students accepted	Yes
Evening division offered	No
Part-time accepted	No
CAS accepted	Yes

International Students

TOEFL recommended of international students.	Yes

FINANCIAL FACTS

Annual tuition	$50,106
Books and supplies	$8,342
Fees	$2,294
Room & Board (on/off campus)	$10,708/$12,478
Financial aid application deadline	3/1
% first-year students receiving some sort of aid	94
% all students receiving some sort of aid	89
% of aid that is merit based	34
% receiving scholarships	61
Average grant	$26,501
Average loan	$45,975
Average total aid package	$52,527
Average debt	$116,660

EMPLOYMENT INFORMATION

Career Rating	95	**Prominent Alumni**
Total 2014 JD Grads	136	Leon Jaworski, Special Prosecutor for the
% for whom you have useable information	99	Watergate trials; William Sessions
% grads employed ten months out	86	**Grads Employed by Field (%)**
Median starting salary	$70,000	Academic (3)
# employed full-time	106	Business/Industry (10)
# employed part-time	11	Government (11)
# employed bar required	100	Judicial Clerkship (3)
# employed JD preferred	10	Private Practice (57)
# employed professional/other	5	Solo: (0)
# employed non-professional	2	2-10: (21)
# pursuing advanced degree	1	11-25: (12)
# unemployed and seeking employment	8	26-50: (10)
# not seeking employment	4	51-100: (3)
% grads employed by school	3	101-250: (4)
State for bar exam	TX	251-500: (2)
Pass rate for first-time bar	92.0	501+: (3)
		Size Unknown: (1)
		Public Interest (1)

BOSTON COLLEGE
LAW SCHOOL

INSTITUTIONAL INFORMATION

Public/private	Private
Affiliation	Roman Catholic
Student-faculty ratio	11:1
% faculty part-time	32
% faculty female	38
% faculty underrepresented minority	11
Total faculty	119

SURVEY SAYS...
Good social life

STUDENTS

Enrollment of law school	716
% male/female	53/47
% from out-of-state	71
% part-time	0
% underrepresented minority	29
% international	2
# of countries represented	9
Average age of entering class	24

ACADEMICS

Academic Experience Rating	**87**
Profs interesting rating	85
Profs accessible rating	85
Hours of study per day	3.88

Academic Specialties
Civil Procedure, Commercial, Constitutional, Corporation Securities, Criminal, Environmental, Human Rights, International, Labor, Legal History, Legal Philosophy, Property, Taxation, Intellectual Property

Advanced Degrees Offered
JD 3 yrs; LLM, 1 year

Combined Degrees Offered
JD/MBA, 4 yrs; JD/MSW, 4 yrs; JD/MEd., 3 yrs; JD/MA Philosophy 3.5 yrs; JD/MA Environmental law, 4 yrs; JD/MPH, 4 yrs

Academics

The future barristers of Boston College Law School rave that their "academic experience has been better than I ever expected law school to be." The academic facilities "are excellent. Many are state of the art with appropriate media, and some have advanced recording capabilities for lectures/student participation (pending professor permission and advance notice)."

While facilities, the "very nice" library, and "the 'campus' feel with multiple buildings and a courtyard in the middle" all contribute to the "ideal learning environment;" the professors are "the best part of being a BC Law student." Many students cite their professors as "experts" who "focus on teaching practical skills." Possibly more importantly, a transfer student offers that most professors "are great at the art of teaching." The pep of professors who are "excited about the material they teach" is contagious and makes many "excited for class (even when it was at 8:30 A.M.)."

Professors also get high marks for their willingness to put forth "a strong effort to make themselves available during office hours, by appointment, or they have an open door policy." That kind of personal attention is evident in stories from one 3L "After speaking to [my property professor] about my goals and ambitions, she connected me with three of her former students who had taken similar career paths."

The kinds of connections with professors that lead to "helping to find summer employment" or "assist students in job search processes or career-related mentoring" are invaluable when some students describe the career services as making "a great effort to help students, but in this tough job market they can be spread pretty thin." Some students feel the office "runs off the notion that BC law will sell itself in the market." But "there has been a lot of turnover in the Career Services department" recently as well as the implementation of "a '1L Bootcamp' where there are monthly (well attended) seminars on specific aspects of building a career (they included, interviewing, résumé workshops, breaking down the financial structure of law firms, appropriate dress for the legal professional, etc)." Students can always avail themselves of the "fantastic" alumni network that is "very enthusiastic about helping fellow Eagles." Alums "are more than happy to talk" as well as participate in the "numerous panel discussions and networking events with BC alumni working in Boston."

Students speak very highly of the clinical opportunities offered as part of the experiential learning programs. These programs "can be taken advantage of early on" at BC Law. One 2L excitedly runs down their experience as including "a clinic, competed in Moot Court and Negotiations, and volunteered with local organizations, all set up through BC Law."

Living

One thing we hear from BC law students over and over again is "the camaraderie of the student body is a huge advantage." The general consensus seems to be "everyone at school is motivated and wants to do well, but not at the expense of others." There are a few who contend that the "collegial" atmosphere may have taken a hit in recent years. "Yes, we are friendly and outgoing. But this doesn't translate to a 'collegial atmosphere,'" states one 3L. Still, it seems likely that the collegial manner is still in play when another student can offer "a student's computer had crashed a few weeks before finals causing all their outlines to be lost. Within a few hours, other 1Ls had sent over their outlines with notes of consolations and wishing the student luck. That was awesome!"

RITA JONES SIMPSON, ASSISTANT DEAN ADMISSIONS AND FINANCIAL AID
885 CENTRE STREET, NEWTON, MA 02459
TEL: 617-552-4351 • FAX: 617-552-2917
E-MAIL: BCLAWADM@BC.EDU • WEBSITE: WWW.BC.EDU/LAW

The location in the Boston suburb of Newton is viewed as a kind of double edged sword by some. The "remote location really does facilitate student bonding and relationship building, as during breaks between classes, it is not feasible to leave the campus or go home." However, this also means there are "not very many dining options" and "there is no public transit nearby and there is no direct law school shuttle in the afternoons."

The administration is credited as more "approachable and receptive to student input" than in recent years. Students cite initiatives such as a "list of opportunities for improvement" presented to the Dean "who then appointed an administrative advisor to each department to work with students to implement the changes the students wanted to see (for example, more transparency in the exam rescheduling process)." The administration is even open to adding classes! When "only one corporations class was being offered which filled up fairly quickly on registration day, students petitioned the administration to add another section of corporations for those who didn't get in and within a few days the administration had added another section."

Getting In

Only about one in five applicants is admitted to BC Law, but the school offers prospective students some nice application options. The admissions process opens in mid-September and runs through March 15th. Applicants are admitted on a rolling basis. One may also reactivate an application submitted in the previous year by submitting a new application form, personal statement, CAS report, and application fee.

Clinical program required	No
Legal writing course requirement	Yes
Legal methods course requirement	Yes
Legal research course requirement	Yes
Moot court requirement	No
Public interest law requirement	No

ADMISSIONS

Selectivity Rating	88
# applications received	3,717
% applicants accepted	44
% acceptees attending	14
Median LSAT	162
LSAT Range (25th to 75th percentile)	161–164
Median undergrad GPA	3.52
Application fee	$75
Regular application deadline	3/31
Transfer students accepted	Yes
Evening division offered	No
Part-time accepted	No
CAS accepted	Yes

International Students

TOEFL required of international students.   Yes

FINANCIAL FACTS

Annual tuition	$46,790
Books and supplies	$1,300
Room & Board	$11,300
Financial aid application deadline	3/15
% first-year students receiving some sort of aid	86
% all students receiving some sort of aid	86
% of aid that is merit based	60
% receiving scholarships	65
Average grant	$20,000
Average loan	$38,282
Average total aid package	$47,158
Average debt	$74,264

EMPLOYMENT INFORMATION

Career Rating	95	Prominent Alumni
Total 2014 JD Grads	273	John Kerry, U.S. Secretary of State;
% for whom you have useable information	98	Francis X. Spina, MA Supreme Judicial Court Justice; Edward Markey, U.S.
% grads employed ten months out	90	Senator
Median starting salary	$75,000	**Grads Employed by Field (%)**
# employed full-time	238	Academic (1)
# employed part-time	8	Business/Industry (11)
# employed bar required	210	Government (12)
# employed JD preferred	33	Judicial Clerkship (11)
# employed professional/other	3	Federal: (5)
# employed non-professional	0	State or local: (5)
# pursuing advanced degree	4	Private Practice (48)
# unemployed and seeking employment	13	2-10: (6)
		11-25: (4)
# not seeking employment	4	26-50: (2)
% grads employed by school	1	51-100: (4)
State for bar exam	MA, NY, NJ, FL, CA	101-250: (8)
Pass rate for first-time bar	90.2	251-500: (6)
		501+: (19)
		Size Unknown: (0)
		Public Interest (7)

BOSTON UNIVERSITY
SCHOOL OF LAW

INSTITUTIONAL INFORMATION

Public/private	Private
Affiliation	No Affiliation
% faculty part-time	61
% faculty female	33
% faculty underrepresented minority	11
Total faculty	148

SURVEY SAYS...
Students love Boston, MA, Diverse opinions accepted in classrooms, Abundant externship/internship/ clerkship opportunities, Law school well run

STUDENTS

Enrollment of law school	646
% male/female	45/55
% part-time	0
% underrepresented minority	30
# of countries represented	16
Average age of entering class	24

ACADEMICS

Academic Experience Rating	**89**
Profs interesting rating	99
Profs accessible rating	97
Hours of study per day	4.04

Academic Specialties
Corporation Securities, International, Intellectual Property

Advanced Degrees Offered
LLM Taxation; LLM Banking and Financial Law; Executive LLM in International Business Law; LLM American Law; LLM Intellectual Property Law

Combined Degrees Offered
JD/LLM in Banking and Financial Law; JD/LLM in Taxation; JD/MA in English; JD/M.A .in History; JD/MA in International Relations; JD/MA in Law and Preservation Studies; JD/MA in Philosophy; JD/MBA in Law and Health Sector Management; Accelerated Three-Year JD/MBA in Law & Management; JD/MBA in Management; JD/MD in Law and Medicine; JD/MPH in Public Health;

Academics

Among much to praise at BU's seriously competitive law school, students report almost universally that "the dedication of the faculty and administration has to be the greatest strength" of the program. BU was one of the first law schools to admit women and minorities, and continues its commitment to diversity with a stunningly broad range of specialized programs for law students: six concentrations, eighteen dual-degree programs, eighteen study abroad options in both English and foreign languages, a transactional law program, and a fleet of clinical programs and externships in the professionally target-rich surrounding city of Boston. In addition, "the school encourages faculty-student interaction through numerous mentorship and social programs." These, obviously, aid job placement for students in Boston and elsewhere, and while there can be a "sometimes uphill battle to receive the initial offers for summer employment," students report that they're equipped to compete with the best: "My classmates and I are consistently considered the top summer interns at our jobs."

Students appreciate BU's practice-oriented curriculum, including "the great moot court opportunities beyond 1L, with 2L moot court competitions and 3L teams." While BU students have sometimes suffered from a reputation, many are eager to counteract this image: "Some of us were admitted to Harvard but chose BU due to its focus on teaching, its small class size, and its generous financial aid."

Few law schools elicit as much praise from students for both the "top notch" professors and the "absolutely wonderful" administration. "Everything runs very smoothly" as a result of the combined efforts of "the administration and professors," who "are extremely friendly, intelligent, and accommodating." While the Career Development & Public Service Office (CDO) "is still scrambling with the recession/jobs market," it excels at tuning in to students' needs: "I have been impressed by how open they are to feedback—from the Dean down." Similarly, BU's professors, who are at "the top of their field," "love their areas of law, and they love teaching. They go out of their way to be accessible—even offering their home phone numbers." Thanks to a recent $18 million donation from alumnus Summer Redstone, a new building that houses most law school classes opened in 2014, and the renovated Law Tower reopened in Fall 2015.

Boston University School of Law, Office of Admissions
765 Commonwealth Avenue, Boston, MA 02215
Tel: 617-353-3100 • Fax: 617-353-0578
E-Mail: bulawadm@bu.edu • Website: www.bu.edu / law

Life

While BU's graduates are prepared to compete with the best, they pride themselves on avoiding the typically competitive law student portrait: students say BU has "managed to get together a good group of people who are intelligent and competitive but fun-loving and caring." Another reports, "I came to law school expecting to jump into a shark tank, and have been delightfully surprised by the smart, funny, thoughtful students I have found instead." "The community at BU is very accepting and encourages personal growth," many students agree, without sacrificing the "drive of the students." In addition to the demands of law school, some notable BU lawyers-to-be find the time to participate in Legal Follies, the law school's "regionally (some might say nationally) well-known sketch comedy group": "The fact that some students are willing to practice 15–20 hours a week to put on a great show really speaks to the type of people that attend BU."

While they're smart, BU students also resist being characterized as nerds: "Sure we may be the 'bright' kids, but we're not an excessively nose to the book school." The average age upon entrance is twenty-four, but students are anxious to point out that "the community is by no means monolithic and includes directors of non-profits, former Marines, and students that have never gone to a bar review."

Getting In

Admission to BU's law school is extremely competitive, with a high median LSAT score of 163. Each year, BU Law enrolls a class of students characterized by extraordinary academic achievement and diverse life experiences. Applicants whose first choice is BU Law can apply via the Boston University School of Law Distinguished Scholar Binding Early Decision Programs. Students admitted via the binding early decision process will receive a full-tuition scholarship.

EMPLOYMENT INFORMATION

Career Rating	**97**	**Prominent Alumni**
Total 2014 JD Grads	246	Alan Change, Deputy General Counsel, VP
% for whom you have useable		Legal Affairs, New York Yankees; David M.
information	99	Zaslav, President and CEO, Discovery
% grads employed ten months out	89	Communications
# employed full-time	207	**Grads Employed by Field (%)**
# employed part-time	13	Business/Industry (14)
# employed bar required	196	Government (14)
# employed JD preferred	20	Judicial Clerkship (4)
# employed professional/other	4	Federal: (2)
# employed non-professional	0	State or local: (3)
# pursuing advanced degree	9	Private Practice (49)
# unemployed and seeking		2-10: (6)
employment	11	11-25: (3)
% grads employed by school	8	26-50: (2)
State for bar exam	MA, NY, CA, IL, TX	51-100: (3)
Pass rate for first-time bar	94.7	101-250: (2)
		251-500: (8)
		501+: (24)
		Public Interest (8)

JD/MS in Mass Communication; JD/LLM in Asian Legal Studies; JD/LLM in Chinese Law; JD/LLM in European Law; JD/LLM in International and European Business Law; JD/LLM in Finance

Clinical program required	No
Legal writing course requirement	Yes
Legal methods course requirement	No
Legal research course requirement	Yes
Moot court requirement	Yes
Public interest law requirement	No

ADMISSIONS

Selectivity Rating	**91**
# applications received	4,218
% applicants accepted	39
% acceptees attending	13
Median LSAT	163
LSAT Range (25th to 75th percentile)	160–165
Median undergrad GPA	3.66
Application fee	$85
Regular application deadline	4/1
Early application deadline	11/17
Early application notification	12/20
Transfer students accepted	Yes
Evening division offered	No
Part-time accepted	No
CAS accepted	Yes

International Students

TOEFL required of international students.	Yes

FINANCIAL FACTS

Annual tuition	$48,170
Books and supplies	$1,462
Room & Board	$12,620
Financial aid application deadline	3/1
% first-year students receiving some sort of aid	99
% all students receiving some sort of aid	92
% of aid that is merit based	49
% receiving scholarships	97
Average grant	$20,747
Average loan	$37,736
Average total aid package	$47,547
Average debt	$107,850

BRIGHAM YOUNG UNIVERSITY
J. REUBEN CLARK LAW SCHOOL

INSTITUTIONAL INFORMATION

Public/private	Private
Affiliation	Church of Jesus Christ of Latter-day Saints
Student-faculty ratio	15:1
% faculty part-time	37
% faculty female	24
% faculty underrepresented minority	6
Total faculty	115

SURVEY SAYS...

Great research resources, Abundant externship/internship/clerkship opportunities, Conservative students

STUDENTS

Enrollment of law school	427
% male/female	64/36
% part-time	1
% underrepresented minority	20
% international	2
# of countries represented	8
Average age of entering class	26

ACADEMICS

Academic Experience Rating	**95**
Profs interesting rating	86
Profs accessible rating	84
Hours of study per day	4.21

Advanced Degrees Offered

International Comparative Law, one school year

Combined Degrees Offered

JD/MBA; JD/MPA; JD/MAcc; JD/MEd (education); JD/MPP each 4 yrs; JD/EdD (education) 5 yrs.

Academics

Brigham Young University's J. Reuben Clark Law School in Provo, Utah is known for "excellent externship program" and low tuition, which creates a value that "simply cannot be beat." Affiliated with the Church of Jesus Christ of Latter-day Saints, the school "is not nearly as religious or conservative as I was expecting," one student, who also earned an undergraduate degree from BYU, told us. Students would still characterize the school as "conservative," but "debate is encouraged and frequent," and "a growing segment seems to be leaning left, which has likely helped increase dialogue."

Students appreciate that their professors "all have very impressive experience—many having previously clerked at the Supreme Court." Even the 1L "faculty is top-notch," including "a current Utah Supreme Court Justice" who teaches "statutory interpretation in my 1L year." Attending a religious institution, students enjoy that their professors "discuss and bring in religion where appropriate," but that they also "maintain the legitimacy of the academic experience by not drowning it in religion." Faculty create close relationships with students, "handing out phone numbers" in their classes and having "lunch with every student in small groups." These lunch meetings are financed by the school "to foster an open-door policy between professors and students."

Students have also been enjoying "more practical and clinical opportunities" than they had in the past, including "courses for negotiation, transactional law, legal drafting, [and] litigation." In addition, "a robust externship program that allows for more practical experience." However, students say that "the system isn't set up for specializations," and they would like to see "better course offerings." While most students say that "many more graduates go to firms than, for example, to the government," those looking for non-firm jobs find support, too. "Sure, lots of firms come to interview," one student who was pursuing public-sector work said, "but some government offices come as well. . . . The career services office has been very helpful and proactive in setting me up with alumni contacts in government offices." Recent renovations to the law building means that the "law school is slowly but surely improving aesthetically." Yet, "spotty" Internet connections are common, and the problem "is frankly one of the most frustrating parts of the library." The Career Services office is generally "incredibly helpful when it comes to [job leads in] Utah," and students who "place well (top 30 percent) at BYU and reach out to alumni . . . can get into major firms throughout the country."

Life

Students abide by a strict honor code on- and off-campus. "Almost everyone is a member of the LDS Church, and many are already married," which creates a "family-friendly" environment: "Everyone is very nice and . . . there's even a reading room with toys and children's books." But that is not to say that there is no social scene for the school's single population. There is no drinking, but "the singles still get together for sports, movie nights, and dinner parties." This isn't to suggest that there is no social contact between the single and married students. One student explained, "You find your people, and we support each others' lifestyles. I've become good friends with a few of the spouses of my married classmates."

GaeLynn Kuchar, Director of Admissions
340 JRCB, Brigham Young University Law School, Provo, UT 84602
Tel: 801-422-4277 • Fax: 801-422-0389
E-Mail: kucharg@law.byu.edu • Website: www.law.byu.edu

Additionally, "Provo is paradise for the active, outdoor type." Situated "at the mouth of rock canyon," students enjoy "hikes to waterfalls and hot springs," rock-climbing and spelunking, and even "mountain-side paragliding." In the winter months, "this area is home to some of the greatest skiing and snowboarding on earth." One student said that "BYU students are also known for long boarding down Provo Canyon," adding that "Law school is stressful; it's nice to live in a place where you can let loose and decompress on the weekends."

Students are competitive but "because we are religious we are not cut-throat." One student clarifies, saying, "It's very competitive in that the students are all very smart and on top of things, but no one is going to sabotage your work, and everyone is willing to help out if you need notes, have a question." Because many students "have served LDS missions which requires working for the church at like eighty to ninety hour weeks for eighteen to twenty-four months," students "are used to working longer hours." Students say they have no cliques or exclusive study groups. They keep the atmosphere "very collegial and congenial," and "many study groups are a combination of people in the top of the class and people in the bottom."

Getting In

Recently admitted students at BYU Law at the 25th percentile have LSAT scores of 158 and GPAs in the 3.52 range. Admitted students at the 75th percentile have LSAT scores of 165 and GPAs of roughly 3.85.

Clinical program required	No
Legal writing course requirement	Yes
Legal methods course requirement	No
Legal research course requirement	Yes
Moot court requirement	Yes
Public interest law requirement	No

ADMISSIONS

Selectivity Rating	95
# applications received	753
% applicants accepted	29
% acceptees attending	64
Median LSAT	162
LSAT Range (25th to 75th percentile)	158–165
Median undergrad GPA	3.75
Application fee	$50
Regular application deadline	3/1
Transfer students accepted	Yes
Evening division offered	No
Part-time accepted	No
CAS accepted	Yes

International Students

TOEFL recommended of international students.	Yes

FINANCIAL FACTS

Annual tuition (in-state/out-of-state)	$10,950/$21,900
Books and supplies	$1,724
Fees	included
Room & Board	$11,412
% first-year students receiving some sort of aid	92
% all students receiving some sort of aid	90
% of aid that is merit based	35
% receiving scholarships	42
Average grant	$7,388
Average loan	$25,067
Average total aid package	$24,026
Average debt	$57,080

EMPLOYMENT INFORMATION

Career Rating	94
Total 2014 JD Grads	147
% for whom you have useable information	68
% grads employed ten months out	91
Median starting salary	$70,750
# employed full-time	120
# employed part-time	13
# employed bar required	107
# employed JD preferred	24
# employed professional/other	2
# pursuing advanced degree	1
# unemployed and seeking employment	7
# not seeking employment	6
% grads employed by school	5
State for bar exam	UT, CA, NV, AZ, TX
Pass rate for first-time bar	94.0

Prominent Alumni
Mike Lee, US Senator; N. Randy Smith, US Court of Appeals, Ninth Circuit; Jay Bybee, US Court of Appeals, Ninth Circuit; Dee V. Benson, Senior Judge, Federal District Court, Utah; Steve Young, Former quarterback, San Francisco 49ers

Grads Employed by Field (%)
Academic (3)
Business/Industry (18)
Government (10)
Judicial Clerkship (16)
Private Practice (37)
Public Interest (2)

BROOKLYN LAW SCHOOL

Academics

Praising its proximity to one of the biggest law markets in the world, as well as the "very wide ranging" scope of its clinic programs, Brooklyn Law School students enjoy the multiple flexible options the school offers for them to earn their law degrees. As far as rankings go, "BLS knows that it's not the #1 . . . school in the most saturated legal market in the world, and as a result its focus on helping students carve out their niche in something other than Big Law is both smart and admirable." Brooklyn Law also has four academic journals—"a decent percentage of our student body writes for a journal," says one student—and an award-winning moot court program. For those students looking to pursue careers in public interest law, Brooklyn Law offers the Edward V. Sparer Public Interest Law Fellowship Program; Sparer Fellows aim to bring adequate legal services to under-represented constituencies.

Professors on the whole are "accessible, attentive, and eager to challenge students to reach their potential" and students praise the recent appointment of Dean Nicholas Allard, "a great addition to the school [who] has provided much of the stability and forward-thinking that the school needed." While a small minority note that some professors "often lack actual real world experience" or "could use a pedagogy refresher," most Brooklyn Law students "cannot say enough great things about the faculty at BLS," noting that the "faculty members here are the greatest asset of Brooklyn Law." The school's prime location near both the Southern and Eastern District Courts of New York mean that "many judges and prosecutors...work as...adjunct[s]," with one student noting that "I've been taught by academics, public defenders, prosecutors, judges, and niche field experts." Students also praise Brooklyn Law's "vast and diverse alumni" network and school's extensive externship program. The school's clinic program is unique in that students are allowed to take as many as 30 clinical credits, which means a clinic per semester. At Brooklyn Law School, opportunities for students to gain practical experience while attending school include In-House Clinic programs taught by full-time faculty, as well as programs supervised by adjunct faculty at law offices, government agencies, and non-profits. Students also enroll in Externships that allow them to work in both public and private sector placements in the five boroughs and beyond (enrollment in either a clinic or an externship is a graduation requirement).

Students consistently note the need for expanded options for evening classes: "The school should expand and improve its evening program by making the hours more favorable, adding more class offerings at night, and expanding clinics to evening hours." Others note that specific career counselors assigned to part-time students would be beneficial and that Brooklyn Law "need[s] to develop more resources into the part-time program which was, at one point, amongst the best in the nation." The administration in general gets mixed reviews, with some students describing the school as "highly responsive," while others lament the "understaffed" career center, where some would "like more support...especially help geared towards students that want to pursue transactional work, rather than litigation or public interest work."

EULAS G. BOYD JR., DEAN OF ADMISSIONS
250 JORALEMON STREET, BROOKLYN, NY 11201
TEL: 718-780-7906 • FAX: 718-780-0395
E-MAIL: ADMITQ@BROOKLAW.EDU • WEBSITE: WWW.BROOKLAW.EDU

Life

Most students seem over "the whole 'Brooklyn is so cool!' line of gushing" when it comes to location ("look where NYU and Cardozo are located—the shopping and dining options are pretty comparable") but concede that "for the starry-eyed 22-year-old, Brooklyn sounds like the coolest place to live and study." It seems to come down to whether students attend Brooklyn Law directly from college or are part of the not insignificant number of older students or those with families; the latter "feel a little incongruent, but are nevertheless part of the group and are made to feel included when possible." Not all students associate the school with a "work hard/play hard" ethic, or "frat culture," though it's generally agreed that Brooklyn Law students "take their studies (and their Moot Court, and their externships and clinical placements) very seriously." The environment is such that one student was pleasantly surprised to discover that "I've found myself reading and researching and processing the material independently and continuing debate and discussion of the issues with my friends out of sheer interest—and my classmates have done the same." In terms of diversity on campus, according to some, Brooklyn Law's student clubs "cater to the diversity of the students," and there are "many ethnicity/religion-based clubs, as well as political groups and social justice groups."

Getting In

Acceptance to Brooklyn Law is competitive. Accepted students at the 25th percentile have an LSAT score of 153 and GPA of approximately 3.05, while accepted students at the 75th percentile have an LSAT score of 159 and a GPA of approximately 3.54.

Clinical program required	No
Legal writing course requirement	Yes
Legal methods course requirement	Yes
Legal research course requirement	Yes
Moot court requirement	Yes
Public interest law requirement	No

ADMISSIONS

Selectivity Rating	83
# applications received	3,376
% applicants accepted	53
% acceptees attending	22
Average LSAT	156
Median LSAT	156
LSAT Range (25th to 75th percentile)	153–159
Average undergrad GPA	3.28
Median undergrad GPA	3.31
Application fee	$0
Early application deadline	12/1
Early application notification	12/31
Transfer students accepted	Yes
Evening division offered	Yes
Part-time accepted	Yes
CAS accepted	Yes

FINANCIAL FACTS

Annual tuition	$ 1,526 p/c
Books and supplies	$1,300
Fees	same
Room & Board	$23,058
Financial aid application deadline	5/30
% first-year students receiving some sort of aid	96
% all students receiving some sort of aid	93
% of aid that is merit based	41
% receiving scholarships	79
Average grant	$29,810
Average loan	$42,656
Average total aid package	$57,540
Average debt	$114,956

EMPLOYMENT INFORMATION

Career Rating	78
Total 2014 JD Grads	382
% grads employed ten months out	88
# employed full-time	283
# employed part-time	52
# employed bar required	257
# employed JD preferred	55
# employed professional/other	22
# pursuing advanced degree	2
# unemployed and seeking employment	30
# not seeking employment	4
% grads employed by school	9
State for bar exam	NY
Pass rate for first-time bar	84.5

Prominent Alumni

David Dinkins, former Mayor, City of New York; Larry A Silverstein, Chairman, Silverstein Properties (Freedom Tower builder); Barry Salzberg, CEO, Deloitte & Touche Tohmatsu Ltd; Lonn A. Trost, CEO and General Counsel, NY Yankees; Gary Kesner, Executive VP of Silvercup Studios; Geraldo Rivera, Fox News; Matthew Swaya, Chief Ethics & Compliance Officer, Starbucks Coffee Company; Avery Fischer, General Counsel & Secretary, Ralph Lauren; Lee Sporn, General Counsel, Michael Kors.

Grads Employed by Field (%)

Business/Industry (22)
Government (12)
Judicial Clerkship (6)
Federal: (2)
State or local: (3)
Other: (1)
Private Practice (36)
Public Interest (11)

CAMPBELL UNIVERSITY
NORMAN ADRIAN WIGGINS SCHOOL OF LAW

INSTITUTIONAL INFORMATION

Public/private	Private
Affiliation	Baptist
Student-faculty ratio	15:1
% faculty part-time	17
% faculty female	56
% faculty underrepresented minority	12

SURVEY SAYS...

Students love Raleigh, NC, Great research resources

STUDENTS

Enrollment of law school	432
% from out-of-state	19
% part-time	0
% underrepresented minority	10
Average age of entering class	25

ACADEMICS

Academic Experience Rating	82
Profs interesting rating	78
Profs accessible rating	88
Hours of study per day	5.16

Advanced Degrees Offered

JD 3 yr program, 90 semester hours. JD 4 yr, Campbell Flex Program, 90 semester hours.

Combined Degrees Offered

JD/Campbell MDiv 5 yrs. JD/Campbell MBA 3 yrs. JD/Campbell MTWM 3 yrs. JD/Campbell MSPH 4 yrs. JD/NC State MBA 4 yrs. JD/NC State MPA 4 yrs.

Academics

Campbell University School of Law is a small, Baptist-affiliated school in North Carolina that offers a Christian perspective on law and boasts a stellar bar-passage rate. Also, small class sizes prevent you from getting lost in a sea of people. The curriculum is decidedly focused on the actual practice of law "instead of relying on theory." The trial and appellate advocacy programs here are some of the most extensive in the country. "A Campbell lawyer can walk into any courtroom and never feel lost," proclaims a 2L. "Campbell is a hard law school," though. "It over-prepares you," suggests a 1L, "so that when you get out, you are not as surprised as most first-year lawyers." Most professors are dyed-in-the-wool believers in the Socratic Method, so you'll be able to breathe easy only if you've read and actually thought about the assignment for that day. "The pressure lets up after your 1L year," but "course work is extremely rigorous, and the school is not afraid to fail students who perform poorly." Student complaints generally center on the very limited range of available courses. In short, Campbell needs to "offer more electives." Also, the massive number of required courses is "ridiculous."

Despite their hardcore approach, professors at Campbell are generally beloved by students. The faculty is reportedly "dedicated" and "always happy to answer questions." "Professors are very engaged and take time to get to know students individually." "The accessibility of our professors is one of the greatest strengths of Campbell Law," beams a 1L. "Their open-door policy makes it easy to slip in after class to ask a quick question or stay even longer to discuss legal issues." Critics call the top brass "out of touch with reality," but most students say that the administration is "extremely responsive and attentive." "They really strive to make themselves available to the students."

According to many students, the Career Center is "great for the students who utilize it." They say the staff "does an impressive job" and is "much more efficient and effective than at most law schools." Other students charge that this aspect of Campbell Law "is in need of vast improvement." Whatever the case, this school is located "in the heart of the state capital," "a hop, skip, and a jump away from" a bevy of state courts and government buildings. "Externships and internships (though most are unpaid) can easily be had," and there are "hundreds of attorneys within just a few miles" if you're looking to pad your résumé with part-time employment. The "vicious" grading curve is "a hindrance in finding a job," and it's tough "to find jobs outside of North Carolina," but most students seem pretty confident about their career prospects.

Students tell us, "Resources and facilities are fantastic" at Campbell. "There could be additional space for individual study," but the shiny, newer building here is "gorgeous" and technologically "state-of-the-art." Another perk is the fact that "active" state court proceedings "reside at Campbell Law" as well, making Campbell one of the few law schools with a functioning court inside its walls.

Dexter A. Smith, MEd, JD, Assistant Dean of Admissions and Financial Aid
225 Hillsborough St. Raleigh, NC 27603
Tel: 914-865-5988 • Fax: 914-865-5992
E-Mail: admissions@law.campbell.edu • Website: www.law.campbell.edu

Life

Students spend a great deal of time together, and the overwhelming sentiment is that there's "a strong community feeling" at Campbell Law. "The size allows you to form close working and personal relationships, not only with your fellow classmates, but also with the professors, deans, and administration," explains a 1L. "You will never be a number at Campbell." "I am able to leave my laptop and purse in the commons area while I attend class," adds a 3L. But some students say there's "no sense of camaraderie at Campbell Law. According to them, many students "go to school, go home, and hang out with a completely unique set of friends."

Opportunities for meaningful participation in extracurricular activities are reportedly plentiful. Social activities are also quite common. Beyond the law school realm, the local area has a lot to offer. In addition to being North Carolina's capital city, Raleigh is the state's second largest city (behind Charlotte). It's also among a rapidly growing city in a geographic region that has burgeoned economically over the past few decades. The metropolitan area here, which encompasses Raleigh, Durham, and Chapel Hill, as well as three huge research universities, offers very adequate amounts of culture and urban energy.

Getting In

Admitted students at the 25th percentile have LSAT scores in the low-150s and undergraduate grade point averages approaching 3.0. At the 75th percentile, LSAT scores are in the mid-150s, and GPAs are close to 3.6.

Clinical program required	No
Legal writing course requirement	Yes
Legal methods course requirement	Yes
Legal research course requirement	Yes
Moot court requirement	Yes
Public interest law requirement	No

ADMISSIONS

Selectivity Rating	80
# applications received	834
% applicants accepted	55
% acceptees attending	26
Median LSAT	152
LSAT Range (25th to 75th percentile)	151–156
Median undergrad GPA	3.26
Application fee	$50
Regular application deadline	5/1
Early application deadline	11/15
Early application notification	12/15
Transfer students accepted	Yes
Evening division offered	No
Part-time accepted	Yes
CAS accepted	Yes

International Students

TOEFL recommended of international students.	Yes

FINANCIAL FACTS

Annual tuition	$36,500
Books and supplies	$2,300
Fees	$560
Room & Board	$8,500
Financial aid application deadline	7/2
% first-year students receiving some sort of aid	100
% all students receiving some sort of aid	96
% of aid that is merit based	52
% receiving scholarships	51
Average grant	$14,000
Average loan	$26,000

EMPLOYMENT INFORMATION

Career Rating	76
Pass rate for first-time bar	81.0

Prominent Alumni

Elaine Marshall, North Carolina Secretary of State; John Tyson, Judge, North Carolina Court of Appeals; Richard Thigpen, General Counsel, Carolina Panthers NFL Franchise; Ann Marie Calabria, Judge, North Carolina Court of Appeals; Laura Bridges, North Carolina District Court Judge

CAPITAL UNIVERSITY
LAW SCHOOL

INSTITUTIONAL INFORMATION

Public/private	Private
Affiliation	Lutheran
Student-faculty ratio	23:1
% faculty part-time	36
% faculty female	21
% faculty underrepresented minority	14
Total faculty	29

SURVEY SAYS...
Students love Columbus, OH

STUDENTS

Enrollment of law school	683
% male/female	54/46
% from out-of-state	27
% part-time	39
% underrepresented minority	9
% international	1
# of countries represented	9
Average age of entering class	25

ACADEMICS

Academic Experience Rating	**84**
Profs interesting rating	76
Profs accessible rating	82
Hours of study per day	3.53

Academic Specialties
Corporation Securities, Environmental, Government Services, International, Labor, Taxation

Advanced Degrees Offered
LLM in Taxation (1-6 yrs), LLM in Business (1-6 yrs), LLM in Business & Taxation (1-6 yrs), MT (1-6 yrs)

Combined Degrees Offered
JD/MBA-3.5-6 yrs; JD/MSN-3.5-6 yrs; JD/MSA-3.5-4 yrs; JD/MTS-4-6 yrs

Academics

It's a simple fact: Capital University Law School is "an underrated gem." Boasting "one of the highest Bar passage rates in Ohio," a "good practical skills program," "small classes" and "abundant" resources, it's easy to understand how the program attracts so many future JDs. Students greatly benefit from "a strong mandatory legal research and writing program, including a mandatory drafting class for 3Ls." Moreover, beyond the general clinic program, students can take advantage of a fabulous "Foster Youth Advocacy Clinic." Additionally, those prospective students hoping/needing to work while attending law school will be delighted to discover that Capital "offers [that] rare alternative in legal education, a high-quality part-time evening program." Students really appreciate the "opportunity to take courses with people who have work experience gives a unique diversity to course discussions."

Impressively, Capital's faculty is comprised of "scholars who are nationally known in the areas of family, children's, environmental, and regulatory law." Further, a number of professors have "[practical] experience in litigation, negotiation, and public service." Accessibility is another common attribute of Capital's faculty and, typically, they are "more than willing to meet with students out of class when necessary." Students here also find that their professors are "motivated and engaged in the material." Their "love for teaching is infectious" and they continually find ways to be "creative" in the classroom. And, as one sage third-year explains, "the dedicated professors make all the difference."

Students certainly have a difference of opinion when it comes to Capital's administration. As one third-year laments, "The registar's office needs a lot of help." He further elaborates, "[A]lmost every semester I attended Capital, it cancelled classes after I registered. During my fall semester of last year four out of five of the classes I wanted to take got cancelled. This semester, a class got cancelled abruptly, with over eighty students registered, because of 'unforeseen changes in the professor's personal life.'" However, a second-year argues that the "administration is generally quick to address problems," and a first-year asserts that they "make great efforts to accommodate the needs of [their] students."

Life

Capital is able to foster a "strong student community." This can largely be attributed to the fact that it's "not overly competitive, and the students at the school are all friends." As a knowing third-year tells us, "We share notes, study suggestions, even outlines. I've NEVER seen any underhanded or mean competitive actions." While there tends to be a divide between full-time first-years and part-time students, another third-year informs us that "as soon as you hit 2L year (even as a full-time day student) you almost always have to take a night course or two." He continues, "I can't underscore how valuable this is to class discourse, diversity or students, and networking. CULS also has a number of veterans in the night program, which brings the conversation to a whole different level."

CASSANDRA B. JETER-BAILEY, ASSISTANT DIRECTOR OF ADMISSIONS, JD & GRADUATE LAW
PROGRAMS
303 E. BROAD STREET, COLUMBUS, OH 43215-3200
TEL: 614-236-6310 • FAX: 614-236-6972

Outside the classroom, students benefit from CULS's prime Columbus location. Indeed, the program's great reputation and proximity to the capital virtually guarantees "amazing externship opportunities." A third-year explains, "Varieties of positions are available at the Supreme Court of Ohio, the Legislature, Executive branch, numerous agencies, or lobbying organizations." And, given the "current evolving legal market, public service work continues to be one of the more stable practice areas. [Attending] CULS provides outstanding preparation and networking opportunities." Beyond the legal world, students can take advantage of all the great entertainment options Columbus offers—from the zoo and aquarium to NHL hockey, the symphony, opera, and numerous restaurants and cafes.

Getting In

The admissions office at Capital takes a fairly straightforward approach. There's a healthy balance of qualitative and quantitative assessment so expect your undergraduate GPA, test scores, personal statements, recommendations and work history to all be closely vetted and considered. The median GPA for accepted students is 3.14 and the average LSAT score is 153. Therefore, if you're a solid student and a decent test taker you'll likely be considered a competitive applicant.

Clinical program required	No
Legal writing course requirement	Yes
Legal methods course requirement	Yes
Legal research course requirement	Yes
Moot court requirement	No
Public interest law requirement	No

ADMISSIONS

Selectivity Rating	83
# applications received	1,575
% applicants accepted	40
% acceptees attending	41
Average LSAT	153
LSAT Range (25th to 75th percentile)	151–156
Average undergrad GPA	3.21
Application fee	$40
Early application deadline	5/1
Transfer students accepted	Yes
Evening division offered	Yes
Part-time accepted	Yes
CAS accepted	Yes

International Students

TOEFL required of international students.	Yes

FINANCIAL FACTS Annual tuition
$24,795

Books and supplies	$898
Room & Board	$10,580
Financial aid application deadline	4/1
% first-year students receiving some sort of aid	94
% all students receiving some sort of aid	93
% of aid that is merit based	40
% receiving scholarships	40
Average grant	$8,000
Average loan	$23,570
Average total aid package	$28,737
Average debt	$70,806

EMPLOYMENT INFORMATION

Career Rating	82
% grads employed ten months out	95
Median starting salary	$59,849
Pass rate for first-time bar	87.0

Prominent Alumni
David Tannenbaum, Partner, Fulbright Jaworski - Patent Law; Deborah Pryce, U.S. Congress Woman; Paul McNulty, Deputy Attorney General, U.S. Dept. of Justice; Robert Schottenstein, Chairman, CEO, and President of M/I Homes, Inc.; Thomas Baruch, Founder & Managing Director, CMEA Ventures

Grads Employed by Field (%)
Academic (4)
Business/Industry (19)
Government (21)
Judicial Clerkship (3)
Private Practice (46)
Public Interest (6)

CARDOZO SCHOOL OF LAW
BENJAMIN N. CARDOZO SCHOOL OF LAW

INSTITUTIONAL INFORMATION

Public/private	Private
Affiliation	Jewish
% faculty part-time	60
% faculty female	16
% faculty underrepresented minority	9
Total faculty	153

SURVEY SAYS...
Students love New York, NY

STUDENTS

Enrollment of law school	1,022
% male/female	50/50
% from out-of-state	48
% part-time	7
% underrepresented minority	26
% international	4
# of countries represented	20
Average age of entering class	24

ACADEMICS

Academic Experience Rating	86
Profs interesting rating	86
Profs accessible rating	77
Hours of study per day	3.57

Academic Specialties
Commercial, Constitutional, Corporation Securities, Criminal, International, Legal Philosophy, Property, Taxation, Intellectual Property

Advanced Degrees Offered
JD, 3 yrs; LLM (Intellectual Property Law, Comparative Legal Thought, Dispute Resolution and Advocacy, or General Studies), 1–3 yrs.

Combined Degrees Offered
JD/LLM Intellectual Property Law, JD/LLM Dispute Resolution and Advocacy, 7 semesters; JD/MSW, 4 yrs.

Academics

Situated in New York City's Greenwich Village, the Benjamin N. Cardozo School of Law offers students "exceptional practical experience" throughout the city and "a strong sense of community between the students and the faculty." Students find their experience "extremely fulfilling," and praise the faculty as being "near top in their field," "passionate about their own work," and caring "about student progress." These "SCOTUS clerks, Ivy League grads [and] White House [counsels]" "know how to take command of the classroom and effectively teach hard material," so students leave Cardozo having "had an extremely challenging and enlightening experience." Beyond the classroom professors "know most students by name, participate in many out of classroom activities, and are very responsive to student concerns."

The administration earns equal praise, but students note that "there has been a lot of turnover recently in the Office of Career Services." One 3L told us, "Although I was able to find a good job I will start right out of school, I think I am the exception and not the norm." Another current student who expressed concern about the quality of her job prospects told us, "I know many others who worry about getting a job, and I know that career services is, for lack of a better word, inept." However, students are also quick to note "that career services HAS been improving" with several new hires including a new dean and two new career counselors "and has begun forays into firm outreach and programs designed to help students find jobs." For one, Cardozo has launched the Resident Associate Mentors Program (RAMP) through which students work for one year at a fellowship salary at small and medium sized firms in New York. In fact, there is a "culture of prioritizing practical experience" that is "pervasive" at Cardozo. "Between in-house clinics, field clinics and externships," students "gain a broad range of legal skills and interests," and, as one says, "almost every single person I know at Cardozo has participated in a clinic or an externship." Additionally, the Alexander Fellows Program allows students to work "full-time for credit as a junior clerk in the chambers of a federal judge" and attend a weekly seminar "also taught by a federal judge."Other notable opportunities include externships through the FAME Center in fashion, arts, media, and entertainment, the Carodozo Startup Tech Clinic, and the Indie Film Clinic.

Students say "the library, research resources, professional and academic clinics, and access to networking events are all incredibly impressive." However, while "the library is beautiful and overlooks Fifth Avenue," students are quick to complain about its hours of operation and the availability of facilities in general. "In addition to closing prohibitively early on Fridays and remaining closed all day on Saturdays," one student notes, "the building also doesn't stay open past midnight Sunday through Thursday."

DAVID G. MARTINIDEZ, DEAN OF ADMISSIONS
55 FIFTH AVENUE, NEW YORK, NY 10003
TEL: 212-790-0274 • FAX: 212-790-0482
E-MAIL: LAWINFO@YU.EDU • WEBSITE: WWW.CARDOZO.YU.EDU

Life

The law building at Cardozo is surrounded by "record stores, book stores, concert venues [and] thrift stores," and it is only a block away from The New School where students "take advantage of some of the graduate level classes . . . for credit." And the school sits "between Union Square Park and Washington Square Park" with "seventeen subways within very convenient walking distance" that take students to every corner of New York City. There are also "tons of networking opportunities because the school has a wide-range of clubs and activities that provide panel discussions and networking events outside of school." On campus, Cardozo stays as busy as the city: "There are almost always events in the third floor lounge or in the lobby." Some students bristle when these events mean "there is no place for students to hang out/do work" because "the lounge is always the best atmosphere for a mix of studying and socializing." Students say that, "despite the undeniably competitive atmosphere in law school, I had no trouble finding a welcoming group of friends who help me prepare for exams and prepare me with notes whenever I'm absent from class." And when it comes time for the job search, the supportive "environment fostered by its students" comes in handy. One student described the "very rigorous hiring process" at the city's District Attorney's office, where he and "other students going through the same process used each other to help ourselves advance through the multiple rounds of interviews."

Getting In

Cardozo accepts students three times annually, for the fall, January, and May terms, but prospective students can only apply to the program once per calendar year. Recently, the incoming full-time class had a median GPA of 3.5 and LSAT scores range from 157–163.

Clinical program required	No
Legal writing course requirement	Yes
Legal methods course requirement	Yes
Legal research course requirement	Yes
Moot court requirement	Yes
Public interest law requirement	No

ADMISSIONS

Selectivity Rating	86
# applications received	2,592
% applicants accepted	49
% acceptees attending	20
Median LSAT	160
LSAT Range (25th to 75th percentile)	157–163
Median undergrad GPA	3.50
Application fee	$75
Regular application deadline	4/1
Transfer students accepted	Yes
Evening division offered	No
Part-time accepted	Yes
CAS accepted	Yes

FINANCIAL FACTS

Annual tuition	$53,000
Books and supplies	$6,701
Room & Board	$19,700
Financial aid application deadline	4/15
% first-year students receiving some sort of aid	89
% all students receiving some sort of aid	87
% of aid that is merit based	43
% receiving scholarships	74
Average grant	$30,388
Average loan	$42,339
Average total aid package	$56,642
Average debt	$121,644

EMPLOYMENT INFORMATION

Career Rating	89
Total 2014 JD Grads	392
% for whom you have useable information	100
% grads employed ten months out	83
Median starting salary	$62,750
# employed full-time	286
# employed part-time	39
# employed bar required	256
# employed JD preferred	49
# employed professional/other	12
# employed non-professional	8
# pursuing advanced degree	5
# unemployed and seeking employment	48
# not seeking employment	8
% grads employed by school	4
State for bar exam	NY, NJ
Pass rate for first-time bar	85.5

Prominent Alumni
Randi Weingarten '83, President, American Federation of Teachers; Hon. Sandra J. Feuerstein '79, Federal Judge, U.S. District Court, Eastern District of NY; David Samson '93, President, Florida Marlins

Grads Employed by Field (%)
Academic (2)
Business/Industry (21)
Government (13)
Judicial Clerkship (4)
  Federal: (2)
  State or local: (2)
Private Practice (40)
  2-10: (18)
  11-25: (4)
  26-50: (3)
  51-100: (4)
  101-250: (2)
  251-500: (2)
  501+: (7)
Public Interest (8)

CASE WESTERN RESERVE UNIVERSITY
SCHOOL OF LAW

INSTITUTIONAL INFORMATION

Public/private	Private
% faculty part-time	48
% faculty female	35
% faculty underrepresented minority	7
Total faculty	68

SURVEY SAYS...
Abundant externship/internship/ clerkship opportunities

STUDENTS

Enrollment of law school	398
% male/female	52/48
% from out-of-state	64
% part-time	0
% underrepresented minority	18
% international	9
# of countries represented	32
Average age of entering class	24

ACADEMICS

Academic Experience Rating	**88**
Profs interesting rating	80
Profs accessible rating	78
Hours of study per day	4.62

Academic Specialties
Commercial, Constitutional, Corporation Securities, Criminal, Government Services, Health, Human Rights, International, Legal History, Taxation, Intellectual Property

Advanced Degrees Offered
MPP; MA in Patent Practice; LLM in U.S. & Global Legal Studies; LLM in Intellectual Property Law; LLM in International Business Law; LLM in International Criminal Law.

Combined Degrees Offered
JD/MBA(Management) 4 yrs; JD/ MA (Art History & Museum Studies) 3.5 yrs; JD/MSSA (Social Work) 4 yrs; JD/MA (Legal History) 3.5 yrs; JD/MA (Bioethics) 3 yrs; JD/MD 7 yrs; JD/MPH 4 yrs; JD/MS (Biochemistry) 4 yrs; JD/MA (Political Science) 3.5 yrs

Academics

Well known for its professional schools and status as a world-class research institution, Case Western Reserve University's School of Law only fortifies the school's reputation. All students follow the school's unique practical legal curriculum, LLEAP, which one student calls "the greatest strength of our school." This integrated skills program brings together legal theory, leadership, and fundamental practice skills with traditional classroom methods, putting students in the role of a practicing lawyer. Second and third year students have a wide discretion in selecting their courses, and with seven areas of concentration and 10 dual-degree and certificate programs, there are many choices, and there is "not much difficulty in getting into any class you'd like." All students are required to complete a Capstone semester of real-world experience in an externship or the law clinic. The law clinic, which allows students to handle a broad range of civil, criminal, health, and business matters "is the greatest experience I've had in law school," according to one student. It "really increases the value of the classroom experience." "Few law schools mandate so many practical courses, and provide so many elective options in various specialty areas."

Beyond the strength of the academics and the great "breadth of its specialty programs and classes," the school has a "highly respected" faculty that "provide a first-rate legal education," though a few students mention their experience is "lacking in one on one attention." All of the professors have at least a decade of experience in practice, and the faculty boasts attorneys with backgrounds from the WTO, World Bank, and corporate law, as well as "national public sector international scholars." Most professors are "excellent teachers who match up well against the best in any of [the] top tier law school[s]," and "lots of them have written the textbooks and know their subjects inside and out." Many have also moved beyond the traditional Socratic method, in order "to find what works for their subject and students."

Aside from faculty, "the staff clearly cares about the school and the students," and "the school's administration is very accessible and knowledgeable." It "learns from its mistakes...if something isn't working, they try to fix it." Research facilities are also "really amazing," especially "the access to international law information through the War Crimes Portal and through all of the database access in the library." "I worked on a journal and the librarians were literally the largest sources of knowledge I've ever encountered," says a student.

Truly, it is the school's curriculum that shines through for students. One student proclaims, "[It] has allowed me to hit the ground running in my legal summer work." Another states, "[It] provides opportunities that I know other schools don't," such as an exchange program with Chinese law schools and "the ability to extern at an international war crimes tribunal for a semester instead of taking classes." "When I was participating in [the international tribunal externship], I had students from Yale, Harvard, and Georgetown doing summer internships at the tribunals who were very envious and surprised that we had this opportunity to continue on in the fall for credits." Some do say that the Career Services Office "needs to improve its relationship between the school and the alumni" and "to focus on expanding its influence into legal markets such as New York, Chicago, and Washington, D.C." However, nearly all agree that "Case does a great job of giving students the resources they need to succeed, [and] everything else is (and should be) up to the individual."

KELLI CURTIS, ASSISTANT DEAN FOR ADMISSIONS
11075 EAST BOULEVARD, CLEVELAND, OH 44106
TEL: 800-756-0036 • FAX: 216-368-0185
E-MAIL: LAWADMISSIONS@CASE.EDU • WEBSITE: WWW.LAW.CASE.EDU

Life

As the school is housed in a building "a bit too small for the number of students," a lot of courses "have to be offered at night," which is great for adjuncts and people who work. The students are the best part of the school. Case students "aren't competitive, but rather friendly and helpful, and always looking out for each other." In Cleveland, "you make your own fun," so "it's a great environment to study without getting distracted." "You can have as much of a social life as you want. Some weeks, I go out three or four times a week. Other times not at all," says a student. Cleveland itself "isn't horribly dangerous, but you do have to be careful about where you go."

Case has "more than a fair amount of diversity" in this "very friendly, cohesive community," and "there are many students who represent many different communities," with strong student associations for African Americans, Jewish students, and South Asian students, among others.

Getting In

With little over 150 spots in Case Western Reserve's entering law school class, competition is high. While the selection process is rigorous, it is not rigid. According to the school's website, "We insist upon diversity in our student body because we believe that the entire law school community benefits from it." The admissions committee evaluates applicants holistically, "looking carefully at the candidate's undergraduate grade point average and LSAT score as well as other, non-quantitative factors, such as level and difficulty of undergraduate course work, writing ability, and work experience." The majority of students come from outside of Ohio.

Clinical program required	No
Legal writing course requirement	Yes
Legal methods course requirement	Yes
Legal research course requirement	Yes
Moot court requirement	No
Public interest law requirement	No

ADMISSIONS

Selectivity Rating	88
# applications received	1,913
% applicants accepted	33
% acceptees attending	23
Median LSAT	159
LSAT Range (25th to 75th percentile)	157–162
Median undergrad GPA	3.44
Application fee	$40
Regular application deadline	4/1
Early application deadline	2/1
Transfer students accepted	Yes
Evening division offered	No
Part-time accepted	No
CAS accepted	Yes

International Students

TOEFL required of international students.	Yes

FINANCIAL FACTS

Annual tuition	$47,600
Books and supplies	$1,700
Fees	$128
Room & Board	$18,044
Financial aid application deadline	5/1
% first-year students receiving some sort of aid	94
% all students receiving some sort of aid	93
% of aid that is merit based	100
% receiving scholarships	89
Average grant	$29,114
Average loan	$39,949
Average total aid package	$70,372
Average debt	$131,724

EMPLOYMENT INFORMATION

Career Rating	90	
Total 2014 JD Grads	168	
% for whom you have useable information	100	
% grads employed ten months out	90	
Median starting salary	$62,000	
% job accepting grads providing useable salary information	40	
# employed full-time	149	
# employed part-time	2	
# employed bar required	116	
# employed JD preferred	27	
# employed professional/other	8	
# pursuing advanced degree	1	
# unemployed and seeking employment	14	
# not seeking employment	2	
% grads employed by school	11	
State for bar exam	OH, NY, PA, IL, CA	
Pass rate for first-time bar	86.7	

Prominent Alumni
Janet Donovan '83, Admiral, Commander Navy Reserve Forces Command; Mohamed Ibn Chambas '84, UN Special Representative for Darfur

Grads Employed by Field (%)
Academic (2)
Business/Industry (19)
Government (19)
Judicial Clerkship (2)
Federal: (1)
State or local: (1)
Private Practice (42)
 2-10: (20)
 11-25: (4)
 26-50: (4)
 51-100: (2)
 101-250: (7)
 501+: (5)
 Size Unknown: (1)
Public Interest (8)

THE CATHOLIC UNIVERSITY OF AMERICA
COLUMBUS SCHOOL OF LAW

INSTITUTIONAL INFORMATION
Public/private	Private
Affiliation	Roman Catholic
% faculty part-time	115
Total faculty	161

SURVEY SAYS...
Students love Washington, DC

STUDENTS
Average age of entering class	25

ACADEMICS
Academic Experience Rating	**84**
Profs interesting rating	81
Profs accessible rating	82
Hours of study per day	3.27

Academic Specialties
Civil Procedure, Corporation Securities, Criminal, International, Labor, Intellectual Property

Advanced Degrees Offered
JD, 3 yrs (full-time) or four yrs (part-time). LLM degrees offered in Communications Law, Securities Law, or Comparative and International Law. Master of Legal Studies, 26 credits required. A non-JD Master of Legal Studies (MLS) Degree Program is available for part time students in the areas of Intellectual Property, Compliance, Labor and Employment, and General Studies.

Combined Degrees Offered
JD/MA programs in accounting, canon law, history, philosophy, psychology, politics, library science, economics, and social work.

Academics

Catholic University of America's Columbus School of Law combines the professional opportunities and legal resources of Washington, D.C. with the intimate, student-friendly atmosphere of a private law school. Drawing from the surrounding city's large legal community, many CUA professors are "full-time practicing attorneys" with a "deep understanding of their particular field." Here, professors come from "interesting and diverse legal backgrounds," including "younger faculty already making names for themselves in areas like civil procedure, First Amendment conscience protection, and protecting children from sexual abuse." While the school attracts top-notch names, the atmosphere is "warm" and accommodating, with professors described as "intelligent, sympathetic, approachable, and caring." While the JD program is not overly easy, "the emphasis is on creating successful students," with ample support services to promote that goal. For instance, "there is a program for individuals in [the] lower 15 percent of the class with additional lectures, and study technique assistance—they don't let people slip through the cracks." The accommodating culture extends to the administrative offices and staff, too. From financial aid to the program dean, "the administration is very helpful and will address student concerns promptly."

Legal education extends beyond the classroom at CUA, and the administration puts a lot of "emphasis on the school's moot court, arbitration, and trial teams, as well as journals and clinics." Plus, "all of the professors are more than willing and able to help connect students with internships, clerkships, and eventual jobs." Research is also a major component of the academic program, and "the research librarians bend over backwards to help any student who asks." If they cannot find what they need at CUA, the school provides "access to all major research databases as well as catalogs from most major libraries in Washington, D.C. through the interlibrary loan program." When it comes to the job hunt, many would love to see CUA's Career Services department significantly enhanced. A current student details, "While the people working there currently do a very good job, that office needs more funding and larger staff so they can help students learn about and apply for jobs." However, "the connections to government and legislative opportunities" are strong at CUA, and the "very active alumni network" helps students make inroads in D.C.'s legal community. On that note, students point out that the school "focuses primarily on D.C. and government jobs, so if you're a student looking to work elsewhere after graduation, Catholic may not be the best option."

Catholic University of America's religious affiliation is more than just in name alone, and, depending on their own background, students either praise or deride the Catholic influence on their law school education. Prospective students should be aware that, even in strict legal discussion, "you don't get away from that Catholic perspective" at CUA. For example, "the school's connection to the Catholic church prevents student groups from participating in certain activities, and makes some journal-writing topics off limits." Others explain that because of the school's stringent standards, "there can sometimes be trouble in getting outside speakers approved in a timely manner." Excluding religious affiliations, most students are happy to note that the school's Catholic values are wonderfully demonstrated in its "commitment to public service and pro bono" work.

SHANI BUTTS, DIRECTOR OF ADMISSIONS
3600 JOHN MCCORMACK ROAD, NE, WASHINGTON, DC 20064
TEL: 202-319-5151 • FAX: 202-319-6285
E-MAIL: ADMISSIONS@LAW.EDU • WEBSITE: WWW.LAW.EDU

Life

Described as "a great place to learn and study," CUA offers a comfortable campus environment, which also affords access to the many events, venues, and recreational opportunities in greater Washington, D.C. Within the law school, the "facilities are phenomenal," offering classrooms that are "large, technologically current, and well-kept." Per the school's recommendation, "Every student has a laptop," and there is "wireless internet and power outlets at each desk." When students need a quiet place to concentrate, the "vast and beautiful" law library "is well-lit and expansive; and it has a great view of the Catholic University campus."

Taking a cue from the school's friendly teaching staff, "students tend to be much more collegial at Catholic compared with the more cutthroat competition you find at other area schools." This student body is a convivial crew who are instilled with the knowledge that "the people in our classes are going to be our colleagues when we are done with school, so everyone is willing to work together if someone needs help." When they are not convening for study groups, CUA students also get together for clubs, association meetings, and school social events. Among other happenings, "the school provides the opportunity for a vast number of happy hours both on and off campus."

Getting In

When evaluating candidates at CUA Law, a prospective student's academic record and performance on the LSAT are the two most important factors in any admissions decision; however, the admissions committee will also consider other elements of an applicant's history, such as previous leadership or professional experience, letters of recommendation, and one's personal statement. Recent students who enrolled had an LSAT range (in the 25th–75th percentile) of 151–157. Incoming students join the program from more than 28 U.S. states and internationally.

Clinical program required	No
Legal writing course requirement	Yes
Legal methods course requirement	Yes
Legal research course requirement	No
Moot court requirement	No
Public interest law requirement	No

ADMISSIONS

Selectivity Rating	83
# applications received	1,869
Median LSAT	154
LSAT Range (25th to 75th percentile)	151–157
Median undergrad GPA	3.21
Application fee	$0
Regular application deadline	3/16
Early application deadline	11/1
Early application notification	12/20
Transfer students accepted	Yes
Evening division offered	Yes
Part-time accepted	Yes
CAS accepted	Yes

International Students

TOEFL required of international students.	Yes

FINANCIAL FACTS

Annual tuition	$44,900
Books and supplies	$1,500
Room & Board	$17,000
% first-year students receiving some sort of aid	91
% all students receiving some sort of aid	86
% of aid that is merit based	99
% receiving scholarships	60
Average grant	$12,989
Average loan	$46,845
Average total aid package	$49,770
Average debt	$142,960

EMPLOYMENT INFORMATION

Career Rating	73
Total 2014 JD Grads	238
% grads employed ten months out	83
# employed full-time	182
# employed part-time	15
# employed bar required	117
# employed JD preferred	65
# employed professional/other	10
# employed non-professional	5
# pursuing advanced degree	1
# unemployed and seeking employment	33
# not seeking employment	5
State for bar exam	MD, VA, CA, NY, FL

Prominent Alumni
Robert Casey, US Senator, Pennsylvania; Michael Bidwill, President, Arizona Cardinals NFL Team; Charlene Barshefsky, (former) US Trade Ambassador; Peggy Quince, Justice, Florida Supreme Court; Daniel M. Gallagher Jr., Commissioner, Securities and Exchange Commission

Grads Employed by Field (%)
Business/Industry (26)
Government (29)
Judicial Clerkship (12)
Private Practice (30)
Public Interest (3)

CHAPMAN UNIVERSITY
DALE E. FOWLER SCHOOL OF LAW

Academics

Located in the heart of Southern California, Chapman University Dale. E. Fowler School of Law is a "welcoming place to be a student" and impresses many with its "hospitality" and "personalized community experience." While Chapman is "heavily focused on students going to big firms or the Orange County DA's Office, there are a number of smaller niches that are available and pushed. For example, the broad availability of tax courses and clinics as well as the ability to have an emphasis in the ENLURE program (Environmental, Land Use, and Real Estate Law) offer a diversity of educational opportunities. Professors as well as the administration clearly have spent years developing connections with employers, scholars, agencies, etc. within and without of the area for the purpose of benefiting the students." As for the classroom experience and professor teaching quality, students say they "could not have found a better law school. Each professor understands the topics they are teaching and teach the classes in exactly the way they could be best taught." One student says that "overall, my experience at Chapman has been amazing. I have successfully found a great job for after graduation and feel prepared for [the] real [lawyer's] life thanks to Chapman."

Students report that the facilities at Chapman are "top notch," with "state-of-the-art classrooms and both a trial courtroom and appellate court room," while the library "is constantly updated, and the library staff all hold at least a master's degree in library sciences, while the research librarians all have a JD." As for that staff, one student notes that "the research librarians at Chapman are extremely skilled, proactive, knowledgeable, helpful, friendly, and so resourceful. They are also well-versed in cutting edge legal research tools and methods that have been a huge benefit to me as a student."

However, despite the students wonderful feelings towards the faculty and facilities, several Chapman students note a "disconnect" between the administration and the students. Others would like to see "increased diversity in faculty who teach 1L classes, a greater variety in elective courses" and the "[elimination of] the curve in practical classes like trial practice." One student notes that the school's grading curves make progress difficult for some. Yet, despite these remarks, nearly all students agree that the faculty and their peers are without compare.

Life

Located "in the beautiful city of Orange just down the block from historic downtown," "the law building is classic and elegant." One student notes that they "attended many law school orientations and Chapman clearly impressed me the most with their hospitality, faculty, staff, and just the positive overall vibe from the other students." Another student explains that the school itself "is beautiful and the resources available in the library or through the professors continue to astound me. The location of the school is incredible too. Being located in Orange is great; the city is centrally located in the Los Angeles basin (about 45 to 60 minutes from the four county seats in the area) and provides great access to courts in both Orange County (Santa Ana—about a five minute drive the school) and Los Angeles." Additionally, Chapman finds itself "located between multiple DA offices and courthouses allowing for ample intern, extern, and clerkship opportunities." At Chapman, everyone "pushes each other to success." There is certainly the feeling that students do compete for grades, and there are definitely "competitive undertones."

KARMAN HSU, ASSISTANT DEAN OF ADMISSION AND DIVERSITY INITIATIVES
ONE UNIVERSITY DRIVE, ORANGE, CA 92866
TEL: 714-628-2500 • FAX: 714-628-2501
E-MAIL: LAWADMISSION@CHAPMAN.EDU • WEBSITE: WWW.CHAPMAN.EDU/LAW

Out here, "the weather is always perfect." "There is a club for everyone." Students note that "the school is also very successful in bringing in high-level speakers, including judges and well-known academics." The most consistent response is "I have thoroughly enjoyed my time at Chapman Law."

Getting In

Enrolled students at the 75th percentile have LSAT scores of about 158 and GPAs of 3.56. Enrolled students at the 25th percentile have LSAT scores of approximately 153 and GPAs of 3.17. It's also worth noting that the admissions staff will look at all of your LSAT scores, not just your best one.

Clinical program required	No
Legal writing course requirement	Yes
Legal methods course requirement	Yes
Legal research course requirement	Yes
Moot court requirement	Yes
Public interest law requirement	No

ADMISSIONS

Selectivity Rating	70
# applications received	1,505
% applicants accepted	52
% acceptees attending	22
Average LSAT	156
Median LSAT	156
LSAT Range (25th to 75th percentile)	153–158
Average undergrad GPA	3.34
Median undergrad GPA	3.41
Application fee	$75
Regular application deadline	4/15
Early application deadline	11/30
Early application notification	12/31
Transfer students accepted	Yes
Evening division offered	No
Part-time accepted	Yes
CAS accepted	Yes

FINANCIAL FACTS

Annual tuition	$46,300
Books and supplies	$1,800
Fees	$446
Room & Board	$19,092
Financial aid application deadline	3/2
% first-year students receiving some sort of aid	91
% all students receiving some sort of aid	91
% of aid that is merit based	31
% receiving scholarships	58
Average grant	$30,780
Average loan	$49,331
Average total aid package	$61,007
Average debt	$148,421

EMPLOYMENT INFORMATION

Career Rating	73	
Total 2014 JD Grads	138	
% for whom you have useable information	97	
% grads employed ten months out	76	
Median starting salary	$65,025	
# employed full-time	85	
# employed part-time	20	
# employed bar required	77	
# employed JD preferred	19	
# employed professional/other	4	
# employed non-professional	5	
# pursuing advanced degree	2	
# unemployed and seeking employment	23	
# not seeking employment	2	
% grads employed by school	1	
State for bar exam	CA, AZ, CT, HI, IL	
	MA, MD, NV, WA	
Pass rate for first-time bar	76.5	

Prominent Alumni
Katie Rodin, Assistant General Counsel, Anaheim Ducks; Jason Rednour, Partner, Paul Hastings

Grads Employed by Field (%)
Academic (1)
Business/Industry (21)
Government (4)
Judicial Clerkship (1)
State or local: (1)
Private Practice (47)
 Solo: (1)
 2-10: (26)
 11-25: (7)
 26-50: (4)
 51-100: (6)
 101-250: (1)
 501+: (1)
Public Interest (2)

CHARLESTON SCHOOL OF LAW

Academics

Charleston School of Law is one of the South's premiere legal programs. Armed with a "challenging curriculum" and "emphasis on practical skills," the School of Law has managed to attract "some of the biggest legal influences in the state of South Carolina." Students greatly benefit from studying with professors who have incredibly diverse professional backgrounds including "retired Deans from top law schools, district attorneys, former partners, and associates in 'Big Law' firms in large cities, and some of the top local attorneys in South Carolina." Not surprisingly, these professors "do a great job of bringing practical and 'real life' issues to the classroom." And while teachers here certainly "keep you on your toes in class with the Socratic method," students can breathe a sigh of relief knowing that they "[won't] belittle you."

In addition to their impressive credentials and towering intellect, it's obvious that professors at Charleston "truly care about their students." Importantly, they "do an excellent job in making themselves available outside of the classroom." A first-year student elaborates, "The faculty employ an open door policy in which students can come to their office hours to get help if they are falling behind or simply to clarify a minor topic. The professors actually get upset if students don't come and take advantage of their openness. They don't try and hide the ball from you and want their students to be the best lawyers they can be."

This friendliness and accessibility also extends to the administration. The deans, who "are a pleasure to work with," really "take the time to get to know the students personally." They "portray a positive attitude at all times and are dedicated to making the school the best it can be." A second-year wholeheartedly supports this notion exclaiming, "A large majority of the administrators know my name and year before I walk through the door, and everyone works hard to cultivate a welcoming and encouraging atmosphere."

Charleston's infrastructure and amenities do leave a little bit to be desired. As a third-year student admonishes, "Facilities need upgrading, for a more professional experience/appearance." A first-year student quickly adds, "The library is small and lacks the print resources of some other law schools." Of course, a more understanding peer counters, "With today's growing dependency on technology and the increasing availability of online material, I don't find these issues to be a problem. I always have a quiet seat in the library when I go to study and enough room in my classes to comfortably take notes and follow along."

Life

Charleston School of Law prides itself on the fact that it "doesn't have the cutthroat mentality that so many law schools are rumored to [possess]." Indeed, "people generally seem very willing to help one another out, send each other outlines, and review material together." As one relieved third-year shares, "It certainly has made the otherwise intimidating culture of law school more of a non-factor so that students can concentrate on studies more." Moreover, "we work hard in Charleston to cultivate an atmosphere of civility and camaraderie within the student body, and I believe that will continue to be achieved…. I am thankful that our student body is helpful, encouraging, and genuinely happy to hear about my success." A classmate concurs adding, "The overall environment is collegiate, cooperative, stimulating, and above all else, welcoming."

P.O. Box 535, Charleston, SC 29402
Tel: 843-329-1000
E-Mail: info@charlestonlaw.edu • Website: www.charlestonlaw.edu

These future JDs can also take advantage of "great connections with the Charleston legal community, and surrounding cities." What's more, these lucky students have access to "amazing speakers and potential opportunities for externships, internships, and various other programs." Students also rave about hometown Charleston, a "fantastic," "beautiful," and "historic" city. As a second-year student boasts, "The location is also second to none. I don't know if [there] is a better place to go to law school than in Charleston. With its world class restaurants, bars, history, culture, white sand beaches, and gorgeous weather, Charleston has everything a law student could desire while taking a break from the stress of classes."

Getting In

Charleston's admission committee gives each application a thorough vetting. Both undergraduate GPA and LSAT performance are of primary importance. After all, those are the strongest indicators of law school success. Charleston also gives consideration to military service, employment history, community service, leadership experience, and extracurricular involvement. The only prerequisite is an undergraduate degree from an accredited university. No pre-law curriculum necessary.

Clinical program required	No
Legal writing course requirement	Yes
Legal methods course requirement	No
Legal research course requirement	Yes
Moot court requirement	No
Public interest law requirement	Yes

ADMISSIONS

Selectivity Rating	70
# applications received	1,108
% applicants accepted	83
% acceptees attending	16
Average LSAT	148
Median LSAT	148
LSAT Range (25th to 75th percentile)	144–152
Average undergrad GPA	2.99
Median undergrad GPA	3.03
Application fee	$50
Regular application deadline	3/1
Transfer students accepted	Yes
Evening division offered	No
Part-time accepted	Yes
CAS accepted	Yes

International Students

TOEFL required of international students.	Yes

FINANCIAL FACTS

Annual tuition	$39,096
Books and supplies	$1,250
Fees	$120
Room & Board	$12,609
Financial aid application deadline	5/15
% first-year students receiving some sort of aid	87
% all students receiving some sort of aid	86
% of aid that is merit based	9
% receiving scholarships	67
Average grant	$11,582
Average loan	$48,587
Average total aid package	$48,057
Average debt	$139,256

EMPLOYMENT INFORMATION

Career Rating	73	Grads Employed by Field (%)
Total 2014 JD Grads	201	Academic (2)
% for whom you have useable information	97	Business/Industry (13)
% grads employed ten months out	79	Government (5)
# employed full-time	147	Judicial Clerkship (14)
# employed part-time	11	Federal: (2)
# employed bar required	113	State or local: (12)
# employed JD preferred	27	Private Practice (42)
# employed professional/other	16	Solo: (4)
# employed non-professional	2	2-10: (30)
# pursuing advanced degree	7	11-25: (3)
# unemployed and seeking employment	25	26-50: (1)
		51-100: (1)
# not seeking employment	4	101-250: (1)
State for bar exam	SC, NC, VA, TN, GA	501+: (1)
Pass rate for first-time bar	72.4	Size Unknown: (3)
		Public Interest (1)

CITY UNIVERSITY OF NEW YORK
SCHOOL OF LAW

INSTITUTIONAL INFORMATION

Public/private	Public
Student-faculty ratio	7:1
% faculty part-time	7
% faculty female	69
% faculty underrepresented minority	30
Total faculty	54

SURVEY SAYS...
Students love Long Island City, NY, Liberal students, Strong sense of community

STUDENTS

Enrollment of law school	327
% male/female	35/65
% from out-of-state	22
% part-time	2
% underrepresented minority	42
% international	1
# of countries represented	23
Average age of entering class	28

ACADEMICS

Academic Experience Rating	**83**
Profs interesting rating	80
Profs accessible rating	89
Hours of study per day	3.63

Academic Specialties
Civil Procedure, Commercial, Constitutional, Criminal, Environmental, Government Services, Human Rights, International, Labor, Property

Advanced Degrees Offered
JD, 3 yrs, F/T only

Combined Degrees Offered
None

Academics

The City University of New York School of Law is an "academically rigorous" school that "also [provides] heavy academic support to help students succeed." Known as "the capital of public interest," CUNY is "the ideal law school for anyone interested in public service from government to LGBT rights to environmental law." The school is very affordable, and the administration works hard to help students financially. For example, "all required books are included in tuition [and] are ordered by CUNY for each student." The school promotes "progressive values" and the faculty and students "take their idealism into the practical real world and don't let 'law school' (typically dehumanizing and alienating) taint their mission to help social justice causes." "The public interest world in New York City respects CUNY" and students say that "CUNY's academic reputation as a '3rd tier' school wholly underestimates its quality."

Academically, CUNY is "both challenging and stimulating" with "great professors" who are "very dedicated to social justice and the school's public interest mission." If there is any issue with the classes, it is in "the breadth of classes offered" as "most classes are public interest oriented and there is a lack of tax and business related courses." CUNY's faculty really stands out in its "diversity." This "diverse and highly skilled faculty" includes many who "were public interest practitioners before joining the faculty." "All the professors at CUNY" are approachable and willing "to meet with you outside of the classroom." CUNY professors "not only have remarkable public interest law careers" but are "effective educators" who don't engage in "terrifying exercises of the Socratic method, just for the sake of using the Socratic method." Rather, the professors use techniques that "engender vibrant discussions of the cases and the law, usually framed within the context of social justice."

Students love the "sleek," "amazing," and "gorgeous" "new building," which provides "so many areas for sitting and talking or studying." While the CUNY law "library is modest," students have access to the massive "interlibrary loan" program at CUNY and "extensive database subscriptions." The most common complaint among students is the administration, which "is by far the weakest part of the school." "The administration is at best a train wreck" and "run by very well-meaning, but very backward-minded people." Others say the administration "is supportive of students" and that there is a great "sense of community among the student body, faculty & administration." One happy student sums up CUNY as having "a unique supportive environment, among students and between students and the administration and faculty. It is a great place to learn!"

DEGNA P. LEVISTER, INTERIM ASSISTANT DEAN OF ADMISSIONS
2 COURT SQUARE, LONG ISLAND CITY, NY 11101-4356
TEL: 718-340-4210 • FAX: 718-340-4435
E-MAIL: ADMISSIONS@LAW.CUNY.EDU • WEBSITE: WWW.LAW.CUNY.EDU

Life

Located in Long Island City, Queens, CUNY is "easily accessible by subway, Long Island Rail Road, and by car." New York City is a haven of diversity, and this is reflected in CUNY's student body. "The school is diverse in age, race, and socioeconomic background" and "students bring with them diverse work experiences which greatly enhance the overall community." The student body is "filled with students of various backgrounds, life styles and ambitions," and skews "slightly older" than many law schools. Students describe CUNY as a "safe space" "where differences in opinions are tolerated."

"The amount of school events is staggering" and "student groups are very active and supportive of each other." CUNY law itself provides "the benefits and burdens of belonging to a small community" and it's "not possible to blend into the woodwork" here. However, if a student "desires a bit of anonymity" all of New York City is only a short subway ride away! "Besides, someone you know is always going to a bar or a nice long walk or an art show and inviting you along," one student adds.

Getting In

CUNY's mission as a public interest law school means that it seeks applicants who are interested in working for historically underserved communities. CUNY also aims to have a diverse student body, and is especially interested in students who are from New York or have a special interest in New York City and its many diverse communities. The average GPA and LSAT for the 2014 entering class were 3.27 and 155 respectively.

Clinical program required	Yes
Legal writing course requirement	Yes
Legal methods course requirement	Yes
Legal research course requirement	Yes
Moot court requirement	No
Public interest law requirement	Yes

ADMISSIONS

Selectivity Rating	84
# applications received	1,236
% applicants accepted	40
% acceptees attending	19
Average LSAT	155
Median LSAT	154
LSAT Range (25th to 75th percentile)	151–158
Average undergrad GPA	3.27
Median undergrad GPA	3.33
Application fee	$60
Regular application deadline	5/15
Regular notification	6/15
Transfer students accepted	Yes
Evening division offered	Yes
Part-time accepted	Yes
CAS accepted	Yes

International Students

TOEFL recommended of international students.	Yes

FINANCIAL FACTS

Annual tuition (in-state/ out-of-state)	$13,430/$22,310
Books and supplies	$1,764
Fees	$363
Room & Board	$19,984
Financial aid application deadline	5/1
% first-year students receiving some sort of aid	90
% all students receiving some sort of aid	87
% of aid that is merit based	23
% receiving scholarships	27
Average grant	$8,384
Average loan	$37,677
Average total aid package	$36,619
Average debt	$82,415

EMPLOYMENT INFORMATION

Career Rating	82	
Total 2014 JD Grads	151	
% for whom you have useable information	100	
% grads employed ten months out	75	
Median starting salary	$50,000	
# employed full-time	81	
# employed part-time	32	
# employed bar required	88	
# employed JD preferred	16	
# employed professional/other	6	
# employed non-professional	2	
# pursuing advanced degree	1	
# unemployed and seeking employment	21	
# not seeking employment	1	
% grads employed by school	9	
State for bar exam	NY	
Pass rate for first-time bar	79.2	

Prominent Alumni
Rita Mella, Manhattan Surrogate Court Judge; William Massey, Partner at Gladstein, Reif & Meginniss LLP; Judith C. McCarthy, U.S. Magistrate Judge, Erica McHale Buckley, Bureau Chief, NYS Attorney General

Grads Employed by Field (%)
Academic (4)
Business/Industry (13)
Government (17)
Judicial Clerkship (7)
  Federal: (2)
  State or local: (5)
Private Practice (19)
  Solo: (5)
  2-10: (6)
  11-25: (1)
  51-100: (2)
  501+: (1)
  Size Unknown: (4)
Public Interest (40)

CLEVELAND STATE UNIVERSITY
CLEVELAND-MARSHALL COLLEGE OF LAW

Academics

Students at Cleveland State University's Cleveland-Marshall College of Law call their school "a diamond in the rough." The focus here is squarely on bar preparation and practical training. "The greatest strengths are the opportunities for real-world experience," says a 3L. There are a half dozen clinics and they cover a wide range of legal areas. Externships with judges, government entities, and public interest groups are "readily available" in Cleveland and the greater metropolitan area. The moot court program is strong. The legal writing program thoroughly emphasizes "advocacy skills." If students run into academic difficulties, they can take advantage of Cleveland-Marshall's academic support programs, which provide group training and one-on-one assistance to help students with their course work. Areas of concentration are available in business law, civil litigation and dispute resolution, criminal law, employment law, health law, and international law. There are five dual-degree programs and three journals. Cleveland-Marshall Law is also quite a bargain, particularly if you are an Ohio resident.

"On average, Marshall professors are knowledgeable, passionate, and approachable," relates a 2L. "I have never been taught something as inherently boring as civil procedure in such an invigorating manner," beams a 1L. Professors are also generally accessible outside the classroom. The "excellent" administration is "extremely open to student interaction and answers questions and concerns promptly." However, "heading to the main campus to get administrative stuff done can be tedious." Students' biggest academic complaint involves the distribution of grades. The curve here, which permits faculty members to give over 50 percent of all 1Ls a grade of C+ or lower, can be pretty rough.

Cleveland-Marshall Law is located in downtown Cleveland on the main campus of the larger university, which means that part-time work at local firms is easy to come by throughout the year. According to some students, "the facilities could be a little fancier." Most say that the layout of the law school is "not only aesthetically pleasing but functional," though. "The library is great." "The new addition is modern and beautiful," relates a 1L. "It's eye-catching from the street and a great place for students to study or relax between classes."

More than 75 percent of all newly minted graduates take jobs in either private practice or the corporate world. The overwhelming majority of Cleveland-Marshall's alumni practice in Ohio and the school's reputation is very solid throughout the northeastern part of the state. Students rave about Cleveland-Marshall Law's "connection to the Cleveland legal community" as well as "a supportive, active alumni base that extends opportunities to anyone who seeks them."

CHRISTOPHER LUCAK, ASSISTANT DEAN FOR ADMISSION AND FINANCIAL AID
2121 EUCLID AVENUE, LB 138, CLEVELAND, OH 44115-2214
TEL: 866-687-2304 • FAX: 216-687-6881
E-MAIL: LAW.ADMISSIONS@CSUOHIO.EDU • WEBSITE: WWW.CSULAW.ORG

Life

The part-time program at Cleveland-Marshall is pretty large and "evening and day students do have very different experiences." As you would expect, full-timers are generally younger while part-timers are older and have "more time in the real world" already under their belts. "In my class, we have architects, engineers, law enforcement officials, researchers, bankers, and people with other varying careers," says a part-time 2L. Some part-time students complain that they are "excluded from a lot of school activities and classes." Others assert that "the full- and part-timers are treated equally." "I am a full-time 3L who frequently takes night classes due to my part-time work schedule and I haven't noticed a divide between night and day professors' focus on the students," explains one student. "Some of the best professors I have had in law school teach night classes."

Student opinion concerning the academic atmosphere is mixed. Some students flatly call it "competitive." Others, staking something of a middle ground, say that "people are friendly and willing to help, most of the time." Still others describe "a great sense of camaraderie." "Students here help one another better than at any institution I've ever encountered," declares a 3L. Socially, clubs and extracurricular activities are abundant. "The student bar association plans fun socials at least once a month with free food and drinks for students to unwind." "Everyone seems to fall into whatever groups make them happy and things move right along." "Most of the students know one another," explains a 3L. "We have lockers, prom (Barrister's Ball), socials, drama, and tons of drinking." Beyond the law school orbit, Cleveland isn't generally listed among the greatest cities in the United States but there really are a lot of charming neighborhoods and the cost of living is comparatively low.

Getting In

Enrolled students at the 75th percentile at Cleveland-Marshall have LSAT scores around 156 and grade point averages of 3.55. At the 25th percentile, LSAT scores are 151, and GPAs are 3.00.

Clinical program required	No
Legal writing course requirement	Yes
Legal methods course requirement	No
Legal research course requirement	Yes
Moot court requirement	No
Public interest law requirement	No

ADMISSIONS

Selectivity Rating	86
# applications received	1,768
% applicants accepted	35
% acceptees attending	34
Average LSAT	156
LSAT Range (25th to 75th percentile)	153–157
Average undergrad GPA	3.38
Regular application deadline	5/1
Transfer students accepted	Yes
Evening division offered	Yes
Part-time accepted	Yes
CAS accepted	Yes

International Students

TOEFL required of international students.	Yes

FINANCIAL FACTS

Annual tuition (in-state/ out-of-state)	$16,478/$22,608
Books and supplies	$1,400
Fees	$25
Room & Board	$11,000
Financial aid application deadline	5/1
% first-year students receiving some sort of aid	90
% all students receiving some sort of aid	95
% of aid that is merit based	90
% receiving scholarships	40
Average grant	$6,457
Average loan	$24,070
Average total aid package	$24,906
Average debt	$59,458

EMPLOYMENT INFORMATION

Career Rating	74

% grads employed ten months out
90 Median starting salary $81,823
State for bar exam OH, NY, MD, MA, FL

Prominent Alumni
Tim Russert, The late Sr. VP, NBC News and moderator of; Hon. Louis Stokes, US House of Representatives, Rtd.; Hon. Maureen O'Connor, Justice, Supreme Court of Ohio; Christopher Vasil, Chief Deputy Clerk, US Supreme Court; Elizabeth Pugh, General Counsel, Library of Congress

Grads Employed by Field (%)
Academic (3)
Business/Industry (24)
Government (12)
Judicial Clerkship (5)
Private Practice (53)
Public Interest (3)

THE COLLEGE OF WILLIAM & MARY

MARSHALL-WYTHE LAW SCHOOL

INSTITUTIONAL INFORMATION

Public/private	Public
Affiliation	No Affiliation
Student-faculty ratio	13:1
% faculty part-time	52
% faculty female	30
% faculty underrepresented minority	9
Total faculty	103

SURVEY SAYS...

Diverse opinions accepted in classrooms, Great research resources, Abundant externship/internship/clerkship opportunities

STUDENTS

Enrollment of law school	631
% male/female	48/52
% from out-of-state	73
% part-time	0
% underrepresented minority	13
% international	4
# of countries represented	10
Average age of entering class	24

ACADEMICS

Academic Experience Rating	94
Profs interesting rating	93
Profs accessible rating	90
Hours of study per day	3.96

Advanced Degrees Offered

JD, 3 yrs and LLM in the American Legal System, 1 yr

Combined Degrees Offered

JD/MPP, 4 yrs; JD/MBA, 4 yrs; JD/MA in American Studies, 4 yrs

Academics

William & Mary, in Williamsburg Virginia, has enjoyed a long and successful history since its founding in 1693, and its public law school, the William & Mary Law School, still "offers a great value for the quality of education." William & Mary faculty are celebrated by students as "fantastic and willing to help the students rather than focusing on their own research," though many are "oftentimes the preeminent experts in their field." "Learning the Erie doctrine," one student explained, "from the man that pioneered the theory of horizontal Erie is a once in a lifetime experience." Nonetheless, they "routinely hang out in the lobby and discuss classes or just to interact causally with the students," and students rarely find them intimidating. There is a "great mix of seasoned faculty and younger faculty who are all at the top of their respective legal fields," which contributes to the school's "forward thinking and innovative approaches to legal education" with "a great balance of both theory and the practical hands-on."

There is a wealth of opportunities here for practical development. Students love "the very specialized electives where you can surprise yourself by how much you learn while at the same time possibly discovering a new passion." Additionally, "there are countless opportunities to get practical experience via externships and clinic experiences" that become "integral in getting summer internships." Students report leaving "first year having experience doing client intake and client interviews." Students say that the school's Legal Practice Program, "including 'Legal Writing' and oral presentation skills, has taken great strides evolving over the past few years in order to best suit students' needs and prepare us for the world of practice." The program includes "numerous adjunct professors" who provide "interesting insight." And while "the legal writing program has its problems," "the administration truly wants to hear feedback from students and continues to make successful changes to provide meaningful training for practice." These efforts "to give students an opportunity to become great writers and practitioners" seem to be paying off. One student reported that, "during my 1L summer externship, my supervising attorneys were very impressed with how advanced my legal argumentation and writing skills were."

Students are pleased with facilities and resources, finding that "there are always available seats in the library, and study room reservations are easy to make." Technologically equipped classrooms help to "create a comfortable learning environment," and "the actual law school building is also lovely with great nooks and crannies for studying."

FAYE SHEALY, ASSOCIATE DEAN FOR ADMISSION
WILLIAM & MARY LAW SCHOOL, OFFICE OF ADMISSION, P.O. BOX 8795, WILLIAMSBURG, VA 23187-8795
TEL: 757-221-3785 • FAX: 757-221-3261
E-MAIL: LAWADM@WM.EDU • WEBSITE: LAW.WM.EDU

Life

William & Mary "has a great community feel and a lot of opportunities to get involved—including five reputable law journals." The school emphasizes the "idea of a Citizen-Lawyer," Thomas Jefferson's founding mission to create lawyers who contribute to society and live up to a high moral code, and "is exemplified by faculty and upper-classman." Students remain close "despite being graded on a curve," and create a friendly "cooperative atmosphere," without "cut-throat" competition. They develop a close "community (which isn't a word often associated with law school)," and "the upperclassmen are supportive" and provide "outlines, career advice, [and] networking" opportunities." While it is impossible to "really eliminate competition at law schools ([full of] a bunch of type-A weirdos who are graded on a mandatory curve)," one student jokes, "William & Mary really has reduced the competition significantly." Yet, this collective fondness and involvement in each other's lives sometimes develops a penchant for gossip: "Since we're such a small school, people learn each other's business very quickly," and "we are pretty gossipy." While Williamsburg may be small with " only three to four 'law school' bars," students make up for it "with Public Service Fund and school-sponsored events." "If you want a place that you can focus on law school but still have an outlet for fun, this is the place to be."

Getting In

William & Mary accepts applications for the fall semester on a modified rolling basis between September 1 and March 1. Admission is competitive with the acceptance rate at 32 percent. In 2015, 4,407 students applied for 213 spots in the incoming class. For the class of 2017, students had a median GPA of 3.79 and a median LSAT score of 163. Over 50 percent had professional experience before entering the program.

Clinical program required	No
Legal writing course requirement	Yes
Legal methods course requirement	Yes
Legal research course requirement	Yes
Moot court requirement	No
Public interest law requirement	No

ADMISSIONS

Selectivity Rating	92
# applications received	4,407
% applicants accepted	32
% acceptees attending	15
Average LSAT	161
Median LSAT	163
LSAT Range (25th to 75th percentile)	157–165
Average undergrad GPA	3.68
Median undergrad GPA	3.79
Application fee	$50
Regular application deadline	3/1
Regular notification	4/1
Transfer students accepted	Yes
Evening division offered	No
Part-time accepted	No
CAS accepted	Yes

FINANCIAL FACTS

Annual tuition (in-state/ out-of-state)	$24,544/$32,987
Books and supplies	$1,545
Fees	$5,813
Room & Board	$10,980
Financial aid application deadline	2/15
% first-year students receiving some sort of aid	97
% all students receiving some sort of aid	96
% of aid that is merit based	71
% receiving scholarships	85
Average grant	$11,552
Average loan	$33,972
Average total aid package	$39,493
Average debt	$97,705

EMPLOYMENT INFORMATION

Career Rating	94
Total 2014 JD Grads	215
% for whom you have useable information	100
% grads employed ten months out	90
Median starting salary	$65,000
# employed full-time	186
# employed part-time	8
# employed bar required	161
# employed JD preferred	26
# employed professional/other	7
# employed non-professional	0
# pursuing advanced degree	3
# unemployed and seeking employment	16
% grads employed by school	11
State for bar exam	VA, CA, MD, NY, PA
Pass rate for first-time bar	92.4

Grads Employed by Field (%)
Academic (1)
Business/Industry (11)
Government (22)
Judicial Clerkship (13)
Federal (6)
State or local (7)
Private Practice (39)
  Solo: (1)
  2-10: (13)
  11-25: (4)
  26-50: (3)
  51-100: (3)
  101-250: (2)
  251-500: (2)
  501+: (11)
  Size Unknown: (0)
Public Interest (6)

COLUMBIA UNIVERSITY
SCHOOL OF LAW

INSTITUTIONAL INFORMATION

Public/private	Private
% faculty part-time	44
% faculty female	37
% faculty underrepresented minority	11
Total faculty	323

SURVEY SAYS...

*Students love New York, NY,
Abundant externship/internship/
clerkship opportunities*

STUDENTS

Enrollment of law school	1,170
% male/female	54/46
% underrepresented minority	34
% international	9
# of countries represented	45
Average age of entering class	24

ACADEMICS

Academic Experience Rating	97
Profs interesting rating	87
Profs accessible rating	74
Hours of study per day	3.19

Academic Specialties

Civil Procedure, Commercial, Constitutional, Corporation Securities, Criminal, Environmental, Government Services, Human Rights, International, Labor, Legal History, Legal Philosophy, Property, Taxation, Intellectual Property

Advanced Degrees Offered

LLM, 1 yr; JSD, two semesters in residence and a dissertation.

Combined Degrees Offered

JD/PhD; JD/MA; JD/MBA; JD/MFA (Arts Administration); JD/MS Urban Planning, JD/MS Social Work; JD/MS Journalism; JD/MIA in International Affairs; JD/MPA in Public Administration with Columbia; JD/MPA in Public Affairs with Woodrow Wilson School at Princeton; JD/MPH in Public Health

Academics

Columbia Law School is "a very exciting and dynamic place." The curriculum is very heavy on legal theory "with a dash of practical, just for show," and the "breadth of course offerings" is staggering. There are countless centers and programs specializing in everything from law, media, and the arts to European legal studies to tax policy to gender and sexuality law. "Getting on a journal is remarkably noncompetitive." "Being in New York affords the opportunity to participate in almost any internship you could imagine." Programs in international law and intellectual property law are reportedly excellent. Columbia is also "a corporate lawyer factory" and the "best place in the country for budding transactional lawyers." Public interest law is yet another strong suit here. Students who are involved are "a bit clique-ish" but, if you are in the clique, you'll have access to a wealth of opportunities as well as a tremendously generous loan repayment assistance program.

The "unbelievable," "unmatched" faculty at Columbia is "amazing" "across the board." "Columbia does a good job mixing the young, relatable rising superstars with older, more practiced professors." Virtually all of them "make class interesting," and "they're the number-one reason to come to CLS (besides the prestige, of course)." Professors also "make a huge effort to be approachable" and "are happy to give career-related advice or answer questions." The administration isn't as beloved. Happier students note that there are some "really caring people" on staff. However, the general sentiment seems to be that management is somewhat "disdainful."

When the time comes to find a real job, "employment prospects are unbeatable and the alumni network is extraordinarily strong." Career Services is "very helpful in offering support in a variety of capacities." Columbia boasts a "high placement rate in big law firms" and "the opportunities for working in prestigious government and sought-after public interest positions are unparalleled." "It's Columbia," candidly explains a 2L. "The name buys you a lot." About the only complaint we hear is the contention that "the employment focus is a little too New York–centric."

The facilities here are far from great. "Everything is very modern" and "the building is serviceable and clean, but it is ugly." Classrooms "aren't terribly comfortable," and "They're not as pretty as what you'll find at other Ivy League law schools." "The library is one of the best in the country" as far as the resources on offer are concerned, but its aesthetic "is absolutely hideous," says an appalled 2L.

Life

The population of future lawyers at Columbia is "extremely diverse," generally young, and "quite national." Students describe this place as "a nerd paradise," full of "geniuses" who are "brilliant and accomplished but surprisingly cool." "There are spoiled brats, and awkward types, and public interest people, and friendly people, and inflated egos, and social people," reports a 3L. A few students say there is a "divide between students of different economic and academic" backgrounds. However, many others insist that personal circumstances don't matter at all. "There isn't any sort of conspicuous divide between the student body on socioeconomic or geographic factors until you realize that most of the Ivy kids are terrible at beer pong," quips a 1L.

NKONYE IWEREBON, DEAN OF ADMISSIONS
435 WEST 116TH STREET, BOX A-3, NEW YORK, NY 10027
TEL: 212-854-2670 • FAX: 212-854-1109
E-MAIL: ADMISSIONS@LAW.COLUMBIA.EDU • WEBSITE: WWW.LAW.COLUMBIA.EDU

Academically, "There is an atmosphere of [intensity] here." Students are "constantly assessing how they stack up, which feeds into the collective neurosis." Some students assert that the struggle for top grades is pretty brutal. "People in general are not happy to share notes," claims a 2L. "They are, in fact, very secretive about their notes." "Our reputation for gunning, competitive jerks is unfortunately true for about 5 percent of the class," laments a 1L. Other students tell us, "People are extremely generous about sharing their outlines and studying together." "If you miss a class," they say, "your neighbors will e-mail you their notes without you even asking."

Columbia's location in a "safe, relatively quiet" neighborhood on Manhattan's Upper West Side provides few distractions when you are trying to study. When students put down their casebooks, though, they can take advantage of a "vibrant student community." "You'll be happy socially here unless you are a complete tool," promises a 2L. "Everyone is fairly involved in all sorts of organizations." "There are multiple lunch events every day, and there's some sort of lecture or panel or firm event with dinner almost every evening." There are "plenty of students who want to party like it's college," too, and "no shortage of happy hours." Living in the Big Apple is also a massive plus. "It's hard to explain the type of magnetic force this place can be unless you've lived here and worked here," reflects a 1L. "New York City means students can do anything they please (with the free hours they have)."

Getting In

Getting into any Ivy League law school is exceedingly difficult and Columbia is certainly no exception. Entering students at the 25th percentile have LSAT scores of about 170 and undergraduate grade point averages of almost 3.7. At the 75th percentile, LSAT scores are a whopping 174 or so and GPAs are around 3.8.

Clinical program required	No
Legal writing course requirement	Yes
Legal methods course requirement	Yes
Legal research course requirement	Yes
Moot court requirement	Yes
Public interest law requirement	Yes

ADMISSIONS

Selectivity Rating	98
# applications received	6,188
% applicants accepted	19
% acceptees attending	32
Average LSAT	171
Median LSAT	172
LSAT Range (25th to 75th percentile)	170–174
Average undergrad GPA	3.69
Median undergrad GPA	3.71
Application fee	$85
Regular application deadline	2/15
Early application deadline	11/15
Early application notification	1/1
Transfer students accepted	Yes
Evening division offered	No
Part-time accepted	No
CAS accepted	Yes

FINANCIAL FACTS

Annual tuition	$58,292
Books and supplies	$1,568
Room & Board	$21,300
Financial aid application deadline	3/1
% first-year students receiving some sort of aid	74
% all students receiving some sort of aid	74
% of aid that is merit based	42
% receiving scholarships	43
Average grant	$19,750
Average loan	$58,440
Average total aid package	$42,750
Average debt	$154,076

EMPLOYMENT INFORMATION

Career Rating	99
Total 2014 JD Grads	468
% for whom you have useable information	100
% grads employed ten months out	97
Median starting salary	$160,000
# employed full-time	454
# employed part-time	1
# employed bar required	441
# employed JD preferred	9
# employed professional/other	3
# employed non-professional	1
# pursuing advanced degree	1
# unemployed and seeking employment	9
# not seeking employment	0
% grads employed by school	7
State for bar exam	NY, CA, NJ, VA, MA
Pass rate for first-time bar	91.2

Prominent Alumni
Ruth Bader Ginsburg, Justice/U.S. Supreme Court; George Pataki, Governor/New York State; Franklin D. Roosevelt, former President of U.S.; Paul Robeson, performing artist/civil rights activist

Grads Employed by Field (%)
Business/Industry (4)
Government (6)
Judicial Clerkship (6)
Federal: (5)
State or local: (1)
Private Practice (79)
  11-25: (0)
  26-50: (1)
  51-100: (1)
  101-250: (4)
  251-500: (9)
  501+: (64)
  Size Unknown: (0)
Public Interest (7)

CORNELL UNIVERSITY
LAW SCHOOL

INSTITUTIONAL INFORMATION

Public/private	Private
Student-faculty ratio	10:1
Total faculty	53

SURVEY SAYS...

Abundant externship/internship/ clerkship opportunities

STUDENTS

Enrollment of law school	578
% part-time	0
Average age of entering class	25

ACADEMICS

Academic Experience Rating	94
Profs interesting rating	93
Profs accessible rating	81
Hours of study per day	3.98

Academic Specialties

International

Advanced Degrees Offered

JD, 3 yrs; LLM, 1 year; JD/LLM in International and Comparative Law, 3 yrs; JD/Maitrise en Driot French Law degree, 4 yrs; JSD, 2 yrs; JD/ MLLP, Master of German and European Law and Legal Practice, 4 yrs.

Combined Degrees Offered

JD/MBA (3 and 4-yrs), JD/MPA, JD/MA, JD/PhD, JD/MRP, JD/MILR

Academics

Cornell University is a small school with a big name. Cornell University's Law School works hard to keep up its reputation for producing quality lawyers. The law school places a big emphasis on cultivating a diverse student body, from work background and race to hometown. This "great and unique" law school stands out due to its smaller size since there are less than 200 students in each year's class, which means sections consist of about 30-35 students, and "you get a real sense of community being here." Every Wednesday, the school has a student/faculty coffee hour called "The Weekly Perk," where all of the students and professors "can mingle and have some coffee and cookies." The Deans also host a monthly breakfast for the leaders of the student organizations "so they can hear concerns and suggestions from the students themselves." In case it is not clear from all of the food-based collaboration, the "eager to help" administration "works hard to provide as many opportunities as they can, including public interest grants for summer work." Students who want to be involved in the Cornell community have plenty of opportunities, and "faculty take a genuine interest in student's ideas and research goals."

Much of the high tuition at Cornell goes to maintaining the excellence in the faculty. The "rock star" professors here are "amazing" and "truly want every student to succeed and excel." Some say "the ability to take classes with some of the leading professionals and thinkers in a particular area is one of the best aspects of a Cornell Law education." "They are like legal celebrities." Others say that it is "the ease with which graduates can land a big law job in NYC." "Our career services department made the process both painless and simple, and most students had their summer employment locked down by the beginning of Fall 2011," according to one student. The rest of Cornell Law School also "runs like a well-oiled machine." "I have had the opportunity to see my legal writing published in national magazines, and I have been given chances to do things I never thought I could achieve, through the guidance of the staff and faculty at Cornell," says one student.

Students are required to take thirteen credits per semester, leaving many wishing for "more mandatory pass/fail one credit classes," since many students are left "scrambling for that extra credit" in the second semester. Still, the focus on the practical experience is what firms are looking for in this economy, and "the clinical classes give students a chance to apply what they've learned to real world problems." "It's refreshing to have theory classes taught by individuals who also have real-world experience in the field," says one student. "For example, my Public International Law professor helped to draft the new constitution for Kenya and [has a working relationship] with Kofi Annan." One huge benefit of the school's size includes the opportunities to schedule a directed reading or supervised writing. With a directed reading, if a student is interested in taking a course in something that is not currently offered, that student can contact the professor and set up a directed reading or supervised writing to receive credit and study a particular topic.

Though students frequently admit, "Ithaca is a lovely place," they are also keenly aware that "there aren't the same type of part-time externship opportunities that one would find in New York City, Washington, D.C., or even the smaller cities." Luckily, networking opportunities and reputation can help compensate, and "just having 'Cornell' on your résumé can open certain doors."

HOPE JAMISON, ASSOCIATE DIRECTOR OF ADMISSIONS
226 MYRON TAYLOR HALL, ITHACA, NY 14853-4901
TEL: 607-255-5141 • FAX: 607-255-7193
E-MAIL: JDADMISSIONS@CORNELL.EDU • WEBSITE: WWW.LAWSCHOOL.CORNELL.EDU

Life

"Because we study in a small town, we all know each other well and work together as much as possible," says one student of Ithaca. Of course there are still some gunners and "a few overly type-A individuals," but for the most part Cornell students make up a "tightly knit community that seems to care more about getting through this together rather than a bunch of individuals doing anything to make sure they are the best in the class." The town may not be the best place to live for three years "if you're used to a much more cosmopolitan area," but "many students do visit NYC/Boston on weekends," and the nightlife can be "quite active." Additionally, each semester there are usually two formal events that many students attend, and if you "really put yourself out there by initiating study groups (which double as dinner and drinking groups) or get involved in volunteer activities/sports/religion," then you can have a decent social life.

With construction completed in December 2013, the new wing of Cornell Law School opened in time to host spring 2014 classes. The library is particularly "state-of-the-art." The campus is "beautiful," and students often remark, "We attend school in a castle." This castle is "a very insular community," and many law students don't venture far off of the hill. The student body is understandably "extremely close." "I know the names of the majority of my fellow students in my class year," says one; however, the small population can "create a bubble of stress that can sometimes be hard to overcome."

Getting In

Admission to Cornell is highly competitive. The Admissions Committee weighs all aspects of an applicant's background, including extracurricular and community activities, graduate work, LSAT scores, letters of recommendation, and undergraduate transcripts. Applicants are also encouraged to submit a separate document that details how their ethnic, cultural, or linguistic background will contribute to the diversity of the school community. The median LSAT score for the 2014 entering class was 167 and the median undergraduate GPA was 3.66.

Clinical program required	No
Legal writing course requirement	Yes
Legal methods course requirement	Yes
Legal research course requirement	Yes
Moot court requirement	No
Public interest law requirement	No

ADMISSIONS

Selectivity Rating	94
# applications received	4,006
Median LSAT	167
LSAT Range (25th to 75th percentile)	166–169
Median undergrad GPA	3.68
Application fee	$80
Regular application deadline	2/1
Transfer students accepted	Yes
Evening division offered	No
Part-time accepted	No
CAS accepted	Yes

FINANCIAL FACTS

Annual tuition	$59,360
Books and supplies	$8,738
Fees	$81
Room & Board	$11,250
Financial aid application deadline	3/15
% first-year students receiving some sort of aid	50

EMPLOYMENT INFORMATION	
Career Rating	90
State for bar exam	NY
Pass rate for first-time bar	92.0

CREIGHTON UNIVERSITY
SCHOOL OF LAW

INSTITUTIONAL INFORMATION

Public/private	Private
Affiliation	Roman Catholic
Student-faculty ratio	13:1
% faculty part-time	49
% faculty female	16
% faculty underrepresented minority	7
Total faculty	66

SURVEY SAYS...
Great research resources

STUDENTS

Enrollment of law school	361
% male/female	61/39
% from out-of-state	56
% part-time	2
% underrepresented minority	18
% international	1
# of countries represented	4
Average age of entering class	24

ACADEMICS

Academic Experience Rating	79
Profs interesting rating	85
Profs accessible rating	96
Hours of study per day	3.74

Academic Specialties
Commercial, Corporation Securities, Criminal, International

Combined Degrees Offered
JD/MBA; JD/MA International Relations; JD/MS Government and Leadership; JD/MS Negotiation and Conflict Resolution: 3 yrs with summer study.

Academics

Founded in 1878, Creighton is a Jesuit-affiliated university that "will uplift you rather than scare you." The Jesuit tradition is embodied in the School of Law's motto: "educating for service and justice." Creighton looks to produce attorneys that are not only skilled and knowledgeable, but who work to service society at large. The school offers four areas of concentration as well as four joint-degree programs. Supreme Court Justice Thomas even co-teaches a class at Creighton on a biannual basis. The school has a "dedicated alumni base." "Located in an economically strong region," Creighton University offers students many opportunities in Omaha, "one of the best business cities in the United States." Students rave about the "networking if you plan to stay in Omaha," although "the Career Development Office is not optimized for students wanting to practice outside Nebraska."

One thing that is important at any law school is the library, and Creighton students rave about the "beautiful," "large, and well-equipped" library that is replete "with plenty of available study rooms, computer labs, and private workstations." "The resources available in the library are fantastic," and "the research librarians are always there to help with finding anything and teach you how to find it on your own." If there is a primary complaint about Creighton, it is "Cost. Cost. Cost." "It's quite expensive, especially considering the earning potential in the rural areas of the Midwest," a 3L explains. However, another student says that despite being on "the high end for the cost of tuition," "most people who end up in law firms will be making anywhere from 50k to 80k."

The cost of Creighton is offset by the "awesome professors" without whom "Creighton Law wouldn't be worth it." These "dedicated, knowledgeable, passionate educators," are "all well versed in law and have accomplished backgrounds." "I love my professors!" a 3L declares. "They have very diverse viewpoints and methods of teaching, yet most of them seem very invested in our education." The administration is also "always helpful and friendly." "I cannot imagine needing something that the school does not already offer," one student says. The dean of the law school is "accessible to the entire student body and sees herself as the 'mom' of the school." "The education I receive is tailored to me," a 2L says. "The practical experiences available at Creighton are unreal" including "trial teams [that] are competitive nationally" as well as a Negotiations team "taught by the man who wrote the book on Negotiations competitions—quite literally." Students are very pleased with the school's "open door policy" which encourages students to interact with professors one-on-one. Perhaps most importantly, the professors "provide numerous opportunities to learn about and make connections with potential employers in the Omaha area." Although Creighton is not ranked as highly as many other schools, students say they "have never felt that I was at a disadvantage or less prepared for practical law work than students from more 'prestigious' law schools." One student sums his experience up thusly: "I do not know if I could say enough wonderful things about Creighton Law School and how pleased I have been with my experience here."

Andrea D. Bashara, Assistant Dean
2500 California Plaza, Omaha, NE 68178
Tel: 402-280-2586 • Fax: 402-280-3161
E-Mail: lawadmit@creighton.edu • Website: creighton.edu/law

Life

Being situated in Omaha, the largest city in Nebraska, provides Creighton students with plenty of job and social opportunities. "Everyone is friendly and social" and "tend to skew a little older with much more work experience than I thought coming in." "As far as politics, it appears to me that professors and students alike are right down the middle," a 3L says. The school is "lacking, and visibly so" in racial and cultural diversity though. "I can literally count the number of non-white students," one student says, and another thinks "the school needs more female students/applicants." Students do report that the school is making strides on both fronts. It would be remiss of us not to note the "top ranked basketball team" which is a huge "selling point and attracts high attendance from undergrad and law students."

Getting In

Applicants are required to send two letters of recommendation, a personal statement, résumé, and a Credential Assembly Service Report. The entering 2014 class had an average GPA of 3.24 and an average LSAT of 152. The school leans heavily on the LSAT and GPA scores when evaluating applications, so if your scores match up well with those you have a strong shot at getting in.

Clinical program required	No
Legal writing course requirement	Yes
Legal methods course requirement	No
Legal research course requirement	Yes
Moot court requirement	Yes
Public interest law requirement	No

ADMISSIONS

Selectivity Rating	**76**
# applications received	884
% applicants accepted	71
% acceptees attending	18
Average LSAT	152
Median LSAT	152
LSAT Range (25th to 75th percentile)	148–154
Average undergrad GPA	3.24
Median undergrad GPA	3.31
Application fee	$50
Regular application deadline	5/1
Transfer students accepted	Yes
Evening division offered	No
Part-time accepted	Yes
CAS accepted	Yes

International Students

TOEFL recommended of international students.	Yes

FINANCIAL FACTS

Annual tuition	$33,936
Books and supplies	$1,355
Room & Board	$14,400
Financial aid application deadline	7/1
% first-year students receiving some sort of aid	92
% all students receiving some sort of aid	86
% of aid that is merit based	26
% receiving scholarships	58
Average grant	$19,327
Average loan	$44,027
Average total aid package	$50,945
Average debt	$126,586

EMPLOYMENT INFORMATION

Career Rating	**85**
Total 2014 JD Grads	133
% grads employed ten months out	90
Median starting salary	$58,000
# employed full-time	108
# employed part-time	11
# employed bar required	88
# employed JD preferred	19
# employed professional/other	7
# employed non-professional	5
# pursuing advanced degree	0
# unemployed and seeking employment	9
# not seeking employment	1
State for bar exam	NE, IA, CO, UT, MO
Pass rate for first-time bar	70.0

Prominent Alumni
Michael O. Johanns, Former United States Senator and former Secretary of Agriculture; Laura Duffy, US Attorney for the Southern District of California

Grads Employed by Field (%)
Academic (1)
Business/Industry (23)
Government (14)
Judicial Clerkship (8)
Federal: (3)
State or local: (5)
Private Practice (40)
Solo: (4)
2-10: (21)
11-25: (5)
26-50: (2)
51-100: (5)
251-500: (2)
501+: (2)
Public Interest (4)

DePaul University
College of Law

Academics

DePaul University College of Law makes great uses of its bustling urban location, near major courthouses and law offices, and students laud their "access to the Chicago legal community, number of alumni in the judiciary, business, and private practice in the Chicagoland area." Current students note that there are some changes afoot, reflected both administratively and academically. Faculty-wise there have been "lots of retirements and also new hires" which have "changed up the look of the faculty but the core, which was great, [has] remained." Also, students say, "The administration, while in a transition period, still runs the school pretty smoothly." One student sums up: "I feel that the school is still working to keep up with a changing legal atmosphere. Before, students would go through three years of school with very little writing or practical experience under their belts, with the understanding that they would be trained to do the writing and client work at whatever firm they were hired by. Today, however, firms are demanding that students come to them with those skills already in place. That meant that most law schools had to re-tool, revamp, and re-energize their legal writing programs. DePaul is no different, and puts a great deal of emphasis on the importance of legal research and writing." Still, this student says, the writing classes at DePaul "only meet once per week, instead of twice as doctrinal classes do. Not that it is bad, but that it can be far better than it is." This sentiment, that the legal writing program could, students admit, be "tweaked," is echoed throughout the students we surveyed.

Regardless of these criticisms, students have found the professors here to be "generally outstanding": "Whether they are part of the older faculty who have been specializing in their fields for a long time, part of the younger faculty who know their subjects and are passionate about becoming leaders in the administration, or the adjuncts who are practicing in their fields and can give a new perspective on their subjects, with few exceptions, the faculty have been incredibly good at teaching their subjects, and being available outside of class as well as in to contact, ask questions of, and ask for help with non-academic issues (such as letters of recommendation)." DePaul has "a strong staff, which does a good job of making sure that we are prepared outside the classroom, and tries to guide students in such a way that they are prepared to get jobs during or immediately after school." Students feel that "the tax program is great," and that there is a "strong family law center." "The law school has a very strong alumni network," with students noting that DePaul graduates "are willing to go above and beyond to help you find a job or practice in an area that they are familiar with." Overall, "the greatest strength of the law school is the faculty, and both their skill at teaching, and willingness to try new ideas. The fact that the faculty and administration allow themselves to be in a constant state of small improvements is a welcome relief from schools which have found their one way to do things, and stick with it no matter what."

MICHAEL S. BURNS, ASSOCIATE DEAN OF ADMISSIONS & STUDENT ADMINISTRATION
25 EAST JACKSON BOULEVARD, CHICAGO, IL 60604
TEL: 312-362-6831 • FAX: 312-362-5280
E-MAIL: LAWINFO@DEPAUL.EDU • WEBSITE: WWW.LAW.DEPAUL.EDU

Life

In addition to its wonderful location in downtown Chicago, DePaul boasts a "robust and diverse set of student organizations, covering nearly any topic." Students feel that the "overall academic experience at DePaul has been fantastic." The tuition is "very affordable, and I feel like I'm getting a ton for my money." One students cites access to "opportunities" as an example, "i.e. service immersion trips to two different parts of the country, study abroad programs to nine different countries, covering different fields of study, clinics to learn direct client work, massive volunteer and outreach programs to get students into the community using their legal skills, and the list goes on and on." Some students note that "elevator service in the building is inadequate, but elevator improvements seem to be on the horizon in the near future." One student states that "the students, myself included, often complain about the physical condition of the school and the classrooms," although this sentiment is not necessarily universal.

Getting In

Students admitted for the fall entering class of 2014 at the 25th percentile had an LSAT score of 148 and an average GPA of 2.98, while admitted students at the 75th percentile had an LSAT score of 155 and a GPA of 3.56. Like many law schools, DePaul offers rolling admissions, but first-year students may only be admitted for the fall semester.

Clinical program required	No
Legal writing course requirement	Yes
Legal methods course requirement	No
Legal research course requirement	Yes
Moot court requirement	No
Public interest law requirement	No

ADMISSIONS

Selectivity Rating	78
# applications received	2,087
% applicants accepted	65
% acceptees attending	17
Average LSAT	152
Median LSAT	153
LSAT Range (25th to 75th percentile)	148–155
Average undergrad GPA	3.24
Median undergrad GPA	3.32
Application fee	$0
Regular application deadline	3/1
Transfer students accepted	Yes
Evening division offered	Yes
Part-time accepted	Yes
CAS accepted	Yes

International Students

TOEFL required of international students.	Yes

FINANCIAL FACTS

Annual tuition	$44,515
Books and supplies	$1,480
Fees	$484
Room & Board	$13,962
% first-year students receiving some sort of aid	99
% all students receiving some sort of aid	97
% of aid that is merit based	30
% receiving scholarships	90
Average grant	$16,252
Average loan	$42,171
Average total aid package	$49,843
Average debt	$125,895

EMPLOYMENT INFORMATION

Career Rating	84	
Total 2014 JD Grads	286	
% for whom you have useable information	100	
% grads employed ten months out	80	
Median starting salary	$55,000	
# employed full-time	211	
# employed part-time	18	
# employed bar required	166	
# employed JD preferred	47	
# employed professional/other	12	
# employed non-professional	4	
# pursuing advanced degree	3	
# unemployed and seeking employment	46	
# not seeking employment	5	
State for bar exam	IL, NY, CA, OH, MI	
Pass rate for first-time bar	85.5	

Prominent Alumni
Richard M. Daley, Former Mayor, City of Chicago; Mary Dempsey, Commissioner for Chicago Public Library

Grads Employed by Field (%)
Business/Industry (21)
Government (7)
Judicial Clerkship (1)
State or local: (1)
Private Practice (47)
 Solo: (2)
 2-10: (24)
 11-25: (9)
 26-50: (3)
 51-100: (1)
 101-250: (2)
 251-500: (1)
 501+: (4)
Public Interest (4)

DRAKE UNIVERSITY
LAW SCHOOL

INSTITUTIONAL INFORMATION

Public/private	Private
Affiliation	No Affiliation
Student-faculty ratio	11:1
% faculty part-time	38
% faculty female	44
% faculty underrepresented minority	11
Total faculty	55

SURVEY SAYS...

Great research resources, Abundant externship/internship/clerkship opportunities

STUDENTS

Enrollment of law school	333
% male/female	54/46
% from out-of-state	33
% part-time	2
% underrepresented minority	8
% international	1
# of countries represented	6
Average age of entering class	25

ACADEMICS

Academic Experience Rating	80
Profs interesting rating	86
Profs accessible rating	88
Hours of study per day	3.84

Academic Specialties

Civil Procedure, Commercial, Constitutional, Corporation Securities, Criminal, Environmental, Government Services, Human Rights, International, Labor, Property, Taxation, Intellectual Property

Advanced Degrees Offered

JD, 3 yrs; LLM, 1 yr; MJ, 1 yr

Combined Degrees Offered

JD/MBA(6sem 2sum); JD/MPA(6sem 2sum); JD/PharmD; JD/MA Political Science(6sem 1sum); JD/MS Ag. Econ.(6sem 1sum); JD/MSW; JD/MPH; JD/MHA

Academics

Located in Des Moines, Drake University is a "small school" where the professors are "kind and patient" but also "demand a lot out of students." Drake offers "world-class caliber" instruction and is known for its "legal research and writing program" that "none of the other schools in the region seem to have," says one student. Drake's Career Opportunity Program (COP) allows "for qualified law students to pursue their law degree on a part-time basis." The research program at Drake Law "allows students to experience a variety of research sources and methods," many of which "students at other law schools don't touch until after they graduate." For example, in their first year students "watch the entirety of a trial," and are able "to discuss various aspects of the trial with professors, the judge, jurors, and practicing attorneys"—an invaluable learning experience. Students also praise Drake's legal clinic, in which students give "legal aid to people who couldn't other-wise afford it," and cite it as a "great opportunity for practical experience."

Classes are "small enough" that students feel they can "engage effectively, but large enough that there are always competing points of view." Though class sizes are small, physical "classrooms are large but feel comfortable" and many have been "recently reno-vated." Students find Drake Law "the perfect amount of challenging." They are "continu-ously pushed" to their "intellectual limits" and their "academic skills have flourished under the pressure." Though some professors may be "intimidating" in the classroom, they are "very open to meeting with students" during their office hours, and will "fre-quently stop and talk with students in the halls." They "also attend social events so you can get to know them better." You definitely "get what you put in," notes one student, but "professors, peers, staff, and administrators always want to help each other." The school's administration is "absolutely amazing." The "staff learns your name right away," and "it's very easy to find answers to questions."

Students also find the location and networking opportunities quite beneficial. Drake is "very in touch with the legal community" and the "opportunities for employment and networking are endless." Since "Drake Law is situated in a capitol city," students are "able to obtain internships with state-level governmental entities" and in a "diverse range of businesses and practice fields." The alumni network is also quite robust. As one student notes, "nearly every lawyer and judge in the area went to Drake, so it has a very strong network."

KARA BLANCHARD, DIRECTOR OF ADMISSIONS AND FINANCIAL AID
2507 UNIVERSITY AVENUE, DES MOINES, IA 50311
TEL: 515-271-2782 • FAX: 515-271-1990
E-MAIL: LAWADMIT@DRAKE.EDU • WEBSITE: WWW.LAW.DRAKE.EDU

Life

The small class size "helps the school feel like a family," and students have many opportunities to bond and network outside of the classroom. The city of Des Moines, "has a plethora of cultural opportunities, festivals, activities, bars, and restaurants," for students to enjoy. The university also hosts several networking events each year for its students. "If you show up to the networking events," notes one student, "you will know many of the attorneys in the area and most of the Iowa Supreme Court by the time you have completed your 2L year." Many attorneys in the "Des Moines area graduated from Drake and love coming back to volunteer their time with the students." Drake also boasts "two student law review bodies," and practice teams are that are "nationally ranked and frequently in the top five to ten."

Drake University has also recently undergone some major renovations to their facilities to improve student learning and life including the addition of "large, multi-media classrooms, new furniture, podcasted lectures," and a "large communal area with floor-to-ceiling windows and microwaves and refrigerators to accommodate [students'] busy schedules." "The classrooms are all technologically modern," notes one student "and the students have easy access to the most recent research systems." What the library may lack "in physical sources, it makes up for through online sources."

Getting In

At the 25th percentile, students recently admitted to Drake Law have LSAT scores of 148 and GPAs in the 2.97 range, while admitted students at the 75th percentile have LSAT scores of 156 and GPAs of roughly 3.5.

Clinical program required	No
Legal writing course requirement	Yes
Legal methods course requirement	Yes
Legal research course requirement	Yes
Moot court requirement	Yes
Public interest law requirement	No

ADMISSIONS

Selectivity Rating	75
# applications received	487
% applicants accepted	78
% acceptees attending	27
Average LSAT	153
Median LSAT	152
LSAT Range (25th to 75th percentile)	148–156
Average undergrad GPA	3.21
Median undergrad GPA	3.25
Application fee	$50
Early application deadline	4/1
Transfer students accepted	Yes
Evening division offered	Yes
Part-time accepted	Yes
CAS accepted	Yes

International Students

TOEFL required of international students.	Yes

FINANCIAL FACTS

Annual tuition	$38,754
Books and supplies	$1,500
Fees	$112
Room & Board	$20,040
Financial aid application deadline	4/1
% first-year students receiving some sort of aid	86
% all students receiving some sort of aid	91
% of aid that is merit based	77
% receiving scholarships	66
Average grant	$19,441
Average loan	$37,115
Average total aid package	$49,115
Average debt	$108,857

EMPLOYMENT INFORMATION

Career Rating	90	**Prominent Alumni**
Total 2014 JD Grads	130	Dwight D. Opperman, CEO, West
% for whom you have useable information	99	Publishing Company; Mark Cady, Current Chief Justice of Iowa Supreme Court
% grads employed ten months out	89	**Grads Employed by Field (%)**
Median starting salary	$52,540	Academic (2)
# employed full-time	106	Business/Industry (19)
# employed part-time	9	Government (9)
# employed bar required	88	Judicial Clerkship (4)
# employed JD preferred	23	Federal: (1)
# employed non-professional	3	State or local: (3)
# pursuing advanced degree	2	Private Practice (49)
# unemployed and seeking employment	9	Solo: (2)
		2-10: (34)
# not seeking employment	1	11-25: (6)
State for bar exam	IA, MO, CA, CO, MN	26-50: (3)
Pass rate for first-time bar	90.6	51-100: (4)
		Public Interest (5)

DREXEL UNIVERSITY
SCHOOL OF LAW

INSTITUTIONAL INFORMATION

Public/private	Private
Affiliation	No Affiliation
% faculty part-time	19
% faculty female	50
% faculty underrepresented minority	20

SURVEY SAYS...

Diverse opinions accepted in classrooms

STUDENTS

Enrollment of law school	404
% male/female	54/46
% from out-of-state	42
% part-time	0
% underrepresented minority	14
% international	2
# of countries represented	4
Average age of entering class	25

ACADEMICS

Academic Experience Rating	84
Profs interesting rating	83
Profs accessible rating	86
Hours of study per day	3.74

Academic Specialties

Criminal, Intellectual Property

Advanced Degrees Offered

JD 3-year and 2-year options; LLM in American Legal Practice 1-year

Combined Degrees Offered

JD/MBA 4 yrs; JD/PhD Psychology 7 yrs; JD/MPH 4 yrs; JD/MSPP (Master of Science in Public Policy) 3 yrs

Academics

Drexel's brand-new law school was established in 2006, and "as a new school, everything is modern and state of the art." Students name the school's newness as one of its strengths: the professors are passionate and dedicated to making a name for the school, all the facilities are up to date, and the school offers competitive financial aid packages to attract legal talent. "This school may not have the long-standing reputation of many other schools throughout the country, but the fact that it is so new makes the faculty and staff strive to help the students achieve success." The "very accessible" faculty, particularly, impress Drexel's students: Drexel "has the most invested administration and faculty of any of the law schools I considered" because they "went out and recruited some of the best of the best to be members of the faculty." Budding lawyers revere the ethical grounding of the school, too: "The Dean of Students is one of the most amazing people I've ever met and his ethos of honesty, integrity and passion for the law can be found throughout the Administration and the Faculty."

Drexel's graduates feel well-prepared for the job market due to the program's "emphasis on gaining practical experience," and creating "'work-ready' graduates." "Drexel does an excellent job making networking easy." "Gone are the days where employment waits for every single one of those who complete a JD program. With this truth in mind, Drexel Law equips its students to be practicing attorneys before even taking a bar exam." Indeed, "the law school strongly encourages students to co-op for a semester," and requires a measure of pro-bono legal work: "Drexel offers so many experiential learning opportunities through co-op, clinics, fellowships, the pro-bono requirement, and internships/externships." It seems the university has taken seriously its obligation to measure up to older highly-ranked schools, which students notice and appreciate: "Drexel's commitment to building a top-notch law school shows not only in its staffing and funding levels, but in the strong extra-curricular support and skills training they make available to us."

Students also feel that because Drexel's law school isn't old, it hasn't struggled to break free of the values of the old guard in the way that other programs may: "I think the diversity and academic learning environment are this school's strong suit. I briefly attended a highly ranked school and I quickly realized that tolerance and diversity were not as prevalent as I had expected."

ISABEL "ISSA" DISCIULLO, ASSISTANT DEAN FOR ADMISSIONS
3320 MARKET STREET, ROOM 102, PHILADELPHIA, PA 19104
TEL: 215-895-1529 • FAX: 215-571-4769
E-MAIL: LAWADMISSIONS@DREXEL.EDU • WEBSITE: DREXEL.EDU/LAW

Life

Drexel escapes the shark-tank reputation of many of its competitors in social atmosphere: "The student body is extremely friendly despite the competitive atmosphere that law school creates through its use of the curve." One student credits the university for having "made the process of being in law school relaxed." As the school's roots have grown, so has the social network of the law school: "People hang out all the time. There is a bar right across the school where you can find law students every evening." While some students "do commute from New Jersey or from the suburbs," "many people live a trolley, bus, or train ride away" and find plenty to do socially around the Philadelphia campus, especially in nearby Center City. A common complaint congeals around the fact that the law school's new facilities are still integrating with the rest of the campus: "The library is very nice, however we have to share it with Drexel's undergraduates after 6:00 P.M. on weeknights and all weekend long. The undergrads do not have the same respect for our space that we do." Many students echo that it "would be nice if we did not have to share the library with the undergraduate students at certain hours." Overall, though, Drexel's students credit its "small community" for creating "a great student life here."

Getting In

For the 140 students in Drexel's class of 2016, the median LSAT range was 152–157 and the median GPA was 3.35, placing the school among the best, but not quite the best of the best, in American law school rankings. However, Drexel poises itself to compete with financial aid offers: all applicants are automatically reviewed for financial aid candidacy, and 91 percent of the class of 2015 received academic merit scholarships between $2,500 and $32,000 a year.

Clinical program required	Yes
Legal writing course requirement	Yes
Legal methods course requirement	Yes
Legal research course requirement	Yes
Moot court requirement	No
Public interest law requirement	Yes

ADMISSIONS

Selectivity Rating	82
# applications received	0
% applicants accepted	50
% acceptees attending	20
Average LSAT	154
Median LSAT	154
LSAT Range (25th to 75th percentile)	151–156
Average undergrad GPA	3.25
Median undergrad GPA	3.28
Application fee	$0
Regular application deadline	8/1
Transfer students accepted	Yes
Evening division offered	No
Part-time accepted	No
CAS accepted	Yes

International Students

TOEFL required of international students.	Yes

FINANCIAL FACTS

Annual tuition	$38,359
Books and supplies	$8,356
Fees	$840
Room & Board	$13,026
Financial aid application deadline	3/1
% first-year students receiving some sort of aid	98
% all students receiving some sort of aid	95
% of aid that is merit based	18
% receiving scholarships	82
Average grant	$21,979
Average loan	$32,982
Average total aid package	$46,871
Average debt	$91,915

EMPLOYMENT INFORMATION

Career Rating	93	Grads Employed by Field (%)
Total 2014 JD Grads	141	Academic (1)
% grads employed ten months out	85	Business/Industry (13)
# employed full-time	108	Government (16)
# employed part-time	12	Judicial Clerkship (13)
# employed bar required	101	Private Practice (36)
# employed JD preferred	13	Public Interest (5)
# employed professional/other	4	
# employed non-professional	2	
# pursuing advanced degree	3	
# unemployed and seeking employment	14	
# not seeking employment	2	
% grads employed by school	4	
State for bar exam	PA, NJ, NY	
Pass rate for first-time bar	86.8	

DUKE UNIVERSITY
SCHOOL OF LAW

INSTITUTIONAL INFORMATION

Public/private	Private
Affiliation	No Affiliation
Student-faculty ratio	9:1
Total faculty	119

SURVEY SAYS...

Students love Durham, NC, Diverse opinions accepted in classrooms, Great research resources, Abundant externship/internship/clerkship opportunities, Law school well run, Strong sense of community, Good social life

STUDENTS

Average age of entering class	23

ACADEMICS

Academic Experience Rating	98
Profs interesting rating	99
Profs accessible rating	99
Hours of study per day	3.31

Advanced Degrees Offered

JD 3 yrs; LLM 1 year, for international students only; LLM in Law and Entrepreneurship 1 year; SJD 1 year, for international students only

Combined Degrees Offered

JD/LLM in International & Comparative Law (3 yrs); JD/LLM in Law & Entrepreneurship (3 yrs); JD/MA in Bioethics and Science Policy (3 yrs); JD/MBA, JD/MPP, JD/MEM, JD/MTS (4 yrs); JD/MD (6 yrs); JD/PhD (7 yrs)

Academics

Despite its ranking as one of country's top law schools, students describe Duke University School of Law as "friendly and uncompetitive as a highly selective law school could be," praising its "fantastic atmosphere" and "excellent" professors. Students highlight professors who "see as more than our grades and really care about us as individuals," noting that "graduating without forming strong relationships with professors is the exception here." The close-knit feeling of the law school—Duke Law enrolls a little over 200 first-years annually—despite Duke's not insubstantial total student population—roughly 15,000 total—is one of the school's best features, according to students. Duke Law is "a small school community with the vast resources you would expect from a major research university." Most students fondly remember dinner, brunches, or even bowling parties with their various professors and "almost all of them have non-stop, open door office hours, and you can go in and talk to them about anything you want." This goes beyond just clarifying a point from an earlier seminar: "Students are not only welcome to discuss course material with professors, but are encouraged to discuss their broader interests, their careers, and their lives. Professors are always willing to lend a helping hand." Other students note the lengths that professors, and the Duke administration are willing to go for students: "My career counselor jumped through hoops to help me get a job at a top Washington, DC firm as a 1L." This willingness to lend a helping hand—or, as one student puts it, "Duke Law values—no talking about grades, no intimidating other students, no bragging"—adds to the collegial, communal atmosphere that "allows students to develop their own path at school and chart their own career choice," which "wouldn't be possible without our stellar, diverse faculty."

Duke Law's facilities get high marks. They are "extremely modern and able to handle anything from simple seminars to Federal Circuit Court arguments," and the law school building is "beautiful and comfortable with a lot of space to study, both inside and outside." Goodson Library has "ample space, is always open, and the seating is very comfortable." Of particular note to law students perpetually in research mode, the "research assistants in the library are helpful not only throughout the school year but also during the summer when students are working at internships."

While some students say that "more resources" could be put into the clinical programs at Duke Law and "wish there was a bit more emphasis on practical/experiential learning (especially in the third year)," others say that the "clinics are very well resourced." The Duke Legal Clinics, which operates collectively as a public interest law firm with ten distinct practice areas, is housed in its own wing of the law school and aims to provide students with opportunities to makes experiential connections between what they learn in the classroom and legal work in the Durham community.

WILLIAM J. HOYE, ASSOCIATE DEAN FOR ADMISSIONS AND STUDENT AFFAIRS
P.O. BOX 90393, DURHAM, NC 27708-0393
TEL: 919-613-7020 • FAX: 919-613-7257
E-MAIL: ADMISSIONS@LAW.DUKE.EDU • WEBSITE: LAW.DUKE.EDU / ADMIS /

Student Life

"Durham is an incredible place to live. I would live here permanently if it had the caliber of legal jobs that New York had," says one wistful student. Other students note Duke Law's "vibrant culture" of extra curricular activities—"it is a small school, but we have SO MANY activities to get involved in because students do like to spend their free time on such pursuits"—and the school's "general positive vibe." One student notes, "I feel completely comfortable being 'out' at Duke, even though Duke is located in the South;" another echoes that "we have a strong LGBT community." While other students do see the need to increase the "diversity of the student population and faculty," others want "emphasize that there is really a space for everyone at Duke Law." There is a "balance of married students, some with children, and many who went straight through or took less than three years off." Off campus, "the local food scene and brewery scene is incredible" and "Durham punches above its weight when it comes to food / drink." For basketball fans, you "have a professional sports team in [your] backyard," and "season tickets are easy for grad students to get."

Getting In

In addition to a regular admissions program, Duke Law also operates a binding early admissions program. The median GPA for accepted students is 3.77 and the median LSAT score for accepted students is 169. Duke Law receives roughly 5,550 applications and enrolls less than 225 students.

Clinical program required	No
Legal writing course requirement	Yes
Legal methods course requirement	Yes
Legal research course requirement	Yes
Moot court requirement	Yes
Public interest law requirement	No

ADMISSIONS

Selectivity Rating	**97**
# applications received	5,358
% applicants accepted	21
% acceptees attending	20
Median LSAT	169
LSAT Range (25th to 75th percentile)	166–170
Median undergrad GPA	3.77
Application fee	$70
Regular application deadline	2/15
Early application deadline	11/14
Early application notification	12/31
Transfer students accepted	Yes
Evening division offered	No
Part-time accepted	No
CAS accepted	Yes

International Students

TOEFL required of international students.	Yes

FINANCIAL FACTS

Annual tuition	$54,460
Books and supplies	$1,326
Fees	$1,088
Room & Board	$12,324
Financial aid application deadline	3/15

EMPLOYMENT INFORMATION	
Career Rating	**91**
Total 2014 JD Grads	215
% for whom you have useable information	100
% grads employed ten months out	93
# employed full-time	207
# employed part-time	0
# employed bar required	200
# employed JD preferred	6
# employed professional/other	1
# pursuing advanced degree	1
# unemployed and seeking employment	3
# not seeking employment	3
% grads employed by school	5
State for bar exam	NY, VA, CA, NC, TX
Pass rate for first-time bar	95.4

ELON UNIVERSITY
ELON UNIVERSITY SCHOOL OF LAW

INSTITUTIONAL INFORMATION

Public/private	Private
Affiliation	No Affiliation
Student-faculty ratio	12:1
% faculty part-time	33
% faculty female	33
% faculty underrepresented minority	11
Total faculty	45

SURVEY SAYS...

Diverse opinions accepted in classrooms

STUDENTS

Enrollment of law school	281
% male/female	46/54
% from out of state	45
% part-time	0
% underrepresented minority	21
% international	0
# of countries represented	0
Average age of entering class	24

ACADEMICS

Academic Experience Rating	**72**
Profs interesting rating	79
Profs accessible rating	79
Hours of study per day	4.60

Advanced Degrees Offered
JD; 2.5-year full-time program

Combined Degrees Offered
JD/MBA; 3 to 3.5 year program.
JD/MELP, 2.5 year program.

Academics

Established in 2006, Elon University School of Law "is an emerging talent" that "emphasizes leadership in the community" and developing practical skills. Situated in downtown Greensboro, North Carolina, a location that students say "is perfect to be able to connect with lawyers, judges, and legal professionals outside of the classroom," Elon strives to provide "practical experience" and to stand on the "front line of innovation in the legal education field." Students praise the school's ability "to adapt to change" as well as "its focus on experiential education" and innovative approaches.

The recent arrival of a new dean, who will be ushering in "a new curriculum starting within the next year," has spurred many of these developments. But it also means that the program is in flux. "I think Elon is still finding itself," one student explained, "which can be challenging at times when you are a student, but it is also very exciting." Students say that they are confident that the administration has a "progressive understanding of what the profession wants from law students," and "is not hesitant about accommodating those needs in the curriculum." Largely, students "strongly believe Elon's new push for experiential education is cutting edge, and will put Elon at the forefront of legal education in the next ten to twenty years."

One of these approaches is Elon's "preceptor program." The preceptorship—a term Elon borrowed from medical education—pairs a student with a working professional to gain technical skill and industry insight. There are more changes and new approaches coming down the pipe for Elon students, including guaranteed full-time residencies-in-practice. One student says that the new dean "seems to be making drastic changes," some of which "have already had a positive impact on the school and my experience" by helping students to develop "personal and professional relationships with my professors." Students remain confident in Elon, knowing that "students' success is in their best interest." The administration has been cultivating "relationships with firms, internships, externships" to help students gain "practical hands on experience."

Students speak warmly about their professors who "genuinely care about the students' success and grasp of the subject matter" and "make sure they are accessible outside the classroom for questions." Some even "go out of their way to develop mentoring relationships with students." One student enthusiastically endorses the "handful of professors who are extremely invested in their students: in making sure that we have a full understanding of the subject matter, that we are prepared to practice, and that we remain successful even after finishing their classes." Yet, some think that Elon has trouble "[recognizing] how to help students that seem to struggle. Elon is trying but there is still more they can do for students that are trying to understand but constantly fall short."

When interacting with the administration some students feel like all of their needs are met and concerns are addressed. "I have never found a door to a professor or administrator closed to me, nor have I ever felt as if my questions or concerns were not given someone's full attention." Others note that "the school suffers from a lack of transparency and a lack of accountability." And while some students say the school has a good track record of "aiding students in getting real-world experience with actual attorneys in the community," others report that "professional development mentors here are not helpful," adding that students struggle to secure "internships or jobs." One 3L warns, "I only know a few people out of my small graduating class who have employment lined up for next year, and I think this should be a huge concern." The school has implemented four-person advising teams to aid students in their professional and career develop-

ALAN WOODLIEF, SENIOR ASSOCIATE DEAN FOR ADMISSIONS & ADMINISTRATION
201 N. GREENE STREET, GREENSBORO, NC 27401
TEL: 336-279-9200 • FAX: 336-279-8199
EMAIL: LAW@ELON.EDU • WEBSITE: LAW.ELON.EDU

ment, and it reports that almost 70 percent of graduates are employed within ten months of graduation.

Life

This "small school with a strong sense of community" boasts "a ton of student orgs," and "growth every year in terms of diversity." Students say that "despite the serious talent at Elon, there is an overwhelming humility," without the "toxic environment" that some may associate with law programs. People "of all walks [of life] are welcome," one current student told us, "as are diverse viewpoints." "The Elon University undergraduate campus has a slogan of 'bELONg,'" one student recalls, "and I think that has carried over to the law school."

Getting In

Recently accepted students had LSAT scores averaging between 145 and 151 and a median GPA of 3.03. Early decision consideration is available to students who submit their application before December 1st.

Clinical program required	No
Legal writing course requirement	Yes
Legal methods course requirement	Yes
Legal research course requirement	Yes
Moot court requirement	No
Public interest law requirement	Yes

ADMISSIONS

Selectivity Rating	72
# applications received	599
% applicants accepted	75
% acceptees attending	25
Median LSAT	148
LSAT Range (25th to 75th percentile)	145–151
Median undergrad GPA	3.03
Application fee	$0
Regular application deadline	6/30
Early application deadline	11/15
Early application notification	12/30
Transfer students accepted	Yes
Evening division offered	No
Part-time accepted	No
CAS accepted	Yes

International Students

TOEFL required of international students.	Yes

FINANCIAL FACTS

Annual tuition	$37,924
Books and supplies	$12,950
Fees	$0
Room & Board	$12,500
Financial aid application deadline	7/1
% first-year students receiving some sort of aid	95
% all students receiving some sort of aid	93
% of aid that is merit based	25
% receiving scholarships	77
Average grant	$15,808
Average loan	$44,850
Average total aid package	$53,157
Average debt	$132,444

EMPLOYMENT INFORMATION

Career Rating	74	**Grads Employed by Field (%)**
Total 2014 JD Grads	104	Academic (3)
% for whom you have useable information	99	Business/Industry (17)
% grads employed ten months out	67	Government (6)
Median starting salary	$52,000	Judicial Clerkship (3)
% job accepting grads providing useable salary information	34	Federal: (3)
# employed full-time	64	State or local: (0)
# employed part-time	6	Other: (0)
# employed bar required	44	Private Practice (41)
# employed JD preferred	18	Solo: (2)
# employed professional/other	7	2-10: (33)
# employed non-professional	1	11-25: (5)
# pursuing advanced degree	4	26-50: (1)
# unemployed and seeking employment	25	51-100: (0)
# not seeking employment	4	101-250: (0)
% grads employed by school	1	251-500: (0)
State for bar exam	NC, VA, SC, MD, NY	501+: (0)
Pass rate for first-time bar	66.0	Size Unknown: (0)
		Public Interest (0)

EMORY UNIVERSITY
SCHOOL OF LAW

Academics

"Everyone is generally very welcoming and understanding" at Emory Law, and "every type of person who is dedicated to the legal profession can thrive in this environment." The professors are "incredible" and "unbelievably smart;" "they are the heart and soul of the institution [and] I would not be where I am now without their kinds hearts and dedication to the field." Students praise professors overall who "seem to truly enjoy teaching," though say that "some of the adjuncts shouldn't be there." Whether students are looking to pursue a traditional academic path or a take a more specialized route, Emory Law offers a wide range of options with its multiple academic programs, from the Center for Transactional Law and Practice, which educates students on topics related to business transactions, to the Global Health Law and Policy Project, a multidisciplinary platform for developing global healthcare initiatives, and the Child Rights Project, which aims to teach students about advocating for juveniles in the court system. Students praise Emory's externship program, which "gives you lots of options" in these specialized areas within the Atlanta legal community and is "easily the best part about Emory." For students "interested in the private sector, the opportunity to get experience working in-house at places like Coca-Cola, The Home Depot, and GE, to name a few, is invaluable." Public sector opportunities exist as well, "such as working at the FTC, the SEC, and a host of other government and non-profit options." Emory Law "provides a very wide range of legal education." In addition to externship opportunities, there are "extracurricular activities such as Mock Trial, Moot Court, Journal, and diversity practice societies/organizations," all of which help foster "a great [sense] of community among students." With the help of professors and Emory's alumni network, one student confidently says, "I feel like I am ready to wow potential employers both in formal interviews and informal networking occasions."

Despite a "strong alumni network," students have few positive things to say about Emory Law's career center, which "seems to do the bare minimum" and might be "great when you're a 1L and need resume advice but they don't really help you find jobs." While one student calls the administration "a near-constant bureaucratic frustration," others describe it as "accessible and friendly," noting that "the school is very well run [and the] administration does a lot to cater to the students." Some students would like the school to devote more energy "helping the students who are not in the top of the class realize that they still have great opportunities to find work," noting that "sometimes the middle-of-the-road students feel like the opportunities for career [development] are less because the focus is not on mid-size and small firms." Facilities are "up-to-date" and "up to par with competitive law schools," though one student regrets that the "library the law school is not open often enough," particularly on the weekends.

ETHAN ROSENZWEIG, ASSISTANT DEAN FOR ADMISSION
1301 CLIFTON ROAD, ATLANTA, GA 30322-2770
TEL: 404-727-6801 • FAX: 404-727-2477
E-MAIL: LAWINFO@LAW.EMORY.EDU • WEBSITE: WWW.LAW.EMORY.EDU

Student Life

Students praise the "strong sense of community" at Emory Law and point to a top-notch faculty that "tend to be engaged with the law school community." One student, "after hearing experiences of my friends at other law schools," was "so surprised how welcoming everyone was," underscoring that "this was by far the aspect that has set Emory apart for me." With a plethora of student activities, from academic endeavors like the Student Bar Association to social events like the Harvest Moon Ball and the Barristers Ball, "there is always something to look forward to" at Emory. In general, the atmosphere at Emory Law is "welcoming" and students under score "the friendliness of the faculty." As one transfer student says, although [Emory Law] was much more expensive, it was the best decision I've ever made," citing the friendly atmosphere on campus and the fact that "the school has so many clubs to cater to any interests." While there are a little over 800 students at the law school, Emory's total enrollment is closer to 14,000, meaning that students can usually find something social to do on campus. Though one student describes fellow Emory Law students as "pretty much rich and uptight," others praise the "diversity of the student body."

Getting In

Emory Law operates on a rolling admissions basis, so it's best for applicants to apply early for this competitive process—the school receives roughly 4,000 applications annually for a class of 245. The median GPA for admitted students is 3.75 and the median LSAT score is 165.

Clinical program required	No
Legal writing course requirement	Yes
Legal methods course requirement	Yes
Legal research course requirement	Yes
Moot court requirement	No
Public interest law requirement	No

ADMISSIONS

Selectivity Rating	**93**
# applications received	3,876
% applicants accepted	32
% acceptees attending	19
Average LSAT	162
Median LSAT	165
LSAT Range (25th to 75th percentile)	157–166
Average undergrad GPA	3.58
Median undergrad GPA	3.75
Application fee	$80
Regular application deadline	3/1
Transfer students accepted	Yes
Evening division offered	No
Part-time accepted	No
CAS accepted	Yes

International Students

TOEFL required of international students.	Yes

FINANCIAL FACTS

Annual tuition	47,500
Books and supplies	$5,696
Fees	$498
Room & Board (on/ off campus)	$18,602/$18,602
Financial aid application deadline	3/1
% first-year students receiving some sort of aid	100
% all students receiving some sort of aid	94
% of aid that is merit based	37
% receiving scholarships	86
Average grant	$18,144
Average loan	$34,261
Average total aid package	$48,343
Average debt	$114,363

EMPLOYMENT INFORMATION

Career Rating	**97**	
Total 2014 JD Grads	292	
% for whom you have useable information	34	
% grads employed ten months out	98	
Median starting salary	$100,000	
% job accepting grads providing useable salary information	42	
# employed full-time	276	
# employed part-time	9	
# employed bar required	252	
# employed JD preferred	31	
# employed professional/other	1	
# pursuing advanced degree	3	
# unemployed and seeking employment	3	
# not seeking employment	1	
% grads employed by school	23	
State for bar exam	GA	
Pass rate for first-time bar	96.6	

Prominent Alumni

Hon. Sanford Bishop, U.S. Congressman; Hon. Leah Sears, Former Chief Justice, Georgia Supreme Court; Hon. Sam A. Nunn, U.S. Senator (ret.), CEO Nuclear Threat Initiative; Raymond McDaniel, CEO, Moody's Investor Services

Grads Employed by Field (%)

Academic (8)
Business/Industry (15)
Government (15)
Judicial Clerkship (8)
Private Practice (47)
Public Interest (5)

FAULKNER UNIVERSITY
THOMAS GOODE JONES SCHOOL OF LAW

INSTITUTIONAL INFORMATION

Public/private	Private
Affiliation	Church of Christ
% faculty part-time	23
% faculty female	17
% faculty underrepresented minority	7
Total faculty	30

SURVEY SAYS...
Conservative students

STUDENTS

Enrollment of law school	282
% male/female	50/50
% underrepresented minority	50
# of countries represented	1
Average age of entering class	26

ACADEMICS

Academic Experience Rating	70
Profs interesting rating	88
Profs accessible rating	88
Hours of study per day	4.33

Academics

Faulkner University's Jones School of Law in Montgomery, Alabama is "a Church of Christ–affiliated school" with "a non-intimidating environment." According to students here, it's "the best-kept secret in Alabama." The "bar-passage rate is very high;" in fact, students report that Faulkner has had "the highest bar-passage rate in the state of Alabama." "The trial advocacy program is top-notch." "The faculty and administration actually care about you as a person" and "make sure you have practical knowledge for the real world." Many appreciate that professors "treat them like a friend and not a sub-ordinate." Some feel that Jones "could benefit from a broader curriculum." While the "small" campus can mean fewer opportunities, many students find that "the resources of the law school are growing everyday."

The many "very knowledgeable" and "distinguished" professors here "truly are a hidden gem." Their ranks include "some of the most experienced legal minds anywhere." They also "possess a great deal of real-world experience" and "give practical lessons about real-life lawyering." The faculty is pretty big on the "Socratic Method." A student explains that his torts professor "writes everyone's name on a playing card. Before class he draws three cards, and the three people have a roundtable discussion presenting the cases that were assigned. It is by far the most memorable first-year experience." "Small class sizes" "allow for greater participation" and "You are able to get to know your professors better." The intimacy "strongly encourages differing viewpoints and class discussion" as well. Professors here "truly care about your success and take an interest in your life outside of the classroom." "The amount of time each professor is willing to dedicate to each student never fails to impress me," agrees another student. "They genuinely want each student to succeed."

The "professional looking" facilities (featuring "marble and mahogany throughout") are "outstanding." There is also "Internet access throughout the school." "Every class-room is equipped with plenty of electrical outlets," notes one student. Most students would also like to see the library "open later hours."

The well-liked administration here is "always available and extremely helpful." It's worth noting that the Jones School of Law is one of only three fully ABA accredited law schools in Alabama. A significant milestone for the school, it basically means that students can take any bar exam in any state when they graduate just like graduates of all ABA-approved law schools.

JOSHUA M. ROBERTS, DIRECTOR OF ADMISSIONS
5345 ATLANTA HIGHWAY, MONTGOMERY, AL 36109
TEL: 334-386-7210 • FAX: 334-386-7908
E-MAIL: LAW@FAULKNER.EDU • WEBSITE: WWW.FAULKNER.EDU/LAW

Life

"There is a definite sense of community" since "everyone knows everyone," but students insist that "that's a plus." At the same time, "there is a competitive environment, but that's what the real world is like." "We are all in this struggle together, and we help each other to survive," explains a 3L. "This includes saving someone who is drowning in class when briefing a case or forming study groups for exams." Faulkner University is definitively "Christian oriented," and overall, it's "a very conservative campus." The law school is "extremely conservative" as well, but people who aren't on the political right feel welcome here. "Even though I am very liberal and a bit outside the norm, the faculty and staff do not attempt to curtail my individuality," comments a 3L. "I do not hesitate to be vocal in my opinions and viewpoints (both in and out of class) and have never had any repercussions."

Students say that their peers "come from all strata of society and bring varying perspectives based upon their personal, professional and educational experiences." "There are people that are directly out of college as well as people that have been out of undergrad for fifteen to twenty years," explains one student.

Outside of class, there are "seminars, speakers," and "even school parties," but students feel "there should be a few more social opportunities, especially on the weekends." Many students are active in church. "I play basketball with friends," says an athletic 2L. "We also play flag football and get together for poker and other events to take our minds off school."

Getting In

Admitted students at the 25th percentile have LSAT scores in the low 140s and GPAs of about 2.79. Admitted students at the 75th percentile have LSAT scores in the low 150s and GPAs of 3.28. If you take the LSAT more than once, Faulkner will use your highest score.

Clinical program required	No
Legal writing course requirement	Yes
Legal methods course requirement	Yes
Legal research course requirement	Yes
Moot court requirement	Yes
Public interest law requirement	No

ADMISSIONS

Selectivity Rating	72
# applications received	494
% applicants accepted	76
% acceptees attending	28
Average LSAT	147
Median LSAT	146
LSAT Range (25th to 75th percentile)	142–151
Average undergrad GPA	3.09
Median undergrad GPA	3.14
Application fee	$0
Regular application deadline	6/15
Transfer students accepted	Yes
Evening division offered	No
Part-time accepted	No
CAS accepted	Yes

FINANCIAL FACTS

Annual tuition	$34,000
Books and supplies	$2,400
Room & Board (on/ off campus)	$12,000
Financial aid application deadline	7/15
% all students receiving some sort of aid	45
% of aid that is merit based	100
% receiving scholarships	45
Average grant	$13,559

EMPLOYMENT INFORMATION

Career Rating	72	
Total 2014 JD Grads	101	
% for whom you have useable information	99	
% grads employed ten months out	83	
Median starting salary	$44,950	
# employed full-time	75	
# employed part-time	9	
# employed bar required	62	
# employed JD preferred	18	
# employed professional/other	1	
# employed non-professional	3	
# pursuing advanced degree	1	
# unemployed and seeking employment	15	
# not seeking employment	1	
% grads employed by school	1	
State for bar exam	AL, GA, FL, TN, MS	

Prominent Alumni

Greg Allen, Partner of Beasley, Allen, et.al.; Kelli Wise, Associate Justice, Alabama Supreme Court; Ernestine Sapp, Partner of Gray, Langford, Sapp, et.al.; Bobby Bright, Former U.S. Congressman, Former Mayor of Montgomery, Alabama; Tommy Bryan, Associate Justice, Alabama Supreme Court

Grads Employed by Field (%)
Academic (2)
Business/Industry (12)
Government (9)
Judicial Clerkship (3)
Private Practice (56)
Public Interest (0)

FLORIDA INTERNATIONAL UNIVERSITY
COLLEGE OF LAW

INSTITUTIONAL INFORMATION

Public/private	Public
Affiliation	No Affiliation
Student-faculty ratio	11:1
% faculty part-time	42
% faculty female	41
% faculty underrepresented minority	46
Total faculty	79

SURVEY SAYS...

Diverse opinions accepted in classrooms, Great research resources, Abundant externship/internship/clerkship opportunities, Good social life

STUDENTS

Enrollment of law school	487
% male/female	45/55
% part-time	27
# of countries represented	22
Average age of entering class	26

ACADEMICS

Academic Experience Rating	89
Profs interesting rating	88
Profs accessible rating	92
Hours of study per day	3.15

Academic Specialties

Commercial, Criminal, Environmental, Government Services, Human Rights, International, Labor, Taxation, Intellectual Property

Advanced Degrees Offered

LLM for international lawyers; 1 year

Combined Degrees Offered

JD/MSW 4.5 yrs; JD/MPA3.5 yrs; JD/MIB (Master of International Business) 3.5 yrs; JD/MS Psych (Master of Science in Psychology) 4 yrs; JD/MALACS (Master of Latin America and Caribbean Studies) 3.5 yrs; JD/MBA 4 yrs; JD/MSCS (Master of Science in Criminal Justice) 3.5 yrs; JD/MSES (Master of Environmental Studies) 4 yrs.

Academics

Florida International University College of Law is a relatively new school. It received its full accreditation from the ABA in 2006. It was created to provide opportunities for underrepresented groups and to serve the immediate community. Students come from all over the globe, and most agree it's a great educational experience for the cost—truly "an affordable gem." One student says, "The school has surpassed all of my expectations." The school offers eight clinical programs, giving students the chance to gain experience in the courtroom by representing real cases. In the human rights and immigration clinic, they represent clients in political asylum, as well as other immigration cases. This real-world experience is "something employers are always looking for" and is a part of the "hands-on" experience many students refer to. At FIU, education is practical. Community service is required, as well as a three-semester legal writing program. Professors spend time teaching how to write memos, petitions, appeals, and oral arguments. Students are prepared for the tangible world of legal practice and claim they measure up well against those of other more established institutions, performing highly in both national and international moot courtroom competitions. "FIU compares to the top law schools of the country," one student boasts. Students attribute this to the faculty, who are some of the "most qualified and brilliant professors in the field." "They care about our success." Another thing that sets this program apart from others is the school's "focus on international education." There's an international law requirement in the first year. Most classes devote some time to global issues, respecting "current legal trends and the importance of globalization." "The curriculum is challenging but fair and offers a good variety of electives in the second and third years." However, some students would prefer a chance to specialize in areas such as tax, business, or criminal law. They hope FIU will confer the LLM degree in the future, as well.

Students love the "familial atmosphere" of FIU, claiming "the deans and administrators know most students by name." The class sizes are small, and students say professors honestly appear happy when they drop by their offices. The professors "provide real-world insight," and even the administrative body is "committed" to its students. The career development office assists students with writing résumés and cover letters, as well as prepping them for mock interviews. "The administration does not just 'operate' the school, but understands itself to be partners of the students in their journey through law school." There are many opportunities for internships within Miami. Another perk is the school's proximity to both state and federal courts. In addition to the many Miami firms, Florida's Third District Court of Appeals is situated right behind the campus. Furthermore, "the dean and the professors do everything that they can to bring the legal world to us." The school hosts visiting lecturers from across the country. Some students argue the school's newness might hamper their vocational opportunities beyond state lines, citing its lack of recognition outside of Florida. "Not many employers conduct on-campus interviews here," but "the administration is working hard at facilitating networking and externship and internship opportunities that could lead to jobs down the road." Most students feel confident that FIU's reputation as a law school will grow, claiming "it has already made excellent progress in its short history."

ALMA O. MIRÓ, DIRECTOR OF ADMISSIONS AND FINANCIAL AID
FIU COLLEGE OF LAW, OFFICE OF ADMISSIONS AND FINANCIAL AID, RDB 1055, MIAMI, FL 33199
TEL: 305-348-8006 • FAX: 305-348-2965
E-MAIL: LAWADMIT@FIU.EDU • WEBSITE: LAW.FIU.EDU

Life

Students at FIU are "very down-to-earth, easily approachable, and thoroughly diverse." They challenge each other in a way better characterized as "Olympic spirit" rather than "academic Darwinism." The student body is comprised of people from more than twenty-two countries, and "there are student organizations for just about every interest you can imagine."

FIU students enjoy a "beautiful" library, "state-of-the-art facilities," and "courtyards decorated with professional and student art." Students say going to law school in a city is fun for the downtimes when you're not studying. Miami, although admittedly difficult for some transplants, is a true multicultural hub with a population of more than two million people. Students also have access to the Everglades National Park, as well as miles of Florida's beaches.

Getting In

The LSAT and GPA are the most important criteria to the admissions committee, followed by letters of recommendation and personal essay. Admitted students in the 25th percentile have GPAs just under 3.3 and LSAT scores in the low 150s. Admitted students in the 75th percentile have GPAs just under 3.8 and LSAT scores in the high 150s. Transfer students are accepted as long as their current institution is accredited by the ABA and they're in the upper-third tier of their first-year class. A maximum of thirty-one hours can be transferred. Last year, 138 out-of-state applicants were accepted, and the average age of the entering class was twenty-five. Roughly one in five students is admitted.

Clinical program required	No
Legal writing course requirement	Yes
Legal methods course requirement	Yes
Legal research course requirement	Yes
Moot court requirement	No
Public interest law requirement	Yes

ADMISSIONS

Selectivity Rating	88
# applications received	1,823
% applicants accepted	29
% acceptees attending	21
Median LSAT	156
LSAT Range (25th to 75th percentile)	151–158
Median undergrad GPA	3.58
Application fee	$20
Regular application deadline	5/1
Transfer students accepted	Yes
Evening division offered	Yes
Part-time accepted	Yes
CAS accepted	Yes

International Students

TOEFL required of international students.	Yes

FINANCIAL FACTS

Annual tuition (in-state/out-of-state)	$18,398/$31,964
Books and supplies	$8,876
Fees	$4,024
Room & Board	$18,322
Financial aid application deadline	2/15
% first-year students receiving some sort of aid	95
% all students receiving some sort of aid	92
% of aid that is merit based	12
% receiving scholarships	73
Average grant	$9,703
Average loan	$30,626
Average total aid package	$33,254
Average debt	$89,815

EMPLOYMENT INFORMATION

Career Rating	79	**Prominent Alumni**
Total 2014 JD Grads	154	Rebeca Mendez, Atty, Holland & Knight;
% grads employed ten months out	93	Christopher Kokoruda, Atty, Miami-Dade
# employed full-time	131	County Attorney's Office; Katie A. Edwards,
# employed part-time	12	Member, Florida House of Representatives;
# employed bar required	108	Carlos Lago, Atty, Greenberg Traurig;
# employed JD preferred	27	Andrea Canona, Fellow, Dept. of Justice
# employed professional/other	8	Honors Program
# employed non-professional	0	**Grads Employed by Field (%)**
# unemployed and seeking employment	10	Academic (2)
		Business/Industry (18)
State for bar exam	FL, TX, CA, NY, DC	Government (16)
Pass rate for first-time bar	78.9	Private Practice (56)

FLORIDA STATE UNIVERSITY
COLLEGE OF LAW

Academics

At FSU, its students report, prepare for a friendly, individualized law school experience at a state school price. Of the faculty and administration, who "all [have] open door policies," students say, "I never imagined law professors would be so accessible" and "any problems or concerns ranging from externships to the temperature of the classrooms someone is always polite and wanting to help." This is undoubtedly because "there is so much conversation between the stellar faculty and the students" and "the administration is fairly transparent and keeps students informed." Students feel connected to their professors: "All of the professors at FSU Law seem to enjoy teaching here, and I believe that says something about the faculty, facilities, and student body."

Looking beyond law school, while "FSU is very much focused on policy and theory rather than on teaching legal-practice skills from day one," "It's clear that the school places great weight on job placement." "The placement office, deans office, and all other staff here to support the students are phenomenal. They are constantly offering small workshops, résumé reviews, intimate gatherings with local judges and attorneys, and more."

Students offer high praise for FSU's facilities as well: "The classrooms are freshly renovated and the technology is great." "Our new advocacy center, the previous Florida 1st DCA building, has brought five new courtrooms to the law school as well as conference rooms, new classrooms, and interview rooms. I would put the facilities of FSU law up against any law school." Study space is widely available: "The law library is comfortable and spacious enough to fit all the students without overcrowding during exams" and across campus, facilities are "open 24/7 for students with our ID cards so no matter when we want to study we can." Add "very low" tuition, "great" program availability, "openness toward transfer students," and a "location in a capital city," and it's easy to see why FSU's law students are so satisfied with their choice.

Life

Of all the things to love about FSU Law, its "location in Tallahassee is a great asset. Being in the capital city offers opportunities to law students in multiple different disciplines in the legal profession." Faculty and staff are eager to help students maximize these connections, cultivating local firms to host "events for students who are pursuing study in a particular field...because there are so many local lawyers, there are more networking opportunities than any student can possibly participate in." Students benefit from the university's deep roots in Florida, finding that FSU's "alumni base is also great for reaching out and networking." One student puts it strongly: "FSU Law is located in the capital city, literally within the shadow of the Florida Capitol Building. Being so close to the seat of power in Florida means many opportunities to interact with Supreme Court justices, legislators, and others."

JENNIFER L. KESSINGER, DIRECTOR OF ADMISSIONS AND RECORDS
425 WEST JEFFERSON STREET, TALLAHASSEE, FL 32306-1601
TEL: 850-644-3787 • FAX: 850-644-7284
E-MAIL: ADMISSIONS@LAW.FSU.EDU • WEBSITE: WWW.LAW.FSU.EDU

In terms of social culture, "my classmates all seem to get along and there isn't a sense of throat cutting competition." Reports confirm that "the other students are smart and actually nice to each other" and "competition is very low. It's a great combination of hard work and plenty of play." Indeed, "the students here are kind to one another, will email you notes if you are sick, and I've never heard of a book being hidden in the library!" Students register a few complaints about "parking" availability on campus and wishing for "more food options at school," as well as the fact that, as at many large universities "there is often a mismatch between available seats in a class and demand," but as a whole, one student sums it up positively: "I think we're one of the nation's best kept secrets."

Getting In

Don't be fooled by FSU's position as a large state university: getting in takes some chops. FSU's median LSAT is 159, its median GPA is 3.43, and a quarter of its students have two or more years of work experience. However, only 14 percent of entering FSU law students are non-Florida residents, suggesting that out-of-state students might be reviewed kindly. FSU Law has a good reputation for being transfer-friendly; all transfer students must be in the top third of their class to be eligible for admission.

Clinical program required	No
Legal writing course requirement	Yes
Legal methods course requirement	Yes
Legal research course requirement	Yes
Moot court requirement	No
Public interest law requirement	Yes

ADMISSIONS

Selectivity Rating	89
# applications received	1,916
% applicants accepted	41
% acceptees attending	24
Median LSAT	159
LSAT Range (25th to 75th percentile)	156–161
Median undergrad GPA	3.43
Application fee	$30
Regular application deadline	4/15
Transfer students accepted	Yes
Evening division offered	No
Part-time accepted	No
CAS accepted	Yes

International Students

TOEFL required of international students.	Yes

FINANCIAL FACTS

Annual tuition (in-state/out-of-state)	$18,071/$18,071
Books and supplies	$3,000
Fees (in-state/out-of-state)	$2,623/$22,635
Room & Board	$10,000
Financial aid application deadline	3/1
% first-year students receiving some sort of aid	93
% all students receiving some sort of aid	89
% receiving scholarships	58
Average grant	$8,328
Average loan	$28,540
Average total aid package	$27,576
Average debt	$80,375

EMPLOYMENT INFORMATION

Career Rating	89
Total 2014 JD Grads	268
% for whom you have useable information	97
% grads employed ten months out	88
Median starting salary	$50,000
% job accepting grads providing useable salary information	70
# employed full-time	219
# employed part-time	18
# employed bar required	185
# employed JD preferred	41
# employed professional/other	7
# employed non-professional	4
# pursuing advanced degree	7
# unemployed and seeking employment	6
# not seeking employment	9
State for bar exam	FL, GA, TX, CA, NY

Prominent Alumni
Mark Williamson, Alston & Bird LLP; Justice Rick Polston, Florida Supreme Court; Jeffrey A. Stoops, President of SBA Communications Corp.; Peggy Rolando, Shutts & Bowen

Grads Employed by Field (%)
Business/Industry (13)
Government (29)
Judicial Clerkship (4)
 Federal: (2)
 State or local: (3)
Private Practice (39)
 Solo: (1)
 2-10: (2)
 11-25: (7)
 26-50: (4)
 51-100: (1)
 101-250: (3)
 251-500: (2)
 501+: (1)
 Size Unknown: (2)
Public Interest (3)

FORDHAM UNIVERSITY
SCHOOL OF LAW

Academics

New York City's Fordham University School of Law carries a "strong reputation and hardworking, practical students," who benefit from "[the school's] connection and location within the strong NYC job market." With "lots of experiential opportunities" and a "loyal and large alumni network," students leave with practical job skills and connections within top firms. Students hold many of their "higher caliber " professors in high regard, saying that they are "active in our lives" and meet with students on "their own time to help . . . with everything from in-class questions, to drafting cover letters for internships and clerkships, and doing mock interviews." Students are especially keen on the Fordham adjuncts, who are "partners" and "practitioners at premier law firms." Fordham also keeps students in contact with the NYC legal community through campus events like the "three days of meet and greets with the 1L class" and top firms, and networking opportunities with alumni who serve as "lawyers at big firms," in "government agencies" and on the federal bench, and who "are always excited to meet Fordham students."

Recent decisions by the administrations regarding the curve have largely soured students on their school's leadership. While students say they are "not opposed to a curve in theory," they tell us that a 2014 "mandatory upper level class curve for all courses with more than 4 JD students, including seminars and clinic work," was "instituted with essentially no warning or consultation with students." They say that this "immediate," "dead of night" change damaged student morale and "penalized" "current students who chose classes in an unlucky order." However, while some feel that "the result was an increasingly unworkable system which has caused at least as many problems as it has purported to solve," others say that "the debacle over the upper level curve implementation helped convince the administration it was finally time to join a number of our peer institutions and place student representatives on faculty governance committees," and they remain hopeful about the new dean who arrived in Summer 2015. Despite this hiccup, the "administration has been quick to respond" to other issues and "proactive in getting students . . . the help they need."

Students say that they have "always found [the research librarians] extremely helpful," and the new, beautiful facility provides plenty of resources and technological tools. Students universally praise the Public Interest Resource Center as "probably the best center at Fordham." While the new building has had some issues with long lines at the elevator banks, students generally think it "is gorgeous and looks and feels like a hotel."

STEPHEN BROWN, ASSISTANT DEAN FOR ENROLLMENT SERVICES
33 WEST 60TH STREET, NINTH FLOOR, NEW YORK, NY 10023
TEL: 212-636-6810 • FAX: 212-636-7984
E-MAIL: LAWADMISSIONS@LAW.FORDHAM.EDU • WEBSITE: LAW.FORDHAM.EDU

Life

Fordham fosters a "competitive but cooperative" environment by attracting students who "conduct themselves professionally, but don't take themselves too seriously." One student jokes, "Compared to our neighbor schools on the Upper West Side and near Washington Square, Fordham is practically a social paradise." Students enjoy informal "bar nights" and outings hosted by the school, like museum visits and alumni mentoring events. The Student Bar Association also hosts frequent events, which "ensures that there are many social and community-building events among the student body." Students say that the first year helps to knit the community together and that "the social life is good . . . especially if you join one of the journals or competition societies." Students say that "the journals are widely respected and near uniformly acknowledge as something which one wants to be a part of," and not as merely a line on their résumé. Students also come to Fordham with a "wide range of work experience" and educational backgrounds. One student described an evening section that included former professional athletes, "various PhDs, MDs, and a wide range of master's degrees." This helps to create "a strong networking opportunity within the class itself" while adding interest and color to peer interactions. Fordham has thriving "affinity groups," like Latin American Law Student's Association and OutLaws—an LGBT organization, though many students say that the school suffers from a lack of diversity. One student explains that, while "students from different [racial] and ethnic backgrounds and different sexual orientations" are represented at the school, "many of us have had similar experiences and offer little substantive diversity. The affinity groups are much more focused on gaining access to privileged spaces (clerkships and firms) rather than challenging the status quo."

Getting In

Admitted students have LSAT scores that average between 160 and 165 and a median undergraduate GPAs of 3.54. Grade and score distributions for evening division students are slightly lower.

Clinical program required	No
Legal writing course requirement	Yes
Legal methods course requirement	Yes
Legal research course requirement	Yes
Moot court requirement	No
Public interest law requirement	No

ADMISSIONS

Selectivity Rating	91
# applications received	4,645
% applicants accepted	35
% acceptees attending	22
Median LSAT	163
LSAT Range (25th to 75th percentile)	160–165
Median undergrad GPA	3.54
Application fee	$70
Regular application deadline	3/15
Early application deadline	10/15
Early application notification	12/15
Transfer students accepted	Yes
Evening division offered	Yes
Part-time accepted	Yes
CAS accepted	Yes

FINANCIAL FACTS

Annual tuition	$51,880
Books and supplies	$1,816
Room & Board	$19,494
Financial aid application deadline	4/1
% first-year students receiving some sort of aid	78
% all students receiving some sort of aid	76
% receiving scholarships	49
Average grant	$12,500

GEORGE MASON UNIVERSITY
SCHOOL OF LAW

INSTITUTIONAL INFORMATION

Public/private	Public
Affiliation	No Affiliation
% faculty part-time	71
% faculty female	25
% faculty underrepresented minority	15
Total faculty	129

SURVEY SAYS...

Students love Arlington, VA, Abundant externship/internship/ clerkship opportunities, Conservative students

STUDENTS

Enrollment of law school	490
% male/female	57/43
% part-time	31
% underrepresented minority	19
% international	2
Average age of entering class	26

ACADEMICS

Academic Experience Rating	**88**
Profs interesting rating	83
Profs accessible rating	72
Hours of study per day	3.71

Academic Specialties

Corporation Securities, Criminal, Government Services, International, Legal Philosophy, Taxation, Intellectual Property

Advanced Degrees Offered

LLM - a post-JD degree specializing in (a)Intellectual Property or (b) Law and Economics.

Combined Degrees Offered

JD/MPP; JD/MA or PhD in Economics

Academics

George Mason University's law students agree that "the professors are brilliant" and "Mason is a hidden gem that prepares students for actual practice better than any other law school out there." However, there's plenty more to say about the school that incites a disagreement typical of students who are being taught to argue for a living. Some contend that "one of the school's strengths is the four-semester legal writing requirement" while some refer disparagingly to "the nightmare of a writing program that the school has instituted." Others synthesize the two arguments: "The students often complain about the [legal writing] program, but most recognize that it is tremendously useful and will help them with future legal opportunities." Students are similarly divided on GMU's pedagogical ethos: some assert that "there is a very good blend of theory and practical knowledge conveyed" in the curricula, while others maintain that "the emphasis on economics in many ways is distracting from understanding the black letter law" or that "this is a patent law heavy school with unequal opportunities for students with social science rather than hard science backgrounds." GMU is stringent about its graduation requirements, leading some students to complain about "too many required courses," yet students also appreciate that "there are many classes available to practice both courtroom advocacy and writing skills, and taking part in these classes has given me invaluable experience for litigation."

In terms of faculty, administration, and other on-campus support, students feel that GMU's "administration is vested in student outcomes" and that "the staff is unbelievably open to outside discussion and help providing high government contacts and networking." The university's ten minutes away from Washington, D.C., provides a major asset to job-seeking graduates "with ready access to fabulous internships and other educational opportunities at a public school price." This proximity also creates a culture of working lawyers amongst its faculty: "most of the professors aren't just professors. They're also practicing attorneys or policy specialists who have major influences on their respective fields, and on the development of those fields." Students find the school's facilities "extremely up to date" and "outstanding," and extol the librarians: "The librarians are perhaps the most wonderful people on campus." There are some complaints about the law school's relationship to the rest of the university: students claim "the law school is like the estranged step-child to the main campus," that they "could use better amenities," and that they sometimes "feel like nothing more than a cash cow to the main campus in Fairfax" due to rising tuition prices in the last few years. That said, Virginia locals appreciate the "in-state tuition rate," which is "relatively cheap."

ALISON PRICE, SR. ASSOCIATE DEAN AND DIRECTOR OF ADMISSIONS
3301 FAIRFAX DRIVE, ARLINGTON, VA 22201
TEL: 703-993-8010 • FAX: 703-993-8088
E-MAIL: APRICE1@GMU.EDU • WEBSITE: WWW.LAW.GMU.EDU

Life

Even as they argue about, well, everything, GMU students seem to like each other, reporting that the school's culture has a "down-to-earth personality" and that "George Mason invites very bright and hard working students." "There is a social scene if you want it but most prefer to keep it to the weekends," and students observe a "Great community." They attribute this to the intimacy of the program: "GMU has small class sizes. This leads to more approachable professors and a greater camaraderie between the students. Though it is still competitive, I have not seen any animosity or heard about nefarious acts by students." This supportive social atmosphere is mirrored in the "Safe, well-lit campus," which is "metro accessible" to D.C. and the other surrounding areas. This, as well as the school's wide offering of evening classes, makes GMU a good choice for working or commuting students: "Being an evening student I appreciate the fact that the night courses are taught by the same faculty as the day classes."

GMU hardly conveys that liberals need not apply, but prospective students are well-advised to know that "the school has a noticeable libertarian (not necessarily conservative) bias, but the faculty and students are accepting of other viewpoints and willing to engage in respectful debate." Some attest that "there is no ideological diversity" and that the school could use "more diversity of viewpoints on the faculty," but many others value the school's "conservative perspective deriving from its focus on law and economics." In general, though, GMU's law students feel "camaraderie" in their peer community, and like that GMU is "not a cutthroat environment."

Getting In

Many students feel that GMU's ranking isn't consummate with its quality of education; its high admissions standards underscore this. For the students matriculating in 2014, the median LSAT was 161 and median GPA was 3.60.

Clinical program required	No
Legal writing course requirement	Yes
Legal methods course requirement	No
Legal research course requirement	Yes
Moot court requirement	Yes
Public interest law requirement	No

ADMISSIONS

Selectivity Rating	90
# applications received	2,163
% applicants accepted	38
% acceptees attending	20
Median LSAT	161
LSAT Range (25th to 75th percentile)	156–163
Median undergrad GPA	3.60
Application fee	$0
Regular application deadline	4/1
Regular notification	4/15
Early application deadline	12/15
Early application notification	1/31
Transfer students accepted	Yes
Evening division offered	Yes
Part-time accepted	Yes
CAS accepted	Yes

FINANCIAL FACTS

Annual tuition (in-state/ out-of-state)	$22,698/$38,084
Books and supplies	$6,634
Fees	$2,653
Room & Board	$16,710
Financial aid application deadline	3/1
% first-year students receiving some sort of aid	97
% all students receiving some sort of aid	86
% of aid that is merit based	20
% receiving scholarships	60
Average grant	$11,556
Average loan	$41,994
Average total aid package	$39,767
Average debt	$104,188

EMPLOYMENT INFORMATION

Career Rating	73
Total 2014 JD Grads	184
% grads employed ten months out	96
Median starting salary	$63,046
% job accepting grads providing useable salary information	67
# employed full-time	153
# employed part-time	22
# employed bar required	106
# employed JD preferred	65
# employed professional/other	3
# employed non-professional	1
# pursuing advanced degree	2
# unemployed and seeking employment	2
# not seeking employment	2
% grads employed by school	9
State for bar exam	VA, MD, DC, NY, CA

Prominent Alumni

Congressman David Jolly, Florida's 13th Congressional District; Maureen Ohlhausen, Commissioner, Federal Trade Commission; The Hon. Scott Clarkson, U.S. Bankruptcy Court, Central District of California; The Hon. Wesley G. Russell, Jr., Virginia Court of Appeals; Kelly McNamara Corley, Executive Vice President & General Counsel, Discover Financial Services

Grads Employed by Field (%)

Academic (5)
Business/Industry (21)
Government (19)
Judicial Clerkship (11)
Private Practice (38)
Public Interest (6)

INSTITUTIONAL

THE GEORGE WASHINGTON UNIVERSITY
LAW SCHOOL

INFORMATION

Public/private	Private
Affiliation	No Affiliation
Student-faculty ratio	15:1
% faculty part-time	73
% faculty female	33
% faculty underrepresented minority	11
Total faculty	394

SURVEY SAYS...
Students love Washington, DC

STUDENTS

Average age of entering class	25

ACADEMICS

Academic Experience Rating	**69**
Profs interesting rating	75
Profs accessible rating	69
Hours of study per day	NR

Academic Specialties
Civil Procedure, Commercial, Constitutional, Corporation Securities, Criminal, Environmental, Government Services, Human Rights, International, Labor, Legal History, Legal Philosophy, Property, Taxation, Intellectual Property

Advanced Degrees Offered
JD full-time 3 yrs; JD part-time 4 yrs; Master of Laws 1-2 yrs; Doctor of Juridical Science 3 yrs

Combined Degrees Offered
JD/MBA; JD/MPA; JD/MA International Affairs; JD/MA History; JD/MA Women's Studies JD/MPH, all can be completed in 4 yrs with full-time and summer attendance

Academics

The caliber of the "limitless" resources available to a George Washington University law students are outstanding, and the location cannot be beat; its various connections to federal agencies, lobbyists, firms, and judges in the area make it easy to find some area of law that will interest any student, as well as allowing for a wealth of outside placement and internship possibilities. "I have enough room in my schedule to go hear oral arguments at the Supreme Court or the Federal Circuit Court," says a student. "Nearly everyone I know has had the opportunity to intern in the federal or D.C. courts or some federal agency," says another. Even if students aren't happy with the Career Development office (and many outside of the top 15 percent of the class are not), there's the matter of the upstanding reputation with employers. "People that don't get jobs that attend GW either (1) didn't try hard enough to diversify where they were applying (particularly, geographically—people seem to forget there are jobs outside D.C., New York, and the coasts), or (2) aren't trying hard enough period," says a 3L. Add to that stellar academics, and this "close knit, high energy" school is definitely on the move, though the price tag can be steep. The somewhat high enrollment means "at times it feels a bit crowded" at GW, but the law school complex is very big, and the school has done a good job of expanding spaces, having recently developed a café for students and enlarging student conference spaces. In addition to the excellent law library, at one's fingertips on any given day there are lectures, panels, and workshops.

The Student Bar Association is one of the best in the nation, which is a reflection of the close relationship between the students and the administration, who "make a clear effort to engage students on the decisions of the law school." GW Law's Dean is a "terrific fundraiser and cheerleader," and even normally teaches a 1L Criminal Law class. The emphasis placed upon professors' teaching abilities is reflected in the inclusion of a student panel on the Faculty Appointments Committee, where students' views as reflected in their reports to the faculty are "given serious consideration during the appointment process." It shows, too, as the professors at GW are first-rate; there are "so many 'must-takes' here that you are guaranteed a great professor (at least by reputation) for each major doctrinal course." Indeed, GW Law professors are well-known locally and nationally, and "it's not unusual to attend a professor's class, and then later see him or her on the television that evening." These superstars are approachable as well, and "you would be hard-pressed to go to a student function and not find a friendly face from the faculty and staff enjoying time away from the formal school setting and lending their wisdom and wit to the outside student life." Classes mix theory and practice, placing an emphasis on didactic ability, and "there can be a little tough love involved" if needed. Each lecture "is an experience," and while the Socratic Method is used, it is used "very gently, and tends to create more of an open discussion format than a fear-invoking grilling process." However, students would like to see their torts class expanded to two semesters. The student culture and atmosphere at GW Law rounds out the experience, as "people actually like each other and enjoy a good conversation, whether studying or not."

ANNE M. RICHARD, ASSOCIATE DEAN FOR ADMISSIONS & FINANCIAL AID
700 20TH STREET, NW, WASHINGTON, DC 20052
TEL: 202-994-7230 • FAX: 202-994-3597
E-MAIL: JDADMIT@LAW.GWU.EDU • WEBSITE: WWW.LAW.GWU.EDU

Life

At this large law school, "there is a group (or clique) for everyone," and while "most law students are naturally type-A," the school is not competitive, possibly because most students have a job when graduating. There is a genuine atmosphere of camaraderie, where "students are colleagues not just in the classroom, but in the outside world as well." Only a few blocks from the National Mall and a short walk to Georgetown and Dupont Circle, GW has the perfect location for the social, career, and academic needs of students. It "is expensive to live here," but "the benefits far outweigh the costs." Students are all business for the most part in the classroom, but "relaxed and laid-back outside of it," and most "tend to be social and well-adjusted." The school is a social paradise, with "beautiful people, [a] 200-student ski trip, weekly special events at local bars, formal dances at luxury hotels, intra-class dating, and every other extracurricular activity necessary for keeping your sanity in law school is provided for in healthy amounts." Despite the more visible liberal element at the school, "liberals and conservatives, atheists, Jews, Mormons, the occasional Evangelical, and kids of all different backgrounds and ethnicities get together and enjoy each others' company on a regular basis." Tons of student groups help bring together the already diverse student body, and a huge percentage attend SBA events like the Halloween party and Barrister's Ball.

Getting In

Admission to George Washington is highly competitive. You should have an LSAT score at or above the 90th percentile and an A-minus average to be seriously considered.

Clinical program required	No
Legal writing course requirement	Yes
Legal methods course requirement	Yes
Legal research course requirement	Yes
Moot court requirement	No
Public interest law requirement	No

ADMISSIONS

Selectivity Rating	95
# applications received	8,652
Average LSAT	167
LSAT Range (25th to 75th percentile)	162–168
Median undergrad GPA	3.82
Application fee	$80
Regular application deadline	3/1
Early application deadline	1/5
Early application notification	1/30
Transfer students accepted	Yes
Evening division offered	Yes
Part-time accepted	Yes
CAS accepted	Yes

FINANCIAL FACTS

Annual tuition	$40,100
Books and supplies	$1,185
Room & Board	$13,600
% first-year students receiving some sort of aid	85
% all students receiving some sort of aid	87
% of aid that is merit based	48
% receiving scholarships	47
Average grant	$13,000
Average loan	$35,000
Average total aid package	$35,000
Average debt	$107,000

EMPLOYMENT INFORMATION

		Grads Employed by Field (%)
Career Rating	96	Academic (7)
% grads employed ten months out	95	Business/Industry (12)
Median starting salary	$136,643	Government (18)
State for bar exam	NY, VA, MD, CA	Judicial Clerkship (9)
Pass rate for first-time bar	94.0	Private Practice (43)
		Public Interest (9)

GEORGETOWN UNIVERSITY
LAW CENTER

INSTITUTIONAL INFORMATION

Public/private	Private
Affiliation	Roman Catholic-Jesuit
Student-faculty ratio	11:1
% faculty female	42
% faculty underrepresented minority	13

SURVEY SAYS...

Students love Washington, DC, Diverse opinions accepted in classrooms, Great research resources, Abundant externship/internship/clerkship opportunities, Good social life

STUDENTS

Enrollment of law school	580
% male/female	49/51
% part-time	8
% underrepresented minority	24
# of countries represented	15
Average age of entering class	24

ACADEMICS

Academic Experience Rating	97
Profs interesting rating	89
Profs accessible rating	82
Hours of study per day	3.56

Academic Specialties

Civil Procedure, Commercial, Constitutional, Corporation Securities, Criminal, Environmental, Government Services, Human Rights, International, Labor, Legal History, Legal Philosophy, Property, Taxation, Intellectual Property

Advanced Degrees Offered

SJD. LLM Taxation; Securities and Financial Regulation; International Business and Economic Law; Global Health Law; Global Health Law and International Institutions; National Security Law; Individualized Program; Environmental Law; Executive LLM in Taxation. LLM General Studies or International Legal Studies. LLM Advocacy; Executive LLM Securities and Financial Regulation; Dual Master of International Affairs and Law

Academics

The "prestigious," "ridiculously large," and tangentially Jesuit Georgetown University Law Center is "a choose-your-own-adventure school" in "a prime downtown D.C. location." "The sheer variety of the offerings is stunning," declares a 2L. "If you are looking to do something, odds are there is a club, or a class, or a journal, or some other event on this campus that is targeted at that." The range of courses is "extremely impressive and covers a broad spectrum of subjects." Georgetown is "a particularly great choice for students looking for opportunities in public interest or government." "Its international focus is without par," and there are several study abroad programs offered. In addition to the traditional first-year curriculum, you can take an alternative set of 1L courses that emphasize the interconnected impact of government regulation and "concentrates on making law school applicable to the legal world." The clinics "cover a breathtaking array of topics." Internships and externships galore on Capitol Hill and all over D.C. during the academic year give students "a leg up on summer internships and future employment." Another fabulous feature here is the Supreme Court Institute's moot court program. Attorneys who are about to appear before the U.S. Supreme Court routinely practice their oral arguments on Georgetown's campus "in front of professors" in "a perfect, scaled-down replica of the actual Supreme Court (right down to the carpeting)." "It's remarkably educational to see an advocate's dry run" and "then, a week later, actually go watch the same argument" for real.

Some of the "classes are very large [during the] first year" but faculty members are "very accessible" and they generally manage to "turn dull information into lively debate." "The professors make all the reading and writing worthwhile," encourage "diverse points of view, and [take] an interest in students' academic, professional, and personal lives," gushes a 3L. Professors are also "extremely accomplished" and they "bring fantastic experience and knowledge to the classroom." Often, though, "the 'big-name' professors are the worst teachers because they just tell war stories that are irrelevant to the exam, albeit interesting." Some students tell us that the top brass is "hard-working" and "surprisingly accessible for a big school." "They definitely make a very conscious effort to make the school seem smaller," opines a 1L. Other students say that "a ton of red tape" plagues Georgetown. "It seems like nothing is ever done on time," they say, and the registrar is "sloppy and inefficient."

Career Services staffers are "far from uber-helpful life coaches," and "there is a general feeling among the student body that Career Services is more interested in statistics (e.g., how many students went to big firms) than in helping students find paths that will make them happy." An optional first year program titled The Search Before the Search (SBTS) encourages students to reflect on their own strengths and interests while providing insight into the myriad opportunities available to Georgetown law graduates. The Georgetown brand has "an amazing domestic and international presence," though. "A huge range of firms and government agencies" recruits on campus each year. The pool of alumni is colossal. "Georgetown has amazing support for public interest students" as well, including a stand-alone office tailored to help them "pursue careers and co-curricular options." The biggest chunk of graduates stay in Washington, D.C., or head to New York City or California. About 50 percent go into private practice.

"The facilities are comfortable and more than adequate" here. Classrooms "are in great condition." The five-story law library is "enjoyable to spend time in and has plenty of nooks and crannies." The law school is located "away from the main campus." But " the

ANDREW P. CORNBLATT, DEAN OF ADMISSIONS
600 NEW JERSEY AVENUE, NW, ROOM 589, WASHINGTON, DC 20001
TEL: 202-662-9010 • FAX: 202-662-9439
E-MAIL: ADMIS@LAW.GEORGETOWN.EDU • WEBSITE: WWW.LAW.GEORGETOWN.EDU

proximity to SCOTUS (The Supreme Court), the Capitol, the White House, and the many international institutions in D.C. make for a special experience."

Life

Students at Georgetown Law are "very nice and good-natured, but really busy." Minority representation clocks in at about 28 percent and people come from all over the planet and all manner of backgrounds. "There is truly a diversity of opinions" as well. "When you put together students from many different walks of life," says a 2L, "you're bound to have an eclectic environment which makes the law school experience more tolerable."

Academically, there are "those few students with an exceptionally competitive attitude" but, for the most part, "students share notes, help each other, and actually want to work together." "I would say the level of competition is moderate," estimates a 1L. Outside of class, "extracurriculars are very popular." "There are plenty of student organizations and there are always more activities on campus than are possible to attend." "Famous speakers" are ubiquitous. Supreme Court justices "pop by all the time," for example. The swanky, "state-of-the-art" fitness center is a "great escape from studying" and it's exclusively for law students. Amenities include a swimming pool, racquetball courts, a full-size basketball court, and whirlpools. You can also take classes in spinning, yoga, dance, boxing, and much else. "A lot of the student body commutes from a good distance to school," but "there is a buzzing social scene, particularly among 1Ls." On the weekends, "students tend to go en masse to Dupont Circle and other parts of D.C."

Getting In

Overall, students at the 25th percentile have LSAT scores in the low 160s and GPAs just over 3.5. At the 75th percentile, LSAT scores are in the high 160s and GPAs are approximately 3.8. Part-time students have somewhat less intimidating numbers.

Combined Degrees Offered

JD/MBA, JD/MPH, JD/MPP, JD/MSFS, JD/MAAS: 4 yrs. JD/MAGES 4 yrs. JD/MALAS, JD/MAREES, JD/MASSP: 4 yrs. JD/PhD Government, JD/PhD or MA Philosophy: 4+ yrs. JD/LLM Taxation; International Business and Economic Law; National Security Law; Environmental Law; or Securities and Financial Regulation: 3.5 yrs.

Clinical program required	No
Legal writing course requirement	Yes
Legal methods course requirement	Yes
Legal research course requirement	Yes
Moot court requirement	No
Public interest law requirement	No

ADMISSIONS

Selectivity Rating	96
# applications received	7,793
% applicants accepted	29
% acceptees attending	23
Average LSAT	165
Median LSAT	167
LSAT Range (25th to 75th percentile)	163–168
Average undergrad GPA	3.67
Median undergrad GPA	3.76
Application fee	$85
Regular application deadline	3/1
Early application deadline	3/1
Transfer students accepted	Yes
Evening division offered	Yes
Part-time accepted	Yes
CAS accepted	Yes

FINANCIAL FACTS

Annual tuition	$53,130
Books and supplies	$1,200
Room & Board	$25,470
Financial aid application deadline	3/15
% first-year students receiving some sort of aid	84
% all students receiving some sort of aid	78
% of aid that is merit based	52
% receiving scholarships	47
Average grant	$20,750
Average loan	$58,972
Average total aid package	$65,379
Average debt	$150,529

EMPLOYMENT INFORMATION

		Grads Employed by Field (%)
Career Rating	98	Academic (3)
Total 2014 JD Grads	626	Business/Industry (5)
% grads employed ten months out	94	Government (15)
Median starting salary	$160,000	Judicial Clerkship (9)
# employed full-time	563	Federal: (4)
# employed part-time	26	State or local: (5)
# employed bar required	516	Private Practice (52)
# employed JD preferred	63	2-10: (2)
# employed professional/other	8	11-25: (2)
# employed non-professional	2	26-50: (1)
# pursuing advanced degree	5	51-100: (2)
# unemployed and seeking employment	18	101-250: (3)
# not seeking employment	8	251-500: (8)
% grads employed by school	14	501+: (34)
State for bar exam	MD, NY, CA, VA	Size Unknown: (1)
Pass rate for first-time bar	87.8	Public Interest (12)

GEORGIA STATE UNIVERSITY
COLLEGE OF LAW

INSTITUTIONAL INFORMATION

Public/private	Public
Affiliation	No Affiliation
Student-faculty ratio	10:1
% faculty part-time	38
% faculty female	52
% faculty underrepresented minority	18
Total faculty	102

SURVEY SAYS...
Diverse opinions accepted in classrooms

STUDENTS

Enrollment of law school	646
% male/female	55/45
% from out-of-state	10
% part-time	31
% underrepresented minority	37
% international	3
# of countries represented	6
Average age of entering class	25

ACADEMICS

Academic Experience Rating	**90**
Profs interesting rating	91
Profs accessible rating	83
Hours of study per day	3.32

Academic Specialties
Civil Procedure, Commercial, Constitutional, Corporation Securities, Criminal, Environmental, Human Rights, International, Labor, Property, Taxation, Intellectual Property

Advanced Degrees Offered
LLM

Combined Degrees Offered
JD/MBA 4 yrs; JD/MBA/MHA 4 yrs; JD/MPA(Masters in Public Administration) 4 yrs; JD/MA Philosophy 4 yrs; JD/MCRP 4 yrs; JD/MHA 4 yrs; JD/MSHA 4 yrs; JD/MPA 4 yrs; JD/BA (through Honors College) 6 yrs; JD/MPH 4 yrs

Academics

According to its students, Georgia State University's College of Law offers "a top-quality law school education without the aggressive environment." Of particular note is the school's "top-notch part-time program full of talented students." "GSU COL offers an incredible value to students—strong academic reputation with a low cost of attendance," says a 2L. "Tuition is unbelievable," adds a 1L. "[With] only about $10,000 a year for a very strong education, you can graduate with minimal debt, enabling you to begin a law career of your choice." The "amazing" professors are "diverse and open-minded." "Impressively, professors believe in the program and voluntarily teach evening classes," says a 2L. "I am challenged every day by brilliant professors who make me think in ways I never thought possible," explains a 1L. Most students find that the administration is "very responsive" and committed to ensuring quality instruction and improving academic instruction." Others students note, "They are always willing to go the extra mile and show concern for the success of their students."

Students appreciate GSU COL's "flexible class hours," particularly those involved in the very popular part-time program. Some feel that, due to this program, there is "a weighting toward evening classes" and that those evening classes are "where the best adjuncts teach." That said, others believe the "emphasis on the part-time program is a bit overstated." "It's available and great, but the full-time day classes are on par with any you will find," says a 3L. Regardless of which program students partake in, the "effective" courses offered are roundly praised. "The health law program is dynamic and first-rate," says a 2L. "Charity Scott is a legend in this city and any future health care attorney would be lucky to take a class with her." "The school is not afraid to try new ideas," adds another 2L. "I've taken 'Law and the Internet,' which is all about legal issues and the online community," says one student, and another tells us, "I'm now in a new non-traditional class that combines Wills, Trusts, Estates, and Taxes, in which the students form their own law firms and actually prepare all of the documents as if in the real-world."

By and large, students are very happy with their decision to attend GSU COL. However, when it comes to the school's Career Services Office, some believe "they could do a better job." Despite this, "the access to the Atlanta legal community" that GSU's location offers goes a long way in making up for any career office shortcomings. "I have clerked for a year with a Superior Court judge, worked for a professor as a GRA, competed in a National Moot Court competition, become president of numerous societies, and have a job lined up after graduation," says a 3L.

With a prime spot in downtown Atlanta, GSU's location allows students to "walk to the 11th Circuit, Supreme Court, and Northern District of Georgia courthouses." On campus, the law school's buildings aren't quite as appreciated as the university's metropolitan location. "The technology available in the classrooms and libraries [is] high quality, but the classrooms themselves are not," says a 1L. "The current law school is old, and was never meant to be used for anything aside from administrative purposes." However, construction has been completed on a new—and "much more aesthetically pleasing"—building. "We are all looking forward to . . . the new law school," which opened in Summer 2015, "because a new building will give the professors and students more opportunities to show just how amazing the school really is!" says a 2L.

DR. CHERYL JESTER-GEORGE, DIRECTOR OF ADMISSIONS
P.O. BOX 4049, ATLANTA, GA 30302-4049
TEL: 404-413-9200 • FAX: 404-413-9203
E-MAIL: LAWADMISSIONS@GSU.EDU • WEBSITE: LAW.GSU.EDU

Life

Thanks to GSU COL's non-traditional student population, "the school [has] a more diverse student body than most other schools" since "the introduction of older students with more work experience adds a great deal to the classroom experience." While "the part-time (evening) students work well together," among full-time students, "the competition is still severe," though it is "not as cutthroat as it is at other law schools." Students attribute this "to the evening students being older, with full-time jobs." "The younger students tend to be more social with one another," explains a 2L. "The older students, who come from the working world, are almost entirely focused on school." A 3L gives a more specific breakdown: "First year is difficult and competitive. However, the second and third years are much more cooperative and fun. Students begin to help each other out in terms of outlines, readings, etc." Regardless of whether students are part of the part-time or full-time programs, all agree that their "fellow classmates have been the best thing about law school—they're a great bunch of people."

"On the social side, there is a substantial group of part-time students that get together monthly on an ad-hoc basis, purely for social time, usually with spouses or significant others," says a 2L. "I was pleasantly surprised." Others find that the urban campus has a negative effect on socializing. "So many people are spread out all over the city…that no one stays around to socialize after class" says a 1L. "If you just go to class and go home I think you will miss out on the social life," says a 2L. "If you make an effort to meet people then it is easy to make friends."

Getting In

Recently admitted students at Georgia State University College of Law have median GPAs of 3.41 and LSAT scores of 158. Though 90 percent of GSU COL students are in-state residents, the admissions committee "considers each student's credentials regardless of residence."

EMPLOYMENT INFORMATION		
Career Rating	**95**	
Total 2014 JD Grads	198	**Prominent Alumni**
% for whom you have useable		Ronald J. Freeman, Founding Partner at
information	98	Johnson and Freeman; Former Judge
Median starting salary	$72,564	Cynthia J. Becker, Superior Court of
% job accepting grads providing		Georgia Stone Mountain Judicial Circuit;
useable salary information	85	Lynne R. O'Brien, Director of Corporate
# employed full-time	169	Real Estate, the Coca Cola Company; Scott
# employed part-time	11	M. Frank, President, AT&T Intellectual
# employed bar required	152	Property; Linda K. DiSantis, General
# employed JD preferred	17	Counsel, C.A.R.E.
# employed professional/other	11	**Grads Employed by Field (%)**
# pursuing advanced degree	5	Academic (3)
# unemployed and seeking		Business/Industry (21)
employment	8	Government (11)
# not seeking employment	2	Judicial Clerkship (8)
% grads employed by school	0	Private Practice (56)
State for bar exam	GA	Public Interest (4)
Pass rate for first-time bar	92	

Clinical program required	No
Legal writing	
course requirement	Yes
Legal methods	
course requirement	No
Legal research	
course requirement	Yes
Moot court requirement	No
Public interest	
law requirement	No

ADMISSIONS

Selectivity Rating	**89**
# applications received	1,821
% applicants accepted	29
% acceptees attending	36
Average LSAT	158
Median LSAT	158
LSAT Range (25th to	
75th percentile)	155–160
Average undergrad GPA	3.41
Median undergrad GPA	3.41
Application fee	$50
Priority application deadline	3/15
Transfer students accepted	Yes
Evening division offered	Yes
Part-time accepted	Yes
CAS accepted	Yes

International Students

TOEFL recommended of	
international students.	Yes

FINANCIAL FACTS

Annual tuition (in-state/	
out-of-state)	$16,378/$35,986
Books and supplies	$1,500
Fees	$1,121
Room & Board	$12,410
Financial aid application	
deadline	4/1
% first-year students receiving	
some sort of aid	81
% all students receiving	
some sort of aid	78
% of aid that is merit based	12
% receiving scholarships	7
Average grant	$5,051
Average loan	$19,497
Average total aid package	$20,500
Average debt	$39,246

GONZAGA UNIVERSITY
SCHOOL OF LAW

INSTITUTIONAL INFORMATION

Public/private	Private
Affiliation	Roman Catholic
Student-faculty ratio	5:1
% faculty part-time	38
% faculty female	40
% faculty underrepresented minority	10
Total faculty	40

SURVEY SAYS...
Great research resources

STUDENTS

Enrollment of law school	339
% male/female	58/42
% from out-of-state	54
% part-time	0
% underrepresented minority	17
% international	2
# of countries represented	3
Average age of entering class	26

ACADEMICS

Academic Experience Rating	**76**
Profs interesting rating	75
Profs accessible rating	88
Hours of study per day	3.79

Advanced Degrees Offered
None

Combined Degrees Offered
JD/MBA, JD/MAcc, JD/MSW; 3–4 yrs.

Academics

"Smaller classes, smaller community, close-knit school identity." Much at Gonzaga University, a small Jesuit school in Spokane, Washington, is couched in terms of size, but size does not define the school. With a "very accessible" administration, an "amazing" classroom environment, and "intellectual property professors who are experts in their field," Gonzaga's impact on students is larger than its size would suggest. Perhaps that's because its size affords students a chance to work closely with administrators and instructors alike. "Communication between faculty and students is pretty good," students note, with leadership that is "very accessible and approachable but respectable." The same is said about the "great" professors here. "All seem qualified, engaging, and effective instructors," a group who "come from excellent schools from around the country and have many years of professional experience."

Technology and access to information is paramount at Gonzaga. The "top notch" facilities and "incredibly helpful library assistants" make research a breeze. "There is a concerted effort to familiarize students with every online resource that is available (as well as) with information in more traditional formats." In addition, "the library and staff work very hard to ensure students have access to the most relevant and up to date materials." This works hand-in-hand with the accolades the legal research and writing program receives. This four-semester program, with an optional fifth semester, gives students "an ability to research better than most and have experience drafting multiple legal memorandums, motions to the court, and appellate briefs."

The new required skills labs during 1L year "need drastic improvements," due in part to an inconsistent approach between professors, but this is balanced by the two-year LRW program, "which really helps a student compete for hard to get internships and compete with bigger schools like University of Washington." The idea is to give students practical, hands-on experience that will allow them to succeed in the real world. The school also has "an excellent mentorship program that they do not force the students to participate in even though it is an excellent opportunity." In addition, "the clinic and externship requirements are great. They require real world experience so you are practice ready when you graduate." Overall, the "wonderful facilities, faculty that cares about the students, and very helpful professional development office" make Gonzaga stand taller than its size would seem to allow.

Life

Comfortable and inviting, the "collegial, friendly, laid back atmosphere" of Gonzaga "is definitely a plus." The "small, close-knit law school environment" fits well with the "modern and pleasant" facilities and "beautiful" building with a student lounge completed in 2013. "It has been a great place to spend the last three years." In some ways, the easygoing atmosphere is designed to offer balance to the "difficult" classes. As one student notes, "The law school experience is challenging enough without having to deal with difficult people and difficult conditions."

SUSAN LEE, DIRECTOR OF ADMISSIONS
P.O. BOX 3528, 721 N. CINCINNATI STREET, SPOKANE, WA 99220-3528
TEL: 800-793-1710 • FAX: 509-313-3697
E-MAIL: ADMISSIONS@LAWSCHOOL.GONZAGA.EDU • WEBSITE: WWW.LAW.GONZAGA.EDU

That said, "there is a glaring lack of diversity at the school." As a Jesuit school, a certain conservative atmosphere comes as no surprise, but some students complain about an "overall sense of intolerance" in some areas. "While I recognize that it is a Jesuit Catholic school," one student said, "this is counter to the school's mission of tolerance and respect for all." Those who do fit into the atmosphere here, though—and most do—find that "students are encouraged to work together and have good relations with each other." Indeed, "it is easy to standout, get personalized attention, and get involved at Gonzaga Law." This kind of camaraderie is welcome, since many students complain that Spokane is a "boring" town. Students must often create their own distractions, which tend to focus on outdoor activities like biking, rock climbing, and more. Thankfully, Glacier National Park, Banff, Seattle, Northern Idaho, and lower British Columbia are all within a few hours, making weekend getaways varied and easily accessible.

Getting In

Among admitted students at the 25th percentile, Gonzaga's students have LSAT scores in the range of 151 and GPAs hovering around 3.0. Meanwhile, admitted students at the 75th percentile have LSAT scores of about 155 and GPAs of roughly 3.6.

Clinical program required	Yes
Legal writing course requirement	Yes
Legal methods course requirement	No
Legal research course requirement	Yes
Moot court requirement	No
Public interest law requirement	Yes

ADMISSIONS

Selectivity Rating	77
# applications received	886
% applicants accepted	67
% acceptees attending	21
Average LSAT	154
Median LSAT	153
LSAT Range (25th to 75th percentile)	151–155
Average undergrad GPA	3.28
Median undergrad GPA	3.25
Application fee	$50
Regular application deadline	4/15
Early application deadline	2/1
Transfer students accepted	Yes
Evening division offered	No
Part-time accepted	No
CAS accepted	Yes

International Students

TOEFL required of international students.	Yes

FINANCIAL FACTS

Annual tuition	$36,360
Books and supplies	$5,327
Fees	$150
Room & Board	$11,205
Financial aid application deadline	2/1
% first-year students receiving some sort of aid	98
% all students receiving some sort of aid	88
% of aid that is merit based	21
% receiving scholarships	94
Average grant	$13,500
Average loan	$33,370
Average total aid package	$41,918
Average debt	$124,345

EMPLOYMENT INFORMATION

Career Rating	83	
Total 2014 JD Grads	162	
% for whom you have useable information	99	
% grads employed ten months out	81	
Median starting salary	$53,090	
# employed full-time	119	
# employed part-time	12	
# employed bar required	99	
# employed JD preferred	23	
# employed professional/other	7	
# employed non-professional	2	
# pursuing advanced degree	4	
# unemployed and seeking employment	16	
# not seeking employment	5	
State for bar exam	WA, CO, ID, CA, UT	
Pass rate for first-time bar	74.5	

Prominent Alumni
Christine Gregoire, Governor, State of Washington, former; Barbara Madsen, Chief Justice, Washington Supreme Court; Mike McGrath, Chief Justice, Montana Supreme Court; Paul Luvera, Plantiffs Attorney, lead in tobacco litigation; Kelly Cline, Executive VP, Fox Cable Legal Affairs

Grads Employed by Field (%)
Academic (2)
Business/Industry (15)
Government (9)
Judicial Clerkship (5)
Federal: (1)
State or local: (4)
Private Practice (44)
Solo: (4)
2-10: (31)
11-25: (6)
26-50: (1)
51-100: (3)
101-250: (1)
Public Interest (6)

HAMLINE UNIVERSITY
SCHOOL OF LAW

INSTITUTIONAL INFORMATION

Public/private	Private
% faculty part-time	0
% faculty female	52
% faculty underrepresented minority	12
Total faculty	35

SURVEY SAYS...

Diverse opinions accepted in classrooms

STUDENTS

Enrollment of law school	536
% male/female	46/54
% part-time	29
% underrepresented minority	10
% international	3
Average age of entering class	28

ACADEMICS

Academic Experience Rating	81
Profs interesting rating	83
Profs accessible rating	83
Hours of study per day	4.04

Academic Specialties

Commercial, Criminal, Government Services, International, Labor, Property, Intellectual Property

Advanced Degrees Offered

JD 3 yrs of study; LLM for international lawyers 1 year of study

Combined Degrees Offered

JD/MAPA (Master of Public Administration) 4 yrs; JD/MANM (Master Nonprofit Mgmt) 4 yrs; JD/MAOL (Master of Arts in Organizational Leadership) 4 yrs; JD/MBA 4 yrs; JD/MFA (Master of Fine Arts - Creative Writing)

Academics

In addition to the traditional full-time program, the excellent and "extremely underrated" Hamline University School of Law in Minnesota's Twin Cities offers a unique part-time, four-year weekend program that "truly creates flexibility for people who want to keep their present job." "Hamline takes a practical approach to legal education that has…a regional reputation for creating graduates who are strong legal writers and are ready to work Day One," explains a 2L. "Hamline graduates end up being the attorneys who like getting their hands dirty and who are probably the most realistic and practical of the law school [graduates] in the area." There are eleven clinics and twelve specialized areas of focus on offer. Hamline does health law "exceptionally well," but the crown jewel is the Dispute Resolution Institute, where students learn the art of the deal. Other perks include an Academic Success Program, which offers structured study groups, workshops, and one-on-one tutoring for free. Study abroad options include programs in Hungary, Israel, and Norway. According to many students, "the writing program is also fantastic." Not everyone loves it, though. "It feels really self-taught," grouses a 1L.

Classes at Hamline are usually conducted in "a semi-Socratic atmosphere." "The majority of professors use the Socratic Method or some sort of system that includes calling on unsuspecting students, but not in a bad way," relates a 3L. Students have very few negative comments about the faculty. "The professors are great." They are "outstanding educators who are passionate about their work," and they "provide a diverse range of expertise and experiences." Once class is over, profs are "highly accessible outside of the classroom" and "individual attention" is plentiful if you seek it out. Some students love the top brass as well. "The administration keeps everything running very smoothly," says a 1L, "such that I don't need to waste any of my time untangling messes." "The administration is strongly focused on the law school experience from start to graduation," emphasizing "bar passage and career development," adds a 2L. Other students complain that management is "unwilling to respond to student problems with course registration or student complaints."

According to students, "The appearance of the law school building is lackluster." "The interior of the building is comfortable but could be updated." "Some new carpet here and there wouldn't be a bad thing." However, "the classrooms are all up-to-date with the latest technology, including plug-ins for your laptop." Opinions regarding Career Services are decidedly mixed. Critics charge that the staff "hardly does anything worthwhile to help students with their job searches or career issues." Other students counter that Career Services is "incredibly helpful, open, and dedicated to helping students find jobs, internships, and develop skills of professionalism," as well as careers after graduation. A strong alumni network also helps in this regard. "Hamline alumni have been very helpful in connecting me with other attorneys and notifying me when they hear of opportunities that [they] know I am interest[ed] in," notes a 2L.

ROBIN INGLI, DIRECTOR OF ADMISSIONS
1536 HEWITT AVENUE, ST. PAUL, MN 55104-1284
TEL: 800-388-3688 • FAX: 651-523-3064
E-MAIL: LAWADM@GW.HAMLINE.EDU • WEBSITE: WWW.HAMLINE.EDU/LAW

Life

A "community atmosphere" is pervasive at Hamline, though the student body is really composed of two very different subgroups. The younger students in the full-time day program here are "competitive but not cutthroat." "Generally, the students are friendly toward each other and are willing to help each other out," relates a 2L. "There are a few zealots, but they tend to identify themselves quickly so you know who to avoid." "I am very comfortable providing my classmates with help and frequently receive assistance in return," adds a 1L. Meanwhile, students in the part-time, weekend program say their program has its own "very special, very communal essence." "The weekend program students have a wealth of experience and are extremely welcoming," explains a 1L. "Law school is merely one important component in our lives."

Socially, "there are cliques and 'in' groups," but "common courtesy" and Midwestern affability is ubiquitous. Intramural sports are pretty popular. There are over two dozen clubs and organizations. The location provides plenty of options for culture and nightlife as well. "The campus is within walking distance of several great ethnic restaurants" and bar review on Thursday nights "at different bars in the Twin Cities area" is pretty well attended.

Getting In

Enrolled full-time students at the 25th percentile have LSAT scores of about 148 and GPAs near 3.2. Enrolled students at the 75th percentile have LSAT scores close to around 156 and GPAs near 3.6.

Clinical program required	No
Legal writing course requirement	Yes
Legal methods course requirement	Yes
Legal research course requirement	Yes
Moot court requirement	No
Public interest law requirement	Yes

ADMISSIONS

Selectivity Rating	**80**
# applications received	966
% applicants accepted	61
% acceptees attending	21
Average LSAT	153
Median LSAT	153
LSAT Range (25th to 75th percentile)	148–156
Average undergrad GPA	3.33
Median undergrad GPA	3.38
Application fee	$35
Transfer students accepted	Yes
Evening division offered	Yes
Part-time accepted	Yes
CAS accepted	Yes

International Students

TOEFL required of international students.	Yes

FINANCIAL FACTS

Annual tuition	$36,066
Fees	$230
Room & Board (on/ off campus)	$12,786/$20,339
Financial aid application deadline	4/1
% first-year students receiving some sort of aid	97
% all students receiving some sort of aid	96
% receiving scholarships	63
Average grant	$19,126
Average loan	$34,337
Average total aid package	$43,933
Average debt	$104,647

EMPLOYMENT INFORMATION

Career Rating	**81**	
Total 2014 JD Grads	190	**Grads Employed by Field (%)**
% grads employed ten months out	91	Academic (2)
Median starting salary	$55,000	Business/Industry (36)
# employed full-time	157	Government (8)
# employed part-time	14	Judicial Clerkship (10)
# employed bar required	92	Private Practice (26)
# employed JD preferred	63	Public Interest (5)
# employed professional/other	10	
# employed non-professional	5	
# pursuing advanced degree	2	
# unemployed and seeking employment	7	
# not seeking employment	5	
State for bar exam	MN, WI, IL, NY, CA	
Pass rate for first-time bar	87.7	

HARVARD UNIVERSITY
HARVARD LAW SCHOOL

INSTITUTIONAL INFORMATION
Public/private   Private
% faculty female   22
% faculty underrepresented
  minority   15
Total faculty   110

SURVEY SAYS...
Great research resources, Abundant externship/internship/clerkship opportunities

STUDENTS
Enrollment of law school   1,752
% part-time   0
# of countries represented   70

ACADEMICS
Academic Experience Rating   96
Profs interesting rating   80
Profs accessible rating   71
Hours of study per day   3.62

Academic Specialties
Civil Procedure, Commercial, Constitutional, Corporation Securities, Criminal, Environmental, Government Services, Human Rights, International, Labor, Legal History, Legal Philosophy, Property, Taxation, Intellectual Property

Advanced Degrees Offered
LLM 1 yr; SJD - course work, exam, and dissertation.

Combined Degrees Offered
JD/MBA, JD/MPP, JD/MPA-ID, JD/PhD, JD/MPH, JD/MUP, JD/MALD, JD/LLM (with Cambridge University)

Academics

Harvard Law School—perhaps you've heard of it?—is like the land of Oz for aspiring lawyers, where "anything you want exists." Indeed, the school has plenty of funding for student scholarships, interests, and activities, and the opportunities for "public service, research and publication, faculty mentor relationships, editorial, moot court, or legal aid experience, and international study and service options are endless." The "you name it, it's on the menu" mentality is definitely present for most students, and humility can (understandably) be a bit short in supply. "Harvard is Harvard. This is…simply a reinforcing circle of virtue, i.e., you get brilliant professors, amazing students, interesting courses, great opportunities, attracting brilliant professors and amazing students, etc."

The "abundance of resources" available here lends itself to excellent support for public interest law, including a formidable public interest advising group, who "do a lot to build the community." "Though there's a lot of pressure to take a firm job, the counselors at [the public interest office] do a heck of a job fighting back. They'll chase you down in the hall and tell you it's time to start applying for fellowships, clerkships, and jobs," says a student. "When employers start cutting their recruiting classes, the last place they cut is HLS," says another. Everyone agrees that the economy has taken its toll, though—the ice skating rink closed—still have to put in work and make sure that they are putting their best foot forward."

Though each HLS class is hefty in size, it actually creates an "atmosphere of conversation and collaboration." "Because our class is so big, there is always a critical mass for any interest, activity, or cause students want to pursue," says a 2L. "I was a little concerned entering this school that its size would be intimidating or overwhelming, but in fact I've found that its size is one of its greatest strengths," agrees a 1L.

As expected, the courses offered are top-notch, with "a lot of very random options" to diversify the curriculum, though many students wish there was "more emphasis on practical lawyering skills," not to mention an alternative to the "arcane and mysterious" registration system. Though in recent years, a sizeable portion of the faculty has "fled to Washington, D.C., to work on Change," students are "still terribly spoiled to have as many wonderful professors as we do." According to a student, "O[bama] left us a couple of our best profs," and plenty of "superstar" professors remain at Harvard, and "everyone is extremely accomplished and an expert in his/her field." "Not everyone is a natural teacher," but "most of them are approachable and have interesting insights into the law (and many other areas)." There are also many research assistant and student writing opportunities offered.

The administration is "very flexible and willing to work with students as circumstances arise," and the school "really strives to please students, even in tough economic times." In 2012, a new academic building opened with the Caspersen Student Center and new classroom space that "are nicely equipped," research facilities "could not be better," and the library—the largest law library in the world, by the way—is "huge and lovely, with a staggering quantity of books." In other words, don't come to this corner of Boston if you're looking for the entire package of "sunshine, butterflies and architectural triumphs"—"There are reasons to come here; aesthetic bliss is not one of them."

JESSICA SOBAN, ASSISTANT DEAN AND CHIEF ADMISSIONS OFFICER
1515 MASSACHUSETTS AVENUE, CAMBRIDGE, MA 02138
TEL: 617-495-3109
E-MAIL: JDADMISS@LAW.HARVARD.EDU · WEBSITE: WWW.LAW.HARVARD.EDU

Life

There is most definitely "a lot of underlying stress and tension" at HLS, but "it's never about beating your classmates." While Harvard isn't the same cutthroat school of the Paper Chase era, "there are still quite a few gunners"; however, once you hit your second year, "everyone has relaxed a bit and gotten comfortable with their law school identities."

It's "very easy to find a great group of friends" because people are "generally fun and good-humored (in addition to being extremely smart and accomplished)." There is a Bar Review every week, and "the student government and other organizations host happy hours and other social events." While the size of the school means that students "wouldn't say the school as a whole has a strong general sense of community," it does provide a larger potential pool for friends, and students "are able to find a sense of community by joining various organizations." Be careful—students often "overwhelm themselves with extracurricular activities."

Students tend to be "quite liberal," but "one of the biggest surprises at HLS is how acceptable it is to be a conservative," as students here "tend to be tolerant and accepting of people despite their gender, race, religion, ethnicity, or sexual orientation." "It's very cooperative—there's a definite feeling of 'we're all in this together,'" says a 1L.

Getting In

When students arrive at law school to hear the dean say, "The competition is over. You've won," it's safe to say that getting in wasn't what most would call easy. Admitted students at the 25th percentile have LSAT scores of 170 and GPAs of about 3.77. Admitted students at the 75th percentile have LSAT scores of 175 and GPAs of about 3.95. (Note that Harvard looks at all LSAT scores in their contexts.) The school also aggressively seeks applicants from underrepresented minority groups.

Clinical program required	No
Legal writing course requirement	Yes
Legal methods course requirement	Yes
Legal research course requirement	Yes
Moot court requirement	Yes
Public interest law requirement	Yes

ADMISSIONS

Selectivity Rating	**99**
# applications received	5,943
% applicants accepted	15
% acceptees attending	61
Median LSAT	173
LSAT Range (25th to 75th percentile)	170–175
Median undergrad GPA	3.87
Application fee	$85
Regular application deadline	2/1
Transfer students accepted	Yes
Evening division offered	No
Part-time accepted	No
CAS accepted	Yes

FINANCIAL FACTS

Annual tuition	$54,850
Books and supplies	$5,330
Fees	$992
Room & Board	$20,728
% first-year students receiving some sort of aid	76
% all students receiving some sort of aid	79
% of aid that is merit based	0
% receiving scholarships	45
Average grant	$22,561
Average loan	$54,328
Average total aid package	$67,533
Average debt	$137,599

EMPLOYMENT INFORMATION

Career Rating	**98**	**Prominent Alumni**
Total 2014 JD Grads	586	Barack H. Obama, President of the United States
% for whom you have useable information	100	**Grads Employed by Field (%)**
% grads employed ten months out	97	Academic (1)
Median starting salary	$160,000	Business/Industry (5)
# employed full-time	565	Government (4)
# employed part-time	3	Judicial Clerkship (18)
# employed bar required	528	Federal: (15)
# employed JD preferred	29	State or local: (3)
# employed professional/other	10	Other: (1)
# employed non-professional	1	Private Practice (59)
# pursuing advanced degree	4	2-10: (1)
# unemployed and seeking employment	12	11-25: (1)
# not seeking employment	2	101-250: (4)
% grads employed by school	5	251-500: (7)
State for bar exam	NY, CA, MA, TX, MD	501+: (46)
Pass rate for first-time bar	94.9	Size Unknown: (0)
		Public Interest (10)

HOFSTRA UNIVERSITY
MAURICE A. DEANE SCHOOL OF LAW

INSTITUTIONAL INFORMATION

Public/private	Private
Affiliation	No Affiliation
Student-faculty ratio	14:1:1
% faculty part-time	38
% faculty female	38
% faculty underrepresented minority	7
Total faculty	81

SURVEY SAYS...
Diverse opinions accepted in classrooms

STUDENTS

Enrollment of law school	793
% male/female	50/50
% part-time	3
% underrepresented minority	29
% international	4
Average age of entering class	24

ACADEMICS

Academic Experience Rating	**81**
Profs interesting rating	74
Profs accessible rating	76
Hours of study per day	4.01

Academic Specialties
Criminal, Environmental, Family, Health, International, Labor,Intellectual Property

Advanced Degrees Offered
JD: full-time 3 yrs, part-time 4 yrs; LLM: full-time 1 yr, part-time 2 yrs, in the following areas: Family Law and American Legal Studies (for foreign lawyers)

Combined Degrees Offered
JD/MBA: full-time, 4 yrs; JD/MPH: full-time, 4 yrs

Academics

There is a "professional, collaborative environment" at Hofstra Law, where the school's students are huge fans of the "outstanding" administration, who, in many cases, "are willing to bend over backwards to accommodate you." "The administration is great because they are very accessible and interested in our success as lawyers and as students," says a 1L. The Career Center here is similarly involved, "not only [in] our futures, but also in helping alumni find new jobs." Right from the first week of class, Hofstra Law is big on helping students to network with attorneys and alumni and putting a realistic perspective on the possibilities out there (Note: The school does rank students within classes.), though a few students do lament the school's rather intense focus on work in the public sector. An expanded internship and externship program began in 2013 offering semester long experience in Washington D.C.."I've had the opportunity to learn about how much work and how many different areas of law you can practice...now I actually know what I can do with a JD," says a first-year law student. Though not every single person leaves a satisfied customer, the school certainly shows a "desire to improve," and all who go here pretty much generally agree, "If you are proactive and work hard, Hofstra will work hard for you as well."

Its location close to New York City helps the school to attract "some legendary professors at the top of their fields," most of whom are "readily available outside of class, and...seem to genuinely care about the students' success." "Not a single one stands on ceremony," says a student. Most "do not implement harsh variations of the Socratic Method"; they have "real-world experience that they bring to their lectures" and use "practical methods that help students to try [to] learn, rather than simply memorize the material." Hofstra Law's focus on practical and legal writing skills "never ceases to pay off during internships/clerkships." "I thought that Hofstra would not offer the same kind of academic experience as those in the top schools. I was very pleasantly surprised," says a student. "They are constantly trying to...help develop the students into lawyers."

Some bigger picture gripes include that tuition is not easy on the wallet. "Lower tuition please. I don't have a money tree in my backyard," begs a 1L. Classrooms "are adequate for the purpose they serve"; though the technology is up-to-date (lectures are webcast, Wi-Fi is readily available), the facilities as a whole could use a face-lift. Also, as one weary student puts it, "Not to beat a dead horse, but parking is always an issue."

Life

First-year students have all their classes with the same section, so "there is a sense that we are all getting through together." This instantly creates a nice community for incoming students, who also appreciate their access to 2Ls and 3Ls that "are more than happy to help with information about classes and professors." "There is some small amount of competition, but that is what keeps us on our toes. It shouldn't be frowned upon," says a student. Students are encouraged to work in study groups (and the overwhelming majority do), and "there is a strong desire to help others understand"; students "get lots of support from...fellow law school brothers and sisters." "We actually like one another!" says a 1L.

JOHN CHALMERS, ASSOCIATE DEAN FOR ENROLLMENT MANAGEMENT
108 HOFSTRA UNIVERSITY, HEMPSTEAD, NY 11549
TEL: 516-463-5916 • FAX: 516-463-6264
E-MAIL: LAWADMISSIONS@HOFSTRA.EDU • WEBSITE: LAW.HOFSTRA.EDU

While the school's location on the edge of the somewhat tucked-away neighborhood of Hempstead is far from ideal, "security on campus is very efficient." Long Island is "a little boring," but "there is ample opportunity for social activities," as the law school itself has many different student organizations, "so it's easy to find a group of people you can relate to and who have interest[s] in common with you." Commuting to and from New York City, for school or for fun, is also an option. The school offers a free shuttle to the local train station and its a thirty-five minute ride on the train. Law students here do tend to be a bit "stressed out," but the school as a whole still remains a "very friendly environment that the students really enjoy." It is a "laid-back atmosphere, [where students are] serious about work but not competitive."

Getting In

Hofstra Law is not the toughest school to get into, but it's not a cakewalk, either. As with almost every school, there's no set minimum score required for admission here, but the entering class of 2014 had LSAT scores of 151 at the 25th percentile and 157 at the 75th percentile. The average undergraduate GPA was 3.15.

Clinical program required	No
Legal writing course requirement	Yes
Legal methods course requirement	Yes
Legal research course requirement	Yes
Moot court requirement	No
Public interest law requirement	No

ADMISSIONS

Selectivity Rating	79
# applications received	2,155
% applicants accepted	64
% acceptees attending	13
Average LSAT	154
Median LSAT	152
LSAT Range (25th to 75th percentile)	151–157
Average undergrad GPA	3.15
Median undergrad GPA	3.35
Application fee	$0
Regular application deadline	4/15
Early application deadline	11/15
Early application notification	12/15
Transfer students accepted	Yes
Evening division offered	No
Part-time accepted	Yes
CAS accepted	Yes

International Students

TOEFL recommended of international students.	Yes

FINANCIAL FACTS

Annual tuition	$51,474
Books and supplies	$1,400
Room & Board (on/ off campus)	$16,756/$17,105
Financial aid application deadline	4/1
% first-year students receiving some sort of aid	85
% all students receiving some sort of aid	90
% of aid that is merit based	95
% receiving scholarships	52
Average grant	$24,947
Average loan	$48,893
Average total aid package	$48,000
Average debt	$133,861

EMPLOYMENT INFORMATION

Career Rating	82
Total 2014 JD Grads	317
% for whom you have useable information	92
% grads employed ten months out	83
Median starting salary	$59,000
% job accepting grads providing useable salary information	41
# employed full-time	231
# employed part-time	32
# employed bar required	198
# employed JD preferred	58
# employed professional/other	4
# employed non-professional	3
# pursuing advanced degree	4
# unemployed and seeking employment	20
# not seeking employment	2
% grads employed by school	4.6
State for bar exam	NY
Pass rate for first-time bar	72.9

Prominent Alumni
Maurice A. Deane, President, Bama Equities, Inc.; Hon. Maryanne Trump Barry, Judge, US Court of Appeals for the Third Circuit; Brad Eric Scheler, Senior Partner and Chairman, Bankruptcy and Restructuring, Fried Frank; Hon. David A. Paterson, Former Governor of New York; Randy L. Levine, President, New York Yankees

Grads Employed by Field (%)
Academic (2)
Business/Industry (12)
Government (9)
Judicial Clerkship (1)
Private Practice (44)
Public Interest (4)

ILLINOIS INSTITUTE OF TECHNOLOGY
CHICAGO-KENT COLLEGE OF LAW

INSTITUTIONAL INFORMATION

Public/private	Private
Affiliation	No Affiliation
Student-faculty ratio	11:1
% faculty part-time	65
% faculty female	30
% faculty underrepresented minority	11
Total faculty	194

SURVEY SAYS...

Students love Chicago, IL, Abundant externship/internship/clerkship opportunities

STUDENTS

Enrollment of law school	799
% male/female	53/47
% from out-of-state	44
% part-time	13
% underrepresented minority	19
% international	4
# of countries represented	21
Average age of entering class	25

ACADEMICS

Academic Experience Rating	**85**
Profs interesting rating	82
Profs accessible rating	81
Hours of study per day	2.86

Academic Specialties
Criminal, Environmental, International, Labor, Intellectual Property

Advanced Degrees Offered
JD, 3 yrs full-time, 4 yrs part-time; LLM, 2–8 semesters.

Combined Degrees Offered
JD/MBA, 3.5–5 yrs; JD/LLM, 4–5 yrs; JD/MS in Finance, 4–5 yrs; JD/MPA, 3.5–5 yrs; JD/MS in Environmental Management & Sustainability, 3.5–5 yrs; JD/MPH, 3.5 yrs.

Academics

At the Illinois Institute of Technology's Chicago-Kent College of Law, an emphasis on legal research and writing skills combines with an excellent career services office that pledges to provide individualized guidance for each student to support their career goals. Students can gain practical experience through externships, clinics, and any number of pro bono opportunities found at the Public Interest Resource Center, and there is "a distinct group of alumni who make a great effort to ensure students have as many opportunities as possible."

The faculty is composed of "great young professors that bring practical knowledge of the changing legal environment." Chicago-Kent "has a great presence in Chicago" and has many adjunct professors who bring practical experience and real world advice to the classroom. "Overall I have had an excellent experience at Chicago—Kent College of Law," says a 2L. An "extremely comprehensive/thorough" legal writing program gets high marks, as does the excellent Trial Advocacy program, which includes a popular 8-day intensive course during which students learn the basic principles of trial advocacy (and conduct two trials). "Taking the course was one of the best experiences I have had during law school and I would recommend it to anyone interested in pursuing a career in litigation," says a student. The professors of this course (and other trial advocacy courses) include "trial attorneys with 10+ years experience, state court judges, federal court judges, prosecutors from the ARDC, and many more"; the wealth of experience they are able to offer is "unparalleled." It should be unsurprising that the professors are "great at connecting what we're learning in class to applications in actual law practice." "I've had many professors conclude lessons with phrases like 'And this will be important to know when you're a lawyer because...'" says a student. "Often, I feel like I have an edge because of the passion and dedication of my professors."

The administration is also lauded as "phenomenal." They "respond to emails promptly and always do their best to help solve your problems and accommodate your needs." There is a great flexibility in the evening program in catering to working professionals and professors are "sympathetic to busy work schedules," as displayed by the helpful lead time given for assignments. "Even first-years" are given opportunities to engage with the way Chicago-Kent is run, through student organizations, student government, or simple feedback.

The career counselors are similarly "very well-informed, well-connected, and skilled," and this trickles into the real world. "I have consistently been able to hit the ground running at each of my internships, which proves to be a great asset for future positions and even for post-grad employment," says a student. "I've been told during externship applications that I don't need to provide a writing sample saying, 'Oh, I don't need that, you go to Kent,'" says another student.

NICOLE VILCHES, ASSISTANT DEAN FOR ADMISSIONS
565 WEST ADAMS STREET, CHICAGO, IL 60661
TEL: 312-906-5020 • FAX: 312-906-5274
E-MAIL: ADMISSIONS@KENTLAW.IIT.EDU • WEBSITE: WWW.KENTLAW.IIT.EDU

Life

As a school affiliated with a technological institute, the law school is "extremely techno-logically advanced"; however, "some of the older classrooms and study areas (including the library) could use a facelift." The student body is "very inclusive." "There is something for everyone and everyone supports one another." Chicago-Kent students originate from all over the world, so "many newcomers to Chicago bond closely and spend pretty much every day, including weekends, with each other." The SBA puts on a decent number of social events (like the "Conviser Bash" every semester), and there is "an extensive array of extra-curricular clubs and societies at Kent." "No matter what you're interested in there's a club for it, and if not you can start one very easily," says a 1L. The various panels, film screenings, and networking opportunities organized by the school every semester also help to enrich one's time here. "I've had a professor bring breakfast and champagne for the class on the last day of class," says a student. "Small gestures like that add to the students' experience and their knowledge that the people around care for them."

Getting In

Admissions are on a rolling basis. Recently enrolled students at the 25th percentile had an LSAT score of 152 and a GPA of 3.20, while enrolled students at the 75th percentile had an LSAT score of 159 and a GPA of 3.62.

Clinical program required	No
Legal writing course requirement	Yes
Legal methods course requirement	No
Legal research course requirement	Yes
Moot court requirement	Yes
Public interest law requirement	No

ADMISSIONS

Selectivity Rating	82
# applications received	1,729
% applicants accepted	64
% acceptees attending	17
Average LSAT	156
Median LSAT	157
LSAT Range (25th to 75th percentile)	152–159
Average undergrad GPA	3.38
Median undergrad GPA	3.43
Application fee	$0
Regular application deadline	3/15
Transfer students accepted	Yes
Evening division offered	Yes
Part-time accepted	Yes
CAS accepted	Yes

FINANCIAL FACTS

Annual tuition	$46,350
Books and supplies	$2,048
Fees	$1,911
Room & Board	$14,274
Financial aid application deadline	3/1
% first-year students receiving some sort of aid	95
% all students receiving some sort of aid	93
% of aid that is merit based	37
% receiving scholarships	83
Average grant	$17,119
Average loan	$27,624
Average total aid package	$45,237
Average debt	$121,236

EMPLOYMENT INFORMATION

Career Rating	73
Total 2014 JD Grads	292
% for whom you have useable information	96
% grads employed ten months out	85
Median starting salary	$65,000
# employed full-time	222
# employed part-time	26
# employed bar required	171
# employed JD preferred	57
# employed professional/other	18
# employed non-professional	2
# pursuing advanced degree	5
# unemployed and seeking employment	22
# not seeking employment	3
% grads employed by school	1
State for bar exam	IL, CA, NY, TX, FL

Prominent Alumni

The Honorable Ilana Diamond Rovner, U.S. Court of Appeals for the 7th Circuit; The Honorable Anne Burke, Illinois Supreme Court; Thomas Demetrio, Partner, Corboy & Demetrio

Grads Employed by Field (%)

Academic (2)
Business/Industry (18)
Government (9)
Judicial Clerkship (2)
Private Practice (52)
  Solo: (2)
  2-10: (25)
  11-25: (10)
  26-50: (4)
  51-100: (2)
  101-250: (4)
  251-500: (1)
  501+: (4)
Public Interest (3)

INDIANA UNIVERSITY—BLOOMINGTON
MAURER SCHOOL OF LAW

INSTITUTIONAL INFORMATION

Public/private	Public
Affiliation	No Affiliation
% faculty part-time	32
% faculty female	40
% faculty underrepresented minority	10
Total faculty	96

SURVEY SAYS...
Great research resources, Good social life

STUDENTS

Enrollment of law school	586
% male/female	55/45
% from out-of-state	63
% underrepresented minority	29
% international	7
# of countries represented	15
Average age of entering class	24

ACADEMICS

Academic Experience Rating	**90**
Profs interesting rating	87
Profs accessible rating	73
Hours of study per day	3.77

Academic Specialties
Civil Procedure, Commercial, Constitutional Democracy, Corporations and Securities, Criminal, Cybersecurity, Environmental, Government Services, Human Rights, Intellectual Property, International, Labor, Legal History, Legal Philosophy, Property, Taxation, Intellectual Property

Advanced Degrees Offered
SJD; LLM Thesis; LLM Practicum; MCL; PhD in Law & Social Science; PhD in Law & Democracy

Combined Degrees Offered
JD/MPA Public Affairs; JD/MS Telecommunications; JD/MA Telecommunications; JD/MA Journalism; JD/MLS (School of Library Science); JD/MSES (Pub./ Environmental Affairs); JD/MBA (Business) (3- and 4-year

Academics

Students at the Indiana University Maurer School of Law enjoy "first-rate resources and education" at "an excellent value." The law school boasts no fewer than nineteen clinical programs and projects including a community legal clinic, an entrepreneurship law clinic, and an inmate legal assistance project. Externship programs include the Semester Public Interest Program, which allows 3Ls to earn credit for public interest internships with government agencies and nonprofits in Washington, D.C. Students can study in Paris, Florence, Barcelona, Beijing, Auckland, and a host of other international cities, and they can apply for summer internships in Argentina, India, Brazil, China, Korea, Japan, and Thailand through the school's Center on the Global Legal Profession. An unusual 1L course in the legal profession helps students discover their strengths while they explore career options. Several interesting dual-degree programs, including a three-year JD/ MBA and a bevy of specialization programs in taxation, international and comparative law, and intellectual property round out IU's "excellent" academic options.

The "extremely knowledgeable and accessible" faculty at IU "is really impressive." "When you go to class, you get the sense that your professors want to be in the class-room, and that makes engaging yourself in the material much easier," says a 2L. "There's a nice balance between professors who try to scare the pants off of you and the ones who really encourage you to take risks and push yourself, even if you turn out to be wrong." Even "boring" professors "really have a lot of important things to say." Outside the classroom, professors "participate in the law school social events" and "will go to great lengths to help students publish, research, and get placed" in jobs.

IU's administration "is genuinely concerned about students as individuals," and its "helpful and nice" Financial Aid Office "is the best in the country." Though in the past students have noted that "Career Services, while improving, has a long way to go," the Office of Career and Professional Development has since created an alternative career series, alumni mentoring programs, and two alumni career service committees as well as expanded off campus interviews, hired new staff and hosted alumni-sponsored welcome-to-the-city events in key cities around the country. Many students tell us that the Career Services Office "does all it can to assist students in obtaining jobs." "I think they're great," declares a 1L. "They're not going to get a job for you, but they'll do pretty much everything else." "If you are near the top of the class," "you'll have the Indy firms drooling all over you," and you won't have a problem working at "any of the best firms in Chicago" "or even Washington, D.C."

Everyone here agrees that the campus surrounding the law school is "beautiful." Classrooms once described as "uncomfortable," have been renovated. "The entire building has wireless Internet," and "there are electrical outlets at each seat." The gem of IU is the law library, which students claim is "without equal in the world, in part because of its staff." "With large windows that look out on the forest in the middle of campus, it's easy to forget that you're in the middle of a Big Ten school."

Life

IU's Midwestern location helps encourage a collegial attitude that frowns on aggressive competition." Students "simply do not let the abstract, competitive nature of the grading system affect their outward nature or the way they see their classmates." "If there is a more laid-back group of students at any law school in the country, I'd like to see it," challenges a 2L. "Students find their groups and comfort zones relatively quickly." Smaller class sizes "contribute to some minor drama at times," but students "get to know each

GREG CANADA, ASSISTANT DEAN OF ADMISSIONS
211 SOUTH INDIANA AVENUE, BLOOMINGTON, IN 47405-1001
TEL: 812-855-4765 • FAX: 812-855-1967
E-MAIL: LAWADMIS@INDIANA.EDU • WEBSITE: WWW.LAW.INDIANA.EDU

other better and have a closer relationship with the faculty." "You can learn as much law as well here as at Harvard or Yale," promises a 3L. "But you will pay less, will see people being nicer to each other, and don't have to live in a grungy New England city."

The law school is "settled into a big university" "far away from the real-world" in "one of the greatest college towns in America." "The school is great for young undergraduates who appreciate a small-town environment." "Moving from a city to the boonies is still taking some getting used to," says one urbanite, "but the school offers some phenomenal cultural opportunities." There are "at least thirty ethnically diverse restaurants within a three-minute walk from the law school." Students here "work hard," but "there is great balance between the social life and the academic life." "The fitness and recreation facilities are superb," and "There are law school teams for intramurals." The Law and Drama Society "puts on a play in the school's moot court room." "The annual Women's Law Caucus Auction" is a big hit, as is an annual basketball game in IU's beloved Assembly Hall, which pits students against professors. Mostly, though, "the social environment is aimed at those who like to go out and party." "We're very social, very involved, and very fun," boasts a 2L. "The school is the focal point around which life spins, but there's always something to do, somewhere to go, someone to talk to." "There are after-hours activities sponsored by the school or a student group almost each week, and if there's nothing going on students will always congregate somewhere to have fun."

Getting In

Admitted students at the 25th percentile have LSAT scores of about 154 and GPAs hovering around 3.31. Admitted students at the 75th percentile have LSAT scores of approximately 163 and GPAs of approximately 3.9.

EMPLOYMENT INFORMATION

Career Rating	93
Total 2014 JD Grads	222
% grads employed ten months out	91
Median starting salary	$65,000
# employed full-time	188
# employed part-time	13
# employed bar required	151
# employed JD preferred	45
# employed professional/other	2
# employed non-professional	3
# pursuing advanced degree	3
# unemployed and seeking employment	12
# not seeking employment	1
% grads employed by school	5
State for bar exam	IN, IL, CA, NY, TX
Pass rate for first-time bar	91.4

Prominent Alumni
Loretta Rush, Chief Justice, Indiana Supreme Court; Catherine A. Conway, Partner, Gibson Dunn; Alecia DeCoudreaux, President, Mills College; Michael S. Maurer, Chairman, IBJ Media Corporation; Chairman, The National Bank of Indianapolis; John Tinder, Judge, U.S. Court of Appeals, 7th Circuit

Grads Employed by Field (%)
Academic (5)
Business/Industry (15)
Government (16)
Judicial Clerkship (6)
Private Practice (42)
Public Interest (7)

---

programs); JD/MBA Accounting; JD/MS Accounting; JD/MPH Public Health; JD/MA Russian & East European Studies; JD/MA Latin American and Caribbean Studies; JD/LLB O.P. Jindal Global University

Clinical program required	No
Legal writing course requirement	Yes
Legal methods course requirement	No
Legal research course requirement	Yes
Moot court requirement	No
Public interest law requirement	No

ADMISSIONS

Selectivity Rating	90
# applications received	1,812
% applicants accepted	62
% acceptees attending	16
Average LSAT	159
Median LSAT	161
LSAT Range (25th to 75th percentile)	154–163
Average undergrad GPA	3.57
Median undergrad GPA	3.72
Application fee	$50
Early application deadline	11/15
Early application notification	12/15
Transfer students accepted	Yes
Evening division offered	No
Part-time accepted	No
CAS accepted	Yes

International Students

TOEFL required of international students.	Yes

FINANCIAL FACTS

Annual tuition (in-state/ out-of-state)	$29,820/$48,676
Books and supplies	$1,800
Fees	$1,301
Room & Board	$13,396
Financial aid application deadline	3/10
% first-year students receiving some sort of aid	97
% all students receiving some sort of aid	96
% of aid that is merit based	52
% receiving scholarships	94
Average grant	$25,006
Average loan	$31,857
Average total aid package	$47,161
Average debt	$89,785

INDIANA UNIVERSITY
ROBERT H. MCKINNEY SCHOOL OF LAW

INSTITUTIONAL INFORMATION

Public/private	Public
% faculty part-time	32
% faculty female	44
% faculty underrepresented minority	12
Total faculty	85

SURVEY SAYS...

Students love Indianapolis, IN, Diverse opinions accepted in classrooms

STUDENTS

Enrollment of law school	857
% male/female	55/45
% part-time	38
% underrepresented minority	16
% international	1
# of countries represented	4
Average age of entering class	26

ACADEMICS

Academic Experience Rating	82
Profs interesting rating	81
Profs accessible rating	76
Hours of study per day	3.62

Academic Specialties

Environmental, Government Services, Human Rights, International, Intellectual Property

Advanced Degrees Offered

SJD 3–5 yrs; LLM 1 yr full-time or up to 3 yrs part-time; MJ 1 yr full-time or up to 3 yrs part-time

Combined Degrees Offered

JD/MPA 4 yrs; JD/MBA 4 yrs; JD/MHA 4 yrs; JD/MPH 4 yrs; JD/MPhil 4 yrs; JD/MLS 4 yrs; JD/MSW 4 yrs; JD/MD 6 yrs

Academics

Indiana University Robert H. McKinney School of Law is a relatively large school on an "urban campus" in "a great downtown location." The "lovely," spacious, and "comfortable" facility here is "a beautiful, high-tech place to learn." "Classrooms are modern and large and sport electric outlets at every seat," and "There are many places, such as the reading room, where students can go to study." Eight joint-degree programs are available. There are three law reviews, eight clinics, and summer study abroad programs in China. Opportunities to specialize include intellectual property law and international law as well as a "particularly strong" health law curriculum. Students can choose from five different graduate certificates.

The faculty as a whole is "excellent" and "engaging." They "do their best to make sure the material is as interesting as possible" and "take a very practical tack in their approach to teaching." "The atmosphere at McKinney is such that, while the work is intense, I've never felt like not wanting to go to class," beams a 2L. "Ever." Outside of class, "Professors are accessible and students are not afraid to approach them for help on a concept or to share a joke." The two-semester legal writing program (with optional third semester) generally receives high marks. Student opinion concerning the administration is mixed. Defenders of it tell us that the top brass is student-friendly and "does a fairly good job." "The administration always tries its best to help us succeed," says a happy 2L. Detractors complain that "the administration has no idea what's going on." One complaint is that registration can be difficult for 2Ls and 3Ls. "Too many classes clumped at the same time make it difficult" to take all the courses you want (or need). A few professors are "not interested in teaching at all."

McKinney is the lesser known of the two IU law schools (the other one is in Bloomington), but students say that attending the only law school in Indiana's state capital and commercial hub definitely has its perks. The school is close to "all of the large firms" in the city and "within blocks of city, state, and federal government offices, and courthouses." "This enables us to work at some of the state's best and largest firms throughout the school year," explains a 3L. "It also provides us with the opportunity to do externships with all of the state's major courts and organizations." "Being in downtown Indianapolis is excellent for networking opportunities with the legal community," too. Some students applaud the efforts of the "hardworking" staff in the Office of Professional Development to secure career opportunities. Other students are less than thrilled. "They don't help anyone get jobs," gripes a 3L, "and they don't respond to phone calls or e-mails, either." Also, while the school's reputation in the state is very good, "it's an uphill battle to find employment outside of Indiana."

Life

Students here describe themselves as "quite friendly." "Animosity is pleasantly absent." "Students generally get along quite well with one another and are collegial in the classroom," relates a 1L. While there's "a decent amount of diversity" and McKinney is "very welcoming environment to students of all backgrounds," a pretty vast chasm exists between the full-time day students and the part-time evening students. A large percentage of the full-timers come "straight out of undergrad" and "chose to attend Indianapolis for its proximity to firm, corporate, and political experiences." The part-time program constitutes about one-third of the student body, and it's mostly "older, nontraditional" students who already have occupations, families, and their own social lives.

PATRICIA KINNEY, ASSISTANT DEAN FOR ADMISSIONS
530 WEST NEW YORK STREET, INDIANAPOLIS, IN 46202-3225
TEL: 317-274-2459 • FAX: 317-278-4780
E-MAIL: LAWADMIT@IUPUI.EDU • WEBSITE: MCKINNEYLAW.IU.EDU

McKinney is located on the campus of Indiana University—Purdue University Indianapolis (where "parking is absolutely atrocious"). "The school's central location is used to its fullest advantage through symposiums, networking functions, alumni activities, and other gatherings where members of the Indianapolis legal community mingle with students," relates a 2L. Life beyond academics gets mixed reviews. By all accounts, Indianapolis is "a great city" with lots to see and do. Some students tell us that the school provides many social outlets. "There are a lot of activities," and you can "relive high school all over again" "with more drinking." Others give the campus "a mediocre rating for social life." "The problem is that it's a commuter school and people are coming from all over the place." "People do their work and go home." "As a result, there is not a whole lot of socializing."

Getting In

Enrolled full-time students at IU Robert H. McKinney School of Law have a median LSAT score of 152 and a GPA of about 3.39. Admissions statistics for part-time students are lower.

Clinical program required	No
Legal writing course requirement	Yes
Legal methods course requirement	No
Legal research course requirement	Yes
Moot court requirement	No
Public interest law requirement	No

ADMISSIONS

Selectivity Rating	80
# applications received	620
% applicants accepted	70
% acceptees attending	46
Median LSAT	152
LSAT Range (25th to 75th percentile)	148–155
Median undergrad GPA	3.39
Application fee	$0
Regular application deadline	7/31
Transfer students accepted	Yes
Evening division offered	Yes
Part-time accepted	Yes
CAS accepted	Yes

International Students

TOEFL required of international students.	Yes

FINANCIAL FACTS

Annual tuition (in-state/ out-of-state)	$24,892/$45,193
Books and supplies	$1,500
Fees	incld. above
Room & Board	$11,646
Financial aid application deadline	7/31
% receiving scholarships	54
Average grant	$13,895
Average loan	$31,576
Average total aid package	$0
Average debt	$96,651

EMPLOYMENT INFORMATION

Career Rating	86	**Prominent Alumni**
Total 2014 JD Grads	279	Ann Slaughter Andrew, Former US
% for whom you have useable information	97	Ambassador to Costa Rica; Susan Brooks, United States Congresswoman; Mike
% grads employed ten months out	87	Pence, Governor, State of Indiana
Median starting salary	$55,000	**Grads Employed by Field (%)**
% job accepting grads providing useable salary information	59	Academic (1) Business/Industry (20)
# employed full-time	232	Government (6)
# employed part-time	12	Judicial Clerkship (2)
# employed bar required	180	State or local: (2)
# employed JD preferred	44	Private Practice (43)
# employed professional/other	16	Solo: (2)
# employed non-professional	4	2-10: (20)
# pursuing advanced degree	4	11-25: (7)
# unemployed and seeking employment	15	26-50: (3) 51-100: (2)
# not seeking employment	7	101-250: (2)
% grads employed by school	1	251-500: (3)
State for bar exam	IN, TX, GA, MD, I	501+: (3)
Pass rate for first-time bar	82.5	Public Interest (3)

THE JOHN MARSHALL LAW SCHOOL

INSTITUTIONAL INFORMATION

Public/private	Private
Affiliation	No Affiliation
Student-faculty ratio	16:1
% faculty part-time	73
% faculty female	33
% faculty underrepresented minority	10
Total faculty	227

SURVEY SAYS...
Students love Chicago, IL

STUDENTS

Enrollment of law school	1,138
% male/female	50/50
% part-time	27
% underrepresented minority	27
% international	4
Average age of entering class	23

ACADEMICS

Academic Experience Rating	**72**
Profs interesting rating	73
Profs accessible rating	71
Hours of study per day	3.96

Academic Specialties
Alternative Dispute Resolution, Elder Law, Health Law, Intellectual Property Law, International Human Rights Law, Sustainability, Trial Advocacy

Advanced Degrees Offered
LLM: Employee Benefits, Estate Planning, U.S. Legal Studies (for foreign lawyers), Information Technology & Privacy Law, Intellectual Property Law, International Business & Trade Law, Real Estate Law, Tax Law, Trial Advocacy & Dispute Resolution. MJ: Education (pending), Estate Planning, Employee Benefits, Healthh (pending), Information Technology & Privacy Law, Intellectual Property Law, Real Estate Law, and Tax Law.

Combined Degrees Offered
JD/LLM: Employee Benefits, Information Technology & Privacy

Academics

Located in Chicago, The John Marshall Law School is a relatively large, independent law school with options for both daytime and evening programs. The intellectual property program is strong, and the writing program is one of the school's greatest strengths and a cornerstone of the practice-ready curriculum, which ensures that "when the students are ready to practice, they can hit the ground running." "Everyone really works with you to make sure you understand what you are doing," says a student. John Marshall provides work study opportunities for students to get paid for legal work in any nonprofit or government agency, and a variety of clinical internship/externship opportunities "geared towards teaching students the practical skills needed to successfully practice law in a variety of settings."

In addition to the "really quite strong" academics, the faculty comprises "very knowledgeable professors who have considerable real world experience that benefits their ability to relate material to students." Professors are "very welcoming when you come to see them" and "they enjoy working through issues with students." As one might expect from a school designed for students at all points of their careers, the incredibly flexible school "is willing to accommodate each student's individual academic interests/goals." The law librarians and staff are also "extremely helpful." "Although there are more required courses than other law schools, at the end of the day they are valuable and allow a student to explore the type of attorney they want to be," says a 2L. "There are no undeserved grades awarded at our school and it prompts each of us students to give our best performance."

The school has "extensive resources" including the writing center, and a helpful alumni network "practicing in just about every area of law you can think of" that aids the Career Services Office in getting students into jobs. "If you plan on working in the northern Illinois region, you should strongly consider attending JMLS," says a student of the school's mainly regional reputation. Many students say that "at times the school could be more organized" and "information could be distributed to students in a more timely manner, so things aren't so rushed." Still, "the school really cares about the students, and it shows." "I have always felt that every single employee at JMLS is rooting for me to thrive professionally and personally," says a 1L.

WILLIAM B. POWERS, ASSOCIATE DEAN FOR ADMISSION & STUDENT AFFAIRS
315 SOUTH PLYMOUTH COURT, CHICAGO, IL 60604
TEL: 800-537-4280 • FAX: 312-427-5136
E-MAIL: ADMISSION@JMLS.EDU • WEBSITE: WWW.JMLS.EDU

Life

About half of the students are full-time students who tend to be more "outgoing" and make friends with one another; the other half is composed of commuters who, "though friendly people, have to spend more time elsewhere." Many see this diversity of the student population as "the school's greatest strength" and "school pride is always fostered and witnessed each day." Student organizations are very active and "there are always ways to get involved and social gatherings."

The law school has been undergoing "almost constant renovation over the last few years so the school facilities are very new," and the campus's location in the heart of Chicago's loop means you are only a short walk away from various courts, government offices, and private firms. "You can see the 7th Circuit federal building from the classrooms, the Cook County circuit building is down the street, and the City of Chicago offices are right there as well...the Chicago Bar Association is next door."

Getting In

Admitted students at the 25th percentile have an LSAT score of 146 and a GPA of 2.97. Admitted students at the 75th percentile have an LSAT score of 151 and a GPA of 3.52.

Law, Intellectual Property Law, International Business & Trade Law, Real Estate Law, Tax Law and Trial Advocacy & Dispute Resolution. JD/MBA w/ Dominican University, Elmhurst College, and Benedictine University. JD/MS Public Administration w/ Roosevelt University.

Clinical program required	Yes
Legal writing course requirement	Yes
Legal methods course requirement	Yes
Legal research course requirement	Yes
Moot court requirement	Yes
Public interest law requirement	No

ADMISSIONS

Selectivity Rating	72
# applications received	1,708
% applicants accepted	75
% acceptees attending	22
Median LSAT	149
LSAT Range (25th to 75th percentile)	146–151
Median undergrad GPA	3.05
Application fee	$0
Transfer students accepted	Yes
Evening division offered	Yes
Part-time accepted	Yes
CAS accepted	Yes

International Students

TOEFL required of international students.	Yes

FINANCIAL FACTS

Annual tuition	44,850
Books and supplies	$2,500
Fees	$270
Room & Board	$16,000
Financial aid application deadline	3/28
% first-year students receiving some sort of aid	96
% all students receiving some sort of aid	92
% of aid that is merit based	95
% receiving scholarships	60
Average grant	$12,000
Average loan	$42,784
Average total aid package	$48,698
Average debt	$133,841

EMPLOYMENT INFORMATION

Career Rating	88	
Total 2014 JD Grads	419	
% for whom you have useable information	97	
% grads employed ten months out	86	
Median starting salary	$59,340	
# employed full-time	319	
# employed part-time	43	
# employed bar required	270	
# employed JD preferred	69	
# employed professional/other	14	
# employed non-professional	9	
# pursuing advanced degree	6	
# unemployed and seeking employment	29	
# not seeking employment	4	
% grads employed by school	1	
State for bar exam	IL, NY, CA, TX, MI	
Pass rate for first-time bar	85.0	

Prominent Alumni
Mark Pedowitz, President of The CW Network; Bill Daley, former White House Chief of Staff

Grads Employed by Field (%)
Academic (1)
Business/Industry (18)
Government (12)
Judicial Clerkship (2)
State or local: (1)
Private Practice (51)
  Solo: (2)
  2-10: (31)
  11-25: (7)
  26-50: (4)
  51-100: (3)
  101-250: (1)
  251-500: (1)
  501+: (3)
Public Interest (2)

LEWIS & CLARK COLLEGE
LAW SCHOOL

INSTITUTIONAL INFORMATION

Public/private	Private
Affiliation	No Affiliation
Faculty-student ratio	10:1
% faculty part-time	49
% faculty female	45
% faculty underrepresented minority	14
Total faculty	92

SURVEY SAYS...
Liberal students

STUDENTS

Enrollment of law school	627
% male/female	53/47
% from out-of-state	72
% part-time	29
% underrepresented minority	26
% international	1
# of countries represented	12
Average age of entering class	27

ACADEMICS

Academic Experience Rating	**81**
Profs interesting rating	74
Profs accessible rating	80
Hours of study per day	3.58

Academic Specialties
Animal, Commercial, Corporation Securities, Criminal, Environmental, International, Taxation, Intellectual Property

Advanced Degrees Offered
LLM Environmental & Natural Resources, 12–18 mos; LLM Animal Law, 12–18 mos; MS Environmental Law Studies Program, 12–24 mos

Combined Degrees Offered
JD/LLM Environmental & Natural Resources Law 3.5 yrs

Academics

Students who take the legal plunge at Lewis & Clark Law School in beautiful Portland, Oregon, enjoy professors who are "uniformly excellent and approachable for discussion about class topics and other issues striking your fancy." The small size of the law school allows for an extremely personalized educational experience, and students benefit from this cozy setup on multiple levels, "from an academic perspective as well as from a functional perspective." "I have been lucky enough to develop solid mentor relationships with specific professors that were particularly inspirational," says a second-year student. Practically everyone involved in running the school, from the dean to the cafeteria staff, "seem to truly like each other," and the well-regarded faculty is given an "unusual amount of influence in the way that the school is run, and [in] the school's policies."

Lewis & Clark Law School has a relatively small course load of required classes and offers a night program, bringing a large contingent of older and more experienced students to the classrooms, which "adds a valuable, practical dimension to the learning experience." As one would expect from such an environmentally conscious institution, programs such as environmental and natural resources law and animal law are "unparalleled." No matter what their specialization, the faculty is considered to be "inspirational and knowledgeable enough to stimulate thinking beyond what's required by the curriculum," and the school's size "allows for an ideal student/teacher ratio that goes further to foster a highly effective teaching environment." Lewis & Clark's National Crime Victim Law Institute is another source of pride for the school, "leading the way in an emerging field of law."

Administrators are friendly, and accessible, "always willing to help out a student," and they keep the law school "running very smoothly." The research librarians are cited for being "very knowledgeable," and the Career and Professional Development Center also does its part to make sure students' needs are met, though some would like to see more non-metro area firms on campus. For students who are interested in staying in the area after graduation, there is "heavy support and involvement from the Portland legal community," and for others, "alumni are distributed all around the world."

Since the school and its student body are known for being nature-friendly, it follows that the buildings on campus are all "green" and "tucked into a forested state park." This is nice, students say, because "when you are facing the gut-wrenching pain of law school, a 'walk in the park' goes a long way." Students are quite pleased with the library and the newer building, Wood Hall, but many are clamoring for an update of the other facilities. Portland is universally beloved as "a great place to live," though students say the parking situation could stand some improvements. A graduating student sums up life at the law school this way: "The professors are passionate about what they teach, and the students actually want to help each other get ahead in school. And where else do you get to study while in an overly large tree house?"

SHANNON DAVIS, ASSISTANT DEAN FOR ADMISSIONS
LEWIS & CLARK LAW SCHOOL, 10015 SW TERWILLIGER BOULEVARD, PORTLAND, OR 97219
TEL: 503-768-6613 • FAX: 503-768-6793
E-MAIL: LAWADMSS@LCLARK.EDU • WEBSITE: WWW.LAW.LCLARK.EDU

Life

No one would argue that "liberal" describes the majority of those enrolled at Lewis & Clark, and as one 3L warns, "If you are conservative, religious, or a meat-eating capitalist, be prepared." Fortunately, the laid-back nature of the majority of the student body means that there is "a complete void of competition"; absolutely "no one participates in the awful game of one-upmanship or cutthroat competition," and "the students are genuinely interested in helping and supporting each other." The day and night students don't often interact outside of class, but this doesn't seem to be a source of much tension. There are plenty of clubs in which they can relate if they so choose, and students here "are spoiled with the number of lunchtime events," including speakers and panels. "Everyone is accepted for who they are," coos a 2L. A second-year student puts it in another way: "Good people go here."

Getting In

The typical student has been in the work force for several years, which plays into the amount of weight placed on various admissions factors. GPA will factor in more heavily for recent grads, and applicants should make sure their letters of recommendation come from the appropriate sources (professors or employers). Recently admitted students at the 25th percentile had an LSAT score of 155 and an average GPA of 3.18, while admitted students at the 75th percentile had an LSAT score of 161 and a GPA of 3.67.

Clinical program required	No
Legal writing course requirement	Yes
Legal methods course requirement	Yes
Legal research course requirement	Yes
Moot court requirement	No
Public interest law requirement	No

ADMISSIONS

Selectivity Rating	81
# applications received	1,491
% applicants accepted	67
% acceptees attending	20
Median LSAT	158
LSAT Range (25th to 75th percentile)	155–161
Median undergrad GPA	3.34
Application fee	$50
Regular application deadline	3/15
Transfer students accepted	Yes
Evening division offered	Yes
Part-time accepted	Yes
CAS accepted	Yes

International Students

TOEFL required of international students.	Yes

FINANCIAL FACTS

Annual tuition	$40,114
Books and supplies	$2,800
Room & Board	$19,800
Financial aid application deadline	2/15
% first-year students receiving some sort of aid	99
% all students receiving some sort of aid	92
% of aid that is merit based	89
% receiving scholarships	75
Average grant	$16,628
Average loan	$43,983
Average total aid package	$50,625
Average debt	$107,475

EMPLOYMENT INFORMATION

Career Rating	83	
Total 2014 JD Grads	234	
% for whom you have useable information	99	
% grads employed ten months out	81	
Median starting salary	$55,000	
# employed full-time	175	
# employed part-time	15	
# employed bar required	139	
# employed JD preferred	34	
# employed professional/other	14	
# employed non-professional	3	
# pursuing advanced degree	5	
# unemployed and seeking employment	30	
# not seeking employment	6	
State for bar exam	OR	
Pass rate for first-time bar	78.0	

Prominent Alumni
Earl Blumenauer, US Representative; Phil Schirilo, legislative strategist on Obamacare; Heidi Heitkamp, U.S. Senator, North Dakota; Honorable Robert E Jones, US District Court for the District of Oregon; Kate Brown, Governor of Oregon

Grads Employed by Field (%)
Business/Industry (15)
Government (12)
Judicial Clerkship (14)
Private Practice (31)
Public Interest (10)

LOUISIANA STATE UNIVERSITY
PAUL M. HEBERT LAW CENTER

INSTITUTIONAL INFORMATION

Public/private	Public
Affiliation	No Affiliation
% faculty part-time	33
% faculty female	25
% faculty underrepresented minority	6
Total faculty	69

SURVEY SAYS...
Great research resources,
Conservative students,
Good social life

STUDENTS

Enrollment of law school	601
% male/female	57/43
% from out-of-state	24
% part-time	1
% underrepresented minority	24
% international	1
# of countries represented	4
Average age of entering class	25

ACADEMICS

Academic Experience Rating	88
Profs interesting rating	90
Profs accessible rating	92
Hours of study per day	3.21

Advanced Degrees Offered
Master of Laws (LLM) 1 yr.

Combined Degrees Offered
JD/MPA 3 yrs; JD/MBA 4 yrs; JD/Masters of Mass Communication 4 yrs; JD/MS Finance 4 yrs

Academics

The "very inexpensive" Louisiana State University Law Center boasts "the highest bar-passage rate in the state" pretty much every year and a unique program where graduates may receive both a JD and optional Graduate Diploma in Comparative Law, which becomes a second degree. All students leave LSU Law with exposure to civil law—the law of private relations such as contracts, marriage, property and inheritance, set forth in Louisiana code following the European legal tradition. "The focus on the civil law at LSU is a definite plus because most of us remain in Louisiana to practice," explains a 2L. "It's a much different approach to problems than our common law colleagues use, and the training in the civil law happens early and often." The "first-year curriculum is rich and very demanding." Contracts, torts, civil procedure, constitutional law, and all your standard 1L courses are required. First-year students must also take course work in Louisiana's codes of obligations, civilian property, and the history and methods of both civil and common law. After first year, "2Ls and 3Ls [are] more free to specialize and take advantage of the practical law courses available that would be applicable out of state." Some students complain that there aren't nearly enough electives, though. "LSU is small and so the range of courses available isn't very broad, and it's not always clear when a course will be taught." "Some courses offered in the school's course booklet haven't been offered in years," gripes a hardened 3L. However, in 2015 the school adopted scheduling changes that aims to reduce obstacles to scheduling each semester and allow for better planning by students.

"The classrooms and facilities are phenomenal." Class attendance policies are "relatively stringent." It's a good thing, then, that the academic atmosphere is generally "excellent." "The great thing about LSU Law professors is that many of them have been incredibly influential in the development of Louisiana law," observes a 1L. "In preparing cases for classes, you can't help but notice how often the courts have relied on your professor's doctrinal works in formulating their decisions." "While some are intent on using the Socratic Method at all costs, most use it simply to ensure that you are paying attention and can answer their questions when called upon," relates a 3L. Not all faculty members are fabulous, though. "LSU has some of the best," advises a 2L, "but a couple have to be the worst." Outside of class, most faculty members are "more than willing to talk to students." "They are all accessible if you try a little bit." A few students tell us that the administration "emphasizes bureaucracy," but the overwhelming sentiment here is that top brass "truly works for the students" and is "remarkably responsive to the student body."

LSU Law offers "an abundance of opportunities to be involved" in journals and advocacy programs. There are clinical programs in immigration law, family law, mediation, homeless advocacy, parole reentry, and juvenile representation. "A well-connected externship program places second- and third-year students with justices and judges in the Louisiana Supreme Court and the U.S. Fifth Circuit Court of Appeals, among others," adds a 3L. A study abroad program in Lyon, France, is also popular. Over 150 employers recruit here each year, but opinion regarding LSU Law's ability to help students find jobs is split. Critics tell us that the Career Services office displays "callous indifference toward students who are not in the top five to ten percent of the class." Other students say that Career Services is "in touch with you from the beginning" and "goes the extra mile to help students and find opportunity for them." "This school does everything it possibly can to ensure that you pass the bar and get a job," beams a confident 1L.

MICHELE FORBES, DIRECTOR OF STUDENT AFFAIRS AND REGISTRAR
202 LAW CENTER, BATON ROUGE, LA 70803
TEL: 225-578-8646 • FAX: 225-578-8647
E-MAIL: ADMISSIONS@LAW.LSU.EDU • WEBSITE: WWW.LAW.LSU.EDU

Life

"Students are generally serious and hardworking." "The student body and faculty lean conservative, but all walks of life are welcome" and it's a diverse group, "age-wise and experience-wise." LSU Law "has a collegial feel where there is a place for everyone." "The school is just the right size to allow getting to know everyone," explains a 2L. "No one is just a number. Everyone has the opportunity to be an individual." "We have gunners just like every law school," admits a 1L. For the most part, though, there is only "a mild dose" of competition. "There really isn't a lot of the cutthroat behavior." Students frequently "share outlines and help each other learn the law."

"Social life at LSU Law is great from the library to the tailgate." This school is "in the middle of Cajun country—great food, one of the best football teams in the nation, and good Southern people." "LSU is in the greatest location a student could ask for," gloats a 1L. "Baton Rouge is an amazing city, and the Law Center is located in the heart of one of the most vibrant undergraduate campuses in the nation." "There are many social programs running throughout the semester so that you get to know your classmates personally and you aren't just doing law school 24/7." "There are parties all the time." "There are free drinks nearly every weekend." "Intramural tournaments" are pretty popular, too. "Students strap on pads and play a charity football game once a year," just for instance, complete with tackling.

Getting In

Admitted students at the 25th percentile have LSAT scores around 153 and undergraduate grade point averages not much over 3.0. At the 75th percentile, LSAT scores are about 159 and GPAs are approximately 3.7.

Clinical program required	No
Legal writing course requirement	Yes
Legal methods course requirement	No
Legal research course requirement	Yes
Moot court requirement	No
Public interest law requirement	No

ADMISSIONS

Selectivity Rating	85
# applications received	1,045
% applicants accepted	46
% acceptees attending	37
Average LSAT	157
Median LSAT	156
LSAT Range (25th to 75th percentile)	153–159
Average undergrad GPA	3.34
Median undergrad GPA	3.45
Application fee	$50
Regular application deadline	3/1
Transfer students accepted	Yes
Evening division offered	No
Part-time accepted	No
CAS accepted	Yes

International Students

TOEFL required of international students. Yes

FINANCIAL FACTS

Annual tuition	$17,903
Books and supplies	$2,000
Fees	$20,215
Room & Board (on/off campus)	$19,060/$20,968
Financial aid application deadline	7/1
% first-year students receiving some sort of aid	89
% all students receiving some sort of aid	89
% of aid that is merit based	21
% receiving scholarships	63
Average grant	$10,133
Average loan	$22,370
Average total aid package	$24,484
Average debt	$38,827

EMPLOYMENT INFORMATION

		Grads Employed by Field (%)
Career Rating	87	Academic (4)
Total 2014 JD Grads	218	Business/Industry (17)
% for whom you have useable information	98	Government (12)
% grads employed ten months out	92	Judicial Clerkship (13)
Median starting salary	$58,000	Private Practice (51)
% job accepting grads providing useable salary information	59	Public Interest (2)
# employed full-time	192	
# employed part-time	4	
# employed bar required	150	
# employed JD preferred	30	
# employed professional/other	12	
# employed non-professional	4	
# pursuing advanced degree	5	
# unemployed and seeking employment	10	
# not seeking employment	3	
State for bar exam	LA	
Pass rate for first-time bar	73.4	

LOYOLA MARYMOUNT UNIVERSITY
LOYOLA LAW SCHOOL

INSTITUTIONAL INFORMATION

Public/private	Private
Affiliation	Roman Catholic-Jesuit
% faculty part-time	44
% faculty female	41
% faculty underrepresented minority	17
Total faculty	134

SURVEY SAYS...
Diverse opinions accepted in classrooms, Great research resources, Abundant externship/internship/clerkship opportunities, Good social life

STUDENTS

Enrollment of law school	1,095
% male/female	46/54
% from out-of-state	10
% part-time	44
% underrepresented minority	40
% international	2
# of countries represented	7
Average age of entering class	24

ACADEMICS

Academic Experience Rating	**92**
Profs interesting rating	94
Profs accessible rating	89
Hours of study per day	3.70

Academic Specialties
Commercial, Corporate Securities, Criminal, Entertainment, Environmental, Fashion, Human Rights, Immigrant Advocacy, International, Public Interest, Taxation, Intellectual Property

Advanced Degrees Offered
MLS: FT 1 yr, PT 2 yrs. LLM Taxation: FT 1 yr, PT 3 yrs. LLM (Specializations in Civil Litigation & Advocacy, Criminal Justice, Entertainment Law, Intellectual Property, International Business Law), 1 yr; Doctor of Juridical Science, 2 semesters of coursework, max 5 yrs for dissertation.

Academics

With its "close proximity to the finest law firms, [the Los Angeles] court system, and non-profit firms and organizations," Loyola Law School—affiliated with the larger Loyola Marymount University—"has an exceptional reputation amongst the Los Angeles-area law schools, with an amazing bar pass rate, well-connected professors, solid research coming from the school, and a diverse student base." Citing the school's "large local presence," students note that "teaching toward the California bar is important" and "practical orientation" at Loyola Law "toward likely first-year jobs is very strong, particularly in government and litigation." In general, graduates of Loyola Law practice primarily in Los Angeles, and California, so it can seem like the school enjoys a greater reputation—and alumni network—within the state than it does nationally or internationally. The school "puts great emphasis on developing competent attorneys with many opportunities for practical legal experience," with one student noting the "Byrne Trial Team and the Civil Litigation Skills Practicum are the highlights of my law school experience." There are "so many different clinics where students can gain experience in every field from immigration to criminal law to arbitration/mediation to human rights," and students underscore that these clinics not only offer invaluable practical experience but will "[set] you apart from the crowd when it comes time to apply for jobs and internships." Students cite opportunities like Loyola's Project for the Innocent and the school's Corporate Law concentration as areas that have contributed to their "foundation" as attorneys. One student adds, "My participation in the school's Law Review has also been incredibly rewarding."

The professors at Loyola are "amazing" and "extremely accessible," with students saying that they enjoy being pushed "to think critically and do your best inside the classroom. The high caliber of instruction is a clear reason why Loyola consistently maintains strong bar passage rates." Loyola Law professors have "extensive real world experience" and "really care about their students and want to see us succeed." Loyola Law also offers an evening program, which one student describes as "wonderful," noting that "Loyola values its evening students and accommodates us well," though others think the school "could improve in [its] incorporation of evening students."

The administration is a mixed bag, according to most Loyola students, with some describing it as "very attentive and usually responds to student inquiries and concerns very quickly" while others complain that Loyola's administration is "cutting corners" and "not run well." The classrooms "were recently updated and have state of the art technology" and the library—"comfortable, open, [with a] well-organized layout, and always clean"—is popular.

JANNELL LUNDY ROBERTS, ASSISTANT DEAN OF ADMISSIONS
919 ALBANY STREET, LOS ANGELES, CA 90015
TEL: 213-736-1074 • FAX: 213-736-6523
E-MAIL: ADMISSIONS@LLS.EDU • WEBSITE: WWW.LLS.EDU

Student Life

Loyola Law's downtown Los Angeles campus is separate from the parent school hub 15 miles to the west. Students are split on whether the separation creates "isolation" or makes for "a very close and supportive community." Competition among Loyola students is, according to some, "high"—one student points out that it's "stronger among the higher-ranked students, but it is not very noticeable to the rest of the students"—though class notes and outlines are shared. It's nearly unanimous that the food at Loyola Law can use an upgrade in keeping with the school's hefty tuition: "We only have one cafeteria with limited food options." When it comes to making connections outside the classroom, "just because people commute doesn't mean they don't spend all day on campus, so there are plenty of opportunities to socialize," notes one student. In addition to Los Angeles's legal connections, students are quick to point out that "we're in the heart of the greatest city in the world" and even though the campus is not in the heart of downtown, there's a school-run shuttle that "is really useful." Students also praise Loyola's "diverse students and staff" and "a diverse student base." In general, with all the opportunities available to them, students say that "there is something for everyone here. There isn't even time to take advantage of all of the options!"

Getting In

In 2014, Loyola Law received roughly 2,972 applications for its regular day program and enrolled approximately 266 students. Enrolled students in the 25th percentile have a GPA of around 3.21 and an LSAT score of 156. Enrolled students in the 75th percentile have a 3.62 GPA and an LSAT score of 161.

Combined Degrees Offered

JD/MBA, 4 yrs; JD/LLM in Taxation, 3 yrs

Clinical program required	No
Legal writing course requirement	Yes
Legal methods course requirement	Yes
Legal research course requirement	Yes
Moot court requirement	No
Public interest law requirement	Yes

ADMISSIONS

Selectivity Rating	86
# applications received	2,972
% applicants accepted	47
% acceptees attending	19
Median LSAT	159
LSAT Range (25th to 75th percentile)	156–161
Median undergrad GPA	3.48
Application fee	$0
Early application deadline	12/1
Early application notification	12/31
Transfer students accepted	Yes
Evening division offered	Yes
Part-time accepted	Yes
CAS accepted	Yes

FINANCIAL FACTS

Annual tuition	$47,180
Books and supplies	$1,370
Fees	$570
Room & Board	$16,660
Financial aid application deadline	3/2
% first-year students receiving some sort of aid	92
% all students receiving some sort of aid	90
% of aid that is merit based	28
% receiving scholarships	57
Average grant	$24,700
Average loan	$48,665
Average total aid package	$55,043
Average debt	$147,701

EMPLOYMENT INFORMATION

Career Rating	90
Total 2014 JD Grads	396
% for whom you have useable information	100
% grads employed ten months out	81
Median starting salary	$70,000
# employed full-time	298
# employed part-time	23
# employed bar required	257
# employed JD preferred	57
# employed professional/other	5
# employed non-professional	2
# pursuing advanced degree	3
# unemployed and seeking employment	58
# not seeking employment	8
% grads employed by school	3
State for bar exam	CA
Pass rate for first-time bar	80.0

Prominent Alumni

Alejandro Mayorkas, Deputy Secretary of Homeland Security; Bob Myers, Golden State Warriors General Manager

Grads Employed by Field (%)

Academic (0)	
Business/Industry (14)	
Government (4)	
Judicial Clerkship (3)	
Federal: (2)	
State or local: (1)	
Private Practice (55)	
Solo: (1)	
2-10: (26)	
11-25: (8)	
26-50: (4)	
51-100: (2)	
101-250: (2)	
251-500: (2)	
501+: (9)	
Size Unknown: (0)	
Public Interest (6)	

LOYOLA UNIVERSITY CHICAGO
SCHOOL OF LAW

INSTITUTIONAL INFORMATION

Public/private	Private
Affiliation	Roman Catholic
% faculty part-time	64
% faculty female	48
% faculty underrepresented minority	10
Total faculty	188

SURVEY SAYS...
Students love Chicago, IL, Abundant externship/internship/clerkship opportunities

STUDENTS

Enrollment of law school	724
% male/female	46/54
% from out-of-state	34
% part-time	9
% underrepresented minority	26
% international	2
Average age of entering class	24

ACADEMICS

Academic Experience Rating	83
Profs interesting rating	75 Profs
accessible rating	81
Hours of study per day	3.22

Academic Specialties
Civil Procedure, Commercial, Constitutional, Corporation Securities, Criminal, Human Rights, International, Labor, Property, Taxation, Intellectual Property

Advanced Degrees Offered
Campus Programs—LLM: Business Law; Child Law; Health Law; International Law; Tax Law; Trial Advocacy, Appellate Advocacy, and Alternative Dispute Resolution; US Law for Foreign Lawyers; Rule of Law for Development. SJD in Health Law and Policy. Online Programs—LLM: Business Law; Health Law; Global Competition Law. MJ: Business Law; Children's Law and Policy; Health Law, Global Competition Law.

Academics

Loyola University Chicago's School of Law provides a "great well-rounded education" in a "very friendly and welcoming environment" from its location in "one of the most beautiful city blocks in Chicago." Founded in 1909 by the Society of Jesus, the school's "Jesuit values...permeate everything that goes on at the school." "The best thing about Loyola is that for a competitive law school that boasts many of Chicago's most well-known litigators, the personality of the institution is welcoming," a 2L says. This "extremely friendly" atmosphere receives endless praise from Loyola students. "I have heard horror stories of law schools that pit the students against each other," a 1L explains, "[but] it isn't like that at Loyola." "The Loyola name is highly respected in the Chicago area," and the "very good" and "very engaged" alumni "help Loyola Law students and will often hire them."

"Loyola's facilities are excellent," including the "beautiful," "large, and spacious" classrooms that provide "great views of the city which make studying not seem as bad." The law school is located in a "new, state-of-the-art" building, but students point out that "the undergrads share the building with the law students." The "abysmal" law library is actually "out done by [the] undergraduate library" and "could stand to be re-done." However, the "library staff is excellent." Students also complain that "the cost of tuition is quite high." "I am very worried about getting a job after school that will allow me to pay off my debt," one student admits.

Students have praise for the school's "amazing" staff and faculty nearly across the board. "The staff is great!" says one student, while another declares "the administration is unlike any I've ever experienced." "I have been extremely impressed by the level of attention to detail the Loyola professors and non-academic staff place on managing the legal program," a happy 1L says. The "always available" professors will "talk and say hello in the hallways." While some say the professors have a "very broad range" of quality, most "really challenge you" and "are more like friends/mentors." Loyola "offers a wide variety of practical, hands on courses" as well as "great panels, symposiums, and networking events." The administration and faculty "really encourage getting outside experience while in school." Thus, "many students participate in externships" or find other opportunities in Chicago. "I have had a great experience at Loyola thus far and can't say enough good things about it," a 3L proudly says.

Life

The "excellent" student body is filled with "very nice people" that are "very cohesive and social." However, the student body is divided between "day and evening students," and there can be "limited interaction between" the two groups. This may be due to the "different situations...between the older evening students and the younger less experienced day students." Although another student says "day and evening students do interact quite often in social settings and after the first year, there is little distinction between them." In general, the culture at Loyola is "very nurturing" and many miles from "the stereotypical 'highly competitive' environment."

Office of Admission and Financial Assistance, Office of Admission & Financial Assistance
25 East Pearson Suite 1208, Chicago, IL 60611
Tel: 312-915-7170 • Fax: 312-915-7906
E-Mail: law-admissions@luc.edu • Website: www.luc.edu/law

"The school is in the most perfect location one could hope for in an urban campus," giving students access to all of America's Second City. The "social scene" on campus "is very much catered to twenty-two-year-olds" due to the "very young student body." Although the law school facilities are separate from those of other University departments in the building, "undergrad students and overall environment is a constant complaint." "There is plenty to do if you have extra time" on campus or off, and "there are ample opportunities for networking and for job searching while in school." "Loyola is real big on community service which you gotta love, there is always an opportunity to serve," one 3L says.

Getting In

Loyola University Chicago's School of Law is very competitive. The median GPA and LSAT for the 2014 class were 3.3 and 157 respectively, so potential applicants will want to study, study, study. In addition to grades and scores, the Loyola looks closely at letters of recommendation and personal statement, and takes into account work experience as well as a perceived ability to overcome hardships.

Combined Degrees Offered

JD/MBA, JD/MSW, JD/MA Political Science, 4 yrs; JD/MMP, 3 yrs

Clinical program required	No
Legal writing course requirement	Yes
Legal methods course requirement	No
Legal research course requirement	Yes
Moot court requirement	No
Public interest law requirement	No

ADMISSIONS

Selectivity Rating	83
# applications received	2,575
% applicants accepted	52
% acceptees attending	17
Median LSAT	157
LSAT Range (25th to 75th percentile)	155–159
Median undergrad GPA	3.30
Application fee	$0
Regular application deadline	4/1
Early application deadline	1/15
Early application notification	2/15
Transfer students accepted	Yes
Evening division offered	Yes
Part-time accepted	Yes
CAS accepted	Yes

International Students

TOEFL required of international students.	Yes

FINANCIAL FACTS

Annual tuition	$44,450
Books and supplies	$1,500
Room & Board	$22,130
Financial aid application deadline	3/1
% first-year students receiving some sort of aid	90
% all students receiving some sort of aid	87
% of aid that is merit based	80
% receiving scholarships	87
Average grant	$12,000
Average loan	$40,000
Average total aid package	$67,452

EMPLOYMENT INFORMATION

Career Rating	86	
Total 2014 JD Grads	262	
% for whom you have useable information	98	
% grads employed ten months out	89	
Median starting salary	$60,000	
# employed full-time	209	
# employed part-time	25	
# employed bar required	165	
# employed JD preferred	55	
# employed professional/other	12	
# employed non-professional	2	
# pursuing advanced degree	2	
# unemployed and seeking employment	16	
# not seeking employment	3	
% grads employed by school	1	
State for bar exam	IL	
Pass rate for first-time bar	83.5	

Prominent Alumni

Lisa Madigan, Illinois Attorney General; Dan Webb, Chairman, Winston & Strawn; John Cullerton, Illinois Senate President; Michael Madigan, Speaker of the Illinois House of Representatives; Robert Thomas, Illinois Supreme Court Justice

Grads Employed by Field (%)

Academic (2)	
Business/Industry (21)	
Government (12)	
Judicial Clerkship (5)	
Federal: (1)	
State or local: (4)	
Private Practice (44)	
Solo: (1)	
2-10: (22)	
11-25: (3)	
26-50: (3)	
51-100: (3)	
101-250: (3)	
251-500: (3)	
501+: (6)	
Size Unknown: (0)	
Public Interest (6)	

LOYOLA UNIVERSITY—NEW ORLEANS
COLLEGE OF LAW

Academics

Loyola University—New Orleans College of Law is "hands down, the best place to study law" thanks to its "regional reputation, elite professors, great career resources, and guest speakers." Owing to "its location in one of the world's great cultural centers," students here aren't surprised with "the quality and accessibility of the professors," all within an "atmosphere that facilitates learning and making connections." The "top-notch" professors "bring a wealth of practical experience into the classroom" and are "willing to bend over backwards to help students in their career path." It helps that the professors "all have practical experience in their area of law" and "incorporate that [expertise] in the classroom." "It's great to have a professor who helped write the civil code and court opinions teach them to you," says a 3L. The administration can be "very good, very personal, and helpful," and the financial aid department recently acquired new staff, improving the department's efficiency. Those involved in the school's evening program would like to see the administration give them the same "availability of classes and special programs, such as internships or externships," as those in the regular program have. Others appreciate the lack of "long lines" and "red tape." "This law school is completely oriented around the students," says a 1L.

"There are continual opportunities to gain practical legal experience" at Loyola through "constant notices of internships, jobs, volunteer projects, and externships." "Professors share their advice for exam preparation and are very up front with expectations for exams," says a 2L. However, while nearly all students approve of the "moot court and trial advocacy programs," some would like to "have fewer required courses so that students can specialize in a particular area with more ease." Others think that "Loyola needs to do a much better job preparing students to actually practice law." "The odds are severely stacked against a recent graduate arguing anything to an appeals court, as most firms have attorneys with considerably more experience who handle all of the firm's appeals work," explains a 3L. "Therefore, the area in which Loyola could stand to improve the most is offering more trial court advocacy classes and giving those equal, if not greater, focus than moot court."

Opinions on Loyola's career services office range from "fantastic" to "a joke," though which side you'll fall on will likely depend on where you're from. "One area that I think the school could improve on is helping the common law students obtain jobs out of state," says a 3L. "Our career services is terrible if you're not from Louisiana," adds a 2L. That said, most students are happy to stay in New Orleans after graduating. "Loyola's great for people who want to practice in New Orleans," says a 2L. "It offers lots of connections and alumni in the area who like to give back to their own."

"Some of the classrooms, namely the newer ones, are top-notch," says a 1L. Others "are overcrowded and students are relegated to using stand-alone desks along the edges of the classrooms with inadequate surfaces for writing or computer usage." "The facilities could use a drastic update," says a 2L. While the library is "giant" with "many helpful resources," it's in "need of a twenty-first (or even twentieth) century makeover." Students also wouldn't mind having a place where they can "study late at night, segregated from the undergrads," along with "more food options for the law campus."

Life

Students at Loyola "are generally helpful to each other" and "very friendly regardless of whether they are from the New Orleans area or not." "There is some competitiveness

K. MICHELE ALLISON-DAVIS, DEAN OF ADMISSIONS
7214 SAINT CHARLES AVENUE, BOX 904, NEW ORLEANS, LA 70118
TEL: 504-861-5575 • FAX: 504-861-5772
E-MAIL: LADMIT@LOYNO.EDU • WEBSITE: LAW.LOYNO.EDU

amongst the student body, but I would hesitate to say cutthroat," says a 2L. "Every student seems to view your own personal success as their own," adds a 1L. Though there's a lot of talk about "the rift between Civil and Common Law students," most agree, "it is best explained by the fact that students take largely different courses and study very different material over three years." That said, most admit that they "have never seen an argument or any social outcasting based on a student's choice of study." There's a fair amount of diversity in the student population. "I have never had a group of friends as diverse as what I have found here," says a 2L. "There is not another school that I am aware of that could foster such camaraderie among so diverse a population."

When it comes to social life at Loyola, all students have to do is step outside. Located in "Uptown New Orleans," students can readily hop a streetcar that "provides access to the French Quarter and Central Business District." "New Orleans has the best nightlife in the South," says a 3L. "The city environment is perfect for young professionals." "I would say that most students spend a majority of their social time in Uptown or in the Garden District rather than in the belligerent, tourist-packed French Quarter," says a 2L. "The nightlife in Uptown and the Garden District is much more tailored to the academic crowd." According to a 1L, "This year's 1L class hangs out together in a wide variety of ways, [whether it's] going to the Jay-Z concert as a big group or holding our own Mardi Gras party with the whole class invited to come, grab a drink, and watch the parades." Fundamentally, argues a 2L, "The music, food, and social justice opportunities should encourage anyone to come to law school at Loyola."

Getting In

Recently admitted students at Loyola Law have average undergraduate GPAs of 3.14 and LSAT scores of 153. The admissions office operates a unique Early Admit program that allows those who have completed three-fourths of their undergraduate degree requirements to be admitted. Those who take advantage of this option will be expected to have higher entering credentials than those who will be entering law school with an undergraduate degree.

Clinical program required	No
Legal writing	
course requirement	Yes
Legal methods	
course requirement	Yes
Legal research	
course requirement	Yes
Moot court requirement	Yes
Public interest	
law requirement	Yes

ADMISSIONS

Selectivity Rating	78
# applications received	1,014
% applicants accepted	58
% acceptees attending	24
Average LSAT	153
Median LSAT	153
LSAT Range (25th to	
75th percentile)	150–157
Average undergrad GPA	3.14
Median undergrad GPA	3.15
Application fee	$0
Transfer students accepted	Yes
Evening division offered	Yes
Part-time accepted	Yes
CAS accepted	Yes

International Students

TOEFL recommended of	
international students.	Yes

FINANCIAL FACTS

Annual tuition	$42,000
Books and supplies	$1,500
Fees	$1,150
Room & Board	$21,644
% first-year students receiving	
some sort of aid	93
% all students receiving	
some sort of aid	91
% of aid that is merit based	100
% receiving scholarships	61
Average grant	$20,320
Average loan	$20,500
Average total aid package	$40,820
Average debt	$117,892

EMPLOYMENT INFORMATION

Career Rating	82
Total 2014 JD Grads	218
% grads employed ten months out	78
Median starting salary	$65,000
# employed full-time	151
# employed part-time	20
# employed bar required	123
# employed JD preferred	27
# employed professional/other	15
# employed non-professional	6
# pursuing advanced degree	4
# unemployed and seeking	
employment	35
# not seeking employment	7
% grads employed by school	1
State for bar exam	LA, TX, FL, GA, MS

Prominent Alumni
Pascal Calogero, Chief Justice, Louisiana Supreme Court; Moon Landrieu, Secretary of HUD, Mayor of New Orleans, etc.

Grads Employed by Field (%)
Business/Industry (16)
Government (8)
Judicial Clerkship (6)
Federal: (3)
State or local: (3)
Private Practice (44)
Solo: (4)
2-10: (24)
11-25: (7)
26-50: (3)
51-100: (3)
251-500: (1)
Public Interest (2)

MARQUETTE UNIVERSITY
LAW SCHOOL

Academics

Located in Milwaukee, Marquette University is academically "challenging, but very supportive." The school encourages students to challenge themselves through their studies "rather than to compete with others." This creates an environment in which students are a part "of a community, not just a law school." The "normal stereotype of law school being a cut throat environment does not seem to apply" to Marquette. Here "students help each other," and "the administration and faculty really care about" the students and "do everything they can to help" students with "school or their lives outside of school."

In addition to its "peaceful and supportive social environment," Marquette is known for its "experience programs in public service" and "focus on networking in the local legal community." Students at Marquette receive "one of the best, most well-rounded, legal educations available in the country" says one student. Students roundly praised "the caliber of its faculty," "the engaged student body," and "the school's connections to the Milwaukee legal community." Several students noted the Sports Law program as one of the main reasons they were drawn to the university. And Marquette offers a range of "specialty programs (specifically sports law, alternative dispute resolution, and moot court)."

The "practical education" provided "through workshops, seminars, and intern/externships" prepares students "for the workforce." "I feel prepared to become an attorney and start working immediately upon graduation," notes one student. "Even as a 1L you are able to get involved and gain real world experiences through our phenomenal Pro Bono Society," notes another. Students say their "professors truly care about what they are teaching and enjoy teaching law." "They make sure they are engaging," and "work with the students on multiple levels" to make "sure the class actually learns the materials," rather than "just spitting it back out for an exam." Students at Marquette feel truly supported by the faculty, noting that the faculty is actively "engaged in helping their students succeed, whether it's staying late to help a struggling student or helping connect someone with a potential employer."

The "faculty is highly esteemed in their practice areas" and "well connected in local and national markets." Professors "run programs for intern and externships all over the city and country." As one student notes "this resource is invaluable to our legal education and our ability to leave law school with strong practical skills and resumes that make us attractive hires"—which is especially important in a tough job market. Milwaukee also has "a strong and active [legal] community that are always willing to network and meet with outgoing students who take advantage of that opportunity."

As the "only law school in a large city, Milwaukee," Marquette provides "the legal intern work force for the city, which is a huge advantage over cities with several law schools all trying to get the same internships." The school offers "programs to introduce the legal community to the law school through speakers and events" and the "administration and career planning are extremely approachable and receptive to student needs."

SEAN REILLY, ASSISTANT DEAN FOR ADMISSIONS
ECKSTEIN HALL, ROOM 132, P.O. BOX 1881, MILWAUKEE, WI 53201-1881
TEL: 414-288-6767 • FAX: 414-288-0676
E-MAIL: LAW.ADMISSION@MARQUETTE.EDU • WEBSITE: LAW.MARQUETTE.EDU

And, because the law school building is only five years old, its facilities are new and "top notch." As on student notes: "It is very nice to have all your needs met in one building . . . gym, cafe, kitchen, classrooms, library, ping-pong, parking, and social gathering spots." "The research facilities/resources and classrooms are definitely top of the line." The building is "unbelievably beautiful and provides the students, faculty, and guests with any technology and accommodations needed or wanted." The school has "excellent research resources, including a team of librarians who are ready to help day and night."

Life

Students call Marquette's campus "beautiful" and "very accommodating for students," but note that "while the facility is gorgeous," Wisconsin is "always cold." The buildings feature "large windows in all the study rooms" and "the open library" though beautiful, reminds some students of being in a "fish-bowl." Students do feel well taken care of though, and appreciate the "learning seminars that provide free lunch" on a cold day.

Getting In

At the 25th percentile, students recently admitted to Marquette Law have LSAT scores of 149 and GPAs in the 3.12 range, while admitted students at the 75th percentile have LSAT scores of 155 and GPAs of roughly 3.52. Approximately 5 percent of accepted applicants in 2014 held other graduate/professional degrees, while 53 percent of full-time students enrolled directly after college. The school has rolling admissions, which means it is better to apply as early into the admissions seasons as possible.

Clinical program required	No
Legal writing course requirement	Yes
Legal methods course requirement	No
Legal research course requirement	Yes
Moot court requirement	No
Public interest law requirement	No

ADMISSIONS

Selectivity Rating	76
# applications received	1,148
% applicants accepted	76
% acceptees attending	22
Average LSAT	152
Median LSAT	152
LSAT Range (25th to 75th percentile)	149–155
Average undergrad GPA	3.29
Median undergrad GPA	3.33
Application fee	$50
Regular application deadline	4/1
Transfer students accepted	Yes
Evening division offered	No
Part-time accepted	Yes
CAS accepted	Yes

International Students

TOEFL required of international students.	Yes

FINANCIAL FACTS

Annual tuition	$41,040
Books and supplies	$1,248
Fees	$0
Room & Board	$13,770
Financial aid application deadline	3/1
% first-year students receiving some sort of aid	97
% all students receiving some sort of aid	94
% of aid that is merit based	15
% receiving scholarships	57
Average grant	$11,959
Average loan	$45,891
Average total aid package	$48,135
Average debt	$134,533

EMPLOYMENT INFORMATION

Career Rating	**85**	
Total 2014 JD Grads	214	
% for whom you have useable information	94	
% grads employed ten months out	88	
Median starting salary	$55,000	
# employed full-time	165	
# employed part-time	13	
# employed bar required	122	
# employed JD preferred	42	
# employed professional/other	11	
# employed non-professional	3	
# pursuing advanced degree	3	
# unemployed and seeking employment	21	
% grads employed by school	1	
State for bar exam	TX, IL, MN, CA, WI	
Pass rate for first-time bar	93.0	

Prominent Alumni
Hon. Diane Sykes, U.S. Court of Appeals Judge; Hon. Janine Geske, Former WI Supreme Court Justice; Hon. James Wynn, U.S. Court of Appeals Judge; Hon. Annette Ziegler, WI Supreme Court Justice; Lynne Halbrooks, Principal Deputy Inspector Gen., Dept. of Defense

Grads Employed by Field (%)
Academic (1)
Business/Industry (19)
Government (16)
Judicial Clerkship (3)
Private Practice (46)
Public Interest (3)

MERCER UNIVERSITY
WALTER F. GEORGE SCHOOL OF LAW

INSTITUTIONAL INFORMATION

Public/private	Private
Affiliation	Baptist
Student-faculty ratio	14:1
% faculty part-time	58
% faculty female	33
% faculty underrepresented minority	7
Total faculty	86

SURVEY SAYS...

Great research resources, Diverse opinions accepted in classrooms

STUDENTS

Enrollment of law school	427
% male/female	49/51
% from out-of-state	27
% underrepresented minority	29
% international	1
Average age of entering class	25

ACADEMICS

Academic Experience Rating	78
Profs interesting rating	82
Profs accessible rating	88
Hours of study per day	3.77

Academic Specialties
Criminal, International, Labor, Taxation, Intellectual Property

Advanced Degrees Offered
JD, 3 yrs. LLM, Federal Criminal Practice & Procedure, 1 yr.

Combined Degrees Offered
JD/MBA, 3–4 yrs.

Academics

In addition to its beautiful campus southeast of Atlanta, students are drawn to Mercer University's Walter F. George School of Law in Macon, Georgia for "scholarships and aid" as well as a sense of "community and academic success." All student classes are "located in one building." Mercer University has been around for awhile, but the "older building . . . gives it character." Students spend time studying in the "fully stocked" library, and every 1L student has "the opportunity to receive a laptop during their 1L year." The facilities were upgraded over the past few years, but some students feel some things could still be improved, including "upgrading technology "and using a better wireless connection.

The students are fond of many classes and professors at Mercer, but many will tell you that they "particularly love the Legal Writing Certificate Program." One student called the program "one of the best aspects of the school." Another agreed, saying it's "an excellent experience and a worthwhile venture for law students. It refreshes your grammar rules knowledge and provides an opportunity to craft your personal style." Students also have the chance to "participate in mock trial and moot court, the externship program, Habeus Project, a great career service group."

One student applauds having a "female Dean of my law school . . . and the transition was very smooth." Still, several students point out the need for more diverse faculty, staff, students, and administrators: It seems to them that the "school does not value the beliefs and sensitivities of minority students." Other students mention that "the education is top-class, but the administration is condescending and not open to important changes. They will ignore important issues until they explode." Students hope the administration will work on "being more approachable and responding to student's needs," leaving the students concerned about the "atmosphere and climate." One student notes that Mercer "is embedded in the deep South and there needs to be more education/training on diversity and inclusion, especially for future lawyers who will some day have to work with a diverse client-base or [in a] diverse work environment."

As for the faculty, students say their professors "are the best part of the school." Faculty is always accessible to students and keep an "open door policy" which students say is "refreshing and extremely helpful." Students enjoy "the smaller elective classes where there is lively debate and open discussion." Most students point out the "practical application" of their studies as a huge part of their happiness at Mercer. The school is smaller and allows for more "one-on-one with professors," and is "very public service oriented." Law students at Mercer are engaged on campus in their community, and last year organized a "silent protest regarding police brutality." Simply put by one student, "If you want to be a litigator, Mercer is the place to be."

Marilyn E. Sutton, Asst. Dean of Admissions and Financial Aid
1021 Georgia Avenue, Macon, GA 31207
Tel: 478-301-2605 • Fax: 478-301-2989
E-Mail: admissions@law.mercer.edu • Website: www.law.mercer.edu

Life

Students in this small community are happy that the area is growing and that they can now brag about "a football team, driving economic development downtown, and . . . a broader spectrum of social activities." Students like to " study on the porch or have class outside." The student body and student organizations "make a lot of decisions and have a strong voice at the school." Mercer students are also quick to point out the camaraderie between students: "The greatest strength of this law school is how far removed from competition the student body is." Another student says that even with the recent problems, "there is a good mix of conservative and liberal students so classroom discussions will often go both ways." Mercer Law is dependent on "community and solidarity" and students always try to find ways to work together.

Macon itself has "a great selection of restaurants from take-away hibachi to authentic Indian food and Greek." The area is also free from Atlanta's "real traffic." Students often go to "major retail shops" and are grateful that they don't have to endure hours of traffic to get there, and seem especially happy about the amount of "outdoor space."

Getting In

Mercer Law recently admitted students with a median LSAT score of 152. Students' undergraduate GPAs ranged from 3.05 in the 25th percentile, to 3.5 in the 75th percentile.

Clinical program required	No
Legal writing course requirement	Yes
Legal methods course requirement	No
Legal research course requirement	Yes
Moot court requirement	No
Public interest law requirement	No

ADMISSIONS

Selectivity Rating	79
# applications received	829
% applicants accepted	61
% acceptees attending	29
Median LSAT	152
LSAT Range (25th to 75th percentile)	147–155
Median undergrad GPA	3.29
Application fee	$0
Regular application deadline	3/15
Transfer students accepted	Yes
Evening division offered	No
Part-time accepted	No
CAS accepted	Yes

International Students

TOEFL recommended of international students.	Yes

FINANCIAL FACTS

Annual tuition	$36,960
Books and supplies	$1,482
Fees	$300
Room & Board	$19,058
Financial aid application deadline	4/1
% first-year students receiving some sort of aid	95
% all students receiving some sort of aid	94
% of aid that is merit based	20
% receiving scholarships	68
Average grant	$14,400
Average loan	$44,677
Average total aid package	$51,024
Average debt	$125,301

EMPLOYMENT INFORMATION

Career Rating	88	**Prominent Alumni**
Total 2014 JD Grads	143	Griffin Bell, Former Attorney General of the
% for whom you have useable information	99	United States; Honorable Hugh Thompson, Chief Justice, Georgia Supreme Court;
% grads employed ten months out	83	Nathan Deal, Governor of Georgia
Median starting salary	$50,000	**Grads Employed by Field (%)**
% job accepting grads providing useable salary information	43	Academic (1)
		Business/Industry (4)
# employed full-time	114	Government (17)
# employed part-time	5	Judicial Clerkship (13)
# employed bar required	105	Federal: (4)
# employed JD preferred	11	State or local: (10)
# employed professional/other	2	Private Practice (48)
# employed non-professional	1	Solo: (1)
# pursuing advanced degree	4	2-10: (31)
# unemployed and seeking		11-25: (6)
employment	14	26-50: (5)
# not seeking employment	3	51-100: (1)
% grads employed by school	1	101-250: (1)
State for bar exam	GA	251-500: (1)
Pass rate for first-time bar	80.0	501+: (1)
		Public Interest (1)

MICHIGAN STATE UNIVERSITY
COLLEGE OF LAW

INSTITUTIONAL INFORMATION

Public/private	Private
Student-faculty ratio	14:1
% faculty part-time	115
% faculty female	35
Total faculty	182

SURVEY SAYS...

Diverse opinions accepted in class-rooms, Great research resources, Law school well run, Good social life

STUDENTS

Enrollment of law school	791
% male/female	54/46
% from out-of-state	52
% part-time	18
% underrepresented minority	179
% international	6
# of countries represented	19

ACADEMICS

Academic Experience Rating	88
Profs interesting rating	83
Profs accessible rating	92
Hours of study per day	4.92

Academic Specialties

Commercial, Constitutional, Corporation Securities, Criminal, Environmental, Government Services, International, Taxation, Intellectual Property

Advanced Degrees Offered

LLM 1 year, MJ 1 year.

Combined Degrees Offered

JD/MBA 4 yrs, JD/MS 4 yrs (Various Fields), JD/MA 4 yrs (Various Fields).

Academics

When students at Michigan State University say their school offers "the best of both worlds," they really mean it. As a private school affiliated with a large public institution, MSU Law offers "a small academic community where professors remember and really take an interest in their students," while simultaneously providing "access to all the benefits of a world-class Big Ten university." The school maintains an accomplished faculty, and "the professors have, for the most part, attended top schools and have great experience to share." "While all the professors have their own research and other legal work, the emphasis is on teaching" at MSU. Of course, "you'll have some professors that are better than others," but the majority are engaging and student-friendly. If you visit them during office hours or linger around after class, many professors will "talk about work experience, research they've done, [and] interesting cases they've worked on. Some of them will connect on a more personal level" and talk "about their families or cool places they have visited."

The JD curriculum is "quite rigorous," and "you have to be willing to put in the work to get the results"; however, MSU invests in its students' success. One student explains, "The law college is good at providing academic resources for students such as labs, advisement, and TAs for 1Ls." In the library, "the research librarians are great at helping students find what they are looking for," as well as keeping the noise levels reasonable during exams. Highly student-friendly, the law school's administration is praised for their efficiency, friendliness, and contemporary approach to education, especially the school's "great Dean, who understands the current legal market and the changing legal education system." Throughout departments and processes, "the administration at MSU is actively involved in making sure you receive a high-quality legal education," and they "genuinely want to connect with students." For example, "the deans have a free lunch meeting once a month where they explain what is going on in the school and let students ask questions."

There are many ways to put your legal skills into practice at MSU, including the school's "excellent Moot Court and Law Review opportunities." Of particular note, "the emphasis on clinical experience and expansion of the clinical programs at MSU College of Law is second to none." Depending on your area of interest, "there are about seven or eight different clinics that 2Ls and 3Ls can enroll in, ranging from Tax and Housing to Chance at Childhood and Plea and Sentencing." Alternatively, MSU's "geographic location (adjacent to the state capitol, Lansing) enables students to pursue a variety of intern- and externships in lieu of the offered clinics." Those interested in government work can augment these experiences through the school's popular "semester in Washington, D.C.," which combines professional experience at a federal agency coupled with the ongoing course work at MSU.

After graduation, students looking for work in Michigan appreciate the school's great local reputation. Propitiously located in the capital city of Lansing, "there are a lot of opportunities for work within a few miles of school," particularly for those interested in government-related positions. For those planning to practice outside of the Great Lakes state, note the words of one student in particular who affirms that "career services is an extremely useful department for in-state students. However, more could be done to improve the ability of out-of-state students to obtain internships and externships."

Life

Those looking for a lively, well-rounded law school experience will be happy with the atmosphere at MSU. There is "great cooperative attitude among all students," and no lack of activities and events to fill up their free time. Between the law school and the larger university campus, there is "a wide range of extracurricular activities and organizations, from access to intramural sports through the university to law-student-specific groups that encompass just about every background, interest, and practice area." Students love attending college football games with their classmates, and they take advantage of the myriad fitness and recreational facilities on campus. Among other perks, "there are two golf courses on campus, and the driving range is heated so you can hit a bucket late into fall or early in spring."

The law school is located in an "excellent building," which is "newly renovated with wireless throughout." In addition to nice study spaces and common areas, "there are private study rooms for groups that can be reserved in advance." Plus, "Sparty's, the cafe in the law school, is a great spot to get caffeine before late nights or long classes." Located in a bustling "college town," law students benefit from an affordable and relaxed lifestyle in hometown Lansing. When they need a change of scenery, "E. Lansing and Lansing offer a wide range of cuisines and other activities that don't have to revolve around the school."

Getting In

Applications for the fall term are reviewed on a rolling basis starting in November. While the school will accept new applications through April 30, priority is given to students who apply before March 1. As with any rolling admissions program, changes of admission are better earlier in the application cycle. In recent years, the median LSAT score for incoming students was 155; and their median undergraduate GPA was 3.55.

Clinical program required	No
Legal writing course requirement	Yes
Legal methods course requirement	No
Legal research course requirement	Yes
Moot court requirement	No
Public interest law requirement	No

ADMISSIONS

Selectivity Rating	85
# applications received	2,733
% applicants accepted	43
% acceptees attending	22
Average LSAT	154
Median LSAT	155
LSAT Range (25th to 75th percentile)	150–158
Average undergrad GPA	3.46
Median undergrad GPA	3.55
Application fee	$60
Regular application deadline	4/30
Early application deadline	3/1
Transfer students accepted	Yes
Evening division offered	No
Part-time accepted	Yes
CAS accepted	Yes

International Students

TOEFL required of international students.	Yes

FINANCIAL FACTS

Annual tuition	$37,294
Books and supplies	$1,506
Fees	$28
Room & Board	$5,397
Financial aid application deadline	4/1
% first-year students receiving some sort of aid	84
% all students receiving some sort of aid	86
% of aid that is merit based	40
% receiving scholarships	58
Average grant	$25,175
Average loan	$32,445
Average total aid package	$43,351
Average debt	$95,494

EMPLOYMENT INFORMATION

Career Rating	86	Grads Employed by Field (%)
Total 2014 JD Grads	331	Academic (6)
% for whom you have useable information	100	Business/Industry (24)
# employed full-time	304	Government (13)
# employed part-time	15	Judicial Clerkship (6)
# employed bar required	199	Federal: (1)
# employed JD preferred	101	State or local: (5)
# employed professional/other	13	Private Practice (34)
# employed non-professional	6	Solo: (2)
# pursuing advanced degree	7	2-10: (13)
# unemployed and seeking employment	2	11-25: (5)
# not seeking employment	1	26-50: (3)
% grads employed by school	18	51-100: (4)
State for bar exam	MI, IL, OH, CA, NY	101-250: (3)
Pass rate for first-time bar	80.0	251-500: (2)
		501+: (2)
		Size Unknown: (1)
		Public Interest (12)

MISSISSIPPI COLLEGE
SCHOOL OF LAW

INSTITUTIONAL INFORMATION

Public/private	Private
Affiliation	Southern Baptist
% faculty part-time	77
% faculty female	41
% faculty underrepresented minority	8
Total faculty	110

SURVEY SAYS...

Abundant externship/internship/clerkship opportunities, Conservative students

STUDENTS

Enrollment of law school	432
% male/female	55/45
% from out-of-state	56
% part-time	5
% underrepresented minority	22
% international	1
# of countries represented	6
Average age of entering class	26

ACADEMICS

Academic Experience Rating	71
Profs interesting rating	75
Profs accessible rating	82
Hours of study per day	3.16

Academic Specialties
Commercial, Criminal, International

Advanced Degrees Offered
JD, 3 yrs; JD, 2 yrs; LLM, 1 yr (International Students - American Legal Studies), LLM (General); LLM Advocacy

Combined Degrees Offered
JD/MBA; JD (3 yrs), MBA (1 year)

Academics

At Mississippi College, a "positive learning environment" and friendly staff offset the inevitable challenges of a legal education. Rather than promoting cutthroat competition or scary Socratic questioning, "the faculty and staff at MC Law are a unique bunch filled with kindness and enthusiasm." Students praise their school's moderate size, saying it allows for a more rewarding academic experience. While one may have a few large lecture courses, many "smaller classrooms allow for more collaboration because students sit around round tables." Plus, the academic intimacy really pays off at MC, where students can find "MS State Supreme Court justices teaching seminars, Federal District Court judges leading lectures, and practicing attorneys from the city of Jackson and surrounding areas leading our legal writing program." Despite their all-star credentials, "the professors make a wonderful effort to ensure that you understand the concepts, whether you ask in class or out of class." That extra help can really pay off, as "the low GPA curve creates a more competitive environment than most people like to admit."

There is a "very strong emphasis on writing" throughout the MC curriculum, as well as an "exceptional legal research staff" in the library. For those with a specific legal interest, the school also offers several special centers, like the Bioethics and Health Law Center and the Public Service Law Center, which operate both academic and extracurricular programs, as well as the opportunity to earn special certificates at graduation. Nonetheless, a handful of students worry that "some of the professors are too theoretical" in their approach to the course work, while others say, "The school should require more research classes." Fortunately, Mississippi College augments traditional classroom instruction with numerous hands-on learning tools, which "allow everyone an opportunity to see how law is practiced in a variety of fields while taking classroom courses." For example, "the training provided by the Moot Court program provides law students with the practical skills needed to make the transition into effective young attorneys." In addition to moot court, students are eager to point out that "there are other exceptional programs here such as the Adoption Clinic, the Externship Program, and the Pro Bono Certificate program that are rarely discussed." In addition, there is the newly added Small Law and Solo Practice Certificate Program. One area in which the school has improved in recent years is bar passage rate with an 85 percent pass rate for first time test takes in July 2013.

Yet, when it comes to the real world, "being in the state's capital is definitely a huge plus to attending school" at Mississippi College. "As the only law school in the capital city, MC Law students receive a unique opportunity to [receive] practical experience through many clerkships, externships, and internships." Through these practical programs, students make professional connections and have "contact with state and federal bench, bar, and state legislators on a regular basis." Back on campus, "the school strives to keep the classroom technologically updated and recently added a new mock courtroom and several classrooms." These amenities are certainly nice, but they also come at a price. As a private institution, "tuition and books costs are very high" at Mississippi College. The good news is that students feel their investment is respected at MC, where everyone is "incredibly accommodating" and "willing to help you any way they possibly can." From financial aid to registrars, the "administration at MC is extremely friendly," including the school's new dean who is very approachable even scheduling student town meetings and monthly Days with the Dean. Believe it or not, one may even "see the dean weeding the landscaping or picking up trash in the parking lot."

KAREN FLOWERS, DIRECTOR OF ADMISSIONS
151 EAST GRIFFITH STREET, JACKSON, MS 39201
TEL: 601-925-7152 • FAX: 601-925-7166
E-MAIL: KFLOWERS@MC.EDU • WEBSITE: WWW.LAW.MC.EDU

Life

MC Law "provides a comfortable environment conducive to learning," and most students say cooperation trumps competition in the classroom and in the courtroom. At Mississippi College, "everyone is friendly and works together towards the one single goal of graduation and passing the bar...The school is small enough that you know most of the people in your classes, and can recognize everyone in the halls." A student shares, "I think that in any academic setting there will be factions and competition on some level. However, my experience was that most students were cordial, helpful, and conducted themselves as if they were part of one really big team moving toward one common goal—graduation."

Although some would love to see "more campus activities" specifically planned for law students, they say there is a great social atmosphere at Mississippi College. There are parties and other activities organized by the Student Bar Association, as well as student-run clubs and associations. Overall, "the number of student run social events is pretty high, and it does allow for students to branch out and meet others." Nevertheless, one's level of involvement is individualized. "MC Law has a wonderful social base which is just right if you choose to be social, but is not overly pressured." Unfortunately, students note a "lack of quality social events" in surrounding Jackson.

Getting In

Admission to Mississippi College School of Law is attainable, if you have the right balance of grades, LSAT score, and activities. Mississippi College seeks well-rounded applicants, evaluating students based on their academic record and LSAT scores, as well as their professional, military, and leadership experience. The median undergraduate GPA for incoming students is about 3.11. For top applicants, the school offers generous merit-based scholarships, which can help offset the cost of a private education. The admissions office accepts applications on a rolling basis from September 1 to July 15.

EMPLOYMENT INFORMATION		
Career Rating	**82**	
Total 2014 JD Grads	175	**Prominent Alumni**
% for whom you have useable		Robert Hurt, U.S. Congress; Sharion
information	98	Aycock, Federal District Judge; L. Joe Lee,
% grads employed ten months out	71	Chief Judge, MS Court of Appeals; Mike
Median starting salary	$58,008	Parker, Federal Magistrate Judge
% job accepting grads providing		**Grads Employed by Field (%)**
useable salary information	48	Academic (0)
# employed full-time	119	Business/Industry (11)
# employed part-time	7	Government (7)
# employed bar required	96	Judicial Clerkship (9)
# employed JD preferred	20	Federal: (2)
# employed professional/other	5	State or local: (7)
# employed non-professional	5	Private Practice (43)
# pursuing advanced degree	8	Solo: (6)
# unemployed and seeking		2-10: (30)
employment	34	11-25: (2)
# not seeking employment	1	51-100: (2)
State for bar exam	MS, LA, TN, AL	101-250: (2)
Pass rate for first-time bar	76.0	251-500: (1)
		Public Interest (1)

Clinical program required	No
Legal writing	
course requirement	Yes
Legal methods	
course requirement	No
Legal research	
course requirement	Yes
Moot court requirement	Yes
Public interest	
law requirement	No

ADMISSIONS

Selectivity Rating	**71**
# applications received	746
% applicants accepted	79
% acceptees attending	26
Average LSAT	148
Median LSAT	147
LSAT Range (25th to	
75th percentile)	144–153
Average undergrad GPA	3.10
Median undergrad GPA	3.11
Application fee	$0
Regular application deadline	7/15
Early application deadline	11/30
Early application notification	12/19
Transfer students accepted	Yes
Evening division offered	No
Part-time accepted	Yes
CAS accepted	Yes

International Students

TOEFL required of international	
students.	Yes

FINANCIAL FACTS

Annual tuition	$31,100
Books and supplies	$1,200
Fees	$1,520
Room & Board	$12,375
Financial aid application	
deadline	7/1
% first-year students receiving	
some sort of aid	85
% all students receiving	
some sort of aid	83
% of aid that is merit based	100
% receiving scholarships	46
Average grant	$20,400
Average loan	$41,000
Average total aid package	$48,000
Average debt	$102,000

NEW ENGLAND LAW | BOSTON

INSTITUTIONAL INFORMATION

Public/private	Private
Affiliation	No Affiliation
Student-faculty ratio	28:1
% faculty part-time	76
% faculty female	39
% faculty underrepresented minority	9
Total faculty	121

SURVEY SAYS...

Students love Boston, MA, Diverse opinions accepted in classrooms

STUDENTS

Enrollment of law school	852
% male/female	45/55
% from out-of-state	68
% part-time	28
% underrepresented minority	32
% international	2
# of countries represented	8
Average age of entering class	25

ACADEMICS

Academic Experience Rating	**74**
Profs interesting rating	88
Profs accessible rating	86
Hours of study per day	4.06

Academic Specialties
Criminal, Human Rights, International, Taxation, Intellectual Property

Advanced Degrees Offered
JD degree (3–4 yrs); LLM degree (1 year)

Academics

New England Law | Boston provides "a unique and invaluable law school experience" with a "great regional reputation and alumni network." "Since it's small there is a close-knit family feel," although some suggest "the school is cramped" and "can become congested." "The strong sense of community" nurtures "a very supportive upbeat educational experience at every level." "The Boston location gives students a lot of possibilities for employment" although the school could work on "improving its reputation" in the area. New England Law "wants to help you succeed in your law school life and later career," and "goes through great measures to ensure all students have the necessary knowledge and requirements to be successful in the workplace."

By far the most celebrated part of the school is the "exceptional" faculty. These "very approachable" professors "encourage intellectual curiosity and value hard work." "Professors are committed to providing the highest quality academics with the goal of producing top level lawyers," one student explains. "The faculty is always available for consultation and assistance," and New England Law "does not have teaching assistants." "All of the professors have extensive legal background," and many are Harvard graduates. Students really get to know their professors here, as "the comparatively small size of the school means that faculty and students are in constant, casual contact." One 3L says, "I would wager that if our faculty was compared to any other law school in the nation, that our school would win, hands down!"

The students also love the "excellent library and IT staff" that are "always available for research assistance." "The law librarians are indeed wizards & the security staff know everything & everyone," one student explains. While the students love the faculty and staff, "the administration is abysmal" and "the worst part of this entire school." "In my three years at New England I've seen the Dean ONCE," one student says.

Those who attend New England Law are "pretty much guaranteed to pass the bar statistically." Students love the "supportive atmosphere," "strong alumni network, networking opportunities," and how "the small community encourages teamwork, collaboration, and success." "Okay, sure at BC or Harvard you will learn what Thomas Jefferson was thinking when he wrote the Constitution," one student says, "but at New England Law you will learn how to conduct a divorce between a plumber and a nurse."

MICHELLE L'ETOILE, DIRECTOR OF ADMISSIONS
154 STUART STREET, BOSTON, MA 02116
TEL: 617-422-7210 • FAX: 617-422-7201
E-MAIL: ADMIT@NESL.EDU • WEBSITE: WWW.NESL.EDU

Life

"I love my diverse (in both age and background) group of peers," one happy student says. Originally founded as a law school for women, the law school is now co-ed. "The political leaning of the students is roughly 90 percent liberal and 10 percent conservative," although one student was "definitely surprised at the large number of conservatives who attend this school." New England Law "itself is small" and "there is technically only one building with classes." Although "almost totally confined to a single building," the school is "very tech oriented, with WiFi that reaches the food court across the street & plugs at every seat in classrooms and the library." Students do think the "facilities could use an improvement and be modernized." Socially, students "tend to stay within their cliques for day to day studying, talking, and beer drinking." It should be noted that there is "definitely a difference between the full-time day students and the part-time evening students." The evening students "look at law school as an extension of their day job," "seem to form a close bond quickly" and "prefer to stay together and study together than compete and spread rumors." It is easy for students to get off campus and enjoy all that Boston has to offer. "The social life in the middle of downtown Boston/theater district always has something to do," one student says.

Getting In

The Fall 2014 class enrolled 265 students with 58% of them being female. At the 25th percentile, the full-time class had GPA and LSAT scores of 2.85 and 145. The 75th percentile was 3.40 and 152.

Clinical program required	No
Legal writing course requirement	Yes
Legal methods course requirement	Yes
Legal research course requirement	Yes
Moot court requirement	Yes
Public interest law requirement	No

ADMISSIONS

Selectivity Rating	71
# applications received	1,539
% applicants accepted	82
% acceptees attending	16
Median LSAT	149
LSAT Range (25th to 75th percentile)	145–152
Median undergrad GPA	3.13
Application fee	$65
Regular application deadline	3/15
Transfer students accepted	Yes
Evening division offered	Yes
Part-time accepted	Yes
CAS accepted	Yes

International Students

TOEFL required of international students.	Yes

FINANCIAL FACTS

Annual tuition	$43,988
Books and supplies	$1,300
Fees	$80
Room & Board	$18,630
Financial aid application deadline	3/21
% first-year students receiving some sort of aid	96
% all students receiving some sort of aid	95
% of aid that is merit based	98
% receiving scholarships	56
Average grant	$23,775
Average loan	$44,990
Average total aid package	$52,201
Average debt	$132,246

EMPLOYMENT INFORMATION

Career Rating	79
Total 2014 JD Grads	299
% for whom you have useable information	92
% grads employed ten months out	76
Median starting salary	$55,000
# employed full-time	209
# employed part-time	19
# employed bar required	135
# employed JD preferred	61
# employed professional/other	22
# employed non-professional	10
# pursuing advanced degree	10
# unemployed and seeking employment	34
# not seeking employment	1
State for bar exam	MA
Pass rate for first-time bar	79.6

Prominent Alumni
Massachusetts Lt. Gov. Karyn Polito; U.S. Comptroller of the Currency Thomas J. Curry; former Director of the U.S. Secret Service John R. Simpson

Grads Employed by Field (%)
Academic (3)
Business/Industry (22)
Government (10)
Judicial Clerkship (4)
State or local: (4)
Private Practice (31)
 Solo: (4)
 2-10: (18)
 11-25: (3)
 26-50: (3)
 51-100: (1)
 101-250: (1)
 501+: (1)
Public Interest (6)

NEW YORK LAW SCHOOL

INSTITUTIONAL INFORMATION

Public/private	Private
Affiliation	No Affiliation
Student-faculty ratio	13:1
% faculty part-time	48
% faculty female	40
% faculty underrepresented minority	8
Total faculty	139

SURVEY SAYS...

Students love New York, NY, Diverse opinions accepted in classrooms, Great research resources, Abundant externship/internship/clerkship opportunities, Good social life

STUDENTS

Enrollment of law school	968
% male/female	48/52
% from out-of-state	24
% part-time	32
% underrepresented minority	28
% international	1
# of countries represented	6
Average age of entering class	25

ACADEMICS

Academic Experience Rating	81
Profs interesting rating	87
Profs accessible rating	84
Hours of study per day	4.07

Academic Specialties

Civil Procedure, Commercial, Constitutional, Corporation Securities, Criminal, Environmental, Government Services, Human Rights, International, Labor, Property, Taxation, Intellectual Property, Trusts and Estates

Advanced Degrees Offered

JD 3 yrs FT, 4 yrs PT, Accelerated Honors Program 2 yrs. LLM program in Taxation, 1–2 yrs.

Combined Degrees Offered

JD/MBA with Baruch College 4 yrs FT or 6 yrs PT. JD/MA in Forensic Psychology with John Jay College of Criminal Justice, CUNY, 4–5 yrs. JD/LLM in Taxation, 4–5 yrs.

Academics

New York Law School "emphasizes practical legal skills" and a "customized" education to develop students with specialized skills who know "what is to be expected in the real legal world." A private school in lower Manhattan, NYLS is well-situated to connect students with job opportunities throughout the city. Outside the core curriculum, students enjoy small, intimate classes "with fewer than twenty-five students, [and] some as small as twelve." Students praise the faculty as "incredible . . . industry-leading professionals," who take care in explaining the "theory or the policy rationale for the legal rules we learn about." But students are also given plenty of opportunities for practical experience: "By my first year, I drafted full legal documents, contracts, negotiation plans, [and] interview plans . . . I used all of these techniques and papers to help me when it came time to practicing in a firm, and it was incredibly helpful." Additionally, "the school's clinical offerings and the various legal writing and other skills classes" focus on developing the practical skills that effective attorneys need.

Students take a predominantly practical approach when evaluating the administration. They universally praise Dean Oral Hope, Registrar, who "is possibly the most helpful person I've ever met," assisting with everything from scheduling to AV issues. Yet, students admit "there is always room for improvement." The administration is sometimes criticized as "defensive," but students say it is "more open to criticism when the student has a reasoned, intelligible, and evidence-supported argument." Students also appreciate the administration's efforts "to guide and aid students in their writing abilities [and] job applications," as well as the "wide range of programs and info sessions" the administration organizes, which help students develop a "better understanding of which career path" they should pursue.

When it comes to the job search, NYLS students are self-starters who contend, "You get what you put into it, the more work you do to find a job, the more likely success is in finding one." While they admit that "there may be areas in which career resources could improve," they put a large portion of the onus on students to take advantage of the many opportunities career services and the NYC area provide. "Recruitment has gotten better," one student tells us, and "grades are important, but there are opportunities for everyone," even those who are not in the top of their class. "The recruitment efforts are wonderful," another student argues. "Half of my family went to New York Law School, and they all have great jobs." Students are also quick to point out that the school does offer "many job fairs and career opportunities" which afford "students every opportunity that they are willing to accept." Additionally, students have access to "a broad range of clinics, externships, and experiential learning courses, which provide students with the hands-on, practical training that is becoming increasingly required by employers."

ADAM BARRETT, ASSOCIATE DEAN FOR ADMISSIONS AND FINANCIAL AID
NEW YORK LAW SCHOOL, 185 WEST BROADWAY, NEW YORK, NY 10013
TEL: 212-431-2888 • FAX: 212-966-1522
E-MAIL: ADMISSIONS@NYLS.EDU • WEBSITE: WWW.NYLS.EDU

Life

NYLS students value self-advocacy and shun "entitlement," but that doesn't mean groups of students aren't willing to "share notes" and support one another. "Overall," one student said, "I was surprised with the warmth and 'family atmosphere' at NYLS. While law school is always going to be competitive, I have not experienced any of the negative aspects of that competitive environment at NYLS." Knowing that "students who came straight to law school from undergrad are more invested in the social scene" than others who may have "jobs, kids, friends from their pre-law-school lives who also live in the area," most agree that there is general camaraderie among the student population.

Students also benefit from the diversity of New York City that "is inherently built in" to the school. And while some complain of exclusive study groups, others say they "have made some really wonderful friends," and particularly that "upper level students are always more than willing to share advice and insight." And sometimes that advice is given over "a drink at Tribeca Tavern with some fellow students after class" or during "an event at Brooklyn Bowl" organized by the dean. "You can read about Torts anywhere," one student tells us, "but the students, professors, and administration are what make NYLS the wonderful place it is—I wouldn't want to be anywhere else."

Getting In

Admitted students in the 25th percentile had LSAT scores that range from 148 and GPAs of 2.8, while those in the 75 percentile had LSAT scores of 154 and GPAs of 3.48. New York Law School offers a full-time day program and a part-time evening program. NYLS also offers a two-year honors program.

EMPLOYMENT INFORMATION		
Career Rating	81	**Prominent Alumni**
Total 2014 JD Grads	415	Charles E. Phillips, Jr. '93, CEO of Infor,
% for whom you have useable		former President of Oracle.
information	99	**Grads Employed by Field (%)**
% grads employed ten months out	85	Academic (1)
Median starting salary	$70,000	Business/Industry (34)
# employed full-time	320	Government (9)
# employed part-time	33	Judicial Clerkship (4)
# employed bar required	199	Federal: (1)
# employed JD preferred	104	State or local: (3)
# employed professional/other	36	Private Practice (33)
# employed non-professional	14	2-10: (19)
# pursuing advanced degree	3	11-25: (3)
# unemployed and seeking		26-50: (2)
employment	41	51-100: (2)
# not seeking employment	8	101-250: (1)
% grads employed by school	1	251-500: (1)
State for bar exam	NY	501+: (4)
Pass rate for first-time bar	71.2	Size Unknown: (1)
		Public Interest (4)

Accelerated BA/JD with Stevens Institute of Technology, 6 yrs.

Clinical program required	No
Legal writing	
course requirement	Yes
Legal methods	
course requirement	Yes
Legal research	
course requirement	Yes
Moot court requirement	Yes
Public interest	
law requirement	No

ADMISSIONS

Selectivity Rating	**77**
# applications received	2,273
% applicants accepted	58
% acceptees attending	13
Median LSAT	151
LSAT Range (25th to	
75th percentile)	148–154
Median undergrad GPA	3.22
Application fee	$0
Regular application deadline	7/1
Early application deadline	4/1
Transfer students accepted	Yes
Evening division offered	Yes
Part-time accepted	Yes
CAS accepted	Yes

International Students

TOEFL required of international	
students.	Yes

FINANCIAL FACTS

Annual tuition	$47,600
Books and supplies	$1,300
Fees	$1,640
Room & Board	$17,550
Financial aid application	
deadline	7/1
% first-year students receiving	
some sort of aid	98
% all students receiving	
some sort of aid	89
% of aid that is merit based	19
% receiving scholarships	59
Average grant	$19,891
Average loan	$51,214
Average total aid package	$54,589
Average debt	$163,650

NEW YORK UNIVERSITY
SCHOOL OF LAW

INSTITUTIONAL INFORMATION

Public/private	Private
% faculty part-time	32
% faculty female	31
% faculty underrepresented minority	12
Total faculty	248

SURVEY SAYS...
Students love New York, NY, Great research resources, Abundant externship/internship/clerkship opportunities, Law school well run, Liberal students, Good social life

STUDENTS

Enrollment of law school	1,423
% male/female	54/46
% part-time	0
% underrepresented minority	29
% international	6
Average age of entering class	24

ACADEMICS

Academic Experience Rating	98
Profs interesting rating	96
Profs accessible rating	84
Hours of study per day	3.45

Academic Specialties
Civil Procedure, Commercial, Constitutional, Corporation Securities, Criminal, Environmental, Government Services, Human Rights, International, Labor, Legal History, Legal Philosophy, Property, Taxation, Intellectual Property

Advanced Degrees Offered
LLM, JSD, MSL

Combined Degrees Offered
JD/LLM, JD/MBA, JD/MPA, JD/MPP, JD/MUP, JD/MSW, JD/MA, JD/PhD, JD/JD (Melbourne), JD/LLB (NUS)

Academics

New York University School of Law is a "highly ranked" program with "a seemingly bottomless well of resources with which students can explore their academic/career interests." NYU's "academic experience cannot be beat," and the school "provides the best access to practicing lawyers, both in litigation and transactional practices." One of NYU's biggest selling points is its Manhattan location, which is "hands down the best location in the country (or the world) for a law school." They are myriad "opportunities in New York to do pro bono or clinical work" and studying here puts you "right next to many of the most important employers like big law firms." The location also helps the school bring "great guest speakers" on a regular basis. In general, "everything is here and everyone wants to be here; that's why we have the best faculty [and] the most opportunities." The NYU name carries a lot of weight, and even students with only "average grades and decent interviewing ability you can easily get a job at a top firm, especially one in New York." "If you can't get into Harvard, Yale, or Stanford, NYU probably provides the best experience of the Columbia, Chicago, NYU tier," one student explains.

The school has a public interest program that is "the best in the country," but also "NYU has many of the world's foremost international law authorities on its faculty." The "quality of the professors" is astounding at NYU. These "top-notch professors" "are very accessible but also very demanding." "They teach a lot of difficult material in an understandable manner," while remaining "helpful and accessible." Many on the faculty are "famous," and all are "smart and approachable." "The quality of the upper level classes, particularly in intellectual property and constitutional law, have been rigorous and inventive—no easy combination!" The adjunct professors are typically "practicing lawyers, which gives those classes a focus on the practical side of the material." "There is a wide range of interesting philosophical topics and courses available" at NYU, although "the grading curve is tough." "Generally, I have the sense that the administration truly cares about students," one student says. "You can tell they're working hard to make this a very pleasant experience, and students appreciate that," confirms another. Students do often "wish the lines of communication were a little better" between the administration and students.

If there is a downside to NYU, it is "the overwhelming expense." Students really hope the school can "find a way to reduce cost." In addition to the high cost of the school, the area the school is located in is "incredibly expensive." "Living in one of the surrounding boroughs and commuting to Manhattan makes the cost of living much more reasonable," one student points out. The "facilities are excellent" and "the resources are great." Perhaps the most raved about aspect of NYU is the "incredible" career services office. They "can get anyone a job" and "give tons of information about employers and hiring statistics, and are willing to meet with students all the time." "Career center is amazing!!!" is a common exclamation.

OFFICE OF ADMISSIONS
139 MacDougal Street, Suite C-20 New York, NY 10012
Tel: 212-998-6060 • Fax: 212-995-4527
E-Mail: LAW.MOREINFO@NYU.EDU • Website: WWW.LAW.NYU.EDU

Life

"NYU has done a fantastic job assembling a diverse class of strong, motivated individuals with great attitudes" who combine into a student body that is "friendly" and "not competitive." "Before coming to NYU, I was worried that my classmates would be competitive and unfriendly," a 1L says. "The complete opposite is true." "Everyone here knows that because we are all at NYU, we are going to get top notch jobs, and so there is no reason to be so cutthroat," one student explains. Students at NYU "tend to be slightly more laid back and normal" than students at other law schools, "making it a pleasant place to spend a lot of time for three years." On campus, "there is free yoga almost every day, and lots of ways to unwind." The school provides plenty of entertainment and intellectual engagement. One student says "there's so much to do at the school itself with the speakers and student groups—one can't be bored." The school is located in the West Village, which is "one of the more pretentious areas of NYC" and "kind of a big hipster frat party more often than not." Luckily, "NYU is accessible to trains on both the West and East sides" so it is easy to live off campus or access the rest of New York City.

Getting In

NYU Law is one of the most competitive programs in the country, so students will need to bring their A-game to applications. Recent students have had LSAT scores between 167 and 172 at the 25th and 75th percentiles, and GPA scores between 3.56 and 3.87 at the 25th and 75th percentiles.

Clinical program required	No
Legal writing course requirement	Yes
Legal methods course requirement	Yes
Legal research course requirement	Yes
Moot court requirement	No
Public interest law requirement	No

ADMISSIONS

Selectivity Rating	97
# applications received	6,193
% applicants accepted	30
% acceptees attending	24
Median LSAT	170
LSAT Range (25th to 75th percentile)	167–172
Median undergrad GPA	3.75
Application fee	$85
Regular application deadline	2/15
Regular notification	4/30
Early application deadline	11/15
Early application notification	12/31
Transfer students accepted	Yes
Evening division offered	No
Part-time accepted	No
CAS accepted	Yes

FINANCIAL FACTS

Annual tuition	$55,330
Books and supplies	$1,500
Fees	$1,508
Room & Board	$23,064
Financial aid application deadline	4/15
Average grant	$26,100
Average debt	$147,744

EMPLOYMENT INFORMATION

Career Rating	**99**	**Grads Employed by Field (%)**
Total 2014 JD Grads	479	Academic (1)
% grads employed ten months out	97	Business/Industry (4)
Median starting salary	$160,000	Government (5)
# employed non-professional	0	Judicial Clerkship (9)
% grads employed by school	8	Private Practice (67)
State for bar exam	NY	Public Interest (11)
Pass rate for first-time bar	96.2	

NORTH CAROLINA CENTRAL UNIVERSITY
SCHOOL OF LAW

INSTITUTIONAL INFORMATION

Public/private	Public
Affiliation	No Affiliation
Student-faculty ratio	14:1
% faculty part-time	32
% faculty female	62
% faculty underrepresented minority	66
Total faculty	76

SURVEY SAYS...
Diverse opinions accepted in classrooms

STUDENTS

Enrollment of law school	595
% male/female	38/62
% from out-of-state	25
% part-time	17
% underrepresented minority	69
% international	0
# of countries represented	0
Average age of entering class	26

ACADEMICS

Academic Experience Rating	**69**
Profs interesting rating	67
Profs accessible rating	69
Hours of study per day	NR

Academic Specialties
Constitutional, Taxation, Intellectual Property

Advanced Degrees Offered
JD Day Program 6 semesters (3 yrs); JD Evening Program 8 semester and 5 summer sessions (4 yrs)

Combined Degrees Offered
JD/MBA 4 yrs, JD/MLS 4 yrs, JD/MPA 4 yrs, JD/MPP (with Duke University) 4 yrs

Academics

"I rave about my law school," gloats a 3L at the North Carolina Central University School of Law. By all accounts, NCCU is a "great value." It's unquestionably possible to graduate from here with little or no debt. The renovated law school building feels "very new" and it's "always well-kept." The facilities are "state-of-the-art" and "extremely high-tech." "Practical training is strongly encouraged" and readily available. "NCCU has substantial opportunities for practical legal experience outside the classroom," explains a 1L. "Excellent" clinics, pro bono opportunities, externship programs, and hands-on skills courses provide real world experience galore. "The variety of clinics" (eighteen in all) includes criminal litigation, juvenile law, and a small business clinic—just to name a few. There's also a standard JD/MBA program, a JD/MLS program (for future law librarians), and a unique Biotechnology and Pharmaceutical Law Institute, where you can engross yourself in the labyrinth of prescription drug regulation. It's also worth noting that students here have easy access to the state and federal courts in the nearby state capital, Raleigh.

Inside the classroom, the "passionate, knowledgeable," and "very dedicated" faculty brings plenty of "real-world" know-how. For the most part, professors are also "very clear in explaining concepts." "The teachers are really encouraging, and they want to see each student succeed." "Motivation, guidance, and encouragement" are ample. "Faculty accessibility" is another huge plus. "They are tough but there for you in many ways." Faculty members are "very responsive" and "always available and willing to help" if you stay after class or stop by their offices.

Some students call NCCU "the total package" and wouldn't change a thing. Others, however, see areas that could be better. While some students tell us that management is "organized" and "always helpful," for example, others disagree. Also, despite the fact that a loyal alumni base works "to ensure that you have an opportunity to practice" and a recently reorganized Career Services Office has helped students with job placement, "other support services" could still use "an overhaul." A broader selection of electives would be another improvement. "We could offer a wider variety of classes in more concentrated areas," suggests a 3L.

Life

NCCU began in 1939 as North Carolina's only law school for African Americans. Today, it's quite a diverse bastion of legal education, ethnically and otherwise. "Students come from all over the country and all over the world." Ages run the gamut from students straight out of undergrad to those in their fifties who are training for a second (or third) career. "Different perspectives on life and law" are abundant. "Many schools claim to be diverse and accepting of diversity," observes one 3L. "Yet my school proves it every day. We are a family. It includes the good, the bad, and ugly."

LAURA BROOKS, ASSOCIATE DEAN FOR STUDENT SERVICES
640 NELSON STREET, DURHAM, NC 27707
TEL: 919-530-6607 • FAX: 919-530-6030
E-MAIL: SBWILLIAMS@NCCU.EDU • WEBSITE: RECRUITER@NCCU.EDU

NCCU's relatively small size lends an intimacy that you just won't find at larger schools. First-year sections are particularly cozy, and the atmosphere for all students is "very friendly." "We are a strong, supportive community," explains a 3L. "We help each other out and truly want each other to succeed." "Upperclassmen are mentors for new law students," and they offer advice "on a daily basis and on a variety of subjects and experiences." Nevertheless, and all of this social comfort notwithstanding, students are often competing for just a few precious A's. "The curve of our grading system can be devastating to a GPA," cautions a 2L, "but it does force students to work their hardest to achieve good grades."

Students here are very satisfied with their lives outside of law school. "The campus has some problems with crime," but students stress that safety isn't much of an issue at all. Durham is a growing and revitalizing city that offers a low cost of living, some forty annual festivals, and unbeatable medical facilities. With about 15,000 students in town (at NCCU and at nearby Duke University), there are certainly plenty of lively social options. If you prefer laid-back ones, you can find those, too. An array of outdoorsy activities is available in every direction as well.

Getting In

Though the acceptance rate at NCCU is low, you don't necessarily need outstanding grades and test scores to get admitted. Admitted students at the 25th percentile have LSAT scores of 141 or so and their undergraduate GPA is right around 3.0. Admitted students at the 75th percentile typically have LSAT scores around 148 and GPAs in B+ to A– territory.

Clinical program required	No
Legal writing course requirement	Yes
Legal methods course requirement	Yes
Legal research course requirement	Yes
Moot court requirement	No
Public interest law requirement	No

ADMISSIONS

Selectivity Rating	75
# applications received	807
% applicants accepted	55
% acceptees attending	41
Median LSAT	144
LSAT Range (25th to 75th percentile)	141–148
Median undergrad GPA	3.23
Application fee	$50
Regular application deadline	3/31
Transfer students accepted	Yes
Evening division offered	Yes
Part-time accepted	Yes
CAS accepted	Yes

International Students

TOEFL required of international students.   Yes

FINANCIAL FACTS

Annual tuition (in-state/ out-of-state)	$8,998/$24,039
Books and supplies	$2,200
Fees	$3,621
Room & Board (on/ off campus)	$11,310/$15,680
Financial aid application deadline	6/1
% first-year students receiving some sort of aid	98
% all students receiving some sort of aid	98
% of aid that is merit based	21
% receiving scholarships	40
Average grant	$4,485
Average loan	$32,570
Average total aid package	$32,570
Average debt	$55,852

EMPLOYMENT INFORMATION

Career Rating	71
Total 2014 JD Grads	142
% for whom you have useable information	88
% grads employed ten months out	71
Median starting salary	$42,500
% job accepting grads providing useable salary information	35
# employed full-time	92
# employed part-time	9
# employed bar required	68
# employed JD preferred	14
# employed professional/other	16
# employed non-professional	3
# pursuing advanced degree	4
# unemployed and seeking employment	20
% grads employed by school	1
State for bar exam	NC, MD, GA, NJ, VA
Pass rate for first-time bar	72.4

Prominent Alumni

The Honorable Wanda Bryant, N.C. Court of Appeals; The Honorable G. K. Butterfield, U.S. House of Rep.; The Honorable Rick Elmore, N.C. Court of Appeals

Grads Employed by Field (%)

Academic (2)
Business/Industry (18)
Government (12)
Judicial Clerkship (1)
Federal: (1)
Private Practice (31)
Solo: (5)
2-10: (18)
11-25: (1)
26-50: (1)
51-100: (1)
251-500: (1)
501+: (1)
Size Unknown: (4)
Public Interest (4)

NORTHEASTERN UNIVERSITY
SCHOOL OF LAW

INSTITUTIONAL INFORMATION

Public/private	Private
Affiliation	No Affiliation
Student-faculty ratio	13:1
% faculty part-time	39
% faculty female	47
% faculty underrepresented minority	14
Total faculty	72

SURVEY SAYS...

Students love Boston, MA, Abundant externship/internship/clerkship opportunities, Liberal students

STUDENTS

Enrollment of law school	473
% male/female	38/62
% from out-of-state	59
% part-time	1
% underrepresented minority	31
% international	2
# of countries represented	6
Average age of entering class	25

ACADEMICS

Academic Experience Rating	89
Profs interesting rating	81
Profs accessible rating	81
Hours of study per day	4.23

Academic Specialties

Civil Procedure, Commercial, Constitutional, Corporation Securities, Criminal, Environmental, Government Services, Health Law and Policy, Human Rights, International, Labor, Legal History, Legal Philosophy, Property, Taxation, Intellectual Property

Advanced Degrees Offered

LLM Program: 2-Year Dual Degree; LLM+MBA 2-Year Dual Degree; LLM+MA Sustainable Economic Development

Combined Degrees Offered

JD/MA in Sustainable International Development; JD/MELP; Environmental Law and Policy; JD/MPH with Tufts University School of

Academics

In nearly every aspect of the legal education, Northeastern University School of Law sets itself apart as a school that focuses on practical, cooperative education and largely attracts students and faculty who "are committed to public interest and to a legal education that molds intelligent, hardworking and compassionate lawyers." While the school is based in Boston, NUSL's signature co-operative education program allows second- and third-year students to pursue internships and externships "across the world." While 1Ls follow a traditional curriculum, the second two years of education follow a quarter system where students spend alternating quarters on experiential learning assignments. While this can make planning a bit of a struggle, students say that the school does a good job "making sure that every student gets four internship experiences they are excited about." "The co-op program does make your 2nd and 3rd years go by very quickly," but the quarter system "[keeps] it interesting; the co-op opportunities let you practice before your peers" at other institutions might be able to.

While the school maintains a "deserved reputation as a place for people who want to do public interest work to study," "many more corporate, conservative types are in attendance, and programs catering to these interests are being added rapidly." There is also "a good amount of public interest work, clinics and, with the requirement of four internships to graduate, opportunities for practical experience." Students appreciate that "the school has grown with a much more well-rounded curriculum." While many students will follow public interest careers, "getting a big law job isn't hard if you go for it."

Students rave about the co-op program, which they say "truly allows for [each] student to have exposure to the legal practice immediately following the first year [of] classes." One graduating senior boasts, "I [will leave] law school with four diverse practice areas on my résumé, and a lot of practice legal experience to boot." They are a bit colder about "the co-op and professional advising offices," where some find it "difficult to get . . . necessary help." However, other service components of the college seem to be performing well. Despite the library "downsizing a ton," "the law library staff is amazing, able to help with research issues even while you're away on co-op, and the building itself is currently getting a much needed facelift." Many students think that these issues are temporary and say that "the administration has recently made great hires and is on the rise."

NUSL faculty are "famous scholars, judges, and professionals" beloved by students for their openness, accessibility, and practical approaches. "My 1L professors were exceptional at bringing simulations, writing exercises, and a practical focus into the doctrinal subjects," one student explains. "The focus is on learning by doing rather than just listening to lectures." While the faculty generally "lean to the left, it is possible to be a conservative and do quite well at northeastern. Professors are open to many opinions and often look to conservative students for a different viewpoint." They "care about each student's performance in their class," but also help student with "the trajectory of our legal careers based on our interests as well."

NUSL has done away with grades and class ranking. Instead, students receive detailed feedback from their professors and receive honorifics for exemplary work. Students love that the evaluation system provides "meaningful feedback from professors rather than a simple letter grade," and argue that the system cultivates an "environment that is cooperative and supportive instead of competitive and stressful," creating a "community of learners." "Students are focused more on truly learning rather than grades," one student notes.

CARRIE TAUBMAN, ASSISTANT DEAN OF ADMISSIONS
416 HUNTINGTON AVENUE, BOSTON, MA 02115
TEL: 617-373-2395
E-MAIL: LAWADMISSIONS@NEU.EDU • WEBSITE: WWW.NORTHEASTERN.EDU / LAW

Life

The cooperative attitude extends to other parts of campus life as well. "Students here collaborate all of the time, in legal atmospheres and social atmospheres," one student explains. Biweekly "bar events are called 'Bar Reviews'" are well attended "and quite fun." While many students said they "couldn't stress enough how liberal the school is," many pushed back. Some chalk up the perception of an overwhelmingly liberal school to "the most vocal elements of the student body" overshadowing "a sizeable plurality of students who disagree but feel uncomfortable speaking up about it." Either way, "As someone who falls slightly on the right side politically," one student explained, "I've had no problems here and [have] made friends who are much more conservative in differing ways. You do have to watch what you say or you may feel slightly attacked, but as future lawyers we should be ready for confrontation and learn how to handle it productively . . . [and] my very liberal friends remain open minded and interested in debates."

Getting In

For the enrolled students of the Class of 2017, the median LSAT score was 161, and the median GPA was 3.53 as of August 25, 2014. Early action applicants, available to students who take the LSAT by December, who are admitted are not required to attend, as the program is non-binding.

Medicine; JD/MPH in Urban Health; JD/MBA; JD/MBA/MS in Professional Accounting; JD/MS in Law and Public Policy; JD/MS in Music Industry Leadership

Clinical program required	No
Legal writing course requirement	Yes
Legal methods course requirement	Yes
Legal research course requirement	Yes
Moot court requirement	No
Public interest law requirement	Yes

ADMISSIONS

Selectivity Rating	89
# applications received	2,936
% applicants accepted	38
% acceptees attending	11
Median LSAT	161
LSAT Range (25th to 75th percentile)	153–162
Median undergrad GPA	3.53
Application fee	$75
Regular application deadline	3/1
Regular notification	4/15
Early application deadline	11/15
Early application notification	1/15
Transfer students accepted	Yes
Evening division offered	No
Part-time accepted	No
CAS accepted	Yes

International Students

TOEFL recommended of international students.	Yes

FINANCIAL FACTS

Annual tuition	$45,000
Books and supplies	$2,499
Fees	$118
Room & Board	$17,100
Financial aid application deadline	2/15
% first-year students receiving some sort of aid	87
% all students receiving some sort of aid	86
% of aid that is merit based	75
% receiving scholarships	86
Average grant	$18,220
Average loan	$37,811
Average total aid package	$50,031
Average debt	$134,918

EMPLOYMENT INFORMATION

Career Rating	91
Total 2014 JD Grads	216
% for whom you have useable information	95
% grads employed ten months out	79
Median starting salary	$70,000
% job accepting grads providing useable salary information	4
# employed full-time	151
# employed part-time	20
# employed bar required	140
# employed JD preferred	21
# employed professional/other	6
# employed non-professional	4
# pursuing advanced degree	3
# unemployed and seeking employment	23
# not seeking employment	5
% grads employed by school	4
State for bar exam	MA
Pass rate for first-time bar	80.9

Prominent Alumni
Mary Bonauto, Civil Rights Project Director, Gay & Lesbian Advocates & Defenders; Joel Goldberg, General Counsel, PerkinElmer; William "Mo" Cowan, US Senator; Margaret Hassan, Governor, NH

Grads Employed by Field (%)
Academic (4)
Business/Industry (13)
Government (11)
Judicial Clerkship (4)
State or local: (4)
Private Practice (30)
Solo: (3)
2-10: (12)
11-25: (4)
26-50: (2)
51-100: (1)
101-250: (1)
501+: (7)
Size Unknown: (1)
Public Interest (16)

NORTHERN ILLINOIS UNIVERSITY
COLLEGE OF LAW

INSTITUTIONAL INFORMATION

Public/private	Public
Student-faculty ratio	7:1
% faculty part-time	34
% faculty female	48
% faculty underrepresented minority	25
Total faculty	44

SURVEY SAYS...

Diverse opinions accepted in classrooms

STUDENTS

Enrollment of law school	277
% male/female	53/47
% from out-of-state	18
% part-time	1
% underrepresented minority	26
% international	0
# of countries represented	0
Average age of entering class	26

ACADEMICS

Academic Experience Rating	**72**
Profs interesting rating	67
Profs accessible rating	69
Hours of study per day	NR

Academic Specialities

Certificate in Civil Advocacy, Criminal Practice, Business Law, International Law, or Public Interest Law

Combined Degrees Offered

JD/MPA; JD/MPA.

Academics

As the only public school found within the environs of the greater Chicago area, NIUers are released into Illinois' sea of graduating law students equipped with a solid education at a fraction of the price. Known for its commitment to fostering a sense of community and responsibility and pointing its students in the direction of public service jobs, NIU places a high value on pro bono work and makes a number of "public interest stipends" available to its students each summer. The school "has placed a special emphasis on diversity, both amongst its faculty and its student body," and it shows in the number of "divergent viewpoints" that are represented both in and out of the classroom.

Professors are themselves one source of these divergent viewpoints, with many students claiming that "some of the professors are amazing while others clearly enjoy the benefits of tenure." While the vast majority of professors "are well above average" and "do a very good job," offering students a high level of approachability, many students claim to have had a few instructors who were below par. "Simply reciting material straight from the textbook is not teaching," observes a first-year student. For the most part, however, students are happy with the quality of teaching at NIU and say that the school is very good at balancing theory with practice. "A number of the professors go out of their way to expand on topics illustrated in the text and to relate their real-world experiences to the matters at hand. The professors as a group make themselves accessible to students who have issues that need to be discussed," affirms a student. "The faculty and administration practically begs students to come in and talk to them." Other students would like to see a broader spectrum of courses offered.

Although some students have grumbled about "1970s decor," the school recently repainted and refurnished several on-campus buildings, including the law library and the student lounge. One of the greatest resources offered to NIU students, many of whom are older, is the Career Opportunities Office, which "will definitively help you get started toward your career," especially if you're at the top of your class and looking to get into "big law." Though some students speak of the disadvantages facing NIU grads—particularly the distance of the school from Chicago proper—others are reassured by the Career Opportunities Office's strong networking prospects, which complement the school's well-established and reputable clinic and externship programs. "We have a lock on many state attorney and public defenders offices now, and an incredible number of alumni in the judiciary. If you want to be a government trial lawyer in Illinois, this is definitely the school to go to." As an exiting student avers, "The price was right, and if you are willing to do the work you can get a good education."

SARAH E. SCARPELLI, DIRECTOR OF ADMISSIONS & FINANCIAL AID
SWEN PARSON HALL, COLLEGE OF LAW, ROOM 151, DEKALB, IL 60115
TEL: 815-753-8595 • FAX: 815-753-5680
E-MAIL: LAWADM@NIU.EDU • WEBSITE: NIU.EDU / LAW

Life

With a strong contingent of older, "second-career" individuals, "a high bar for maturity and professionalism within the student body" tends to be set on campus. Students are friendly enough, but hometown DeKalb can be a "pretty desolate place to kids accustomed to the party life of Champaign—Urbana, Bloomington—Normal, or other major college towns." DeKalb is "without much of the nightlife and amenities that students were accustomed to having from their undergrad experience." There are two fraternities on campus (one is "clearly the party frat, and the other is the academic frat"), and there are a number of student groups that students can join, though "a few struggle to survive" due to lack of participation. As for competition among students, a second-year student assures us, "The shark-eat-shark mentality of other law schools would not be tolerated here." "For one thing, the student body is too small, and we all know each other too well. For another, there's just more a sense of being practical and real-world here; we're 'type-A' people, surely, but we've also mellowed with more life experience than your average law student straight out of undergrad."

Getting In

Northern Illinois encourages students to submit their application early, though they do accept applications after the suggested priority deadline of April 1. Recently admitted students at the 25th percentile had an LSAT score of 146 and an median GPA of 3.09, while students at the 75th percentile had an LSAT score of 153 and a GPA of about 3.37.

Clinical program required	Yes
Legal writing course requirement	Yes
Legal methods course requirement	No
Legal research course requirement	Yes
Moot court requirement	Yes
Public interest law requirement	No

ADMISSIONS

Selectivity Rating	81
# applications received	561
% applicants accepted	71
% acceptees attending	21
Average LSAT	150
Median LSAT	150
LSAT Range (25th to 75th percentile)	146–153
Average undergrad GPA	3.11
Median undergrad GPA	3.09
Application fee	$0
Early application deadline	4/1
Transfer students accepted	Yes
Evening division offered	No
Part-time accepted	Yes
CAS accepted	Yes

International Students

TOEFL required of international students.	Yes

FINANCIAL FACTS

Annual tuition (in-state/ out-of-state)	$15,936/$31,872
Books and supplies	$1,600
Fees	$5,828
Room & Board	$13,050
% first-year students receiving some sort of aid	95
% all students receiving some sort of aid	98
% of aid that is merit based	82
% receiving scholarships	60
Average grant	$7,968
Average loan	$27,633
Average total aid package	$32,776
Average debt	$77,182

EMPLOYMENT INFORMATION

Career Rating	75	
Total 2014 JD Grads	99	
% grads employed ten months out	88	
Median starting salary	$55,529	
# employed full-time	79	
# employed part-time	8	
# employed bar required	64	
# employed JD preferred	19	
# employed professional/other	4	
# employed non-professional	0	
# pursuing advanced degree	2	
# unemployed and seeking employment	7	
# not seeking employment	1	
State for bar exam	IL, IN, WI	
Pass rate for first-time bar	82.9	

Prominent Alumni
Kathleen Zellner; Cheryl Niro; Dr. Kenneth Chessick; Honorable Patricia Martin-Bishop

Grads Employed by Field (%)
Academic (4)
Business/Industry (15)
Government (23)
Judicial Clerkship (0
Private Practice (56)
Public Interest (2)

NORTHWESTERN UNIVERSITY
SCHOOL OF LAW

INSTITUTIONAL INFORMATION

Public/private	Private
% faculty part-time	34
% faculty female	38
% faculty underrepresented minority	9
Total faculty	180

SURVEY SAYS...

Students love Chicago, IL, Diverse opinions accepted in classrooms, Great research resources, Abundant externship/internship/clerkship opportunities, Law school well run, Good social life

STUDENTS

Enrollment of law school	737
% male/female	53/47
% part-time	0
% underrepresented minority	33
% international	7
Average age of entering class	25

ACADEMICS

Academic Experience Rating	**72**
Profs interesting rating	67
Profs accessible rating	69
Hours of study per day	NR

Academic Specialties
Environmental, Human Rights, International, Taxation

Advanced Degrees Offered
JD 3 yrs; LLM 1 yr; SJD 5 yrs; LLM in Taxation 1 yr; LLM in Human Rights 1 yr; JD for international lawyers 2 yrs; Accelerated JD 2 yrs; MSL 1 yr

Combined Degrees Offered
JD/MBA 3 yrs; JD/PhD 6 yrs; JD/LLM International Human Rights 4 yrs; JD/LLM Tax 4 yrs; LLM/certificate in management (Kellogg) 1 yr

Academics

Located "in the heart of Chicago," Northwestern University School of Law has a first-rate "national reputation" for "developing practical skills" and offering "world-class" clinics that give students "unbelievable" opportunities to work on "real cases." Many here agree, "It's hard to imagine getting a better mix of academic rigor and practical job training anywhere else." Other highlights at NU include study abroad programs all over the world, a highly touted JD/MBA program, and lots of "self-scheduled exams." One demerit is the "legal writing program" that students wish was "a pass/fail class" due to the "incredible amount of work" it requires.

Northwestern's "brilliant" and "very friendly" faculty is made up of "nationally and internationally renowned scholars" who have "a great sense of humor." Students have "an unparalleled opportunity to learn from the best, starting right at the beginning." "My classes and instruction have ranged from very good to simply outstanding," relates a 2L. "I'd go so far as to say that my Constitutional Law class was one of the most intellectually stimulating courses I've encountered." Professors are "accessible" and "seem to really enjoy talking to students outside of class." "It is not uncommon for them to stop me in the hallway and chat about a class topic, my journal comment, or even college football," explains a student. For the most part the administration is "receptive to student concerns" and "always approachable." "Everything goes pretty smoothly," and the atmosphere is "not very bureaucratic," though some note that "change is very slow to come" in regards to "accommodation for disabilities."

Students happily report, "If you do even moderately well in your 1L classes at Northwestern, you're going to have legal employers knocking down your door." "You'd be hard-pressed to find someone coming out of NU to a less-than-excellent job." "Most of us start out at big firms," adds a 1L. "The Chicago firms just love NU students." However, some students complain, "There should be a greater emphasis on public interest career choices," as "not everybody wants to go to a big law firm upon graduation."

The architecture here is "nice, consisting of both old, more traditional buildings, and a newer building." "A quiet atmosphere prevails" and the "gorgeous" library overlooks Lake Michigan. Also, trust us: Lincoln Hall is exactly what a law school classroom should look like. While "good," the classrooms could use some "updating," and "There aren't enough areas to study." Also, "lighting conditions" in the library are "bad," and though "wireless Internet continues to improve," it can still be "insufficient and annoying."

Life

"Northwestern places a huge emphasis on admitting students who have a couple years of work experience after undergrad, and it makes a huge difference," says one student. These future lawyers "come from a variety of backgrounds and offer amazing insights into a range of issues." They "are grounded and have balanced lives." "People have a better sense of the world around them and the realities of life beyond a classroom," observes a 2L. "This keeps the drama to a minimum and also assembles a group of people who've done some pretty interesting things—minor league ball, the military, symphonic bassoon, and so on." "There seems to be the misconception that the students at Northwestern are really old," clarifies another student. "For most students it is only about two years [after undergrad] before we come to law school."

Don Rebstock, Associate Dean of Enrollment
375 East Chicago Avenue, Chicago, IL 60611
Tel: 312-503-8465 • Fax: 312-503-0178
E-Mail: admissions@law.northwestern.edu • Website: www.law.northwestern.edu

"Class sizes are small" and "the school goes to great lengths to create and foster a sense of community among the students." In this "collegial" atmosphere, students are "intelligent, friendly, [and] laid-back." "There are not too many gunners," reports one student. "We're smart, personable people who mix well socially while doing top-notch legal work," says a 2L. However, some students project an "'I-don't-study-at-all' attitude in the middle of the semester, trying to throw others off base. Then, suddenly, the same person who 'never studies' has a 150-page annotated outline with hyperlinks to all of its sections and subsections."

Outside of class, Northwestern is "a very fun place to attend school." "The school sponsors many events for students every week," and there are "free lunches almost every day," along with "random social events put on by the many, many student organizations." "Lunchtime speakers, panels, and club meetings provide great opportunities to explore different facets of the law school experience and the legal profession without taking up too much time." In addition, "Chicago is a great city" with "a great mix of...hustle and bustle and Midwestern friendliness"—all of which starts right "next door" to campus with "Michigan Avenue's Magnificent Mile."

Getting In

Northwestern claims to be the only law school in the country that strongly encourages all applicants to interview as a part of the admissions process. Knowing this, it behooves you to show up for an interview if you apply. With or without an interview, though, admission is unusually competitive. Admitted students at the 25th percentile have LSAT scores of 162 and GPAs of about 3.4. Admitted students at the 75th percentile have LSAT scores of 175 and GPAs of about 3.9.

Clinical program required	No
Legal writing course requirement	Yes
Legal methods course requirement	No
Legal research course requirement	Yes
Moot court requirement	Yes
Public interest law requirement	No

ADMISSIONS

Selectivity Rating	81
# applications received	4,033
% applicants accepted	25
% acceptees attending	24
Median LSAT	168
LSAT Range (25th to 75th percentile)	162–170
Median undergrad GPA	3.75
Application fee	$75
Regular application deadline	2/15
Transfer students accepted	Yes
Evening division offered	No
Part-time accepted	No
CAS accepted	Yes

FINANCIAL FACTS

Annual tuition	$56,134
Books and supplies	$76,740
Room & Board	$14,040
Financial aid application deadline	3/1
% of aid that is merit based	50
% receiving scholarships	57
Average grant	$28,426
Average loan	$65,286
Average debt	$163,065

EMPLOYMENT INFORMATION

Career Rating	75	
Total 2014 JD Grads	291	
% for whom you have useable information	100	
% grads employed ten months out	92	
Median starting salary	$160,000	
% job accepting grads providing useable salary information	96	
# employed full-time	264	
# employed part-time	5	
# employed bar required	241	
# employed JD preferred	27	
# employed professional/other	1	
# pursuing advanced degree	1	
# unemployed and seeking employment	16	
# not seeking employment	1	
% grads employed by school	3	
State for bar exam	IL	
Pass rate for first-time bar	96.0	

Prominent Alumni
John Paul Stevens, Supreme Court Justice; Ada Kepley, First American woman to obtain a law degree; Jerry Reinsdorf, Owner, Chicago Bulls and White Sox

Grads Employed by Field (%)
Academic (1)
Business/Industry (8)
Government (5)
Judicial Clerkship (12)
Federal: (9)
State or local: (2)
Private Practice (63)
 2-10: (1)
 11-25: (1)
 26-50: (2)
 51-100: (3)
 101-250: (3)
 251-500: (7)
 501+: (47)
 Size Unknown: (0)
Public Interest (4)

NOVA SOUTHEASTERN UNIVERSITY
SHEPARD BROAD LAW CENTER

Academics

At the Shepard Broad Law Center, the focus is "more how to be a lawyer right out of school and less about the theoretical practice of law." Students praise the school's "practical application of the law": "Every clerkship I have gone to I was ready for whatever was asked because the school prepares you to be able to do real world stuff." NSU Law emphasizes the importance of clinical education; every student who meets the clinic criteria has the opportunity to participate in one of the school's seven clinical programs, which include the Bankruptcy Clinic, the Environmental and Land Use Law Clinic, and the International Practice Clinic. NSU Law's in-house clinics give qualified students the opportunity to gather practical skills in three specialized areas: alternative dispute resolution; children and family; and veterans law. Students begin their clinical semester with intensive classes that focus on advanced substantive law; for the rest of the term, faculty members supervise students while representing clients in NSU Law clinics, government agencies, nonprofits, and private law offices. Students interested in international law can take advantage of NSU Law's host of study abroad programs, particularly the dual-degree law programs in Barcelona, Rome, or Prague that allow students to study American common law in addition to preparing to take the foreign nation's bar exam (for those students that participate in the Spain and Italy program) or, for students in the Czech program, earn a LLM degree in either international human rights and environmental law or Central European and Czech law and business. Stateside, students generally praise the alumni network but say that the school could improve by paying more attention to its "[rank] and national reputation."

Many students say their professors at NSU Law "are available and have an open-door policy. Their office hours feel like an extension of the classroom [but] much more personal," with one student saying wistfully, "I wish I could clone the vigor and enthusiasm of my civil procedures teacher in all my future courses." But not all NSU Law students speak so highly of the faculty, lamenting that "most of the professors are knowledgeable . . . however, most of them have no teaching skills of whatsoever. They are just proud of who they are and their own achievements." Others wish for a less "sink or swim" attitude when it came to future success. The administration doesn't earn high marks either, with students classifying it as "disorganized" and adding that "registering for classes is a nightmare." One student goes so far as to say "the school administration is non-existent. In fact, I've been here 3 years and I have no idea who the administration is."

The "facilities of the law school need serious work. We pay a lot in tuition that does not appear to be going to the law school." One student notes that "more law students go to the public library than our own," due to poor conditions, although another student counters that the NSU Law library "has all the resources we need but no one (at any law school) truly utilizes libraries anymore. They're outdated and serve less and less any practical purpose." Most research, say students, "is done online on our personal computer[s], not through the library," though "if students want to use the library to go study, that is another matter. There's plenty of study area in our library."

WILLIAM PEREZ, ASSISTANT DEAN FOR ADMISSIONS
3305 COLLEGE AVENUE, FORT LAUDERDALE, FL 33314
TEL: 954-262-6117 • FAX: 954-262-3844
E-MAIL: ADMISSION@NSU.LAW.NOVA.EDU • WEBSITE: WWW.NSULAW.NOVA.EDU

Student Life

As a fairly large law school that's associated with an even larger parent institution—Nova Southeastern University has roughly 27,000 students and the law school has around 925—NSU Law has the potential to offer its students multiple social opportunities, as well as academic ones: "[NSU Law] has strong community ties since it is the only law school in the county." Opportunities to unwind certainly abound in Fort Lauderdale and nearby Miami, which is thirty miles away.

In terms of competition among students, one student was surprised that "there was certainly a cutthroat mentality when I was a 1L" and "plenty of phony outlines" circulated that were "purposely changed with false information. If that's not cutthroat, I don't know what is."

Getting in

NSU Law sees a little over 1,500 applications total for its full-time and part-time programs, and offers spots to approximately 835 students. Admitted students in the 25th percentile have an approximate GPA of 2.86 and an LSAT score of 147, while admitted students in the 75th percentile have a GPA of roughly 3.42 and an LSAT score of 151.

Clinical program required	No
Legal writing course requirement	Yes
Legal methods course requirement	No
Legal research course requirement	Yes
Moot court requirement	No
Public interest law requirement	No

ADMISSIONS

Selectivity Rating	76
# applications received	1,222
% applicants accepted	56
% acceptees attending	29
Average LSAT	149
Median LSAT	149
LSAT Range (25th to 75th percentile)	147–151
Average undergrad GPA	3.11
Median undergrad GPA	3.16
Application fee	$53
Regular application deadline	5/1
Transfer students accepted	Yes
Evening division offered	Yes
Part-time accepted	Yes
CAS accepted	Yes

International Students

TOEFL required of international students.	Yes

FINANCIAL FACTS

Annual tuition	$35,956
Books and supplies	$2,356
Room & Board (on/ off campus)	$15,002/$16,191
Financial aid application deadline	4/15
% first-year students receiving some sort of aid	87
% all students receiving some sort of aid	88
% of aid that is merit based	43
% receiving scholarships	38
Average grant	$10,364
Average loan	$43,606
Average total aid package	$44,500
Average debt	$131,449

EMPLOYMENT INFORMATION

Career Rating	84	
Total 2014 JD Grads	280	
% for whom you have useable information	36	
% grads employed ten months out	86	
Median starting salary	$55,000	
# employed full-time	217	
# employed part-time	25	
# employed bar required	185	
# employed JD preferred	26	
# employed professional/other	16	
# employed non-professional	15	
# pursuing advanced degree	7	
# unemployed and seeking employment	27	
# not seeking employment	4	
State for bar exam	FL	
Pass rate for first-time bar	69.7	

Prominent Alumni
Melanie G. May, Appeals Court Judge; Rob Brzezinski, VP Football Operations, Minnesota Vikings (NFL); Ellyn Setnor Bogdanoff, FLA House of Representative; Rex Ford, US Immigration Judge

Grads Employed by Field (%)
Academic (1)
Business/Industry (19)
Government (10)
Judicial Clerkship (1)
State or local: (1)
Private Practice (51)
Solo: (3)
2-10: (31)
11-25: (7)
26-50: (3)
51-100: (3)
101-250: (4)
251-500: (1)
501+: (1)
Size Unknown: (0)
Public Interest (4)

OHIO NORTHERN UNIVERSITY
PETTIT COLLEGE OF LAW

INSTITUTIONAL INFORMATION

Public/private	Private
Affiliation	Methodist
Student-faculty ratio	11:1
% faculty part-time	40
% faculty female	40
% faculty underrepresented minority	13
Total faculty	30

SURVEY SAYS...
Great research resources

STUDENTS

Enrollment of law school	207
% male/female	52/48
% from out-of-state	65
% part-time	0
% underrepresented minority	15
% international	1
# of countries represented	8
Average age of entering class	26

ACADEMICS

Academic Experience Rating	77
Profs interesting rating	71
Profs accessible rating	82
Hours of study per day	5.00

Academic Specialties
Civil Procedure, Commercial, Constitutional, Corporation Securities, Criminal, Environmental, Government Services, Human Rights, International, Labor, Legal History, Property, Taxation, Intellectual Property

Advanced Degrees Offered
JD 3 yrs

Combined Degrees Offered
JD/LLM in Democratic Governance and Rule of Law, 3rds; JD/MPPA (Masters of Professional Practice in Accounting), 3 yrs

Academics

Nestled in the remote and "extremely small" town of Ada, the Claude W. Pettit College of Law at Ohio Northern University routinely boasts a high bar-passage rate—73 percent of students passed in February 2015. Plus, its "career and internship placement [are] excellent," and in 2013 it lead the state in graduates who went on to land JD-required jobs. ONU is also known for its "congenial atmosphere between students and teachers" and its "small class sizes [that] enable you to interact more and [give] the professors the opportunity to [get to know] you on a first-name basis"—in fact, the school boasts a cozy student-to-faculty ratio of 11:1.

Another plus is ONU's commitment to affordability. As part of The ONU Law Promise, the law school reduced its tuition for the 2014–15 academic year (by a not-too-shabby 25 percent, at that) and a whopping 98 percent of students receive some form of financial aid, making this school a bona fide budget-friendly option.

As for classes, one student listed the "academics themselves" as a strong suit, and tons more expressed wholehearted enthusiasm for ONU's "great teachers" who are "extremely knowledgeable and willing to help students learn as much as they can" and who "genuinely care about the students." Plus, the professors' commitment goes beyond the lecture hall: They "devote more time to getting you networked with the appropriate legal communities" and "are easily accessible . . . outside of class." One student even called the faculty "a hidden gem in rural Ohio." However, some students did wish that the school's 120-plus classes offered "larger variety" and lamented that the "administration can be a bit disorganized at times."

ONU offers a fair amount of opportunities for experiential learning, with an "incredible . . . law review," a moot court that allows students to develop mock trial experience, 10-plus subject-specific clinics (such as bankruptcy, public defense, and family law) that offer guaranteed placement, and externships that pair students with judges, whom they aid with research, writing, or other court-related duties. These and 20-plus additional organizations regularly "[bring] in speakers to network and build connections" and invite "alumni [to] come to the school every year to speak to the current students," who may even "offer jobs to many students here after graduation." One student reported that "most [of] my peers are very happy with the pipeline [that] ONU has built for us into the legal community of our choosing." Another chimed in to say that the revamped career services department does a "fantastic job," with "more people [having] jobs and internships than ever before."

While ONU's classes, professors, and hands-on learning opportunities definitely pass muster, students are quick to point out a slight lag in updates to the facilities: The classrooms are "bland and outdated" and communal spaces are described as "lacking," "but [overall] they meet every need we have." Conversely, "our library and research facilities are extensive and easy to access and understand" and students receive "thorough teaching" on how to make good use of these resources.

Life

Law students looking to bunker down and study free of distraction, look no farther than ONU—for better or for worse. "The small town of Ada offers the atmosphere to focus on your schoolwork," a student confirmed. And while some students find Ada "a depressing, miserable place to live and study" and deem it "way too boring," others say that it has "the most charming small town atmosphere you could dream of," love the

CHAD M. VONDENHUEVEL, DIRECTOR OF LAW ADMISSIONS
PETTIT COLLEGE OF LAW, 119 TILTON HALL OF LAW, ADA, OH 45810-1599
TEL: 877-452-9668 • FAX: 419-772-3042
EMAIL: LAWADMISSIONS@ONU.EDU • WEBSITE: WWW.LAW.ONU.EDU

community's "nice slow pace," and point out the "small family-owned restaurants that offer great food, several bars where law students often meet, a small movie theater and bowling alley, and great pizza places."

The town's tiny size also creates a real sense of community, as there is "not a lot to do, activities-wise, but [the students] really get to know each other" and the town "fosters a more team-like environment." Plus, "the school and the professors … make the atmosphere welcoming as they sponsor and host several social activities for the students." All this coziness can lead to a bit of "drama," "competition," and even "cut-throat" vibes, according to some students. But others report that "the environment is much more healthy than that of other law schools" and that "dirty tricks are not tolerated."

With state capital Columbus just an hour-and-a-half's drive away and a few other mid-size towns even closer, it's certainly possible to seek out entertainment and professional opportunities outside Ada's gates. The key? Know what you're getting into and if it's right for you. "Some people find that they wanted a large city where you can do anything or get anything any time. That is not Ada."

Getting In

Considered a fairly competitive law school, ONU accepts 47 percent of its applicants. Students accepted at the 25th percentile typically had an LSAT score of 144 and a GPA of 2.86, while students at the 75th percentile had an average score of 152 and GPA of 3.58. Good news: If you take the LSAT twice, ONU will consider your higher score.

Clinical program required	No
Legal writing course requirement	Yes
Legal methods course requirement	Yes
Legal research course requirement	Yes
Moot court requirement	No
Public interest law requirement	No

ADMISSIONS

Selectivity Rating	80
# applications received	466
% applicants accepted	49
% acceptees attending	31
Median LSAT	150
LSAT Range (25th to 75th percentile)	144–152
Median undergrad GPA	3.22
Application fee	$0
Regular application deadline	8/15
Transfer students accepted	Yes
Evening division offered	No
Part-time accepted	No
CAS accepted	Yes

International Students

TOEFL required of international students.	Yes

FINANCIAL FACTS

Annual tuition	$24,800
Books and supplies	$2,000
Room & Board (on/off campus)	$11,235/$9,657
Financial aid application deadline	6/1
% first-year students receiving some sort of aid	89
% all students receiving some sort of aid	87
% of aid that is merit based	96
% receiving scholarships	63
Average grant	$16,718
Average loan	$37,576
Average total aid package	$46,382
Average debt	$110,391

EMPLOYMENT INFORMATION

Career Rating	80	
Total 2014 JD Grads	94	
% for whom you have useable information	97	
% grads employed ten months out	79	
Median starting salary	$46,000	
% job accepting grads providing useable salary information	19	
# employed full-time	60	
# employed part-time	14	
# employed bar required	49	
# employed JD preferred	12	
# employed professional/other	2	
# employed non-professional	10	
# pursuing advanced degree	0	
# unemployed and seeking employment	15	
# not seeking employment	1	
% grads employed by school	0	
State for bar exam	OH, FL, PA, NC, IN	
Pass rate for first-time bar	90.0	

Prominent Alumni
Michael DeWine, Ohio Attorney General; Gregory Frost, U.S. District Judge Southern Ohio; Benjamin Brafman, Senior Partner at Brafman & Ross, New York City; Greg Miller, U.S. Attorney for Northwest Florida; Jessica Price Smith, U.S. Bankruptcy Court Northern District of Ohio

Grads Employed by Field (%)
Business/Industry (25)
Government (13)
Judicial Clerkship (7)
 Federal: (2)
 State or local: (5)
Private Practice (31)
 Solo: (2)
 2-10: (24)
 11-25: (0)
 26-50: (2)
 51-100: (1)
 101-250: (1)
 Size Unknown: (1)
Public Interest (0)

THE OHIO STATE UNIVERSITY
MICHAEL E. MORITZ COLLEGE OF LAW

INSTITUTIONAL INFORMATION

Public/private	Public
Student-faculty ratio	15:1
% faculty part-time	28
% faculty female	31
% faculty underrepresented minority	19
Total faculty	83

SURVEY SAYS...
Good social life

STUDENTS

Enrollment of law school	700
% male/female	57/43
% from out-of-state	33
% part-time	0
% underrepresented minority	20
% international	2
# of countries represented	7
Average age of entering class	23

ACADEMICS

Academic Experience Rating	**93**
Profs interesting rating	85
Profs accessible rating	86
Hours of study per day	3.86

Academic Specialties
Civil Procedure, Commercial, Constitutional, Corporation Securities, Criminal, Government Services, International, Labor, Property, Taxation, Intellectual Property

Advanced Degrees Offered
Masters in the Study of Law, 1 yr; LLM International Students 1 yr

Combined Degrees Offered
JD/MBA (4 yrs), JD/MHA (4 yrs), JD/MPA (4 yrs), JD/over 80 different individually designed (4–5 yrs)

Academics

The Ohio State University Moritz College of Law is a "kinder, gentler law school," which "supports creativity." "Through career workshops each week, setting students up with legal professionals as private mentors, and a wide breadth of clinics to satisfy each particular taste, OSU invests in its students. And their offerings keep expanding!" The new Entrepreneurial Business Clinic should ease any student fears arising from a perceived lack of focus on corporate law and "fill the one gap Moritz had." OSU advocates pro bono work, and plenty of clinics allow students to gain practical experience in the legal world. Students love this "hands-on" approach. Additionally, there is a strong criminal law program, and "the alternative dispute resolution program is one of the best in the nation." The legal writing program is also outstanding. Students praise the law school's "connection with the university as a whole." The school offers various joint-degree programs, including a Master of Public Policy that can be completed "for free and in no additional time." Students couldn't be happier with their classroom experience, and professors seem to love what they do. "Almost every professor I've had has been engaging, brilliant, and enthusiastic," says one student. Students agree there's an endless supply of "fantastic educators." Professors are "leaders in their research fields," and "great citizens," who give openly of their time and "have a real passion for instructing." "It's common to see faculty at student events and around the law school." They're "excellent facilitators of class conversation" and create a "friendly environment." "I had no idea how strong the faculty would be," one student proclaims. "I have yet to find a professor, who does not go above and beyond to meet with students and share insight."

The resources at OSU are "focused on student access." The administration doesn't "hesitate to interact with the students to give them advice or even just to have casual conversation." Also, the school is "just a hop, skip, and a jump away from downtown Columbus, home of the Ohio Statehouse, Ohio Supreme Court, and many other courts, organizations, and firms." This is very helpful in acquiring externship opportunities and jobs within the community. Although there are "increasing career outreach opportunities through Career Services," some worry that outside the state of Ohio resources might be "limited." There's a strong "network of alumni," and even though some students did stress their concern over finding jobs out of state, one student offers, "Even if you don't plan to stay in Ohio, OSU has great regional ties throughout the Midwest and a strong national reputation." Another student says the alumni and the Columbus legal community believe in the school's mission and will continue to help out when they can. Still students emphasize concern over the lack of East Coast firms coming to campus to recruit.

Students mention the "primarily left-leaning" nature of the faculty and student body. While some love this aspect, others disputed it as fact. Whichever way the pendulum might swing, at OSU "a strong current of tolerance pervades." In the classroom and outside it, all views are expressed and accepted. Facilities and technology are a worry at OSU. Both are described as "surprisingly lacking." However, they "just finished remodeling the student union and the main library," and one student notes, "The facilities have gotten much better this year."

JIMMI NICHOLSON, ASSISTANT DIRECTOR
104 DRINKO HALL, 55 WEST 12TH AVENUE, COLUMBUS, OH 43210
TEL: 614-292-8810 • FAX: 614-292-1492
E-MAIL: LAWADMIT@OSU.EDU • WEBSITE: MORITZLAW.OSU.EDU

Life

OSU School of Law is referred to as both "supportive" and "surprisingly congenial," and a school in which "people will always share their notes." "While we acknowledge the curve as a fact of life, we have a strong sense of camaraderie." Some students believe competition exists, but that it "does not overshadow a great law school experience." Another student has "never really felt a competitive spirit among the students here." Age at the law school ranges from those just out of undergrad to older students, many of whom "are married and have children."

"The law school is literally right next to the center of campus social life." Most students agree its location is convenient. "Directly across the street is the brand new Ohio Union, twenty restaurants and bars, a concert venue, movie theaters, coffee shops, and more." There are a multitude of places for students to relax and gather before and after class. To further foster a sense of community, "every weekday at noon, there are no classes and an impressive amount of group and club events, guest speaker presentations, debates, and other special events happen every day."

Getting In

The admissions committee considers LSAT scores, undergraduate GPAs, personal essays, and letters of recommendation all very important in the process of admission. Roughly one in three applicants is accepted. Admitted students in the 25th percentile have undergraduate GPAs around 3.4 and LSAT scores in the high 150s. Admitted students in the 75th percentile have GPAs around 3.8 and LSAT scores in the mid-160s.

Clinical program required	No
Legal writing course requirement	Yes
Legal methods course requirement	No
Legal research course requirement	No
Moot court requirement	Yes
Public interest law requirement	No

ADMISSIONS

Selectivity Rating	92
# applications received	2,300
% applicants accepted	39
% acceptees attending	23
Average LSAT	162
Median LSAT	163
LSAT Range (25th to 75th percentile)	159–165
Average undergrad GPA	3.61
Median undergrad GPA	3.63
Application fee	$60
Regular application deadline	3/15
Transfer students accepted	Yes
Evening division offered	No
Part-time accepted	No
CAS accepted	Yes

International Students

TOEFL required of international students.	Yes

FINANCIAL FACTS

Annual tuition (in-state/ out-of-state)	$26,328/$41,278
Books and supplies	$3,980
Fees	$2,300
Room & Board	$15,876
Financial aid application deadline	2/15
% first-year students receiving some sort of aid	76
% all students receiving some sort of aid	81
% of aid that is merit based	77
% receiving scholarships	75
Average grant	$8,132
Average loan	$34,169
Average total aid package	$9,512
Average debt	$87,770

EMPLOYMENT INFORMATION

Career Rating	89	
Total 2014 JD Grads	231	
% grads employed ten months out	97	
Median starting salary	$60,000	
% job accepting grads providing useable salary information	53	
# employed full-time	181	
# employed part-time	32	
# employed bar required	156	
# employed JD preferred	45	
# employed professional/other	10	
# employed non-professional	2	
# pursuing advanced degree	6	
# unemployed and seeking employment	5	
# not seeking employment	7	
State for bar exam	OH, DC, NY, IL, CA	
Pass rate for first-time bar	89.0	

Prominent Alumni
Jack Creighton, Former CEO Weyerhauser Corp. and United Airlines; Brian Sandoval, Governor of Nevada; Erin Moriarity, 48 Hours/CBS News Journalist; Karen Sarjeant, V.P. Legal Services Corp.; George Voinovich, Senator

Grads Employed by Field (%)
Business/Industry (26)
Government (16)
Judicial Clerkship (6)
Private Practice (44)
Public Interest (5)

OKLAHOMA CITY UNIVERSITY
SCHOOL OF LAW

INSTITUTIONAL INFORMATION

Public/private	Private
Affiliation	Methodist
Student-faculty ratio	14:1
% faculty part-time	51
% faculty female	32
% faculty underrepresented minority	15
Total faculty	59

SURVEY SAYS...

*Students love Oklahoma City, OK,
Diverse opinions accepted in class-
rooms, Great research resources,
Abundant externship/internship/
clerkship opportunities,
Good social life*

STUDENTS

Enrollment of law school	453
% male/female	53/47
% from out-of-state	42
% part-time	12
% underrepresented minority	19
% international	1
# of countries represented	6
Average age of entering class	28

ACADEMICS

Academic Experience Rating	**76**
Profs interesting rating	86
Profs accessible rating	85
Hours of study per day	4.17

Academic Specialties

Commercial, Energy and
Environmental, Government
Services, National Security Law,
American Indian Law, Alternative
Dispute Resolution

Advanced Degrees Offered

JD,3 yrs; L.L.M., 1 year.

Combined Degrees Offered

JD/MBA and JD/Masters in Non-
Profit Leadership, 3 yrs.

Academics

While the Oklahoma City University School of Law recently lowered the 1L curve "from a C+ to a B- to match the University of Oklahoma and other law schools" in the region, it maintains rigorous academic standards and a "very strong legal research and writing program" that "is tough but so, so helpful." The school has relocated to "a newly renovated and beautiful" building in the heart of Oklahoma City, which students say "is a vast improvement from the former location." The move seems to have heightened the school's focus on practical experience and creating connections between students, faculty and administrators. With "well-thought-out spaces that integrate technology" and "plenty of places for group work and solo study," this "historic five-story 'castle'" "[brings] everything together" under one roof, and "gives [students] the feeling of an open door policy." Students feel like this harmony and integration is reflected in the curriculum as they have "never experienced school administration and faculty so integrated with student body." One student explains that the "1L faculty seems to have a coordinated approach where overlapping topics are presented very close to the same time in different classes."

OCU Law students are now only "a few blocks from both state and federal courthouses and several large law firms," which "present phenomenal opportunities to get plenty of training." Students are "able to walk to the county courthouse between classes to watch trials." One student added that the new location "is great for networking; I meet Judges and attorneys on a daily basis." Students also appreciate that the school "allows a generous number of credit hours to be satisfied with practical skills [courses]." In fact, most students agree that the "clinical and externship offerings and practical skills courses, like trial practice and pretrial litigation," are among the school's greatest strengths. Clinics like "the school's American Indian Wills Clinic where" students learn "to draft estate planning devices for Native American clients," help students learn "how to understand and conform to" a client's wishes and "translate their oral concerns into artfully drafted legal documents." These clinics help develop "skills that improve attorney-client relationships and performance in any legal office," skills "that most attorneys do not begin to develop until [they are] actually in practice." Students say that "getting this head start" makes them "more marketable and flexible in any work environment."

Some students praise the school for trying "to accommodate even more working adults, moms with children, adults returning for career change, police officers and those with disabilities" by offering night classes. Though, this has caused friction with some traditional students who find "that the class scheduling is very difficult to work with" "because many classes are only offered at night" and "most electives were offered exclusively at night," others enjoy that the schedule is flexible enough to "work with people who have commitments that keep them busy during the day." But students universally applaud the professors of those classes as coming "from some of the most respected schools around the nation and [as being] highly regarded as experts in their specialized fields."

Laurie W. Jones, Associate Dean for Admissions
800 N. Harvey Avenue, Oklahoma City, OK 73102-1493
Tel: 405-208-5354 • Fax: 405-208-5814
E-Mail: lawquestions@okcu.edu • Website: law.okcu.edu

Life

Situated "in the heart of downtown Oklahoma City," students enjoy a host of "local restaurants, [coffee] shops, and other fun places within just a few blocks of the school" as well as "a fantastic outdoor plaza with tables, so students can enjoy sitting outside to study on a pleasant day." Students say "there is ample housing available" nearby, and the central location also "allows the students to be more active in the community that most will be serving when they graduate." And the school encourages that involvement. One student explained that "the cost of attendance is high, but scholarships are readily available, as are school payments for internships/externships in areas that serve the public welfare." Students also keep busy through school organizations and activities: "Club membership is high, and those clubs are active," while "it is rare that a weekend goes by where there is not an event to go to." And the school's connections mean that there is never a shortage of "great guest speakers from the law community" or "connections in the workforce" that "help students gain internships and jobs." A "diverse student body" paired with "passionate and committed" faculty and administrators creates a community where "professors know each student in the 1L class by name [on] the 1st day."

Getting In

Oklahoma City University School of Law considers an applicant's highest LSAT score. Admitted students' LSAT scores range from 135-165.

Clinical program required	Yes
Legal writing course requirement	Yes
Legal methods course requirement	Yes
Legal research course requirement	Yes
Moot court requirement	No
Public interest law requirement	No

ADMISSIONS

Selectivity Rating	73
# applications received	544
% applicants accepted	82
% acceptees attending	35
Median LSAT	148
LSAT Range (25th to 75th percentile)	145–151
Median undergrad GPA	3.19
Application fee	$50
Regular application deadline	7/31
Transfer students accepted	Yes
Evening division offered	Yes
Part-time accepted	Yes
CAS accepted	Yes

International Students

TOEFL required of international students.	Yes

FINANCIAL FACTS

Annual tuition	$30,885
Books and supplies	$1,740
Room & Board	$9,210
Financial aid application deadline	7/31
% first-year students receiving some sort of aid	93
% all students receiving some sort of aid	93
% of aid that is merit based	64
% receiving scholarships	64
Average grant	$16,000
Average loan	$30,729
Average total aid package	$41,279
Average debt	$99,298

EMPLOYMENT INFORMATION

Career Rating	86	**Prominent Alumni**
Total 2014 JD Grads	162	Yvonne Kauger, Oklahoma Supreme Court
% for whom you have useable information	98	Justice; Andrew Benton, President, Pepperdine University; Nona Lee, VP and
% grads employed ten months out	93	General Counsel, Arizona Diamondbacks;
Median starting salary	$55,000	Carl Alexandre, Deputy Special
# employed full-time	147	Representative of the United Nations;
# employed part-time	1	**Grads Employed by Field (%)**
# employed bar required	105	Business/Industry (26)
# employed JD preferred	38	Government (18)
# employed professional/other	3	Private Practice (56)
# employed non-professional	2	Solo: (12)
# pursuing advanced degree	2	2-10: (63)
# unemployed and seeking employment	7	11-25: (6.87)
# not seeking employment	2	26-50: (1)
State for bar exam	OK, TX, MO	51-100: (2)
Pass rate for first-time bar	81.0	101-250: (4)
		501+: (1)
		Public Interest (1)

PACE UNIVERSITY
SCHOOL OF LAW

INSTITUTIONAL INFORMATION

Public/private	Private
Affiliation	No Affiliation
% faculty part-time	47
% faculty female	42
% faculty underrepresented minority	8
Total faculty	103

SURVEY SAYS...
Diverse opinions accepted in classrooms

STUDENTS

Enrollment of law school	557
% male/female	42/58
% part-time	14
% underrepresented minority	28
Average age of entering class	25

ACADEMICS

Academic Experience Rating	**80**
Profs interesting rating	80
Profs accessible rating	82
Hours of study per day	4.32

Academic Specialties
Civil Procedure, Commercial, Constitutional, Corporation Securities, Criminal, Environmental, Government Services, Human Rights, International, Labor, Legal History, Property, Taxation, Intellectual Property

Advanced Degrees Offered
SJD Environmental Law, 1 yr. LLM Environmental Law, 1–2 yrs. LLM Comparative Legal Studies, 1 yr.

Combined Degrees Offered
BA/JD with Pace University Dyson School of Arts and Sciences, 6 yrs. JD/MBA with Pace University, 4–6 yrs. JD/MPA with Pace University, 4–6 yrs. JD/M.E.M. with Yale University, 4–6 yrs. JD/MS with Bard College, 4–6 yrs. JD/MA with Sarah Lawrence College, 4-6 yrs.

Academics

New York's Pace University School of Law has earned a regional reputation as a leader in its field because it has excelled in its specialty of environmental law. The "one-of-a-kind" environmental law curriculum wins praise for offering "a variety of courses" taught by faculty who are "highly respected and known in the environmental community." This "broad" program "offers a unique specialization within the legal profession" taught by "some of the greatest professors available," and one that has proven to be the best known aspect of Pace's law program. However, students point out that Pace is "not just an environmental law school...I think Pace has rested on this reputation for far too long."

Educators at Pace aim to ensure graduates are "readily prepared to enter the working field and perform at a high level." Internships abound, including study abroad opportunities that allow you to work at overseas law firms or intern with a war crime tribunal. The "amazing" professors here "are interested in their students' growth, understanding, and achievement and are for the most part available for help and talking outside of the classroom." Indeed, they will "frequently even give students their home phone numbers if they need to call for questions." Some suggest the quality of professors can be "hit or miss," with some going so far as to say that "the professors are either very good or very poor with very little in between." However, according to most these educators "are intelligent, love their jobs, and are always helpful." These teachers "work hard to help us and are excellent at the subjects they teach and conveying the subjects to us."

Student opinions on the administration are mixed, with some indicating that the administration's unwillingness to confront problems or ideas presented by students "detracts from all the great resources available to those who attend Pace." Other members of the faculty win praise. Many students note that "the librarians are fantastic at helping students and explaining research tools to students." Gripes with the administration aside, overall "the quality of the faculty coupled with the genuine care in preparation of students is unrivaled." The trick is letting people know—students would love to see Pace gain a wider reputation.

Life

With a campus in the Westchester County suburbs of New York City, life at Pace Law School can be as active as you want to make it. It is not cheap to live here—White Plains "is an expensive place to live"—but the school is proximate enough to the five boroughs of New York City, as well as the NYC suburbs, that commuting to school is common. The "extremely professional" and "extremely polite" people on campus, both staff and students alike, create an "intimate atmosphere" in which students feel "close to (their) peers." Student organizations are many, so "social life is there if you want it, but you're not an outcast if you don't."

CATHY ALEXANDER, ASSISTANT DEAN FOR ADMISSIONS
78 NORTH BROADWAY, WHITE PLAINS, NY 10603
TEL: 914-422-4210 • FAX: 914-989-8714
E-MAIL: ADMISSIONS@LAW.PACE.EDU • WEBSITE: WWW.LAW.PACE.EDU

The situation with the campus itself is not as universally beloved. Despite its reputation as a cutting edge environmental law school, "there is nothing particularly cutting-edge about the technology on campus." Students complain that "the wireless is frequently down," and that the "windowless" auditorium-style classrooms lack natural lighting. Despite these complaints, one student summed up a common sentiment: "I consider myself to be very fortunate to be a Pace law student."

Getting In

LSAT scores of approximately 149 and GPAs a little less than 3.0 are typical for enrolled students at the 25th percentile. At the 75th percentile, those scores are close to 153 (LSAT) and about 3.5 (GPA). Pace has an accelerated program that allows students to start in January and graduate in two and a half years, if they are in a hurry to get their JD.

Clinical program required	No
Legal writing course requirement	Yes
Legal methods course requirement	Yes
Legal research course requirement	Yes
Moot court requirement	Yes
Public interest law requirement	No

ADMISSIONS

Selectivity Rating	77
# applications received	1,436
% applicants accepted	62
% acceptees attending	23
Median LSAT	151
Median undergrad GPA	3.28
Application fee	$65
Transfer students accepted	Yes
Evening division offered	No
Part-time accepted	Yes
CAS accepted	Yes

International Students

TOEFL required of international students.	Yes

FINANCIAL FACTS

Annual tuition	$45,376
Books and supplies	$1,600
Fees	$248
Room & Board	$10,460

EMPLOYMENT INFORMATION

Career Rating	82	**Prominent Alumni**
Total 2014 JD Grads	217	John Cahill, Chadbourne & Parker; 02-06
% grads employed ten months out	83	Secretary & Chief of Staff to NY Governor
Median starting salary	$66,500	George Pataki; Robert F. Kennedy Jr.,
# employed full-time	163	Co-Director, Pace Environmental Litigation
# employed part-time	18	Clinic; V. Gerard Comizio, Partner, Paul
# employed bar required	139	Hastings, LLP; Judith Lockhart, Partner,
# employed JD preferred	25	Carter Ledyard & Milburn
# employed professional/other	13	**Grads Employed by Field (%)**
# employed non-professional	4	Business/Industry (23)
# pursuing advanced degree	2	Government (12)
# unemployed and seeking employment	29	Judicial Clerkship (6)
# not seeking employment	2	Private Practice (47)
% grads employed by school	4	Public Interest (10)
State for bar exam	NY	
Pass rate for first-time bar	79.0	

PEPPERDINE UNIVERSITY
SCHOOL OF LAW

INSTITUTIONAL INFORMATION

Public/private	Private
Affiliation	Church of Christ
Student-faculty ratio	13:1
% faculty part-time	49
% faculty female	28
% faculty underrepresented minority	12
Total faculty	99

SURVEY SAYS...

Students love Malibu, CA, Diverse opinions accepted in classrooms, Abundant externship/internship/ clerkship opportunities, Law school well run, Conservative students, Strong sense of community, Good social life

STUDENTS

Enrollment of law school	602
% male/female	51/49
% from out-of-state	45
% part-time	0
% underrepresented minority	28
% international	2
# of countries represented	4
Average age of entering class	24

ACADEMICS

Academic Experience Rating	**91**
Profs interesting rating	95
Profs accessible rating	99
Hours of study per day	3.76

Academic Specialties
Commercial, Corporation Securities, Criminal, Human Rights, International, Property, Intellectual Property

Advanced Degrees Offered
LLM in Dispute Resolution

Combined Degrees Offered
JD/MBA 4 yrs; JD/MDR 3–4 yrs; JD/MPP 4 yrs; JD/MDiv 5 yrs

Academics

It's hard not to lead with the most obvious benefit of choosing Pepperdine for law school: "the panoramic view of the Pacific Ocean and Catalina Island as you enter just about make law school tolerable." Pepperdine's law campus is in fact located in stunning Malibu, CA, just outside Los Angeles, but to emphasize the beauty of its location would "wrongly connote a culture that may lack rigor or seriousness." Indeed, among Pepperdine's legal strengths are "top-notch dispute resolution curricula, wide variety of faculty from myriad professional and ideological backgrounds, and its top-tier student body." "The administration is currently in the process of evolving to update themselves with modern times and beliefs," and students see its recent changes as mostly positive ones that are "not yet complete" but "moving at a promising rate:" "Our new dean is spectacular, and will continue to improve our law school in any way needed." "Dean Tacha could not be more optimistic, outgoing, or encouraging if she tried." Though Pepperdine is historically, and still, a Christian university, they recently instituted an LGBT student group, and students say Pepperdine's "is a growing community of diversity." Despite the fact that "technology has been updated recently," many students do echo the need for further updates: the "WiFi speed" is "miserable," and "the interior of the Law Building looks as though it was plucked straight out of 1985." More importantly, a lot of students feel some lack in the school's career services, saying Pepperdine "could use heavy improvement in its career development office," but there's a "large alumni base in Los Angeles," where there's also an abundance of legal jobs.

Professors, for the most part, receive high marks from students: they're "absolutely excellent," "have a genuine open-door policy," and "have been nothing less than completely exceptional." "They truly invest in and care about the students and it makes law school much less stressful." A few voices dissent with this characterization, noting the prevalence of "very wealthy, conservative men, which makes expressing your (differing) opinions difficult." In spite of that, "I haven't met one professor who didn't seem completely passionate about both teaching law and encouraging every student to succeed." Beyond Malibu, "the overseas study opportunities are numerous and very well run," and students praise Pepperdine's program in "dispute resolution," noting that "classes through the Straus Institute for Dispute Resolution...fill up quickly."

Life

It's hard not to love your time at Pepperdine when the "campus is set in an absolutely beautiful location," and students appreciate their "Wonderful peers as a result of such a warm environment." While "the competition is extremely high," "The student body is generally very warm." The staff also "promotes both personal and intellectual growth:" "The leadership and location are unmatched. Pepperdine's School of Law has been an extremely welcoming environment."

SHANNON PHILLIPS, ASSISTANT DEAN, ADMISSIONS
24255 PACIFIC COAST HIGHWAY, MALIBU, CA 90263
TEL: 310-506-4631 • FAX: 310-506-7668
E-MAIL: SOLADMIS@PEPPERDINE.EDU • WEBSITE: LAW.PEPPERDINE.EDU

As a Christian university, Pepperdine leans right and could, according to some, be "more open to diversity in viewpoints," but "in my three years at Pepperdine I have never once felt out of place as a non-religious, liberal Democrat." Even if higher-ups tend in conservative directions, "there are plenty of conservatives and liberals alike among the students," which creates a vibrant culture of discussion. "Because most students who choose Pepperdine share its religious values, it can create a dividing line among students. That being said, the faculty, staff, and students are all very welcoming and kind to every single student at Pepperdine regardless of their religious and political affiliations." Pepperdine is also "second to none among law schools in America today" in its commitment to making its law education available to veterans: "From being one of three top tier law schools in the country to offer full Yellow Ribbon support, housing allowance based on the Malibu Beach zip code, to dinner at the Dean's house on Veteran's Day, this law school truly strives to serve those who have served their country."

Getting In

Pepperdine's LSAT median is 162 (154–162, 25th–75th percentiles) and GPA median is 3.59 (3.35–3.75, 25th–75th percentiles). As noted above, aspiring lawyers who have served in the U.S. military are very welcome applicants.

Clinical program required	Yes
Legal writing course requirement	Yes
Legal methods course requirement	No
Legal research course requirement	Yes
Moot court requirement	Yes
Public interest law requirement	No

ADMISSIONS

Selectivity Rating	87
# applications received	2,251
% applicants accepted	52
% acceptees attending	17
Median LSAT	160
LSAT Range (25th to 75th percentile)	154–162
Median undergrad GPA	3.59
Application fee	$60
Regular application deadline	4/1
Early application deadline	2/1
Transfer students accepted	Yes
Evening division offered	No
Part-time accepted	No
CAS accepted	Yes

FINANCIAL FACTS

Annual tuition	$48,970
Books and supplies	$1,200
Room & Board	$17,230
Financial aid application deadline	4/1
% first-year students receiving some sort of aid	85
% all students receiving some sort of aid	88
% of aid that is merit based	34
% receiving scholarships	59
Average grant	$21,375
Average loan	$49,863
Average total aid package	$64,400
Average debt	$145,893

EMPLOYMENT INFORMATION

Career Rating	87
Total 2014 JD Grads	198
% for whom you have useable information	99
% grads employed ten months out	79
Median starting salary	NA
# employed full-time	127
# employed part-time	30
# employed bar required	106
# employed JD preferred	43
# employed professional/other	5
# employed non-professional	3
# pursuing advanced degree	4
# unemployed and seeking employment	27
# not seeking employment	2
% grads employed by school	7
State for bar exam	CA, TX
Pass rate for first-time bar	78

Prominent Alumni
Beverly Reid O'Connell, U.S. District Judge for the United States District Court for the Central District of California; Jennie Dorsey, U.S. District Judge for the United States District Court for the District of Neveda; Andre Birotte Jr., U.S. Attorney for the Central District of California; James M. Rishwain, Jr., Firm Chair of Pillsbury Winthrop Shaw Pittman LLP

Grads Employed by Field (%)
Academic (8)
Business/Industry (14)
Government (9)
Judicial Clerkship (8)
Private Practice (39)
Public Interest (2)

QUINNIPIAC UNIVERSITY
SCHOOL OF LAW

INSTITUTIONAL INFORMATION

Public/private	Private
Affiliation	No Affiliation
Student-faculty ratio	12:1
% faculty part-time	45
% faculty female	36
% faculty underrepresented minority	4
Total faculty	53

SURVEY SAYS...

Abundant externship/internship/ clerkship opportunities

STUDENTS

Enrollment of law school	289
% male/female	44/56
% from out-of-state	42
% part-time	20
% underrepresented minority	15
% international	1
# of countries represented	1
Average age of entering class	25

ACADEMICS

Academic Experience Rating	80
Profs interesting rating	78
Profs accessible rating	83
Hours of study per day	3.87

Academic Specialties

Criminal, Environmental, Taxation, Intellectual Property

Advanced Degrees Offered

JD 3 yrs full time, 4 yrs part time
LLM in Health Law

Combined Degrees Offered

JD/MBA, 4 yrs; JD/MELP, 3 yrs; 3+3 Accelerated BA/JD

Academics

The Quinnipiac University School of Law recently moved from its former home on the main campus in Hamden, Connecticut, where it shared space with the undergraduate university, to its "exceptional" new building adjacent to the medical school in nearby North Haven. "Not only is [the new building] equipped with the most advanced state of the art technology, but it is spacious, and comfortable." Quinnipiac Law is a "small school" that "has a vibrant, tight-knit community," and it's the school's small size that "allows all the faculty and administration to learn the names of students, and vice versa." When it comes to Quinnipiac's faculty, "Many professors remain in practice and are able to offer real world training in order to prepare students for what is to be expected in practice." One student says that "the clinic and externship opportunities are immense, and an important focus at the school." Quinnipiac offers six areas of concentration—civil advocacy and dispute resolution, criminal law and advocacy, family law, health law, intellectual property, and tax—and all include a writing component while most include a clinic component. While some say that "the school could improve by offering a wider selection in courses and by integrating the clinical experience into the classroom," another student counters, "I personally couldn't take all the classes I was interested in just because there were too many to fit into my schedule." Students praise the "good balance between theory and practical application in the classroom," as well as the "excellent use of seasoned practitioners as adjuncts in practically-based elective courses." Professors on the whole are "extremely knowledgeable and extremely personable"— they are "extremely well qualified, accessible and act [as] amazing sources of support to the students."

Resources and alumni connections are most helpful for "[Connecticut] or New England students who plan on staying there for their career," with one student lamenting that "the administration and career services personnel were little to no help for me, a student who wanted internships and a future job in the Midwest." In terms of resources, one student notes, "It seems like the full-time students have a lot more opportunities than the part-time students." Another part-time student puts it more bluntly: "We work full-time during the day and all the 'practical' experiences are not available. We can't do clinics or internships, and we have no time to put into law review. We come to campus for class each night and then leave. That's it." The overall consensus seems to be for "more class options" for night school students.

As one student puts it, "The school administration means well, but there are not enough resources," though another student points out that "each Tuesday, our Dean hosts an open forum for students called 'doughnuts with the Dean'; she also holds weekly luncheons for small groups of 1Ls." Communication between the administration and the student body gets mixed reviews, with some students praising the "extremely dedicated and personable administration" and others observing that "a lot of students feel like they have no idea what's happening at the law school because the administration doesn't communicate with us."

EDWIN WILKES, ASSOCIATE VICE PRESIDENT AND DEAN OF LAW SCHOOL ADMISSIONS
MAILING ADDRESS: 275 MOUNT CARMEL AVENUE, HAMDEN, CT 06518-1908
TEL: 203-582-3400 • FAX: 203-582-3339
E-MAIL: LAW@QUINNIPIAC.EDU • WEBSITE: LAW.QUINNIPIAC.EDU

Student Life

The move away from the undergraduate campus to the graduate campus with the medical school seems to suit most Quinnipiac law students just fine, though "there isn't much to [do] around campus. But as a 1L I haven't found that to be too much of a negative since you're mostly studying all the time anyway." Luckily, "New Haven is all of five minutes away, and you are within one to two hours of both New York and Boston, which should be a plus." Closer still, "locally North Haven, Wallingford and Hamden in their town centers offer great delis, cafes, Italian eateries and local taverns, [and] two movies theaters are close by." Of course, as one student is quick to point out, "if someone is going to law school for fun things to do in their spare time, they should probably look elsewhere." Other popular activities include "apple picking, corn mazes and the Connecticut Wine trail" in the fall and skiing in the winter. For a serious dose of city life, students will make the trek to New York or Boston.

Getting In

Admitted students at the 25th percentile have roughly a 3.00 GPA and an LSAT score of 151, while admitted students at the 75th percentile have roughly a 3.57 GPA and an LSAT score of 155. In recent years, Quinnipiac received a little over 800 applications and accepted around 290.

Clinical program required	No
Legal writing course requirement	Yes
Legal methods course requirement	Yes
Legal research course requirement	No
Moot court requirement	Yes
Public interest law requirement	No

ADMISSIONS

Selectivity Rating	80
# applications received	722
% applicants accepted	58
% acceptees attending	18
Average LSAT	153
Median LSAT	153
LSAT Range (25th to 75th percentile)	151–155
Average undergrad GPA	3.32
Median undergrad GPA	3.38
Application fee	$65
Transfer students accepted	Yes
Evening division offered	Yes
Part-time accepted	Yes
CAS accepted	Yes

International Students

TOEFL recommended of international students.	Yes

FINANCIAL FACTS

Annual tuition	$47,190
Books and supplies	$1,200
Fees	$859
Room & Board (on/ off campus)	$0/$15,172
Financial aid application deadline	4/15
% first-year students receiving some sort of aid	92
% all students receiving some sort of aid	93
% of aid that is merit based	55
% receiving scholarships	81
Average grant	$25,567
Average loan	$31,448
Average total aid package	$48,886
Average debt	$99,872

EMPLOYMENT INFORMATION

Career Rating	80
Total 2014 JD Grads	113
% for whom you have useable information	98
% grads employed ten months out	82
Median starting salary	$50,000
% job accepting grads providing useable salary information	61
# employed full-time	80
# employed part-time	13
# employed bar required	54
# employed JD preferred	26
# employed professional/other	9
# employed non-professional	4
# pursuing advanced degree	2
# unemployed and seeking employment	14
# not seeking employment	1
% grads employed by school	3
State for bar exam	CT, NY, NJ, MA, RI
Pass rate for first-time bar	86.0

Prominent Alumni
Melanie Schnoll-Begun '94, Alan Abramason '85, Christa Dommers '97, Betty Ryberg '94, Joseph Tacopina '95

Grads Employed by Field (%)
Academic (4)
Business/Industry (25)
Government (15)
Judicial Clerkship (3)
Federal: (0)
State or local: (3)
Private Practice (48)
Solo: (0)
2-10: (18)
11-25: (7)
26-50: (6)
51-100: (4)
101-250: (3)
251-500: (0)
501+: (0)
Size Unknown: (1)
Public Interest (2)

REGENT UNIVERSITY
SCHOOL OF LAW

INSTITUTIONAL INFORMATION

Public/private	Private
Affiliation	Nondenominational
Student-faculty ratio	15:1
% faculty part-time	0
% faculty female	35
% faculty underrepresented minority	15
Total faculty	26

SURVEY SAYS...

Abundant externship/internship/ clerkship opportunities, Law school well run, Conservative students, Strong sense of community

STUDENTS

Enrollment of law school	312
% male/female	47/53
% part-time	8
% underrepresented minority	25
% international	<1
Average age of entering class	26

ACADEMICS

Academic Experience Rating	**85**
Profs interesting rating	95
Profs accessible rating	94
Hours of study per day	5.01

Academic Specialties

Constitutional, Human Rights, International, Labor

Advanced Degrees Offered

LLM American Legal Studies, 1yr. LLM in Human Rights, 1yr.

Combined Degrees Offered

JD/MBA 4yrs; JD/MA in Management 4yrs; JD/MA in Communication 4yrs; JD/MA in Journalism 4yrs; JD/MA in Counseling 4yrs; JD/MA in Divinity 4yr; JD/MDiv 4–5yrs; JD/MA in Government 4yrs

Academics

Tucked away in beautiful Virginia Beach, Regent University is molding the next generation of Christian lawyers and legal scholars. The program works diligently to maintain "a good sense of community" and the school as a whole feels "very cohesive." Academically, Regent places "a strong emphasis on legal research and writing." And while the course is "extremely rigorous and challenging," students admit they find it "incredibly useful" as they begin to tackle summer internships. Additionally, Regent boasts "first-class" moot court and ADR facilities. Even better; the "buildings and grounds are beautiful" to boot!

Moreover, Regent manages to attract some stellar professors. The vast majority are "very engaging in the classroom and are always available for one-on-one discussions." One third-year student agrees, remarking that "accessibility" is a common attribute of the faculty here. Indeed, "each professor, including the Dean, leaves their door open and students drop by all the time." Many professors also come to the classroom armed with "practical legal experience" which helps students thoroughly understand how to apply legal concepts within real-world settings. Students also greatly appreciate that professors use "multiple teaching techniques, methods and forms of evaluation."

Beyond the classroom, the "research librarians are always helpful with journal work and general library questions." As a pleased third-year shares, "They demonstrated a knowledge and skill in research I have never seen before." Another 3L expounds, "The law library staff is a tremendous help in guiding students to the right resources using Westlaw, Lexis, Bloomberg, and online resources like Google scholar. And the interlibrary loan program is extraordinarily helpful and fast when working on journal related items." However, some students do bemoan the fact that the law library is simply "the third floor of the general school library." This results in students frequently having to deal with loud, boisterous undergraduates.

By and large, students also speak highly of the "very nice" Career Services. The office "regularly hold[s] events and [counselors] are always willing to meet with you regarding internships, résumés, cover letters, etc." They also "active[ly] provide students with opportunities to network." However, a first-year does caution that "they are extremely busy and you must book about two weeks in advance."

Finally, the "great" administration continually proves themselves to be "very responsive to students' needs." Generally, Regent's administrators are "well organized," "provide clear, succinct communication" and offer many "opportunities for student feedback." Overall, "the people who comprise the Regent School of Law make attending law school an absolute pleasure. The school embraces a motto "iron sharpening iron" as it seeks to fulfill a mission of service and leadership in the practice of law."

Jᴀᴍᴇꜱ E. Mᴜʀᴘʜʏ, Iɴᴛᴇʀɪᴍ Aꜱꜱɪꜱᴛᴀɴᴛ Dᴇᴀɴ ᴏꜰ Aᴅᴍɪꜱꜱɪᴏɴꜱ
1000 Rᴇɢᴇɴᴛ Uɴɪᴠᴇʀꜱɪᴛʏ Dʀɪᴠᴇ, Rᴏʙᴇʀᴛꜱᴏɴ Hᴀʟʟ, Vɪʀɢɪɴɪᴀ Bᴇᴀᴄʜ, VA 23464
Tᴇʟ: 757-352-4584 • Fᴀx: 757-352-4139
E-Mᴀɪʟ: ʟᴀᴡꜱᴄʜᴏᴏʟ@ʀᴇɢᴇɴᴛ.ᴇᴅᴜ • Wᴇʙꜱɪᴛᴇ: ᴡᴡᴡ.ʀᴇɢᴇɴᴛ.ᴇᴅᴜ/ʟᴀᴡ

Life

An atmosphere of compassion and camaraderie certainly permeate Regent's campus. Indeed, it's truly evident that the "faculty and administration genuinely care about student success in the classroom as well as success in the future and in their personal lives." This definitely extends to the student body as well. As one third-year shares, "It's amazing how people pull together to help others whether it's related to school work or a personal issue." A pleased first-year pipes in, "Students are not at each other's throats[; instead] there is an atmosphere of teamwork and community for collective learning. Law school is stressful enough, but at Regent you have a village to support you." Additionally, the law school really "encourages personal development in scholarship, leadership, moral character formation, and skills practice." Therefore, not surprisingly, "opportunities for skills development, and exposure to guest speakers including state, federal, and community leadership" abound.

Getting In

Certainly, the admissions committee at Regent University's School of Law takes the typical factors into account. So, you can rest assured your undergraduate GPA and LSAT score will be closely considered. However, beyond the standard facets, Regent is also deeply interested in each candidate's relationship to his/her faith. Admissions officers favor applicants who are committed to incorporating Christian principles into their practice of law.

Clinical program required	No
Legal writing course requirement	Yes
Legal methods course requirement	Yes
Legal research course requirement	Yes
Moot court requirement	Yes
Public interest law requirement	No

ADMISSIONS

Selectivity Rating	81
# applications received	570
% applicants accepted	51
% acceptees attending	36
Average LSAT	153
Median LSAT	152
LSAT Range (25th to 75th percentile)	148–156
Average undergrad GPA	3.26
Median undergrad GPA	3.23
Application fee	$50
Regular application deadline	7/1
Early application deadline	2/1
Transfer students accepted	Yes
Evening division offered	Yes
Part-time accepted	Yes
CAS accepted	Yes

International Students

TOEFL required of international students.	Yes

FINANCIAL FACTS

Annual tuition	$34,200
Books and supplies	$1,500
Fees	$640
Room & Board	$17,745
Financial aid application deadline	7/1
% first-year students receiving some sort of aid	100
% all students receiving some sort of aid	100
% of aid that is merit based	100
% receiving scholarships	100
Average grant	$14,712

EMPLOYMENT INFORMATION

Career Rating	80	
Total 2014 JD Grads	122	
% for whom you have useable information	93	
% grads employed ten months out	80	
Median starting salary	$51,000	
# employed full-time	83	
# employed part-time	15	
# employed bar required	64	
# employed JD preferred	24	
# employed professional/other	2	
# employed non-professional	8	
# pursuing advanced degree	1	
# unemployed and seeking employment	12	
# not seeking employment	3	
% grads employed by school	1	
State for bar exam	VA, CA, TX, FL, NY	
Pass rate for first-time bar	75.7	

Prominent Alumni
Joe Migliozzi, Norfolk Circuit Court Judge; Scott Dupont, North Carolina Circiut Court Judge; Ron Pahl, Oregon Circuit Court Judge; Teresa Hammons, Virginia Beach General District Court Judge

Grads Employed by Field (%)
Academic (2)
Business/Industry (20)
Government (11)
Judicial Clerkship (8)
  Federal: (4)
  State or local: (4)
Private Practice (24)
  Solo: (3)
  2-10: (16)
  11-25: (1)
  251-500: (1)
  Size Unknown: (3)
Public Interest (7)

ROGER WILLIAMS UNIVERSITY
SCHOOL OF LAW

INSTITUTIONAL INFORMATION

Public/private	Private
Affiliation	No Affiliation
Student-faculty ratio	13:1
% faculty part-time	55
% faculty female	41
% faculty underrepresented minority	7
Total faculty	56

SURVEY SAYS...

Great research resources, Abundant externship/internship/clerkship opportunities

STUDENTS

Enrollment of law school	370
% male/female	52/48
% from out-of-state	69
% part-time	0
% underrepresented minority	22
% international	0
# of countries represented	2
Average age of entering class	25

ACADEMICS

Academic Experience Rating	**77**
Profs interesting rating	92
Profs accessible rating	94
Hours of study per day	5.16

Academic Specialties

Civil Procedure, Commercial, Constitutional, Criminal, Environmental, Human Rights, International, Property, Taxation, Intellectual Property

Advanced Degrees Offered

JD 3 yrs full-time

Combined Degrees Offered

JD/MMA Masters Marine Affairs, 3.5 yrs; JD/MS Masters of Science in Labor Relations & Human Resources, 4 yrs; JD/MSCJ Masters of Criminal Justice, 3.5 yrs. JD/MS Historic Preservation, 4 yrs.

Academics

Rhode Island may only have one law school in the state, but the stellar faculty and strong academics of the student body, make Roger Williams an impressive law school to attend. The small size draws students in, who are comforted "that everybody knows your name, whether it's a librarian, your professor, or the dean." Students are "encouraged to practice conscious lawyering" and the coursework is "innovative and creative." Students have access to "experiential learning opportunities" and professors work to create "a name and legacy." Roger Williams' students brag that the faculty helps students "succeed in a personalized manner. They take the time to get to know you and truly understand your idea of law."

The professors are just a small part of what makes Roger Williams so successful. Students get to meet "with the hiring partners of the biggest law firms in Providence," and RWU makes sure their students are ready for careers once they graduate. As one student told us, "Every student is guaranteed at least one semester of clinic or externship placement, if they choose, and students are able to spend a full semester in practice through these programs."

Every law school is constantly improving and Roger Williams is no different. Students say that the school can do more to "improve diversity in opinion . . . that not only promotes healthy debate but encourages and integrates it into our learning." Other students mention they'd like "more diverse networking opportunities beyond the public interest realm." And, while one student mentions the program is "on the forefront of ethnic diversity," others say the school should "become more open about addressing diversity in the classroom as well as in the real world."

Many students mention the Marine Affairs Institute as another huge help in creating positive experiences and opportunities for students. The school has "a strong relationship with NOAA (National Oceanic and Atmospheric Association), where they reserve one internship with their general counsel for a RWU student." Roger Williams also connects to other schools: "There is an option to get a dual degree with a JD and a Masters of Marine Affairs from the University of Rhode Island." This expands student options, so they can be more experienced lawyers, or continue work in law-adjacent fields.

Roger Williams is "very public interest oriented, so it is refreshing to be in an environment that is dedicated to 'giving back.'" The Feinstein Center is also a great way for students to "explore options in public interest law and helps to facilitate a student's interest in the field." Many students also talk about the stellar Financial Aid department, which is "straightforward and dedicated to helping us find ways to pay for our education."

MICHAEL DONNELLY-BOYLEN, ASSISTANT DEAN OF ADMISSIONS
10 METACOM AVENUE, BRISTOL, RI 02809-5171
TEL: 401-254-4555 • FAX: 401-254-4516
E-MAIL: ADMISSIONS@LAW.RWU.EDU • WEBSITE: LAW.RWU.EDU

Life

Students enjoy Bristol, Rhode Island's "relaxing" and "beautiful view[s]." "RWU is in a great location . . . close to several high profile law schools, the local bar association" and the "opportunity to bring big name speakers to our campus, such as U.S. Supreme Court justices, and international speakers." The city allows easy access to Boston as well as Providence. Even so, one student told us "having a car is definitely an advantage" to travel to other cities, and another student mentioned the law school should simply relocate to the capital.

A few other students point out that a social divide seems to appear between liberal and conservative students: "It's a very liberal leaning school, far beyond the average, which provides great camaraderie for those on the left but not so much on the right." Some students are concerned about how money is allocated, since they feel "the law school societies no longer have available student funds," but another student simply mentions that before, "there was free pizza everywhere." Over thirty campus clubs are assets to students who say they "want our peers to emerge as our colleagues and we are encouraged to have amicable relationships with each other."

Getting In

Roger Williams demands excellence from its students and accepts many of its applicants. The Admissions Office makes offers based on LSAT scores, GPAs, letters of recommendation, and personal essays. The median GPA for the incoming class in Fall 2014 was 3.2, and the median LSAT score was 148.

Clinical program required	No
Legal writing course requirement	Yes
Legal methods course requirement	Yes
Legal research course requirement	Yes
Moot court requirement	Yes
Public interest law requirement	Yes

ADMISSIONS

Selectivity Rating	73
# applications received	957
% applicants accepted	72
% acceptees attending	20
Average LSAT	149
Median LSAT	148
LSAT Range (25th to 75th percentile)	145–152
Average undergrad GPA	3.15
Median undergrad GPA	3.15
Application fee	$60
Regular application deadline	4/1
Transfer students accepted	Yes
Evening division offered	No
Part-time accepted	No
CAS accepted	Yes

International Students

TOEFL required of international students.	Yes

FINANCIAL FACTS

Annual tuition	$33,792
Books and supplies	$1,500
Fees	$730
Room & Board (on/ off campus)	$17,316/$15,886
Financial aid application deadline	3/31
% first-year students receiving some sort of aid	99
% all students receiving some sort of aid	94
% of aid that is merit based	25
% receiving scholarships	55
Average grant	$18,836
Average loan	$20,723
Average total aid package	$55,712
Average debt	$128,543

EMPLOYMENT INFORMATION

Career Rating	81	**Prominent Alumni**
Total 2014 JD Grads	173	Eugene Bernardo, Partner, Partridge Snow
% for whom you have useable information	94	Hahn LLP, Providence, RI; Peter Kilmartin, RI Attorney General, Providence, RI; Lucy
% grads employed ten months out	73	Holmes Plovnick, Partner, Mitchell
Median starting salary	$49,960	Silberberg & Knupp LLP, Washington DC
# employed full-time	107	**Grads Employed by Field (%)**
# employed part-time	12	Academic (2)
# employed bar required	88	Business/Industry (21)
# employed JD preferred	20	Government (8)
# employed professional/other	16	Judicial Clerkship (8)
# employed non-professional	3	State or local: (8)
# pursuing advanced degree	4	Private Practice (32)
# unemployed and seeking employment	24	Solo: (2)
# not seeking employment	4	2-10: (20)
State for bar exam	MA	11-25: (5)
Pass rate for first-time bar	80.0	26-50: (2)
		51-100: (2)
		101-250: (0)
		251-500: (1)
		501+: (1)
		Size Unknown: (0)
		Public Interest (3)

RUTGERS, THE STATE UNIVERSITY OF NEW JERSEY—CAMDEN
SCHOOL OF LAW

INSTITUTIONAL INFORMATION
Public/private	Public
Student-faculty ratio	7:1
% faculty part-time	30
% faculty female	48
% faculty underrepresented minority	7
Total faculty	71

SURVEY SAYS...
Abundant externship/internship/ clerkship opportunities

STUDENTS
Enrollment of law school	501
% male/female	66/34
% part-time	17
% underrepresented minority	21
% international	0
# of countries represented	2
Average age of entering class	25

ACADEMICS
Academic Experience Rating	**86**
Profs interesting rating	81
Profs accessible rating	75
Hours of study per day	3.68

Academic Specialties
Commercial, Constitutional, Criminal, Environmental, Human Rights, International, Labor, Intellectual Property

Combined Degrees Offered
JD/MBA, School of Business-Camden or Rutgers Business School: Graduate Programs-Newark and New Brunswick; JD/Master of City and Regional Planning, Edward J. Bloustein School of Planning and Public Policy; JD/MSW, School of Social Work; JD/Master of Public Affairs and Politics, Edward J. Bloustein School of Planning and Public Policy; JD/MPA, Graduate School-Camden; JD/MPH, Rutgers Biomedical and Health Sciences-School of Public Health; JD/MD, Rutgers Biomedical and Health

Academics

If going to law school gives you the jitters, your fears will quickly be assuaged at Rutgers, The State University of New Jersey—Camden School of Law. Sure, just like other prestigious JD programs, Rutgers will treat you to a dose of the "Socratic thunderstorm approach," and there is the typical "never-ending workload" throughout the first year. However, Rutgers maintains a remarkably friendly and supportive academic environment. Students insist, "First-year classes don't intimidate you, as there's no fear of speaking your mind in class, and diversity in thinking is highly encouraged." Outside the classroom, Rutgers professors are personable, to say the least: "Every Wednesday afternoon, there's a veritable party in our torts professor's office during his office hours. So many students go to discuss both academic and non-textbook-related topics that there aren't enough chairs and people sit on the floor," recalls one 2L. In fact, "it's common for professors to take students out to lunch, to conferences, and even to show up at student-sponsored pub crawls." The administration draws similar praise from students, who believe it "tries to be very open-door and available for anything we could possibly need." A 1L jokes, "I came to Rutgers expecting to witness students getting 'burned' by professors every day in class. Instead the only burn I got was on the roof of my mouth while eating pizza with the dean."

Students are impressed with the caliber of the Rutgers faculty, describing them as "knowledgeable and passionate about their subjects" and able pedagogues to boot. In the lecture hall, "the faculty is as intelligent as they are witty. Anecdotes from [their] real-world experiences are common in the classroom and make some of the drudgery more interesting." Many also point out the strength of the adjunct staff, who "come from varied fields, providing a unique and practical perspective to current topics." Indeed, a practical approach is emphasized at Rutgers, and classes may even include "spontaneous field trips to the federal courthouse across the street from the campus just so we can view real-world motions to dismiss, jury selection, and final arguments." The school's active alumni network is also called on to contribute to the JD experience, and students tell us that "in many courses, alumni return to give lectures on the practical aspects of the subject, and they have been willing to assist any student [who] has a question."

Among the greatest perks of Rutgers—Camden is its low tuition, offering a "fantastic and highly respected education at a very reasonable price." As a result, students do not experience the financial anxiety common to law students today. "Due to a scholarship and a summer internship at a Philadelphia law firm," reports one 2L, "I will graduate with a top-rate legal education and virtually no debt. That combination is hard to beat, and I expect it will free up my career options considerably."

The school takes advantage of the resources in the surrounding community to instruct students in the playing out of law in the real world. "The federal courthouse is literally around the corner, the county courthouse a couple of blocks [away]," and Rutgers students "have tremendous access to the judges in the area and several teach as adjuncts." Students also praise the fact that "the law school is very involved in the community through its pro bono clinics."

Rutgers is "located close to Philly, Trenton, and New York, so there are plenty of job opportunities." On that note, "Career Services are always on the job helping students get placed for both summer and permanent positions. They also expose students to the different options available to attorneys by having guests come to the law school to provide experiences in different areas." Rutgers is somewhat unique among law schools in that almost half of the graduating class takes judicial clerkship positions, more students than those who take positions in private practice.

Ass. Director Maureen O'Boyle, Assistant Director of Admissions
406 Penn Street, 3rd floor, Camden, NJ 08102
Tel: 800-466-7561 • Fax: 856-225-6537
E-Mail: admissions@camlaw.rutgers.edu • Website: www.camden.rutgers.edu

Life

Attracting students from all across the nation and the world, the Rutgers student body is "extremely diverse in all aspects, including gender, socioeconomics, age, and interests." On this multicultural campus "there is an organization for just about any interest a person may have, [and] the SBA and other clubs do a great job of providing numerous social functions nearly every week." A 2L explains, "The environment is positive and students are involved with the school. Whether it be moot court, law journals, or politics, students are engaged in society and provide for a very strong sense of community." Off campus, "people are always looking to get together to study or to just go out socially," though most prefer hanging out in Philly to hitting the bars in the surrounding town of Camden. While some describe Camden as "the pit of despair," others tell us that "the waterfront on both sides of the Delaware River is beautiful." In addition, many appreciate the fact that "Philadelphia is exactly a mile away and provides for plenty of social opportunities."

Students warn that there are "a handful of students who are hell-bent on getting a certain GPA." Most, however, value kindness and cooperation over competition. A 3L explains, "My school is both cooperative and competitive. Students here care deeply about being successful, but everyone is quick to lend a hand to bring someone else along for the ride." Indeed, many students praise the fact that "you can always find a good conversation outside after class."

Getting In

The Law school recognizes that the LSAT and UGPA may not be the best predictors of success in law school and the legal profession for all applicants. Therefore, approximately one-fourth of the class is admitted based on other factors, including educational and employment experience, leadership ability, maturity, a history of overcoming disadvantage, extraordinary accomplishment or success in a previous career. For other prospective students, the admissions process is standard fare: Rutgers admits student who have demonstrated a high level of academic achievement, as well as strong standardized test scored.

Sciences, length varies; JD/MA in Philosophy, Rutgers-New Brunswick Department of Philosophy.

Clinical program required	No
Legal writing course requirement	Yes
Legal methods course requirement	Yes
Legal research course requirement	Yes
Moot court requirement	Yes
Public interest law requirement	No

ADMISSIONS

Selectivity Rating	85
# applications received	1,233
% applicants accepted	42
% acceptees attending	35
Average LSAT	155
Median LSAT	155
LSAT Range (25th to 75th percentile)	152–158
Average undergrad GPA	3.18
Median undergrad GPA	3.23
Application fee	$65
Early application deadline	4/15
Early application notification	4/15
Transfer students accepted	Yes
Evening division offered	Yes
Part-time accepted	Yes
CAS accepted	Yes

International Students
TOEFL required of international students.   Yes

FINANCIAL FACTS

Annual tuition (in-state/ out-of-state)	$23,201/$35,168
Books and supplies	$1,350
Fees	$2,989
Room & Board (on/ off campus)	$12,750/$18,090
Financial aid application deadline	8/9
% all students receiving some sort of aid	71
% of aid that is merit based	38
% receiving scholarships	43
Average grant	$12,335
Average loan	$33,117
Average total aid package	$37,333
Average debt	$91,223

EMPLOYMENT INFORMATION

		Grads Employed by Field (%)
Career Rating	84	Academic (1)
Total 2014 JD Grads	296	Business/Industry (11)
% for whom you have useable information	98	Government (3)
% grads employed ten months out	81	Judicial Clerkship (36)
Median starting salary	$46,096	Federal: (3)
# employed full-time	224	State or local: (33)
# employed part-time	17	Private Practice (29)
# employed bar required	200	Solo: (1)
# employed JD preferred	24	2-10: (16)
# employed professional/other	15	11-25: (1)
# employed non-professional	2	26-50: (2)
# pursuing advanced degree	9	51-100: (2)
# unemployed and seeking employment	34	101-250: (2)
# not seeking employment	7	251-500: (2)
State for bar exam	NJ	501+: (3)
Pass rate for first-time bar	83.8	Public Interest (1)

Rutgers, The State University of New Jersey—Newark
School of Law

Academics

According to students, the Rutgers School of Law in Newark "is more than a law school; it is a family." As a public university, Rutgers offers in-state tuition to New Jersey residents, and students say that "the school prepares [us] as well as the highest ranking law schools in the country." "The reputation Rutgers carries in the tri-state area, and especially in New Jersey, is outstanding. I am proud to tell people where I go to law school." The location is an unparalleled draw in terms of potential employment prospects, as it "provides a great opportunity for students to see Federal and State courts in action. There is no shortage of opportunity for the student in Newark ranging from prestigious private firms to branches of the state and federal government." Newark itself doesn't draw the biggest raves, with some students citing "public safety concerns" around the university, but this is outweighed by the legal market in the tri-state area and the fact that "the school has a great reputation in New Jersey." Students praise wide range of courses available at RU–N, saying that "it's a struggle every semester to pick my classes because there are just so many options." One of the school's greatest strength's "is the emphasis on real world practice skills" and students emphasize that RU–N is "very big on providing students with practical experience," saying that "the clinic program is very good," and it "seems to be expanding." "Rutgers is known for public interest" and one student elaborates that the school's "huge commitment to public interest law . . . shows in the public interest backgrounds of the professors, the school's curriculum, and the various programs and community engagement opportunities that are coordinated by the school."

Professors at RU–N are a "great mix" of those from "a traditional academic background and also adjunct faculty with strong backgrounds in practicing law." Students say that "it is easy to get to know your professors, and everyone is approachable and supportive." Of course, "there are some bad professors just like anywhere else," but others stand out, in particular one professor's "knowledge and passion for the 4th Amendment in his Criminal Procedure class has made it my favorite subject and strengthened my dream of being a criminal prosecutor." Students generally praise RU–N's "exceptionally diverse faculty who are committed to teaching and their students." "Whether it be extended office hours, staying late after class . . . the faculty aims for the success of the students." The administration, on the other hand, does not earn such high praise, with students noting that it "takes forever to post grades, which puts the students at a disadvantage when applying for jobs that have hard deadlines" and "the administration can be a bit slow in sending notifications (about class registration and school closings)." But one student highlights the strengths of the school's administration, saying, "I am a student veteran and the school's coordination with the VA has been flawless thus far. Additionally, the administration and professors have been very attentive and responsive during a recent family emergency." When it comes to facilities, students note that "the library is public, so it can be difficult to compete for study space with the undergraduates and general public that come in" and when it comes to aesthetics, "the school and library look like what they are—public facilities." But "the library staff will bend over backwards to help you with research and we also have access to all Rutgers libraries via interlibrary loan services and online journal subscriptions."

ANITA WALTON, ASSISTANT DEAN FOR ADMISSIONS
CENTER FOR LAW AND JUSTICE, 123 WASHINGTON STREET, NEWARK, NJ 07102
TEL: 973-353-5554 • FAX: 973-353-3459
E-MAIL: LAWINFO@ANDROMEDA.RUTGERS.EDU • WEBSITE: LAW.NEWARK.RUTGERS.EDU

Student Life

"The diversity of our law school cannot be beat," one student tells us, while another echoes, "The things I love the most about this school are the racial and cultural diversity of the student body and faculty, the school's focus on public interest and giving back to communities." There is a "supportive community atmosphere" on campus and "the Minority Student Program (MSP) is also one of the school's greatest strengths, providing students with a close-knit network of students and alumni that are eager to help one another and make law school the meaningful experience it should be."

Getting In

Admitted students have LSAT scores between 153 and 159, and an approximate undergraduate GPA of 3.30. RU–N does a rolling admissions program, so it's to a student's advantage to apply early.

Clinical program required	No
Legal writing course requirement	Yes
Legal methods course requirement	Yes
Legal research course requirement	Yes
Moot court requirement	Yes
Public interest law requirement	No

ADMISSIONS

Selectivity Rating	84
# applications received	1,710
% applicants accepted	44
% acceptees attending	25
Average LSAT	156
Median LSAT	156
LSAT Range (25th to 75th percentile)	153–159
Average undergrad GPA	3.30
Median undergrad GPA	3.33
Application fee	$65
Regular application deadline	3/15
Transfer students accepted	Yes
Evening division offered	Yes
Part-time accepted	Yes
CAS accepted	Yes

FINANCIAL FACTS

Annual tuition (in-state/ out-of-state)	$22,746/$34,478
Books and supplies	$1,550
Fees	$2,711
Room & Board (on/ off campus)	$13,022/$17,194
Financial aid application deadline	3/15
% all students receiving some sort of aid	98
% of aid that is merit based	9
% receiving scholarships	38
Average grant	$8,319
Average loan	$30,090
Average total aid package	$29,687
Average debt	$89,417

EMPLOYMENT INFORMATION

Career Rating	87	**Prominent Alumni**
Total 2014 JD Grads	270	Robert Menendez, US Senator; Jaynee
% grads employed ten months out	87	LaVecchia, NJ State Supreme Court
Median starting salary	$55,316	Justice; Louis Freeh, Former FBI Director;
# employed full-time	209	Virginia Long, NJ State Supreme Court
# employed part-time	26	Justice
# employed bar required	163	**Grads Employed by Field (%)**
# employed JD preferred	38	Academic (3)
# employed professional/other	32	Business/Industry (19)
# employed non-professional	2	Government (7)
# pursuing advanced degree	2	Judicial Clerkship (25)
# unemployed and seeking employment	18	Private Practice (31)
# not seeking employment	4	Public Interest (2)
% grads employed by school	3	
State for bar exam	NJ, NY, PA	
Pass rate for first-time bar	81.0	

SAINT LOUIS UNIVERSITY
SCHOOL OF LAW

INSTITUTIONAL INFORMATION

Public/private	Private
Affiliation	Roman Catholic
Student-faculty ratio	13:1
% faculty part-time	0
% faculty female	55
% faculty underrepresented minority	8
Total faculty	61

SURVEY SAYS...

Students love St. Louis, MO, Great research resources, Abundant externship/internship/clerkship opportunities

STUDENTS

Enrollment of law school	165
% male/female	54/46
% from out-of-state	47
% part-time	8
% underrepresented minority	13
% international	0
# of countries represented	1
Average age of entering class	25

ACADEMICS

Academic Experience Rating	**82**
Profs interesting rating	75
Profs accessible rating	83
Hours of study per day	2.82

Academic Specialties

Criminal, Environmental, International, Labor, Property, Taxation, Intellectual Property

Advanced Degrees Offered

LLM Health Law, 1 yr full-time, 2 yrs part-time; LLM for Foreign Lawyers, 1 yr full-time

Combined Degrees Offered

JD/MBA, 3.5 yrs; JD/MA in Public Administration, 4 yrs; JD/M.H.A., 4 yrs; JD/MPH, 4 yrs, JD/PhD in Health Care Ethics, 4–6 yrs; JD/MSW, 4 yrs; JD/MA in Sociology and anthropology, 4 yrs; JD/MA in Public Health-Health Policy, 4 yrs; JD/MA Accounting 4 yrs; JD/MS in Health Outcomes Research & Evaluation Sciences, 4 yrs

Academics

Not only do students at the Saint Louis University School of Law say the school's plum new downtown Saint Louis location is unbeatable, but "the opportunities for practical experience at SLU Law make it so that we are part of the legal community before we even graduate." Says one grateful student, "I truly feel like each professor wants great success for each student. They believe in us and want to help equip is with the best skills for the real world." The diverse curriculum at SLU Law is designed to prepare students for all areas of legal practice. After the first thirty hours of required core curriculum, where students are introduced to the building blocks of law and develop basic legal analysis, upperclassmen are able to essentially design their own curriculum from a wide variety of courses that include specialized offerings and foundational bar preparation courses. In addition, students have the option of pursuing a concentration in specialized areas such as employment law, health law, intellectual property law, or urban development, land use and environmental law. Notes one student, the "Health Law program has a national reputation that makes it easy to find a health law position" after graduation. Qualified students also have the opportunity to write and edit for one of SLU Law's three prestigious law journals. SLU Law also offers a part-time JD program for working adults.

When it comes to the Saint Louis community, students say that "our professors are active in legal issues throughout the St. Louis area and their ideas are invaluable in community discourse. It is a great feeling to attend and work with faculty and students so involved and respected in the area." Not only that, "[we] can walk across the street and watch a trial in their free time" at the civil courthouse, and "the criminal and federal courthouses are less than a quarter mile away." When it comes to connecting with SLU Law alumni, "SLU has a good reputation in the St. Louis area and it is great at providing information and networking events that connect you with the alumni." One student points out that SLU Law "seems to be doubted for academic quality because of the rankings and the fact that a top 20 law school [Washington University] is the other school in the city;" rankings aside, students say they "wish people could now take the opportunity to see how awesome [SLU Law] is."

The professors at SLU Law "are overall great, and class sizes makes professors accessible. They are always willing to help students outside of the classroom." The fact that "teachers and faculty know virtually everyone working the St. Louis legal community" leads to "introductions" and "internships." Students appreciate that "practically ever professor has practiced law before becoming an academic, so they know what to teach you to be successful. They train lawyers not professors, unlike many elite schools." Unlike at many law schools, students say that on the whole "the administration staff, including career services, are excellent" and that "since the first day that I interacted with SLU Law administration and faculty, I have always felt welcomed and that they had an open door for me, whatever the issue." Some wish, however, that "the Career Services office would be more useful if it gave equal attention to all students regardless of class rank." Others add that, in the current economy, it might be beneficial for the Career Services office to "provide more resources for alternative career paths for law graduates." In terms of facilities, students say, "The modernization at the school is unbelievable and really maximizes the learning experience."

MICHAEL J. KOLNIK, ESQ., ASSISTANT DEAN AND DIRECTOR OF ADMISSIONS
100 NORTH TUCKER BLVD (AS OF AUGUST 1, 2013), ST. LOUIS, MO 63101
TEL: 314-977-2800 • FAX: 314-977-1464
EMAIL: ADMISSIONS@LAW.SLU.EDU • WEBSITE: LAW.SLU.EDU

Student Life

Students value the "sense of community" at SLU Law, saying the school "is like a mini community where everyone knows everyone and wants them all to succeed." SLU Law "fosters a sense of unity among students from the beginning, which makes the transition to law school a lot easier. Students will share outlines with each other, study together, and create lasting friendships." This isn't a "a crazy competitive school—nobody hides books in the library." In terms of finding activities on campus, "SLU Law's student organizations do a great job at facilitating social events outside of the law school. There is always something going on, or something to look forward to."

Getting In

SLU Law receives roughly 850 applications and makes admission offers to approximately 525 students. Admitted students at the 25th percentile have an approximate GPA of 3.19 and an LSAT score of 151. Admitted students at the 75th percentile have roughly a 3.65 GPA and an LSAT score of 158.

Clinical program required	No
Legal writing course requirement	Yes
Legal methods course requirement	No
Legal research course requirement	Yes
Moot court requirement	No
Public interest law requirement	No

ADMISSIONS

Selectivity Rating	**82**
# applications received	808
% applicants accepted	63
% acceptees attending	32
Average LSAT	155
Median LSAT	155
LSAT Range (25th to 75th percentile)	151–159
Average undergrad GPA	3.45
Median undergrad GPA	3.47
Application fee	$55
Regular application deadline	5/1
Transfer students accepted	Yes
Evening division offered	Yes
Part-time accepted	Yes
CAS accepted	Yes

International Students

TOEFL required of international students.

FINANCIAL FACTS

Annual tuition	$37,990
Books and supplies	$1,500
Fees	$445
Room & Board	$10,380
% first-year students receiving some sort of aid	97
% all students receiving some sort of aid	91
% receiving scholarships	84
Average grant	$19,449
Average loan	$35,679
Average total aid package	$44,657
Average debt	$128,764

EMPLOYMENT INFORMATION

Career Rating	**79**	**Prominent Alumni**
Total 2014 JD Grads	267	Gary Rutledge, Vice President, Secretary
% grads employed ten months out	88	and General Counsel of Anheuser-Busch
# employed full-time	235	Companies Inc.; Francis G. Slay, Mayor,
# employed part-time	8	City of St. Louis; Kevin O'Malley, U.S.
# employed bar required	178	Ambassador to Ireland; Keith Ebling,
# employed JD preferred	44	Executive Vice President & General
# employed professional/other	11	Counsel, Express Scripts
# employed non-professional	1	**Grads Employed by Field (%)**
# pursuing advanced degree	6	Business/Industry (19)
# unemployed and seeking employment	20	Government (12)
		Judicial Clerkship (2)
# not seeking employment	7	Private Practice (49)
% grads employed by school	0	Public Interest (3)
State for bar exam	MO	
Pass rate for first-time bar	91.5	

SAMFORD UNIVERSITY
CUMBERLAND SCHOOL OF LAW

INSTITUTIONAL INFORMATION

Public/private	Private
Affiliation	Southern Baptist
Student-faculty ratio	18:1
% faculty part-time	56
% faculty female	29
% faculty underrepresented minority	17
Total faculty	52

SURVEY SAYS...

Students love Birmingham, AL, Diverse opinions accepted in classrooms, Great research resources, Law school well run, Conservative students, Strong sense of community

STUDENTS

Enrollment of law school	411
% male/female	57/43
% from out-of-state	44
% part-time	0
% underrepresented minority	10
% international	0
# of countries represented	1
Average age of entering class	24

ACADEMICS

Academic Experience Rating	83
Profs interesting rating	94
Profs accessible rating	96
Hours of study per day	3.99

Academic Specialties

Constitutional, Corporation Securities, Criminal, Environmental, International, Taxation, Intellectual Property, and Trial Advocacy.

Advanced Degrees Offered

Master of Comparative Law

Combined Degrees Offered

JD/Master of Accountancy, JD/MBA, JD/MDiv, JD/MPA, JD/MPH, JD/MS in Environmental Management, JD/MA in Theological Studies, and JD/MS in Bioethics: all 3.5–4 years. JD/MDiv, 5 yrs.

Academics

Students at Samford University's Cumberland School of Law say their school is "a little bit of a hidden gem" and "a great place to become a lawyer." The bar-passage rate is stellar. There are eight joint-degree programs and a "diverse array" of available courses. "Practical skills are the strength" here, though. The legal writing program is reportedly outstanding. Students have an "incredible amount of opportunity to get experience in trial competition." "As far as trial advocacy goes, you cannot find a better school in the country," vaunts a 3L. "Practicing litigation attorneys train students in specialized trial advocacy programs, and the trial teams consistently win major national tournaments." Externships and a wealth of community service programs also provide "unmatched" opportunities to gain practical experience.

Cumberland is a small school with small class sizes, and it is home to "a diverse faculty with impeccable credentials." The professors are "an amazing group." "There is always going to be that jerk who is a complete know-it-all and thinks he hung the moon in any law school," and Cumberland is no exception. As a rule, though, these professors are "extremely knowledgeable" and "hilarious yet simultaneously intimidating." They "have practice experience, which is helpful in class because it allows for personal experiences to be introduced," and they "emphasize what will actually be useful and necessary" when you are representing clients. "A wonderful open-door policy" is another plus. "Professors are willing to meet with students and discuss the subject matter at any point outside of class," and they "genuinely want to help students in whatever way they can." "I don't even know why they put 'office hours' in their syllabi," adds a happy 2L. Students also rave about their "hands-on," accessible, and "very personable" administration. "They actually know students' names and want to help." And if you want to "shoot the breeze" with the dean, you can.

Students report that "the campus is beautiful and is extremely convenient to all areas of Birmingham." The "comfortable" and "awesome" library is "a great place to study." "Also, the library resources are exceptional," and the librarians are "wonderful" if you are in a bind. However, the "outdated" classrooms aren't the greatest. They "can feel a little cramped," and they are "windowless." "In some ways, that is a good thing because it keeps you from getting distracted," explains a 1L. "The technology in the classrooms isn't the best," either.

Students are pretty satisfied with their career prospects, although the "extremely helpful" Career Development Office "could do a better job marketing the school's graduates outside of the Birmingham legal market," laments a 2L. "The alumni network of this school is incredible," beams a 2L. "Cumberland alums are always looking to hire the bright young Cumberland graduates. And if an alum can't help you out, they are always willing to refer you to someone who can."

KENNETH ENLAND, DIRECTOR OF ADMISSIONS AND ADMINISTRATION
800 LAKESHORE DRIVE, BIRMINGHAM, AL 35229
TEL: 205-726-2702 • FAX: 205-726-2057
E-MAIL: LAWADM@SAMFORD.EDU • WEBSITE: CUMBERLAND.SAMFORD.EDU

Life

Politically, liberals are seen occasionally, but the overall population leans "pretty far to the right." Academically, there may be "a behind-the-scenes competitiveness," but the atmosphere looks and feels "cooperative and collegial." "Most students are more than willing to help their classmates succeed."

Socially, Cumberland is a decidedly "Southern school." Hospitality is paramount, and "even the slightly awkward students are still warmly received." "There is a real community at Cumberland," relates a 2L. "We study together, hang out together, and have formed a tight bond with each other," adds another 2L. "There is a friendliness and warmth that you just won't find at other schools." "We interact with each other like friendly colleagues; we compete with each other like sibling rivals; and we support each other through the trials of life and death like family," reflects an already wistful 3L. "The school creates a 'work hard' culture but constantly has entertaining social events." Weekly bar reviews around the affordable, growing city of Birmingham are reportedly well attended. In the spring, Cumberland celebrates Rascal Day in honor of its long-deceased canine mascot from the 1930s. There's food and live music, and the dean and the school president lead a march through campus.

Getting In

Enrolled students at the 25th percentile at Cumberland have LSAT scores around 148 and GPAs at just about 2.88. At the 75th percentile, LSAT scores are approximately 154 and GPAs just about 3.5. If you want to get started on your law school career a few months early, Cumberland School of Law allows admitted students to take two law school electives during the summer before 1L courses begin.

Clinical program required	No
Legal writing course requirement	Yes
Legal methods course requirement	Yes
Legal research course requirement	No
Moot court requirement	Yes
Public interest law requirement	No

ADMISSIONS

Selectivity Rating	77
# applications received	688
% applicants accepted	76
% acceptees attending	28
Average LSAT	152
Median LSAT	151
LSAT Range (25th to 75th percentile)	148–154
Average undergrad GPA	3.20
Median undergrad GPA	3.38
Application fee	$50
Regular application deadline	7/1
Early application deadline	2/28
Transfer students accepted	Yes
Evening division offered	No
Part-time accepted	No
CAS accepted	Yes

International Students

TOEFL required of international students.	Yes

FINANCIAL FACTS

Annual tuition	$35,876
Books and supplies	$2,000
Room & Board (on/off campus)	$0/$13,500
Financial aid application deadline	3/1
% first-year students receiving some sort of aid	91
% all students receiving some sort of aid	87
% of aid that is merit based	92
% receiving scholarships	49
Average grant	$15,662
Average loan	$43,224
Average total aid package	$45,865
Average debt	$124,106

EMPLOYMENT INFORMATION

Career Rating	89	
Total 2014 JD Grads	136	
% for whom you have useable information	99	
% grads employed ten months out	80	
Median starting salary	$53,054	
# employed full-time	96	
# employed part-time	13	
# employed bar required	85	
# employed JD preferred	13	
# employed professional/other	4	
# employed non-professional	7	
# pursuing advanced degree	7	
# unemployed and seeking employment	14	
# not seeking employment	3	
State for bar exam	AL	
Pass rate for first-time bar	84.3	

Prominent Alumni
Charles J. Crist, Jr., Former Governor of Florida; Cordell Hull, Founder of United Nations; Howell E. Jackson, U.S. Supreme Court; Horace H. Lurton, U.S. Supreme Court

Grads Employed by Field (%)
Business/Industry (24)
Government (10)
Judicial Clerkship (6)
Private Practice (55)
Public Interest (1)

SANTA CLARA UNIVERSITY
SCHOOL OF LAW

INSTITUTIONAL INFORMATION

Public/private	Private
Affiliation	Roman Catholic-Jesuit
Student-faculty ratio	12:1
% faculty part-time	36
% faculty female	50
% faculty underrepresented minority	21
Total faculty	66

SURVEY SAYS...

Students love Santa Clara, CA,
Diverse opinions accepted in
classrooms

STUDENTS

Enrollment of law school	880
% male/female	53/47
% part-time	21
% underrepresented minority	41
% international	4
# of countries represented	10
Average age of entering class	25

ACADEMICS

Academic Experience Rating	**75**
Profs interesting rating	79
Profs accessible rating	79
Hours of study per day	4.07

Academic Specialties

Constitutional, Criminal, Environmental, Human Rights, International, Labor, Taxation, Intellectual Property

Advanced Degrees Offered

LLM in U.S. Law for Foreign Lawyers, 1 yr. LLM in International and Comparative Law, 1 yr. LLM in Intellectual Property Law, 1–3 yrs

Combined Degrees Offered

JD/MBA, 3.5–4 yrs; JD/MSIS, 3.5–4 yrs

Academics

Jesuit-affiliated Santa Clara University School of Law "in the heart of Silicon Valley" is a smaller school that manages to offer "a wide range" of courses across a host of legal areas. As you would expect given the location, Santa Clara Law boasts "one of the top-ranking high-tech programs in the nation." The course work in patent and intellectual property law is "tremendous," and students regularly intern with "the vast array" of existing mammoth corporations as well as the next generation of mammoth corporations here "in the venture-capital capital of the country." The international law program is also extensive and "incredible." Study abroad opportunities are mind-blowing. There are a dozen different programs in twenty cities around the globe including—just to cite a few—Istanbul, Budapest, and Shanghai. In addition, there are several unique international judicial externships and international internships available. Still another perk here is the prominent focus on public interest and social justice law. SCU is teeming with institutes, centers, and programs that allow students to do "great things for people."

"Real-world experience" is one of the hallmarks of the professors at Santa Clara Law. "Some are brilliant savants, but you just can't learn from them." On the whole, though, faculty members are "top-notch," "dedicated to teaching," and "obviously committed to their students." Professors are "approachable" as well. They "really engage students" outside of class" "about their past experiences and future hopes." Administratively, lower-level staff can be "somewhat surly," and sometimes the decisions of the top brass "leave much to be desired," but the general consensus is that management is "extremely accommodating" and "very concerned with student feedback." "It would be difficult to find another law school that cares so much about [its] students and actually does something about it," beams a 1L.

Santa Clara's lush, "peaceful" campus is "simply gorgeous and kept very nicely." It's also home to some "great facilities." The law school facilities are pretty mundane, though. "The classrooms are classrooms," says a 3L. The law library is "certainly adequate," but it's "fairly depressing." It's "dark, and the temperature controls suck." On the bright side, the undergrad library "right next door" is "incredibly awesome," and it's a regular haunt for law students.

Santa Clara has a stellar reputation in the Bay Area, and career prospects are solid. More than 80 percent of all newly minted graduates head off to the private sector, where median starting salaries are very impressive. Quite a few students take jobs in Silicon Valley. San Francisco is another common destination. Santa Clara Law's "very accessible, passionate, successful, and helpful alumni network" is a huge advantage when students are looking for work. They are "very willing to give back to the school and provide advice and opportunities to current students." "Sometimes it feels like the entire community of attorneys in the South Bay graduated from Santa Clara," explains a 3L, "especially when it comes to district attorneys, public defenders, and judges." The alumni base and the SCU brand name aren't as strong nationally, though. "Nobody knows about it outside of the San Francisco area," laments another 3L.

JEANETTE J. LEACH, ASSISTANT DEAN FOR ADMISSIONS & FINANCIAL AID
500 EL CAMINO REAL, SANTA CLARA, CA 95053
TEL: 408-554-5048 • FAX: 408-554-7897
E-MAIL: LAWADMISSIONS@SCU.EDU • WEBSITE: LAW.SCU.EDU

Life

"The school's location allows it to attract a diverse group of highly educated students." In terms of ethnicity, Santa Clara Law is among the most diverse schools in the country. "Varying ages," radically different life experiences, and a solid geographic distribution also make for "a good mix." Academically, a few students "are jerks and should be quarantined," but "there usually is a positive vibe around the school." "It is a very welcoming environment that engenders very happy students." "We're a social tribe," explains a 1L. "We might be graded on a curve but you'd never know it from how everyone treats each other."

"Student life is collaborative." "There's a club or society for everything under the sun." "Stimulating" speakers including local corporate bigwigs are frequent, and "The school makes a real effort to engage its alumni and host events where students can meet them." "Social activities and opportunities for students to get together" are also commonplace. "We study hard, but we also go out a lot on the weekends and form some close-knit friendships," says a 3L. The cost of living in Silicon Valley is very high, and the city of Santa Clara is "decidedly not a college town." The locale is "green and sunny most of the year," though, and the Bay Area offers quite a bit to do. When students need a break from their casebooks or law school in general, heading up to San Francisco is pretty common.

Getting In

Enrolled full-time students at the 25th percentile have LSAT scores of 156 and grade point averages right around 3.02. At the 75th percentile, LSAT scores are 160 and GPAs are around 3.47. Stats for the part-time program are somewhat lower.

Clinical program required	No
Legal writing course requirement	Yes
Legal methods course requirement	Yes
Legal research course requirement	Yes
Moot court requirement	Yes
Public interest law requirement	No

ADMISSIONS

Selectivity Rating	83
# applications received	2,940
% applicants accepted	53
% acceptees attending	13
Average LSAT	158
Median LSAT	158
LSAT Range (25th to 75th percentile)	156–160
Average undergrad GPA	3.23
Median undergrad GPA	3.23
Application fee	$75
Regular application deadline	2/1
Early application deadline	11/1
Early application notification	12/20
Transfer students accepted	Yes
Evening division offered	Yes
Part-time accepted	Yes
CAS accepted	Yes

FINANCIAL FACTS

Annual tuition	$45,000
Books and supplies	$1,286
Room & Board	$14,582
Financial aid application deadline	2/1
% first-year students receiving some sort of aid	92
% all students receiving some sort of aid	87
% of aid that is merit based	94
% receiving scholarships	51
Average grant	$13,753
Average loan	$47,565
Average total aid package	$46,263
Average debt	$129,621

EMPLOYMENT INFORMATION

Career Rating	85
Total 2014 JD Grads	298
% grads employed ten months out	76
Median starting salary	$90,000
# employed full-time	179
# employed part-time	46
# employed bar required	154
# employed JD preferred	60
# employed professional/other	4
# employed non-professional	7
# pursuing advanced degree	4
# unemployed and seeking employment	24
# not seeking employment	28
% grads employed by school	6
State for bar exam	CA, FL, OR, TX, NY
Pass rate for first-time bar	70.0

Prominent Alumni
Leon Panetta, Political Leader; Zoe Lofgren, Congresswoman, U.S. House of Representatives; Sam O'Rourke, Deputy General Counsel, Intellectual Property at Facebook; Dorian Daley, General Counsel, Oracle; Robert Durham, Oregon Supreme Court Associate Justice

Grads Employed by Field (%)
Academic (1)
Business/Industry (19)
Government (5)
Private Practice (42)
Public Interest (2)

SEATTLE UNIVERSITY
SCHOOL OF LAW

INSTITUTIONAL INFORMATION

Public/private	Private
Affiliation	Roman Catholic-Jesuit
Student-faculty ratio	12:1
% faculty part-time	42
% faculty female	50
% faculty underrepresented minority	31
Total faculty	107

SURVEY SAYS...
Liberal students

STUDENTS

Enrollment of law school	793
% male/female	49/51
% part-time	21
% underrepresented minority	33
% international	<1
Average age of entering class	27

ACADEMICS

Academic Experience Rating	**81**
Profs interesting rating	74
Profs accessible rating	74
Hours of study per day	3.68

Academic Specialties
Commercial, Corporation Securities, Criminal, Environmental, Human Rights, International, Labor, Property, Taxation, Intellectual Property

Advanced Degrees Offered
Law School offers JD degrees in 2 and a half yrs, 3 yrs, and 3 and a half yrs.

Combined Degrees Offered
JD /MBA, Master of International Business (JD /M.I.B), JD /MS Finance, JD/MPA. JD/Master of Sports Administration and Leadership (JD/MSA.L.); JD/ Masters in Transformational Leadership (JD/M.TL) with the School of Theology and Ministry. All programs 4 yrs.

Academics

Seattle University "[offers] a great academic experience" while fostering "a challenging but supportive environment." The "great faculty, tremendous core values, [and] excellent course selection," are influenced by the school's Jesuit tradition. This "mission of social justice" divides the opinions of students. Some praise it as "one of the greatest strengths of this school." The school's location in one of America's hippest cities "affords many opportunities for externships and doing pro bono work." Seattle offers many benefits, both socially and career-wise, to students. The school is very "connected to the local legal community."

"The facilities are outstanding" at Seattle University, with a "bright and open" building that is "really nice, modern, and inviting." The law school is "always a comfortable temperature," has "excellent wireless access," and features "plenty of places to study and plenty of plug ins for laptops." There are "tons of places to meet in groups or hide to study alone," especially in the library where you can even "eat and drink" while hitting the books. "The library staff [is] very accessible and helpful" and "even the custodial staff and the baristas are sweethearts."

Academically, the most constantly praised program is easily the "top notch" "number one-ranked legal writing program." "The legal writing program really shines and local employers take that into account when making hiring decisions," a 1L explains. "It's the only reason anyone that has a job after graduation got that job," says a 3L. "One of the highlights really has to be the center for professional development," and students also praise the law clinics. The "very passionate" professors "literally beg students to come to office hours." Some do suggest professors can be "a mixed bag." "The professors and deans are very accessible and willing to talk to/work with students to solve any problems," and they work to ensure classes are "always a collaborative and encouraging but challenging environment." A 2L elaborates: "The teaching focus is traditional with modern twists: how would this rule of evidence apply to text messages? Is opening an email an unlawful search? What free sources of research are available on the internet?" However, one 2L fears that "the theme of 'social justice' has overrun the theme of creating employable lawyers." "I loved every class and for the first time in my educational career, I actually WANTED to do my homework!" one pleased student declares. The "very down to earth" administration also receives praise for being "more than capable of answering just about every question you could have." Some students do think the administration should work to make "the night program more equal to the day program," and in general the administration should "focus more on preparing students for employment following graduation." A 2L sums up their experience thusly: "The entire focus of the program, from top to bottom, is: You CAN do this and you CAN be amazing at it."

CAROL COCHRAN, ASSISTANT DEAN FOR ADMISSION
901 12TH AVENUE, SULLIVAN HALL, P.O. BOX 222000, SEATTLE, WA 98122-1090
TEL: 206-398-4200 • FAX: 206-398-4058
E-MAIL: LAWADMIS@SEATTLEU.EDU • WEBSITE: WWW.LAW.SEATTLEU.EDU

Life

Seattle University "hosts frequent events both social and otherwise," which fosters "camaraderie between students." The student body is somewhat divided "between the day and evening students," two groups that are "different and [do] not socialize with each other." This may be exacerbated by the fact that "most of the school events, activities, and classes are geared towards day-students." The school's location "the midst of a great Seattle neighborhood" provide plenty of nightlife and off-campus activities. "Seattle is definitely gray and rainy, but that is part of the package," and students enjoy "being located in such a progressive city."

Getting In

The 2014 class had a GPA range (25th to 75th percentile) of 3.07 to 3.54. The same LSAT range was 151 to 157. In addition to these scores, Seattle University says that personal accomplishments are heavily weighted in admission decisions. Applicants with a history of community service, individual talents, of other extracurricular activities should note this in their personal statements.

Clinical program required	No
Legal writing course requirement	Yes
Legal methods course requirement	No
Legal research course requirement	Yes
Moot court requirement	No
Public interest law requirement	No

ADMISSIONS

Selectivity Rating	81
# applications received	1,460
% applicants accepted	61
% acceptees attending	29
Average LSAT	154
Median LSAT	154
LSAT Range (25th to 75th percentile)	151–157
Average undergrad GPA	3.33
Median undergrad GPA	3.29
Application fee	$60
Regular application deadline	3/1
Regular notification	Rolling
Transfer students accepted	Yes
Evening division offered	Yes
Part-time accepted	Yes
CAS accepted	Yes

International Students

TOEFL required of international students.	Yes

FINANCIAL FACTS

Annual tuition	$41,010
Books and supplies	$1,300
Fees	$78
Room & Board	$16,416
Financial aid application deadline	2/15
% first-year students receiving some sort of aid	98
% all students receiving some sort of aid	98
% of aid that is merit based	63
% receiving scholarships	62
Average grant	$13,748
Average loan	$47,213
Average total aid package	$53,177
Average debt	$139,518

EMPLOYMENT INFORMATION

Career Rating	82
Total 2014 JD Grads	295
% grads employed ten months out	75
# employed bar required	167
# employed JD preferred	35
# employed professional/other	16
# employed non-professional	3
# pursuing advanced degree	9
# unemployed and seeking employment	40
# not seeking employment	7
State for bar exam	WA, CA, OR, TX, NY
Pass rate for first-time bar	75

Prominent Alumni
Angela Rye, T.V. Analyst and Commentator; Justice Charles Johnson, Washington State Supreme Court; Bill Walker, Governor of Alaska; William Marler, Food Safety Advocate; Catherine Walker, General Counsel, REI

Grads Employed by Field (%)
Academic (1)
Business/Industry (16)
Government (9)
Judicial Clerkship (5)
Private Practice (38)
Public Interest (5)

SETON HALL UNIVERSITY
SCHOOL OF LAW

INSTITUTIONAL INFORMATION

Public/private	Private
Affiliation	Roman Catholic
% faculty part-time	63
% faculty female	37
% faculty underrepresented minority	16
Total faculty	111

SURVEY SAYS...
Diverse opinions accepted in classrooms

STUDENTS

Enrollment of law school	571
% male/female	48/52
% from out-of-state	29
% part-time	33
% underrepresented minority	15
% international	1
Average age of entering class	24

ACADEMICS

Academic Experience Rating	84
Profs interesting rating	78
Profs accessible rating	82
Hours of study per day	3.68

Academic Specialties
Intellectual Property

Advanced Degrees Offered
JD: 3 yrs full-time, four yrs part-time. LLM: 1 yr full-time, 2 yrs part-time MSJ: 1 yr full-time, 2 yrs part-time

Combined Degrees Offered
JD/MD: 6 yrs MD/MSJ: 5 yrs JD/MBA: 4 yrs JD/MADIR: (Int'l Relations): 4 yrs BS/JD: 3+3

Academics

Seton Hall University School of Law is a private, mid-size bastion of legal education, where you'll get an excellent foundation in both the theoretical and the practical aspects of law. Concentrations are available in health law and intellectual property. The Center for Social Justice is "a great resource" that provides "ample opportunities to get hands-on legal experience." It consists of five clinics, and it's among the most comprehensive clinical and pro bono programs in the region, which is quite impressive considering the competition. Opportunities to participate begin during first year. "Very cool study abroad trips" in places such as Cairo, Zanzibar, and Geneva are another nice perk.

The classroom environment at Seton Hall Law is "very conducive to discussion." "There aren't many horrible professors," and "Most rave about their professors." Students say the faculty is full of some of "the wittiest, most passionate, brilliant, best-looking legal minds in the country." "Each of the first-year professors I've had has been really impressive," reports a 1L. "Some of them are pretty idiosyncratic, which provides for some good entertainment outside the classroom, and behind their backs." The faculty is "very accessible," as well. Many students also find the administration "generally helpful." The support staff goes out of its way to accommodate and even anticipate student needs," says a 2L. "It is reliable and makes few mistakes." Other students charge, "The administration at this school is a tsunami of disorganization." We also hear a number of complaints about the legal writing program, which a 3L calls "abhorrent."

"There's very much an on-your-own-feel to finding a job," and some students with middling grades feel "left out in the cold." Nevertheless, most students are pretty satisfied with their job prospects. State and federal court houses "are very close," and "the school has a strong connection to the New Jersey judiciary, so a lot of students get judicial clerkships at graduation." The alumni network is notably loyal, and "Seton Hall Law has a good networking system set in place." "We have the run of New Jersey," boasts a 2L. However, students who want to work in Manhattan have only moderate success. "You can see the city from the library," observes a 1L, "but it seems more like a beautiful dream than a reality for most students." That's not necessarily a drawback, though. "There are plenty of pretty great law firms right here in Newark."

The facilities here are definitely above average. "There can be no debate about that." Not everyone loves "the modern-esque style of the interior," and "The classrooms are more functional than aesthetically pleasing," but upgrades are "constant," and students have few serious grievances. Technology is "particularly smooth." "The library is fantastic," declares a 3L. "It provides especially good electronic resources, even in obscure areas." "I love how everything is in one place," adds a 2L.

Life

The population of future attorneys at Seton Hall Law is reasonably diverse in pretty much every respect except geography. Students report that they have "serious drive, ambition, and talent." While the curve is "severe" and "things get a little competitive during finals time," the academic atmosphere is generally "friendly, fun, and helpful." "Student life at Seton Hall Law delicately balances that line between competition and teamwork," explains a 1L.

Ms. Gisele Joachim, Asst. Dean of Admissions and Financial Aid
One Newark Center, Newark, NJ 07102
Tel: 888-415-7271 • Fax: 973-642-8876
E-Mail: admitme@shu.edu • Website: law.shu.edu

Outside of class, there are frequent seminars and tons of organizations and activities. Attitudes concerning the surrounding city of Newark are seriously mixed. Detractors call it "a notoriously terrible city" that's "lacking in sophistication and charm." "Newark may be the least desirable place to go to law school in the country," reckons a 2L. Other students insist that the Brick City's reputation is unwarranted. "Just because Newark looks crappy doesn't mean it's dangerous," they say. "I feel like a lot of the kids from New Jersey just hate Newark because they bring their prejudices with them," claims a 2L. "Downtown Newark is as safe—if not safer—than any block in NYC. It is a professionally developed area" full of courts and multiple government offices. Whatever the case, the school is "about two blocks from Penn Station, so it's easy enough to commute from a nice area." Despite the commuter ambience, students tell us that there's "a very vibrant social community" at Seton Hall Law. Events sponsored by the student bar association are "pretty awesome," and students "regularly" go out en masse in Hoboken or New York City.

Getting In

Overall, admitted students at the 25th percentile have LSAT scores around 156 and undergraduate GPAs of approximately 3.46. At the 75th percentile, LSAT scores are 161, and GPAs are around 3.6. Stats for the evening division are somewhat lower across the board.

Clinical program required	No
Legal writing course requirement	Yes
Legal methods course requirement	No
Legal research course requirement	Yes
Moot court requirement	Yes
Public interest law requirement	No

ADMISSIONS

Selectivity Rating	85
# applications received	1,327
% applicants accepted	54
% acceptees attending	15
Average LSAT	158
Median LSAT	157
LSAT Range (25th to 75th percentile)	156–161
Average undergrad GPA	3.48
Median undergrad GPA	3.55
Application fee	$65
Regular application deadline	4/1
Transfer students accepted	Yes
Evening division offered	Yes
Part-time accepted	Yes
CAS accepted	Yes

International Students

TOEFL recommended of international students.	Yes

FINANCIAL FACTS

Annual tuition	$49,194
Books and supplies	$1,500
Room & Board	$13,950
Financial aid application deadline	4/1
% first-year students receiving some sort of aid	98
% all students receiving some sort of aid	94
% of aid that is merit based	60
% receiving scholarships	82
Average grant	$27,981
Average loan	$40,322
Average total aid package	$52,000
Average debt	$128,100

EMPLOYMENT INFORMATION

Career Rating	**90**	**Prominent Alumni**
Total 2014 JD Grads	285	Michael Chagares, Judge on Third US
% for whom you have useable information	35	Circuit Court of Appeals; Christopher Christie, Governor of the State of New
% grads employed ten months out	93	Jersey
Median starting salary	$50,707	**Grads Employed by Field (%)**
% job accepting grads providing useable salary information	82	Business/Industry (17)
# employed full-time	257	Government (5)
# employed part-time	9	Judicial Clerkship (43)
# employed bar required	210	Federal: (2)
# employed JD preferred	37	State or local: (41)
# employed professional/other	14	Private Practice (27)
# employed non-professional	5	Solo: (1)
# pursuing advanced degree	1	2-10: (13)
# unemployed and seeking employment	17	11-25: (3)
# not seeking employment	1	26-50: (3)
State for bar exam	NJ	51-100: (2)
Pass rate for first-time bar	90.9	101-250: (2)
		251-500: (1)
		501+: (2)
		Public Interest (3)

SOUTH TEXAS COLLEGE OF LAW

INSTITUTIONAL INFORMATION

Public/private	Private
Affiliation	No Affiliation
% faculty part-time	42
% faculty female	32
% faculty underrepresented minority	16
Total faculty	92

SURVEY SAYS...
Great research resources

STUDENTS

Enrollment of law school	1,116
% male/female	54/46
% from out-of-state	8
% part-time	24
% underrepresented minority	38
% international	1
# of countries represented	4
Average age of entering class	27

ACADEMICS

Academic Experience Rating	**76**
Profs interesting rating	83
Profs accessible rating	77
Hours of study per day	3.74

Combined Degrees Offered
JD/MBA

Academics

South Texas College of Law "is a school for litigators." Arming students with the tools they need to succeed in the courtroom, "the school has great advocacy programs in several different fields of law," with a mock trial program that is considered "one of the best in the nation." The regular JD program incorporates intensive training in trial and appellate advocacy, and the school additionally operates a "Summer Trial Academy, as an additional option for practical preparation for those not able to compete or who don't have time in their schedule to do the regular advocacy courses." In addition, "there are a lot of clinics that will place you in a firm or court to gain experience" in the real world. The lively, litigious environment is a huge draw for many STCL students, who warn that quieter types "will be eaten alive" at this competitive school. But do not be startled, as one current student reassures, "Many come to the school for its mock and moot programs, but as a member of the law review's editorial board, I can assure you that opportunities exist in all areas of practice and academia."

As "a down and dirty trade school rather than a school for philosophers," South Texas's academic curriculum "provides a well-reasoned balance between theoretical and practical education," emphasizing critical thinking skills as well as hands-on applications. Through discussion, Socratic questioning, and assignments, "the professors truly try to get you to start thinking like a lawyer from day one. They ask you the right questions to lead you down the path to the answer on your own, without giving you the answer." A cadre of accomplished attorneys, "the professors are all extremely qualified, and only a few are purely academic." They will also give you a broad understanding of the law, as "the school has strategically sought out professors from a wide range of backgrounds: some the typical academics (Harvard-educated, brilliant résumé of publications), some working for the Government (such as the SEC or the EPA), and some as experts of their fields in Private Practice (such as the oil and gas fields, and the energy transactional fields)." Law school is a challenge anywhere, but South Texas students tell us that those that apply must be prepared to work especially hard at their school. A current student recounts, "You have God awful amounts of reading to do all day and all night, you learn more material in the first six months than entire undergrad experience." For anyone who is struggling to keep up, "the professors are, for the most part, extremely accessible and ready to help with clarifications or advice on how to study or understand the material."

When it comes to the nuts and bolts, the program runs smoothly, especially when you consider that it's split between the daytime and evening divisions. Evening students, who attend part-time, are pleased to report, "Almost every class is offered during the day and at night using the same professors." Attentive to students' needs, "the Dean and Associate Deans are accessible and work diligently to ensure we receive a first-rate legal education." Plus, "when some offices/groups within the administration do not uphold their responsibilities, the leadership has made great strides in correcting any problem areas swiftly." After graduation, South Texas students say it's best to look for a job locally. "South Texas is well respected in the Houston community," and "the networking availability is unparalleled" in the region. On the flip side, many students complain that the national rankings do not reflect the true quality of the law school, and that these rankings can have a negative influence on employment opportunities. When looking for a job outside Houston, students admit that, "In other cities, competition is harder." They further note, "The prestigious firms which recruit tier 1 students also recruit at STCL. The big firms may not take as many first year associates, but every firm still appears at on campus interviews."

ALICIA K. CRAMER, ASSISTANT DEAN OF ADMISSIONS
1303 SAN JACINTO STREET, HOUSTON, TX 77002
TEL: 713-646-1810 • FAX: 713-646-2906
E-MAIL: ADMISSIONS@STCL.EDU • WEBSITE: WWW.STCL.EDU

Life

Despite the fact that South Texas has produced more championship advocacy teams than any other law school in the United States, students reported that they do not feel like minnows in a tank of trial sharks at South Texas College of Law. "Students at this college are extremely competitive," yet most agree that, "The student body is very friendly…the students help each other out and want to see each other succeed." With its dual daytime and evening programs, "One of the greatest strengths of this school is the diversity of experience in its student body, especially the part-time students. You have people from many different walks of life and careers. People with families. Single people. People in their 40s and 50s. People in their 20s."

Regular full-time students will get the full law school experience at South Texas College of Law. From Amnesty International to the Environmental Law Society, the student body maintains a range of "clubs and organizations that are either fun, competitive, or fun and competitive." Socially, students further benefit from an active community, where "there is always some group throwing a party during lunch or happy hour and plenty of students show up to enjoy good food, cheap drinks, and good company." On the flip side, evening students lament the fact that most "Socials and activities are scheduled during our class times or are scheduled so that we will get out 15 minutes before the social ends."

Getting In

Students are admitted to the full-time program during both the fall and spring semesters. Students entering the part-time program are admitted during the fall semester only. Both paper and online applications are accepted for either program. Students are accepted primarily on the basis of their LSAT and undergraduate GPA. However, a segment of each incoming class is selected on the basis of additional factors. Every attempt is made to evaluate each applicant as an individual, a prospective student, and a future professional.

Clinical program required	No
Legal writing course requirement	Yes
Legal methods course requirement	Yes
Legal research course requirement	Yes
Moot court requirement	No
Public interest law requirement	No

ADMISSIONS

Selectivity Rating	76
# applications received	1,631
% applicants accepted	66
% acceptees attending	34
Average LSAT	151
Median LSAT	151
LSAT Range (25th to 75th percentile)	148–154
Average undergrad GPA	3.08
Median undergrad GPA	3.12
Application fee	$55
Regular application deadline	2/15
Regular notification	5/25
Transfer students accepted	Yes
Evening division offered	Yes
Part-time accepted	Yes
CAS accepted	Yes

International Students

TOEFL required of international students.	Yes

FINANCIAL FACTS

Annual tuition	$28,680
Books and supplies	$8,130
Fees	$600
Room & Board	$13,770
Financial aid application deadline	5/1

EMPLOYMENT INFORMATION

Career Rating	89
Total 2014 JD Grads	390
% for whom you have useable information	25
% grads employed ten months out	89
Median starting salary	$70,000
# employed full-time	310
# employed part-time	24
# employed bar required	247
# employed JD preferred	53
# employed professional/other	27
# employed non-professional	7
# pursuing advanced degree	5
# unemployed and seeking employment	26
# not seeking employment	10
State for bar exam	TX
Pass rate for first-time bar	83.6

Prominent Alumni
Richard H. Anderson, CEO and Chairman, Delta Airlines; Eva M. Guzman, Justice, Texas Supreme Court

Grads Employed by Field (%)
Academic (1)
Business/Industry (20)
Government (9)
Judicial Clerkship (1)
State or local: (1)
Private Practice (54)
Solo: (7)
2-10: (30)
11-25: (7)
26-50: (3)
51-100: (2)
101-250: (2)
251-500: (2)
501+: (1)
Public Interest (1)

SOUTHERN ILLINOIS UNIVERSITY
SCHOOL OF LAW

INSTITUTIONAL INFORMATION

Public/private	Public
Affiliation	No Affiliation
Studen-faculty ratio	12:1
% faculty part-time	37
% faculty female	52
% faculty underrepresented minority	20
Total faculty	54

SURVEY SAYS...

Diverse opinions accepted in classrooms, Abundant externship/ internship/clerkship opportunities

STUDENTS

Enrollment of law school	349
% male/female	60/40
% from out-of-state	34
% part-time	0
% underrepresented minority	20
# of countries represented	0
Average age of entering class	26

ACADEMICS

Academic Experience Rating	**73**
Profs interesting rating	79
Profs accessible rating	92
Hours of study per day	3.52

Academic Specialties
International, Intellectual Property

Advanced Degrees Offered
JD, 3 yrs; MLS, 2 yrs; LLM, 2 yrs

Combined Degrees Offered
JD/MD 6 yrs, JD/MBA 4 yrs, JD/ MPA 4 yrs, JD/MAcc 4 yrs; JD/ MSW varies, JD/MSEd varies

Academics

Southern Illinois University is a "small school" where "the tuition is low" yet the "quality of education" is "high." From professors to staff, the school fosters a "friendly / familial feel" that includes "personal attention" to students' needs. "The atmosphere" at SIU "is friendly and respectful." "I'd say the best aspect is the rapport between the students, faculty, and administration," a 1L says. "You can tell the day that you start, that everyone [wants] you to succeed." The school's small size appeals to many, but can also cause "a significant amount of 'little school syndrome.'" The "great facilities" provide plentiful resources for "legal research, IT help, and assistance from librarians." "From adequate parking space, to on-site tech support," "there are all of the resources" students at a law school need. "In the library there are computers and all of the rooms have outlets for our laptops," and the school is open to students "twenty-four hours a day."

The friendly atmosphere and "small" size means the "helpful, insightful, and always accessible" administration "knows nearly all the students by name from day one." "Students are very close with the administration" and the overall experience is "great and friendly." Although some students say the administration can be "quite disorganized and disorderly," most say that "when there is a problem, it is fixed before anyone notices." "[The administration is] willing to sit down and explain the law school process, as well as help in any way to balance law school, family, and social life," says one 2L. Students do wish that the school offered "more diverse classes." Academically, there is strong "emphasis on practical skills" and "emphasis on legal writing." "We gain practical skills that prepares us well for outside employment," one student reports. SIU makes sure to work with the local community, and "the volunteer hours the local attorneys give to talk with students, coach students, and mentor students is phenomenal." As for the faculty themselves, they "are amazingly approachable and supportive" professors that "care deeply about their students" and "always open to conversation, whether it was about law school or not." "The professors at SIU have an open door policy and encourage one-on-one encounters," leading students to be impressed by "how accessible they are to meeting with students outside of class." The professors here are "freely willing to give students their personal contact information." "It is very nice to have instructors that have not only written texts but also model rules and the current law in the state," a happy 1L says. In general, the faculty and staff work to foster a culture that "minimizes competition and promotes collaboration."

AKAMI MARIK, DIRECTOR OF ADMISSIONS & FINANCIAL AID
SIU SCHOOL OF LAW WELCOME CENTER, 1150 DOUGLAS DRIVE, MAIL CODE 6804
CARBONDALE, IL 62901
TEL: 618-453-8858 • FAX: 618-453-8921
E-MAIL: LAWADMIT@SIU.EDU • WEBSITE: WWW.LAW.SIU.EDU

Life

Your experience at SIU is influenced greatly by whether you are "a city-slicker" or someone who will like "the great outdoors" and "the small town feel of Carbondale." Carbondale, with a population of around 25,000, has "some beautiful scenery" but otherwise is "blah." However, "there are some of the most beautiful state parks and federal lands in the Midwest within [a] 20 minute drive of the law school." Some students report "cabin-fever," but many come to SIU specifically for "the slower pace of the small town life." As one student says: "some come, love it, and never leave." The student body has a Midwest feel, being mostly composed of students "from across the region, with about 15 percent coming from outside the region." While some feel the student body is "not racially diverse," students agree that everyone gets along. SIU is a place where "students can actually interact with each other instead of competing with each other." "We are a small community and we all care a lot for each other," a 1L explains. "Everyone is friendly and I truly think that relationships that I have formed are unique and special to our school."

Getting In

A recent entering class at SIU had an average GPA of 3.08 and an average LSAT score of 148. In addition to these scores, the administration says they look heavily at the letters of recommendation, personal statement, and work history shown on applicant résumés.

Clinical program required	No
Legal writing course requirement	Yes
Legal methods course requirement	Yes
Legal research course requirement	Yes
Moot court requirement	No
Public interest law requirement	Yes

ADMISSIONS

Selectivity Rating	71
# applications received	433
% applicants accepted	85
% acceptees attending	34
Average LSAT	148
Median LSAT	147
LSAT Range (25th to 75th percentile)	144–151
Average undergrad GPA	3.08
Median undergrad GPA	3.09
Application fee	$0
Regular application deadline	4/1
Transfer students accepted	Yes
Evening division offered	No
Part-time accepted	No
CAS accepted	Yes

International Students

TOEFL required of international students.	Yes

FINANCIAL FACTS

Annual tuition (in-state/ out-of-state)	$14,325/$36,975
Books and supplies	$1,150
Fees	$3,828
Room & Board	$13,064
Financial aid application deadline	4/1
% first-year students receiving some sort of aid	100
% all students receiving some sort of aid	98
% of aid that is merit based	25
% receiving scholarships	76
Average grant	$9,321
Average loan	$27,000
Average total aid package	$32,288

EMPLOYMENT INFORMATION

Career Rating	87
Total 2014 JD Grads	105
% for whom you have useable information	98
% grads employed ten months out	79
Median starting salary	$46,000
# employed full-time	78
# employed part-time	3
# employed bar required	70
# employed JD preferred	9
# employed professional/other	2
# unemployed and seeking employment	20
% grads employed by school	1
State for bar exam	IL, MO
Pass rate for first-time bar	87.8

Prominent Alumni

Ray Wood, Chief Patent Officer for ZTE USA; Karen Kendall, Partner, Heyl, Royster, Voelker & Allen; Hon. William E. Holdridge, Illinois Appellate Court, 3rd District

Grads Employed by Field (%)

Academic (2)
Business/Industry (11)
Government (17)
Judicial Clerkship (2)
Federal: (1)
State or local: (1)
Private Practice (45)
Solo: (3)
2-10: (30)
11-25: (8)
26-50: (3)
51-100: (1)
101-250: (1)
Public Interest (0)

SOUTHERN METHODIST UNIVERSITY
DEDMAN SCHOOL OF LAW

Academics

Boasting "a great program...great size...in a city with great opportunity," the Dedman School of Law at Southern Methodist University has it all. "The local legal community draws heavily from the law school, and with a little initiative, a law student can easily network with numerous lawyers and judges in the area and beyond." "Diverse course offerings" in "everything from the philosophical to the tediously practical" define the curriculum here, and "The legal clinics are absolutely amazing." Externships and scholarly journals are abundant. Students say there are plenty of opportunities to get involved: "We have consistently won national moot court and mock trial competitions over the past two years, and the school has a great Trial Advocacy program co-taught by practitioners and judges." A unique JD/MA program allows students to study economics as well as law, and students have the opportunity to study abroad in Oxford each summer.

Academic complaints often revolve around the legal writing program, which "needs a massive overhaul" and, "while informational, [can] feel more like fifth grade English in the way [it is] approached." Fortunately, the "very distinguished" yet "easily approachable" professors "are very receptive to students and concerned with [their] learning" and "make an effort to be available." They are "demanding of their students," but "interesting and entertaining in the classroom."

Professors "make the classroom experience fun," gushes one student. "My civil procedure exam was one of the funniest things I have ever read, with witty undercurrents and subtle political satire." Opinions of the administration vary considerably. Some students say the deans seem "distant at times, but whenever you need them, they're available and helpful." Others tell us that the administration "does not care about the students" and gripe about "bureaucratic inefficiencies."

Job prospects are very promising for SMU grads. Career Services is "actually concerned with helping you find a job." "Dallas is a wonderful market that pays salaries on par with New York, but the quality of life is so much better," according to students. "If you want to stay and practice in Dallas, you could not go to a better school." SMU's "exceptionally strong relationship with the Dallas legal market" provides an "extensive network of attorneys" "in every field imaginable." "The alums are very supportive and willing to help out." "A lot of doors are opened by attending the SMU Dedman School of Law, regardless of your class rank." "I was able to secure a six-figure job without being on law review or moot court," says a 3L. "There is definitely a huge hurdle" for students to face who do not want to practice in Texas, though.

The "gorgeous" campus is full of "very pretty, collegiate-looking brick buildings" and "nestled in one of the nicest, most affluent neighborhoods in the Dallas area." "The law school itself is further cloistered away from the rest of the university and, once inside, it is easy to forget you are sitting in the middle of a bustling metropolis." "Large oak trees provide shady walkways, and outdoor study places are ample." "The majority of classrooms are "very comfortable and accommodating," and the "nearly flawless" wireless signal is "strong in every corner of the law school." The library is "amazing," "both with regard to holdings and ease of use."

Jill Nikirk, Assistant Dean of Admissions
P.O. Box 750110, Dallas, TX 75275-0110
Tel: 214-768-2550 • Fax: 214-768-2549
E-Mail: lawadmit@smu.edu • Website: www.law.smu.edu

Life

"Students in the full-time day program tend to be younger—either directly out of their undergraduate program or with only a year or two of work experience. Nevertheless, there are still many full-time students in their thirties or older." Most are "Texas natives," and all are "fun, attractive, and smart." Some students are "cooperative, collegial, and very supportive of one another." Others are "very competitive." "There are definitely a few trust fund kids, but a lot of us are living off student loans as well," says one student. "The parking garage does boast an unusual concentration of BMWs and Hummers," agrees a 2L. "But as a non-Texan who shares a beat-up Honda with my wife, I've never felt out of place." "Political views run the gamut, but the large majority of students are tolerant of opposing views." SMU is also "remarkably LGBT-friendly."

Regarding social events on campus, students say, "There's a club for everyone, whether you're a gun-toting Second Amendment crusader or a die-hard liberal." "The students put together a lot of fun activities," ranging from happy hours to baseball games to tailgating events. "The highlight of everyone's week is Bar Review where the Student Bar Association gets drink specials at a different local bar every Friday." There's also "a picnic/sports spectacular every semester." SMU's ritzy location is "great" in terms of safety but "can make finding student housing right next to school virtually impossible." Beyond the neighborhood surrounding campus, "Big D" is one of the liveliest cities in the South and "a fun place to live." "You get a great all-around legal education and have the resources of the Dallas–Fort Worth Metroplex right at your doorstep."

Getting In

For a recent entering class the median LSAT score among applicants to the full-time program was 164 and the median GPA was 3.73. Applicants to the part-time evening program posted slightly lower numbers: the median GPA was 3.49 and the median LSAT score was 160.

Clinical program required	No
Legal writing course requirement	Yes
Legal methods course requirement	No
Legal research course requirement	Yes
Moot court requirement	Yes
Public interest law requirement	Yes

ADMISSIONS

Selectivity Rating	89
# applications received	1,518
% applicants accepted	46
% acceptees attending	32
Median LSAT	161
LSAT Range (25th to 75th percentile)	156–163
Median undergrad GPA	3.58
Application fee	$75
Regular application deadline	2/15
Regular notification	5/15
Early application deadline	11/1
Early application notification	1/31
Transfer students accepted	Yes
Evening division offered	Yes
Part-time accepted	Yes
CAS accepted	Yes

FINANCIAL FACTS

Annual tuition	$43,626
Books and supplies	$2,000
Fees	$5,170
Average loan	$24,199

EMPLOYMENT INFORMATION

Career Rating	95	**Prominent Alumni**
Total 2014 JD Grads	254	Michael Boone, Founding partner, Haynes
% for whom you have useable information	100	& Boone; Nathan Hecht, Chief Justice, Texas Supreme Court; Wayne Watts, Sr.
% grads employed ten months out	93	Executive VP and General Counsel, AT&T;
Median starting salary	$85,000	Edward B. Rust Jr., Chairman & CEO, State
% job accepting grads providing useable salary information	70	Farm Insurance
# employed full-time	227	**Grads Employed by Field (%)**
# employed part-time	10	Academic (2)
# employed bar required	186	Business/Industry (24)
# employed JD preferred	41	Government (5)
# employed professional/other	9	Judicial Clerkship (4)
# employed non-professional	1	Federal: (3)
# pursuing advanced degree	1	State or local: (1)
# unemployed and seeking employment	14	Private Practice (58)
# not seeking employment	1	Public Interest (1)
State for bar exam	TX	
Pass rate for first-time bar	85.5	

SOUTHERN UNIVERSITY
LAW CENTER

INSTITUTIONAL INFORMATION

Public/private	Public
Student-faculty ratio	14:1
% faculty part-time	34
% faculty female	46
% faculty underrepresented minority	74
Total faculty	67

SURVEY SAYS...
Diverse opinions accepted in classrooms

STUDENTS

Enrollment of law school	644
% male/female	47/53
% from out-of-state	21
% part-time	21
% underrepresented minority	59
% international	0
# of countries represented	0
Average age of entering class	26

ACADEMICS

Academic Experience Rating	**71**
Profs interesting rating	71
Profs accessible rating	78
Hours of study per day	3.06

Academic Specialties
Civil Procedure, Commercial, Criminal, Environmental, Government Services, International, Taxation, Intellectual Property

Combined Degrees Offered
JD/MPA 4yrs

Academics

With roughly 600 full-time and part-time students, Southern University Law Center is "small and personable." "I don't feel like just another number at my school," says a 1L. "You feel that the people around you want you to be successful." SULC is also "ridiculously affordable." "While others will be coming out of law school hundred of thousands of dollars in debt, Southern grads will have debt that is approximately one fifth of the cost." Additional perks here include a decently broad selection of courses and six clinics that provide hands-on experience with the realities of practicing law for a very good percentage of students. If you want to pursue both a JD and MPA, the school offers a joint-degree program in cooperation with Southern's Nelson Mandela School of Public Policy and Urban Affairs. There's also a study abroad program in London, in which students take courses in international law.

Louisiana is a civil law jurisdiction (in the tradition of France and Continental Europe), while law in every other state is based on the common law tradition (of England). While SULC students learn both, the required curriculum focuses on civil law both substantively and procedurally. If you plan to practice in the Pelican State, Southern is a great choice. The "wealth of alums" doesn't hurt when it comes to finding a job, either. However, if you want to practice in another state, learning Louisiana's unique system of law and trying to apply it to another state's bar exam won't be the easiest thing in the world.

"Some profs can be very intimidating," but the full-time faculty is full of "sincere, challenging, intelligent people" who are "downright awesome." The faculty is notoriously approachable as well. Most professors are "always willing to help." "I have a great amount of respect for 90 percent of my professors," explains a 2L. "I feel that all of them have been knowledgeable in the subject matter." The "generally excellent" part-time program tends to have more adjunct professors. They're more of a mixed bag. "Some of the evening professors are practicing attorneys during the day and are not as accessible or as devoted as the full-time day professors." Students offer considerable praise for the "very professional" administration. Deans are "approachable and available," and they "work diligently in their efforts to help the students succeed" and to "know who their students are." Some students tell us that the financial aid process can be a "nightmare," though. The legal writing program is another complaint. Students say that it "could use a lot of improvement." SULC's "somewhat new facilities" are "very poorly maintained." Otherwise, they are "really good" and "very hospitable." Classrooms have wireless Internet and plenty of electrical outlets. The library is "stocked with great resource materials."

LENA JOHNSON, COORDINATOR OF ADMISSION
A.A. LENOIR HALL, P.O. BOX 9294, 2 ROOSEVELT STEPTOE STREET, BATON ROUGE, LA 70813
TEL: 225-771-4976 • FAX: 225-771-2121
E-MAIL: ADMISSION@SULC.EDU • WEBSITE: WWW.SULC.EDU

Life

"This school is probably the most diverse school in the country in terms of the student body," gushes a 2L. SULC is a historically black institution, and some 60 percent of the students are African American. Students come here "from all over the country," and they "have very interesting backgrounds." The range of ages is vast as well.

"Southern charm is alive and well at SULC." A "kind and friendly" "family atmosphere" reigns supreme, and "a strong sense of camaraderie and support is evident in every aspect." "Some people are competitive," says a 1L, "but I don't get that extremely competitive vibe from Southern." "It's a smaller law school," explains a 2L, "which allows students to work more cooperatively, instead of against each other as at most law schools." Most everyone "goes out of their way to help." The biggest social divide is probably between the day program, which is generally composed of younger students, and the evening program, which is "mostly older professionals."

During the school day, "the school regularly has speakers and attorneys come in during the noon hour to give practical advice on the practice of law." Students are split when it comes to life beyond the confines of campus. Some tell us that Baton Rouge—the state capital and the second largest city in Louisiana—is a student's Shangri-la, especially if you like music and food. Baton Rouge is home to unique art and culture, tons of festivals, and mouthwatering cuisine of every kind. When students take a break from hitting the books, a good number of bars and clubs and a raging live music scene keep life interesting. Other students aren't feeling the cultural love, though. "The main chances for socialization seem to be at a bar or a church," suggests a 2L. "What if you don't drink or believe?"

Getting In

Admitted students at the 25th percentile have LSAT scores around 142 and GPAs in the 2.6 range. Admitted students at the 75th percentile have LSAT scores of 147 or so and GPAs of around 3.2.

Clinical program required	No
Legal writing course requirement	Yes
Legal methods course requirement	No
Legal research course requirement	Yes
Moot court requirement	No
Public interest law requirement	No

ADMISSIONS

Selectivity Rating	**71**
# applications received	621
% applicants accepted	65
% acceptees attending	48
Average LSAT	146
Median LSAT	144
LSAT Range (25th to 75th percentile)	142–147
Average undergrad GPA	2.91
Median undergrad GPA	2.82
Application fee	$50
Regular application deadline	2/28
Transfer students accepted	Yes
Evening division offered	Yes
Part-time accepted	Yes
CAS accepted	Yes

International Students

TOEFL recommended of international students.	Yes

FINANCIAL FACTS

Annual tuition (in-state/ out-of-state)	$12,054/$21,614
Books and supplies	$3,956
Room & Board	$12,600
Financial aid application deadline	4/15
% first-year students receiving some sort of aid	93
% all students receiving some sort of aid	87
% of aid that is merit based	2
% receiving scholarships	11
Average grant	$5,753
Average loan	$21,639
Average total aid package	$22,070
Average debt	$74,272

EMPLOYMENT INFORMATION

Career Rating	**70**	**Prominent Alumni**	
Total 2014 JD Grads	165	Brian Jackson, Chief U.S. District Judge for the Middle District of LA	
% for whom you have useable information	100	**Grads Employed by Field (%)**	
% grads employed ten months out	76	Academic (2)	
Median starting salary	$0	Business/Industry (13)	
# employed full-time	116	Government (22)	
# employed part-time	10	Judicial Clerkship (7)	
# employed bar required	63	Federal: (2)	
# employed JD preferred	40	State or local: (5)	
# employed professional/other	23	Private Practice (29)	
# pursuing advanced degree	1	Solo: (9)	
# unemployed and seeking employment	38	2-10: (15)	
		11-25: (1)	
State for bar exam	LA	26-50: (2)	
Pass rate for first-time bar	60.5	51-100: (1)	
		101-250: (1)	
		Public Interest (3)	

SOUTHWESTERN LAW SCHOOL

INSTITUTIONAL INFORMATION

Public/private	Private
Affiliation	No Affiliation
% faculty part-time	28
% faculty female	40
% faculty underrepresented minority	26
Total faculty	93

SURVEY SAYS...

Diverse opinions accepted in classrooms, Great research resources

STUDENTS

Enrollment of law school	1,048
% male/female	41/59
% part-time	34
% underrepresented minority	41
% international	2
Average age of entering class	26

ACADEMICS

Academic Experience Rating	**77**
Profs interesting rating	72
Profs accessible rating	75
Hours of study per day	3.93

Academic Specialties

Civil Procedure, Commercial, Constitutional, Corporation Securities, Criminal, Environmental, Government Services, Human Rights, International, Labor, Legal History, Legal Philosophy, Property, Taxation, Intellectual Property

Advanced Degrees Offered

LLM in Entertainment and Media Law; individualized LLM: 1 yr full-time, 2 yrs part-time.

Combined Degrees Offered

JD/MBA; JD/MAM (MA in Management) with The Drucker Graduate School of Management, 3–4.5 yrs. 3+3 BA/JD with California State University, Northridge and Dominguez Hills, 6 yrs.

Academics

Large, private, and independent Southwestern Law School boasts an "emphasis on practical skills" and an impressive array of bells and whistles. In addition to your standard full-time day and part-time evening programs, there's a very intensive two-year program that features small classes and integrates plenty of real-world training. There's also a part-time day program that helps nontraditional students juggle the demands of work, family, and school. A "broad" and "ever-increasing" range of courses includes summer law programs in Argentina and England. Clinics are available in appellate litigation, children's rights, civil rights, entertainment and the arts, immigration law, street law, and youth offender parole hearings. "The externships are amazing and very available to all class ranks." There's a JD/MBA program allied with the Drucker Graduate School of Management. If you are interested in entertainment and media law, Southwestern is home to a huge contingent of professors who specialize in that area, and the school maintains impressive connections "within the entertainment industry." Another perk is Southwestern's unique "three-track approach" to legal writing. As a 1L, you can choose from specialized writing programs in trial practice, negotiation, or appellate advocacy. While Southwestern sort of exists in the shadow of other law schools in the local area with national reputations, students tell us that they are happy with their employment prospects. Career Services has "tons of resources," they say, and Southwestern has a "huge alumni network," "especially in the Los Angeles area."

The faculty is composed of "an array of ages, ethnicities, and eccentricities." There are "some really outstanding teachers" here "who could not be more dedicated to their craft," and the faculty as a whole is "helpful and accommodating." They "genuinely care about your success in law school." "They are engaging and really care about what each student takes away from their class," explains a 3L. "The school is attempting to teach us to be good lawyers," explains a 1L, "with less emphasis on maintaining the 'hide-the-ball' pedagogy of the Socratic Method." There's the stray "incompetent" prof here, though, and some of the older ones are "standard fare." "Most professors are available to students on a regular basis" once class ends. "I was surprised by the support from teachers and access to them outside of the classroom," reports a 1L. "This institution is committed to a student-first ideology." Some students say that the administration "treats everyone like an individual, not just another customer." Others say that there is "too much bureaucracy, in all aspects."

The facilities at Southwestern are within easy commuting distance to the downtown district of Los Angeles. Students say they are "world-class." The crown jewel is a legendary, enormous, and very distinctive Art Deco building. It used to be a fancy department store and now it is listed on the National Register of Historic Places. "The administration clearly takes pride in the campus upkeep." "Everything is new and high-tech." Classrooms are "really nice." "The library is beautiful and basically kicks the ass out of the other law school libraries in Los Angeles," pronounces a 1L. There are also ample study areas, terraces with sweeping city views, and a gigantic fitness center for student use. A new upscale on-campus student residential complex opened in Fall 2013.

LISA GEAR, ASSISTANT DEAN FOR ADMISSIONS
3050 WILSHIRE BOULEVARD, LOS ANGELES, CA 90010-1106
TEL: 213-738-6834 • FAX: 213-383-1688
E-MAIL: ADMISSIONS@SWLAW.EDU • WEBSITE: WWW.SWLAW.EDU

Life

By all accounts, diversity is "great" at Southwestern in every way. Students come here from pretty much every state and all walks of life. Ethnic minorities constitute more than a third of the population. Roughly two-thirds of the students have either previous work experience or some kind of advanced degree already. The academic atmosphere is "very professional and collegiate." "It's very cooperatively competitive," explains a 3L. "Everyone wants to do better than the next person but is always willing to help the next person out." "There's a lot of mentoring that goes on at Southwestern" between 1Ls and upper-division students as well.

While Southwestern's campus in Koreatown is "an oasis," some students contend that social life is pretty dismal. "There is a social disconnect at the school," laments a 1L, who feels that "clubs are not really active and there is a commuter atmosphere." Other students strongly disagree. According to them, Southwestern is "very social" with over fifty organizations on campus. "Everyone is friendly with each other, which has made for a pleasant experience," declares a 3L. "I've created some bonds with certain students that I will cherish forever." Whatever the case, the inexhaustible sprawl of the metropolitan Los Angeles area offers something for every taste and predilection imaginable.

Getting In

Enrolled full-time students at the 25th percentile have LSAT scores in the low 150s and GPAs around 3.2. Enrolled students at the 75th percentile have LSAT scores around 155 and GPAs a little over 3.5. If you enroll in the two-year program, classes start in mid-summer.

Clinical program required	No
Legal writing course requirement	Yes
Legal methods course requirement	Yes
Legal research course requirement	Yes
Moot court requirement	Yes
Public interest law requirement	No

ADMISSIONS

Selectivity Rating	77
# applications received	1,622
% applicants accepted	62
% acceptees attending	26
Median LSAT	151
LSAT Range (25th to 75th percentile)	150–155
Median undergrad GPA	3.22
Application fee	$60
Regular application deadline	4/1
Transfer students accepted	Yes
Evening division offered	Yes
Part-time accepted	Yes
CAS accepted	Yes

FINANCIAL FACTS

Annual tuition	$46,900
Books and supplies	$1,250
Fees	$200
Room & Board (on/ off campus)	$18,000/$20,520
Financial aid application deadline	6/1
% first-year students receiving some sort of aid	90
% all students receiving some sort of aid	93
% receiving scholarships	42

EMPLOYMENT INFORMATION

Career Rating	77	
Total 2014 JD Grads	313	
% for whom you have useable information	96	
% grads employed ten months out	73	
% job accepting grads providing useable salary information	20	
# employed full-time	195	
# employed part-time	34	
# employed bar required	132	
# employed JD preferred	73	
# employed professional/other	17	
# employed non-professional	7	
# pursuing advanced degree	5	
# unemployed and seeking employment	55	
# not seeking employment	7	
State for bar exam	CA, NY, FL, CO, NV	
Pass rate for first-time bar	74.0	

Prominent Alumni

Tom Bradley, LA Mayor for 20 yrs; Stanley Mosk, Longest serving Cal. Sup. Ct. Justice; Hon. Vaino Spencer, 1st Afr-Amer woman Judge in Calif. & 3rd in the US; Gordon Smith, Former US Senator (OR); President of the National Association of Broadcasters; Daniel Petrocelli, Won OJ Simpson civil trial

Grads Employed by Field (%)

Academic (2)
Business/Industry (20)
Government (3)
Judicial Clerkship (1)
Private Practice (45)
Public Interest (2)

St. John's University

School of Law

INSTITUTIONAL INFORMATION

Public/private	Private
Affiliation	Roman Catholic
Student-faculty ratio	16:1

SURVEY SAYS...

Diverse opinions accepted in classrooms

STUDENTS

Enrollment of law school	743
% male/female	54/46
% part-time	16
% underrepresented minority	20
Average age of entering class	23

ACADEMICS

Academic Experience Rating	**86**
Profs interesting rating	78
Profs accessible rating	80
Hours of study per day	3.65

Advanced Degrees Offered

JD, 3 yrs (Full Time Day), 4 yrs (Part Time evening); LLM in Bankruptcy, 1 yr (full time), 2–3 yrs (part time); LLM in US Legal Studies for Foreign Lawyers 1 yr (full time), 2-4 yrs (part time); LLM in Transnational Legal Practice; LLM in International and Comparative Sports Law

Combined Degrees Offered

JD/MBA; JD/MA(MS); BA (BS)/JD; JD/LLM

Academics

St. John's University School of Law's "greatest strength... is its willingness to go to bat for its students." "Friends, alumni, and professors routinely make calls and write letters on behalf of students," one happy student says. St. John's provides a "strong alumni base, especially in the NYC area," and has "a great reputation in the New York Judicial arena." Consequentially, graduates "have an edge in both NYC and Long Island firms." SJU "has a very collegial atmosphere" with "no backstabbing." The friendly atmosphere is created in part by the fact that "each 1L class is divided into three groups that take all of their first year classes together." Students quickly make friends and "camaraderie is pervasive, everyone works hard, [and] most are willing to help each other with outlines or forming study groups."

"The teachers are uniformly excellent," and most "have an Ivy League background" and are "experienced within their respective fields." These "absolutely amazing" professors tend to have an "open door policy" and "are pleasant and willing to help." "The professor student interaction is great," although one student says there is "much too much emphasis on rote memorization of law that leads to cramming and a 'brain dump' on a single final exam." "The professor takes a personal interest in his or her student" and the school "encourages participation in its trial advocacy, moot court and journal programs." "A few (maybe 10 percent) of the Professors seem very unenthusiastic, like they don't want to be there," but overall the teachers are "excellent" and "accessible beyond belief."

Student opinion on the administration is more divided. Some say that the "helpful" administration "works like clockwork." Others say "the right hand never knows what the left is doing, and you can go to five different people with the same question and get five different answers." A 2L says, "I would say the administration has your back. It's not 'us and them;' it's 'us.'" Students are friendly with the Dean, who "tries to get to know everyone" and is frequently seen "walking around." By far the most common complaint is a rather unusual one: "temperature regulation." The "climate problem in the classrooms" means that "it can be fifty degrees in a room one day and ninety degrees the next day." "Seriously, why is blazing hot in every other room?" one sweaty student bemoans. Otherwise, "the facilities are nice" and "classrooms have all been re-done in recent years and utilize current technology." "The library is well organized and has a good variety of quiet areas and common areas for group work," when students need to study. "The most valuable resource so far has been the Career Development Office," a 1L tells us. "I was able to get instant feedback on cover letters and résumés. In the end, this led to me landing a desirable summer internship rather quickly."

ROBERT M. HARRISON, ASSISTANT DEAN FOR ADMISSIONS
8000 UTOPIA PARKWAY, QUEENS, NY 11439
TEL: 718-990-6474 • FAX: 718-990-2526
E-MAIL: LAWINFO@STJOHNS.EDU • WEBSITE: WWW.LAW.STJOHNS.EDU

Life

"Stop by the cafeteria at lunch time and the noise and energy make it obvious these students ACTUALLY LIKE each other!" one student boasts. SJU students "are helpful, friendly, and the competition is not cutthroat." Instead, students treat each other "like family" although "it is a bit cliquey at times." "The admissions department does a great job of recruiting bright, thoughtful, dynamic and diversified groups of students." That said, they do a poor job in "ethnic diversity" and the student body is "an utter white wash, though I think the school has improved that aspect over the last couple years."

Despite being located in the NYC city limits, students say "you need a car at St. John's" if you want to get anywhere. "The train ride to Manhattan is NOT reasonable," taking about an hour to get from campus to Times Square. "There is practically nothing 'within walking distance,' if you consider 'walking distance' less than twenty minutes away," one student grumbles. Still, if you can brave the ride then all of New York City is at your disposal. "Everything is what you make of it," one student muses, "and St. John's has a very large amount of opportunities to join groups that are highly involved, social, and supportive."

Getting In

SJU takes over 200 full time students per class and is easier to get into than other schools in the NYC area. Admitted students at the 25th percentile have LSAT scores in the low 150s and undergraduate GPAs close to 3.2. At the 75th percentile, LSAT scores are in the high 150s, and GPAs are around 3.6.

Clinical program required	No
Legal writing course requirement	Yes
Legal methods course requirement	Yes
Legal research course requirement	Yes
Moot court requirement	Yes
Public interest law requirement	No

ADMISSIONS

Selectivity Rating	85
# applications received	2,810
% applicants accepted	46
% acceptees attending	16
Median LSAT	157
LSAT Range (25th to 75th percentile)	153–159
Median undergrad GPA	3.45
Application fee	$60
Regular application deadline	4/1
Transfer students accepted	Yes
Evening division offered	Yes
Part-time accepted	Yes
CAS accepted	Yes

FINANCIAL FACTS

Annual tuition	$53,290
Books and supplies	$3,357
Room & Board (on/off campus)	$19,730/$17,429
Financial aid application deadline	2/1
% first-year students receiving some sort of aid	98
% all students receiving some sort of aid	94
% of aid that is merit based	43
% receiving scholarships	68
Average grant	$32,352
Average loan	$42,707
Average total aid package	$58,485
Average debt	$113,353

EMPLOYMENT INFORMATION

Career Rating	90
Total 2014 JD Grads	257
% for whom you have useable information	100
% grads employed ten months out	90
Median starting salary	$65,000
% job accepting grads providing useable salary information	54
# employed full-time	201
# employed part-time	30
# employed bar required	176
# employed JD preferred	44
# employed professional/other	6
# employed non-professional	5
# pursuing advanced degree	3
# unemployed and seeking employment	20
# not seeking employment	1
% grads employed by school	2
State for bar exam	NY
Pass rate for first-time bar	86.0

Prominent Alumni

Judge P. Kevin Castel, United States District Judge, Southern District of New York; Elisa D. Garcia, Executive Vice President and Chief Legal Officer, Office Depot Inc.; Steven J. Gartner, Co-Chairman, Willkie Farr & Gallagher LLP

Grads Employed by Field (%)

Academic (2)
Business/Industry (20)
Government (14)
Judicial Clerkship (2)
Federal: (1)
State or local: (1)
Private Practice (53)
　Solo: (1)
　2-10: (37)
　11-25: (17)
　26-50: (13)
　51-100: (13)
　101-250: (4)
　251-500: (4)
　501+: (10)
　Size Unknown: (0)
Public Interest (5)

ST. MARY'S UNIVERSITY

INSTITUTIONAL INFORMATION

Public/private	Private
Affiliation	Roman Catholic
Student-faculty ratio	20:1
% faculty part-time	59
% faculty female	40
% faculty underrepresented minority	22
Total faculty	109

SURVEY SAYS...
Diverse opinions accepted in classrooms

STUDENTS

Enrollment of law school	769
% male/female	57/43
% from out-of-state	10
% part-time	23
% underrepresented minority	48
# of countries represented	2
Average age of entering class	24

ACADEMICS

Academic Experience Rating	**72**
Profs interesting rating	79
Profs accessible rating	78
Hours of study per day	4.14

Academic Specialties
Alternative Dispute Resolution, Advocacy, Clinical, Criminal, International

Advanced Degrees Offered
LLM in International and Comparative Law and LLM in International Criminal Law for U.S. educated graduates; LLM in American Legal Studies for foreign educated graduates; Masters in Jurisprudence, concentrations in several areas; each 1 yr.

Combined Degrees Offered
JD/I.R. International Relations; JD/MPA Public Administration; JD/MT Theology; JD/MS Computer Science; JD/MBA; 3.5–4 yrs.

Academics

Located in San Antonio, the St. Mary's University School of Law boasts a strong commitment to public service and pro bono work, and students praise it's "service-oriented mission." In fact, "St. Mary's dominates in pro bono work in Texas." "St. Mary's has a new dean who has already done amazing things for the school, including increasing the number and size of scholarships available, and bringing new focus to the school in more modern areas of law" although one student adds that "the rest of administration is fairly inaccessible, or if you manage to get a request across their desk, it is usually summarily shot down." The professors at St. Mary's "are an amazing group who are really trying to prepare us for the world of law practice, while at the same time being incredibly supportive and helpful." Another student adds that "the professors at St. Mary's University School of Law are the School's best assets. They are welcoming, honest and have many voices to share. Most, if not all, of them offer practical experience in class and a good portion are also quite entertaining."

St. Mary's may be a Catholic and Marianist institution, but "it is very welcome[ing] to people of all faiths or no faith at all." Additionally. St. Mary's Law Journal is "one of the most cited law journals in the country, and [the school] also boasts a second law journal, The Scholar, which is the only one in the country that focuses on social and race issues in the law." The first-year curriculum is "tough," and St. Mary's curve "isn't as forgiving as other more prestigious law schools. St. Mary's doesn't artificially inflate grades, but this means if you get a high grade, you really did earn it." The "Mock Trial/Moot Court/Negotiations Programs . . . consistently produce national ranked teams and provide students with practicable skills."

Overall, students "feel fortunate to have attended St. Mary's Law School," but note the "disadvantage when it comes to 'big law' and judicial internships & clerkships (as compared to University of Texas students)," although there are "opportunities St. Mary's students have because of particular professors who have forged relationships with federal and Texas judges." Students at St. Mary's "benefit greatly from professors who impart the practicalities of practicing law, not just the theory, and administrators who strive to provide as many opportunities to gain practical skills as possible. Regardless of whether it is more difficult to obtain post-grad employment because of St. Mary's ranking, I think these aspects (and the tremendous faculty) are well worth it."

Life

"What sets St. Mary's apart is the collective spirit. Students are not afraid of working together to accomplish a similar goal," but "while some cliques can form, it is more a separation of people who participate and people who don't. Those that don't go to events may feel excluded in classroom discussions because some students simply know each other better." And while "the competitive nature of the grades creates a sense of urgency in some students who feel they are constantly looking over their shoulder to see who may be trying to gain an edge over the others," many students nonetheless "feel free to share their notes and outlines with others." Students applaud the "availability of various student organizations, which open up doors to anything from an interview with the Supreme Court of Texas to lasting friendships."

Ms. Catherine Casiano, Director of Recruitment
One Camino Santa Maria, San Antonio, TX 78228-8601
Tel: 866-639-5831 • Fax: NULL
Email: lawadmissions@stmarytx.edu • Website: www.stmarytx.edu/law

Although "the facilities could use some improvement," students note that "the university recently upgraded a few classrooms, which have been received very well, but other elements, such as the library study rooms, could use expansion and renovation. Additionally, the law school does not have many on-campus food locations or student lounge areas that encourage students to stay after classes have ended."

Getting In

Falling well below the median LSAT score of 150 or median GPA 3.02 doesn't necessarily result in rejection at St. Mary's. The committee carefully considers intangibles, such as maturity derived from previous career experience, the ability to overcome challenges, and cultural competence. They are looking for rigorous undergraduate course work and an inclination toward public service. It is best to get applications in soon after the Admissions Office starts accepting them in November.

Clinical program required	No
Legal writing course requirement	Yes
Legal methods course requirement	Yes
Legal research course requirement	Yes
Moot court requirement	Yes
Public interest law requirement	No

ADMISSIONS

Selectivity Rating	74
# applications received	1,154
% applicants accepted	70
% acceptees attending	31
Average LSAT	150
Median LSAT	150
LSAT Range (25th to 75th percentile)	148–152
Average undergrad GPA	3.02
Median undergrad GPA	3.02
Application fee	$0
Regular application deadline	3/1
Regular notification	5/1
Transfer students accepted	Yes
Evening division offered	Yes
Part-time accepted	Yes
CAS accepted	Yes

International Students

TOEFL recommended of international students.	Yes

FINANCIAL FACTS

Annual tuition	$32,340
Books and supplies	$1,500
Fees	$670
Room & Board	$11,830
Financial aid application deadline	3/31
% first-year students receiving some sort of aid	88
% all students receiving some sort of aid	90
% of aid that is merit based	11
% receiving scholarships	38
Average debt	$116,782

EMPLOYMENT INFORMATION

Career Rating	88	
Total 2014 JD Grads	218	
% for whom you have useable information	100	
% grads employed ten months out	80	
Median starting salary	$65,500	
% job accepting grads providing useable salary information	19	
# employed full-time	162	
# employed part-time	13	
# employed bar required	132	
# employed JD preferred	33	
# employed professional/other	10	
# employed non-professional	0	
# pursuing advanced degree	4	
# unemployed and seeking employment	30	
# not seeking employment	8	
% grads employed by school	0	
State for bar exam	TX, FL, MO, OK, NM, NV, WA	
Pass rate for first-time bar	83.0	

Prominent Alumni

John Cornyn, United States Senator from Texas; Charles Gonzalez, Congressman; Alma L. Lopez, Former Chief Justice of the Texas Court of Appeals; Thomas Mummert, U.S. Magistrate Judge; Nelson Wolff, Former Mayor of San Antonio

Grads Employed by Field (%)

Academic (1)
Business/Industry (11)
Government (8)
Judicial Clerkship (1)
Federal: (0)
State or local: (1)
Other: (0)
Private Practice (55)
Solo: (8)
2-10: (34)
11-25: (6)
26-50: (3)
51-100: (1)
101-250: (1)
251-500: (1)
Public Interest (4)

ST. THOMAS UNIVERSITY
SCHOOL OF LAW

INSTITUTIONAL INFORMATION

Public/private	Private
Affiliation	Roman Catholic
% faculty part-time	46
% faculty female	50
% faculty underrepresented minority	30
Total faculty	91

SURVEY SAYS...
Diverse opinions accepted in classrooms, Abundant externship/ internship/clerkship opportunities, Strong sense of community, Good social life

STUDENTS

Enrollment of law school	659
% male/female	45/55
% from out-of-state	20
% part-time	0
% underrepresented minority	80
% international	2
# of countries represented	9
Average age of entering class	26

ACADEMICS

Academic Experience Rating	**78**
Profs interesting rating	89
Profs accessible rating	97
Hours of study per day	4.25

Academic Specialties
Human Rights, International, Taxation, Immigration. Certificate Programs in Tax, Elder Law, Environmental, Sustainability, Intercultural Human Rights.

Advanced Degrees Offered
LLM in Intercultural Human Rights, 1 yr. JSD in Intercultural Human Rights, 2–5 yrs.

Combined Degrees Offered
JD/MS in Marriage & Family Counseling (3 yrs); JD/MS in Sports Administration (3 yrs); JD/MBA in Sports Administration (3 yrs); JD/MBA in Accounting (3 yrs); JD/MBA in International Business (3 yrs); JD/BA 3+3 Program (6 yrs).

Academics

St. Thomas University School of Law offers "a small, tight-knit community" that truly wants to see its students thrive and succeed. The school takes a practical approach to teaching law and students are quick to highlight the legal writing department, which they view as an "asset." Indeed, the in-depth curriculum requires "a closed memo, open memo, motion for summary judgment, client letter, affidavit, service lists, statement of the facts, complaint and answer to the complaint, interrogatories, request for admissions, request for documents, summons, and appeals brief (and argument in the presence of three judges)." As one second-year continues, "Legal writing [is] the cornerstone of [your] career. Therefore, the standards for memos, motions, etc. are high."

Moreover, law students here speak glowingly about their "tremendously helpful and supportive" professors. The vast majority seems to maintain "an open door policy," which really "allows students to visit professors freely to ask questions and review problems." Additionally many truly appreciate how STU professors "push their students to achieve legal and social excellence." Indeed, "they are always there to offer whatever they can to help students, which is always well researched or spoken from their extensive experience." This praise also extends to the administration, which tends to "greet the students with open arms and typically by first name." Impressively, they also operate under an open door policy, which "helps cater to the needs of students (ex: extending library hours during final exams)." As a second-year brags, "Anything the students want/need, the students feel free to bring up to the administration for their consideration."

STU also provides "great" research facilities and on-campus resources. One second-year elaborates, "Not only do we have Westlaw and LexisNexis, we have access to other great databases such as JSTOR and HeinOnline. Campus offers unlimited, free printing which is helping when writing your law review comment and/or seminar paper." Even better, "The staff in the library is ALWAYS around to help. They will meet with you for however long you need; it is like having your own personal library assistant there for you along the way."

Students here are also extremely grateful for the professional opportunities a St. Thomas education affords them. As one second year elaborates, "The externship programs and on-campus interviews brought in from career services is phenomenal. The school places students in trial, appellate, and supreme courts for both state and federal systems." Another pleased student agrees, "The reputation that our school has in South Miami has helped place these students in the judicial clerkships and various public offices (state attorney and public defenders)." Further, St. Thomas has "a unique relationship with the Pax Romana of the United Nations. Therefore, students can be selected to go to New York to the UN headquarters for a unique experience with ambassadors and diplomats."

Life

"This law school is very diverse." In fact, it's one of the most ethnically diverse bastions of legal education in the country. There is a very high Hispanic student enrollment. There is also "a substantial number of second-career types as well as attorneys from Latin American and other countries who are revalidating their degrees" in the United States. "About half of the student body came to St. Thomas via the 'traditional' student method," estimates a 1L, "and the other half is a little older and brings a wide range of practical understandings. This dichotomy leads to some truly enlightening classroom discussions." Some students explain, "There is a good deal of competition" academically. Others say that students "join forces" and share notes regularly and copiously at exam time.

STU is situated on the main campus of the larger university in a suburb between Fort Lauderdale and Miami. Some students tell us the location is "not so good." The cost of living in these parts isn't the cheapest, either. On the plus side, the weather in South Florida is "very relaxing" virtually year-round, and the Floridian campus boasts palm trees, ponds, and tennis courts. The area also offers tons of activities and nightlife. Bars, restaurants, shopping and cuisine are all world-class and, of course, "you always have the beaches." Perhaps more importantly, students at STU are privy to "rich experiences" and "fantastic events." A pleased third-year proudly shares, "Our Law Review [has] hosted a tremendous symposium on Media and the Law, in which Harvard Law Professor Charles Nesson was the keynote speaker." Additionally, "[one] semester, Justice Scalia came and talked to our school." St. Thomas Law hosts many alumni networking opportunities, affording students chances to network with the bench and bar. Socially, there are "enough student organizations to find something you like." This law school is a pretty tight-knit place too. "Close relationships" are easily formed, and students know pretty much everyone in their class year. Also, "The school design invites socialization." "There is a breezeway always full of students talking and hanging out, sharing thoughts, and talking about the professors and classes."

Getting In

St. Thomas University School of Law nets a competitive applicant pool. Admitted students in the 25th percentile scored a 145 on the LSAT and achieved a GPA of 2.71 Admitted students in the 75th percentile scored a 151 on the LSAT and achieved a GPA of 3.36. The overall median LSAT score was 149 and the median GPA was 3.08.

Clinical program required	No
Legal writing course requirement	Yes
Legal methods course requirement	Yes
Legal research course requirement	Yes
Moot court requirement	Yes
Public interest law requirement	Yes

ADMISSIONS

Selectivity Rating	73
# applications received	1,318
% applicants accepted	62
% of acceptees attending	30
Average LSAT	149
Median LSAT	148
LSAT Range (25th to 75th percentile)	145–151
Median undergrad GPA	3.06
Application fee	$40
Regular application deadline	5/1
Transfer students accepted	Yes
Evening division offered	No
Part-time accepted	No
CAS accepted	Yes

International Students

TOEFL recommended of international students.	Yes

FINANCIAL FACTS

Annual tuition	$38,458
Books and supplies	$1,250
Room & Board (on/ off campus)	$17,200/$14,072
Financial aid application deadline	5/1
% of all students receiving some sort of aid	90
% of aid that is merit based	46
Average grant	$15,000
Average total aid package	$55,416
Average debt	$150,166

EMPLOYMENT INFORMATION

Career Rating	**77**	**Prominent Alumni**
Total 2014 JD Grads	230	Brett Barfield, Partner, Holland & Knight;
% grads employed ten months out	76	Mark Romance, Partner, Richman Greer;
Median starting salary	$45,000	Jose Baez, The Baez Law Firm; The
# employed full-time	159	Honorable Margaret T. Courtney, 13th
# employed part-time	13	Judicial Circuit,FL; The Honorable Pedro
# employed bar required	111	Dijols, 17th Judicial Circuit, FL
# employed JD preferred	39	**Grads Employed by Field (%)**
# employed professional/other	8	Academic (2)
# employed non-professional	1	Business/Industry (17)
# pursuing advanced degree	7	Government (13)
# unemployed and seeking employment	41	Judicial Clerkship (1)
# not seeking employment	4	Private Practice (60)
% grads employed by school	1	Public Interest (7)
State for bar exam	FL, NY, GA, CA	
Pass rate for first-time bar	75.0	

STANFORD UNIVERSITY
SCHOOL OF LAW

INSTITUTIONAL INFORMATION

Public/private	Private
Affiliation	No Affiliation
% faculty female	35
% faculty underrepresented minority	17
Total faculty	60

SURVEY SAYS...

Students love Stanford, CA, Diverse opinions accepted in classrooms, Great research resources, Abundant externship/internship/clerkship opportunities, Law school well run, Liberal students, Strong sense of community

STUDENTS

Enrollment of law school	577
% male/female	55/45
% underrepresented minority	35
Average age of entering class	24

ACADEMICS

Academic Experience Rating	99
Profs interesting rating	98
Profs accessible rating	93
Hours of study per day	3.69

Academic Specialties

Civil Procedure, Commercial, Constitutional, Corporation Securities, Criminal, Environmental, Government Services, Human Rights, International, Labor, Legal History, Legal Philosophy, Property, Taxation, Intellectual Property

Advanced Degrees Offered

MLS 1 yr; JSM 1 yr; LLM 1 yr; JSD 4 yrs

Combined Degrees Offered

JD/MBA 3 2/3–4 yrs; JD/MA 3 yrs; JD/PhD 6 yrs

Academics

"People are happy" at Stanford Law School, and why wouldn't they be? There are "tons of programs," an array of specialized centers, and a couple dozen joint-degree options. The eleven clinics here include a Supreme Court litigation clinic and an IP Innovation clinic, just to list a couple. "The resources available to us at Stanford are fantastic, and sometimes unbelievable," gushes a 2L. The "amazingly brilliant" and "diverse" faculty is "a great mix of practically minded and experienced—professors and wild-minded theorists." Professors are "incredible lecturers and easy to approach outside of the classroom." "I have yet to meet a professor who is not only doing something amazing but is completely approachable and dying to help us get jobs and do research," gloats a 2L. Moreover, Stanford is "so small that everything is very easy to do." "All of my seminars have had fewer than ten people," gloats a 2L. "The university as a whole has a lot of red tape," but the law school's administration is "very receptive" and accessible at almost every level. "It's the opposite of the 'factory' feeling at large professional schools," explains a 3L. "If you want to do something new or nontraditional, just ask. Usually you can work something out."

The Stanford campus is "sprawling" and "beautiful," with "acres of rolling green hills for hiking, and palm trees everywhere." "The law school is hideous from the outside but, inside, it's quite nice." The library is a world-class research facility "and all law students have twenty-four-hour access to study there." "I can't study in any other university library," admits a comfortable 1L, "because I have become too accustomed to the law school's Aeron chairs."

A few students call Career Services "underwhelming," but "pretty much everyone can get a firm job if they want one." They can get that job anywhere in the country, too. Less than 50 percent of all newly minted Stanford Law grads take jobs in California. Stanford is also "seriously committed to public interest law," and the "great loan repayment program" here is arguably the best in the country. Also worth noting is the impressive historical fact that more than 100 Stanford law graduates have clerked for one of the Supreme Court Justices.

Of course, nothing is perfect, even at Stanford. Some students love the pass/fail grading system while others say it provides little incentive to work hard. Despite these complaints, though, students call Stanford "the best law school west of the Appalachians," and they "have a hard time seeing why anyone would choose to go to law school anywhere else."

Life

"Small size makes for a more personal experience" at Stanford. Here, "you really get to know your classmates, and there is consequently no competitive behavior." The academic atmosphere is "very collaborative." There are "study groups galore." Students describe themselves as "ridiculously smart people" who are "highly ambitious" and "work extremely hard." "It easy to feel like you must have been admitted by mistake," confesses an awed 1L. There is "lots of diversity" in terms of age, background, ethnicity, and pretty much every other attribute. Some students call the political environment "overwhelmingly liberal." Other students say "there's a critical mass of right-of-center students," and they point out that you definitely won't see too many protests among law students. "Perhaps that's because everyone harbors secret Supreme Court ambitions and wouldn't want to pigeonhole their position on an issue somewhere the Senate Confirmation Committee could find it," suggests a 1L.

OFFICE OF ADMISSIONS
559 NATHAN ABBOTT WAY, STANFORD, CA 94305-8610
TEL: 650-723-4985 • FAX: 650-723-0838
E-MAIL: ADMISSIONS@LAW.STANFORD.EDU • WEBSITE: WWW.LAW.STANFORD.EDU

Certainly, "you won't have to contend with snow or gloomy weather" at this school. "The weather is perfect 90 percent of the time." Some students call Palo Alto "a cultural wonderland" that has everything you need including "incredibly nice" graduate student housing located right next to the law school. Other students gripe, "Living in Palo Alto is like living in a suburb, which to anyone who is coming from an urban area will be a shock." "A big percentage of Stanford students are married, or commute from San Francisco, so they have their own lives away from the school." Extracurricular activity is constant for everyone, though. "Having the law school right in the middle of Silicon Valley allows for many practitioners, general counsels, venture capitalists," and the like to drop by. Student organizations are profuse. "Everyone at Stanford is president of a club, editor of a journal, director of a pro bono, and a board member of a society," claims a 2L. "Social events are plentiful," and they are "always a hoot." There is something of a fraternity-like culture if that's what you are looking for, but it's "not [an] overwhelming scene," and we aren't talking about people doing multiple keg stands. "You have to remember that everyone had to be pretty studious and dorky in order to get in here," says a 1L.

Getting In

Admission to Stanford Law is very competitive. Enrolled students at the 25th percentile have LSAT scores of about 169 and GPAs of roughly 3.8. Enrolled students at the 75th percentile have LSAT scores above 174 and GPAs pretty close to 4.0.

Clinical program required	No
Legal writing course requirement	Yes
Legal methods course requirement	No
Legal research course requirement	Yes
Moot court requirement	No
Public interest law requirement	No

ADMISSIONS

Selectivity Rating	99
# applications received	4,482
% applicants accepted	9
% acceptees attending	44
Average LSAT	171
LSAT Range (25th to 75th percentile)	169–174
Average undergrad GPA	3.87
Application fee	$100
Regular application deadline	2/1
Regular notification	4/30
Transfer students accepted	Yes
Evening division offered	No
Part-time accepted	No
CAS accepted	Yes

FINANCIAL FACTS

Annual tuition	$52,350
Books and supplies	$1,470
Room & Board (on/ off campus)	$21,399/$21,735
Financial aid application deadline	3/15
% first-year students receiving some sort of aid	89
% all students receiving some sort of aid	80
% of aid that is merit based	0
% receiving scholarships	49
Average grant	$23,164
Average loan	$43,886
Average total aid package	$55,773
Average debt	$128,137

EMPLOYMENT INFORMATION

Career Rating	99
Total 2014 JD Grads	187
% for whom you have useable information	100
% grads employed ten months out	96
# employed full-time	179
# employed part-time	1
# employed bar required	170
# employed JD preferred	5
# employed professional/other	5
# employed non-professional	0
# pursuing advanced degree	2
# unemployed and seeking employment	3
# not seeking employment	0
% grads employed by school	5
State for bar exam	CA, NY, VA, MA, GA
Pass rate for first-time bar	91.0

Prominent Alumni

Sandra Day O'Connor, First female Supreme Court Justice (1981 to 2006); Warren Christopher, Former Secretary of State (1993 to 1997); Anthony Romero, Executive Director of ACLU (2001 to present); Max Baucus, US Senator (1979 to Present); Ron Noble, Secretary General of Interpol and law professor

Grads Employed by Field (%)

Academic (3)
Business/Industry (5)
Government (2)
Judicial Clerkship (32)
Private Practice (48)
Public Interest (9)

THE STATE UNIVERSITY OF NEW YORK
UNIVERSITY AT BUFFALO LAW SCHOOL

INSTITUTIONAL INFORMATION

Public/private	Public
Affiliation	No Affiliation
Student-faculty ratio	10:1
% faculty part-time	40
% faculty female	36
% faculty underrepresented minority	8
Total faculty	105

SURVEY SAYS...
Diverse opinions accepted in classrooms

STUDENTS

Enrollment of law school	557
% male/female	50/50
% from out-of-state	8
% part-time	1
% underrepresented minority	16
% international	4
# of countries represented	5
Average age of entering class	25

ACADEMICS

Academic Experience Rating	**82**
Profs interesting rating	77
Profs accessible rating	72
Hours of study per day	4.69

Academic Specialties
Criminal, Cross-Border, Environmental, Family, International, Intellectual Property

Advanced Degrees Offered
LLM in Criminal Law, 1 yr; LLM General 1 yr; Double LLM with the Catholic University of Lyon, 1 yr; Advanced Standing JD for Internationally-Trained Lawyers, 2 yrs

Combined Degrees Offered
JD/MSW, 4 yrs; JD/MBA, 4 yrs; JD/MS in Library Studies, 4 yrs; JD/MA Applied Economics, 3.5 yrs; JD/MUP, 4 yrs; JD/Pharm.D., 6 yrs; JD/PhD, 6+ yrs;

Academics

SUNY Buffalo Law School is a practical and affordable option for future New York State lawyers. The school's three-year JD begins with a series of required classes in contracts, torts, and other basic areas. In the next two years, law students have the "ability to create a unique curriculum" through a "nice array of courses," including "timely classes that are relevant to the world and cover cutting edge legal issues (examples: class on international piracy, class on counterterrorism law, etc.)." The school offers curricular concentrations in nine fields, including civil litigation and intellectual property, and students note the array of "great human rights and international law classes." While they like the course diversity, many Buffalo students feel the school could dig even deeper into specialty topics and "incorporate more courses which teach practical lawyering skills in specific areas of the law." Fortunately, curricular improvements are being implemented with attention and efficiency. "The current administration is making a concerted effort to improve the look of the school and the opportunities available to students." In addition, many students praise the schools' supervisors and staff and attest, "School administrators seem to genuinely care about you from the moment you step in the door all the way up to graduation and beyond."

Buffalo offers "plenty of opportunity to get hands-on experience in legal jobs during law school." Traditional academics are augmented by "diverse opportunities for experiential learning," including "non-traditional course offerings like clinics and externships." Within the law school, "there are countless opportunities for moot court, trial team, and journal work," and "the law school's clinic program is excellent." Of particular note, "the school goes out of its way to help those interested in Public Interest work," with numerous clinics devoted to affordable housing, community economic advocacy, and social justice. Over 50 percent of each graduating class works in private practice. Even so, some would also like to see the school build a "stronger presence in the greater Buffalo community," and point out the campus's isolated location in a northern suburb of the city. The events and culture generated from having over 24,000 undergraduate and graduate students on Buffalo's campus should not be discounted, though.

When it comes to the teaching staff, students praise Buffalo's "terrific adjunct professors," saying they love being taught by "faculty members who are still trying cases, rather than those who have been out of court for years." The school attracts a number of accomplished attorneys, and "some of the faculty [are] at the very pinnacle of their fields, with reputations that span the country." A current student enthuses, "On multiple occasions, my professors have actually worked on the cases we cover in class." Despite their many accolades, "faculty is hit or miss" in the classroom. Because SUNY is a "great research institution," it tends to attract "professors that are experts in their field with a significant amount of publishing in their background, but have no teaching skills and no ability to relate to the students." Outside of the classroom, teachers are diverse in the same manner. Some professors are friendly and student-oriented, while others "are not always accessible because they are busy."

Buffalo is a great choice for local lawyers, and the school maintains a great "reputation in New York, particularly in western New York." For many local students, cost was also a major factor in their decision to attend SUNY Buffalo. New York state residents not surprisingly, comprise more than 90 percent of the school's population, but the Law School offers competitive scholarships for qualified applicants whether in-state or out-of-state residents.

LILLIE V. WILEY-UPSHAW, VICE DEAN FOR ADMISSIONS AND FINANCIAL AID
309 O'BRIAN HALL, BUFFALO, NY 14260
TEL: 716-645-2907 • FAX: 716-645-6676
E-MAIL: LAW-ADMISSIONS@BUFFALO.EDU • WEBSITE: WWW.LAW.BUFFALO.EDU

Life

Students seeking a "serious, but not overly competitive environment" will find a good match at SUNY Buffalo, where academic rigors are balanced by a "strong sense of community and camaraderie among the students." Most students are serious about their education and "come ready to work every day." However, that sense of purpose never overrides the generally low-key and friendly atmosphere within the law school. A current student elaborates, "While we are all competitive, there is a "no 1L left behind," feeling to all of the classes. If you are having trouble with the material there are always countless students willing to sit down and thoroughly discuss the material until you grasp it." Both socially and professionally, the collegial atmosphere pays off. Here, "networking is easy at UB because everyone is already your friend."

Within the law school, there are "myriad, valuable student organizations." Socially, one student proclaims, "There are always SO many events going on, it is literally impossible to keep up," especially since the law school is located on the University at Buffalo campus with an enrollment of over 24,000. In contrast, there isn't much happening in the surrounding area. Located in "suburban hell," campus is north of Buffalo proper with "nothing in walking distance. You have to drive everywhere to get or do anything." Not only is "there is no 'college town' feel," students remind us that "the heart of Buffalo's legal community, including the state and federal courthouses and the major law firms, remains in downtown Buffalo."

Getting In

In addition to LSAT scores and GPA, the most important components of any law school application, SUNY Buffalo Law also considers the personal statement, recommendation, and professional or volunteer experience. In the most recent incoming class, the median LSAT score was 154 and the median GPA was 3.43.

EMPLOYMENT INFORMATION

Career Rating	85	
Total 2014 JD Grads	191	
% for whom you have useable information	98	
% grads employed ten months out	88	
Median starting salary	$65,000	
% job accepting grads providing useable salary information	60	
# employed full-time	153	
# employed part-time	15	
# employed bar required	29	
# employed JD preferred	30	
# employed professional/other	7	
# employed non-professional	2	
# pursuing advanced degree	1	
# unemployed and seeking employment	15	
# not seeking employment	4	
State for bar exam	NY, NJ, MA, CT, GA	
Pass rate for first-time bar	78.2	

Prominent Alumni
Hon. Julio M. Fuentes '75, US Court of Appeals for the 3rd Circuit

Grads Employed by Field (%)
Academic (3)
Business/Industry (17)
Government (13)
Judicial Clerkship (4)
  Federal: (2)
  State or local: (2)
Private Practice (48)
  Solo: (1)
  2-10: (19)
  11-25: (5)
  26-50: (7)
  51-100: (2)
  101-250: (5)
  251-500: (1)
  501+: (1)
  Size Unknown: (7)
Public Interest (5)

Clinical program required	No
Legal writing course requirement	Yes
Legal methods course requirement	No
Legal research course requirement	Yes
Moot court requirement	No
Public interest law requirement	Yes

ADMISSIONS

Selectivity Rating	82
# applications received	1,065
% applicants accepted	56
% acceptees attending	24
Average LSAT	154
Median LSAT	154
LSAT Range (25th to 75th percentile)	151–157
Average undergrad GPA	3.35
Median undergrad GPA	3.43
Application fee	$85
Regular application deadline	3/1
Early application deadline	11/15
Early application notification	12/15
Transfer students accepted	Yes
Evening division offered	No
Part-time accepted	No
CAS accepted	Yes

International Students

TOEFL required of international students.	Yes

FINANCIAL FACTS

Annual tuition (in-state/out-of-state)	$26,111/$43,100
Books and supplies	$1,438
Fees	$2,276
Room & Board (on/off campus)	$7,680/$10,906
Financial aid application deadline	3/1
% first-year students receiving some sort of aid	94
% all students receiving some sort of aid	86
% of aid that is merit based	12
% receiving scholarships	56
Average grant	$6,240
Average loan	$31,486
Average total aid package	$31,475
Average debt	$76,010

STETSON UNIVERSITY
COLLEGE OF LAW

INSTITUTIONAL INFORMATION

Public/private	Private
% faculty part-time	56
% faculty female	46
% faculty underrepresented minority	14
Total faculty	111

SURVEY SAYS...
Students love Gulfport, FL, Diverse opinions accepted in classrooms, Great research resources

STUDENTS

Enrollment of law school	865
% male/female	51/49
% from out-of-state	23
% part-time	23
% underrepresented minority	24
% international	1
# of countries represented	5
Average age of entering class	24

ACADEMICS

Academic Experience Rating	**84**
Profs interesting rating	78
Profs accessible rating	85
Hours of study per day	3.74

Academic Specialties
Environmental, International

Advanced Degrees Offered
JD 3 yrs full-time, 4 yrs part-time; LLM Advocacy, Elder Law, and International Law, typically 1–2 yrs

Combined Degrees Offered
JD/MBA, 3 yrs full-time; JD/LLM in Advocacy, 3.5 yrs full-time; JD/MPH with University of South Florida, approx. 4–5 yrs; JD/MIEL (French Graduate Degree through University of Toulouse) min. 4 yrs; JD/MEBL (Spanish Graduate Degree through Universidad Pontificia Comillas, Madrid) min. 4 yrs

Academics

Stetson University College of Law in Florida offers "a good mix of practicality and theory." Points of pride here include a serious first-year emphasis on research and writing. "The pace and the intensity of it are not matched by other schools," declares a 1L. There's a "wide variety of" "excellent" internships and clinics as well, and pro bono opportunities abound." While five certificate programs are available (in advocacy, elder law, international law, social justice, and environmental law), advocacy is far and away the principal focus here. Students gloat that Stetson is home to "the best trial advocacy school in the country." "Every week, a different trial team is out competing and winning something." "For a litigator who wants to practice in Florida, or an appellate practitioner who wants access to judicial internships in the area," counsels a 2L, "Stetson is ideal." "You will know your way around a courtroom long before graduating." However, some students say that this school overemphasizes litigation, despite a variety of electives, including state-specific topics such as Florida Criminal Procedure and Florida Civil Procedure. Students also note that Stetson isn't cheap. "I had considered transferring just to save money," admits a 3L, "but I had such a great environment at Stetson. I couldn't leave."

There are quite a few adjunct professors, who teach one or two classes per year while maintaining their practice as attorneys or judges. Some full-time professors "can make a semester seem unbearable," but by and large, the faculty at Stetson Law is "caring," "very dedicated," "and eager to make your learning experience successful." Professors are "knowledgeable in both their areas of expertise and general law and life." They're also "available and approachable." Students brag that Stetson has "one the most accessible faculties imaginable." "Despite their busy schedules, they always make time for students and are happy to do so," relates a 3L. Some members of the administration "go to great lengths to get to know students on a personal basis." Others are "arrogant [and] incompetent" and "seem to manage to screw over their students on biweekly basis."

On the employment front, "one of the biggest assets is that Stetson is one of two of the only law schools in the Tampa Bay Area." Students tell us that Stetson has an excellent reputation locally. "Judges rave about Stetson's professionalism," asserts a 3L. The name carries some weight throughout the Sunshine State as well, though "there just are not too many firms that are recruiting" on campus. Views concerning Career Development are conflicting. Some students call the staff "outstanding."

The facilities here are generally impressive. "The campus is exclusively a law school," and the hacienda-style architecture creates a kind of "old resort" vibe, which "takes away some of the sting of having to go to class." "The school has plenty of room, with large classrooms that are modern and comfortable and several gorgeous, usable courtrooms on campus." Library resources are "very impressive," and "the librarians are the best around." A 2L likens them to "fairy godmothers of legal research." Technology is a bit of sore spot, though. The server "seems to be down once a week," and "there are constant problems" with various gadgetry. Also, bring a sweater because "the air conditioning is freezing cold."

LAURA ZUPPO, ASSISTANT DEAN OF ADMISSIONS & STUDENT FINANCIAL PLANNING
1401 61ST STREET SOUTH, GULFPORT, FL 33707
TEL: 727-562-7802 • FAX: 727-343-0136
E-MAIL: LAWADMIT@LAW.STETSON.EDU • WEBSITE: WWW.LAW.STETSON.EDU

Life

Students tell us that there's "a family-like atmosphere" here. "Stetson is very open," relates a 1L. "There is a great sense of community between the students, faculty, and staff." The academic atmosphere is amicable. "Students are generally very helpful to each other, and the environment is friendly and noncompetitive for the most part. Competition is healthy rather than cutthroat or underhanded."

When students aren't hitting the books, it's easy "to get involved in organizations," and everyone here is pretty social. Students also say that they're situated in an ideal place to learn the law. "You cannot beat the location," wagers a 1L. Obviously, this is a "year-round warm place," which has numerous advantages. Stetson's "affordable, tranquil" suburban environs make for an ideal atmosphere to work, study, and play. World class beaches are a short drive away. The reasonably lively city of St. Petersburg is also close, and the broader Tampa Bay Area is a growing, bustling region of close to three million people.

Getting In

Admitted students at the 25th percentile have LSAT scores in the mid-150s and under-graduate GPAs close to 3.2. At the 75th percentile, LSAT scores approach 257, and GPAs are close to 3.7.

Clinical program required	No
Legal writing course requirement	Yes
Legal methods course requirement	Yes
Legal research course requirement	Yes
Moot court requirement	Yes
Public interest law requirement	Yes

ADMISSIONS

Selectivity Rating	**82**
# applications received	1,857
% applicants accepted	52
% acceptees attending	22
Median LSAT	155
LSAT Range (25th to 75th percentile)	152–157
Median undergrad GPA	3.23
Application fee	$55
Regular application deadline	5/15
Transfer students accepted	Yes
Evening division offered	Yes
Part-time accepted	Yes
CAS accepted	Yes

International Students

TOEFL recommended of international students.

FINANCIAL FACTS

Annual tuition	$38,584
Books and supplies	$1,300
Fees	$320
Room & Board	$14,288
% first-year students receiving some sort of aid	95
% all students receiving some sort of aid	91
% receiving scholarships	64
Average grant	$15,877
Average loan	$39,246
Average total aid package	$44,854
Average debt	$147,788

EMPLOYMENT INFORMATION

Career Rating	**82**
Total 2014 JD Grads	307
% for whom you have useable information	100
% grads employed ten months out	91
Median starting salary	$43,250
# employed full-time	266
# employed part-time	12
# employed bar required	191
# employed JD preferred	76
# employed professional/other	8
# employed non-professional	3
# pursuing advanced degree	7
# unemployed and seeking employment	18
# not seeking employment	2
% grads employed by school	9
State for bar exam	FL, GA, AL, NY, WV
Pass rate for first-time bar	80.1

Prominent Alumni
Chief Justice Carol Hunstein, Supreme Court of Georgia; Hon. Elizabeth Kovachevich, USDC Middle District Florida

Grads Employed by Field (%)
Academic (2)
Business/Industry (14)
Government (20)
Judicial Clerkship (6)
Federal: (1)
State or local: (1)
Other: (4)
Private Practice (45)
Solo: (3)
2-10: (24)
11-25: (6)
26-50: (3)
51-100: (4)
101-250: (2)
251-500: (3)
501+: (1)
Size Unknown: (1)
Public Interest (4)

SUFFOLK UNIVERSITY
LAW SCHOOL

INSTITUTIONAL INFORMATION

Public/private	Private
% faculty part-time	38
% faculty female	42
% faculty underrepresented minority	13
Total faculty	149

SURVEY SAYS...
Students love Boston, MA, Great research resources

STUDENTS

Enrollment of law school	1,706
% male/female	46/54
% from out-of-state	37
% part-time	26
% underrepresented minority	28
% international	1
# of countries represented	42
Average age of entering class	26

ACADEMICS

Academic Experience Rating	**70**
Profs interesting rating	79
Profs accessible rating	77
Hours of study per day	3.04

Academic Specialties
Commercial, Corporation Securities, Criminal, Environmental, Government Services, Human Rights, International, Labor, Property, Taxation, Intellectual Property

Advanced Degrees Offered
JD, 3 yrs FT, 4 yrs PT. LLM iGlobal Technology, LLM in General Law, 1 yr FT, 3 yrs PT. SJD, 1–3 yrs.

Combined Degrees Offered
JD/MBA, JD/MPA, JD/MS in International Economics, JD/MS in Finance, JD/MS in Criminal Justice, JD/LLM in Taxation. Each program can be completed in four yrs of full-time study or five yrs of part-time study. There also are three-year accelerated JD/MBA or JD/LLM in Taxation programs.

Academics

A very strong evening program, "high level of pro bono participation," and a fantastic bar passage rate are just a few of the many attributes that make Suffolk Law students love their school. Students say the peer-mentoring program, Academic Support Services, and specialized tutoring, as well as the school's top clinic programs, many journals, and student organizations "make for a rich law school experience." "I participated in the Juvenile Defenders Clinic, and…have been able to appear in court nearly a dozen times on behalf of my clients," says a 3L. "The practical experience you can acquire, should you desire such experience, is unparalleled." Because of the school's connection with the legal community of greater Boston, Suffolk "has a large number of current and former judges on its faculty, which provides for an excellent learning experience."

The school offers a "vast array" of different courses in all specialty areas of the law (as well as a thorough legal writing program), and the "tough but understanding" professors are "consummate professionals and experts in their field." "I have found that respectful dissenting opinions, even radical ones, are met with enthusiasm and serious consideration," says a student. These teachers are the "best part" of Suffolk, "come from all walks of life," and "are not using their positions to launch their career somewhere else." "I even had a tax law professor (a subject I dreaded) who made tax interesting and, dare I say, exciting," says a 3L.

The administration here receives similar kudos for its "fair" treatment of student concerns, particularly the Registrar's Office. "Everyone is willing to work with you [administration, registrar, faculty], but no one is going to work for you," sums up a student. Academic support and bar prep are both "excellent," though Career Services "needs to do better about reaching out to students and professionals in the field to actually place students while in law school," by "building alumni connections within private employers in the city."

Another perk of Suffolk Law is the strong alumni network, which, "in a city with so many law schools…is very important." "Anywhere you go, anywhere you work, there will be a Suffolk grad," says a 1L. A 2L puts it a little less delicately: "I think we're all aware that we're probably not getting by on the name of the school like other Boston schools, so everybody is really focus[ed] on building their networks and learning the skills they need."

The facilities here are brand-new and "outstanding." "I feel like I am part of a grand tradition of lawyers, yet have access to state-of-the-art classrooms," says a 3L. Still, many students wish the school's reputation had more of a "national presence," as the name "doesn't immediately curry the same sort of respect as a more highly ranked school." "Something is holding the school back from being respected as a top law school. It is not the faculty and it is not the students," says one of many puzzled students.

Life

The "fairly large student body" is divided into 1L sections upon entrance to the school, which does a lot "to create close friendships and collaborative relationships between new students." The school is pretty much composed of "nice, young people, mostly from the Boston area," which makes for "a cohesive bunch—none of that *Paper Chase* nonsense." "I am so happy to be at a school where I feel challenged by my classmates, but not threatened," says a student. A surprising number of students refer to the "professionalism" of their classmates, possibly due to the frequent intermingling of day and evening students

MATTHEW GAVIN, INTERIM ASSISTANT DEAN OF ADMISSIONS
120 TREMONT STREET, BOSTON, MA 02108-4977
TEL: 617-573-8144 • FAX: 617-523-1367
E-MAIL: LAWADM@SUFFOLK.EDU • WEBSITE: WWW.SUFFOLK.EDU/LAW

in evening classes, which "is of benefit to both, with the evening students bringing a lot of real-world experience to class discussions." On the flip side, "it's hard to get involved in the social side of life at Suffolk when you're in the evening program."

The central Boston location "couldn't be better," and lends to the school the quality of a "social paradise, with frequent events at school and local bars." "You're [a] ten-minute walk from the Prudential Center, a five-minute walk from Faneuil Hall, a two-minute walk from Pemberton Square, ten minutes from the BMC, and thirty seconds from the Boston Common or the State House." Most first-year students "gather at the local watering hole on Friday afternoon to let off steam and talk trash about the other sections" in a good-natured way. There are also "consistent events throughout the academic year" involving clubs, job opportunities, networking seminars, political groups, and more.

Getting In

Admission to Suffolk Law School is based on individual consideration of each applicant's academic achievement, character and fitness, commitment to a legal education, life experience and potential contribution to the future of the legal profession. The Admissions Committee also considers an applicant's potential contribution to the enrichment and diversity of the law school community. While no quotas or goals are set, such contributing factors may include cultural or ethnic background, geographic origin, personal interests and talents, special achievements, life experience, leadership qualities, maturity, and individuals who have overcome adversity.

Clinical program required	No
Legal writing course requirement	Yes
Legal methods course requirement	Yes
Legal research course requirement	Yes
Moot court requirement	Yes
Public interest law requirement	No

ADMISSIONS

Selectivity Rating	73
# applications received	2,416
% applicants accepted	78
% acceptees attending	24
Average LSAT	149
Median LSAT	149
LSAT Range (25th to 75th percentile)	145–153
Average undergrad GPA	3.24
Median undergrad GPA	3.27
Application fee	$60
Regular application deadline	3/1
Early application deadline	3/1
Transfer students accepted	Yes
Evening division offered	Yes
Part-time accepted	Yes
CAS accepted	Yes

International Students

TOEFL required of international students.	Yes

FINANCIAL FACTS

Annual tuition	$42,540
Books and supplies	$1,000
Room & Board	$18,890
Financial aid application deadline	3/1
% first-year students receiving some sort of aid	86
% all students receiving some sort of aid	85
% of aid that is merit based	49
% receiving scholarships	40
Average grant	$15,054
Average loan	$42,405
Average total aid package	$50,845
Average debt	$119,096

EMPLOYMENT INFORMATION

Career Rating	77
Total 2014 JD Grads	479
% for whom you have useable information	20
% grads employed ten months out	69
Median starting salary	$55,000
% job accepting grads providing useable salary information	55
# employed full-time	292
# employed part-time	40
# employed bar required	199
# employed JD preferred	85
# employed professional/other	35
# employed non-professional	13
# pursuing advanced degree	9
# unemployed and seeking employment	96
# not seeking employment	10
% grads employed by school	1
State for bar exam	MA, NY, RI
Pass rate for first-time bar	83.0

Prominent Alumni
Hon. Linda S. Dalianis, Chief Justice, New Hampshire Supreme Court; Robert A. DeLeo, Speaker of the Mass. House of Representatives; Kristen Kuliga, Principal, K Sports and Entertainment, NFL and MLB sports agent; William Galvin, Mass. Secretary of State; Hon. Gustavo Gelpi Jr., U.S. District Court Judge (D-Puerto Rico); President of the Federal Bar Association

Grads Employed by Field (%)
Academic (2)
Business/Industry (19)
Government (7)
Judicial Clerkship (5)
Private Practice (35)
Public Interest (2)

SYRACUSE UNIVERSITY
COLLEGE OF LAW

Academics

Syracuse University College of Law is an institution that "offers many resources [to ensure] that...students fulfill their potential." The school emphasizes "the importance of acquiring research skills" and many stress the uniqueness of the legal writing and research program. "The LCR staff come from different professional backgrounds making our legal communication and research skills adaptable." Students also value the school's connection to the "fast-rising business school (Whitman School of Management), the Maxwell School of Citizenship and Public Affairs, [along with] other departments as part of [the larger university system.]" They can also take advantage of joint-degree programs with the State University of New York—College of Environmental Science and Forestry, earning a Master in environmental sciences or natural resources management. Additionally, the "international program is fantastic." A handful of respondents also highlight "the National Security and Counterterrorism Program [along with the myriad of] opportunities for clinics/externships."

By and large, students declare that "the faculty is incredible" and represents some of the "preeminent scholars in their respective fields"; however, what they value most is just how "accessible and completely dedicated to their students success" professors have demonstrated themselves to be. As one second year explains, "They go to extreme lengths to ensure that their students understand the material. Further they are available all the time to help students." A pleased classmate adds, "They are really here to make sure students learn, not just to do research." The administration is also "extremely helpful and supportive." They take "student concerns serious[ly] and provide a lot of programming to keep us all balanced." Though a few do caution that there is "a lot of bureaucracy, which can be quite annoying to deal with if you are not a traditional law student (I am a JD/MBA). I often feel like I have to jump through hoops and fill out form after useless form just to do what is required by my program."

Syracuse opened its new 200,000-square foot, LEED-certified law facility, Dineen Hall, in Fall 2014. The new building includes all College of Law classrooms, instructor offices and clinics, a 352-seat ceremonial appellate courtroom, and houses the Law Library. Students assure us that the library "packs a punch," and many appreciate how "there are places to study if you are feeling social and places for when you need to study alone." Perhaps more importantly, the "library staff is incredible. They are knowledgeable, accessible, and helpful."

Students here are also incredibly grateful for their alumni network, which is a "fabulous resource." As one pleasantly surprised second-year elaborates, "I have found that many alumni genuinely care and are willing to go above and beyond what they are asked to help ensure that my goals are given their best chance to succeed." Many also applaud the efforts of the Office of Professional and Career Development. "They connect you with alumni, provide fast but thorough critiques of résumés and cover letters, and do a whole host of trainings to help you prepare for internship and job searches." However, others complain that "the resources available to the students seem to be limited." A 1L suggests, "Improving programming, on-campus networking events, and developing a larger database for off-campus job opportunities would strengthen this department."

Life

Many students at Syracuse proclaim that the school manages to foster "a fun environment." Indeed, the "law school holds ample events, and the university is a Division I

NIKKI S. LAUBENSTEIN, DIRECTOR OF ADMISSIONS
OFFICE OF ADMISSIONS, SUITE 340, SYRACUSE, NY 13244
TEL: 315-443-1962 • FAX: 315-443-9568
E-MAIL: ADMISSIONS@LAW.SYR.EDU • WEBSITE: WWW.LAW.SYR.EDU

athletics school and competitive in the ACC in most sports." There are also organized weekly social nights as well as a seasonal flag football league. A handful of people also socialize through the student-run Syracuse Law Review. Moreover, there are a multitude of law journals for them to join as well as moot court competitions. The surrounding area also offers "great bars [and] great restaurants." As one knowledgeable third-year expounds, "Syracuse is affordable. There is enough to do on the one night a weekend you venture out as a law student, including some really great local restaurants. [Additionally, it's only a] short drive to larger cities like Rochester and New York. Summers [in] Syracuse are the best: sunshine, moderate temperatures, and tons of festivals!" Though one pragmatic student does counter that Syracuse can be "trying in the winter."

When it comes to their peers, law students at Syracuse are decidedly mixed. Some steadfastly assert that their fellow students are "competitive." However, others assure us that they "[are] not cutthroat" and blame the competitive nature on a curve "which can be unforgiving." And plenty more outright disagree, confidently stating that their peers are "generous and helpful to others." One happy student goes as far as saying that "it feels like a family." Further, for older students who might have children or separate lives, the school attempts to foster "a sense of community" by "organizing monthly get-togethers." Whether you attend is up to you, and essentially, "the experience is what you make of it."

Getting In

Accepted students in the 25th percentile earned an LSAT score of around 153 and had an undergraduate GPA around 3.10. Accepted students in the 75th percentile earned an LSAT score of around 157 and had an undergraduate GPA of 3.56. The median LSAT score is 155 and the median GPA is 3.37.

Clinical program required	No
Legal writing course requirement	Yes
Legal methods course requirement	Yes
Legal research course requirement	Yes
Moot court requirement	No
Public interest law requirement	No

ADMISSIONS

Selectivity Rating	82
# applications received	1,927
% applicants accepted	56
% acceptees attending	16
Average LSAT	155
Median LSAT	155
LSAT Range (25th to 75th percentile)	153–157
Median undergrad GPA	3.37
Application fee	$75
Regular application deadline	4/1
Transfer students accepted	Yes
Evening division offered	No
Part-time accepted	No
CAS accepted	Yes

International Students

TOEFL required of international students.	Yes

FINANCIAL FACTS

Annual tuition	$44,000
Books and supplies	$1,622
Room & Board	$12,374
Financial aid application deadline	2/16
% first-year students receiving some sort of aid	96
% all students receiving some sort of aid	95
% of aid that is merit based	84
% receiving scholarships	91
Average grant	$21,715
Average loan	$38,816
Average total aid package	$53,997
Average debt	$139,753

EMPLOYMENT INFORMATION

Career Rating	**86**	
Total 2014 JD Grads	211	
% for whom you have useable information	95	
% grads employed ten months out	82	
Median starting salary	$59,694	
# employed full-time	160	
# employed part-time	14	
# employed bar required	133	
# employed JD preferred	37	
# employed professional/other	2	
# employed non-professional	2	
# pursuing advanced degree	3	
# unemployed and seeking employment	22	
# not seeking employment	2	
% grads employed by school	1	
State for bar exam	NY, PA, MD, FL, TX	
Pass rate for first-time bar	82.0	

Prominent Alumni
Joseph R. Biden, Jr., Vice President of the United States; Theodore A. McKee, Chief Judge, Third Circuit Court of Appeals

Grads Employed by Field (%)
Academic (1)
Business/Industry (22)
Government (11)
Judicial Clerkship (10)
Federal: (2)
State or local: (6)
Private Practice (47)
  2-10: (23)
  11-25: (5)
  26-50: (3)
  51-100: (5)
  101-250: (6)
  251-500: (5)
  501+: (1)
Public Interest (8)

TEMPLE UNIVERSITY
JAMES E. BEASLEY SCHOOL OF LAW

INSTITUTIONAL INFORMATION

Public/private	Public
Affiliation	No Affiliation
% faculty female	43
% faculty underrepresented minority	20
Total faculty	70

SURVEY SAYS...
Diverse opinions accepted in classrooms

STUDENTS

Enrollment of law school	723
% male/female	53/47
% from out-of-state	35
% part-time	22
% underrepresented minority	27
% international	1
# of countries represented	6
Average age of entering class	25

ACADEMICS

Academic Experience Rating	**89**
Profs interesting rating	86
Profs accessible rating	84
Hours of study per day	3.86

Academic Specialties
Commercial, Constitutional, Corporation Securities, Criminal, Environmental, Government Services, Human Rights, International, Taxation, Intellectual Property

Advanced Degrees Offered
JD, 3 yrs full time/4 yrs part time; LLM in Trial Advocacy 1 yr; LLM in Taxation, 1 semester to 1 yr; LLM in Transnational Law, 1 semester to 1 yr; Graduate Teaching Fellowships, 2 yrs; LLM for Graduates of Foreign law schools, 1 yr; SJD; LLM in Asian Law, 1 yr.

Combined Degrees Offered
JD/MBA (3–4 yrs), JD/MPH (3–4 yrs), JD/LLM degree programs in Taxation and Transnational Law (3.5 yrs), JD/Individually designed joint degrees

Academics

Founded in the late nineteenth century, Temple University's James E. Beasley School of Law is known for its a commitment to practical learning, skills classes, and clinicals, a goal which is achieved through hands-on courses and makes for "an enjoyable place to study law." Lots of "capable, intelligent people walking through these halls" pay "very affordable in-state tuition" to get "the biggest bang for your buck in Pennsylvania/New Jersey." "Given its low cost and its plentiful regional connections, if you intend to practice in the Philadelphia area it's probably the most sensible school to attend," says a student.

The school understands that law school must go beyond the theoretical, and to that end "helps students find internships for the summers or for the academic year, even giving students a chance to earn academic credit for unpaid internships." The heavy emphasis on practical experience means that by the time a student is out of law school, they have likely had "two summer internships, a part-time legal job or internship during the school year, and have been exposed to many areas of law in school." The trial advocacy department is "pretty amazing" and "gives students an opportunity to gain extremely important skills in both civil and criminal litigation that makes us stand out to employers." The school also has a Federal Judicial Clinical program that places 3L students in a Federal Judge's chambers and allows them to do substantive legal work on real cases.

The professors "are exceptional, both personally and professionally" and "are always willing to accommodate a student's schedule," which is especially important to students in the evening division. The Career Planning Office "is not the most helpful place, and "most students feel that they get more out of going to certain professors for career advice than they do to career planning." Luckily, this system works out well. "Numerous professors of mine have offered to help my friends and I find summer jobs and have provided excellent guidance," says a 2L. Fear not, though: even though students have to compete with other area law schools for summer positions, "the Temple Law alumni network is quite extensive throughout the city." "Temple has a strong presence in Philadelphia, so if you do well your first year, you should be able to find a great summer job."

JOHANNE L. JOHNSTON, ASSISTANT DEAN FOR ADMISSIONS & FINANCIAL AID
1719 NORTH BROAD STREET, PHILADELPHIA, PA 19122
TEL: 800-560-1428 • FAX: 215-204-9319
E-MAIL: LAWADMIS@TEMPLE.EDU • WEBSITE: WWW.LAW.TEMPLE.EDU

Life

The atmosphere at Temple is "extremely congenial," and the" faculty, administration, the students, and even the security guard at the front door are all immensely friendly, supportive, and community-minded." Unfortunately, the physical building is "outdated" and "not as comfortable as it could be," but the library and research facilities are "ample and available" and "the library staff are amazingly knowledgeable." "What Temple lacks in flash it makes up in grit and determination!"

While most law students do not live on campus, there are specific neighborhoods in which students concentrate. Day students (which make up the vast majority of each class) are "typically in their twenties or thirties," and there is "definitely a sense of community in the evening students" as well. "Temple Law has a family feel, which helps during the dark days of finals," says a 3L. "Section bonding" is quite common, and the school has weekly to bi-weekly social events with a few more popular annual events (such as Barristers Ball and Lunar Banquet). There are "tons of social opportunities at Temple because of the myriad clubs," and these "offer both social bonding and networking, as many attorneys attend these, as well."

Getting In

At Temple, enrolled students at the 25th percentile have LSAT scores of 156 and GPAs in the 3.17 range. At the 75th percentile, the LSAT score is 162 and GPAs are about 3.64. Be warned, however: Temple's highly competitive admission process is designed to look at the whole person. Your personal statement and recommendation letters will be carefully considered by the admissions committee.

Clinical program required	No
Legal writing	
course requirement	Yes
Legal methods	
course requirement	No
Legal research	
course requirement	Yes
Moot court requirement	No
Public interest	
law requirement	No

ADMISSIONS

Selectivity Rating	**88**
# applications received	2,127
% applicants accepted	42
% acceptees attending	24
Average LSAT	159
Median LSAT	160
LSAT Range (25th to	
75th percentile)	156–162
Average undergrad GPA	3.41
Median undergrad GPA	3.49
Application fee	$60
Regular application deadline	3/1
Transfer students accepted	Yes
Evening division offered	Yes
Part-time accepted	Yes
CAS accepted	Yes

International Students

TOEFL recommended of	
international students.	Yes

FINANCIAL FACTS

Annual tuition (in-state/	
out-of-state)	$20,906/$34,032
Books and supplies	$2,000
Fees	$690
Room & Board	$11,865
Financial aid application	
deadline	3/1
% all students receiving	
some sort of aid	84
% of aid that is merit based	96
% receiving scholarships	51
Average grant	$9,544
Average loan	$30,207
Average total aid package	$33,755
Average debt	$97,323

EMPLOYMENT INFORMATION

Career Rating	87	Grads Employed by Field (%)
Total 2014 JD Grads	253	Business/Industry (15)
% grads employed ten months out	88	Government (9)
Median starting salary	$60,000	Judicial Clerkship (14)
% job accepting grads providing		Federal: (5)
useable salary information	77	State or local: (9)
# employed full-time	204	Other: (0)
# employed part-time	18	Private Practice (40)
# employed bar required	164	Solo: (1)
# employed JD preferred	37	2-10: (15)
# employed professional/other	16	11-25: (4)
# employed non-professional	3	26-50: (1)
# pursuing advanced degree	4	51-100: (2)
# unemployed and seeking		101-250: (6)
employment	20	251-500: (2)
# not seeking employment	2	501+: (10)
% grads employed by school	6	Size Unknown: (0)
State for bar exam	PA	Public Interest (8)
Pass rate for first-time bar	84.4	

TEXAS TECH UNIVERSITY
SCHOOL OF LAW

INSTITUTIONAL INFORMATION

Public/private	Public
Affiliation	No Affiliation
Student-faculty ratio	14:1
% faculty part-time	37
% faculty female	31
% faculty underrepresented minority	15
Total faculty	68

SURVEY SAYS...

Diverse opinions accepted in classrooms, Great research resources, Abundant externship/internship/ clerkship opportunities, Conservative students, Strong sense of community

STUDENTS

Enrollment of law school	629
% male/female	52/48
% from out-of-state	12
% part-time	0
% underrepresented minority	28
% international	1
# of countries represented	6
Average age of entering class	25

ACADEMICS

Academic Experience Rating	86
Profs interesting rating	85
Profs accessible rating	99
Hours of study per day	3.83

Academic Specialties

Commercial, Constitutional, Corporation Securities, Criminal, Environmental, International, Property, Taxation, Intellectual Property

Advanced Degrees Offered

LLM-1 year

Combined Degrees Offered

JD/MBA 3–4 yrs, JD/MPA 3 yrs, JD/MS Agricultural and Applied Economics 3–4 yrs, JD/MS Accounting (Taxation) 3–4 yrs, JD/ MS Environmental Toxicology 3–4 yrs, JD/PFP Personal Financial Planning 3–4 yrs; JD/MS Biotechnology 3–4 yrs; JD/MEngr 3–4 yrs; JD/MD 6 yrs.

Academics

Students dole out praises for Texas Tech's rigorous and practical JD program, which really "teaches you what you need to know to be a good lawyer." From day one, real-world principles are incorporated into the learning experience, and throughout the program "the instruction [features] a good balance of the Socratic Method with practical advice." During the 1L curriculum, "emphasis is put on legal writing and research so that we are able to go straight into practice during the summer of our first year." 1Ls have a "year-long legal practice requirement," which "gives you a fantastic foundation before you step your foot in the real world." In addition to curricular offerings, the school offers an incredible breadth of "opportunities to gain practical experience through procedure classes, barrister competitions, clinics, and national competitions."

While the JD curriculum is "rigorous and demanding," it would be very difficult to slip through the cracks at Texas Tech. When they start the program, students are grouped into sections that serve as a support network during 1L, and "all of the first-year classes have upper-level students as tutors to supplement your classroom hours." The teaching staff is also committed to student success, and maintains consistent office hours so that students "can stop by and talk to professors at any time." A totally user-friendly experience, "the resources provided by the school are top-notch and they've designed everything to revolve around the student and their schedule." To top it all off, the construction of the Lanier Professional Development Center building, added 34,000 square feet to the law school building. The school is already equipped with a first-rate library, and "the library staff is amazing and always available."

When it's time to start looking for a job or clerkship, Texas Tech maintains "a great reputation in the Texas legal markets as producing hard-working, effective lawyers." Students choose Tech precisely for this reputation and are proud of the results. One new initiative, the Regional Externship Program, places students in other metro areas in Texas where they work 30-35 hours per week and earn a full semester of credit. A third-year student asserts, "I've been told on several occasions that a firm would rather pick up a Tech Law graduate who knows what to do when he steps foot in the office than some Ivy League grad who knows more about theory and less about how to get the job done." While career placement is highly successful in Texas, many students feel that the school could improve its national reputation and help "out-of-state students find jobs in their home states." In general, students would like their top school to take a more leading role in the national legal community, urging the administration to "spend more money to attract more nationally known . . . guest speakers and employers." One step in this direction is the Academy for Leadership in the Legal Profession's lecture series, which has brought in national speakers such as the GC of Kia Motors.

Life

The surprisingly friendly and open atmosphere at Texas Tech is all due to students who aren't afraid to "help one another, encourage one another, and be kind to one another." No need for first-year jitters. You'll quickly feel at home at Texas Tech, thanks to a "tremendous student-run mentoring program for incoming students." Within the law school, there are a number of students clubs and organizations—plus many more in the larger university—and if you're married, there are "resources and social networking opportunities for students with spouses and their families." Conservative politics predominate, but students reassure us that "you can survive as a liberal." In fact, "the Tech democrats are more active than the republicans," and everyone listens to and respects different opinions.

STEPHEN M. PEREZ, ASSISTANT DEAN FOR ADMISSIONS & RECRUITMENT
TEXAS TECH UNIVERSITY SCHOOL OF LAW 1802 HARTFORD AVENUE, LUBBOCK, TX 79409
TEL: 806-742-3990 • FAX: 806-742-4617
E-MAIL: ADMISSIONS.LAW@TTU.EDU • WEBSITE: WWW.LAW.TTU.EDU

If you've never been to West Texas, a student dryly describes it for us as "a vast, treeless, invariably flat expanse of dirt. They even have tumbleweeds here—like out of a John Wayne movie or *Looney Tunes*." Although it sounds a bit inhospitable, students say the advantage to Lubbock's small city environment and arid landscape is that there are fewer distractions, which makes it easier to focus on your homework. More importantly, "Lubbock is a great environment for law students to partner with local lawyers and learn the ropes." "The Lubbock legal community is extremely strong and polite, and the relationship is emphasized over the case," one student says. "Lubbock is not the most exciting town on the universe" in terms of nightlife; however, the law school's friendly students "have managed to carve out a pretty decent social life. The bars here are okay, but the law students will sponsor various events and they are typically very fun."

Getting In

Texas Tech evaluates students based on their previous academic performance, LSAT scores, letters of recommendation, and personal statements. While no specific pre-law curriculum is required, the admissions committee favors students who have reading and writing skills, an understanding of public institutions and government, and the ability to think both creatively and critically.

Clinical program required	No
Legal writing course requirement	Yes
Legal methods course requirement	Yes
Legal research course requirement	Yes
Moot court requirement	No
Public interest law requirement	No

ADMISSIONS

Selectivity Rating	83
# applications received	1,240
% applicants accepted	57
% acceptees attending	32
Average LSAT	154
Median LSAT	154
LSAT Range (25th to 75th percentile)	151–157
Average undergrad GPA	3.38
Median undergrad GPA	3.45
Application fee	$50
Regular application deadline	3/1
Early application deadline	11/1
Early application notification	1/15
Transfer students accepted	Yes
Evening division offered	No
Part-time accepted	No
CAS accepted	Yes

International Students

TOEFL required of international students.	Yes

FINANCIAL FACTS

Annual tuition (in-state/out-of-state)	$18,388/$24,202
Books and supplies	$1,200
Fees	$4,196
Room & Board	$9,760
Financial aid application deadline	4/15
% all students receiving some sort of aid	95
% of aid that is merit based	100
% receiving scholarships	63
Average grant	$10,000
Average loan	$28,310
Average total aid package	$28,641
Average debt	$81,543

EMPLOYMENT INFORMATION

Career Rating	88
Total 2014 JD Grads	213
% for whom you have useable information	100
% grads employed ten months out	80
Median starting salary	$60,000
# employed full-time	163
# employed part-time	8
# employed bar required	136
# employed JD preferred	26
# employed professional/other	5
# employed non-professional	4
# pursuing advanced degree	2
# unemployed and seeking employment	36
# not seeking employment	1
State for bar exam	TX, NM, CA, UT, WA
Pass rate for first-time bar	85.7

Prominent Alumni
Mary Alice McLarty, Litigator in Dallas, Texas; Pres. Amer. Assn. for Justice; Brian Quinn, Chief Justice, 7th Court of Appeals for Texas; Philip Johnson, Texas Supreme Court Justice; Mark Lanier, Litigator in Houston, Texas; Rob Junell, Federal Judge

Grads Employed by Field (%)
Academic (1)
Business/Industry (18)
Government (11)
Judicial Clerkship (4)
Federal: (2)
State or local: (2)
Private Practice (46)
Solo: (2)
2-10: (24)
11-25: (8)
26-50: (4)
51-100: (2)
101-250: (2)
251-500: (2)
501+: (1)
Size Unknown: (0)
Public Interest (0)

THOMAS M. COOLEY LAW SCHOOL
WESTERN MICHIGAN UNIVERSITY COOLEY LAW SCHOOL

Academics

The Thomas M. Cooley Law School in Michigan is "the largest law school" in the United States in terms of enrollment. There are four Michigan campuses—one in the state capital of Lansing, one in the northern suburbs of Detroit, one in Grand Rapids and one in Ann Arbor. Cooley's newest campus in Tampa Bay, Florida opened in May 2013. Cooley prides itself on "flexible" and "accommodating" scheduling. There are "daytime, nighttime, and weekend" classes. There are "three terms year-round" as well, and you can start in January, May, or September. Students tell us the price tag is "very affordable." Either way, Cooley offers "a lot of financial aid and scholarship opportunities." Technology is also "cutting-edge," and the law library is one of the most extensive in the country.

Students here describe Cooley as an "underrated" "lawyer-making machine." It's not the place for you if you want to imbibe legal theory, though. "The school promotes practical application so you are ready to jump into your career" immediately upon graduation. Real legal experience "is required." Every student must complete a clinic, internship, externship, or otherwise demonstrate the equivalent in work experience. "Lectures are practical and grounded instead of theoretical." Course selection is broad and specializations are available but the number of mandatory courses is "a little ridiculous," and it "may prevent you from taking many electives and delving deeply into a particular area of interest." Basically, "Cooley's thinking is that if it is tested on the bar, it should be a required class." "This law school prepares you for the bar exam." Period.

Some students love the "hard-working" administration. Others say that the top brass is "frigid." Far and away, the biggest administrative complaint is that Cooley takes its sweet time posting grades. Like, "forever." The faculty is "interesting, entertaining, and knowledgeable," and it's full of professors who have "actually practiced law." There are also "many adjunct professors." They're typically judges, partners at big law firms, or general counsel for major corporations. Outside of class, faculty members are very approachable. "The accessibility of the professors is second to none," beams a 3L.

The "rigorous" academic atmosphere here is "not for the faint hearted." "Class sizes tend to be quite large." Professors generally "employ the Socratic Method and are always seeking to test your knowledge of the material." "The majority of students get C's." "Exams are tough, and an A is well earned." "Cooley lowers the bar for admissions, but after that you are on your own to sink or swim," warns a 1L. "Cooley is very hard to stay in." Although the school has a fully staffed academic support resource center, students uniformly promise that "you will struggle to survive through all three of your years here." "You better know the law," they say. "If you slack off, you'll fail out."

Life

Cooley "accepts just about anyone and everyone." The student population is "a mixture of students who didn't get in any place else and students who are on full scholarships because their LSAT and GPA were so high." An overwhelming majority of students are enrolled part time. Diversity of all kinds is a fabulous strength. Well more than half the future attorneys here come from some state other than Michigan. About one-third represent an ethnic minority. There are "nontraditional students from many different professions." "Age, background, and socioeconomic status" really run the gamut. "Cooley is so diverse that one could not even attempt to discriminate without confusing him- or herself," declares a 3L. On the one hand, the vast assortment of students "makes for excellent class discussions." On the other hand, "people divide into cliques easily" outside the classroom.

MOHAMMAD SOHAIL, ACTING DIRECTOR OF ADMISSIONS
P.O. BOX 13038, 300 SOUTH CAPITOL AVENUE, LANSING, MI 48901
TEL: 517-371-5140 • FAX: 517-334-5718
E-MAIL: ADMISSIONS@COOLEY.EDU • WEBSITE: WWW.COOLEY.EDU

The five campuses each have their own identity. In Lansing, students have a "beautiful" building downtown "by the capitol." However, the surrounding area is largely "bleak" and "depressing." The Grand Rapids campus is similarly located in "a refurbished old building in the heart of downtown," and it's not in the greatest neighborhood, either. The decidedly suburban Auburn Hills campus is a nice and new facility "tucked away in a wooded compound" that feels like "a generic corporate headquarters." Ann Arbor's building was designed by renowned architect and Frank Lloyd Wright apprentice, Alden B. Dow. The stunning new Tampa Bay campus is situated on 8.8 acres in suburban Riverview.

Social life can be hit or miss. Cooley is home to a tremendous number of student organizations," and "most students are nice people." However, there isn't much of a community. "A lot of people come to class and then leave immediately after," explains a 1L. "Building a social life takes effort." The fact that "grades are impossible during the first few terms" certainly doesn't help. "Those who are social butterflies mostly ended up failing out after one or two semesters," cautions a 2L. "People get along, but it's best to focus on studying."

Getting In

Cooley is one of the easiest law schools to get admitted to in the country. The acceptance rate hovers at about 70 percent annually. Admitted students at the 25th percentile have LSAT scores around 141 and GPAs of roughly 2.6. Admitted students at the 75th percentile have LSAT scores of 149 or so and their undergraduate GPA is about 3.3.

Clinical program required	Yes
Legal writing course requirement	Yes
Legal methods course requirement	Yes
Legal research course requirement	Yes
Moot court requirement	No
Public interest law requirement	No

ADMISSIONS

Selectivity Rating	69
# applications received	1,481
% applicants accepted	85
% acceptees attending	35
Median LSAT	145
LSAT Range (25th to 75th percentile)	141–149
Median undergrad GPA	2.90
Application fee	$0
Transfer students accepted	Yes
Evening division offered	Yes
Part-time accepted	Yes
CAS accepted	Yes

International Students

TOEFL required of international students.	Yes

FINANCIAL FACTS

Annual tuition	$44,950
Books and supplies	$2,000
Fees	$40
Room & Board	$9,000
Financial aid application deadline	9/1
% receiving scholarships	58

EMPLOYMENT INFORMATION

Career Rating	69
Total 2014 JD Grads	871
% for whom you have useable information	34
% grads employed ten months out	71
Median starting salary	$47,025
# employed full-time	507
# employed part-time	67
# employed bar required	282
# employed JD preferred	158
# employed professional/other	93
# employed non-professional	41
# pursuing advanced degree	13
# unemployed and seeking employment	211
# not seeking employment	11
% grads employed by school	0

Prominent Alumni
John Engler, Former Governor of Michigan; Bart R. Stupak, U. S. Representative; Jane Markey, Judge, Michigan Court of Appeals; Hon. Hiroe Makiyama, Councillor, House of Councillor, Diet of Japan; Bill Neilsen, Director of Industry Outreach, Developer of XBOX360 and Bing for Microsoft

Grads Employed by Field (%)
Academic (3)
Business/Industry (29)
Government (15)
Private Practice (45)
Public Interest (5)

TOURO COLLEGE
JACOB D. FUCHSBERG LAW CENTER

INSTITUTIONAL INFORMATION

Public/private	Private
Affiliation	Jewish
Student-faculty ratio	19:1
% faculty part-time	37
% faculty female	45
% faculty underrepresented minority	9
Total faculty	80

SURVEY SAYS...

Great research resources, Abundant externship/internship/clerkship opportunities

STUDENTS

Enrollment of law school	658
% male/female	51/49
% part-time	31
% underrepresented minority	32
Average age of entering class	27

ACADEMICS

Academic Experience Rating	**75**
Profs interesting rating	85
Profs accessible rating	85
Hours of study per day	3.69

Academic Specialties
Commercial, Criminal, Environmental, Human Rights, Intellectual Property

Advanced Degrees Offered
JD , 2–3 yrs full-time, 3.5–6 yrs part-time; LLM for Foreign law graduates, 1 yr full-time, 3 semesters part-time; LLM General Studies, 1 yr full-time; 3 semesters part-time.

Combined Degrees Offered
Dual Degree Programs: JD/MBA; JD/MPA; JD/MSW

Academics

Long Island's Touro may not receive national accolades, but "the quality of the education at Touro is exceptionally better than the school's reputation." Students say there is "no difference" between professors here and those at more prestigious schools; they are "of the same caliber as professors of top tier law schools." "Brilliant and caring," these "passionate" professors "convey not only legal theory, but the practical points which are necessary to know in the new legal economy." Even outside the classroom, they make the time necessary to guide you through the curriculum. "I have never had a problem with scheduling a meeting with a professor," one student notes. Though TLC is "not too large," it boasts "excellent library resources" and a staff who "are always there to help." Overall, at Touro, students feel the "helpful, kind, and compassionate" administration "is committed to the success of each and every student."

Touro's Long Island location may not seem like a prime destination for law students, but in fact, the school's location is one of its great strengths. Having a "close proximity to the state and federal court houses" means that students here enjoy "opportunities that are unavailable to most other law schools." That access to real law being practiced in real courts, as well as its "great relationship with the judges and attorneys," means "it feels like the courts are part of our educational experience on a daily basis because we frequently visit them to watch trials, and we also have some of the judges teaching in our school."

That access is important to the primary goal here: providing you with the framework necessary to have a thriving career. Faculty members "want to ensure that every student has an opportunity to achieve a solid job opportunity after graduation." The "challenging but fruitful" education students enjoy at Touro "fosters academic and professional development" that, when coupled with the access students have to lawyers and judges—"we can get clerkships much easier than many other schools," one student notes—allows graduates to quickly be on course for their career pursuits. As one student boasts, "lawyers who graduate from our school are more competent and better equipped to practice law than most other third and fourth tier schools."

Life

When making "awesome new friends" is set alongside meeting "some excellent attorneys, district attorneys, assistant U.S. attorneys and judges," it's easy to see why students appreciate life at Touro, even if opportunities for good times on the weekend are relatively limited in the quiet community of Central Islip. (New York City is an hour away, and is a prime destination for those looking for excitement.) Though everyone here is working hard, don't expect a cutthroat atmosphere. Those at Touro "share a spirit more of camaraderie than competition." Your fellow students will not be homogenous, either. "TLC encompasses a diverse student body—not just in terms of race and gender, but also diversity of backgrounds, walks of life, and stages of life."

SUSAN THOMPSON, DIRECTOR OF ENROLLMENT
225 EASTVIEW DRIVE, CENTRAL ISLIP, NY 11722
TEL: 631-761-7010 • FAX: 631-761-7019
E-MAIL: ADMISSIONS@TOUROLAW.EDU • WEBSITE: WWW.TOUROLAW.EDU

The people and atmosphere may be inviting, but there are complaints about the facilities. The elevators are "a nightmare," and "horrible acoustics" and "obstructed view seats" make lectures halls less than pleasant places to be. Even the layout wins some scorn for being unnecessarily complex; "going from the third floor in the library to third floor in the school, ten feet away, you must travel six flights of stairs." In addition, be prepared to work around a schedule influenced by the college's Jewish affiliation. Though the school promotes non-secular activities, "the school and library are closed at 2:30 P.M. on Friday afternoons" and most Saturdays, which for some "makes it extremely hard to put in 100 percent." That said, the building is "relatively new," with wireless available "everywhere."

Getting In

Students recently admitted to Touro Law Center at the 25th percentile have LSAT scores of approximately 145 and GPAs of approximately 2.8. Meanwhile, admitted students at the 75th percentile have LSAT scores of 150 and GPAs of roughly 3.4.

Clinical program required	Yes
Legal writing course requirement	Yes
Legal methods course requirement	Yes
Legal research course requirement	Yes
Moot court requirement	No
Public interest law requirement	Yes

ADMISSIONS

Selectivity Rating	72
# applications received	1,038
% applicants accepted	73
% acceptees attending	27
Median LSAT	148
LSAT Range (25th to 75th percentile)	145–150
Median undergrad GPA	3.02
Application fee	$0
Early application deadline	5/1
Transfer students accepted	Yes
Evening division offered	Yes
Part-time accepted	Yes
CAS accepted	Yes

International Students

TOEFL recommended of international students.	Yes

FINANCIAL FACTS

Annual tuition	$44,300
Books and supplies	$1,840
Fees	$220
Room & Board	$20,526
Financial aid application deadline	6/13
Average grant	$7,650

EMPLOYMENT INFORMATION

Career Rating	85
Total 2014 JD Grads	221
% for whom you have useable information	44
Median starting salary	$66,742
# employed full-time	153
# employed part-time	17
# employed bar required	144
# employed JD preferred	15
# employed professional/other	10
# employed non-professional	1
# pursuing advanced degree	1
# unemployed and seeking employment	41
# not seeking employment	3
State for bar exam	NY, NJ, CT
Pass rate for first-time bar	77.4

Prominent Alumni
Lewis Lubell, Justice, NYS Supreme Court; Kathleen Rice, Nassau County District Attorney; Seymour Liebman, Corporate Counsel, Canon USA; Jothy Narendran, Partner, Certilman, Balin, Adler & Hyman; Jo Christine Reed Miles, Partner, Sonnenschein, Nath & Rosenthal

Grads Employed by Field (%)
Academic (1)
Business/Industry (14)
Government (19)
Judicial Clerkship (5)
Private Practice (58)
Public Interest (3)

TULANE UNIVERSITY
LAW SCHOOL

INSTITUTIONAL INFORMATION

Public/private	Private
Affiliation	No Affiliation
Student-faculty ratio	14:1
% faculty part-time	40
% faculty female	31
% faculty underrepresented minority	6
Total faculty	84

SURVEY SAYS...

Students love New Orleans, LA

STUDENTS

Enrollment of law school	743
% male/female	50/50
% from out-of-state	62
% part-time	0
% underrepresented minority	18
% international	3
# of countries represented	20
Average age of entering class	24

ACADEMICS

Academic Experience Rating	**76**
Profs interesting rating	67
Profs accessible rating	69
Hours of study per day	3.75

Academic Specialties

Environmental, International, Intellectual Property

Advanced Degrees Offered

SJD, 2–3 yrs depending on length of time to complete dissertation; Master of Laws, 1 yr FT, 2 yrs PT; Master of Laws in Admiralty, 1 yr FT, 2 yrs PT; Master of Laws in Energy and Environment, 1 yr FT, 2 yrs PT; Master of Laws in Int'l and Comparative Law, 1 yr FT, 2 yrs PT; Master of Laws in American Law, 1 yr FT.

Combined Degrees Offered

JD/MBA 4 yrs; JD/MHA 4 yrs; JD/MPH 4 yrs; JD/MSW 4 yrs; JD/MAcc 4 yrs; JD/MS Int'l Devel 4 yrs

Academics

Tulane University Law School is "extremely enjoyable because it provides you with the same resources as all the top law schools, with a more laid-back atmosphere." "The quality of teaching is superb." The "world-renowned faculty" here is full of "experts and kick-ass attorneys" who are "funny, extremely smart, and extremely approachable." "They are highly qualified and accomplished but remain accessible and down-to-earth." Some students call the administration "ridiculously awesome," too. The deans are "nice and helpful," they say, "and most of them teach a 1L or 2L class, which gives you the opportunity to be exposed to them early on in your career." More critical students call the management merely "vaguely competent."

Tulane is home to "quite a few unique programs and strengths." In addition to "exceptional clinical opportunities" and a host of dual-degree programs, students edit no fewer than eight journals. Tulane also offers certificates in international and comparative law, admiralty law, environmental law, sports law, and civil law. Also, Louisiana is a civil law state (whereas every other state is a common law state), so students are exposed to two very different legal systems. "The ability to follow a common law or civil law track not only opens up opportunities in Louisiana, but it also makes an international law career more feasible." The big academic complaint here is the research and writing program. "I am not sure whoever designed it has ever heard the term 'best practices,'" speculates a 1L. "If you came as a strong technical writer, you will leave with no new skills. If you did not, you are on your own."

Students note that the academic program is competitive and challenging, and it is important to maintain strong performance if you want to gain the interest of local employers. Tulane is "extremely active in helping everyone secure summer employment and beyond." Students also note that their school's brand name is often a real advantage on a résumé. "We're the best law school in Louisiana, and the firms know it," brags a 2L. "We are not all competing for the same thirty spots at the top law firm in our city because our goals are incredibly diverse," adds a 2L.

Facilities wise, Tulane has "a wonderful library." Some students say that "classrooms are nice." Others disagree. "The actual building and classrooms are forgettable," they tell us. "The horrid ergonomics of it all!" bemoans a 2L. "To plug in your laptop can take two minutes and can set the stage for an awkward encounter with the person sitting next to you while you fumble around under the table like a teenager on a first date."

Life

New Orleans is located in "the American South, and many students come from the South." Geographic diversity is pretty abundant, though. Some 85 percent of the students come from a state other than Louisiana. About 20 percent of the students represent an ethnic minority. There's a "wide range of International Students" and plenty of "diversity of opinion and background." Some students insist that "there's no cutthroat competition here." They say that the typical student is as "friendly, cooperative, and as laid-back as a stressed law student could possibly be." Others tell us that competition exists "but it's not as prevalent until exam time."

ADAM KANCHER, ASSISTANT DIRECTOR
WEINMANN HALL, 6329 FRERET STREET, NEW ORLEANS, LA 70118
TEL: 504-865-5930 • FAX: 504-865-6710
E-MAIL: ADMISSIONS@LAW.TULANE.EDU • WEBSITE: WWW.LAW.TULANE.EDU

Outside of class, Tulane students are an "extremely social," "fun-loving bunch." There are "plenty of cliques, largely organized according to special interests areas of law, ethnicity, and age." At the same time, the environment is "very collegial." "The community atmosphere is a definite plus." Quite a few students "enjoy a good party." There are "a lot of the smart kids who had fun in undergrad" here, and their good times continue unabated in law school. "Socializing is in overdrive at TLS," cautions a 2L, "which can be a distraction from your studies if you let it." "Most people go out at least once or twice a week." "Whether it's a run-of-the-mill bar review or renting out a restaurant on the Mardi Gras parade route, there's always a social event on the horizon."

Off campus, the Big Easy is reportedly "the most relaxed city in the U.S." and "a perfect place to unwind on weekends or after finals." Students love the food, the nightlife, and the "warm winter weather." There's the debauchery of Bourbon Street, of course, but there's also an array of "incredible" streets and neighborhoods. "The sidewalk bistros and beautiful, lush scenery add significant character to your day-to-day experience as a law student." Beyond the city of New Orleans, "there are lots of good places for weekend trips in the area" as well.

Getting In

Tulane has a fabulous regional reputation and a very good national reputation. Admitted students at the 25th percentile have LSAT scores around 156 and GPAs not much less than 3.4. Admitted students at the 75th percentile have LSAT scores of 163 or so and GPAs around 3.7.

Clinical program required	No
Legal writing course requirement	Yes
Legal methods course requirement	No
Legal research course requirement	Yes
Moot court requirement	Yes
Public interest law requirement	Yes

ADMISSIONS

Selectivity Rating	87
# applications received	2,271
% applicants accepted	48
% acceptees attending	23
Average LSAT	160
Median LSAT	161
LSAT Range (25th to 75th percentile)	156–163
Average undergrad GPA	3.44
Median undergrad GPA	3.46
Application fee	$60
Transfer students accepted	Yes
Evening division offered	No
Part-time accepted	No
CAS accepted	Yes

FINANCIAL FACTS

Annual tuition	$41,500
Books and supplies	$7,550
Fees	$3,780
Room & Board	$13,440
% first-year students receiving some sort of aid	88
% all students receiving some sort of aid	88
% receiving scholarships	59
Average grant	$19,452
Average loan	$47,399
Average total aid package	$58,005
Average debt	$115,029

EMPLOYMENT INFORMATION

Career Rating	70	Prominent Alumni
Total 2014 JD Grads	269	Edith Clement, US Ct of Appeals judge;
% grads employed ten months out	87	Jacques Wiener, US Court of Appeals
# employed full-time	215	judge; John Minor Wisdom, judiciary;
# employed part-time	19	William Suter, US Supreme Court clerk;
# employed bar required	185	William Pryor, US Ct of Appeals judge
# employed JD preferred	31	**Grads Employed by Field (%)**
# employed professional/other	11	Academic (2)
# employed non-professional	7	Business/Industry (20)
# pursuing advanced degree	12	Government (8)
# unemployed and seeking employment	15	Judicial Clerkship (11)
# not seeking employment	2	Private Practice (42)
State for bar exam	NY, LA, TX, FL, CA	Public Interest (4)

THE UNIVERSITY OF AKRON
SCHOOL OF LAW

INSTITUTIONAL INFORMATION

Public/private	Public
Affiliation	No Affiliation
Student-faculty ratio	10:1
% faculty part-time	40
% faculty female	35
% faculty underrepresented minority	12
Total faculty	57

SURVEY SAYS...
Diverse opinions accepted in classrooms

STUDENTS

Enrollment of law school	405
% male/female	57/43
% from out-of-state	22
% part-time	28
% underrepresented minority	12
% international	2
# of countries represented	4
Average age of entering class	27

ACADEMICS

Academic Experience Rating	**70**
Profs interesting rating	68
Profs accessible rating	71
Hours of study per day	3.68

Academic Specialties
Business Law, Constitutional Law, Criminal Law, Family Law, Health Law, Intellectual Property and Technology Law, International and Comparative Law, Wealth Management Law, and Trial Advocacy

Advanced Degrees Offered
LLM in Intellectual Property: 1 year FT, 2–3 yrs PT

Combined Degrees Offered
JD/MBA; JD/Master in Taxation; JD/MPA; JD/Master in Applied Politics; JD/MS in Accountancy-Financial Forensics. JD/LLM in Intellectual Property Law 3–4 yrs.

Academics

The University of Akron School of Law is an "undervalued," "regional law school" that offers a lot of perks. "The tuition is very reasonable"; in fact, non-residents and international students can benefit from resident tuition rates from day one. The bar-passage rate is solid. Course load options are "extremely flexible." It's very easy to switch between the full-time and part-time programs. The four specialized centers here "are very well-known." The "high-powered" certificate program in intellectual property and Joint JD/LLM are particularly notable. There's also a certificate in litigation and areas of concentration galore. Akron Law also boasts five joint-degree programs, a couple of "pretty freaking amazing" journals, and the chance to study abroad in Japan and South Korea. The curriculum here focuses primarily on the hard-boiled application of law. "If you want a legal education that emphasizes practical skills needed in the real-world," declares a 1L, "Akron Law is for you." The trial advocacy program is "outstand-ing" and the trial team is "one of the best" in the nation, routinely bagging trophies at national tournaments. Clinics are "very strong" and reportedly a cinch to get into. One of the clinics is the Clemency Project, which aids low-income people who have been con-victed of crimes in securing pardons from the state governor. Another is the new business legal clinic, which helps people start businesses in the Akron area. As far as academic complaints, some students have called the legal writing program "poor." Luckily, Akron now has five full-time legal writing faculty.

Students heap praise on both the faculty and the administration. "The professors at Akron are the crown jewel of the school," beams a 1L. "They make even esoteric, archaic concepts like the rule against perpetuities interesting and understandable." "It is evident that they are passionate about teaching." "Many could probably make double or triple their salary by working in a big-city law firm." Faculty accessibility outside of class is "great," too. Professors here are "really interested in helping you find your way as a lawyer." They are "constantly walking the halls and willing to chit-chat." "Every profes-sor I have had in class knows my name," reflects a 3L. The "ultra-helpful" and "very flexible" administration is "also very accessible and interested in the students" and "will-ing to work with" them.

While you can find Akron Law graduates all over the country, the great mass of alumni ends up practicing in northeast Ohio. While critics charge that the Office of Career Planning "does not do a great job at placing students," most students seem pretty happy with their post-law school employment prospects, and the employment rate is consis-tently around 90 percent. The school has a "good reputation in the region." "The local bar association has a very close relationship with Akron Law," and "the school provides countless opportunities for" mentoring and networking.

Akron Law has started a complete renovation of its facilities, including the construc-tion of a state-of-the art wing with a new courtroom and interactive classrooms In the meantime, the current facility is "less than stellar" and it just "doesn't feel like a law school." "The physical plant is a mess," explains a 3L. "The law school is actually two buildings that were combined in the cheapest way possible." "Areas of the building can seem cramped." "The heating and cooling system is consistently broken." On the plus side, classrooms are adequate. "They are all equipped for wireless Internet access and have plug-ins for every student laptop." Also, the location is excellent. City, county, state, and federal courts "are all steps from the door of the school."

BARBARA C.S. WEINZIERL, ASSISTANT DEAN FOR ADMISSIONS AND STRATEGIC INITIATIVES
THE UNIVERSITY OF AKRON SCHOOL OF LAW, 302 BUCHTEL COMMON, AKRON, OH 44325-2901
TEL: 800-425-7668 • FAX: 330-258-2343
E-MAIL: LAWADMISSIONS@UAKRON.EDU • WEBSITE: WWW.UAKRON.EDU/LAW

Life

The vast majority of students at Akron Law are residents of Ohio. They describe themselves as "pretty outgoing and friendly." "The biggest surprise about law school is the fact that the other students are normal," relates a 1L. "I was expecting snobs and nerds but I have found people that I look forward to seeing every day." Student opinion concerning the academic atmosphere is decidedly split. Some students perceive "healthy amounts of competition." Others don't. "You see your fellow classmates as colleagues," says a 1L. "Students here aren't that competitive," adds a 3L. "I have helped several students and others have helped me study for exams." Beyond the confines of the classroom, a respectable number of speakers come to campus and the student bar association is "very active." Socially, "there is quite a divide between day and evening students" and "there are a lot of cliques." The city of Akron is "a small, insular community." It's not the worst place in the world, but it's certainly not a world-class city, either. "Downtown Akron is not, shall we say, appealing in many ways," explains a 2L. "Some areas are nice, but some areas abutting campus are sketchy."

Getting In

Akron Law offers both a regular fall admission date as well as a spring start which allows students to begin law school in January. Admitted full-time students have an average LSAT score of 152 and an average undergraduate GPA of 3.30.

Clinical program required	No
Legal writing course requirement	Yes
Legal methods course requirement	No
Legal research course requirement	Yes
Moot court requirement	No
Public interest law requirement	Yes

ADMISSIONS

Selectivity Rating	**80**
# applications received	766
% applicants accepted	64
% acceptees attending	24
Average LSAT	152
Median LSAT	153
LSAT Range (25th to 75th percentile)	148–155
Average undergrad GPA	3.30
Median undergrad GPA	3.41
Application fee	$0
Regular application deadline	3/31
Regular notification	within 3 wks
Early application deadline	NA
Spring Start deadline	10/15
Transfer students accepted	Yes
Evening division offered	Yes Part-time accepted
	Yes
CAS accepted	Yes

International Students

TOEFL required of international students.	Yes

FINANCIAL FACTS

Annual tuition	$21,376
Books and supplies	$1,000
Fees	$3,064
Room & Board	$11,524
Financial aid application deadline	3/1
% first-year students receiving some sort of aid	90
% all students receiving some sort of aid	95
% of aid that is merit based	47
% receiving scholarships	95
Average grant	$14,724
Average loan	$26,104
Average total aid package	$29,795
Average debt	$72,926

EMPLOYMENT INFORMATION

Career Rating	**80**
Total 2014 JD Grads	126
% for whom you have useable information	98
% grads employed ten months out	89
Median starting salary	$52,500
% job accepting grads providing useable salary information	48
# employed full-time	100
# employed part-time	12
# employed bar required	69
# employed JD preferred	30
# employed professional/other	9
# employed non-professional	4
# pursuing advanced degree	1
State for bar exam	OH, TX, IL
Pass rate for first-time bar	84.0

Prominent Alumni
Deborah Cook, Federal Judge, U.S. Court of Appeals-Sixth Circuit; Rochelle Seide, VP, Intellectual Property & Business Affairs, Sancilio & Company, Inc.

Grads Employed by Field (%)
Private Practice (48)
 Solo: (4)
 2-10: (15) 11-25: (7)
 26-50: (4)
 51-100: (2) 101-250: (1)
 251-500: (1)
 501+: (1)
 Size Unknown: (3)
Public Interest (2)

THE UNIVERSITY OF ALABAMA—TUSCALOOSA
SCHOOL OF LAW

INSTITUTIONAL INFORMATION

Public/private · Public

SURVEY SAYS...

Diverse opinions accepted in classrooms, Great research resources, Abundant externship/internship/clerkship opportunities, Law school well run, Conservative students, Good social life

STUDENTS

ACADEMICS

Academic Experience Rating	96
Profs interesting rating	90
Profs accessible rating	98
Hours of study per day	3.21

Advanced Degrees Offered
LLM Concentrations in Taxation and Business Transactions, 2 yrs PT; International LLM Program 1yr FT

Combined Degrees Offered
JD/MBA 3.5–4 yrs. Several dual enrollment with various university graduate programs.

Academics

Alabama prides itself on offering a tremendous legal education at an affordable price. Though the school definitely places an "emphasis...on corporate law," students are grateful that there are also "amazing faculty members with interests in academia, public interest and environmental law." And according to one-second year, these professors are "huge assets to students with no desire to go to a big firm or to vote Republican." Overall, many find their academic experience to be "exceptional." As another second year notes, "The quality of classes I've taken has been amazing, especially compared to classes I sat in on at other (higher ranked) law schools prior to enrolling. There are incredible academics willing to oversee guided research topics and help you get published." Students also highlight Alabama's international programs, which offer "even more opportunities to work with professors in different areas of law in different countries." Moreover, they note that "the school's administrators and professors have an open door policy and are always amenable to speaking with students. The administrators and professor genuinely care about the students and their success in the classroom and beyond."

One gripe students at UA do have is with the perceived "bias against students with low GPAs." As a frustrated second-year notes, "While I had hoped that a lower GPA might merit extra attention, especially since I am paying full-price to attend the Law School, I have found that students with high GPAs by far receive the most praise and attention from administrators." Another student concurs adding, "Furthermore, like many law schools, my school's administration and faculty tends to place favor and preference upon those with higher GPAs, a practice that outcasts those of us with a strong work ethic who fell victim to the mandatory curve." Fortunately, the low student to teacher ratio means struggling students can meet individually with their professors if they need extra help. In addition, the school hosts several skills workshops open to the entire law school.

Students feel that there remains room for improvement when it comes to career services. However, they appreciate the strides the office has made. "Our career services are still adjusting to our improving national reputation. They are making increased efforts at providing useful business contacts outside of Alabama, but could still improve." A frustrated second year adds, "We do not attract a lot of attention from prestigious firms because they assume we are all uninformed rednecks—an assumption that is both unfortunate and inaccurate." However, another more content second-year counters, "As a native Alabamian, I am interested in finding long-term employment either in my home state or in Washington, D.C. The school has been very helpful in creating connections for me, both through UA Law alumni and through the D.C. externship program."

Life

UA manages to foster a warm and welcoming environment and this collegial atmosphere certainly extends to the law students. Indeed, "Alabama has heart, ambition, and an attitude that really encourages teamwork. Outlines and notes circulate through so many students—there is no required "quid pro quo" in that regard. We just believe in each other." A second year student concurs stating, "Everyone operates with a sense of respect and professionalism toward one another...with a little 'Southern Hospitality,' everyone always lends a helping hand, so the competition is outweighed by our southern charm."

Ms. Becca Brady Arrington, Assistant Dean
Box 870382, Tuscaloosa, AL 35487
Tel: 205-348-5440 • Fax: 205-348-5439
E-Mail: admissions@law.ua.edu • Website: www.law.ua.edu

"The average student is young and direct from college," and "usually" comes directly from Alabama "or from a neighboring state." Students describe themselves as "very smart" and "down-to-earth." Politically, it is a pretty conservative atmosphere, though you will nonetheless find students with a range of interests and viewpoints. While the UA law population is "not very diverse," "in recent years, racial and geographic diversity has been a priority of the law school. The average age of law students has increased as well." One ecstatic third year buoys this sentiment sharing, "I'm a Yankee, but the people down here are second to none. I wouldn't trade any of them for anything."

While most students here are diligent workers, one 2L also assures us that they "know how to have a little fun" as well. A fellow student agrees adding, "It has been very easy for me to make several good friends among very diverse individuals with differing interests. While we study a great deal we also find time to hit up the bars in large groups." Additionally, "The Student Bar Association throws parties every other week, and the students all socialize together." Tuscaloosa offers "great weather" and "it's a great college town." Be forewarned though, for those not "super interested" in football "[it is considered] sacrilegious down here." Indeed, Alabama's social scene generally "revolves around sports," and "football is a near-religious experience." Devotion to the Crimson Tide certainly extends to the law school. In fact, students have their own cheering section, "right there with the fraternities." As a first year student admits, "We schedule our work so we can attend Crimson Tide ball games." If you "don't like football you'll probably have a harder time finding your niche." However, others assure us that "it is possible to escape and do your own thing." "Birmingham is an awesome city a mere forty-five minutes away from Tuscaloosa and it offers everything an urbanite could need," including "fantastic shopping, excellent restaurants, lots of young singles, a sense of community, and even a little bit of the hipster scene (somewhat of a rarity in Alabama)."

Getting In

Admitted applicants in the 25th percentile earned an LSAT score around 157 and a GPA around 3.37. Admitted applicants in the 75th percentile earned an LSAT score around 165 and a GPA around 3.94. The median LSAT score is 163 and the median GPA 3.77.

Clinical program required	No
Legal writing course requirement	Yes
Legal methods course requirement	No
Legal research course requirement	Yes
Moot court requirement	Yes
Public interest law requirement	No

ADMISSIONS

Selectivity Rating	93
# applications received	1,896
% applicants accepted	27
% acceptees attending	26
Median LSAT	163
LSAT Range (25th to 75th percentile)	157–165
Median undergrad GPA	3.77
Application fee	$40
Transfer students accepted	Yes
Evening division offered	No
Part-time accepted	No
CAS accepted	Yes

International Students

TOEFL required of international students.	Yes

FINANCIAL FACTS

Annual tuition (in-state/ out-of-state)	$21,320/$36,000
Books and supplies	$1,400
Room & Board	$12,066

EMPLOYMENT INFORMATION		
Career Rating	**84**	**Grads Employed by Field (%)**
Total 2014 JD Grads	171	Academic (2)
% grads employed ten months out	94	Business/Industry (15)
# employed full-time	154	Government (14)
# employed part-time	6	Judicial Clerkship (10)
# employed bar required	131	Private Practice (48)
# employed JD preferred	23	Public Interest (5)
# employed professional/other	4	
# employed non-professional	2	
# pursuing advanced degree	3	
# unemployed and seeking employment	4	
# not seeking employment	2	
State for bar exam	AL, GA, FL, TX, TN	
Pass rate for first-time bar	96.4	

UNIVERSITY OF ARIZONA
JAMES E. ROGERS COLLEGE OF LAW

Academics

The University of Arizona James E. Rogers College of Law offers "small class sizes"; "a very friendly, welcoming environment"; and "a price tag that lets students pursue careers in public service and nonprofit organizations" without racking up a gargantuan debt. Opportunities to gain practical experience are plentiful. The "strong" judicial externship program "can accommodate students interested in everything from bankruptcy court to superior court to district court." Clinics offer "hands-on experience" in eight areas including immigration, child advocacy, and indigenous peoples' law.

"This school is the most student-focused academic institution I have ever attended," says a happy 3L. Faculty members "truly care about their students" and "are available constantly." In the classroom, professors "make every effort to make the classes interesting and enjoyable," and "the small-section format during first year allows students to build a relationship with at least one professor." "They encourage discussion before and after class and are more than willing to provide letters of recommendation and reference." "They are approachable, friendly, and most even greet you by name as they pass you in the lobby or going to and from class." "Most are around campus all day and not just available during their office hours." "I e-mailed my property professor on a Sunday at roughly 10:30 P.M., with a pretty lengthy question," describes a 2L. "The question was answered at length by 10:45 P.M." "The administration is great too," enthuses a 1L. "Everyone is very helpful and interested in you getting a good education." "The quality of instruction is outstanding, and the responsiveness of the faculty and staff are remarkable. I am so very happy that I ended up at the U of A," sums up one pleased student.

Some students tell us that the "very helpful" Career and Professional Development Office at the U of A is "active in helping students connect with amazing internship and job opportunities in both the public sector and in law firms" in Arizona, California, and other Western states. If a student "is clear about where she wants to live or what she wants to do, the Career Office will give that student personal attention to strategize a plan to get there," although some complain that "they don't care what job you get, as long as you get one somewhere."

Facilities on campus are impressive. "The new building is gorgeous, especially the library. Tons of technology and connectivity. Little things like plugs at every desk and the latest projectors for classrooms make a big difference." Another student concurs, "The classrooms are brand-new and state-of-the-art—in my Family Law Class last semester we were able to video conference with a teacher in Canada to talk about divorce law without any extraneous equipment. Everything we needed to video chat was in the classroom!"

Life

There is a "relaxed Arizonan attitude" among the "amazingly friendly, smart" students at the U of A. "There is definitely competition here, as is unavoidable, but the school has a very laid-back atmosphere that allows you to keep things in perspective." "The second- and third-year students are very active in assisting the first-years adapt to law school through tutorials for all first-year classes," and teaching assistants "help with briefing and outlining." "Despite the curve, grades are not a big issue among students, and we tend to be excited for others' successes," declares a 1L. "This place is the opposite of cutthroat." Small sections for first-year students "are really conducive to forming lasting friendships." "I became very close with the other twenty-six students in my small section and continue to be good friends with several of them," says a 2L. "There is an overriding sense

JAMES E. ROGERS, ASSISTANT DEAN FOR ADMISSION AND FINANCIAL AID
P.O. BOX 210176, COLLEGE OF LAW, UNIVERSITY OF ARIZONA, TUCSON, AZ 85721-0176
TEL: 520-621-3477 • FAX: 520-626-3436
E-MAIL: ADMISSIONS@LAW.ARIZONA.EDU • WEBSITE: WWW.LAW.ARIZONA.EDU

that everyone, from faculty to administration to students, really wants to be at the school and wants to see the school succeed."

The social atmosphere is "very vibrant." "There are thirty-plus student organizations that cover different religious, political, social and ethnic categories." That translates into lots of events. " "I have had so much fun in law school," gushes a 1L. "Almost every day, there are informative and thought-provoking guest speakers, panel discussions, or film screenings, especially during the lunch hour." Intramural sports are also popular. Social life tends to be "polarized between younger people coming straight out of college and older students with families." "The crowd divides into three groups," elaborates a 3L, "the married/serious relationship/older crowd, the nerds who rarely go out, and those who are trying to extend their undergraduate experience by going to law school." Without question, if you are "interested in partying, you cannot beat the University of Arizona bar scene."

The U of A campus itself is "beautiful, complete with palm trees and a gigantic, ideal student union." "The weather is ideal." The low cost of living is "fabulous, especially from a student's perspective." If you like outdoor activity, there are "myriad" activities within minutes of campus, including hiking, biking, swimming, and rock climbing.

Getting In

Admitted students at the 25th percentile have LSAT scores in the range of about 155 and GPAs in the range of 3.3 or so. Admitted students at the 75th percentile have LSAT scores of about 163 and GPAs approaching 3.8.

Clinical program required	No
Legal writing course requirement	Yes
Legal methods course requirement	No
Legal research course requirement	Yes
Moot court requirement	No
Public interest law requirement	No

ADMISSIONS

Selectivity Rating	89
# applications received	1,243
% applicants accepted	40
% acceptees attending	21
Median LSAT	160
LSAT Range (25th to 75th percentile)	155–163
Median undergrad GPA	3.57
Application fee	$65
Regular application deadline	2/15
Early application deadline	12/3
Early application notification	12/23
Transfer students accepted	Yes
Evening division offered	No
Part-time accepted	No
CAS accepted	Yes

International Students

TOEFL required of international students.	Yes

FINANCIAL FACTS

Annual tuition (in-state/ out-of-state)	$24,607/$29,000
Books and supplies	$10,572
Fees	$0
Room & Board	$12,451
Financial aid application deadline	3/1
% first-year students receiving some sort of aid	100
% all students receiving some sort of aid	100
% of aid that is merit based	50
% receiving scholarships	66
Average grant	$15,643
Average loan	$47,436
Average total aid package	$53,195
Average debt	$90,898

EMPLOYMENT INFORMATION

Career Rating	91	
Total 2014 JD Grads	147	
% for whom you have useable information	68	
% grads employed ten months out	80	
Median starting salary	$56,496	
% job accepting grads providing useable salary information	46	
# employed full-time	113	
# employed part-time	5	
# employed bar required	90	
# employed JD preferred	22	
# employed professional/other	6	
# employed non-professional	0	
# pursuing advanced degree	2	
# unemployed and seeking employment	21	
State for bar exam	AZ, CA, WA, NV, VA	
Pass rate for first-time bar	90.0	

Prominent Alumni
Morris K. Udall, Former Congressman; Stewart Udall, Former Congressman & Sec'y of Interior; Dennis DeConcini, Former Senator; Stanley Feldman, Az Supreme Court Justice; John Kyl, U.S. Senator

Grads Employed by Field (%)
Business/Industry (12)
Government (15)
Judicial Clerkship (20)
Private Practice (31)
Public Interest (2)

UNIVERSITY OF ARKANSAS—FAYETTEVILLE
SCHOOL OF LAW

INSTITUTIONAL INFORMATION

Public/private	Public
Affiliation	No Affiliation
Student-faculty ratio	11:1
% faculty part-time	25
% faculty female	48
% faculty underrepresented minority	18
Total faculty	56

SURVEY SAYS...

Students love Fayetteville, AR,
Good social life

STUDENTS

Enrollment of law school	361
% male/female	61/39
% underrepresented minority	19
% international	0
Average age of entering class	25

ACADEMICS

Academic Experience Rating	**83**
Profs interesting rating	82
Profs accessible rating	86
Hours of study per day	2.88

Advanced Degrees Offered

LLM in Agricultural & Food Law, one academic year

Combined Degrees Offered

JD/MBA 3/1.5 yrs; JD/MPA 3/1 yrs; JD/MA 3/1.5 yrs

Academics

The University of Arkansas School of Law in Fayetteville is "a smaller school" that offers a "five-star, New York restaurant quality education for a McDonald's price." "In choosing a school that has very low in-state tuition, I gained an extremely valuable education at a fraction of the cost I would have paid at other institutions," brags a frugal 3L. "It's a pretty unbelievable education for the cost." "Various trial and counseling competitions are a few of the greatest strengths" here. Clinical courses and certified skills courses offer "excellent opportunities to get hands-on experience with the actual practice of law." In addition to traditional judicial externships, there are legislative externships and corporate counsel externships. A "strong legal writing program" is another plus. "You'll hear the students whining about it around the time appellate briefs are due," promises a 3L, "but we finish the program with excellent practical writing skills."

"The faculty is comprised of both older professors using more traditional teaching styles such as the Socratic Method, and younger professors that bring helpful insight[s] into today's practice of law into the classroom," explains a 2L. While a few professors here "would be better suited to write articles all day long and not get anywhere near the classroom," "the quality of the instruction is fantastic" overall. "Most of the professors are really energetic and relevant," says a 1L, "and they encourage lively discussion." This faculty is also "devoted" and "almost always accessible" outside of class. The "very accessible and accommodating" administration is "always putting the students first" and "committed to raising the school's profile." "I have never had a problem too big or too small for them to address," reminisces a 3L. "It has been great." Upper-level students can choose from a range of elective courses in fields like health law, refugee and asylum law, entertainment law, and immigration policy, though some students would like the school to "add more electives" to the program.

The Career Services staff is generally "wonderful," and employment prospects are reportedly excellent. Starting salaries are lower than what you'll find in more populous places. Arkansas is very inexpensive, though, and it's one of those states where everybody seems to know everybody else. Consequently, "the networking abilities within the city and state" are definitely a strength. Also, with Walmart and gargantuan food conglomerate Tyson "just down the road," Northwest Arkansas is a relatively booming area of the country that "provides many unique opportunities for employment with both law firms and major corporations." "We have some students who go 'big law' in the major cities; we have some students who set up shop in rural Arkansas; we have some who go in-house; and we have a lot of government employees, too," says a 3L.

"The facilities are old in some areas but brand-new in others," and there are "lots of small nooks to study in." The old classrooms that are still used for nearly all of the first-year classes are "okay" at best. "The wood paneling is dark and depressing and reminiscent of an old station wagon," describes a 2L. A newer wing has "ergonomic and aesthetically pleasing" classrooms that are "technology-friendly." "The research facilities are great" in the "comprehensive" library. There's an onsite coffee shop, too, "which is great for study breaks when you need to recaffeinate."

JAMES K. MILLER, ASSOCIATE DEAN FOR STUDENTS
UNIVERSITY OF ARKANSAS SCHOOL OF LAW, FAYETTEVILLE, AR 72701
TEL: 479-575-3102 • FAX: 479-575-3937
E-MAIL: JKMILLER@UARK.EDU • WEBSITE: LAW.UARK.EDU

Life

Some students describe the academic atmosphere as "very competitive." It's "cutthroat" during the first year, they allege. Other students dispute that characterization. "Students here are pretty laid-back," rejoins a 1L. "We work hard but it's not a cutthroat environment where people are trying to claw their way to the top of the class no matter what."

According to one view, social life can be hard for transplants because a lot of students come pre-equipped with their own cliques. "People who went to undergraduate school here seem to hang out with each other," says a 3L. "Many of the groups do not appear to be very inclusive of other students not in their normal social circle." Other students describe the environment as "very communal." "You get to know your fellow students and professors very well," says a 2L. Socially satisfied students also point to the "wide availability" of clubs and organizations and the fact that the student bar association is "active in providing events outside of the law school to…[help] get your mind off of classes." Campus sporting events are another big draw—especially football—and the surrounding Ozarks provide plenty of options for adventure activity. Fayetteville is very much a college town with "a unique feel that allows for people of many different cultures and backgrounds to feel at home." Dickson Street, the hub of Fayetteville nightlife, adjoins the campus, so you can revel with party-hardy undergrads any time you want to blow off your cases.

Getting In

Admitted students at the 25th percentile have LSAT scores around 151 and undergraduate grade point averages of about 3.19. At the 75th percentile, LSAT scores approach 157 and GPAs are 3.7 or so.

EMPLOYMENT INFORMATION

Career Rating	82
Total 2014 JD Grads	129
% for whom you have useable information	98
% grads employed ten months out	87
# employed full-time	111
# employed part-time	1
# employed bar required	73
# employed JD preferred	34
# employed professional/other	5
# pursuing advanced degree	5
# unemployed and seeking employment	7
# not seeking employment	2
% grads employed by school	2
State for bar exam	AR, MO, TX, OK, CA
Pass rate for first-time bar	78.0

Prominent Alumni
Rodney Slater, Former US Secretary of Transportation; George Haley, Former Ambassador to Gambia

Grads Employed by Field (%)
Academic (2)
Business/Industry (22)
Government (15)
Judicial Clerkship (4)
Federal: (3)
State or local: (1)
Private Practice (40)
Solo: (2)
2-10: (24)
11-25: (5)
26-50: (2)
51-100: (2)
101-250: (2)
251-500: (2)
501+: (2)
Public Interest (3)

Clinical program required	No
Legal writing course requirement	Yes
Legal methods course requirement	No
Legal research course requirement	Yes
Moot court requirement	No
Public interest law requirement	No

ADMISSIONS

Selectivity Rating	82
# applications received	624
% applicants accepted	60
% acceptees attending	33
Median LSAT	154
LSAT Range (25th to 75th percentile)	151–157
Median undergrad GPA	3.43
Application fee	$0
Regular application deadline	4/15
Transfer students accepted	Yes
Evening division offered	No
Part-time accepted	No
CAS accepted	Yes

International Students

TOEFL required of international students.	Yes

FINANCIAL FACTS

Annual tuition (in-state/ out-of-state)	$13,018/$28,538
Books and supplies	$1,400
Fees	$1,490
Room & Board	$17,128
Financial aid application deadline	4/1
% first-year students receiving some sort of aid	88
% all students receiving some sort of aid	85
% of aid that is merit based	16
% receiving scholarships	42
Average grant	$7,372
Average loan	$22,708
Average total aid package	$23,157
Average debt	$61,140

UNIVERSITY OF ARKANSAS—LITTLE ROCK
WILLIAM H. BOWEN SCHOOL OF LAW

INSTITUTIONAL INFORMATION

Public/private	Public
Affiliation	No Affiliation
Student-faculty ratio	15:1
% faculty part-time	63
% faculty female	40
% faculty underrepresented minority	15
Total faculty	123

SURVEY SAYS...
Great research resources

STUDENTS

Enrollment of law school	424
% male/female	58/42
% from out-of-state	6
% part-time	28
% underrepresented minority	15
% international	4
# of countries represented	3
Average age of entering class	27

ACADEMICS

Academic Experience Rating	79
Profs interesting rating	71
Profs accessible rating	80
Hours of study per day	3.23

Academic Specialties
Civil Procedure, Commercial, Constitutional, Criminal, Government Services, Labor, Property, Taxation

Combined Degrees Offered
JD/MBA 3–4 yrs, JD/MPA 3–4 yrs, JD/MPH 3–5 yrs, JD/MPS 2–3 yrs, JD/PharmD 3.5–4 yrs

Academics

The "perfectly sized" University of Arkansas—Little Rock William H. Bowen School of Law is located "right in the heart of downtown Little Rock"—"the economic and government center of the state"—and it is thoroughly "tied into the local community through its connections with legislators, judges, government agencies, and private firms." Clerkships and externships are "bountiful." Access to part-time jobs at law firms is "second to none." Other perks at UALR include four clinical programs, five dual-degree programs, and "a bargain-basement price." There are around twenty different areas of concentration here and some students tell us that "the overall breadth of course choices makes it possible to study almost any topic you find particularly interesting." Others grumble that course selection is actually pretty limited. "Students here get a strong, basic legal education," says a 2L. "However, if you want more variety in more subject-specific courses, you won't really find them at this school."

Professors "expect you to come to class prepared." The faculty is "highly qualified, and there is a great mix of" adjuncts who teach specialized courses. Not every professor is great but most are "dedicated" teachers "who really want to see their students learn." "They make sure we understand," says a 1L, "and if we don't, they go back over it." Students also laud the legal writing program and say that the "writing instructors epitomize true excellence in their fields." Outside of class, faculty members are reportedly "very approachable." "The student body is small enough that you can have ample one-on-one time with the profs after hours," reports a 3L, "if you're brave enough." Student opinion concerning the administration is drastically split. Some students call management "incompetent." "The school is run like a low-budget movie set," charges a 2L. Other students contend that UALR is "very well-run." "The administration is very helpful and accessible," they contend, and the deans make "an effort to hear student comments and feedback, and implement changes accordingly."

The law school itself is "ugly-looking from the outside" and it's "in a rough section of town." The facility is "very pretty" on the inside, though, "with great marble stairs" and "nice views" from the upper levels. Incidentally, we think the "haunted floors" are just a legend. "Classrooms are top-notch" "with plenty of outlets" for laptops. "This law school is one of the only schools in the nation with state-of-the-art video lecture capture in nearly every room," beams a 3L. "Missed something in class? Watch it again, including any slides or videos that were shown." The building is also "fully equipped for WiFi access and remote printing." There's a fabulous student lounge, too. Even "parking is awesome," which is something law students at many schools complain about to high heaven. "Overall, our school works to provide us with a comfortable environment," says a 2L. The spacious library is "the law library for the state of Arkansas, so it is excellent," too. The staff is "phenomenal." It's a public library, though, and "there are definitely some *pro se* misfits who can be distracting."

Life

Some students call UALR "a diverse school." Others argue, "There is not much diversity," beyond a solid contingent of nontraditional, older students. Views of the academic atmosphere also vary. "There are some students who are very competitive," relates a 3L, "and there are others like me who do the best that I can regardless of what others do." Other students say, "There is no rivalry" when it come to grades. "There is a definite sense that we are all in this together," says a 1L, "and most everyone is willing to help out a fellow student if that students asks."

VALERIE N. JAMES, ASSISTANT DEAN FOR ADMISSIONS
1201 MCMATH AVENUE, LITTLE ROCK, AR 72202-5142
TEL: 501-324-9903 • FAX: 501-324-9433
E-MAIL: LAWADMISSIONS@VALR.EDU • WEBSITE: UALR.EDU/LAW

Socially, it's "a very congenial atmosphere." "There are plenty of student organizations." In addition, there are "wonderful lunch meetings and seminars, as well as dinner programs on a regular basis that accommodate both part-time and full-time students." "The school is intimate and definitely allows for getting acquainted with people," reports a 2L, though "if you're not from Arkansas it is a lot harder to find a social niche." Also, "there does seem to be a line" between the students who find it "hard turning down the temptation of going out" and those who would rather crack the books all day, every day. Beyond the confines of the law school, Little Rock is "the largest city in Arkansas," but it's "still a small town" that approximates "a suburb" when compared to a lot of bigger cities. "There is not a whole lot to do in Little Rock outside of school," explains a 2L. "There is a downtown area with bars and shops, but nothing huge."

Getting In

For admitted students at the 25th percentile, LSAT scores hover at 146 and undergraduate grade point averages are in the 3.0 range. At the 75th percentile, LSAT scores are around 155 and GPAs are a little under 3.6.

Clinical program required	Yes
Legal writing course requirement	Yes
Legal methods course requirement	No
Legal research course requirement	Yes
Moot court requirement	No
Public interest law requirement	No

ADMISSIONS

Selectivity Rating	**77**
# applications received	451
% applicants accepted	66
% acceptees attending	42
Average LSAT	151
Median LSAT	150
LSAT Range (25th to 75th percentile)	146–155
Average undergrad GPA	3.29
Median undergrad GPA	3.24
Application fee	$0
Regular application deadline	3/15
Early application deadline	1/15
Early application notification	2/15
Transfer students accepted	Yes
Evening division offered	Yes
Part-time accepted	Yes
CAS accepted	Yes

International Students

TOEFL required of international students.	Yes

FINANCIAL FACTS

Annual tuition (in-state/ out-of-state)	$12,030/$22,058
Books and supplies	$1,250
Fees	$1,395
Room & Board (on/ off campus)	$14,673/$15,139
Financial aid application deadline	7/1
% all students receiving some sort of aid	92
% of aid that is merit based	27
% receiving scholarships	58
Average grant	$20,835
Average loan	$7,009
Average total aid package	$20,137
Average debt	$65,709

EMPLOYMENT INFORMATION

Career Rating	**84**	
Total 2014 JD Grads	125	
% for whom you have useable information	82	
% grads employed ten months out	82	
Median starting salary	$50,000	
# employed full-time	97	
# employed part-time	6	
# employed bar required	78	
# employed JD preferred	18	
# employed professional/other	4	
# employed non-professional	3	
# pursuing advanced degree	3	
# unemployed and seeking employment	13	
# not seeking employment	2	
State for bar exam	AR, TX, GA, NY	
Pass rate for first-time bar	85.0	

Prominent Alumni
Colette Honorable, Member, Federal Energy Regulatory Commission; James M. Moody, U.S. District Judge, Eastern District of AR; Phyllis Moore Jones, U.S. Bankruptcy Judge, Eastern & Western District; Randi Fredholm Hutchinson, Partner, Dickstein Shapiro, Washington, D.C.; Charles W. "Bill" Burton, Attorney, Jones Day, Houston, TX

Grads Employed by Field (%)
Academic (8)
Business/Industry (11)
Government (23)
Judicial Clerkship (3)
Private Practice (42)
Public Interest (5)

UNIVERSITY OF CALIFORNIA—BERKELEY
BERKELEY LAW

INSTITUTIONAL INFORMATION

Public/private	Public
% faculty female	36
% faculty underrepresented minority	20
Total faculty	144

SURVEY SAYS...

Students love Berkeley, CA, Great research resources, Abundant externship/internship/clerkship opportunities, Liberal students, Good social life

STUDENTS

Enrollment of law school	916
% male/female	47/53
% from out-of-state	44
% part-time	0
% underrepresented minority	47
Average age of entering class	25

ACADEMICS

Academic Experience Rating	**97**
Profs interesting rating	86
Profs accessible rating	80
Hours of study per day	3.40

Academic Specialties

Corporation Securities, Environmental, International, Intellectual Property

Advanced Degrees Offered

LLM, 1 yr; JSD, varies; PhD in Jurisprudence and Social Policy, approx. 6 yrs.

Combined Degrees Offered

JD/MA Economics; JD/MBA School of Business; JD/MA Asian Studies; JD/MA International Area Studies; JD/MCP Department of City and Regional Planning; JD/MJ Graduate School of Journalism; JD/MPP School of Public Policy; JD/MSW School of Social Welfare; JD/MS Energy and Resources Group

Academics

The UC Berkeley School of Law is indisputably one the nation's most respected centers of legal education. Students praise the breadth of the specialized courses in areas such as "intellectual property/technology law, environmental law, entertainment, and human rights" and say their time at Berkeley Law "hasn't always been easy by any means" but they are "surrounded by the top academics in their fields of expertise [who] are not only great professors but great human beings." One student notes, however, that Berkeley Law's desire to "get profs with fancy accomplishments" doesn't always translate to better courses: "I much prefer a better classroom environment and ease of learning over 'prestige.'" Outside the classroom, "there are a lot of experiential learning opportunities (e.g. clinics, externships, and skills courses) and [if] a student has a genuine interest in doing focused research, he or she can often find faculty to work with on an independent project." Berkeley Law has nearly a dozen journals and unlike at most law schools, all of them (except for the Law Review) are open membership and students are allowed to participate immediately. While "the school does provide tremendous opportunity for 1Ls to get involved through journals and other groups," 1Ls don't participate in "clinics" the way the term is traditionally used in a law school setting. Instead, 1Ls may take part in "Student-Initiated Legal Services Projects (SLPS) through which students do legal work under the direction of attorney (rather than professor) supervision." Upperclassmen praise Berkeley Law's "strong public-interest law community, excellent clinical offerings, and great access to [the] Bay Area legal market" but say that "often students must show initiative to take full advantage."

Professors at Berkeley Law are, for the most part, "incredible" and "accommodating," and "even the older professors—who tend to have more traditional styles—impart progressive views and attitudes about the law." Other students say the school's professors are "not great," even "cold"; they say that while "professors are certainly brilliant, they are not good teachers." While some students praise Berkeley Law's pass/fail grading system for cutting down on law school's inherent cutthroat attitude, others lament that "giving 60 percent of the class the same grade (P for 'pass') diminishes the incentive for people not to completely check out once they have a job. The grading system is not informative enough. The lowest score in the class gets the same grade as several above-average scores." Students who describe their professors as "top-notch" say that the faculty "genuinely care[s] about their students and make time to help them with questions both related to the course and issues outside the scope of the class." Classrooms at Berkeley Law are "awesome and newly renovated" and "after the renovation, [Boalt's] exterior isn't amazing, but it is pretty nice." The resources at a school like Berkeley Law are, as expected, world-class, and the library has research librarians who "are passionate and proud of what they do and look forward to helping students and make themselves available."

The administration, according to some, "is highly responsive and that might be largely due to the fact that students are incredibly involved in school policy decisions." Others say, "The administration seems disorganized and not very communicative. I have no idea what to do most of the time." Some students would like more administrative support when it came to career counseling, particularly "setting up field placements (i.e. externships, study abroad, and [the] UC-DC program). Right now, the process is largely left up to the students."

EDWARD TOM, ASSISTANT DEAN OF ADMISSIONS
396 SIMON HALL, BERKELEY, CA 94720-7220
TEL: 510-642-2274 • FAX: 510-643-6222
E-MAIL: ADMISSIONS@LAW.BERKELEY.EDU • WEBSITE: WWW.LAW.BERKELEY.EDU

Student Life

Students are split on whether their fellow Berkeley attendees are "incredibly friendly" and "mutually supportive of each other" or if they are "highly competitive and egotistical," with a "tendency to [err] on the side of [being] overly politically correct." While there's no doubt that the school leans left—its progressive values are not in doubt—some express concern that "students who are just average liberal to conservative often feel ridiculed for their ideologies." Students live in various spots in the surrounding region, which "limits the social life," making it so that "clubs and organizations are the backbone of student life. . . . Students are extremely active in clubs because that's necessary to make friends." Even with the rigors of law school, students find time to unwind, with "beer Olympics, organized cabin weekend trips to Tahoe, party buses to Napa, bar crawls in San Francisco, (also taco crawls in San Francisco, which are BOMB)." Students also underscore that "social justice is not a fringe thing" at Berkeley Law.

Getting In

It's incredibly competitive to get into Berkeley Law. Admitted students at the 25th percentile have an approximate GPA of 3.67 and an LSAT score of 164, while those at the 75th percentile have a GPA around 3.88 and LSAT score of 169.

Clinical program required	No
Legal writing course requirement	Yes
Legal methods course requirement	Yes
Legal research course requirement	Yes
Moot court requirement	Yes
Public interest law requirement	No

ADMISSIONS

Selectivity Rating	**98**
# applications received	5,699 %
applicants accepted	20
% acceptees attending	25
Median LSAT	167
LSAT Range (25th to 75th percentile)	164–169
Median undergrad GPA	3.79
Application fee	$75
Regular application deadline	2/1
Regular notification	4/1
Transfer students accepted	Yes
Evening division offered	No
Part-time accepted	No
CAS accepted	Yes

International Students

TOEFL required of international students.	Yes

FINANCIAL FACTS

Annual tuition (in-state/ out-of-state)	$48,226/$52,117
Books and supplies	$1,495
Fees	$3,154
Room & Board	$18,560
Financial aid application deadline	3/2
% first-year students receiving some sort of aid	79
% all students receiving some sort of aid	79
% of aid that is merit based	10
% receiving scholarships	60
Average grant	$17,270
Average loan	$52,807
Average total aid package	$60,075
Average debt	$143,546

EMPLOYMENT INFORMATION

Career Rating	98	Grads Employed by Field (%)
Total 2014 JD Grads	287	Academic (2)
# employed full-time	275	Business/Industry (3)
# employed part-time	2	Government (10)
# employed bar required	266	Judicial Clerkship (16)
# employed JD preferred	11	Private Practice (54)
# employed professional/other	0	Solo: (<1)
# employed non-professional	0	2-10: (<1)
# pursuing advanced degree	3	11-25: (3)
# unemployed and seeking		26-50: (1)
employment	5	51-100: (1)
# not seeking employment	2	101-250: (4)
State for bar exam	CA	251-500: (6)
Pass rate for first-time bar	91.6	501+: (39)
		Size Unknown: (0)
		Public Interest (12)

UNIVERSITY OF CALIFORNIA—DAVIS
SCHOOL OF LAW

INSTITUTIONAL INFORMATION

Public/private	Public
Affiliation	No Affiliation
Student-faculty ratio	10:1
% faculty part-time	20
% faculty female	46
% faculty underrepresented minority	42
Total faculty	69

SURVEY SAYS...

Diverse opinions accepted in classrooms, Liberal students, Strong sense of community, Good social life

STUDENTS

Enrollment of law school	513
% male/female	48/52
% from out-of-state	16
% part-time	0
% underrepresented minority	43
% international	6
# of countries represented	21
Average age of entering class	25

ACADEMICS

Academic Experience Rating	92
Profs interesting rating	87
Profs accessible rating	89
Hours of study per day	3.47

Academic Specialties
Criminal, Environmental, Human Rights, International, Taxation, Intellectual Property

Advanced Degrees Offered
JD 3 yrs; LLM 1 year

Combined Degrees Offered
JD/MBA, 4 yrs; JD/MA or JD/MS, 4 yrs

Academics

The School of Law at the University of California, Davis is one of the smallest law schools in California and offers a community balanced with an "atmosphere of excellence." King Hall (as students refer to it, named after Martin Luther King, Jr.) is well-known for its strong environmental law and public interest programs, and the "fantastic" clinical programs give students fantastic "incredible opportunities to gain practical lawyering skills." UC Davis also recently added the California Supreme Court Clinic to its list of clinical experiences, making it the first law school to have a clinic focus on its State Supreme Court. Needless to say, the opportunities for those who are self-starters "are clearly also present."

The seminars given here "are one of, hands-down, the best academic and intellectual opportunities offered at the law school." These small group settings (anywhere from three to twenty-one students) are "true diamonds:" "collaborative, organic environments where extremely high-level, student-driven discussion and thought can flourish." Each first year class is also given an upper level law student tutor to help guide students through the courses and achieve success.

Most large classes are run on the Socratic method, but there is plenty of variance in teaching methods and many professors "have a more conversational style approach, which is refreshing." Professors here are "staggeringly, incredibly helpful, and genuinely dedicated to students learning." They are "extremely approachable and there are various social events such as Coffee Hours where you can interact in a more informal manner." "In my smallest class every student had a one-on-one or two-on-one lunch with the professor at some point during the semester," says a 1L. Not only are they accessible, but they "eagerly encourage students to come to office hours and often lament how few students take advantage of that time."

The faculty and administration are "eager to engage with students" and the student body is "deeply involved with the administration in a constant conversation about budget, classes, and events." Students appreciate the name recognition in the Bay Area and Southern California for legal opportunities, and the "accessibility to Sacramento for job opportunities."

KRISTEN MERCADO, ASSISTANT DEAN OF ADMISSION AND FINANCIAL AID
SCHOOL OF LAW-KING HALL, 400 MRAK HALL DRIVE, DAVIS, CA 95616-5201
TEL: 530-752-6477
E-MAIL: ADMISSIONS@LAW.UCDAVIS.EDU • WEBSITE: WWW.LAW.UCDAVIS.EDU

Life

The community and collegial atmosphere ("We practically do hold hands and sing Kumbaya in the hallways") are "the best things" about UCD according to students, who "genuinely enjoy being law students at King Hall. "The pervasive feeling is that we're all in this together," says one. The diversity in the law school is "very good," with a mix of students from all over the world integrating in the JD/LLM, and visiting and exchange students. The building itself has recently been renovated with several new rooms added on and a library that is "stunning in its beauty," which "shows that your tuition money is going towards making the law school a better place." There are plenty of great student groups which "provide the key for networking and meeting legal professionals and alumni."

Law students also have a lot of fun together outside of the classroom, as well: the school is located in a secure location, "free from distractions and yet close to Sacramento and San Francisco where you can network with legal professionals and build your career and close to Napa and other wine counties and Lake Tahoe where you can visit in a day for recreation." People here tend to be "very liberal" and Davis is "surprisingly bourgeois" for a city "in the middle of nowhere." "I call it the 'Nebraska of California' because it is surrounded by farmland," says a student.

Getting In

Admitted students at the 25th percentile have LSAT scores of 161 and GPAs of 3.41. Admitted students at the 75th percentile have LSAT scores of 167 and GPAs of 3.78. UC Davis will consider all LSAT scores.

Clinical program required	No
Legal writing course requirement	Yes
Legal methods course requirement	Yes
Legal research course requirement	Yes
Moot court requirement	No
Public interest law requirement	No

ADMISSIONS

Selectivity Rating	91
# applications received	3,007
% applicants accepted	35
% acceptees attending	16
Average LSAT	162
Median LSAT	162
LSAT Range (25th to 75th percentile)	160–164
Average undergrad GPA	3.53
Median undergrad GPA	3.60
Application fee	$0
Regular application deadline	3/15
Early application deadline	2/1
Transfer students accepted	Yes
Evening division offered	No
Part-time accepted	No
CAS accepted	Yes

International Students

TOEFL required of international students.	Yes

FINANCIAL FACTS

Annual tuition (in-state/ out-of-state)	$46,460/$55,610
Books and supplies	$1,025
Fees	$1,938
Room & Board	$15,030
Financial aid application deadline	3/2
% first-year students receiving some sort of aid	85
% all students receiving some sort of aid	85
% of aid that is merit based	47
% receiving scholarships	76
Average grant	$25,000
Average loan	$37,864
Average total aid package	$63,064
Average debt	$93,500

EMPLOYMENT INFORMATION

Career Rating	94
Total 2014 JD Grads	169
% for whom you have useable information	99
% grads employed ten months out	88
Median starting salary	$61,000
# employed full-time	142
# employed part-time	6
# employed bar required	137
# employed JD preferred	10
# employed professional/other	1
# employed non-professional	0
# pursuing advanced degree	3
# unemployed and seeking employment	14
# not seeking employment	2
% grads employed by school	12
State for bar exam	CA, NY, MA, NV, OR
Pass rate for first-time bar	86.0

Prominent Alumni
Tani Cantil-Sakauye, Chief Justice, California Supreme Court; Darrell Steinberg, President Pro Tem, California State Senate; George Miller, Member, US House of Representatives, CA 7th district; Sister Simone Campbell, Executive Director, NETWORK, Washington, D.C.; Hon. Dean D. Pregerson, US District Court Judge

Grads Employed by Field (%)
Academic (2)
Business/Industry (8)
Government (20)
Judicial Clerkship (5)
Private Practice (41)
Public Interest (11)

UNIVERSITY OF CALIFORNIA—HASTINGS
COLLEGE OF THE LAW

INSTITUTIONAL INFORMATION

Public/private	Public
Affiliation	No Affiliation
% faculty part-time	53
% faculty female	39
% faculty underrepresented minority	17
Total faculty	158

SURVEY SAYS...

Abundant externship/internship/ clerkship opportunities, Liberal students

STUDENTS

Enrollment of law school	933
% male/female	50/50
% part-time	0
% underrepresented minority	43
% international	2
# of countries represented	10
Average age of entering class	24

ACADEMICS

Academic Experience Rating	87
Profs interesting rating	82
Profs accessible rating	75
Hours of study per day	3.68

Academic Specialties

Criminal, International, Taxation, Intellectual Property

Advanced Degrees Offered

JD, 3 yrs; LLM, 1 year; MSL, 1 year

Combined Degrees Offered

JD, LLM

Academics

UC Hastings is at the forefront of the legal education reformation. Indeed, the program staunchly places an emphasis on "practice [over] theory." This evolution is evident in Hastings' curriculum which only mandates a relatively small number of required courses. In turn, this allows students "to easily specialize and spend their time interning or externing." Additionally, the school provides what is arguably one of the "nation's best" moot courts and offers a "number of clinics" of which students can take advantage.

For the most part, students are impressed with their classroom experience. Although the average class size is fairly large, Hastings manages to accomplish the seemingly impossible and create an "intimate" feel. A first-year explains, "Despite the fact that there are eighty students in my section, I have made personal connections with each of my professors and feel as comfortable with them as I would expect if my section had ten students."

Speaking of professors, Hastings has managed to attract "a number of leaders in their respective fields." One fortunate first-year quickly chimes in, "The professors are not only highly regarded scholars, that many times have written the text for the course, but have also been great teachers with ample time for students." Overall, the faculty offers a "great mix of personalities, interests, backgrounds, credentials, etc." This might offer some insight into why they fervently "encourage and acknowledge different opinions." Finally, just as essential, professors are "always...approachable and willing to engage with students."

Perhaps one of Hastings greatest strengths is its Career Center. Counselors are "always available and work with every student association, and the administration to make getting a job easy and to ensure that students feel prepared for the future." An incredulous first-year quickly adds, "They even have a program to help you determine what kind of LIFE you want to have, and whether it even includes typical lawyering." Beyond the Career Center, students can also tap into a "huge alumni base, particularly in the Bay area" when seeking employment.

Students also happily report that Hastings administrators are a "supportive" bunch. Generally, they "are responsive to any issues and remedy problems as quickly as possible." One particularly pleased third-year student expresses gratitude to them for swiftly "eliminating bad professors upon negative feedback from students." However, there are a handful of students who feel that the administration could "communicate better with students and keep them more informed."

GREG CANADA, ASSISTANT DEAN OF ADMISSIONS
200 MCALLISTER STREET, SAN FRANCISCO, CA 94102
TEL: 415-565-4623 • FAX: 415-581-8946
E-MAIL: ADMISS@UCHASTINGS.EDU • WEBSITE: WWW.UCHASTINGS.EDU

Life

There's a lot of which to take advantage outside the classroom at Hastings. To begin with, "The alumni and career centers put on interesting and informational lawyer and alumni panels on a weekly basis." Additionally, there are also "excellent health and counseling resources" and there "are always lots of social events to attend." A content third-year offers some more insight, "I saw three Supreme Court Justices speak, attended panels and symposiums with top lawyers, even work[ed] with several super lawyers."

Further, Hastings prime location in San Francisco's Tenderloin neighborhood also means that students have a myriad of professional opportunities at their fingertips. As a third-year brags, "we are so close to so many law firms and attorneys- the networking opportunities and proximity to firms/externships is unparalleled." A second-year adds, "UC Hastings is walking distance from both state and federal trial and appellate courts, in addition to numerous government agencies. I can take a class that begins ten minutes after my externship ends at the U.S. Attorney's Office (and not be late)." Finally, yet another classmate confirms declaring, "there is no better legal mecca than our area. It is also centrally located in the city and on main public transportation, making it easy for commuters."

Getting In

Hastings maintains a competitive application process. The median undergraduate GPA for accepted candidates is 3.52 and the median LSAT score is 159. Applicants who think Hastings might be their first choice are encouraged to apply via the program's early commitment option.

Clinical program required	No
Legal writing course requirement	Yes
Legal methods course requirement	No
Legal research course requirement	Yes
Moot court requirement	Yes
Public interest law requirement	No

ADMISSIONS

Selectivity Rating	86
# applications received	3,114
% applicants accepted	49
% acceptees attending	21
Median LSAT	159
LSAT Range (25th to 75th percentile)	155–161
Median undergrad GPA	3.52
Application fee	$75
Regular application deadline	3/1
Regular notification	4/15
Transfer students accepted	Yes
Evening division offered	No
Part-time accepted	No
CAS accepted	Yes

FINANCIAL FACTS

Annual tuition (in-state/ out-of-state)	$43,486/$49,486
Books and supplies	$1,150
Fees	$4,149
Room & Board	$17,325
Financial aid application deadline	3/1
% first-year students receiving some sort of aid	90
% all students receiving some sort of aid	96
% of aid that is merit based	1
% receiving scholarships	86
Average grant	$15,671
Average loan	$46,700
Average total aid package	$57,195
Average debt	$129,178

EMPLOYMENT INFORMATION

Career Rating	91	**Prominent Alumni**
Total 2014 JD Grads	402	Marvin Baxter, Associate Justice, CA
% for whom you have useable information	100	Supreme Court; Willie Brown, Former Mayor, San Francisco
% grads employed ten months out	76	**Grads Employed by Field (%)**
Median starting salary	$80,000	Academic (2)
# employed full-time	272	Business/Industry (13)
# employed part-time	34	Government (14)
# employed bar required	265	Judicial Clerkship (2)
# employed JD preferred	30	Federal: (1)
# employed professional/other	11	State or local: (1)
# pursuing advanced degree	7	Private Practice (40)
# unemployed and seeking employment	71	Solo: (1)
# not seeking employment	9	2-10: (12)
% grads employed by school	6	11-25: (6)
State for bar exam	CA, NY, WA, IL, MD	26-50: (3)
		51-100: (2)
		101-250: (2)
		251-500: (1)
		501+: (10)
		Size Unknown: (1)
		Public Interest (5)

UNIVERSITY OF CALIFORNIA—LOS ANGELES
SCHOOL OF LAW

Academics

At UCLA's law school, "The professors are all studs in their field, and most teach 1L courses. It's pretty cool to have a famous professor as a teacher in your first year." Students feel like a priority to their professors and administrators despite the size of the student population, saying, "Considering UCLA is a large university, the law school feels small and friendly." They laud their professors, especially, for being "some of the most incredible, engaging and intelligent people I have ever met" and appreciate that they've been invited "to meals with or been at the homes of most of my professors." UCLA's "brilliant, renowned, accessible, kind" professors do a great job balancing professional and pedagogical responsibilities: "the number of professors who are considered authorities within their realm of expertise is unreal, and to know that these highly-reputed figures are willing to open their office for you because they truly care about your learning is incredible." Indeed, students perceive their professors to be "completely committed to forming talented attorneys who will contribute to society."

UCLA law is "very progressive" and forward-looking in the legal field, resulting in an "incredibly impressive" "diversity of classes, opinions, [and] extracurricular programs." "The David J. Epstein Program in Public Interest Law and Policy and the Critical Race Studies Program are two very unique and well-run specializations," and many "in-depth classes in particular areas" engage students. "The quality of discussion in the classroom is superb" across the board, and students credit this partially to the program's "ample diversity." When it comes to grading, the curve is kind: "The curve once you're in upper division classes is at a B+, so that's quite nice."

In their interactions with the administration, students often report that they've "greatly benefited from the services and support" of particular programs like "the Public Interest Law Program and the Critical Race Studies Program. I have a post-graduation job already thanks to the advice and support I received from the Public Interest Law Program's office." For budding attorneys looking to practice in California (who may be the best served by a UCLA degree, as some students complain that the school has "no network on the East Coast"), UCLA offers "access to more people and resources in the entertainment industry than any school in the country," as well as "great connections to the legal community and access to jobs and internships." In general, students find that "The administration is unbelievably supportive and communicative," while also encountering that, not unusually for a large, public university, "there is a lot of red tape when trying to do anything out of the ordinary." "In terms of facilities," they critique, "the law school building itself is a bit of a mixed bag. I think they're in the process of renovating rooms continuously, so every semester a new room gets redone, but the two really big lecture halls are pretty outdated." To date, more than half of the lecture-style classrooms have been renovated at UCLA School of Law.

ROBERT SCHWARTZ, DEAN OF ADMISSIONS AND FINANCIAL AID
71 DODD HALL, BOX 951445, LOS ANGELES, CA 90095-1445
TEL: 310-825-2080 • FAX: 310-206-7227
E-MAIL: ADMISSIONS@LAW.UCLA.EDU • WEBSITE: WWW.LAW.UCLA.EDU

Life

Socially, "the culture is competitive (it's law school, after all) while still being friendly and collegial." "Overall, students here are very cooperative and helpful", and value the "community atmosphere" that the program cultivates. They're incredibly proud of the school's "diversity": "The school is full of people who come from different backgrounds and ethnicity, and there is absolutely no barrier between them." Conservative-leaning students sometimes feel the university could do better at "offering a more politically balanced and neutral environment."

Not surprisingly, the perks of UCLA's geographic location are popular: "Though you have no life as a 1L here, there is something amazing about being able to study on the beach in seventy degree weather in the middle of December." "In between classes and at lunch, everyone hangs out in the central courtyard and soaks in the LA sunshine." This contributes, undoubtedly, to the "congenial student body" and a greater environment that students extol as "challenging, diverse, and rewarding."

Getting In

For the class of 2016, the median LSAT spread was 163–169, and the median GPA spread was 3.51–3.88. Students say UCLA does an unusually good job integrating JD and LLM candidates.

Clinical program required	No
Legal writing course requirement	Yes
Legal methods course requirement	Yes
Legal research course requirement	Yes
Moot court requirement	No
Public interest law requirement	No

ADMISSIONS

Selectivity Rating	96
# applications received	5,408
% applicants accepted	28
% acceptees attending	21
Median LSAT	167
LSAT Range (25th to 75th percentile)	163–169
Median undergrad GPA	3.79
Application fee	$75
Regular application deadline	2/1
Early application deadline	11/15
Early application notification	12/31
Transfer students accepted	Yes
Evening division offered	No
Part-time accepted	No
CAS accepted	Yes

FINANCIAL FACTS

Annual tuition (in-state/out-of-state)	$45,226/$51,720
Books and supplies	$1,573
Room & Board	$17,719
Financial aid application deadline	3/2
% first-year students receiving some sort of aid	92
% all students receiving some sort of aid	90
% receiving scholarships	78
Average grant	$23,509
Average loan	$43,605
Average total aid package	$52,463
Average debt	$121,066

EMPLOYMENT INFORMATION

Career Rating	96
Total 2014 JD Grads	336
% for whom you have useable information	100
% grads employed ten months out	83
Median starting salary	$100,000
# employed full-time	302
# employed part-time	8
# employed bar required	284
# employed JD preferred	25
# employed professional/other	1
# pursuing advanced degree	4
# unemployed and seeking employment	17
# not seeking employment	2
% grads employed by school	10
State for bar exam	CA
Pass rate for first-time bar	82.0

Prominent Alumni

Senator Kirsten Gillibrand '91, United States Senator, New York; David Steiner '86, Chief Executive Officer, Waste Management, Inc., Martine A. Rothblatt '81, Chairman & CEO of United Therapeutics Corp.; Kenneth Ziffren '65, Founding Partner, Ziffren Brittenham LLP; Stewart Resnick '62, President and CEO, Roll International Corporation

Grads Employed by Field (%)

Academic (1)
Business/Industry (7)
Government (7)
Judicial Clerkship (6)
Federal: (4)
State or local: (2)
Private Practice (59)
  Solo: (1)
  2-10: (11)
  11-25: (7)
  26-50: (3)
  51-100: (2)
  101-250: (6)

THE UNIVERSITY OF CHICAGO
LAW SCHOOL

251-500: (4)
501+: (25)
Size Unknown: (0)
Public Interest (11)

INSTITUTIONAL INFORMATION

Public/private	Private
% faculty part-time	37
% faculty female	32
% faculty underrepresented minority	15
Total faculty	115

SURVEY SAYS...

Diverse opinions accepted in classrooms, Great research resources, Abundant externship/internship/clerkship opportunities, Law school well run

STUDENTS

Enrollment of law school	604
% male/female	57/43
% from out-of-state	81
% part-time	0
% underrepresented minority	28
% international	6
Average age of entering class	24

ACADEMICS

Academic Experience Rating	99
Profs interesting rating	99
Profs accessible rating	95
Hours of study per day	3.75

Academic Specialties

Civil Procedure, Commercial, Constitutional, Corporation Securities, Criminal, Environmental, Government Services, Human Rights, International, Labor, Legal History, Legal Philosophy, Property, Taxation, Intellectual Property

Advanced Degrees Offered

JD 3 yrs; LLM 1 yr; JSD Depends on Dissertation (up to 5 yrs)

Combined Degrees Offered

JD/MBA, 4 yrs; JD/PhD in conjunction with Graduate School of Business, depends on dissertation;

Academics

It's not exactly a secret that The University of Chicago's Law School is one of the most highly-regarded and academically rigorous law programs in the entire country, with one of the most competitive acceptance rates to boot. UChicago is "invested in each and every student," and the "excellent and responsive" administration goes above and beyond to ensure the highest level of success for every student. Students at Chicago are constantly being held to the highest standard of work and preparedness for class, but are "given full support with interesting programming/research facilities/beautiful building and library." "I'll always be grateful for the tremendous education that I've received here," says a student.

The intimacy of the program (the whole law school is in one building), small class sizes, and the quarter system also make adjusting to law school easier for 1Ls. "Even in required 1L courses like contracts, which I have no natural interest in, I'm blown away by the intellect and teaching skills of our professors," says one first-year. "That definitely makes up for the fact that we only get to choose one elective our 1L year." Many of the 1L doctrinal classes are two quarters long (with a switch halfway between two very different professors), allowing students "to get a more comprehensive understanding of the subject and different ways of looking at it," and once they're in the clear of their second year, students find it easy to take classes in other departments.

The "funny and engaging" faculty is understandably incredible—"There really are no bad professors"—and the school places such a high value on the in-class experience that it "will reject a candidate who is a good scholar but bad teacher." Professors "tolerate pretty much any viewpoint, and will respect your opinion" which "fosters a healthy discussion environment and allows people to be themselves." The fact that their offices are in the student library makes it "incredibly easy to approach them with questions," and "the sheer quantity of preeminent experts who are professors here is staggering." It is "astounding how often you will do a reading and come to find that one of your professors is cited in the reading, or even that they wrote the book." "How often are you taught by federal judges?" asks a 1L. Research librarians are also great and "always available during building hours."

The employment rate of students is "phenomenal" and faculty members are "eager to go to bat for their students when it's time to get clerkships/jobs." "It seems like every week or two, we have major national firms and agencies flying people out to recruit, and almost nobody had any trouble finding a summer job," says a 1L. Because of the strong job prospects for anyone who graduates, "there is not a lot of overt competition." "We were given two pieces of advice during orientation: 'Don't talk about grades' and 'Don't be a jerk,'" says a student. "People here live by that advice and it makes it a great place to be."

ANN PERRY, ASSOCIATE DEAN FOR ADMISSIONS
1111 EAST 60TH STREET, CHICAGO, IL 60637
TEL: 773-702-9484 • FAX: 773-834-0942
E-MAIL: ADMISSIONS@LAW.UCHICAGO.EDU • WEBSITE: WWW.LAW.UCHICAGO.EDU

Life

Facilities are "top-notch" and "the location of the school couldn't be better." The area "maintains a lower than expected cost of living while providing quick and easy access to many of the best law firms in the country." Despite the difficult curriculum, UChicago "does a good job of garnering camaraderie among classmates." There are "a lot of great opportunities for extra-curricular involvement" and so much going on at any given time that "the biggest challenge is just trying to rule out different options." Plenty of school-sponsored bonding activities help cement relationships between students. "People are constantly posting jokes/articles/etc on our class Facebook page. There is probably not a single person my year who I couldn't identify, and there are very few that I haven't at least spoken to once or twice," says one student. The Green Lounge (the main atrium at the law school) is "a very social and fun place to be most of the time," and the social environment is" really fun, especially once 1L finishes and folks move downtown."

Getting In

If you can get admitted here, you can get admitted to virtually any law school in the country. Admitted students at 25th percentile have LSAT scores of about 166 and GPAs of about 3.67. Admitted students at 75th percentile have LSAT scores of 172 and GPAs over 3.95. If you take the LSAT a second time, Chicago will place the most importance on your higher score, but will consider both.

JD/AM Public Policy, 4 yrs; JD/AM International Relations, 4 yrs

Clinical program required	No
Legal writing course requirement	Yes
Legal methods course requirement	Yes
Legal research course requirement	Yes
Moot court requirement	Yes
Public interest law requirement	No

ADMISSIONS

Selectivity Rating	98
# applications received	4,430
% applicants accepted	18
% acceptees attending	23
Median LSAT	170
LSAT Range (25th to 75th percentile)	166–172
Median undergrad GPA	3.90
Application fee	$75
Regular application deadline	2/1
Early application deadline	12/1
Early application notification	12/31
Transfer students accepted	Yes
Evening division offered	No
Part-time accepted	No
CAS accepted	Yes

International Students

TOEFL required of international students.	Yes

FINANCIAL FACTS

Annual tuition	$55,503
Books and supplies	$1,770
Room & Board	$13,590
Financial aid application deadline	2/1
% first-year students receiving some sort of aid	90
% all students receiving some sort of aid	84
% of aid that is merit based	75
% receiving scholarships	76
Average grant	$22,000
Average loan	$55,000
Average debt	$144,695

EMPLOYMENT INFORMATION

Career Rating	99	Grads Employed by Field (%)	
Total 2014 JD Grads	210	Academic (1)	
% for whom you have useable information	100	Business/Industry (6)	
% grads employed ten months out	98	Government (5)	
Median starting salary	$160,000	Judicial Clerkship (17)	
# employed full-time	204	Federal: (16)	
# employed part-time	2	State or local: (1)	
# employed bar required	195	Private Practice (64)	
# employed JD preferred	10	Solo: (1)	
# employed professional/other	1	2-10: (1)	
# unemployed and seeking employment	3	11-25: (1)	
% grads employed by school	6	26-50: (1)	
State for bar exam	IL, NY	51-100: (2)	
Pass rate for first-time bar	95.0	101-250: (2)	
		251-500: (3)	
		501+: (55)	
		Size Unknown: (0)	
		Public Interest (6)	

UNIVERSITY OF CINCINNATI
COLLEGE OF LAW

INSTITUTIONAL INFORMATION

Public/private	Public
Student-faculty ratio	9:1
% faculty part-time	42
% faculty female	39
% faculty underrepresented minority	13
Total faculty	69

SURVEY SAYS...

Diverse opinions accepted in classrooms

STUDENTS

Enrollment of law school	293
% male/female	60/40
% part-time	0
% underrepresented minority	13
% international	1
Average age of entering class	24

ACADEMICS

Academic Experience Rating	83
Profs interesting rating	84
Profs accessible rating	87
Hours of study per day	3.79

Academic Specialties

Commercial, Corporation Securities, Criminal, Environmental, Human Rights, International, Labor, Taxation, Intellectual Property

Advanced Degrees Offered

JD, 3 yrs; LLM, 1 yr

Combined Degrees Offered

JD/MBA, 4 yrs; JD/Master's Community Planning, 4.5 yrs; JD/MA in Women's, Gender, and Sexuality Studies, 4 yrs; JD/MA in Political Science, 4 yrs

Academics

Students at the University of Cincinnati get the "small class sizes" and "intimate environment" typical of a private college while paying the comfortable, low tuition you would expect from a public institution. With roughly one hundred students in each entering class, the school strikes an "excellent" balance with "its affordability, reputation, small class size, and excellent faculty." Students agree that UC professors are an "amazing and diverse group of people who care just as much for teaching and students as they do about publishing their own work." UC is particularly noted for its focus on "public interest" and "international" law; however, "there is no shortage of brilliant legal minds in a broad range of subjects—that goes for students as well as the professors." In addition to the accomplished tenured faculty, students rave about the school's recent acquisition of "exceptional young faculty members that have great teaching skills to match their great scholarship." A 2L sums it up, "As one of the smallest public law schools in the country, I feel my educational experience has been fantastic, and yet, at very little cost. Because our class consists of only 128 people, all of my professors know my name."

University of Cincinnati runs several "amazing" legal institutes and research centers focused on unique topics such as domestic violence, law and psychiatry, and corporate law. Through these centers, students can earn credit hours while doing fulfilling and useful work in the community. Many students make particular note of the Ohio Innocence Project, an institute at the University of Cincinnati through which students conduct substantive work to impact legislative reform, and work on real criminal cases. The institute also brings notable speakers to campus. Students also have the opportunity to research and write for the school's renowned publications, including the Human Rights Quarterly, Law Review, and Freedom Center Journal. While students at other schools might scramble for spots on the school's law review or clinic programs, "since the school is small, each student can participate in and get involved in a number of organizations."

Thanks to an "ambitious but not overly competitive student body," the learning environment is charged, but not cutthroat, at University of Cincinnati. A 3L attests, "While academic achievement is always a numbers game in law school, the atmosphere at UC is nonpretentious and noncontentious." When it comes to the job and internship placements, University of Cincinnati maintains a "deep and well-regarded history as a legal educational institution" both locally and nationally. As a result, most students say the school "is a great place for students with all different kinds of career aspirations, and especially has a public interest/human rights orientation that I think is unparalleled in the Midwest." In fact, "public interest students can actually obtain funding for their summer jobs through the school's Summer Public Interest Fellowship Program." Most UC grads stay in the Cincinnati area and meet with good results while those looking outside the region must do a little extra legwork to find a good placement. "While plenty of our grads go on to excellent careers in major firms, federal clerkships, and other government positions, I don't feel like our school does enough PR work to get out-of-town employers interested in our students," says one student.

Life

For starving students/aspiring lawyers, Cincinnati is an excellent home base offering the unbeatable combination of "small town prices (housing, dining, entertainment) with big city amenities." For both professional and recreational pursuits, the UC campus is pleasantly located "close to downtown so it's easy to get to work, ballgames, and

AL WATSON, ASSISTANT DEAN AND DIRECTOR OF ADMISSION AND FINANCIAL AID
P.O. BOX 210040, CINCINNATI, OH 45221
TEL: 513-556-6805 • FAX: 513-556-2391
E-MAIL: ADMISSIONS@LAW.UC.EDU • WEBSITE: WWW.LAW.UC.EDU

entertainment." While Cincinnati has its charms, students complain that the law school could use "more outlets and better lighting." "Windows would be nice," adds another. However, the school is considering remodeling or re-building the law school along with other campus projects. The good news is that "the new parking garage has been built, and there are brand-new (and attractive) living units pretty much right across the street." Not to mention that a few "ice cream shops have opened within a short walk from school."

Despite the rigors of the academic curriculum, "the students that are here create a suitable balance between academic and social life. There are plenty of opportunities to go out and have fun and not be completely overwhelmed with school." On and off campus, "there are frequently SBA social events for students, such as happy hours at local bars." In fact, the SBA is very active and "most of the students are friends and spend time together outside of the law school." On the other hand, students remind us that Cincinnati also attracts "a large contingent of commuter students who spend little if no time involved in the school outside of actual class."

Getting In

To apply to the University of Cincinnati College of Law, students must submit LSAT scores and register with the Law School Credential Assembly Service Report. If the LSAT was taken more than once, the highest score will be considered by the Admissions Committee. More than 800 hopefuls applied for 100 spots in the JD program. Students in the 25th percentile had LSAT scores of 151 and GPAs of 3.22, while those in the 75th percentile had LSAT scores of 159 and GPAs of 3.7.

Clinical program required	No
Legal writing course requirement	Yes
Legal methods course requirement	No
Legal research course requirement	Yes
Moot court requirement	No
Public interest law requirement	No

ADMISSIONS

Selectivity Rating	82
# applications received	811
% applicants accepted	60
% acceptees attending	15
Median LSAT	155
LSAT Range (25th to 75th percentile)	151–159
Median undergrad GPA	3.45
Application fee	$35
Regular application deadline	3/15
Early application deadline	12/1
Early application notification	1/15
Transfer students accepted	Yes
Evening division offered	No
Part-time accepted	No
CAS accepted	Yes

International Students

TOEFL required of international students.	Yes

FINANCIAL FACTS

Annual tuition (in-state/out-of-state)	$22,332/$27,332
Books and supplies	$1,539
Fees	$1,678
Room & Board	$16,797
Financial aid application deadline	3/1
% receiving scholarships	78
Average grant	$7,539
Average debt	$76,663

EMPLOYMENT INFORMATION

Career Rating	74
Total 2014 JD Grads	125
% for whom you have useable information	99
% grads employed ten months out	88
Median starting salary	$60,000
# employed full-time	104
# employed part-time	6
# employed bar required	83
# employed JD preferred	24
# employed professional/other	1
# employed non-professional	2
# pursuing advanced degree	1
# unemployed and seeking employment	12
State for bar exam	OH, KY, NY, IN, IL

Prominent Alumni
Major General John D. Altenberg, Military; Cris Collinsworth, Journalist; Billy Martin, Wash, DC based high profile case attorney

Grads Employed by Field (%)
Academic (1)
Business/Industry (19)
Government (21)
Judicial Clerkship (5)
Federal: (2)
State or local: (3)
Private Practice (40)
 Solo: (3)
 2-10: (11)
 11-25: (5)
 26-50: (4)
 51-100: (1)
 101-250: (3)
 251-500: (7)
 501+: (6)
Public Interest (2)

UNIVERSITY OF COLORADO
LAW SCHOOL

INSTITUTIONAL INFORMATION

Public/private	Public
Affiliation	No Affiliation
Student-faculty ratio	9:1
% faculty part-time	31
% faculty female	44
% faculty underrepresented minority	18
Total faculty	72

SURVEY SAYS...

Students love Boulder, CO, Great research resources, Abundant externship/internship/clerkship opportunities, Good social life

STUDENTS

Enrollment of law school	509
% male/female	54/46
% from out-of-state	33
% part-time	0
% underrepresented minority	18
% international	1
# of countries represented	5
Average age of entering class	26

ACADEMICS

Academic Experience Rating	90
Profs interesting rating	87
Profs accessible rating	85
Hours of study per day	4.12

Academic Specialties

Constitutional, Corporation Securities, Criminal, Environmental, Labor, Taxation, Intellectual Property

Advanced Degrees Offered

JD, 3 yrs; LLM, 1 yr; MSL, 1 yr

Combined Degrees Offered

JD/MBA, 3.5 to 4 yrs; JD/MPA, 3.5 to 4 yrs; JD/Master of Science and Telecommunications, 3.5 to 4 yrs; JD/PhD in Environmental Science; JD/Master of Environmental Science, 3.5 to 4 yrs; JD/MURP, 3.5 to 4 JD/MURP

Academics

Colorado provides aspiring lawyers with an "intellectually challenging" environment and a myriad of opportunities in which "to begin honing [their] experiential skills." Indeed, the "emphasis on clinical programs and practical experience is second to none." When it comes to environmental law, Colorado is a powerhouse. As one second-year brags, "Our environmental law program is either one of the best or the best in the country depending on who you ask."

Students at Colorado are also privy to "top-notch" facilities and "excellent computer and library resources." A thrilled third-year adds, "The physical building that houses Colorado Law is stunning. It's hard to complain about spending a Saturday studying when you can see the mountains from the library windows." Additionally, the fantastic library staff is always "eager to help with research." They continually "partner with legal writing professors to introduce students to resources early on in the year." The Career Development Office also receives high marks. The office is "comprised of outstanding individuals who always make time to work with students, inform them of opportunities that interest them, and advise whenever required."

However, what "really makes Colorado Law stand out is the accessibility—and quality—of its faculty." For starters, the professors here continually show "genuine... interests in students." Another second-year boasts that, "every professor I have had at CU has known not only who I am, but my academic interests and how they correspond to their own." A deeply satisfied third-year interjects, "Most of the professors here are brilliant intellectuals and wonderful people. I will have lasting relationships with many of them long after I am graduated."

Echoing the care and openness displayed by the faculty, administrators are also heralded as "highly responsive" to the students' needs. A veteran third-year explains, "CU is such a small law school that I see everyone from the Deans to the Registrar, to the office assistants regularly, and I feel comfortable going to any of them with questions or problems that I need help resolving." Moreover, "they also go out of their ways to get to know students, share relevant information, and make it a positive academic experience."

Life

Though one might not associate legal education with the notion of good vibes, the sentiment does ring true for Colorado. Indeed, "the students who comprise CU Law are reflective of the friendly, caring administration and faculty. It's hard to stay cross at CU Law for more than an hour, because the positive atmosphere engulfing you makes you appreciate how good you have it." Truly, "this school's trump card is its quality of life." The "students, faculty, and staff here are all exceptionally friendly, and almost all seem to recognize that being a person should come before being an attorney."

KRISTINE JACKSON, ASSISTANT DEAN FOR ADMISSIONS & FINANCIAL AID
403 UCB, BOULDER, CO 80309-0403
TEL: 303-492-7203 • FAX: 303-492-2542
E-MAIL: LAWADMIN@COLORADO.EDU • WEBSITE: WWW.COLORADO.EDU / LAW

Additionally, Colorado offers many educational opportunities beyond the classroom. As a second-year shares, "The school has gotten great guests during my two years (two Supreme Court justices, the Colorado Supreme Court, the Tenth Circuit, the Federal Circuit, the Colorado Court of Appeals, and countless stars from the public and private sectors)." Of course, there are plenty of opportunities to kick back as well. In fact, "many students arrange their schedules so as not to have class on Friday so they can go skiing all weekend, and I have personally had an adjunct prof cancel a Thursday night class so he could go to Steamboat Springs with his family." Further, "there are loads of people who go out on weekends, whether it be partying, camping, exercising, or travelling. If you want to become a lawyer AND have a good time doing it, this is the place for you."

Getting In

The Colorado admissions office maintains some impressive stats. Amongst accepted applicants, the median undergraduate GPA is 3.62 and the median LSAT score is 161. While the school does not require any specific pre-law curriculum, classes that place an emphasis on analytical and writing skills are highly recommended. Finally, the program operates on a rolling admissions basis. Therefore, the earlier you apply the stronger your chances.

Clinical program required	No
Legal writing course requirement	Yes
Legal methods course requirement	Yes
Legal research course requirement	Yes
Moot court requirement	No
Public interest law requirement	No

ADMISSIONS

Selectivity Rating	89
# applications received	2,174
% applicants accepted	47
% acceptees attending	16
Average LSAT	159
Median LSAT	161
LSAT Range (25th to 75th percentile)	156–163
Average undergrad GPA	3.54
Median undergrad GPA	3.62
Application fee	$65
Regular application deadline	3/15
Regular notification	4/30
Transfer students accepted	Yes
Evening division offered	No
Part-time accepted	No
CAS accepted	Yes

International Students

TOEFL required of international students.	Yes

FINANCIAL FACTS

Annual tuition (in-state/ out-of-state)	$29,718/$36,504
Books and supplies	$1,800
Fees	$2,168
Room & Board (on/ off campus)	$17,486/$18,210
Financial aid application deadline	3/1
% first-year students receiving some sort of aid	93
% all students receiving some sort of aid	92
% of aid that is merit based	26
% receiving scholarships	81
Average grant	$12,999
Average loan	$36,947
Average total aid package	$39,415
Average debt	$116,280

EMPLOYMENT INFORMATION

Career Rating	**93**	
Total 2014 JD Grads	165	
% for whom you have useable information	99	
% grads employed ten months out	93	
Median starting salary	$57,500	
# employed full-time	142	
# employed part-time	12	
# employed bar required	131	
# employed JD preferred	21	
# employed professional/other	2	
# pursuing advanced degree	2	
# unemployed and seeking employment	6	
# not seeking employment	1	
% grads employed by school	11	
State for bar exam	CO, CA, TX, NY, WA	
Pass rate for first-time bar	81.5	

Prominent Alumni
Wiley B. Rutledge, Former Associate Justice, US Supreme Court; Bill Ritter, Jr., former Governor of Colorado; Roy Romer, former Governor of Colorado

Grads Employed by Field (%)
Academic (3)
Business/Industry (11)
Government (17)
Judicial Clerkship (15)
  Federal: (1)
  State or local: (13)
Private Practice (38)
  2-10: (12)
  11-25: (5)
  26-50: (5)
  51-100: (2)
  101-250: (1)
  251-500: (6)
  501+: (6)
  Size Unknown: (1)
Public Interest (10)

UNIVERSITY OF CONNECTICUT
SCHOOL OF LAW

Academics

The University of Connecticut School of Law is located in Hartford, the state's capital. The institution boasts all of "the resources of a large, public institution with the feel of a small, private school." The low in-state tuition is great for Connecticut residents looking for a deal.

The program has cultivated a "strong relationship with pretty much every firm/agency/government office in the state," though most students warn other law school applicants who are looking to practice outside of the state upon graduation to do their research. Career Services at UConn Law has a reputation of being "Connecticut-oriented" and "most of the recruitment is self-selecting/self-motivating," says a 3L.

The administration here is "excellent, very accessible, and very responsive to student needs and concerns." With the exception of the required curriculum, most students find professors to be "approachable" as well, says a 1L.

Once students reach the higher-level courses and specialties, they engage with teachers who possess valuable field experience and provide more practice-oriented instruction to prepare students for their career ahead. "I really get the sense that no one wants me to fail," says a 1L. "Many of the professors have been in the state for a number of years, and many of the lawyers and judges in Hartford, and Connecticut more generally, are alumni, which make opportunities for internships/clerkships very accessible," says a 2L. Overall, many students feel that they have the faculty's full support.

"The University of Connecticut offers a unique program, which allows students to spend a semester working at a federal agency in Washington, D.C. While participating in the program, my fellow classmates and I had exclusive access to the White House, Pentagon, and other various high profile Washingtonian landmarks," says a 3L.

Some students yearn for more evening classes while others just wish for "more classes" overall. In contrast students see the program's opportunities for specialization as its "greatest strength." One student sees this manifested in "the ability to conduct your own research project, as well as [to] compete in trial and appellate competitions across the country and conferences around the world."

However, one aspect of the school that students can agree upon is their love of the clinics offered on campus. "With a little work on your part it is relatively easy to get an externship experience that looks fantastic on a résumé. Attorneys that I talk to look to see experiential learning and UConn gives you that opportunity," says a 3L.

The recent renovation of the school's library has done much to enhance the productivity and esthetic of the UConn Law campus. "The library is absolutely beautiful and we have access to every resource imaginable. The library staff is very friendly and knowledgeable. The classrooms were recently updated and the courtrooms are impressive," informs a 3L.

Students gush about the school's "historic look, with a modern interior." Buildings have "state-of-the-art research capabilities and plenty of private study areas with full Internet access at every desk." "In my last seminar class, the flat screen television started ringing and we began a satellite conference call with someone in England," says a student.

KAREN DeMEOLA, ASSISTANT DEAN FOR ADMISSIONS AND STUDENT FINANCE
45 ELIZABETH STREET, HARTFORD, CT 06105
TEL: 860-570-5100 • FAX: 860-570-5153
E-MAIL: ADMISSIONS@LAW.UCONN.EDU • WEBSITE: WWW.LAW.UCONN.EDU

Life

Students at UConn Law value the school's small size despite the fact that it's a public institution. The campus "really fosters a sense of community among students." "The community of students at UConn Law are some of the most diverse and friendly people I have met," says one 3L. "Every student is incredibly bright, but except for a couple students, each student supports his/her classmates. That is, the environment highly fosters friendship and support for one another's achievements. It also enhances the learning environment." The "student body [is] deeply involved in student organization [and is] deeply involved in the greater Hartford area," says a 1L.

The city of Hartford is academically rich and is home to both UConn and Trinity College. The school has worked to improve the safety of its students on and around the school area.

On campus there is plenty to do in one's spare time despite the large number of commuter and part-time students. "Many activities [are] both structured and informal, in which the younger, full-time students make time to participate."

UConn Law also makes a concerted effort to be "very welcoming to LGBT students," displaying diversity in its student body as well as in its faculty. This, students say, enhances classes and "makes for very lively and interesting discussions."

Getting In

Students are admitted to UConn School of Law once annually, for entry in the fall semester. No numeric index is used to rank applicants to UConn School of Law (though the LSAT is required) and each applicant is considered individually; the school is also veteran-friendly. Connecticut residents receive special consideration in an admissions decision, though no absolute preference is given. Of the 182 1Ls accepted for a recent entering class, the undergraduate GPA was median 3.45 and the LSAT score was median 159.

EMPLOYMENT INFORMATION		
Career Rating	91	**Grads Employed by Field (%)**
Total 2014 JD Grads	179	Academic (4)
% for whom you have useable		Business/Industry (18)
information	52	Government (9)
% grads employed ten months out	83	Judicial Clerkship (12)
Median starting salary	$65,000	Private Practice (50)
% job accepting grads providing		Public Interest (4)
useable salary information	66	
# not seeking employment	6	
% grads employed by school	0	
State for bar exam	CT, NY, MA	
Pass rate for first-time bar	90.0	

Clinical program required	No
Legal writing	
course requirement	Yes
Legal methods	
course requirement	Yes
Legal research	
course requirement	Yes
Moot court requirement	Yes
Public interest	
law requirement	No

ADMISSIONS

Selectivity Rating	**89**
# applications received	1,897
% applicants accepted	31
% acceptees attending	23
Average LSAT	159
Median LSAT	159
LSAT Range (25th to	
75th percentile)	157–163
Average undergrad GPA	3.42
Median undergrad GPA	3.45
Application fee	$60
Regular application deadline	3/15
Transfer students accepted	Yes
Evening division offered	Yes
Part-time accepted	Yes
CAS accepted	Yes

International Students

TOEFL required of international	
students.	Yes

FINANCIAL FACTS

Annual tuition (in-state/	
out-of-state)	$22,416/$43,632
Books and supplies	$1,390
Fees	$876
Room & Board (on/	
off campus)	$12,160
Financial aid application	
deadline	3/15
% first-year students receiving	
some sort of aid	87
% all students receiving	
some sort of aid	80
% of aid that is merit based	7
% receiving scholarships	76
Average grant	$12,645
Average loan	$23,354
Average total aid package	$36,024
Average debt	$65,639

UNIVERSITY OF DAYTON
SCHOOL OF LAW

INSTITUTIONAL INFORMATION

Public/private	Private
Affiliation	Roman Catholic
Student-faculty ratio	13:1
% faculty part-time	43
% faculty female	47
% faculty underrepresented minority	13
Total faculty	47

SURVEY SAYS...

Great research resources

STUDENTS

Enrollment of law school	276
% male/female	52/48
% from out-of-state	46
% part-time	0
% underrepresented minority	19
% international	1
# of countries represented	2
Average age of entering class	25

ACADEMICS

Academic Experience Rating	**71**
Profs interesting rating	71
Profs accessible rating	83
Hours of study per day	3.39

Academic Specialties

Cyber Law; Intellectual Property

Advanced Degrees Offered

JD, 3 yrs; JD accelerated, 2 years

Combined Degrees Offered

JD/MBA, 3–4 yrs; LLM, 1 yr; MSL, 1 yr

Academics

A small, Catholic-affiliated private school with a strong reputation in Ohio, the University of Dayton School of Law offers two JD options: a traditional three-year program and an accelerated two-year degree. No matter which course of study one chooses, the curriculum begins with ten core courses, followed by elective classes and upper-level seminars. When evaluating their academic experience, students dole out praises for the "incredible writing program," often citing the writing course work as the school's greatest strength. They also love the fact that "classes are small," so students feel like "more than just a number to your professors"; although, they would love to see a "wider range of courses" offered to upper-level students.

Those who choose this "serious" school should come prepared to work hard. At this fast-paced program, students insist, "We study just as hard as any first year law student possibly could—the bar is set high, and those who do not meet it after their first semester are asked not to return." The good news is that "professors are extremely accessible" and "genuinely concerned with the success of their students," often "more than willing to meet with students outside of office hours and [to] make previous exams available." A 1L shares this rather reassuring advice, "If you do not study (the workload is considerable) you will fail, but if a person wants to be here, they just need to put in the work and they will be fine."

While UDSL recruits accomplished faculty, "the professors vary as far as quality" in the classroom. The majority of students maintain that "the professors are, for the most part, wonderful. They are all very knowledgeable and are willing to provide as much outside assistance as necessary." Many will even "incorporate trending interests such as pop, music, movies into their teaching materials." Unfortunately, a few UDSL professors love the sound of their own voice, making it "very difficult to learn and share opinions in class." Still, a few bad classes amount to "a small and limited experience" when measured up against the program as a whole. Students dispute the administration's effectiveness in managing the program, though they agree that the school's deans and officers are "quick to respond to student concerns and are very personable." Here, "both the Dean of Students and the Dean of the Law School know most of the students by name."

Throughout the program, there is a "strong emphasis on real world preparation and bar passage." Traditional academics are complemented by courses in writing and research, clinical experience, and a capstone course, in which students must apply their skills to a real-world situation. Through the school's clinical programs, students also get experience "preparing all aspects of a case, from the initial client interview to preparing for trial and possibly even participating in a trial"; plus, "every student is required to take an externship [or clinic] somewhere in a legal office so that we get hands-on legal training." When it comes to hiring, students say the school has a "mostly regional appeal," with most students seeking employment in surrounding Dayton. A big benefit in the job market is that "the alumni are very involved," and the "school's alumni base stretches past the Midwest," reaching as far as western New York and other states.

Life

In contrast to the rigors of the academic program, one student asserts, "There is a pervasive, pleasant, [and] professional atmosphere at this small school, and my fellow students tend to help one another out rather than compete with each other." Unlike some law programs, "people support one another here—those Midwestern values of honesty, decency,

CLAIRE SCHRADER, ASST. DEAN, DIR. OF ENROLLMENT MANAGEMENT & MARKETING
UNIVERSITY OF DAYTON SCHOOL OF LAW, 300 COLLEGE PARK, 112 KELLER HALL,
DAYTON, OH 45469-2760 • TEL: 937-229-3555 • FAX: 937-229-4194
E-MAIL: LAWINFO@NOTES.UDAYTON.EDU • WEBSITE: WWW.UDAYTON.EDU / LAW

forthrightness, and fairness one hears about in the abstract have an actual, everyday existence here in Dayton." Beyond academics, "students are involved in student organizations," and "there are always school and non-school gatherings to attend" when you want to blow off steam. A 3L remembers, "Most (and I mean most) students went out numerous nights a week, partying and drinking at bars close to the law school." Though some choose the school for its Catholic affiliation, the school's Marianist ties are "downplayed" in most cases. For those who would like to incorporate Catholic ethics into their educational experience, "rich opportunities are present to get involved with the Catholic mission of the university."

Throughout the law school, students love the University of Dayton's atmosphere. "The building at UDSL is spectacular in terms of the library, classrooms, and the ease at using computers." Around them, "the undergraduate school is expanding; new buildings are sprouting all around campus." Sadly, some students feel that "Dayton is a dying city," which offers fewer social and recreational activities than some students would like; however, "the surrounding area, such as Kettering or Oakwood, are very safe and classy." Adjacent to the University, Brown Street offers an eclectic row of restaurants and coffeehouses, and there is an array of nightlife options in the historic Oregon District.

Getting In

Every year, University of Dayton strives to admit a diverse incoming class, comprised of students from a range of professional and personal backgrounds. While LSAT scores and undergraduate GPA are important factors, the school also looks at an applicant's professional experience, interests and extracurricular activities, graduate work, volunteer history, and background. The school operates a rolling admissions program from November 1 to April 1, and most applicants will receive a response in two to six weeks of submitting a completed application. For the most recent incoming class, the median undergraduate GPA was 3.1, with a 25th-75th percentile range of 2.78-3.37.

Clinical program required	Yes
Legal writing course requirement	Yes
Legal methods course requirement	Yes
Legal research course requirement	Yes
Moot court requirement	No
Public interest law requirement	No

ADMISSIONS
Selectivity Rating	73
# applications received	762
% applicants accepted	58
% acceptees attending	26
Median LSAT	148
LSAT Range (25th to 75th percentile)	145–151
Median undergrad GPA	3.15
Application fee	$0
Regular application deadline	5/1
Transfer students accepted	Yes
Evening division offered	No
Part-time accepted	No
CAS accepted	Yes

International Students
TOEFL recommended of international students.	Yes

FINANCIAL FACTS
Annual tuition	$34,875
Books and supplies	$1,500
Fees	$398
Room & Board	$16,000
Financial aid application deadline	5/1
% first-year students receiving some sort of aid	99
% all students receiving some sort of aid	89
% of aid that is merit based	20
% receiving scholarships	72
Average grant	$13,386
Average loan	$35,083
Average total aid package	$41,413
Average debt	$113,045

EMPLOYMENT INFORMATION

Career Rating	85
Total 2014 JD Grads	140
% grads employed ten months out	82
Median starting salary	$54,000
# employed full-time	109
# employed part-time	6
# employed bar required	72
# employed JD preferred	32
# employed professional/other	3
# employed non-professional	3
# pursuing advanced degree	2
# unemployed and seeking employment	15
State for bar exam	OH, KY, IL, IN, VA
Pass rate for first-time bar	63.0

Prominent Alumni
Hon. Frank P. Geraci, Chief U.S. District Judge, W.D.N.Y; Hon. Elizabeth McClanahan, Justice, Virginia Supreme Court; Michael Coleman, Mayor, Columbus, Ohio; Richard Apostolik, CEO, Global Association of Risk Professionals; Hinton Lucas, Vice President, DuPont Company

Grads Employed by Field (%)
Academic (3)
Business/Industry (16)
Government (9)
Judicial Clerkship (5)
Private Practice (45)
Public Interest (4)

UNIVERSITY OF DENVER
STURM COLLEGE OF LAW

INSTITUTIONAL INFORMATION

Public/private	Private
Affiliation	No Affiliation
% faculty part-time	52
% faculty female	39
% faculty underrepresented minority	13
Total faculty	157

SURVEY SAYS...

Students love Denver, CO, Great research resources, Abundant externship/internship/clerkship opportunities

STUDENTS

Enrollment of law school	863
% male/female	50/50
% part-time	16
% underrepresented minority	17
% international	1
# of countries represented	2
Average age of entering class	26

ACADEMICS

Academic Experience Rating	84
Profs interesting rating	82
Profs accessible rating	82
Hours of study per day	3.67

Academic Specialties
Commercial, Constitutional, Corporation Securities, Environmental, Human Rights, International, Labor, Taxation, Intellectual Property

Advanced Degrees Offered
LLM Taxation; LLM Environmental and Natural Resources Law; LLM International Business Transactions; LLM American Law Practice; LLM Clinical Legal Education

Combined Degrees Offered
Business, Health Leadership, History, International Studies, Legal Administration, Mass Communications, Professional Psychology, Psychology, Social Work, Sociology. Program lengths vary.

Academics

The University of Denver's Sturm College of Law is "an outstanding school" in "a beautiful building in a beautiful city." The city of Denver provides a great boon to students, as there are "great networking events and close ties with the greater Denver law community." "Our greatest strength is that we feed into the city of Denver with our only other real competition being a smaller class from CU [University of Colorado] every year," a 1L brags. The "gorgeous" and "modern" law building has up-to-date technology "including wireless throughout, power and cable Ethernet hookups at each desk." Most classrooms have "lots of light" although "those with no windows feel like caverns." "The library is pretty well equipped" and there are "lots of places to study alone, converse with others, work on projects—whatever you need." Did we mention the "awesome views of the Rockies from third and fourth floors"?

The Sturm College of Law "places a large emphasis on experiential learning" although "there are many opportunities to explore the theoretical as well." This "focus on practical skill and real life application" means students are ready to work as soon as they graduate. While "the available courses are fairly diverse," one student says there is "too much focus on firms/corporate rather than government work, public interest, non-traditional, or novel/up-and-coming areas of law." The "focus on experiential learning...sets [Denver] students ahead of others in terms of being able to practice law" upon graduation. The "friendly, accessible, and helpful" professors "love working with students," even going so far as to "share their personal cell phone numbers for last minute questions before finals." Several students did feel that many of the first year professors "need to be re-evaluated" but empathized that the "upper level writing profs are great!" These professors are "not only knowledgeable about the theory of law, they are passionate and require students to apply the law in practical ways" with a focus on "hands on learning" such as the "mock trial program. Denver has a "really good faculty/student ratio and the classes are usually no more than twenty once you get past your first year." "The Academic Achievement Program and accessibility of faculty really bolster the academic success of the students at DU Law," a 1L notes.

"Everything runs smoothly with the administration," and the dean "is particularly accessible." The administration "is very concerned with employability of the students and it shows through the many program offerings available throughout the week." However, the downside to the administration is the "incredibly rude" registrar's office that is not "willing to accommodate student needs." The career services office gets mixed reviews, some saying they are "extremely helpful and accessible" and others saying point blank: "The career services DO NOT HELP in finding a job." Overall, students deem the Denver law experience "excellent. Period." "The bar preparation/success program has helped raise DU's bar passage rates well into 90 percent!" a 3L boasts.

IAIN DAVIS, ASSISTANT DEAN OF ADMISSIONS
2255 E. EVANS AVENUE, DENVER, CO 80208
TEL: 303-871-6135 • FAX: 303-871-6992
E-MAIL: ADMISSIONS@LAW.DU.EDU • WEBSITE: WWW.LAW.DU.EDU

Life

The academic atmosphere "is really friendly and not ultra-competitive" while the "social atmosphere at DU is great." Students work hard, but there are still "many many opportunities to socialize and drink together." Denver fosters a "tight knit community" where "students compete with themselves but not with each other," although "most law students are type-A, stressed out, and cliquey." The party atmosphere with "a lot of drinking (happy hours are a common club social)" appeals to younger students, while some "older students who may have families/spouses" might find less to do. Students love Denver, noting that many opportunities off campus and calling it "a wonderful place to live."

Getting In

Competition is fierce at Denver, with the law school getting almost 2,500 applicants in a recent year. This means students will want to study, study, and study more to achieve the right GPA and LSAT scores. The school weighs those two scores more heavily than any other part of the application. A recent class had an average GPA and LSAT of 3.36 and 156 respectively.

Clinical program required	No
Legal writing course requirement	Yes
Legal methods course requirement	Yes
Legal research course requirement	Yes
Moot court requirement	No
Public interest law requirement	Yes

ADMISSIONS

Selectivity Rating	82
# applications received	1,480
% applicants accepted	63
% acceptees attending	24
Average LSAT	156
Median LSAT	156
LSAT Range (25th to 75th percentile)	153–159
Average undergrad GPA	3.36
Median undergrad GPA	3.40
Application fee	$65
Early application notification	1/1
Transfer students accepted	Yes
Evening division offered	Yes
Part-time accepted	Yes
CAS accepted	Yes

International Students

TOEFL required of international students.	Yes

FINANCIAL FACTS

Annual tuition	$42,120
Books and supplies	$1,800
Fees	$310
Room & Board	$11,646
Financial aid application deadline	2/15
% first-year students receiving some sort of aid	88
% all students receiving some sort of aid	89
% of aid that is merit based	23
% receiving scholarships	53
Average grant	$20,610
Average loan	$43,970
Average total aid package	$49,611
Average debt	$114,916

EMPLOYMENT INFORMATION

Career Rating	**88**
Total 2014 JD Grads	277
% grads employed ten months out	89
Median starting salary	$56,081
# employed full-time	201
# employed part-time	46
# employed bar required	179
# employed JD preferred	58
# employed professional/other	7
# employed non-professional	3
# pursuing advanced degree	1
# unemployed and seeking employment	19
# not seeking employment	4
% grads employed by school	12
State for bar exam	CO, TX, NY, CA, AZ
Pass rate for first-time bar	85.7

Prominent Alumni

Don Sturm, LLB '58, Banking; Doug Scrivner, JD '77, Former General Counsel of Accenture; Secretary Jim Nicholson, JD '72, Secretary of Veterans Affairs

Grads Employed by Field (%)

Academic (6)
Business/Industry (15)
Government (19)
Judicial Clerkship (12)
State or local: (12)
Private Practice (34)
Solo: (1)
2-10: (17)
11-25: (4)
26-50: (3)
51-100: (1)
101-250: (2)
251-500: (2)
501+: (3)
Size Unknown: (1)
Public Interest (3)

UNIVERSITY OF THE DISTRICT OF COLUMBIA
DAVID A. CLARKE SCHOOL OF LAW

INSTITUTIONAL INFORMATION

Public/private	Public
Affiliation	No Affiliation
% faculty part-time	53
% faculty female	55
% faculty underrepresented minority	53
Total faculty	51

SURVEY SAYS...
Students love Washington, DC, Liberal students

STUDENTS

Enrollment of law school	306
% male/female	41/59
% from out-of-state	53
% part-time	47
% underrepresented minority	64
% international	6
# of countries represented	3
Average age of entering class	31

ACADEMICS

Academic Experience Rating	**77**
Profs interesting rating	72
Profs accessible rating	76
Hours of study per day	3.49

Advanced Degrees Offered
JD 3 yrs for full-time students, 4 yrs for part-time students; LLM 2 yrs

Academics

The David A. Clarke School of Law at the University of the District of Columbia is founded on an "enthusiasm for equality and justice." It's a small school, one of only six ABA-accredited law schools at Historically Black Colleges and Universities. The school offers training to those underrepresented at the bar. Its mission is "to serve the public and equip lawyers who will promote social justice." Students don't just study law, but "learn how to make the legal system work for the most vulnerable populations in our society." UDC is "on the cutting-edge of clinical practice." There's a required 700 hours of clinical experience, within which are a "great variety" of fields to choose from. In clinic, students are responsible for their own cases and clients and "have a chance to hone their research and writing skills." Unique to UDC School of Law is a "complete public interest focus and a commitment to serving the impoverished." The school operates by the credo, "Tolerance, service, and commitment to ensuring equal access to justice." After graduation, students say "have an edge over other law students because I will be going into a position knowing how to operate as a lawyer already; not in just a theoretical way."

"Our professors are committed to educating the next generation of public interest lawyers." "They are by far the best thing going for the institution. Their experience and expertise is priceless." Professors choose to teach at UDC School of Law because they believe in its mission. They're "truly passionate" and try to prepare students for the "issues most of us will face as public interest attorneys." "I had the opportunity to learn from a D.C. Superior Court Judge, a nationally renowned civil rights attorney whose record and experience comprise nearly fifty years of service to the profession and to society, and an Ivy League–educated criminal defense superstar from D.C.'s Public Defender Service." These professors represent the "spirit of tolerance, dedication, and advocacy." The curriculum is "designed to equip each graduate with not merely an intellectual grasp of the law, but also the skills required to make practice of the law a reality." Students feel prepared for the real world of law outside the doors of UDC and also praise the professors' "compassion for humanity."

Students are divided on the usefulness of the administration. One says they're both "helpful" and "attentive," and another claims they do a good job "making the school feel like a community." One of the common complaints about the administration is the lack of very strong communication skills when it comes to announcements to the whole school, such as events being held on campus, typically there is not sufficient notice given to students in order to allow the students to change their schedule accordingly." Part-time students would like more opportunities to fulfill the clinical requirement and participate in student organizations. Another claims, "The administration here knows individuals by name, and it is not uncommon for an administrator to e-mail an important deadline reminder to a forgetful student."

With a move to a "beautiful" new building in 2011, UDC alleviated previous concerns about space and facilities. "Our new moot courtroom has amazing resources and nice aesthetics." The law library is "full of resources and staffed with highly trained, friendly librarians. " One student says, "I've never had an instance where I was unable to find a research tool I needed." Another student claims the library as a "second home."

VIVIAN CANTY, ASSISTANT DEAN OF ADMISSION
4200 CONNECTICUT AVENUE, NW, BUILDING 38, WASHINGTON, DC 20008
TEL: 202-274-7336 • FAX: 202-274-5583
E-MAIL: VCANTY@UDC.EDU • WEBSITE: WWW.LAW.UDC.EDU

Life

Students "come in all shades, ages, income levels, and backgrounds." UDC law is left-leaning, and no matter what your ethnicity or sexual orientation may be, you'll fit in well, as diversity is the school's "greatest strength." The atmosphere is "noncompetitive" and, "UDC-DCSL doesn't keep class ranks, because, well, everyone is encouraged to succeed." Students say it's an "extremely positive environment." Fellow classmates "help each other succeed" and, even more, are "invested" in that success. "I never feel isolated," another student adds.

The student body is comprised of a mix of "direct from undergraduate" and those "that are several years removed." Night students typically "drive to school from their jobs in D.C., VA, and MD." Students love D.C. for the location! The school is "minutes from the historic streets and monuments of downtown D.C. The location is great for available transportation, travel to the many other D.C. law schools and colleges, and all types of recreation and entertainment for singles, couples, families, and the young at heart."

Getting In

The admissions committee focuses on work experience, extracurricular activities, letters of recommendation, and the personal essay. Roughly one in four candidates is accepted. Admitted students in the 25th percentile had GPAs around 2.8 and LSAT scores just about 145. Admitted students in the 75th percentile had GPAs just beneath 3.4 and LSAT scores at 153.

Clinical program required	Yes
Legal writing course requirement	Yes
Legal methods course requirement	No
Legal research course requirement	Yes
Moot court requirement	Yes
Public interest law requirement	Yes

ADMISSIONS

Selectivity Rating	80
# applications received	697
% applicants accepted	36
% acceptees attending	36
Average LSAT	145
Median LSAT	148
LSAT Range (25th to 75th percentile)	145–153
Average undergrad GPA	2.93
Median undergrad GPA	3.10
Application fee	$35
Regular application deadline	3/15
Transfer students accepted	Yes
Evening division offered	Yes
Part-time accepted	Yes
CAS accepted	Yes

International Students

TOEFL required of international students.	Yes

FINANCIAL FACTS

Annual tuition (in-state/out-of-state)	$10,753/$21,506
Books and supplies	$1,400
Fees	$735
Room & Board	$20,200
Financial aid application deadline	3/31
% first-year students receiving some sort of aid	94
% all students receiving some sort of aid	92
% of aid that is merit based	10
% receiving scholarships	57
Average grant	$6,233
Average loan	$37,851
Average total aid package	$37
Average debt	$121,130

EMPLOYMENT INFORMATION

Career Rating	72	
Total 2014 JD Grads	103	
% for whom you have useable information	96	
% grads employed ten months out	64	
Median starting salary	$63,000	
% job accepting grads providing useable salary information	37	
# employed full-time	59	
# employed part-time	11	
# employed bar required	33	
# employed JD preferred	23	
# employed professional/other	11	
# employed non-professional	3	
# pursuing advanced degree	3	
# unemployed and seeking employment	21	
# not seeking employment	2	
% grads employed by school	2	
State for bar exam	MD, VA, NY, DC, PA	
Pass rate for first-time bar	46.0	

Prominent Alumni

Thomas Kilbride, Illinois Supreme Court Justice; Kim Jones, Founder and Director, Advocates for Justice in Education; Tom Devine, Legal Whistleblower Attorney and Director, Government Accountability Project; Andrea Lyon, Dean, Valparaiso Law School; Keiffer Mitchell, Baltimore City Councilmember

Grads Employed by Field (%)

Academic (4)
Business/Industry (17)
Government (17)
Judicial Clerkship (6)
State or local: (6)
Private Practice (19)
Solo: (2)
2-10: (15)
11-25: (1)
101-250: (1)
Public Interest (7)

UNIVERSITY OF FLORIDA
LEVIN COLLEGE OF LAW

INSTITUTIONAL INFORMATION

Public/private	Public
Student-faculty ratio	12:1
% faculty part-time	27
% faculty female	51
% faculty underrepresented minority	17
Total faculty	51

SURVEY SAYS...
Great research resources, Good social life

STUDENTS

Enrollment of law school	944
% male/female	58/42
% from out-of-state	8
% part-time	0
% underrepresented minority	30
% international	3
Average age of entering class	22

ACADEMICS

Academic Experience Rating	**86**
Profs interesting rating	82
Profs accessible rating	81
Hours of study per day	3.45

Academic Specialties
Criminal, Environmental, International, Estates & Trusts, Taxation, Intellectual Property

Advanced Degrees Offered
LLM in Taxation, 1 yr; LLM in International Taxation, 1 yr; LLM in Comparative Law, 1 yr; LLM in Environmental and Land Use Law, 1 yr; SJD in Taxation, Multi-Year.

Combined Degrees Offered
More than 30 joint degree programs (JD/Masters & PhD); length of program varies.

Academics

Holding students to "high academic standards," the University of Florida's Levin College of Law offers students an excellent "balance between legal theory and practical courses." Certainly a "well respected institution," many students are quick to assert that the school's "value is very good for [the] price." As a pleased 3L boasts, "The greatest strength is how cheap it is, at least relative to other law schools, for the top law school in Florida." Students also enjoy that "there are several certificate programs" available including environmental and land law use, intellectual property law, criminal justice, estates and trusts, and international and comparative law. Though some wish there were "more practical skills courses," others tell us that "clinics and trial practice classes are very hands-on." Further, students here love the extensive opportunities to study abroad in exotic locales such as Costa Rica and France.

Importantly the "professors are a great mix of race, background, experience, and knowledge. They are very approachable and in their offices any time to answer a question." Indeed, "most have an open door policy and welcome student questions." Fortunately, "many professors seek research assistants, which is a very valuable experience." However, some students do caution that first-year classes are "too large for good interaction and discussion." Therefore, it's sometimes possible to feel "totally lost in the shuffle."

While some students have experienced "the significant red tape" that is often part and parcel with a massive state university, many proclaim the administration here is "very responsive to student requests." As a grateful 3L explains, "The school administration here is very helpful and listens to student concerns and does its best to redress any issues raised. The dean [even] meets regularly over coffee with students." A content 2L echoes these sentiments sharing, "Everyone at the Levin College of Law is extremely helpful. I have gone to various offices on campus for help and have not been let down."

Students are quite happy with the "fantastic facilities," which they find "very well kept and modern." Classrooms "all have great seating, lighting, visual, and audio." What's more, the "new advocacy center is a state-of-the-art new building to practice and learn advocacy skills in a realistic full courtroom." In addition, the library is "first-rate" and definitely conducive to long study sessions; although, some students do gripe that it's starting to become overrun with undergraduates.

Finally, students highlight the alumni network which is "vast and plays a major role in obtaining positions." As a pleased 3L recounts, "The greatest strength is the distinguished alumni pool around the state, region, and country who always come back, give back, and are open to help out students in the employment search. The resources and connections of the school are great as well and completely prepare all students who take advantage of them to build great attorneys and connect them with hiring employers." However, a disgruntled 2L counters, "The school is stuck in a cycle of creating a job placement system that benefits only the top 10 percent of the students and handcuffing the bottom 75 percent. Essentially the bottom 75 percent of the students get no benefit from the career services department and thus must scramble to find their own jobs."

Life

The overwhelming majority of students here are Florida residents. Otherwise, "UF Law is unique in its ability to achieve diverse incoming class." Ethnic minorities make up a pretty considerable contingent, and all kinds of students enroll here. "The best part

ASSISTANT DEAN FOR ADMISSIONS
BOX 117622, GAINESVILLE, FL 32611
TEL: 352-273-0890 • FAX: 352-392-4087
E-MAIL: ADMISSIONS@LAW.UFL.EDU • WEBSITE: WWW.LAW.UFL.EDU

of law school is conversing with people of different backgrounds and history," says a thrilled 2L. "It's fascinating." Some students "can be cutthroat," but for the most part, the law student population is "intelligent and harmonious." Indeed, "there is a nice sense of community." "You will be able to find a friend or two to study with regularly and many friends to interact with socially," promises a 1L. Students do tend to stick to their sections first year, but "there's a lot of cross-section interaction starting second year."

Despite a "problematic" parking situation, "Gainesville is nice." With big-time college sports, the University of Florida is certainly hard to beat. As one proud 3L notes, "[Even] our faculty members appreciate the prominence and breadth of Gator Nation, even though our football team didn't live up to the Gator standard last year." The "sunny weather" is spectacular, provided one enjoys heat and a constant dose of humidity. Hometown Gainesville is a quintessential college town and students can take advantage of numerous restaurants, performing arts venues, cultural events, and, of course, bars. Unfortunately though, the law school is located in a rather remote part of the campus, and some students complain that it is "not within walking distance of any dining options and the on-campus options are paltry." On the positive side, should students ever tire of the scene in Gainesville, within driving distance lie Jacksonville, Orlando, and Tampa—all fairly large cities.

Getting In

Gaining that coveted acceptance letter is no simple feat at the University of Florida. Accepted students in the 25th percentile earned around a 155 on the LSAT and an undergraduate GPA of 3.26. Accepted students in the 75th percentile earned around a 161 on the LSAT and an undergraduate GPA of 3.68. The median LSAT score is 158 and the median GPA is 3.50.

EMPLOYMENT INFORMATION

Career Rating	90
Total 2014 JD Grads	309
% for whom you have useable information	99
% grads employed ten months out	86
Median starting salary	$60,000
% job accepting grads providing useable salary information	62
# employed full-time	250
# employed part-time	17
# employed bar required	220
# employed JD preferred	35
# employed professional/other	9
# employed non-professional	2
# pursuing advanced degree	12
# unemployed and seeking employment	26
# not seeking employment	1
% grads employed by school	2
State for bar exam	FL, KY, NY, MD, TX
Pass rate for first-time bar	89.7

Prominent Alumni
Martha Barnett, Holland & Knight LLP, ABA President 2000; Stephen N. Zack, Boies, Schiller & Flexner LLP, ABA President 2010-2012

Grads Employed by Field (%)
Academic (1)
Business/Industry (10)
Government (20)
Judicial Clerkship (4)
Federal: (2)
State or local: (2)
Private Practice (50)
Solo: (1)
2-10: (20)
11-25: (8)
26-50: (3)
51-100: (4)
101-250: (6)
251-500: (5)
501+: (5)
Public Interest (2)

Clinical program required	No
Legal writing course requirement	Yes
Legal methods course requirement	No
Legal research course requirement	Yes
Moot court requirement	No
Public interest law requirement	No

ADMISSIONS

Selectivity Rating	85
# applications received	1,369
% applicants accepted	61
% acceptees attending	37
Median LSAT	158
LSAT Range (25th to 75th percentile)	155–161
Average undergrad GPA	3.45
Median undergrad GPA	3.50
Application fee	$30
Regular application deadline	3/15
Regular notification	4/30
Transfer students accepted	Yes
Evening division offered	No
Part-time accepted	No
CAS accepted	Yes

FINANCIAL FACTS

Annual tuition (in-state/ out-of-state)	$22,230/$38,835
Books and supplies	$3,210
Fees	$150
Room & Board (on/ off campus)	$10,470/$10,900
Financial aid application deadline	3/15
% first-year students receiving some sort of aid	93
% all students receiving some sort of aid	88
% of aid that is merit based	15
% receiving scholarships	60
Average grant	$8,348
Average loan	$28,733
Average total aid package	$29,810
Average debt	$95,535

UNIVERSITY OF GEORGIA
SCHOOL OF LAW

INSTITUTIONAL INFORMATION

Public/private	Public
Student-faculty ratio	11:1
% faculty part-time	17
% faculty female	40
% faculty underrepresented minority	10
Total faculty	70

SURVEY SAYS...

Students love Athens, GA, Diverse opinions accepted in classrooms, Great research resources, Abundant externship/internship/clerkship opportunities, Strong sense of community, Good social life

STUDENTS

Enrollment of law school	583
% male/female	55/45
% from out-of-state	10
% underrepresented minority	19
% international	1
Average age of entering class	23

ACADEMICS

Academic Experience Rating	**95**
Profs interesting rating	98
Profs accessible rating	89
Hours of study per day	4.56

Academic Specialties

Civil Procedure, Commercial, Constitutional, Corporation Securities, Criminal, Environmental, Government Services, Human Rights, International, Labor, Legal History, Legal Philosophy, Property, Taxation, Intellectual Property

Advanced Degrees Offered

LLM, 1 yr; MSL, 1 yr

Combined Degrees Offered

JD/MBA, 4 yrs; JD/Master of Historic Preservation, 4 yrs; JD/MPA 4 yrs; JD/MSW, 4 yrs; JD/MS in Sport Management and Policy, 4 yrs; JD/MA, various fields, varies; JD/PhD, various fields, varies.

Academics

At the University of Georgia Law, students rave about the education they receive for a "bargain price." Non-resident students may apply for in-state rates after the first year, and many out-of-state residents receive scholarships for their first year, which waive the tuition difference. That's not to mention the school's "great academic reputation" and position as a "feeder to the most prominent city in the South." "It is really nice to be able to afford a JD from a reputable school and not be faced with the 'golden handcuffs,'" says a student not looking to work at a firm. All in all, "the professors, the people, the curriculum, and the facilities contribute to an overall competitive and comprehensive program that still embodies southern hospitality."

The "stellar" teachers at Georgia Law are "compassionate, while still demanding excellence," and it's "very easy to meet with professors and discuss things unrelated to class," as well as many student groups that allow for diverse ideas and discussions among students. "They genuinely care about us as individuals and have never been too busy to assist," says a student. Though students "are definitely left to figure things out on our own in many respects" ("Communication about how to get grades, etc., are somewhat lacking."), the school "provides a wide range of clinical opportunities for its students," as well as its nationally recognized moot court and mock trial programs and three major journals. It also offers study and work abroad programs to help reinforce its focus on global issues, and concurrent enrollment with the university's other programs is an option.

There's a wide variety of courses from which students can choose their electives, and the school has a unique approach to grading in the "intense" first year. Students don't receive grades for the first semester (with the exception of criminal law and civil procedure), and at the end of 1L, fall semester performance counts toward the final grade, but it's weighted significantly less than spring exam scores. The school wants students to focus on their studies and discourages 1Ls from taking jobs during the first year of law school.

Georgia Law has one of the largest law libraries in the nation—students love its "huge, picturesque windows and accommodating seating and tables"—and it's embarking on a renovation and expansion that will only improve the quality of life. Classroom facilities are "also great," and the school produces an enthusiastic alumni base that helps during interview season. Still, many students do wish that more job opportunities outside of Georgia found their way to the UGA Law campus.

Life

Students say that the "small Southern town" of Athens, with its coffee shops and music scene, is the "quintessential college town," but one that can be "somewhat limiting for older students." Though the school is just a couple of blocks from downtown, "Housing options are pretty limited around the law school and most students live two to three miles away," and often must drive to school as "the Athens bus service is not great." Atlanta is about an hour-and-a-half away, so students who must frequently travel for their internships have a bit of a hike, but it's still close enough that its myriad entertainment options can be enjoyed without much trouble. "The camaraderie of the students, an awesome social scene, and proximity to Atlanta make a good educational experience that much better," says a student.

GREG ROSEBORO, EXECUTIVE DIRECTOR OF ADMISSIONS
225 HERTY DRIVE, ATHENS, GA 30602-6012
TEL: 706-542-7060 • FAX: 706-542-5556
E-MAIL: UGAJD@UGA.EDU • WEBSITE: WWW.LAW.UGA.EDU

UGA Law offers a "great balance between traditional legal education and strong social environment." Small class sizes mean everyone is very independently driven," providing at most a "friendly competition," instead of a cutthroat one, but "grabbing a beer with friends after a long Friday full of classes makes law school really bearable." "No one is hiding books; no one is refusing to help. We are all in this together and at the end of the day, the person next to you is a future referral and professional colleague," says a 2L. "One thing that [the Dean] reminds all incoming 1Ls at orientation is that our classmates are our colleagues, not our competition, and students really take this to heart," says another student.

Getting In

Admission to the University of Georgia is selective, and the school prides itself on the diverse backgrounds that its students bring. Members of a recent graduating class include a professional baseball player in Israel, the lead singer of a band, a published author, an intern for the SEC, and a former Miss Georgia. The school has received record numbers of applications in recent years. A recent admitted class had a median LSAT of 163 and a median undergraduate GPA of 3.7.

Clinical program required	No
Legal writing course requirement	Yes
Legal methods course requirement	No
Legal research course requirement	Yes
Moot court requirement	No
Public interest law requirement	No

ADMISSIONS

Selectivity Rating	92
# applications received	2,068
% applicants accepted	31
% acceptees attending	29
Median LSAT	163
LSAT Range (25th to 75th percentile)	158–164
Median undergrad GPA	3.70
Application fee	$50
Regular application deadline	6/1
Transfer students accepted	Yes
Evening division offered	No
Part-time accepted	No
CAS accepted	Yes

FINANCIAL FACTS

Annual tuition (in-state/ out-of-state)	$16,894/$34,564
Books and supplies	$1,800
Fees	$2,246
Room & Board (on/ off campus)	$9,246/$10,450
Financial aid application deadline	7/1
% first-year students receiving some sort of aid	87
% all students receiving some sort of aid	88
% receiving scholarships	51
Average grant	$7,160
Average loan	$29,071
Average total aid package	$28,169
Average debt	$88,825

EMPLOYMENT INFORMATION

Career Rating	95	Grads Employed by Field (%)	
Total 2014 JD Grads	235	Academic (2)	
% for whom you have useable information	100	Business/Industry (12)	
% grads employed ten months out	85	Government (12)	
Median starting salary	$70,500	Judicial Clerkship (11)	
% job accepting grads providing useable salary information	36	Federal: (5)	
# employed full-time	193	State or local: (6)	
# employed part-time	6	Other: (0)	
# employed bar required	174	Private Practice (42)	
# employed JD preferred	19	Solo: (0)	
# employed professional/other	5	2-10: (19)	
# employed non-professional	1	11-25: (5)	
# pursuing advanced degree	3	26-50: (2)	
# unemployed and seeking employment	26	51-100: (1)	
		101-250: (3)	
# not seeking employment	2	251-500: (3)	
State for bar exam	GA	501+: (9)	
Pass rate for first-time bar	93.9	Size Unknown: (0)	
		Public Interest (7)	

UNIVERSITY OF HAWAII—MANOA
WILLIAM S. RICHARDSON SCHOOL OF LAW

INSTITUTIONAL INFORMATION

Public/private	Public
Affiliation	No Affiliation
% faculty part-time	41
% faculty female	51
% faculty underrepresented minority	46
Total faculty	61

SURVEY SAYS...

Students love Honolulu, HI, Abundant externship/internship/clerkship opportunities, Strong sense of community, Good social life

STUDENTS

Enrollment of law school	325
% male/female	46/54
% from out-of-state	18
% part-time	21
% underrepresented minority	68
% international	4
# of countries represented	6
Average age of entering class	26

ACADEMICS

Academic Experience Rating	87
Profs interesting rating	85
Profs accessible rating	85
Hours of study per day	3.57

Academic Specialties
Environmental

Advanced Degrees Offered
Full-Time JD, 3 yrs. Evening, Part-Time JD, 4+ yrs. Advanced JD, 2 yrs. Foreign LLM, 1 yr.

Combined Degrees Offered
JD/MA (varies), JD/MBA (varies), JD/MS (varies), JD/MSW (varies), JD/PhD (varies)

Academics

Located in beautiful Hawaii, the William S. Richardson School of Law is a "regional law school" where students "have access to some of the best faculty in the field." Manoa is known for its "small student body" and "very accessible faculty." Students praise the "collaborative nature of the students and faculty." At Manoa "students are seen as valid contributors to the school and are given broad range to explore and introduce new topics in the field of law." Students appreciate the "large selection of moot court teams to participate in" and the "tight-knit community on the islands," which "allows for amazing access to professionals in the field, such as the judges, big law firms, and politicians."

Being "part of the law school is being part of a family for life," says one student. "We all feel welcomed into the Hawaii legal community from the first day of 1L orientation," says one student. And one of the greatest strengths of the school is the way in which "students in each class support each other. As one student notes, "even 'gunners' are polite and helpful to others." Unlike at so-called "cut-throat schools," at Manoa, "aggressive behavior and sabotage are frowned upon and generally do not happen."

The professors "are all well-versed in their fields" and "active practitioners and scholars." Most teachers "are more than willing to speak with you," and "have open door policies," although not all may not be willing to "engage in mentor-style relationships." While some students rave about the faculty, others wish there were more "heavy hitters" since students "need strong recommenders when they come from lesser known institutions." Given Manoa's "geographic location, however, [it has] some of the finest environmental law professors," and "prestigious guest lecturers and speakers are prevalent because no one minds coming to Hawaii." In courses for specialized fields, the "teacher-to-student ratio is very favorable," sometimes "less than 1:10." The school has a "vibrant international LLM program, which allows law students from all over the globe to collaborate and exchange ideas." There is a "heightened focus on ASEAN through the ASEAN Law Integration Center," "China, Japan, and Korea through [the] Pacific Asian Law and Society Certificate," as well as the "Pacific Asian Law and Society Organization" and the "Asia Pacific Law and Policy Journal." Manoa also features "numerous moot court teams," and "they all do extremely well on a national level (especially [the] Jessup team)." As a 2L notes, "If you want to make changes in the world, this is the law school to come to."

The "administration is wonderful" and "supportive of each student's success and career path." Externships, internships, and jobs are "numerous and relatively easy to procure." It's extremely "easy to get involved" and "networking is very important to the administration and students, so networking events are very common." The "larger legal community [of Hawaii] is actively involved with our education," notes one student. And "lawyers and judges regularly provide guidance and opportunities for [Manoa] students."

ELISABETH STEELE HUTCHISON, DIRECTOR OF ADMISSIONS
2515 DOLE STREET, HONOLULU, HI 96822
TEL: 808-956-3000 • FAX: 808-956-5557
E-MAIL: ESTEELE@HAWAII.EDU • WEBSITE: WWW.LAW.HAWAII.EDU

Life

Students at Manoa have access to all the beauty of Hawaii, from the mainland to beaches and neighboring islands. Island life does have some drawbacks, including slow Internet access. But even though some students bemoan the slow Internet, others note that they "have a very decent computer lab that always has open computers," and "good law librarians who are always willing to help." As one student says, "what we lack in terms of facilities and diversity we make up for in community, support and opportunity." Students feel close to each other here. Everyone at Manoa "recognizes that they're in it together," "not just in school but in the small law community of Hawaii after graduation." The "cohorts are very tight" and they "make it a point to look out for each other."

Getting in

At the 25th percentile, students recently admitted to Manoa Law have LSAT scores of 153 and GPAs in the 3.05 range, while admitted students at the 75th percentile have LSAT scores of 159 and GPAs of roughly 3.59. With only 96 full-time students accepted in 2014, Manoa is considered selective. Each year, the Admissions Committee selects ten to twelve applicants to join the first year class as part of the Ulu Lehua Scholars Program. Criteria include a record of overcoming social, educational, economic, or other sources of adversity; and activities and/or employment manifesting a strong commitment to social justice, the public interest, and service to legally, socially, and economically disadvantaged communities.

Clinical program required	Yes
Legal writing course requirement	Yes
Legal methods course requirement	Yes
Legal research course requirement	Yes
Moot court requirement	No
Public interest law requirement	Yes

ADMISSIONS

Selectivity Rating	87
# applications received	541
% applicants accepted	37
% acceptees attending	48
Average LSAT	156
Median LSAT	156
LSAT Range (25th to 75th percentile)	153–159
Average undergrad GPA	3.35
Median undergrad GPA	3.41
Application fee	$75
Regular application deadline	2/1
Regular notification	3/15
Transfer students accepted	Yes
Evening division offered	Yes
Part-time accepted	Yes
CAS accepted	Yes

International Students

TOEFL required of international students.	Yes

FINANCIAL FACTS

Annual tuition (in-state/ out-of-state)	$19,464/$39,192
Books and supplies	$1,270
Fees	$712
Room & Board (on/ off campus)	$13,284/$13,284
Financial aid application deadline	3/1
% first-year students receiving some sort of aid	69
% all students receiving some sort of aid	71
% of aid that is merit based	3
% receiving scholarships	42
Average grant	$8,014
Average loan	$26,990
Average total aid package	$27,829
Average debt	$56,266

EMPLOYMENT INFORMATION

Career Rating	81
Total 2014 JD Grads	105
% for whom you have useable information	98
% grads employed ten months out	80
Median starting salary	$58,000
% job accepting grads providing useable salary information	100
# employed full-time	81
# employed part-time	3
# employed bar required	58
# employed JD preferred	26
# employed professional/other	5
# pursuing advanced degree	3
# unemployed and seeking employment	15
# not seeking employment	1
State for bar exam	HI
Pass rate for first-time bar	69.0

Prominent Alumni
John Waihee, former Governor of Hawaii; Sabrina McKenna, Associate Justice, Hawaii Supreme Court; Alexa Fujise, Associate Judge, Hawai`i Intermediate Court of Appeals; James Duke Aiona, former Lieutenant Governor, State of Hawai`i; Junichi Yanagihara, COO & Executive Producer, Sprite Animation Studios

Grads Employed by Field (%)
Academic (2)
Business/Industry (7)
Government (19)
Judicial Clerkship (27)
State or local: (27)
Private Practice (17)
  2-10: (10)
  11-25: (4)
  26-50: (3)
  51-100: (1)
Public Interest (7)

UNIVERSITY OF HOUSTON
LAW CENTER

INSTITUTIONAL INFORMATION

Public/private	Public
Student-faculty ratio	9:1
% faculty female	39
% faculty underrepresented minority	15
Total faculty	82

SURVEY SAYS...
Diverse opinions accepted in classrooms

STUDENTS

Enrollment of law school	718
% male/female	61/39
% from out-of-state	9
% part-time	17
% underrepresented minority	34
% international	1
# of countries represented	18
Average age of entering class	25

ACADEMICS

Academic Experience Rating	**87**
Profs interesting rating	82
Profs accessible rating	75
Hours of study per day	3.56

Academic Specialties
Commercial, Criminal, Environmental, International, Labor, Taxation, Intellectual Property

Advanced Degrees Offered
LLM, 24 credit hours: Health, Intellectual Property, Tax, Energy, Environment & Natural Resources, International Law, Foreign Scholars (for Foreign Attorneys)

Combined Degrees Offered
JD/MBA, 4 yrs; JD/MPH, 4 yrs; JD/MA History, 4 yrs; JD/MSW, 4 yrs; JD/MD, 6 yrs; Dual US/Canadian Degree Program, 4 yrs.

Academics

As large and lively as the state of Texas, the University of Houston Law Center enrolls fewer than 900 students in its diverse and challenging JD, LLM, and joint-degree programs. Drawing top names from the Houston legal community, professors are "either extremely accomplished attorneys or nationally renowned experts in a particular field of law." Though they represent the top of their field, "there are no 'bigger than Texas' egos with any of the faculty." In fact, "the entire faculty is very accessible and willing to help students learn in any way they can." Students agree that their professors are "not only available during office hours, many professors host lunches or parties in their homes to learn more about their students."

In the classroom, the professors are "very much focused on teaching us to think creatively" and throughout the JD program the "practical aspects of lawyering are stressed." Things here begin with a bang as "all first-year students are required to take part in a moot court competition, and it's a great experience for everyone." In addition, "there are six different law journals in which a student may participate, including the Houston Law Review, which consistently ranks in the top fifty of all Law Reviews in the country." What's more, the school operates a number of clinics and research institutes that augment classroom experiences with hands-on experience. "I have spent three semesters working at the Immigration [Clinic] and Civil [Practice] Clinic and will always remember this time as the most exciting and rewarding aspect of my law school experience," explains one clinic participant. "We are given enormous responsibility for our clients and the experience has given me an invaluable opportunity to learn actual lawyering skills."

Those looking for great value relative to cost in their education will be extremely satisfied with U of H. Students love that they get a "high-value education for a low cost in a great legal market." If you can manage a "scholarship" or are "a Texas resident" it only sweetens the proverbial deal. Even so, students admit there are some sacrifices associated with a U of H education, particularly with regard to the school's facilities which most agree "need improvement." There are no ivy-lined walls at U of H; instead, think "East German bunker school of architecture." However, most students take the environs in stride. "Students who enter with high expectations of facilities will be disappointed," says one student. "But you learn at this school in an environment conducive to learning." On that note, U of H "fosters a community and not a rivalry among students. Fellow students are always willing to answer a question, share notes, and form study groups."

Outside the classroom, "there are lots of opportunities to work with major law firms and other community organizations during the summer and during the school year," and the Career Development Office "is particularly helpful for summer job opportunities." After graduation, Houston is a well-suited environment for future attorneys, boasting its reputation as one of the "largest legal markets in the country." A current student insists, "If you want to succeed, you can, and you can get a great job when you graduate too—with all the top firms in Texas including all the elite New York satellite offices."

JAMIE WEST DILLON, ASSISTANT DEAN FOR ADMISSIONS
100 LAW CENTER, HOUSTON, TX 77204-6060
TEL: 713-743-2280 • FAX: 713-743-2194
E-MAIL: LAWADMISSIONS@UH.EDU • WEBSITE: WWW.LAW.UH.EDU

Life

Students say the school is a great place to work on your powers of persuasion as there's lots of debate on the U of H campus. A student explains, "Because the student body is fairly conservative, but, at the same time, lawyers generally exhibit liberal thinking (at least in the social realm), you get a nice balance of liberal and conservative, often leading to lively debate absent from more liberal institutions." Even so, don't expect "any cutthroat type of competitive environment" here since students agree that "even if they have polar opposite views in the classroom, afterwards they hang out."

On campus, the prevailing atmosphere is "friendly" with "an awesome SBA that is very active in helping make UHLC a better place." Students tend to form strong friendships in their first-year sections, and when the weekend arrives "Plenty of people...go out on a regular basis." Night students are generally less involved in the campus community, admitting that there is something of a "social divide between part-time and full-time students"; many complain that events and activities take place during the day (while they are working) and that "most of the social events are geared toward single people or those without children."

Unfortunately, the campus isn't much of a social hub because "it is in a part of Houston that nobody really cares to live in, so most people come in for class and then head home." However, the cosmopolitan city of Houston is a great place to live, offering "a standing symphony, opera, and ballet, NFL, NBA, MLB, and MLS sports teams (and minor league ice hockey) a great zoo and museums, and a multitude of golfing opportunities."

Getting In

There is no set minimum LSAT score or undergraduate GPA required for acceptance to the University of Houston Law Center; all applicants are reviewed individually. In a recent application year, the lowest LSAT score accepted was in the lower 140s, while the median score for accepted applicants was 159. The median GPA was 3.47. Non-Texans comprise approximately 7 percent of the student population and the acceptance rate is equally competitive for out-of-state and in-state residents.

EMPLOYMENT INFORMATION		
Career Rating	**93**	
Total 2014 JD Grads	256	**Prominent Alumni**
% for whom you have useable		Richard Haynes, Litigation; John O'Quinn,
information	100	Litigation; Charles Matthews, Vice
% grads employed ten months out	90	President and General Counsel/ExxonMobil
Median starting salary	$90,000	**Grads Employed by Field (%)**
# employed full-time	220	Academic (2)
# employed part-time	12	Business/Industry (19)
# employed bar required	176	Government (9)
# employed JD preferred	52	Judicial Clerkship (2)
# employed professional/other	2	Private Practice (57)
# employed non-professional	2	Public Interest (2)
# pursuing advanced degree	4	
# unemployed and seeking		
employment	18	
State for bar exam	TX	
Pass rate for first-time bar	86.3	

Clinical program required	No
Legal writing course requirement	Yes
Legal methods course requirement	Yes
Legal research course requirement	Yes
Moot court requirement	Yes
Public interest law requirement	No

ADMISSIONS

Selectivity Rating	**87**
# applications received	2,208
% applicants accepted	42
% acceptees attending	25
Average LSAT	158
Median LSAT	159
LSAT Range (25th to 75th percentile)	155–161
Average undergrad GPA	3.42
Median undergrad GPA	3.47
Application fee	$0
Regular application deadline	2/15
Regular notification	5/15
Early application deadline	11/15
Early application notification	2/15
Transfer students accepted	Yes
Evening division offered	Yes
Part-time accepted	Yes
CAS accepted	Yes

International Students

TOEFL recommended of international students.	Yes

FINANCIAL FACTS

Annual tuition (in-state/ out-of-state)	$24,467/$38,727
Books and supplies	$2,900
Fees	$5,317
Room & Board (on/ off campus)	$9,000/$10,800
Financial aid application deadline	4/1
% all students receiving some sort of aid	80
% of aid that is merit based	42
% receiving scholarships	75
Average grant	$7,858
Average loan	$32,835
Average total aid package	$40,693
Average debt	$88,664

UNIVERSITY OF IDAHO
COLLEGE OF LAW

INSTITUTIONAL INFORMATION

Public/private	Public
Affiliation	No Affiliation
% faculty part-time	17
% faculty female	51
% faculty underrepresented minority	11

SURVEY SAYS...
Conservative students

STUDENTS

Enrollment of law school	110
% male/female	56/44
% from out-of-state	53
% part-time	1
% underrepresented minority	18
% international	0
# of countries represented	1
Average age of entering class	27

ACADEMICS

Academic Experience Rating	**74**
Profs interesting rating	69
Profs accessible rating	79
Hours of study per day	4.47

Academic Specialties
Commercial, Corporation Securities, Environmental, Intellectual Property

Combined Degrees Offered
JD/MS or PhD in Water Resources (Law, Management, and Policy): JD/MS 8 semesters, PhD varies. JD/MS Environmental Science: 8 semesters. JD/Professional Masters of Science: 8 semesters. JD/MS Accountancy: 8 semesters. JD/MS Accountancy: 8 semesters. JD/MS Taxation (with Boise State University): 8 semesters. JD/MS Bioregional Planning and Community Design: 8 semesters.

Academics

A "great value," University of Idaho College of Law is a small yet affordable place to get a J.D. citing the school's strong regional ties and low in-state tuition, students declare, "If one wants to practice law in Idaho especially, going to UI makes sense from an educational and financial standpoint." With a total enrollment of about 350, students benefit from a surprisingly small and intimate campus environment. A 2L explains, "Even though this is a public institution, I feel like I get as much attention as if I paid more and went to a private law school. My professors' doors are always open." A first-year student adds, "All five of my professors knew my name by the end of my first week. Most of them sincerely care about our success and are happy to answer questions about life after law school." When it comes to their pedagogical skills, "there are some very good professors and some very poor professors" at UI. However, faculty members are generally accomplished in their fields and "bring a lot of experience" to the classroom. In fact, "for being in a relatively small town, we have faculty from very diverse backgrounds who could definitely teach at more prestigious universities." In that regard, the University of Idaho experience is deeply influenced by its location in the small town of Moscow. Far from the capital in Boise, "the campus and community are very isolated," and some students feel that "the school could improve in diversity and the welcoming of diverse people and diverse viewpoints," both within the student body and within the faculty. It is important to note that qualified students may take classes at the campus in Boise in their third year if they so choose. Fortunately, with the concerted effort of the administration, "there are still some very good speakers and events that come through here."

Academically, the school specializes in environmental law, Native American law, business and entrepreneurship, and litigation and alternative dispute resolution. Students would like to see a greater emphasis on real-world skills, complaining that a number of professors "work too much with theory and not enough with practical application" in the classroom. Fortunately, the school offers "a plethora of opportunities to gain practical legal skills" through clinics, and "the administration also does an excellent job in getting internship opportunities for the students." When it comes to the job hunt, "career services is understaffed" (the size of the staff tripled in 2013) and the largest in-state job market in Boise is far away, but, despite these obstacles, graduates have a lot going for them. A boon to anyone hoping to practice in the region, UI is "the only law school in the state (accredited). That means all the law firms and courts are packed with our graduates and they protect the opportunities for our students." For those who'd like to practice further afield, "the administration is good at recognizing that there are a lot of students that want to practice out of state, so they cater to that diversity in instruction and events we host."

Life

Students differ personally, professionally, and philosophically at UI. There is a "substantial Mormon population" within the law school, which tends to be more politically and socially conservative, offset by a "sizable body of politically moderate students." Clashing political views is a source of tension on campus. According to some students, "If you consider yourself conservative or libertarian in any fashion, you will quickly find yourself outnumbered, politically isolated, and regarded as offensive and problematic to the staff and faculty." Others claim, "There's a large and outspoken religious majority at the school that tends to jump at any comment they feel is disparaging while loudly asserting their own freedom of speech." Idaho residents make up about 47 percent of the student body, with the remaining 53 percent hailing from across the country. Though

CAROLE WELLS, JD, DIRECTOR OF ADMISSIONS
875 PERIMETER DR., MOSCOW, ID 83844-2321
TEL: 208-885-2300 • FAX: 208-885-5709
E-MAIL: LAWADMIT@UIDAHO.EDU • WEBSITE: WWW.LAW.UIDAHO.EDU

most students are just a few years out of college, University of Idaho is "accessible to nontraditional students."

There are around 11,700 undergraduates and 1,700 graduate students on the University of Idaho campus in Moscow, lending a fun, vibrant, student-friendly backdrop to the law school environment. Within the law school itself, "everything is in one building. It gives the students and the faculty easy access to each other." "About half of the students socialize on a regular basis," and there are a range of student groups and recreational activities hosted on the larger campus, as well as through the law school. Home to about 24,000 residents, "Moscow is truly a charming college town that provides decent access to a range of outdoor pursuits." In complement to the school's low tuition, "the cost of living is affordable" in Moscow, and students enjoy the "large food co-op," "impressive farmer's market," and many "great parks" in town. It is "easy to walk anywhere." Students can also cross the state line into Pullman, Washington, another college town that is home to Washington State University, only eight miles away.

Getting In

To be eligible for admission to the University of Idaho, students must have an undergraduate degree from an accredited college, recent LSAT scores, and a Credential Assembly Service account. Dedicated to accepting a diverse entering class, the University of Idaho evaluates each applicant's academic preparedness, test scores, personal statement, and other life experiences when making an admissions decision. The application deadline for the fall semester is March 15; applications are accepted after that date, though chances of admission are smaller.

Clinical program required	No
Legal writing course requirement	Yes
Legal methods course requirement	No
Legal research course requirement	Yes
Moot court requirement	Yes
Public interest law requirement	Yes

ADMISSIONS

Selectivity Rating	80
# applications received	657
% applicants accepted	55
% acceptees attending	30
Median LSAT	152
LSAT Range (25th to 75th percentile)	149–156
Median undergrad GPA	3.24
Application fee	$50
Regular application deadline	3/15
Regular notification	3/30
Early application deadline	12/1
Early application notification	12/15
Transfer students accepted	Yes
Evening division offered	No
Part-time accepted	Yes
CAS accepted	Yes

International Students

TOEFL recommended of international students.	Yes

FINANCIAL FACTS

Annual tuition (in-state/out-of-state)	$15,774/$28,850
Books and supplies	$1,232
Room & Board	$9,412
Financial aid application deadline	6/1
% first-year students receiving some sort of aid	100
% all students receiving some sort of aid	100
% of aid that is merit based	100
Average grant	$8,619
Average debt	$98,008

EMPLOYMENT INFORMATION

Career Rating	85
Total 2014 JD Grads	117
% grads employed ten months out	87
Median starting salary	$52,648
# employed full-time	95
# employed part-time	7
# employed bar required	80
# employed JD preferred	15
# employed professional/other	2
# employed non-professional	5
# unemployed and seeking employment	7
# not seeking employment	4
State for bar exam	ID, WA, UT, OR, CA
Pass rate for first-time bar	78.6

Prominent Alumni
Linda Copple Trout, Past Chief Justice, Idaho Supreme Court; Georgia Yuan, Deputy Under Secretary of Education; Frank Shrontz, Former CEO and Chairman of the Boeing Co.; James A. McClure, Former United States Senator; Nancy Morris, Former Secretary of the Securities & Exchange Commission

Grads Employed by Field (%)
Academic (1)
Business/Industry (16)
Government (14)
Judicial Clerkship (14)
Private Practice (39)
Public Interest (2)

UNIVERSITY OF ILLINOIS
COLLEGE OF LAW

INSTITUTIONAL INFORMATION
Public/private   Public

SURVEY SAYS...
Diverse opinions accepted in classrooms

STUDENTS
Enrollment of law school   510
% male/female   58/42
% from out-of-state   N/A
% part-time   0
% international   10

ACADEMICS
Academic Experience Rating   69
Profs interesting rating   67
Profs accessible rating   74
Hours of study per day   NR
Advanced Degrees Offered
LLM, 1 yr; JSD, minimum 3 yrs;
MSL, 1–2 yrs

Academics

"You'll definitely get the bang for your buck" at the University of Illinois College of Law, "a jewel amid the cornfields [that boasts] the best mix of academic excellence, social interaction, and human decency for the best price available." Tuition is especially affordable for in-state students. The "tireless [administration] is also very accessible" and extraordinarily popular among students.

Students at the U of I tell us emphatically that "the faculty is the school's greatest strength." The "tough but not unreasonable" professors are "prolific writers [who are] clearly brilliant and accomplished." Students say the professors "are, for the most part fantastic, both in and out of the classroom [and] always able to clarify concepts that are confusing. More significant, they are completely available [and] genuinely interested in teaching and working with students." The professors make an effort to be reached in that they "have open-door policies and are available for discussions with students about class, a job, or just life in general." Students also note that the school "employs a nice mix of tenured and adjunct faculty, which makes for a perfect balance of legal theory and real-world experience. The primary complaint that students have with regard to the faculty is "keeping the good professors around." One student explains, "There's not much reason for them to stay in central Illinois. The school really needs to make an effort to not let the good ones get away."

Graduates enjoy "a great employment rate" thanks to an aggressive Office of Career Planning and Professional Development. As one transfer student attests, "I'm in a unique position in that I've seen how two different law schools operate. I was blown away by the quality of the Career Services Department at the University of Illinois. The administration goes to great lengths to make sure that not only do all University of Illinois College of Law graduates get jobs, but that they get the jobs they want." "If you do well here, nothing in Chicago will be off limits." However, students complain that the college "needs to broaden its resources [and] expand beyond the Midwestern market." Until that happens, "it is difficult to get much traction" on either coast "when searching for jobs in Champaign."

The facilities at the U of I "are good"in that everything has been converted to WiFi, and the research resources of the library are as abundant as you'll find anywhere. Overall, though, the "rather Spartan [College of Law] could use some serious help." Suffice it to say, the "incredibly ugly and cheap-looking [building] does not give anyone goose bumps for the grand study of the law." One student writes, "There are no windows in any of the rooms." It's like going to school in a casino." Students note, "Sometimes seats are scarce [in the] crowded" classrooms, as well as in the "cramped" library, though now that the school has reduced the size of the incoming class, this should help to alleviate the problem. Also, wear layers because "there also seems to be a bit of a temperature control problem" no matter what the season.

REBECCA RAY, ASSISTANT DEAN FOR ADMISSIONS AND FINANCIAL AID
504 EAST PENNSYLVANIA AVENUE, ROOM 201, MC-594, CHAMPAIGN, IL 61820
TEL: 217-244-6415 • FAX: 217-244-1478
E-MAIL: LAW-ADMISSIONS@ILLINOIS.EDU • WEBSITE: WWW.LAW.ILLINOIS.EDU

Life

If they do say so themselves, the students at the U of I are "very amiable, noncompetitive, [and] very intellectually minded, yet not stuck on themselves." These are the "brightest [and] most fun" people—"all the cool, smart kids." Students at the U of I are also "a bit neurotic [and] love to hear their own voices." The student population "has a wonderful mix of student ethnicities, religions, sexual orientation, and gender." There is also a laid-back atmosphere on campus. "Everybody really cares about you. They want you to succeed, and it's almost difficult not to."

"The school truly is a community because of its manageable size. Lunches with the dean" are common, and there are "endless other ways to connect with the other students and, more important, the faculty." One content student writes, "The cafeteria has good food and, best of all, they carry Starbucks coffee." Students also say, "Although U of I is located in the corn fields of Illinois, it is impossible to feel isolated" because the administration "is constantly bringing in lecturers, symposiums, and guest speakers." In addition, the College of Law sponsors a "weekly" get-together "for law students, faculty, and administrators."

Life outside the classroom has many positive aspects. Students are very "sports-oriented" and say, "It is great to be on a Big Ten campus and be able to devote yourself to the study of law full time." Surprising though it seems, "there is actually a lot to do in Urbana-Champaign." There are "great bars, coffee houses, [and] centers for the arts." There is also "a progressive music scene." Some students gripe that "social life can seem dominated by a frat/sorority type atmosphere," even at the law school level. "The town is basically designed for college students, so it gets a little dullsville at times." Many students would "prefer to be in a larger city," with Chicago being the example of choice. "Socially, we do the best we can with the town we're in," asserts one student. "That means we drink a lot [and] go en masse to football and basketball games."

Getting In

The median LSAT score for admitted students is 161. The median GPA is 3.43. Those numbers are serious but not forbidding. Note also that, while it's cheaper for Illinois residents to attend the college, residency in the Land of Lincoln will not get you one iota of special treatment from the admissions office.

Clinical program required	No
Legal writing course requirement	Yes
Legal methods course requirement	No
Legal research course requirement	Yes
Moot court requirement	No
Public interest law requirement	No

ADMISSIONS

Selectivity Rating	**88**
# applications received	1,462
% applicants accepted	42
% acceptees attending	26
Median LSAT	161
LSAT Range (25th to 75th percentile)	158–163
Median undergrad GPA	3.43
Application fee	$0
Regular application deadline	3/15
Regular notification	Rolling
Early application deadline	None
Transfer students accepted	Yes
Evening division offered	No
Part-time accepted	No
CAS accepted	Yes

International Students

TOEFL required of international students.	Yes

FINANCIAL FACTS

Annual tuition (in-state/ out-of-state)	$38,250/$46,000
Books and supplies	$4,550
Fees	$3,845
Room & Board	$13,350
Financial aid application deadline	3/15
% receiving scholarships	97

THE UNIVERSITY OF IOWA
COLLEGE OF LAW

INSTITUTIONAL INFORMATION

Public/private	Public
Student-faculty ratio	8:1
% faculty part-time	27
% faculty female	33
% faculty underrepresented minority	11
Total faculty	55

SURVEY SAYS...

Diverse opinions accepted in classrooms, Great research resources, Abundant externship/internship/ clerkship opportunities, Good social life

STUDENTS

Enrollment of law school	390
% male/female	56/44
% from out-of-state	48
% part-time	0
% underrepresented minority	17
% international	3
# of countries represented	5
Average age of entering class	24

ACADEMICS

Academic Experience Rating	**92**
Profs interesting rating	89
Profs accessible rating	85
Hours of study per day	4.07

Academic Specialties
Human Rights, International

Advanced Degrees Offered
LLM, JD, SJD

Combined Degrees Offered
JD/MBA, 4 yrs; JD/MA, 4 yrs; JD/ MHA, 4 yrs; JD/MSW, 4 yrs; JD/ MPH, 3.5 yrs; JD/MS, 4 yrs; JD/MD, 6 yrs

Academics

Students at the affordable University of Iowa College of Law are unanimous on one point: Iowa is "the most underrated school in the country." "If you want to learn from the best without giving an arm and a leg for tuition," they say, "come to this school." The "sympathetic" faculty at Iowa is "very concerned with providing the best academic experience." "Professors are demanding in a way that I know will make me a better lawyer," relates 2L. "They are brilliant yet not egomaniacs." "Some scare the crap out of you, and some create a warm classroom environment." Outside of class, "the professors are, for the most part, interesting and cool people," and interaction between students and professors is exceedingly common. Sure, they are "awkward socially," but "even the most distinguished professors welcome you into their offices, and it's not uncommon to go out to dinner with your professor and a few classmates."

Classes here "tend toward the theoretical." "Iowa presents kind of a contradiction," proffers a 2L. "It is a theory-driven program that produces mostly practicing attorneys." Iowa's ten practice clinics are "very strong," "and there are plenty of slots available" (though you do have to lottery into them). "The Iowa City/Cedar Rapids area has opportunities to practice while in law school, but those opportunities are somewhat limited." The legal writing program garners mixed reviews. "We are learning to write legal briefs and memos from the best," contends a satisfied 1L. Others feel "cheated." "We could use a lot more hands-on training with writing and research," says one student. Pretty much everyone who mentions the moot court program is unhappy with it. "The faculty can't be bothered to provide meaningful coaching or instruction," laments one student.

The Career Services staff here "is a group of all-stars" that provides "all of the assistance you need." "The top 25 to 30 percent of students don't seem to have any trouble finding work in cities across the country, including New York, San Francisco, Los Angeles, and Boston." By and large, though, students end up practicing in one of "several large markets" throughout the Midwest. Some students complain that "Iowa could do better in attracting and encouraging employers outside of the Midwest." "If you want to work in the Midwest, this school is considered good, and employers are eager to interview you," advises a 2L. "If you want to work anywhere else, go to law school in that region."

The "really space-constrained" law school building is "functional, though it looks pretty awful." "It was built in the early '80s, and I think at that time people thought it was cool and futuristic," adds a 2L, "but now it just looks like something out of *Star Trek IV*." "Classrooms are pretty typical," though students "appreciate the plentiful outlets and wireless Internet." "There is no shortage of PCs available in the computer labs," and "the school also has very friendly tech gurus." The "extensive" law library is "a little bubble of greatness." It's "open late" and "always staffed by friendly librarians who know more about the law than anyone ever should."

Life

Students are "mostly white and from Iowa or Illinois," but there is also "a surprisingly large number of kids from the coasts." "I was actually surprised by how many non-Midwestern students are currently at the school," admits a 1L. Overall, it's "a good mix of people from all walks of life." There are "some very conservative points of view" but "young crazy liberals" predominate. There are "a lot of do-gooders who are very socially conscious and commit a tremendous amount of time to community and national issues."

Jan Barnes, Admissions Coordinator
320 Melrose, Iowa City, IA 52242
Tel: 319-335-9095 • Fax: 319-335-9646
E-Mail: law-admissions@uiowa.edu • Website: www.law.uiowa.edu

"U of I law students and most of the professors have a definite liberal slant," says a 2L. "If you're conservative and not articulate and able to defend your opinions, you'll never survive classroom discussion."

"Students at Iowa are competitive, certainly." "I was surprised by how many gunners there actually are," relates a 3L. It's "friendly" gunning, though. Iowa students are "a group of people who have their priorities in order, who are willing to lend a hand, and who are remarkably grounded in reality." "There's an earnestness and commitment to integrity and excellence that Iowa students, faculty, and staff all share," enthuses a 3L. "It makes Iowa a unique place, and it makes me hopeful for the legal profession as a whole. As a jaded California native and East Coast private college graduate, I never cease to be surprised by the quality and professionalism I've found here in the heartland."

Socially, though "people tend to buckle down when it is demanded," "You can be sure to find friends out at a bar" on virtually any given weekend night. "Everyone is very good friends with each other," and Iowa City is "a fun town." Coffee shops, libraries, bookstores, and great restaurants abound. There are "weekly Law Nights held at a local drinking establishment." "There's no such thing as a grad student bar in Iowa City," and there is "a pretty big divide between people who took time off and people who came straight from undergrad."

Getting In

Admitted students at the 25th percentile have LSAT scores of 157 and GPAs in the range of 3.5. Admitted students at the 75th percentile have LSAT scores of 162 and GPAs of around 3.8.

Clinical program required	No
Legal writing course requirement	Yes
Legal methods course requirement	Yes
Legal research course requirement	Yes
Moot court requirement	Yes
Public interest law requirement	No

ADMISSIONS

Selectivity Rating	89
# applications received	1,483
% applicants accepted	41
% acceptees attending	23
Average LSAT	160
Median LSAT	160
LSAT Range (25th to 75th percentile)	157–162
Average undergrad GPA	3.60
Median undergrad GPA	3.64
Application fee	$0
Regular application deadline	5/1
Transfer students accepted	Yes
Evening division offered	No
Part-time accepted	No
CAS accepted	Yes

International Students

TOEFL required of international students.	Yes

FINANCIAL FACTS

Annual tuition (in-state/ out-of-state)	$21,964/$39,500
Books and supplies	$2,300
Fees	$1,796
Room & Board	$10,260
% first-year students receiving some sort of aid	93
% all students receiving some sort of aid	94
% of aid that is merit based	27
% receiving scholarships	76
Average grant	$25,336
Average loan	$32,034
Average total aid package	$46,437
Average debt	$92,373

EMPLOYMENT INFORMATION

Career Rating	94	
Total 2014 JD Grads	176	
% for whom you have useable information	100	
% grads employed ten months out	95	
Median starting salary	$57,600	
# employed full-time	160	
# employed part-time	8	
# employed bar required	139	
# employed JD preferred	22	
# employed professional/other	6	
# employed non-professional	1	
# pursuing advanced degree	4	
# unemployed and seeking employment	3	
% grads employed by school	2	
State for bar exam	IA, IL, MN, NY, CA	
Pass rate for first-time bar	88.0	

Prominent Alumni
Luke Yeh, Legal, Snapchat, Venice, CA

Grads Employed by Field (%)
Academic (4)
Business/Industry (18)
Government (8)
Judicial Clerkship (11)
Federal: (3)
State or local: (8)
Private Practice (48)
Solo: (1)
2-10: (18)
11-25: (7)
26-50: (3)
51-100: (5)
101-250: (7)
251-500: (2)
501+: (6)
Size Unknown: (0)
Public Interest (5)

UNIVERSITY OF KANSAS
SCHOOL OF LAW

INSTITUTIONAL INFORMATION

Public/private	Public
Affiliation	No Affiliation
% faculty part-time	32
% faculty female	46
% faculty underrepresented minority	12
Total faculty	57

SURVEY SAYS...
Abundant externship/internship/ clerkship opportunities

STUDENTS

Enrollment of law school	376
% male/female	58/42
% from out-of-state	14
% part-time	0
% underrepresented minority	15
% international	2
# of countries represented	8
Average age of entering class	25

ACADEMICS

Academic Experience Rating	**79**
Profs interesting rating	82
Profs accessible rating	86
Hours of study per day	3.57

Academic Specialties
Commercial, Constitutional, Corporation Securities, Criminal, Environmental, International, Property, Taxation, Intellectual Property

Advanced Degrees Offered
LLM in Elder Law, 1 yr; SJD, 3 yrs.

Combined Degrees Offered
JD/MBA; JD/ Master of East Asian Languages and Cultures; JD/MA in Economics; JD/MA in Global Indigenous Nations Studies; JD/ Master of Health Services Administration; JD/MS in Journalism; JD/MA in Philosophy; JD/MPA; JD/MA in Political Science; JD/MA in Russian, East European and Eurasian Studies; JD/MSW; JD/ Master of Urban Planning. All combined-degree programs are 4 yrs.

Academics

Kansas Law is certainly considered a legal powerhouse in the Midwest. The university "offers a wide variety of classes that suit all types of students interested in an array of legal areas." As one third-year shares, "I've never found it challenging to find classes I'm interested in taking. [In fact,] there are usually too many classes and I have to narrow it down to what fits into my schedule the best." Moreover, students benefit from a curriculum that manages to deftly balance a "mix of traditional legal theory with practical skills." Another satisfied third-year adds, "The clinical programs are numerous and diverse. A student could have practical experience in every semester as an upperclassman, just through the clinics and externships provided by the school." However, some students do grumble that "the mandatory grade curve puts KU students at a disadvantage compared to other law schools within the region."

Students at KU seem to fully enjoy their time in the classroom. This can certainly be attributed to "absolutely fantastic professors" who are "brilliant, approachable, and want to be there." It's readily apparent that they "genuinely love their job and love the university." As one knowing third-year succinctly states, "They are very knowledgeable in their subject areas, friendly, accessible, and willing to help each student succeed."

One area that could use a little improvement is the actual law school building. Many say that it feels "dated" and a first-year colorfully suggests that it resembles an "old airport." Further, a disgruntled second-year laments that it's "crowded with print resources no one uses, lacking moot court space, lacking group study space [and] lacking effective air conditioning." Fortunately, though the law building might leave some wanting, the university's "research resources are also quite simply, wonderful." A first-year explains, "Our library is well stocked, and our librarians are very helpful, as well as available to us at all times. KU Law also provides us with Westlaw, LexisNexis, and Bloomberg research trainings, and representatives from those companies are available 24/7."

Finally, students also greatly appreciate the fact the administration is "very hands on." In fact, even the "Dean teaches classes and takes the time to mingle with the students constantly." As one excited first-year pleasantly sums up, "KU Law is still the most welcoming, diverse, inclusive, and supportive group of individuals I've yet to meet, and I would recommend it to anybody looking to law as a profession."

Life

Students at Kansas speak highly of their peers, finding them (among other choice adjectives) friendly, caring and helpful. As a second-year emphatically states, "The greatest strength of KU Law is that it is very congenial among the students. You hear these horror stories when you apply to law school of students stealing notes or destroying each other's outlines for a competitive edge, but the experience here at KU is much different. While people are still competing for rank, they are still willing to help each other out and compete in an honest and fair way. This, I believe, leads to a much more conducive environment for learning and excelling." A first-year concurs adding that "all of the 2Ls and 3Ls are very kind and supportive to new 1Ls and everyone looks out for one another."

STEVEN FREEDMAN, ASSISTANT DEAN OF ADMISSIONS
1535 W. 15TH STREET, LAWRENCE, KS 66045-7577
TEL: 785-864-4378 • FAX: 785-864-5054
E-MAIL: ADMITLAW@KU.EDU • WEBSITE: WWW.LAW.KU.EDU

Beyond a warm and welcoming vibe, KU Law also provides students with a myriad of professional opportunities. As one proactive third-year delights in sharing, "I have had the opportunity to participate in an externship/clinic, serve on a legal publication, and work as a research assistant for a professor." Moreover, due to "KUs geographical location, it is midway between Kansas City and Topeka, there is an extensive range of externship options, either in a big city or in a state capital." Of course, fear not; these future JDs are also able to indulge in a little R & R every now and again. Indeed, we've been assured that KU offers a "great balance of school and fun" and students find plenty of time to "go out and socialize with [their] law school friends." Not surprisingly, everyone loves supporting the Jayhawks!

Getting In

KU's admissions process is fairly by the book. First and foremost, the committee considers each applicant's undergraduate GPA and LSAT score. Following these quantitative assessments, admissions officers carefully analyze personal statements, recommendations and employment history. The only admissions requirements are an undergraduate degree from an accredited university, sitting for the LSAT and registering with the Law School Admissions Council Credential Assembly Service.

Clinical program required	No
Legal writing course requirement	Yes
Legal methods course requirement	Yes
Legal research course requirement	Yes
Moot court requirement	No
Public interest law requirement	No

ADMISSIONS

Selectivity Rating	85
# applications received	797
% applicants accepted	58
% acceptees attending	27
Average LSAT	157
Median LSAT	158
LSAT Range (25th to 75th percentile)	153–161
Average undergrad GPA	3.41
Median undergrad GPA	3.47
Application fee	$55
Regular application deadline	4/1
Transfer students accepted	Yes
Evening division offered	No
Part-time accepted	No
CAS accepted	Yes

International Students

TOEFL required of international students.	Yes

FINANCIAL FACTS

Annual tuition (in-state/ out-of-state)	$19,084/$33,189
Books and supplies	$1,200
Fees	$900
Room & Board (on/ off campus)	$11,108/$11,908
Financial aid application deadline	4/1
% of aid that is merit based	90
Average debt	$74,890

EMPLOYMENT INFORMATION

Career Rating	92
Total 2014 JD Grads	173
% for whom you have useable information	58
% grads employed ten months out	86
# employed full-time	135
# employed part-time	13
# employed bar required	122
# employed JD preferred	24
# employed professional/other	3
# employed non-professional	1
# pursuing advanced degree	2
# unemployed and seeking employment	20
# not seeking employment	1
% grads employed by school	1
State for bar exam	KS, MO, CA, CO, TX
Pass rate for first-time bar	92.9

Prominent Alumni
Hon. Mary H. Murgia, 9th Circuit Judge; Gov. Sam Brownback, State of Kansas Governor; Mary Beck Briscoe, 10th Circuit Judge; Sen. Jerry Moran, United States Senate; Major General Clyde Tate, Deputy JAG of the U.S. Army (ret'd)

Grads Employed by Field (%)
Academic (2)
Business/Industry (16)
Government (15)
Judicial Clerkship (7)
Private Practice (49)
Public Interest (3)

UNIVERSITY OF KENTUCKY
COLLEGE OF LAW

INSTITUTIONAL INFORMATION

Public/private	Public
Affiliation	No Affiliation
Student-faculty ratio	11:1
% faculty part-time	0
% faculty female	41
% faculty underrepresented minority	12
Total faculty	34

SURVEY SAYS...
Diverse opinions accepted in classrooms

STUDENTS

Enrollment of law school	388
% male/female	57/43
% from out-of-state	24
% part-time	<1
% underrepresented minority	8
% international	0
# of countries represented	1
Average age of entering class	25

ACADEMICS

Academic Experience Rating	**82**
Profs interesting rating	77
Profs accessible rating	81
Hours of study per day	3.44

Advanced Degrees Offered
JD only: No LLM or Masters of Law programs offered

Combined Degrees Offered
JD/MPA, 4 yrs; JD/MBA, 3 yrs; JD/Masters in Diplomacy and International Commerce, 4 yrs; JD/MHA, 4 yrs

Academics

"Camaraderie" and "the accessibility of [their] professors" are frequently cited by students at the University of Kentucky College of Law as their school's greatest strengths. The professors here are "wonderful, very experienced in their fields, great in the classrooms and always willing to meet with students outside of class," and "have a broad range of backgrounds in real practice." A few students note that many professors "are on phased retirement and there seems to be a shortage of professors available to teach certain (key) courses." But, fret not, for "this will only be a problem for the next two or three years until the retiring professors are phased out. There are many new professors, with very impressive CVs, that are on the faculty and they are great resources for the students." One student sums up: "Hands down, the faculty is the greatest strength of the UK Law School. Many are nationally (and some internationally) [renowned] experts in their law practice areas. So far, three of my core classes have been taught by Harvard Law grads. I feel as if I am getting an Ivy League education without the Ivy League price tag!"

Some students say that "when issues around administration (example: registration) arise, the academic dean immediately takes action," though others feel that, while "the administrators are very nice," they are also "not always very efficient. Not all student concerns are addressed, and others feel that there should be "more transparency between the students and the administration," and better consideration by the administration "of how students will be affected by their decisions." Still, another student gushes, "The UK Administration is part of the reason I chose to come to UK. The former Dean of Admissions wrote me a personalized acceptance letter and was an absolutely amazing person and a tremendous help in making my decision."

While the facilities are not very "aesthetically pleasing" (with one student noting, "The building is decades old and all complaints about it are put off by saying, 'it's going to be rebuilt'"), "the quality of the faculty more than makes up for this." Also, the law school has its own dedicated IT department "right in the library, and the IT department is an authorized Dell repair center, which is really handy." Some students feel that there could be more focus on "academic success for 1L students (i.e. weekly review sessions, etc.,) and overall attitudes of inclusion and personal growth." Finally, in terms of practical experience, "the externship opportunities and clinics [at UK] are great strengths and provide students with a broad range of hands-on learning experience."

TONI M. ROBINSON, DIRECTOR
209 LAW BUILDING, LEXINGTON, KY 40506-0048
TEL: 859-257-8321 • FAX: 859-323-1061
E-MAIL: TONI.ROBINSON@UKY.EDU • WEBSITE: WWW.LAW.UKY.EDU

Life

"Being in Kentucky is a blessing" is not an uncommon sentiment to find here in Lexington. Students feel that "the greatest strength of UK Law is its collegial atmosphere," and make such bold claims as, "I definitely feel like I have gained lifelong friends and mentors." The greatest strength of UK is "the close-knit community feeling fostered by the students. The students make a concerted effort to create an open and inclusive society of scholars, and are mostly successful in this endeavor. Only on one occasion can I remember not feeling at home at the University of Kentucky." One student succinctly sums up the prevailing attitude regarding the school's facilities with, "The building is . . . well, we need a new building."

Getting In

The University of Kentucky starts with a prospective student's LSAT scores and GPA when making an admissions decision. However, all applications are reviewed in full and other academic factors (such as writing ability, grade trends, and letters of recommendation) are also considered. Last year, the school extended just 547 offers of admission to more than 900 candidates. The median LSAT score for the entering class was 155 and their median GPA was 3.5.

Clinical program required	No
Legal writing course requirement	Yes
Legal methods course requirement	No
Legal research course requirement	Yes
Moot court requirement	Yes
Public interest law requirement	No

ADMISSIONS

Selectivity Rating	83
# applications received	672
% applicants accepted	59
% acceptees attending	29
Average LSAT	155
Median LSAT	155
LSAT Range (25th to 75th percentile)	152–158
Average undergrad GPA	3.45
Median undergrad GPA	3.49
Application fee	$50
Regular application deadline	3/15
Regular notification	Rolling
Transfer students accepted	Yes
Evening division offered	No
Part-time accepted	No
CAS accepted	Yes

International Students

TOEFL required of international students.	Yes

FINANCIAL FACTS

Annual tuition (in-state/ out-of-state)	$19,890/$37,410
Books and supplies	$4,406
Fees	$1,098
Room & Board	$10,506
Financial aid application deadline	3/15
% first-year students receiving some sort of aid	92
% all students receiving some sort of aid	91
% of aid that is merit based	100
% receiving scholarships	68
Average grant	$8,313
Average loan	$27,757
Average total aid package	$29,129
Average debt	$76,746

EMPLOYMENT INFORMATION

Career Rating	91	**Prominent Alumni**
Total 2014 JD Grads	124	Mitch McConnell, U.S. Senator; Steve
% for whom you have useable information	100	Beshear, Governor; Angela Edwards, Partner, Dinsmore & Shohl; Jim Woolery,
% grads employed ten months out	92	Founding Partner, Hudson Executive
Median starting salary	$48,000	Capital; Karen Caldwell, Federal Judge
% job accepting grads providing useable salary information	49	**Grads Employed by Field (%)**
# employed full-time	114	Academic (1)
# employed part-time	0	Business/Industry (10)
# employed bar required	100	Government (11)
# employed JD preferred	10	Judicial Clerkship (19)
# employed professional/other	2	Federal: (8)
# employed non-professional	2	State or local: (11)
# pursuing advanced degree	3	Private Practice (49)
# unemployed and seeking employment	2	Solo: (1)
# not seeking employment	5	2-10: (25)
State for bar exam	KY	11-25: (6)
Pass rate for first-time bar	90.2	26-50: (7)
		51-100: (1)
		101-250: (5)
		251-500: (2)
		501+: (2)
		Public Interest (2)

UNIVERSITY OF MAINE
SCHOOL OF LAW

INSTITUTIONAL INFORMATION

Public/private	Public
Affiliation	No Affiliation
Student-faculty ratio	9:1
% faculty part-time	45
% faculty female	38
% faculty underrepresented minority	3
Total faculty	40

SURVEY SAYS...
Students love Portland, ME, Diverse opinions accepted in classrooms

STUDENTS

Enrollment of law school	252
% male/female	51/49
% part-time	4
% underrepresented minority	10
% international	2
Average age of entering class	27

ACADEMICS

Academic Experience Rating	**84**
Profs interesting rating	88
Profs accessible rating	90
Hours of study per day	4.00

Advanced Degrees Offered
LLM, SJD

Combined Degrees Offered
JD/MBA, 4 yrs

Academics

The University of Maine School of Law is "a small school with many opportunities to develop personal, professional relationships." Students tell us there's a nice balance of academic legal subjects and practical lawyering skills. In addition to the standard tenets of legal theory, there's a pretty good selection of clinics. Internships and externships are ample, as well. There is a notable marine law institute. While "the cost of tuition is not low for out-of-state students," it's worth noting that Maine Law accepts a limited number of students from New Hampshire, Rhode Island, and Vermont at a reduced tuition rate.

Students tell us, "The very small class size—as compared to other law schools—is a great advantage." Small class sizes let students "become familiar with the entire student body and the faculty" and "encourage class participation, which in turn encourages thoughtful interaction with the subject matter of the class." By virtually all reports, the faculty is "absolutely amazing." Professors are "very interactive and caring." "The professors are as talented as they are accessible and make students feel like they are names instead of numbers," says a 1L. Outside of class, faculty members are "easily accessible." The "lovely" administration "likewise is very approachable." There's some red tape, though. Sometimes, students have "no idea what is going on, which is not a good thing for such a small school." Registration can be problematic, as well. "There are way too many lottery classes," vents a 2L. "Students are sometimes stuck with taking classes they are not truly interested in taking."

Maine Law is "the only law school in Maine," and if you're looking to hang out your shingle or otherwise find legal work in the Pine Tree State, there's really no question that this school is the place for you. Students enjoy "unparalleled access to externships and jobs in public interest law, private practice, the judiciary, and governmental agencies." "You will make connections and network with your Maine peers in a way that just wouldn't be possible at an out-of-state school," promises a 2L. Career Services is reportedly "very kind, warm, and helpful," as well. You can "ask a question without needing an appointment or waiting in a line."

Despite "significant improvements," the overall state of the accommodations here remains "pretty terrible." "Don't come to Maine expecting top-notch facilities," warns a 2L. "The school itself is a physically strange building." We have to agree with the 3L, who calls it a "concrete toilet-paper roll." Technology is merely adequate, and there's a "lack of community space to chat with students and professors between classes or hold study groups." On the plus side, "library resources are as good as you'll find anywhere."

Life

The student population isn't very ethnically diverse, but "there are individuals from all walks of life and many differing ages and opinions" at Maine Law. Nontraditional students "with families and children and prior careers" are fairly common. "Weirdos abound." The political spectrum runs the gamut. "There is a nice mix at the school," relates a 1L, "conservatives and liberals, environmentalists and capitalists." "Most anybody would feel welcome to engage in a friendly debate here, regardless of their leanings."

CAROLINE WILSHUSEN, DIRECTOR OF ADMISSIONS
246 DEERING AVE, PORTLAND, ME 04102
TEL: 207-780-4341 • FAX: 207-780-4018
E-MAIL: LAWADMISSIONS@MAINE.EDU • WEBSITE: MAINELAW.MAINE.EDU

The "low-competition" academic atmosphere is "warm and inviting." All first-year students "take almost all of their classes together and get to know each other." "There is a real sense of community," and "nothing about the school is cutthroat." "Maine Law is as small as it gets, so it naturally engenders a close-knit community," explains a 1L. "How people present themselves during their three years at Maine Law will very likely carry forward into their future legal careers. There's a good chance that most Maine Law students will practice law in Maine, and the legal community in Maine is small, too. Our classmates of today will be our professional peers of the future."

The social scene at Maine Law is generally solid. Student events are widely attended and opportunities to gather at various bars are common. Portland is the largest city in Maine, but that's not saying much. Portland does have great oceanfront scenery and kind of an old New England feel, and it's a fantastic little city for living and working. The bright lights of Boston are within reasonable driving distance. A handful of ski resorts and a multitude of outdoor activities are also nearby.

Getting In

The admissions profile at Maine Law is slightly more competitive than your average public law school in a sparsely populated state. Admitted students at the 25th percentile have LSAT scores about 149, and undergraduate GPAs average just less than 3.2. At the 75th percentile, LSAT scores approach 156, and GPAs are about 3.6.

Clinical program required	No
Legal writing course requirement	Yes
Legal methods course requirement	No
Legal research course requirement	Yes
Moot court requirement	No
Public interest law requirement	No

ADMISSIONS

Selectivity Rating	81
# applications received	635
% applicants accepted	56
% acceptees attending	23
Average LSAT	153
Median LSAT	153
LSAT Range (25th to 75th percentile)	149–156
Average undergrad GPA	3.36
Median undergrad GPA	3.38
Application fee	$0
Regular application deadline	4/15
Early application deadline	11/15
Early application notification	12/31
Transfer students accepted	Yes
Evening division offered	No
Part-time accepted	Yes
CAS accepted	Yes

International Students

TOEFL required of international students.	Yes

FINANCIAL FACTS

Annual tuition (in-state/ out-of-state)	$22,290/$33,360
Books and supplies	$2,000
Fees	$1,320
Room & Board	$13,708
Financial aid application deadline	2/15
% first-year students receiving some sort of aid	73
% all students receiving some sort of aid	45
% receiving scholarships	56
Average grant	$8,146
Average loan	$32,715
Average debt	$99,106

EMPLOYMENT INFORMATION

Career Rating	78
Total 2014 JD Grads	95
% for whom you have useable information	100
% grads employed ten months out	80
Median starting salary	$50,000
# employed full-time	74
# employed part-time	2
# employed bar required	49
# employed JD preferred	19
# employed professional/other	7
# employed non-professional	1
# pursuing advanced degree	5
# unemployed and seeking employment	12
# not seeking employment	1
State for bar exam	ME
Pass rate for first-time bar	76.1

Prominent Alumni
Hon. John A. Woodcock, Judge, United States District Court of Maine; Hon. Leigh I. Saufley, Chief Justice of the Maine Supreme Judicial Court

Grads Employed by Field (%)
Business/Industry (14)
Government (12)
Judicial Clerkship (12)
 Federal: (4)
 State or local: (7)
Private Practice (37)
 Solo: (4)
 2-10: (25)
 11-25: (1)
 26-50: (3)
 51-100: (3)
 101-250: (0)
 251-500: (0)
Public Interest (6)

UNIVERSITY OF MARYLAND
FRANCIS KING CAREY SCHOOL OF LAW

INSTITUTIONAL INFORMATION

Public/private	Public
Affiliation	No Affiliation
Student-faculty ratio	11:1
% faculty part-time	53
% faculty female	41
% faculty underrepresented minority	14
Total faculty	117

SURVEY SAYS...
Great research resources

STUDENTS

Enrollment of law school	710
% male/female	47/53
% from out-of-state	29
% part-time	19
% underrepresented minority	35
% international	5
Average age of entering class	25

ACADEMICS

Academic Experience Rating	83
Profs interesting rating	73
Profs accessible rating	73
Hours of study per day	3.80

Academic Specialties
Business, Environmental, Intellectual Property, Law and Health Care

Advanced Degrees Offered
JD 3 yrs FT day; 4 yrs evening; LLM 1 year FT

Combined Degrees Offered
JD/PhD Public Policy, 7 yrs; JD/MA Public Policy, 4 yrs; JD/MBA, 4 yrs; JD/MA Criminal Justice, 3.5–4 yrs; JD/MSW, 3.5–4 yrs; JD/MA Liberal Arts, 4 yrs; JD/MCP Community Planning, 4 yrs; JD/Pharm.D. Pharmacy 7 yrs; JD/MPH, 4 yrs

Academics

With "great opportunities for hands-on lawyering," and low in-state tuition for residents, the University of Maryland School of Law is "very well-connected to the Baltimore/Maryland legal community," with a "strong commitment to public service and social justice," and recognized legal specialties in health, environmental law, clinical law, and trial advocacy. The school "has tremendous relationships with organizations in Washington, D.C., the Maryland legislature, and many congressional offices," which makes it "extremely easy" to gain the kind of practical experience legal employers will be looking for come hiring season. The clinical offerings here are both required and "hard to beat:" "Not only was I able to argue before a state appellate court during my second year, but I have also received credit for doing two externships during my third year," says a 3L.

Seven professional schools all share the same campus in Baltimore, which can overburden some of the administrative offices; students cite the financial aid office's lag time, and a career development office that "generally lacks important contacts in the work field." Still, the school boasts an active recruiting program and a high job placement rate, while the main head honchos at the school are very accessible, and "many of the deans also teach classes and are available to all students, even if you don't have them as a professor." The school's great strength is "teaching you how to be a smart and effective lawyer," through a few students say there is relatively little class time devoted to "cutting-edge legal scholarship and critical theory," and complain that "the popular courses are filled so quickly."

Maryland professors are "top-notch," being both "incredibly smart legal thinkers and, more importantly, fantastic teachers in the classroom." Nearly all of the professors "have practiced law for a decade or more before coming to the law school," which not only contributes to their legal experience, but to their sympathy for the demands of the profession. Professors and staff are all "very accommodating" to students trying to get through law school while working—night classes are made available to students in their second and third years—and faculty are "very helpful in advising students on how to mitigate stress and handle the competing interests of law school." "I have had a number of brilliant and committed adjunct professors who understand the burdens associated with working and going to school full-time," says a student. "Even if you are not in their class, they help you with course-related questions, study skills, and exam strategies," says another.

Life

As a whole, there is a presiding "positive attitude" among the "friendly" student body, which is "smart and capable." Cliques do tend to form within sections (as with many law schools), and "day students are way more social than the evening students," but there is definitely a sense of "we're all in it together." The student body is also quite diverse, and people "don't have the sense that cultural groups self-segregate here."

While the law school itself is "beautiful," and "new and gorgeous with all the technical bells and whistles," the location of the law school is "truly the worst...although that is not really the school's fault." "Baltimore is an impressive city in many respects, but the campus is not located in one of the city's many pleasant neighborhoods," says a student of the surrounding area, where "things around school shut down as soon as it is dark." There is "no need to go out and buy a Kevlar vest or anything," but "just be sure to do your research, and if you have a chance to, come look around before signing a lease—I would advise that." Students who live on campus are often disappointed with restaurant and

Susan Krinsky, Assistant Dean For Student Affairs
500 West Baltimore Street, Baltimore, MD 21201
Tel: 410-706-3492 • Fax: 410-706-1793
E-Mail: admissions@law.umaryland.edu • Website: www.law.umaryland.edu

nightlife options, and some students feel that finding entertainment "is difficult if you don't own a car," as the social life at the school struggles "because many students commute…and this damages the sense of community." On-campus activities tend to be based on legal issues and career-building, rather than pure socialization, though law students can take advantage of the gym, pool, and student lounge at the brand new campus center.

The law school curve does incite a bit of competition among students, which is more "collaborative" than cutthroat, but it still creates an atmosphere "with enough competition to encourage a race to the top." "Although we all compete against each other, I do not think that anyone at this law school would sabotage another student in anyway," says one, and everyone seems to agree.

Getting In

The school prides itself on a "holistic review" of each applicant's file, which takes into account the background and experiences that students might bring to help diversify classroom discussions. Students may also transfer to the school after completing a year of law school elsewhere. Admitted students for a recent entering class at the 25th percentile have LSAT scores of approximately 155 and GPAs around 3.3. Admitted students at the 75th percentile have LSAT scores of 162 and GPAs in the 3.75 range.

Clinical program required	Yes
Legal writing course requirement	Yes
Legal methods course requirement	Yes
Legal research course requirement	Yes
Moot court requirement	Yes
Public interest law requirement	Yes

ADMISSIONS

Selectivity Rating	**85**
# applications received	2,011
% applicants accepted	49
% acceptees attending	17
Average LSAT	158
Median LSAT	159
LSAT Range (25th to 75th percentile)	155–162
Average undergrad GPA	3.44
Median undergrad GPA	3.50
Application fee	$70
Regular application deadline	4/15
Transfer students accepted	Yes
Evening division offered	Yes
Part-time accepted	Yes
CAS accepted	Yes

International Students

TOEFL required of international students.	Yes

FINANCIAL FACTS

Annual tuition (in-state/ out-of-state)	$26,902/$39,709
Books and supplies	$1,725
Fees	$1,755
Room & Board (on/ off campus)	$24,317/$30,214
Financial aid application deadline	3/1
% first-year students receiving some sort of aid	87
% all students receiving some sort of aid	92
% of aid that is merit based	14
% receiving scholarships	53
Average grant	$10,000
Average loan	$37,320
Average total aid package	$54,329
Average debt	$102,183

EMPLOYMENT INFORMATION

Career Rating	83
Total 2014 JD Grads	296
% for whom you have useable information	100
% grads employed ten months out	91
Median starting salary	$52,000
% job accepting grads providing useable salary information	93
# employed full-time	251
# employed part-time	17
# employed bar required	185
# employed JD preferred	63
# employed professional/other	19
# employed non-professional	1
# pursuing advanced degree	2
# unemployed and seeking employment	24
# not seeking employment	1
% grads employed by school	7
State for bar exam	MD
Pass rate for first-time bar	79.0

Prominent Alumni
Christine A. Edwards, Partner, Winston & Strawn; Mark D. Bloom, Shareholder, Co-chair, Greenberg Traurig; The Honorable Andre M. Davis, U.S. Court of Appeals for the Fourth Circuit; Benjamin L. Cardin, US Senator for MD

Grads Employed by Field (%)
Academic (4)
Business/Industry (17)
Government (20)
Judicial Clerkship (20)
Federal: (3)
State or local: (17)
Private Practice (27)
2-10: (14)
11-25: (4)
26-50: (2)
51-100: (1)
101-250: (3)
251-500: (1)
501+: (3)
Size Unknown: (0)
Public Interest (4)

UNIVERSITY OF MEMPHIS
CECIL C. HUMPHREYS SCHOOL OF LAW

INSTITUTIONAL INFORMATION

Public/private	Public
% faculty part-time	12
% faculty female	43
% faculty underrepresented minority	20
Total faculty	46

SURVEY SAYS...

Students love Memphis, TN, Diverse opinions accepted in classrooms, Great research resources, Good social life

STUDENTS

Enrollment of law school	334
% male/female	60/40
% from out-of-state	8
% part-time	7
% underrepresented minority	22
% international	0
# of countries represented	0
Average age of entering class	27

ACADEMICS

Academic Experience Rating	**85**
Profs interesting rating	84
Profs accessible rating	88
Hours of study per day	3.79

Academic Specialties

Advocacy, Business, Constitutional, Corporations, Criminal, Health, Intellectual Property, International, Labor, Property, Taxation

Advanced Degrees Offered

JD (6 semesters)

Combined Degrees Offered

JD/MBA,105 credit hrs; JD/MA Political Science 107 credit hrs; JD/MPH, begin after completion of JD

Academics

While it may not have Ivy League name recognition, the University of Memphis Cecil C. Humphreys School of Law's "reputation far exceeds [its] rank." As "the only law school in Memphis," the University of Memphis's students over and over again call it "a gem" and "a diamond in the rough." "I came to this school despite options to go to tier 1 schools in the U.S. News and World Report Rankings. The academic life is as rigorous as any intellectual could want, and the social atmosphere of the school as is team-oriented as it gets." The U of M's professors, who are "down to earth, speak for their chosen fields eloquently, and very respectful", "combine Ivy League educations with real-world experience to create classroom experiences that are both challenging and relevant." "I was surprised at how approachable and genuinely interested the administration and professors were in students' opinions and their overall well-being." While approachable, the faculty is "entrenched in the Socratic method" and rigorous. One student notes the presence of those old-school "'I will haze you by employing the Socratic Method' type profs." Some students say they wish the law program was "more practical," or had more "curriculum diversity:" the "abundance of opportunities to work in criminal law, family law, elder, and housing in Memphis" may make it harder to practice an "area of the law that is not so much in need here (business, intellectual property)."

Also among the U of M's prime features are shining facilities: the school recently "opened in a new, restored historic courthouse and customs building, and all of the facilities, library, and classrooms were (and still are) top notch." Classrooms boast "great wireless internet, acoustics, and seating arrangement," and students take pride in their "beautiful" surroundings, asserting that "since the move into the renovated building downtown, there's no way we can't compete with any school in the country on facilities."

What students arguably love the most, though, is how the University of Memphis competes in "bang for your buck." "The price...is very low compared to the national average, and in my book that meant getting a huge value for my legal education." This value doesn't sacrifice job readiness: students report that the university is "dedicated to ensuring our graduates hit the ground running." Extracurricular and internship opportunities include the "Law Review, Mock Trial (both inter and intra school competitions), clinics, and the school's dynamic Memphis Association of Law and Business," as well as "opportunities to volunteer for first year students, such as the Saturday Legal Clinic and the weekday divorce clinics," and "networking opportunities with local professionals and the Memphis Bar Association."

DR. SUE ANN MCCLELLAN, ASSISTANT DEAN FOR LAW ADMISSIONS
1 N. FRONT STREET, MEMPHIS, TN 38103-2189
TEL: 901-678-5403 • FAX: 901-678-0741
E-MAIL: LAWADMISSIONS@MEMPHIS.EDU • WEBSITE: WWW.MEMPHIS.EDU/LAW

Life

"The school's location in the heart of downtown" Memphis strikes students as "perfect:" "The proximity of the campus to downtown restaurants, national and college sports arenas, and other venues really make the school appealing." There's "a great connection between the school and the city" both socially and professionally; U of M students enjoy a campus situated "within blocks of all the courts and numerous attorney offices which makes for easy field trips or internships." Apart from the job-seeking grind, popular activities and destinations include local "Grizzlies games," and "Beale Street," where it's easy to run into "my boss and other lawyers" and "build relationships." Plenty of amenities are available on campus, as well: "The law building sits right on the Mississippi river and has a great book/food store and also some recreational equipment in the lounge." "Our small class sizes create a friendly atmosphere both inside and outside the classroom," and students "cannot stress enough how awesome it is to live, go to school, gain outside experience, and have a fun social life all within half a mile."

Getting In

For the entering class of 2014, the median LSAT was 153 and the median GPA 3.27. A significant factor in the admission decision process is the admission index, which is based on the undergraduate grade point average and the LSAT score. Interviews are not used to evaluate students but all prospective students are encouraged to visit and meet with a member of the admissions staff as well as visit a class or two.

Clinical program required	No
Legal writing course requirement	No
Legal methods course requirement	Yes
Legal research course requirement	Yes
Moot court requirement	No
Public interest law requirement	Yes

ADMISSIONS

Selectivity Rating	82
# applications received	591
% applicants accepted	49
% acceptees attending	38
Average LSAT	153
Median LSAT	153
LSAT Range (25th to 75th percentile)	150–157
Average undergrad GPA	3.26
Median undergrad GPA	3.27
Application fee	$0
Regular application deadline	3/15
Regular notification	4/1
Transfer students accepted	Yes
Evening division offered	No
Part-time accepted	Yes
CAS accepted	Yes

International Students

TOEFL required of international students.	Yes

FINANCIAL FACTS

Annual tuition (in-state/ out-of-state)	$15,992/$23,852
Books and supplies	$1,969
Fees	$2,055
Room & Board	$9,492
Financial aid application deadline	5/1
% first-year students receiving some sort of aid	86
% all students receiving some sort of aid	88
% of aid that is merit based	10
% receiving scholarships	41
Average grant	$8,489
Average loan	$25,940
Average total aid package	$25,972
Average debt	$74,663

EMPLOYMENT INFORMATION

Career Rating	**84**	
Total 2014 JD Grads	131	
% for whom you have useable information	100	
% grads employed ten months out	80	
Median starting salary	$54,254	
# employed full-time	97	
# employed part-time	8	
# employed bar required	79	
# employed JD preferred	8	
# employed professional/other	9	
# employed non-professional	9	
# pursuing advanced degree	2	
# unemployed and seeking employment	20	
# not seeking employment	3	
State for bar exam	TN, TX, AR, AL, LA	
Pass rate for first-time bar	77.3	

Prominent Alumni
Honorable Bernice Donald, Judge, U.S. 6th Circuit Court of Appeals; Steve Cohen, US Congressman, TN 9th District; Caroline Hunter, Commissioner, Federal Election Commission; Karen Clark, VP & General Counsel, Procter & Gamble Corporation, Global Health Care & Global Beauty Care; Honorable Holly Kirby, Justice TN Supreme Courts

Grads Employed by Field (%)
Academic (2)
Business/Industry (15)
Government (19)
Judicial Clerkship (8)
Private Practice (44)
Public Interest (1)

UNIVERSITY OF MIAMI
SCHOOL OF LAW

INSTITUTIONAL INFORMATION

Public/private	Private
Affiliation	No Affiliation
Student-faculty raio	13:1
% faculty part-time	57
% faculty female	42
% faculty underrepresented minority	20
Total faculty	240

SURVEY SAYS...
Students love Coral Gables, FL, Good social life

STUDENTS

Enrollment of law school	1,011
% male/female	53/47
% from out-of-state	25
% part-time	4
% underrepresented minority	54
% international	4
# of countries represented	9
Average age of entering class	24

ACADEMICS

Academic Experience Rating	**86**
Profs interesting rating	76
Profs accessible rating	72
Hours of study per day	3.66

Academic Specialties
Civil Procedure, Commercial, Constitutional, Corporation Securities, Criminal, Environmental, Government Services, Human Rights, International, Labor, Property, Taxation, Intellectual Property

Advanced Degrees Offered
LLM: International Law (with specializations in: International Arbitration, U.S. and Transnational Law for Foreign lawyers, General International Law, and Inter-American Law); Estate Planning; Ocean and Coastal Law; Real Property Development and Taxation.

Combined Degrees Offered
JD/LLM/MBA; JD/MBA; JD/MPH in Public Health; JD/MPS in Marine Affairs; JD/MM in Music Business & Entertainment Industries; JD/MA in

Academics

Students come to University of Miami School of Law for its "amazing resources and faculty" and it's "opportunities for networking," but mostly they come because "it's in Miami." "Location, Location, Location," one student says succinctly. "Miami is a vibrant building city with a lot to offer," and students here have direct "access to Miami's job market." UM enjoys great "name recognition across South Florida" and has "a huge alumni base who are loyal to graduating students." If you want to practice Law in or near Miami, "there's no school that's better rooted in this area." "The campus is absolutely gorgeous—a pleasure to study by the lake, my personal favorite," one student says. "It's sometimes hard to stay in the Law Library all day with such a beautiful and vibrant campus just outside the doors," one 2L explains. "You have to stay really focused."

The "top-notch" professors at UM "cannot be beat." The "genuinely nice" faculty is "a perfect blend of former judges, legal scholars, and adjunct faculty who are at the top of their respective fields in the private sector and judiciary." While "the professors are extremely accessible," since "it is a bigger school" "one-to-one time with the professors is a little difficult to come by." Professors "truly want the students to learn and succeed" and frequently "are national leaders in their field and are greatly respected across the nation." "If you are interested in a few specific areas of law that Miami is known for this is the perfect place." For example, "Miami's litigation skills program has all the major judges and attorneys in Florida," and "UM's resources in Health Law and its reputation as a Health Law up and coming powerhouse should be emphasized!" One student chimes in to say, "I would add art law (with Prof. Urice); maritime law (with Prof. Oxman); and criminal law (with Profs Franks, Rose, Basquez, & Graham) as additional specialties."

While the faculty get high praise, students feel the administration "need to be replaced forthwith if the school hopes not to completely destroy its reputation." Some students say the administration will "nickel and dime you for every penny you have," but "student organizations are poorly funded" and "the Career Development Office does very little to aid in the search for employment." Still, there are ten attorney advisors on staff at the CDO, and Miami Law also provides services like the Student Development Program and the Mindfulness in Law Program with students' personal and professional development in mind. While some students think the dean is "unapproachable" and seems to "prefer to never be bothered," Dean White does hold monthly town hall style meetings to meet with first-year and upper division students and "has used her network and reputation to make big in-roads to the New York and D.C. marketplaces for opportunities for students." "The law library is pretty retro-looking" and "the physical buildings that make up the law school are very old." Still, they are filled with "cutting edge" technology and the campus overall "is beautiful." One highlight that needs to be mentioned is "the Litigation Skills Program." "No other university that I know in the area offers such a well-structured program," one happy student says.

THERESE LAMBERT, DIRECTOR OF STUDENT RECRUITMENT
1311 MILLER DR, ROOM F203, CORAL GABLES, FL 33124-8087
TEL: 305-284-6746 • FAX: 305-284-4400
E-MAIL: ADMISSIONS@LAW.MIAMI.EDU • WEBSITE: WWW.LAW.MIAMI.EDU

Life

The "very intelligent and competitive" students at UM "are drawn from all over the world." "Average student age" at UM "is pretty low compared to most law schools." While the school is diverse "relative to other law schools" (the school reports that 37 percent of the 2014 JD class identified as members of a minority group or as multiethnic), students feel that "it is not diverse at all relative to Miami," "unless you count the many different shades of white." UM has a more a relaxed atmosphere than most law schools. "Everyone wears shorts and the campus has a weekly farmers market." "The university is located where vibrant Miami, beautiful Coral Gables, and quaint Coconut Grove meet," one student explains. "There is always something going on around the university" and the city "has an amazing energy." Students keep busy at studies, but "when you do have free time, you feel like you're on vacation." The undergraduate campus is "a stone's throw away" and the UM "basketball and football teams are excellent and provide a welcome break from studying."

Getting In

If you are interested in practicing law in South Florida, UM should be near the top of your list. The school is on the larger side for a law school, taking over 400 students a class. Recent students have had GPAs between 3.19 and 3.63 at the 25th and 75th percentiles. LSAT scores range between 155 and 160 at those same percentiles.

EMPLOYMENT INFORMATION

Career Rating	89
Total 2014 JD Grads	418
% grads employed ten months out	87
Median starting salary	$58,000
# employed full-time	353
# employed part-time	9
# employed bar required	298
# employed JD preferred	54
# employed professional/other	12
# employed non-professional	3
# pursuing advanced degree	9
# unemployed and seeking employment	22
# not seeking employment	10
% grads employed by school	1
State for bar exam	FL, IL, TX, NC, MD
Pass rate for first-time bar	81.0

Prominent Alumni
The Honorable Fred Lewis, Former Chief Justice, Florida Supreme Court; Carolyn B. Lamm, Partner, White & Case (D.C); Former ABA President; Roy Black, Prominent Criminal Defense Attorney, Legal Expert; Dennis Curran, Sr. VP/Gen. Counsel, NFL Management Council; Horacio Gutierrez, Corporate Vice President and Deputy General Counsel, Microsoft Corporation

Grads Employed by Field (%)
Academic (1)
Business/Industry (17)
Government (13)
Judicial Clerkship (3)
Private Practice (54)
  Solo: (6)
  2-10: (112)
  11-25: (38)
  26-50: (13)
  51-100: (13)
  101-250: (12)
  251-500: (5)
  500+: (25)
Public Interest (3)

ADMISSIONS

Selectivity Rating	**84**
# applications received	2,765
% applicants accepted	52
% acceptees attending	16
Average LSAT	158
Median LSAT	157
LSAT Range (25th to 75th percentile)	155–160
Average undergrad GPA	3.41
Median undergrad GPA	3.42
Application fee	$60
Regular application deadline	7/31
Regular notification	Rolling
Early application deadline	2/3
Transfer students accepted	Yes
Evening division offered	No
Part-time accepted	No
CAS accepted	Yes

Arts Presenting & Live Entertainment Management; JD/MA in Communications; JD/MSEd in Law, Community and Social Change; JD/LLM in International Law; JD/LLM in Ocean and Coastal Law; JD/LLM in Real Property Development; JD/LLM in Taxation; JD/MD; JD/PhD in Environmental Science and Policy

Clinical program required	No
Legal writing course requirement	Yes
Legal methods course requirement	Yes
Legal research course requirement	Yes
Moot court requirement	No
Public interest law requirement	No

FINANCIAL FACTS

Annual tuition	$45,200
Books and supplies	$1,700
Fees	$966
Room & Board	$15,966
Financial aid application deadline	3/1
% first-year students receiving some sort of aid	91
% all students receiving some sort of aid	78
% of aid that is merit based	19
% receiving scholarships	37
Average grant	$24,003
Average loan	$56,076
Average total aid package	$59,316
Average debt	$143,845

UNIVERSITY OF MICHIGAN
LAW SCHOOL

INSTITUTIONAL INFORMATION

Public/private	Public
Student-faculty ratio	13:1
% faculty part-time	34
% faculty female	30
% faculty underrepresented minority	7
Total faculty	131

SURVEY SAYS...

Diverse opinions accepted in classrooms, Great research resources, Abundant externship/internship/ clerkship opportunities, Law school well run, Strong sense of community, Good social life

STUDENTS

Enrollment of law school	1,001
% male/female	55/45
% from out-of-state	77
% underrepresented minority	11
% international	4
# of countries represented	32
Average age of entering class	24

ACADEMICS

Academic Experience Rating	**98**
Profs interesting rating	93
Profs accessible rating	87
Hours of study per day	3.99

Academic Specialties

Civil Procedure, Commercial, Constitutional, Corporation Securities, Criminal, Environmental, Government Services, Human Rights, International, Labor, Legal History, Legal Philosophy, Property, Taxation, Intellectual Property

Advanced Degrees Offered

LLM Master of Laws; International Tax LLM; M.C.L. Master of Comparative Law; and SJD Doctor of the Science of Law

Combined Degrees Offered

JD/MBA; JD/PhD Economics; JD/ MA in Modern Middle Eastern and North African Studies; JD/MPP (MPP); JD/MS in Natural Resources; JD/ MHSA, 4 yrs;

Academics

As a consistently top ten law school, the University of Michigan has a lot to brag about in terms of "name recognition, academic reputation, [and] alumni network." That said, even though "everyone at Michigan is really proud to be here," they're not really bragging types: the "Michigan Difference" provides "a superior legal education while avoiding the snootiness that ordinarily accompanies it—and employers recognize it." U of M professors "are brilliant, accessible, and committed to the classroom," and "frequently attend happy hours or invite us into their homes. They are seriously wonderful, friendly people." Indeed, many students underscore the fact that professors represent "a fantastic array of . . . theoretical and political perspectives" and are "more friendly or open with students at other top law schools." Some students express a desire for "more diversity in course offerings," and their comments frequently reflect the opinion that the "Transnational Law course requirement is a waste," but they generally agree that the "academic experience at Michigan has been out of this world."

Though "the alumni network is massive," job placement is "top notch," and "if you throw a rock in a big law firm, you're likely to hit a Michigan Law grad excited to dish about the school," some students argue that the "school needs a better career services office that is better adapted to the post-recession legal market." Significant investments in the Office of Career Planning since 2014, include reorganizing the office, and adding more resources like counselors and fellowships, as well as building stronger links between students and the alumni network. Equally do they report, though, that the "administration is phenomenal," "friendly, accessible, and responsive," and "responds to emails with amazing promptness and a willingness to help." Students looking to cast a wide net in job placement benefit from Michigan's Midwestern location: "I love how well Michigan places nationally—it is very nice to not be married to one market."

U of M's students adore the law school facilities, which "are not only functionally amazing but spectacular to look at as well. Easily the most aesthetically pleasing law school in the country, and [very recent] renovations to the Lawyers Club should make it better than ever." "Classrooms are well-equipped, with the newer facilities providing nine whiteboards, hydraulic podiums, and individual microphones for every student," and "the buildings are architectural gems, especially the Reading Room." This, of course, comes at a cost: Michigan doesn't give as significant an in-state tuition break as many other state universities (though they do give a competitive amount of financial aid), and "Like any law school, debt is a huge problem." Broadly speaking, students express a high degree of satisfaction with the education they're paying for: "Michigan students rarely want for anything in terms of opportunities, experiences, or facilities."

SARAH C. ZEARFOSS, ASSISTANT DEAN AND DIRECTOR OF ADMISSIONS
701 SOUTH STATE STREET, ANN ARBOR, MI 48109-1215
TEL: 734-764-0537 • FAX: 734-647-3218
E-MAIL: LAW.JD.ADMISSIONS@UMICH.EDU • WEBSITE: WWW.LAW.UMICH.EDU

Life

Michigan students, "genuine and decent people who are simply fun," take pride in their humility: "Everyone here is smart, but nobody is a jerk about it. Employers know that, too." "The friendly, relatively noncompetitive atmosphere is why I chose Michigan Law, and I am so grateful for it every single day." Many of them picked Michigan over other choices because "the cutthroat, unhappy reputation of other schools is the exact opposite of what you find at Michigan" and "the collegiality of the students and professors here is so refreshing." The university encourages this dynamic: "the school seems to make life, especially during finals period, as easy as possible, going the length of increasing/making free printing, keeping facilities open longer, etc."

They're also delighted by their surroundings, joking that the "law quad" is so "gorgeous" it's like "we basically go to school at Hogwarts." The excellent facilities augment quality of life on campus, offering "ample room to study, relax, socialize, and bask in the awe of one of the most beautiful academic buildings on the planet."

Getting In

Though Michigan follows ABA requirements to consider the highest score of any applicant who has taken the LSAT more than once, they do consider the average score as well. Its LSAT range (25th to 75th percentile) is 165–170 and median GPA range is 3.58-3.83. It's possible to start in the summer if you apply accordingly, and as a Teach for America partner school, TFA corps members or alumni can have their application fees waived by contacting the school.

JD/MA in Russian and East European Studies; JD/MA in World Politics; JD/MSW; JD/MS in Information; JD/MPH; JD/MA in Japanese Studies; JD/Master of Urban Planning (MUP), 4 yrs; JD/MA in Chinese Studies, 3.5–4 yrs. Students may design their own dual degrees.

Clinical program required	No
Legal writing course requirement	Yes
Legal methods course requirement	Yes
Legal research course requirement	Yes
Moot court requirement	No
Public interest law requirement	No

ADMISSIONS

Selectivity Rating	96
# applications received	4,751
% applicants accepted	27
% acceptees attending	25
Median LSAT	168
LSAT Range (25th to 75th percentile)	165–170
Median undergrad GPA	3.74
Application fee	$75
Regular application deadline	2/15
Early application deadline	11/15
Early application notification	12/15
Transfer students accepted	Yes
Evening division offered	No
Part-time accepted	No
CAS accepted	Yes

FINANCIAL FACTS

Annual tuition (in-state/ out-of-state)	$51,154/$54,154
Books and supplies	$4,620
Fees	$244
Room & Board	$13,410
% first-year students receiving some sort of aid	96
% all students receiving some sort of aid	92
% receiving scholarships	71
Average grant	$17,205
Average loan	$47,647
Average total aid package	$50,243
Average debt	$132,473

EMPLOYMENT INFORMATION

Career Rating	97	**Grads Employed by Field (%)**
Total 2014 JD Grads	390	Academic (1)
% for whom you have useable information	100	Business/Industry (4)
% grads employed ten months out	96	Government (11)
Median starting salary	$130,000	Judicial Clerkship (18)
# employed full-time	370	Federal: (11)
# employed part-time	4	State or local: (7)
# employed bar required	360	Other: (0)
# employed JD preferred	12	Private Practice (51)
# employed professional/other	1	Solo: (0)
# employed non-professional	1	2-10: (2)
# pursuing advanced degree	6	11-25: (2)
# unemployed and seeking employment	6	26-50: (1)
# not seeking employment	3	51-100: (2)
% grads employed by school	10	101-250: (4)
State for bar exam	NY, IL, CA, MI, MD	251-500: (5)
Pass rate for first-time bar	93.2	501+: (34)
		Size Unknown: (1)
		Public Interest (11)

UNIVERSITY OF MINNESOTA
LAW SCHOOL

INSTITUTIONAL INFORMATION

Public/private	Public
Student-faculty ratio	10:1
% faculty female	39
% faculty underrepresented minority	12
Total faculty	67

SURVEY SAYS...
Great research resources

STUDENTS

Enrollment of law school	698
% male/female	58/42
% from out-of-state	62
% part-time	2
% underrepresented minority	20
% international	12
# of countries represented	31
Average age of entering class	25

ACADEMICS

Academic Experience Rating	**92**
Profs interesting rating	84
Profs accessible rating	72
Hours of study per day	3.82

Academic Specialties

Criminal, Environmental, Human Rights, International, Labor, Intellectual Property

Advanced Degrees Offered

JD, LLM for Foreign Lawyers, 1 yr; MS in Patent Law,1 yr

Combined Degrees Offered

JD/MBA, 4 yrs; JD/MPA, 4 yrs; JD/MA; JD/MD; JD/MPP, 4 yrs; JD/MURP, 4 yrs; JD/MS, 4 yrs; JD/PhD; JD/MBT; JD/MBS; JD/MPH

Academics

The "world class" faculty of the University of Minnesota Law School are "dedicated to the students" and tend to be "very helpful, especially the professors' assistants." Styles vary. "Some professors prefer a more Socratic style, some a more discussion based approach," but regardless of whether they prefer lectures, discussion, or a mixture of both, "all are available to talk to students whenever." One 1L noted that they have "always felt completely welcome to talk to all my professors, and that has continued on as a 2L."

In part because "the professors are experts and heavily published in their fields," the program here is "very research driven." However, the professors having successful outside-of-school pursuits causes some students to complain that "professors care more about their research than their teaching." By and large, however, they are "well-respected in their fields and usually great teachers to boot." Their real-world experience means for many, "they've been very helpful in learning the nuts and bolts of the profession." Regardless of what other distractions they have, professors are "universally welcoming and eager to work with students."

That said, the "dated" facilities can be "gloomy and depressing." Being educated in the basement "feels oppressive in the dead of winter," but it's not all bad when it comes to the facilities. "U of M takes pride in the size of the law library," one student notes, "and I think that pride is well-earned." The school also makes it a point to give students a sense for how their studies will apply to the real world. A mock trial competition team, for example, "is an example of how the school makes sure to promote the practical aspects of the law and integrate the scholastic elements of the education."

Opportunities in the Twin Cities abound. From a wide range of classes to the "large number of journals" to mock courts, an "active student organization community," and a legal community that embraces those in the U of M program, "there are more opportunities than I have time in which to partake." Because this is a top twenty school, "there is a strong drive among students for big firm jobs." At one time that was reflected in the curriculum, too, but these days the school "has made significant progress in recognizing and meeting the needs of students interested in public interest, government, and policy or research oriented positions."

Life

The city of Minneapolis is "amazing," with a bustling nightlife–the music scene is legendary, arts and culture abound, and it's a growing Mecca for craft beer–and "many opportunities to get out there" when it comes to networking with those in the profession. "The legal community is very approachable and welcomes 1Ls (and 2L/3Ls) to many of their events," offering "numerous opportunities to network." If the people and city win accolades, the facilities, which are "unfortunately located in a basement," do not. They "are clean and well-kept, but not attractive." Still, while the "lack of natural light in most classrooms" has resulted in the facilities being nicknamed "the dungeon," they are still "modern" and "tech-equipped," with "comfortable seats, and plugs for everybody's laptops."

NICK WALLACE, DIRECTOR OF ADMISSIONS
290 MONDALE HALL, 229 19TH AVENUE SOUTH, MINNEAPOLIS, MN 55455
TEL: 612-625-3487 • FAX: 612-626-1874
E-MAIL: JDADMISSIONS@UNM.EDU • WEBSITE: WWW.LAW.UMN.EDU

But it is the people who win out in the end. "People are happy to be here" for a reason. The faculty and student body alike "works hard to promote an environment of collegiality, where the students work hard with each other as colleagues instead of against each other as competitors." In fact, "given our career choice … students are not as outwardly assertive as you'd think they'd be." Even though everyone is working hard to succeed, "nobody will flaunt their grades or job prospects." In addition, "diversity is truly valued," especially when it comes to student achievement. Students here "support each other as long as the effort is honest, because it all comes out in finals."

Getting In

Expect competition when trying to gain admission to the University of Minnesota Law School. Interested candidates will need a strong undergraduate record along with excellent LSAT scores, as well as the ability to demonstrate that they can handle rigorous course work and that they've acquired solid communication skills. In addition, the admissions committee will consider factors such as previous work experience, public service, other graduate work, and ethnic background. Because admission is granted on a rolling basis, the earlier an applicant applies the better.

Clinical program required	No
Legal writing course requirement	Yes
Legal methods course requirement	No
Legal research course requirement	Yes
Moot court requirement	No
Public interest law requirement	No

ADMISSIONS

Selectivity Rating	92
# applications received	2,195
% applicants accepted	41
% acceptees attending	21
Average LSAT	162
Median LSAT	164
LSAT Range (25th to 75th percentile)	157–166
Average undergrad GPA	3.63
Median undergrad GPA	3.77
Application fee	$75
Regular application deadline	4/1
Regular notification	4/1
Early application deadline	11/15
Early application notification	12/31
Transfer students accepted	Yes
Evening division offered	No
Part-time accepted	No
CAS accepted	Yes

International Students

TOEFL required of international students.	Yes

FINANCIAL FACTS

Annual tuition (in-state/ out-of-state)	$39,192/$46,680
Books and supplies	$1,700
Fees	$2,102
Room & Board	$10,926
Financial aid application deadline	5/1
% first-year students receiving some sort of aid	92
% all students receiving some sort of aid	91
% of aid that is merit based	0
% receiving scholarships	79
Average grant	$24,470
Average loan	$35,218
Average total aid package	$47,252
Average debt	$104,733

EMPLOYMENT INFORMATION

Career Rating	90
Total 2014 JD Grads	259
% for whom you have useable information	100
Median starting salary	$60,587
# employed full-time	230
# employed part-time	6
# employed bar required	217
# employed JD preferred	15
# employed professional/other	3
# employed non-professional	1
# pursuing advanced degree	5
# unemployed and seeking employment	15
# not seeking employment	3
% grads employed by school	6
State for bar exam	MN
Pass rate for first-time bar	96.5

Prominent Alumni
Walter F. Mondale, Former Vice President of The United States; Keith Ellison, U.S. Representative; Jean E. Hanson, Partner Fried, Frank, Harris, Shriver, & Jacobson

Grads Employed by Field (%)
Academic (1)
Business/Industry (9)
Government (12)
Judicial Clerkship (21)
Federal: (5)
State or local: (16)
Private Practice (41)
  Solo: (1)
  2-10: (12)
  11-25: (7)
  26-50: (3)
  51-100: (2)
  101-250: (5)
  251-500: (4)
  501+: (7)
  Size Unknown: (0)
Public Interest (11)

THE UNIVERSITY OF MISSISSIPPI
SCHOOL OF LAW

INSTITUTIONAL INFORMATION

Public/private	Public
% faculty part-time	30
% faculty female	31
% faculty underrepresented minority	13
Total faculty	52

SURVEY SAYS...
Diverse opinions accepted in classrooms, Good social life

STUDENTS

Enrollment of law school	386
% male/female	60/40
% part-time	0
% underrepresented minority	21
# of countries represented	1
Average age of entering class	24

ACADEMICS

Academic Experience Rating	**84**
Profs interesting rating	87
Profs accessible rating	87
Hours of study per day	2.73

Academic Specialties
Commercial, Corporation Securities, Criminal, Environmental, International, Taxation

Advanced Degrees Offered
None

Combined Degrees Offered
JD/MBA 4 yrs; JD/MA Tax 4 yrs; JD/MA Accounting 4 yrs

Academics

Students at Ole Miss love the combination of "a down-home, small-town atmosphere where everyone knows your name" and a law degree that is "given much credit within the state." Though "academically strenuous," the school's "laid-back atmosphere "prevails, and students praise the "easily accessible" staff, the "large student mall with plenty of couches and chairs for discussions between classes," and the "professors with awesome senses of humor." By all accounts, Ole Miss is not a school that "makes you feel like they are trying to weed you out." As one student explains, "I love the dynamics of the classes and the size of the student body. It is nice to be friends with 2Ls and 3Ls and not feel like a freshman again." "Everyone in the administration is incredibly friendly and helpful," a classmate adds. "If you have any question, even if it has nothing to do with their particular job, they will do everything they can to get you the right answer." Professors here hail from "a broad diversity of backgrounds" and "are all extremely knowledgeable and very experienced." Not only do they "present the material in an entertaining way," they "take a special interest" in students, "which can help build up [students'] confidence and help them to excel."

The professors at Ole Miss are a major reason why its students say the school is a "great value." "It is not nearly as expensive to go to school here as the other schools to which I applied or was accepted," says one student. "I can still get pretty much any job I want coming out of Ole Miss, yet I have zero debt." Other students, however, temper such expectations, noting that while Ole Miss' "Career Services Office is always there to help with a résumé or to provide Tylenol during exams," securing a job outside of Mississippi can be an uphill battle. That said, this situation seems to be on the upswing thanks to the school's "great relationship with alumni" and also in that "Ole Miss changed their grading curve [a few years ago] and that has significantly helped those who are looking to get a job out of state."

Students consistently report that the faculty is one of the school's "greatest strengths." "They take away the mundane, stereotypical experience of law school and present the material in an entertaining way without compromising the integrity of the institution," says one student. Many feel that "there is a lot of potential in the legal writing and research classes"; however, they are damaged by "the lack of communication between... departments." Others would like "more classes to choose from," particularly in the area of entertainment law. Students are divided on the school's aesthetics, finding that the "great library" is "extremely up to date with the latest technology" while the building itself is "not very pretty" and "somewhat outdated." A 1L provides some perspective, explaining that "the law school building would be aesthetically pleasing at most major schools, but when compared to the columned architecture and tree-lined walkways of the rest of the campus, you can immediately tell it is a relic of the early 1970s. Instead of being 'postmodern,' it simply looks out of place." However, "a new state-of-the-art building" "will soon be under construction."

BARBARA VINSON, DIRECTOR OF ADMISSIONS
OFFICE OF ADMISSIONS, P.O. BOX 1848, LAMAR LAW CENTER, UNIVERSITY, MS 38677
TEL: 662-915-6910 • FAX: 662-915-1289
E-MAIL: LAWMISS@OLEMISS.EDU • WEBSITE: WWW.LAW.OLEMISS.EDU

Life

Ole Miss students emphasize that theirs is a "relaxed learning environment," one that "promotes collaboration between students instead of the cutthroat competition that you hear about at other law schools." The school divides 1Ls into sections of "about sixty students." While this can be "good for making friends" and forming "study groups and TV nights," it can at times seem "like high school all over again with the distinct social circles." "In true Southern form," law students at Ole Miss "like to work hard and play hard," and "Life at the law school is very social. Everyone is a part of LSSB (Law School Student Body) and participates in "bar reviews." Also, students attend Ole Miss football games and tailgate every weekend in the fall." When they do take a break, Ole Miss students find themselves in a pleasant location. The university's campus is "beautiful," and hometown Oxford is "a unique place" with "a healthy social scene." Though most will tell you that "drinking is a big part of social life" here, popular opinion states that "you can absolutely have a good time without drinking." "There are two great new movie theaters, and there are plans to open a 'New Square,'" says one student. "Oxford is constantly growing, and hopefully there will be a lot more for students to do soon." One thing that students agree could be improved a more "diverse student body."

Getting In

The early bird gets the worm at Ole Miss since admitted first-year students can begin their studies during the summer. Certain factors, such as "residency, undergraduate institution, difficulty of major, job experience, social, personal or economic circumstances, non-academic achievement, letters of recommendation and grade patterns and progression," can impact your application favorably, according to the school. Admitted students at the 25th percentile have an LSAT score of 151 and a GPA of 3.25. Admitted students at the 75th percentile have an LSAT score of 157 and a GPA of 3.76.

Clinical program required	No
Legal writing course requirement	Yes
Legal methods course requirement	Yes
Legal research course requirement	Yes
Moot court requirement	No
Public interest law requirement	No

ADMISSIONS

Selectivity Rating	81
# applications received	846
% applicants accepted	63
% acceptees attending	24
Median LSAT	155
LSAT Range (25th to 75th percentile)	151–157
Median undergrad GPA	3.47
Application fee	$40
Regular application deadline	4/15
Regular notification	4/30
Transfer students accepted	Yes
Evening division offered	No
Part-time accepted	No
CAS accepted	Yes

International Students

TOEFL required of international students.	Yes

FINANCIAL FACTS

Annual tuition (in-state/ out-of-state)	$14,688/$31,688
Books and supplies	$1,200
Room & Board	$19,198
Financial aid application deadline	3/1
% first-year students receiving some sort of aid	94
% all students receiving some sort of aid	87
% of aid that is merit based	90
% receiving scholarships	60
Average grant	$9,846
Average loan	$23,040
Average debt	$74,523

EMPLOYMENT INFORMATION

Career Rating	85
% grads employed ten months out	96
Median starting salary	$64,025
State for bar exam	MS, TN, GA, FL, TX
Pass rate for first-time bar	90.0

Prominent Alumni
C. Trent Lott, Former U.S. Senator; Thad Cochran, U.S. Senator; John Grisham, Author; Robert C. Khayat, Chancellor, The University of Mississippi

Grads Employed by Field (%)
Academic (3)
Business/Industry (11)
Government (14)
Judicial Clerkship (17)
Private Practice (50)
Public Interest (5)

UNIVERSITY OF MISSOURI
SCHOOL OF LAW

INSTITUTIONAL INFORMATION

Public/private   Public
Affiliation   No Affiliation

SURVEY SAYS...
Diverse opinions accepted in classrooms

STUDENTS
Enrollment of law school   368
% part-time   5

ACADEMICS
Academic Experience Rating   73
Profs interesting rating   67
Profs accessible rating   69
Hours of study per day   NR

Academic Specialties
Commercial, Constitutional, Criminal, Environmental, Government Services, International, Labor, Property, Taxation, Intellectual Property

Advanced Degrees Offered
LLM in Dispute Resolution, which is typically a one-year program.

Combined Degrees Offered
JD/MBA, 4 yrs; JD/MPA (Public Administration), 4 yrs; JD/MHA (Health Administration), 4 yrs; JD/MA (Economics) 4 yrs; JD/MA/MS (Human Development and Family Studies), 4 yrs; JD/MA (Educational Leadership & Policy Analysis), 4 yrs; JD/MA (Journalism), 4 yrs; JD/PhD (Journalism), 6 yrs; JD/MLS (Library and Information Science), 4 yrs; JD/MS (Personal Financial Planning), 4 yrs.

Academics

The University of Missouri School of Law, "provides a high-quality legal education at an affordable price." Its small size, collegial atmosphere and "absolutely outstanding" faculty make Mizzou a "place where you can find all the challenge you want in a law school, without unnecessary stress on top of it." In the words of one student, "If you want to practice in the state of Missouri, there's no better place. Our law school consistently produces the future leaders of Missouri."

Students offer nothing but the utmost praise for their faculty. "The professors are intelligent yet not intimidating; they really care about the students." They "are leading scholars in their field yet available outside the classroom." "Although the Socratic Method is used throughout the first year, and often in other classes, it is used effectively, to help teach students to think like lawyers, but not to embarrass them." Of particular note, one student expresses pleasure in discovering that "classes integrate well with each other, in that professors seem aware of the other classes students are taking, and they draw connections between various fields of the law, thus helping students see how the law comes together." In the words of one particularly enthusiastic student, "The university is the reason I chose MU School of Law, but the faculty is why I would recommend it to any future students. Go Tigers!"

Similar feelings resonate over the administration. One student shares, "The dean of the law school teaches one of my classes. That's probably one of the coolest things about the law school—everyone is so attainable. The administration knows me, and probably every other student in the school, and they genuinely do have our best interests in sight." An older student returning to school after having a family, remarks, "The administration and professors are willing to work with students when those pesky issues of life come along and interfere with the school schedule." Another fan declares, "Law school is hard, MU made it easier."

Academically, students are challenged "within the comfort of a community." Students appreciate "the rigor and intensity of the curriculum" and especially call attention to Mizzou's noteworthy program in alternative dispute resolution. However, of greatest frustration to students are course offerings that conflict with scheduling. One student explains, "Although the course catalog offers a nice variety, students sometimes will have only one opportunity to take a particular class during their student careers, since some 2L/3L classes are offered only every other year." Unfortunately, the wait for in-demand classes can range from a semester to a year, depending on availability.

Career services receive mixed reviews. One student feels that "Career Services does an excellent job with the top 25 percent of the class, but the other three-fourths [of students] could use more attention, in my opinion." Another agrees, remarking that "the career development services are probably the most deserving of attention." Specifically, some feel that "the Career Office could do a better job attracting employers from more geographical areas." Fortunately, it appears that Career Services is addressing some of these issues; as one student reports, due to recent changes, "Career Services has done a much better job at providing job and internship opportunities for the students."

MICHELLE KECK, ASSISTANT DEAN
103 HULSTON HALL, COLUMBIA, MO 65211
TEL: 573-882-6042 • FAX: 573-882-9625
EMAIL: MULAWADMISSIONS@MISSOURI.EDU • WEBSITE: WWW.LAW.MISSOURI.EDU

While instructional technology is current, the facilities have some shortcomings. "The classrooms do not have electrical outlets, which makes it difficult to take notes on a computer when you have class for four hours straight." As a result, "students are commonly seen lugging around extension cords" with them on campus. Additionally, students feel that "physical facilities are starting to show their age and need to be remodeled."

Life

"Mizzou is a great place for law school, the vast majority of people get along well with everyone else, and we all socialize together as well." "As [for] social life—you can get exactly what you want out of it. If you want to be involved, you got it. If you want to be a hermit and just come in for class," go ahead. "It is an environment that allows people to be flexible with their time, but it is also demanding in a sense that it has the proper time constraints to get people motivated." "Furthermore, Columbia is a great city, and the law school is right in the heart of campus with easy access to the recreation center as well as all of the amenities of downtown."

The degree of competition varies depending on who you ask. One student notes, "The thing I like best about this school is that very few individuals are worried about hiding books from each other in the library in order to get that cutthroat best grade." Another explains, "Students are friendly, but not shy about competition. We are here to learn how to be good lawyers, not to tear each other up." "MU is not a lovefest though; people are here because they want to succeed."

Getting In

While application decisions are made on a rolling basis as long as the entering class has openings (class size is 135), the school recommends early application, preferably in the fall of the year prior to enrollment. Admitted students at the 25th percentile have an LSAT score of 154 and a GPA of 3.2. Admitted students at the 75th percentile have an LSAT score of 160 and a GPA of 3.7.

Clinical program required	No
Legal writing course requirement	Yes
Legal methods course requirement	Yes
Legal research course requirement	Yes
Moot court requirement	Yes
Public interest law requirement	No

ADMISSIONS

Selectivity Rating	86
# applications received	633
% applicants accepted	49
% acceptees attending	37
Median LSAT	157
LSAT Range (25th to 75th percentile)	154–160
Median undergrad GPA	3.46
Application fee	$60
Regular application deadline	3/15
Early application deadline	11/15
Early application notification	12/31
Transfer students accepted	Yes
Evening division offered	No
Part-time accepted	Yes
CAS accepted	Yes

International Students

TOEFL required of international students.	Yes

FINANCIAL FACTS

Annual tuition (in-state/ out-of-state)	$19,832/$37,462
Books and supplies	$1,680
Room & Board	$9,828
Financial aid application deadline	3/1

EMPLOYMENT INFORMATION

Career Rating	71	**Prominent Alumni**
Total 2014 JD Grads	135	Claire McCaskill, US Senator; Jay Nixon,
% for whom you have useable information	98	Governor of Missouri; John R. Gibson, US Ct of Appeals-8th Cir; Ted Kulongowski,
% grads employed ten months out	89	Former Governor of Oregon; Ike Skelton,
# employed full-time	112	Former US Congressman
# employed part-time	5	**Grads Employed by Field (%)**
# employed bar required	91	Academic (3)
# employed JD preferred	23	Business/Industry (21)
# employed professional/other	3	Government (19)
# employed non-professional	1	Judicial Clerkship (9)
# pursuing advanced degree	2	Private Practice (45)
# unemployed and seeking employment	11	Public Interest (3)
# not seeking employment	0	
State for bar exam	MO, IL, CA, TX, NY	

UNIVERSITY OF MISSOURI—KANSAS CITY
SCHOOL OF LAW

INSTITUTIONAL INFORMATION

Public/private	Public
Student-faculty ratio	11:1
% faculty part-time	39
% faculty female	37
% faculty underrepresented minority	7
Total faculty	81

SURVEY SAYS...

Students love Kansas City, MO, Diverse opinions accepted in classrooms, Abundant externship/internship/clerkship opportunities, Strong sense of community, Good social life

STUDENTS

Enrollment of law school	468
% male/female	58/42
% from out-of-state	28
% part-time	15
% underrepresented minority	15
% international	1
# of countries represented	7
Average age of entering class	26

ACADEMICS

Academic Experience Rating	**85**
Profs interesting rating	85
Profs accessible rating	96
Hours of study per day	3.52

Academic Specialties
International, Taxation, Intellectual Property

Advanced Degrees Offered
LLM 1–3 yrs

Combined Degrees Offered
JD/MBA 3–4 yrs, JD/MPA 3–4 yrs, JD/LLM 3.5–4 yrs.

Academics

The University of Missouri—Kansas City School of Law offers "relatively low" tuition and boasts a faculty and staff that are "very helpful and accessible." One student notes that "the law school building is somewhat dated, but students have access to adequate technology in the library and each classroom. The library staff goes above and beyond in helping students as well as any visitors of the general public in conducting legal research." Although some students have found the majority of their professors to "have been older, white males," it has also been observed that "while the teaching staff is not very culturally diverse, diversity of opinions is not discouraged in the classroom."

As to that helpful "top-notch" administration and faculty, one student sums up: "I have never found myself in a situation where I wasn't able to get into a specific class or a specific professor's class. The administration team is one of the best I've ever dealt with. Tasks are delegated to various people and myself and other students know exactly where to go if we have any issues. Professors are always accessible and most, if not all, have an open door policy. Additionally, 2L's receive an office for one semester and a carrel for the other semester. The offices and carrels are located right next to professor's offices which is a nice touch. Most professors use the Socratic method, and a few make students stand up when they are talking (I like this touch because it helps with public speaking and is a realistic view of what court will be like for us)."

Six areas UMKC emphasizes include: litigation; business and entrepreneurial law; child and family law; international, comparative and foreign law; urban land use and environmental law; and intellectual property law. There are also three dual-degree options. The clinical programs here include a tax clinic and the Midwestern Innocence Project, which provides pro bono legal and investigative services to wrongfully convicted prisoners, although some students feel the school could place more of an emphasis on human rights law.

Life

The location in the heart of Kansas City is "unbeatable." The alumni "fill this city and because they love UMKC, they are willing to come back and help all of the current students." Students believe "being centered in KC gives [us] the most opportunity to integrate into the KC legal community." As to the state of the facilities, they note that "besides our beautiful courtroom, our décor needs an update. However, that obviously isn't a necessity in an academic environment. Although I do think it might look poor compared to other, newer, beautiful schools that a prospective student might compare UMKC to." To be fair, students say, "Our dean is more worried about keeping our tuition down than updating a sofa and that is a decision I can stand behind."

As to what life at UMKC is like, well, "the people are the greatest strengths: In sum, "the professors are so experienced and approachable, and the staff is so helpful. The students are kind and supportive of each other. The staff and faculty work really hard to intentionally create a positive environment for learning. Also, the location is great. The school is in close proximity to lots of courts, in both Missouri and Kansas, and lots of large and small law firms. The school has a great relationship with the larger legal community which makes it much easier for students to find opportunities for practical experience." The institution "also has three publications in which students can be involved" as well as "spectacular" opportunities to spend the summer abroad. Those options include a program that takes students on a whirlwind tour of Ireland (with a stop in Wales) and an "outstanding" Beijing program "at China's premier university," which offers lectures in the mornings and cultural field trips in the afternoons.

Getting In

Admitted students at the 25th percentile have LSAT scores of 150, and undergraduate GPAs of about 2.9. At the 75th percentile, LSAT scores are around 154 and GPAs are about 3.5. Part-time stats are typically a little lower.

Clinical program required	No
Legal writing course requirement	Yes
Legal methods course requirement	Yes
Legal research course requirement	Yes
Moot court requirement	Yes
Public interest law requirement	No

ADMISSIONS

Selectivity Rating	81
# applications received	566
% applicants accepted	55
% acceptees attending	48
Average LSAT	152
Median LSAT	152
LSAT Range (25th to 75th percentile)	150–154
Average undergrad GPA	3.21
Median undergrad GPA	3.21
Application fee	$60
Transfer students accepted	Yes
Evening division offered	No
Part-time accepted	Yes
CAS accepted	Yes

International Students

TOEFL required of international students.	Yes

FINANCIAL FACTS

Annual tuition (in-state/ out-of-state)	$17,082/$33,726
Books and supplies	$1,145
Fees	$1,384
Room & Board (on/ off campus)	$10,610/$9,402
Financial aid application deadline	3/1
% first-year students receiving some sort of aid	94
% all students receiving some sort of aid	88
% of aid that is merit based	21
% receiving scholarships	51
Average grant	$12,322
Average loan	$1,463
Average total aid package	$35,264
Average debt	$97,139

EMPLOYMENT INFORMATION

Career Rating	87	
Total 2014 JD Grads	143	
% for whom you have useable information	100	
% grads employed ten months out	90	
# employed full-time	122	
# employed part-time	6	
# employed bar required	94	
# employed JD preferred	26	
# employed professional/other	4	
# employed non-professional	4	
# pursuing advanced degree	2	
# unemployed and seeking employment	12	
# not seeking employment	1	
% grads employed by school	1	
State for bar exam	MO, KS, CO, IL, CA	
Pass rate for first-time bar	90.0	

Prominent Alumni
Harry S. Truman, President of the United States; Charles E. Whittaker, U.S. Supreme Court Justice; Clarence Kelley, FBI Director; Lyda Conley, First Native American Woman Lawyer; H. Roe Bartle, Mayor of Kansas City

Grads Employed by Field (%)
Academic (2)
Business/Industry (24)
Government (12)
Judicial Clerkship (10)
Private Practice (40)
Public Interest (1)

UNIVERSITY OF NEBRASKA—LINCOLN
COLLEGE OF LAW

INSTITUTIONAL INFORMATION

Public/private	Public
% faculty part-time	51
% faculty female	36
% faculty underrepresented minority	1
Total faculty	55

SURVEY SAYS...
Great research resources

STUDENTS

Enrollment of law school	392
% male/female	61/39
% from out-of-state	25
% part-time	1
% underrepresented minority	6
% international	1
# of countries represented	3
Average age of entering class	24

ACADEMICS

Academic Experience Rating	**86**
Profs interesting rating	77
Profs accessible rating	91
Hours of study per day	3.43

Academic Specialties
Commercial, Corporation Securities, Environmental, International, Labor, Taxation, Intellectual Property

Advanced Degrees Offered
JD 3 yrs; MLS 1 yr; LLM in Space, Cyber & Telecommunications 1 yr

Combined Degrees Offered
JD/MBA, 4 yrs; JD/MPA, 4 yrs; JD/ MA or PhD Psychology, 4–6 yrs; JD/MRCP (Community & Regional Planning), 4 yrs; JD/MA Journalism, 4 yrs; JD/MA Political Science, 4 yrs; JD/MA Gerontoloty, 4 yrs; JD/ MPH, 4 yrs

Academics

The University of Nebraska College of Law offers a high-quality education at an unbeatable price. With costs and tuition totaling far less than comparable schools, one student incredulously declares, "Where else can you get a top-rate legal education for that cheap?" Students say that Nebraska offers a first-rate education with a "brilliant and very approachable" faculty and staff. "Not only are the professors walking through the library, talking to the students and answering questions, but the staff throughout the college is amazing."

The administration, faculty, and research staff undoubtedly serve as the law school's greatest assets. One student remarks, "Honestly, I don't think that one could find a better school administration or research librarians. They always meet you with a helpful smile," and are willing to do all that they can to assist students. Another notes, "The faculty and staff at Nebraska Law care about the success of each student," and help "student[s] find their place within the law." According to many, professors are "extremely engaging" and "are able to connect the subject matter to practical experience and real-life cases, which makes class more interesting."

Students warn, "The first year is extremely demanding," but one seasoned 3L reassures us, "During my three years at UNL, most of my classes have been very interesting. Some of them have changed my life and outlook on the world." Students rave about Nebraska's prosecutorial clinic, as it is one of the few of its kind amongst an array of defense clinics. One student emphatically declares it "the best class that I took at UNL. Another student is of the opinion that though "there are a lot of classes in varying subjects, [the law school] is lacking in public interest/pro bono–type classes or topics for students wanting a different type of experience," though the school's Pro Bono Initiative has helped ameliorate matters, including an Immigration Clinic where students work with low-income clients.

Students are divided when it comes to the subject of employment after graduation. One student expresses an appreciation for "how UNL is trying to branch out and help students land jobs outside of Nebraska." Another argues that while "the school is great for finding jobs for students with higher grades that want to stay in Nebraska," "there is not enough emphasis on employment after law school if a student wants to work in public interest." One 3L would like "employers more involved in recruiting for clerkships," but in the same breath concedes that "most [students] were able to get clerkships if they wanted them as a 2L."

"It's great having brand new classrooms and facilities, as well as complete access to technology anywhere in the building." The almost fully renovated classrooms are "extremely comfortable" and "all have wireless access and plugs for laptops." Overall, students seem content with the refurbished facilities and as one satisfied 1L affirms, "After six years on the East Coast, the beautiful library and outstanding professors made returning to the Midwest an easy decision."

Tracy Warren, Assistant Dean for Admissions
P.O. Box 830902, Lincoln, NE 68583-0902
Tel: 402-472-2161 • Fax: 402-472-5185
E-Mail: lawadm@unl.edu • Website: law.unl.edu

Life

"UNL recruits some very intelligent and exceptionally talented students," and students agree, "The law school does a really good job of creating community among the students." Specifically, the small class size creates a "close-knit group mentality" and particularly helpful is the practice of scheduling first years "so they have at least one class with most of the students" in their cohort. One reassured student remarks from experience, "I know that if I need any help, albeit from a librarian, administrator, faculty member, or fellow law student, that I will receive it."

There is no shortage of social opportunities at Nebraska. "People take the initiative to organize mixers and activities to help people get to know one another and to keep law school stress at bay as much as possible." The SBA, Women's Law Caucus and American Constitution Society and the law fraternities routinely host speakers, discussion panels and philanthropic events. Academic groups like Moot Court and Client Counseling also bring students together in social-academic environments that don't revolve around the bar scene. The bottom line remains clear as expressed in one student's words, "students aren't just classmates—we're friends."

Getting In

LSAT scores and undergraduate GPA are the main factors that the Admissions Committee considers when evaluating applications. Admitted students at the 25th percentile have an LSAT score of 152 and a GPA of 3.41. Admitted students at the 75th percentile have an LSAT score of 159 and a GPA of 3.88. The law school tries hard to create a class that is diverse.

Clinical program required	No
Legal writing course requirement	Yes
Legal methods course requirement	No
Legal research course requirement	Yes
Moot court requirement	No
Public interest law requirement	No

ADMISSIONS

Selectivity Rating	86
# applications received	825
% applicants accepted	48
% acceptees attending	32
Median LSAT	157
LSAT Range (25th to 75th percentile)	153–159
Median undergrad GPA	3.51
Application fee	$50
Regular application deadline	3/1
Transfer students accepted	Yes
Evening division offered	No
Part-time accepted	No
CAS accepted	Yes

International Students

TOEFL required of international students.	Yes

FINANCIAL FACTS

Annual tuition (in-state/ out-of-state)	$10,783/$26,862
Books and supplies	$1,378
Fees	$3,104
Room & Board (on/ off campus)	$14,310/$13,858
Financial aid application deadline	5/1
% of aid that is merit based	93
% receiving scholarships	51
Average loan	$8,200
Average debt	$22,196

EMPLOYMENT INFORMATION

Career Rating	84
Total 2014 JD Grads	130
% for whom you have useable information	75
% grads employed ten months out	88
Median starting salary	$50,000
% job accepting grads providing useable salary information	63
# employed full-time	106
# employed part-time	8
# employed bar required	82
# employed JD preferred	16
# employed professional/other	8
# employed non-professional	8
# pursuing advanced degree	2
# unemployed and seeking employment	9
# not seeking employment	1
State for bar exam	NE, IA, MO, SD, CO
Pass rate for first-time bar	91.0

Prominent Alumni

Ted Sorensen, Special Counsel to President John F. Kennedy; Harvey Perlman, Chancellor, University of Nebraska—Lincoln; Ben Nelson, U.S. Senator and former Governor of Nebraska; Connie Collingsworth, General Counsel and Secretary for the Bill & Melinda Gates Foundation; Michael Hevican, Chief Justice of the Nebraska Supreme Court

Grads Employed by Field (%)

Academic (2)
Business/Industry (25)
Government (13)
Judicial Clerkship (3)
Private Practice (49)
Public Interest (6)

UNIVERSITY OF NEVADA—LAS VEGAS
WILLIAM S. BOYD SCHOOL OF LAW

INSTITUTIONAL INFORMATION

Public/private	Public
% faculty part-time	5
% faculty female	41
% faculty underrepresented minority	19
Total faculty	58

SURVEY SAYS...
Diverse opinions accepted in classrooms

STUDENTS

Enrollment of law school	157
% male/female	56/44
% from out-of-state	29
% part-time	30
% underrepresented minority	35
% international	0
Average age of entering class	25

ACADEMICS

Academic Experience Rating	**82**
Profs interesting rating	67
Profs accessible rating	72
Hours of study per day	NR

Combined Degrees Offered
JD/MBA 4 yrs; JD/MSW 4 yrs; JD/PhD in Education 4 yrs

Academics

ABA-accredited in 2003, many students feel, "The greatest strength of Boyd is its new-ness," which lends a sense of optimism, excitement, and challenge to the campus. Because it's not "steeped in tradition, there's an entrepreneurial spirit here. Everyone senses we're building something special." With a quality teaching staff, top-notch facili-ties, a talented student body, and reasonable tuition costs, students are confident that their school will continue to climb in the ranks. In fact, this sense of excitement extends throughout the city and state. Boyd is the only law school in Nevada; students report, "The legal community and the community in general are excited to have us here and the whole city [and state] is invested in all of us succeeding."

Professors boast impressive educational and professional backgrounds and are known to be both "intelligent and well-respected in their fields." More important, they are "stimulating individuals who are skilled teachers." Students are "consistently amazed by the ease with which the faculty so effectively employs the Socratic Method, such that the student body...is able to break down even the most complex legal scenarios and digest them as fully understandable rules and concepts." Outside the classroom, "professors are extremely approachable, even for a shy student."

The administration is generally regarded as "accessible and very pro-student." A 2L affirms, "The administrators I deal with on any sort of regular basis are fantastic. Not only do they know their stuff; they are anxious to help and are just all-around fabulous people." Students particularly applaud the efforts the administration has made to help new students make the transition into law school, citing the "optional thirty-minute classes once a week where we are taught exam skills, note-taking, and outlining tips."

Classrooms at Boyd are "new and clean" and very high-tech. The "top quality facili-ties" include "wireless Internet and cable Internet hook-ups throughout the building," as well as "a state-of-the-art library." Off campus, students say, "Being the only law school in Nevada, in the middle of one of the fastest-growing economies in the United States, opportunities abound." For example, UNLV students "have opportunities for something close to eighty-five judicial externships each year (out of a class of 150)" and addition-ally "have extraordinary access to the local, regional, and state governments." When it comes to landing a job after graduation, UNLV is extremely well located. In the city of Las Vegas, "The local law firms are eager to hire graduates, and the private sector oppor-tunities in gaming, hospitality, real estate, corporate, entertainment, and litigation are abundant and highly lucrative."

Elizabeth Karl, Admissions & Records Assistant
4505 Maryland Parkway, Box 451003, Las Vegas, NV 89154-1003
Tel: (702) 895-2440 • Fax: (702) 895-2414
E-Mail: request@law.unlv.edu • Website: www.law.unlv.edu

Life

While located in the heart of Las Vegas, "Most of the students commute into campus… and that can put a strain on the nearby social scene." In lieu of a hopping campus life, "Student organizations are great and have become central to social events at the school." Students have no trouble making friends among their interesting and talented classmates since "The people make the school." One student writes, "I love coming to school because I've made really great friends and don't mind seeing them everyday."

Commuter student or not, "Being in the center of Las Vegas, there is always something to do and somewhere new to go." You may be surprised to learn, however, that law school in Sin City is actually quite serious. Some students feel the competitiveness is a product of the high caliber of the student body. A 1L explains particularly in the school's early years many "of the students in the entering class are in their forties, and several of them are doctors and dentists, so the bar is set quite high." Though the level of commitment remains the same, the profile of the average entrant may have changed over time as the school's applicant pool has widened in terms of age and experience. In addition to their diligence, UNLV students are a fairly homogenous and quite conservative group. One student points out that some of "the faculty is comprised of very liberal individuals from a diverse background, whereas a majority of the students are very conservative and tend to have similar life experiences."

Getting In

When selecting applicants, the Admissions Committee looks for students with demonstrated academic capability, including depth and breadth of undergraduate course work, grades, concurrent work experience, and extracurricular activities. The school also considers non-academic factors, such as community service and work experience. Older students should feel particularly welcomed at Boyd.

Clinical program required	No
Legal writing course requirement	Yes
Legal methods course requirement	Yes
Legal research course requirement	Yes
Moot court requirement	No
Public interest law requirement	Yes

ADMISSIONS

Selectivity Rating	91
# applications received	1,755
% applicants accepted	23
% acceptees attending	39
Average LSAT	158
LSAT Range (25th to 75th percentile)	155–160
Average undergrad GPA	3.44
Application fee	$50
Regular application deadline	3/15
Regular notification	4/30
Transfer students accepted	Yes
Evening division offered	Yes
Part-time accepted	Yes
CAS accepted	Yes

FINANCIAL FACTS

Annual tuition (in-state/ out-of-state)	$18,000/$30,000
Books and supplies	$1,080
Fees	Approx. $500
Room & Board	$8,370
Financial aid application deadline	2/1
% first-year students receiving some sort of aid	88
% all students receiving some sort of aid	86
% of aid that is merit based	90
% receiving scholarships	33
Average grant	$7,400
Average loan	$26,200
Average total aid package	$28,000
Average debt	$55,700

EMPLOYMENT INFORMATION

Career Rating	81	Grads Employed by Field (%)
% grads employed ten months out	94	Academic (2)
Median starting salary	$75,532	Business/Industry (12)
State for bar exam	NV, AZ, UT, CA	Government (10)
Pass rate for first-time bar	75.0	Judicial Clerkship (16)
		Private Practice (55)
		Public Interest (4)

UNIVERSITY OF NEW HAMPSHIRE
SCHOOL OF LAW

INSTITUTIONAL INFORMATION

Public/private	Public
Affiliation	No Affiliation
Student-faculty ratio	15:1
% faculty part-time	42
% faculty female	44
% faculty underrepresented minority	5
Total faculty	57

SURVEY SAYS...
Diverse opinions accepted in classrooms

STUDENTS

Enrollment of law school	273
% male/female	59/41
% from out-of-state	72
% part-time	1
% underrepresented minority	13
% international	2
# of countries represented	9
Average age of entering class	26

ACADEMICS

Academic Experience Rating	87
Profs interesting rating	81
Profs accessible rating	88
Hours of study per day	5.05

Academic Specialties
Commercial, Criminal, Human Rights, International, Intellectual Property

Advanced Degrees Offered
MIP (Intellectual Property), 1 yr; MCT (Commerce & Technology Law), 1 yr; MICL&J (Criminal Law & Justice), 1 yr; LLM Intellectual Property, 1 yr; LLM Commerce & Technology Law, 1 yr; LLM Int'l Criminal Law & Justice, 1 yr; Diploma in Intellectual Property, 6 mos.

Combined Degrees Offered
JD/MBA, 3.5 yrs; JD/MSW, 3.5 yrs; JD/LLM Intellectual Property, JD/LLM in Commerce & Technology Law, and JD/LLM in International Criminal Law & Justice: all 3 yrs.

Academics

The University of New Hampshire is the only law school in the state, yet it attracts a high class of students from all over the country, primarily due to its focus on creating "practice-ready" lawyers and because of its Intellectual Property Program, which "is by far the greatest strength of this school." There are many resources available to students when it comes to IP: the library is the biggest IP library in the U.S., "many graduates are willing to speak to us about their experience," and the program in Commerce and Technology includes a razor edge focus on e-Law.

The school has an "excellent focus on practice," which is buoyed by its externship programs and allows students to work in their fields of interest for up to a full semester while receiving credit. The Daniel Webster Scholar Honors Program "offers every real world experience a future attorney could ask for" and is the only practice-based bar exam alternative in the nation. The emphasis on practical, skills-based lawyering "is not just an advertisement—it really happens in the classroom." There are "endless" internship, externship, and clinical opportunities, as well as a number of classes that focus on what you will do in practice, rather than just theory. "If a student evades a tough question, the professor will often ask 'What would you tell your client?'" "I really enjoy learning how we'll be able to apply what we learn in the real world," says a student.

Small class size means the "dynamic, high energy" faculty "really gets to know the students." Everybody at UNH Law is very accessible. "I even see the Dean walking around in the hallways," says a 1L. "Many professors have an open door policy," and "there are teaching assistants who can help you in the rare times when you can't find the professor." "There was never a time when I needed to locate someone and I just couldn't," says a student. Some professors even give out their phone numbers "just in case," and students "don't have to fight through twenty-three TAs before actually getting in touch with them." One contracts professor even stays until 11 P.M. at times when students need help preparing for finals. Several students take note and appreciate this apparent dedication. Almost all of the professors still practice or have practiced before they begin teaching, which allows them "actual practice-based knowledge to share with the students, [which is] a huge asset to the student body." Similarly, "the administration and overall management of our school is great." "Because it's such a small school, you know all of the administrative staff, and they are very responsive to your needs," says a 2L.

As the main legal game in the state, the school attracts "a wide variety of speakers from judges, governors, senators, to well known commentators in the legal field on a weekly basis," which makes for "endless opportunities for networking as a result." Some externs are sent to the New Hampshire Supreme Court, and students "also have the ability to extern at the first circuit and other federal courts;" however, some feel like other concentrations of law besides IP "could use a little boost." "If one was to practice something else and travel out of state they might not have much luck," says a student.

ROBIN INGLI, ASSISTANT DEAN FOR ADMISSIONS
TWO WHITE STREET, CONCORD, NH 03301
TEL: 603-513-5300 • FAX: 603-513-5234
E-MAIL: ADMISSIONS@LAW.UNH.EDU • WEBSITE: WWW.LAW.UNH.EDU

Life

The school has "a strong sense of community," and although it "has limited facilities" due to its size ("the building is very nice; not too big and not too small"), the facilities the school does have "are pristine, and run very smoothly," including a "beautiful" courtroom that is available for students to use whenever a class is not in session. The "close-knit" Concord coterie means that plenty of campus life takes place off-campus. "I frequently see professors and fellow students working out at the local YMCA," says a student. Concord "doesn't have a great night life, but there are plenty of things to do here." The bars that are here "are enough to keep you satisfied," and "there are also a lot of great things to do around the city that don't involve drinking." Parking can sometimes be problematic, but "most students walk to school."

The "intimate environment" fostered on campus is apparent everywhere. "Professors interact with the students outside of class on a daily basis and seem to generally care about how each student is doing." The student body itself is composed of "diverse groups of students of all ages and from all backgrounds." Although the students are competitive, they "all get along well and work together, creating a strong network in the long term." Most of the students here are right out of undergrad or have spent one to two years outside of school before applying to law school.

Getting In

The school's Intellectual Property program is a huge draw to students from all over the country, so residence is irrelevant and acceptance is fairly easy; around one out of every two students gets in. A B-average and a decent LSAT score should do the trick numerically, but beyond that, UNH Law has a very small admissions department that carefully reviews applications to make sure that the student will bring a fresh perspective and added ambition to the mix. Note: there is no part-time program or spring entry.

Clinical program required	No
Legal writing course requirement	Yes
Legal methods course requirement	Yes
Legal research course requirement	Yes
Moot court requirement	Yes
Public interest law requirement	No

ADMISSIONS

Selectivity Rating	84
# applications received	664
% applicants accepted	54
% acceptees attending	22
Average LSAT	157
Median LSAT	157
LSAT Range (25th to 75th percentile)	153–159
Average undergrad GPA	3.39
Median undergrad GPA	3.39
Application fee	$55
Regular application deadline	4/1
Transfer students accepted	Yes
Evening division offered	No
Part-time accepted	No
CAS accepted	Yes

International Students

TOEFL required of international students.	Yes

FINANCIAL FACTS

Annual tuition (in-state/ out-of-state)	$37,100/$41,100
Books and supplies	$1,448
Fees	$90
Room & Board	$10,998
Financial aid application deadline	3/1
% first-year students receiving some sort of aid	96
% all students receiving some sort of aid	93
% of aid that is merit based	85
% receiving scholarships	83
Average grant	$8,272
Average loan	$43,245
Average total aid package	$60,184
Average debt	$116,234

EMPLOYMENT INFORMATION

Career Rating	95
Total 2014 JD Grads	107
% for whom you have useable information	93
% grads employed ten months out	86
Median starting salary	$83,400
% job accepting grads providing useable salary information	52
# employed full-time	87
# employed part-time	4
# employed bar required	78
# employed JD preferred	8
# employed professional/other	2
# employed non-professional	3
# pursuing advanced degree	2
# unemployed and seeking employment	8
# not seeking employment	5
State for bar exam	NH, MA, NY, VA, TX
Pass rate for first-time bar	80.3

Prominent Alumni

Dawn Buonocore-Atlas, VP-Enforcement and Assistant General Counsel, Calvin Klein; Donna Edwards, US Representative-Maryland; David Koris, General Counsel, Shell International; Tim Ryan, US Representative-Ohio; Douglas Wood, Partner, Reed Smith

Grads Employed by Field (%)

Academic (2)
Business/Industry (21)
Government (7)
Judicial Clerkship (2)
Private Practice (47)
Public Interest (7)

UNIVERSITY OF NEW MEXICO
SCHOOL OF LAW

INSTITUTIONAL INFORMATION

Public/private	Public
Affiliation	No Affiliation
% faculty part-time	50
% faculty female	55
% faculty underrepresented minority	32
Total faculty	66

SURVEY SAYS...
Strong sense of community

STUDENTS

Enrollment of law school	347
% male/female	50/50
% from out-of-state	6
% part-time	0
% underrepresented minority	49
% international	3
# of countries represented	1
Average age of entering class	30

ACADEMICS

Academic Experience Rating	86
Profs interesting rating	81
Profs accessible rating	88
Hours of study per day	3.70

Academic Specialties
Environmental

Advanced Degrees Offered
JD 3 yrs FT, 5 yrs PT

Combined Degrees Offered
JD/MBA, JD/MA in Latin American Studies, JD/MA in Public Administration, JD/MA in Accounting: 4 yrs.

Academics

The University of New Mexico School of Law stands out for how accommodating the program is for its students. With classes in Indian Law and natural resources, and "hands-on" clinical opportunities for students, UNM "takes a supportive and collaborative approach to teaching law." UNM is the only law school in the state, which makes it feel "like the entire legal community is involved in a UNMSOL student's legal education." Students have come to expect "representatives of all areas and levels of the NM legal system to participate in some way." The law school regularly hosts a range of legal professionals: "With the New Mexico Court of Appeals adjacent to the law school, appellate judges sometimes teach classes, coach moot court, and are otherwise uniquely available to students. UNMSOL students have unparalleled opportunity to be directly involved with the state's legal system." Students are continually impressed by UNM's network, including the "accessible" professors. Law students feel as if they can easily discuss issues with the faculty: "Everyone is willing to discuss and answer questions, even if you run into them in the halls," and "almost all employ an open-door policy."

The mentorship continues across the student body as well, since all required 1L courses "have a 2L tutor . . . to answer questions, give reviews throughout the semester, and help in the learning of certain subtopics." The administration "incorporates the student voices into various aspects of the school." Many students are from New Mexico, and most students agree that "UNM is a gem generally hidden to those outside the state."

Students feel happy with the career services office, but feel like they could do more to support students. UNM has "a strong tribal law department, and therefore have a handful of native professors." Even so, some students point out that "diverse perspectives in the faculty will only strengthen those characteristics in the professors who are shaping our learning." And again, no student has to struggle to find their professors when they need them. "No one, not even the Dean, is more than an e-mail or phone call away. The faculty is not only receptive to student needs but welcomes it and solicits it."

As for curriculum, several students point out the need for more legal research and writing access, and say "focusing on legal research earlier in the curriculum might be a good idea to help 1Ls navigate through their first year of school." Most students would like improvement with food ("some of the faculty have tried to alleviate the problem by bringing in food trucks") and the wireless capabilities, and feel that the "building itself could use some upgrades. . . . it shows its age."

JEFFREY DUBINSKI-NEESEN, ASSISTANT DEAN FOR ADMISSIONS & FINANCIAL AID
MSC 11-6070, 1 UNIVERSITY OF NEW MEXICO, ALBUQUERQUE, NM 87131-0001
TEL: 505-277-0958 • FAX: 505-277-9958
E-MAIL: ADMISSIONS@LAW.UNM.EDU • WEBSITE: LAWSCHOOL.UNM.EDU

Life

As one 2L student puts it, "We are competitive . . . but the supportive friends I have made have been at least as much a part of my success as the supportive professors." The law school "is a very special place," where students are taught to be "amazing and strong legal advocates." Everyone's "skills and strengths are analyzed and amplified to the highest degree possible for the individual." Even better, UNM is located in Albuquerque, "one of the coolest places to live, ever."

All told, "UNM is very integrated with the local legal community." Students get to engage with activities and already feel like they're a part of the system before graduation, which makes a huge difference to a student's career. As another student told us, "The community cares about the law students and the school does a great job of fostering the connections." Finally, another student succinctly defined UNM: "In a word, support, support, support."

Getting In

According to current students, "UNM gives a large benefit to applicants from New Mexico." UNM is proud of its diverse population, but considers all students based on LSAT scores, undergraduate GPAs and student essays. The median GPA was 3.43 for the last incoming class, and student LSAT scores ranged from 150 (25th percentile) to 157 (75th percentile).

Clinical program required	Yes
Legal writing course requirement	Yes
Legal methods course requirement	No
Legal research course requirement	Yes
Moot court requirement	No
Public interest law requirement	No

ADMISSIONS

Selectivity Rating	84
# applications received	638
% applicants accepted	44
% acceptees attending	40
Average LSAT	153
Median LSAT	153
LSAT Range (25th to 75th percentile)	150–157
Average undergrad GPA	3.39
Median undergrad GPA	3.43
Application fee	$50
Regular application deadline	2/15
Transfer students accepted	Yes
Evening division offered	No
Part-time accepted	No
CAS accepted	Yes

International Students

TOEFL required of international students.	Yes

FINANCIAL FACTS

Annual tuition (in-state/ out-of-state)	$15,701/$33,971
Books and supplies	$1,187
Fees	$550
Room & Board (on/ off campus)	$8,454/$9,058
Financial aid application deadline	3/1
% first-year students receiving some sort of aid	94
% all students receiving some sort of aid	90
% of aid that is merit based	27
% receiving scholarships	59
Average grant	$7,372
Average loan	$24,211
Average total aid package	$26,268
Average debt	$71,029

EMPLOYMENT INFORMATION

Career Rating	94
Total 2014 JD Grads	111
% for whom you have useable information	100
% grads employed ten months out	96
Median starting salary	$53,000
% job accepting grads providing useable salary information	88
# employed full-time	98
# employed part-time	9
# employed bar required	93
# employed JD preferred	11
# employed professional/other	2
# employed non-professional	1
# pursuing advanced degree	0
# unemployed and seeking employment	4
% grads employed by school	2
State for bar exam	NM, CO, AZ, TX, NV
Pass rate for first-time bar	85.5

Prominent Alumni
The Honorable Barbara J. Vigil, Chief Justice, New Mexico Supreme Court; Tom Udall, U.S. Senator, United States Senate; Michelle Lujan Grisham, U.S. Congresswoman, U.S. House of Representatives; John E. Echohawk, Executive Director, Native American Rights Fund; The Honorable Jimmie V. Reyna, Judge, United States Court of Appeals for the Federal Circuit

Grads Employed by Field (%)
Academic (2)
Business/Industry (8)
Government (34)
Judicial Clerkship (7)
Private Practice (40)
Public Interest (5)

THE UNIVERSITY OF NORTH CAROLINA AT CHAPEL HILL
SCHOOL OF LAW

INSTITUTIONAL INFORMATION

Public/private	Public
% faculty part-time	0
% faculty female	41
% faculty underrepresented minority	14
Total faculty	59

SURVEY SAYS...

*Students love Chapel Hill, NC,
Diverse opinions accepted in classrooms, Good social life*

STUDENTS

Enrollment of law school	737
% male/female	49/51
% from out-of-state	27
% part-time	0
% underrepresented minority	28
% international	1
# of countries represented	11
Average age of entering class	23

ACADEMICS

Academic Experience Rating	**96**
Profs interesting rating	94
Profs accessible rating	84
Hours of study per day	3.71

Academic Specialties

Civil Procedure, Commercial, Constitutional, Corporation Securities, Criminal, Environmental, Government Services, Human Rights, International, Labor, Legal History, Legal Philosophy, Property, Taxation, Intellectual Property

Advanced Degrees Offered

JD, 3 yrs

Combined Degrees Offered

JD/MBA, 4 yrs; JD/MPA, 4 yrs; JD/MPPS, 4 yrs; JD/MPH, 4 yrs; JD/MRP, 4 yrs; JD/MSW, 4 yrs; JD/MA S.A., 4 yrs; JD/MALS or MSIS, 4 yrs; JD/MAMC, 4 yrs

Academics

The School of Law at The University of North Carolina at Chapel Hill is, according to students, "one of the best public law schools in the country." Many claim that "the faculty here couldn't be more down to earth and accessible." They have "a literal 'my-door-is-open-all-the-time policy' and never hesitate to "[take] the time to talk to every single student before class." Still, some students feel that "there is a strong liberal bias at the school" and that professors sometimes "bring their political views with them into the classroom." To correct this, they are calling for the law school to "improve on fostering a more diverse political atmosphere." UNC Law's "excellent" and "accessible" administration is "unparalleled" in its efforts to promote a "positive and supportive environment for the study of law." Everyone here seems to practice "the 'We're all family at UNC' motto to a fault."

Most UNC survey respondents are pleased about their employment prospects. One student credits the Career Services Office as being "the greatest strength of UNC. Even when they are too busy for a brief meeting about résumés or cover letters, you can just leave your stuff under the door, and someone will get it back to you by the next day with recommendations about what you should fix." However, some feel that it could "stand to improve, particularly with communicating jobs to 1Ls." Jobs in North Carolina and neighboring states are fairly abundant, though, in large part because the law school maintains "strong connections" with in-state employers.

Student organizations and learning opportunities are aplenty. According to one student, "There are lots of organizations to get involved in, and the pro bono program is one of the best." About 73 percent of all students do some kind of pro bono work—many during the summer or during winter or spring breaks. Students who have performed more than seventy-five hours of pro bono service receive certificates of acknowledgment from the state bar association, and those who perform more than 100 hours of pro bono service get special shout-outs at graduation. Other notables include UNC's clinical programs, in which students handle more than 350 civil and criminal cases every year and "really get a lot of hands-on experience" along with "solid academic[s]" in the process. Joint-degree programs include the standard JD/MBA as well as Master of Public Policy science and a handful of others. UNC also offers a summer program and semester-long programs in Europe and Mexico.

The general consensus is that facilities at UNC are middling, but in terms of the availability of information, "the resources are outstanding." Also, "The school is improving the technology of each classroom every year." In the meantime, a cry of "more parking!" can be heard throughout campus.

MICHAEL J. STATES, JD, ASSISTANT DEAN FOR ADMISSIONS
CB# 3380, VAN HECKE-WETTACH HALL, UNC SCHOOL OF LAW—ADMISSIONS,
CHAPEL HILL, NC 27599-3380
TEL: 919-962-5109 • FAX: 919-843-7939
E-MAIL: LAW_ADMISSIONS@UNC.EDU • WEBSITE: WWW.LAW.UNC.EDU

Life

"Carolina offers a healthy balance between academic and student life." UNC is home to "diverse, interesting, charming, and intelligent people." One student exclaims, "I am constantly amazed by how interesting my classmates are." Most agree that "everyone gets along" in this "very friendly" and "very cooperative" academic atmosphere. "It is competitive but not necessarily with each other. It seems we all want to see everyone do well," explains one student.

Students insist that "there is no better college town in the United States than Chapel Hill," a Southern hamlet of about 54,000 souls that offers a good supply of part-time jobs, affordable housing, and a mild climate. These fine qualities have not gone unnoticed: *Money* magazine has before named the Raleigh-Durham-Chapel Hill area the "Best Place to Live in the South," in 2000, and *Sports Illustrated* named Chapel Hill "the Best College Town in America" a few years earlier. "It's a great place to live," says one student. "The people are amazing" and the "campus and city are breathtaking." As one student puts it, "While you don't go to law school for the social life, it makes a big difference to have something to do when you actually do find free time."

"Social life is good" at Chapel Hill because "on the whole, students are very social outside of class." There are always a multitude of "school-sponsored social events in town" and "parties being thrown by law students to celebrate a wide array of milestones" (for instance, there is a "we just took our second practice exam" party). However, some students lament that there is little to do "for someone who does not drink."

Getting In

While perhaps easier than you might think, admissions here is no cakewalk. Admitted students at the 25th percentile have an LSAT score of 161 and a GPA of 3.4. Admitted students at the 75th percentile have an LSAT score of 165 and a GPA of 3.8. If applying as a non-resident, keep in mind that you'll want to be ready to dazzle with your academic prowess as around 70 percent of each admitted year at Chapel Hill are residents of North Carolina, and competition for the remaining slots in the class is stiff.

EMPLOYMENT INFORMATION

Career Rating	96	Prominent Alumni
Total 2014 JD Grads	247	Jim Delany, Big 10 Conference Commissioner
% for whom you have useable		Grads Employed by Field (%)
information	39	Academic (1)
% grads employed ten months out	91	Business/Industry (18)
# employed full-time	206	Government (8)
# employed part-time	8	Judicial Clerkship (10)
# employed bar required	178	Federal: (7)
# employed JD preferred	23	State or local: (5)
# employed professional/other	2	Private Practice (48)
# employed non-professional	11	2-10: (14)
# pursuing advanced degree	6	11-25: (3)
# unemployed and seeking		26-50: (2)
employment	14	51-100: (2)
# not seeking employment	5	101-250: (4)
State for bar exam NC, NY, FL, GA, VA		251-500: (2)
Pass rate for first-time bar	93.0	501+: (12)

Clinical program required	No
Legal writing	
course requirement	Yes
Legal methods	
course requirement	No
Legal research	
course requirement	Yes
Moot court requirement	Yes
Public interest	
law requirement	No

ADMISSIONS

Selectivity Rating	95
# applications received	2,576
% applicants accepted	18
% acceptees attending	54
Median LSAT	163
LSAT Range (25th to	
75th percentile)	161–165
Median undergrad GPA	3.51
Application fee	$75
Regular application deadline	3/1
Transfer students accepted	Yes
Evening division offered	No
Part-time accepted	No
CAS accepted	Yes

International Students

TOEFL required of international	
students.	Yes

FINANCIAL FACTS

Annual tuition (in-state/	
out-of-state)	$19,012/$34,120
Books and supplies	$1,150
Room & Board	$14,990
Financial aid application	
deadline	3/1
% first-year students receiving	
some sort of aid	100
% all students receiving	
some sort of aid	92
% of aid that is merit based	11
% receiving scholarships	88
Average grant	$4,636
Average loan	$26,299
Average total aid package	$29,676
Average debt	$76,642

UNIVERSITY OF NORTH DAKOTA
SCHOOL OF LAW

INSTITUTIONAL INFORMATION

Public/private	Public
Student-faculty ratio	14:1
% faculty part-time	39
% faculty female	45
% faculty underrepresented minority	10
Total faculty	31

SURVEY SAYS...

Abundant externship/internship/ clerkship opportunities

STUDENTS

Enrollment of law school	231
% male/female	52/48
% from out-of-state	49
% part-time	0
% underrepresented minority	14
% international	6
# of countries represented	2
Average age of entering class	26

ACADEMICS

Academic Experience Rating	78
Profs interesting rating	77
Profs accessible rating	89
Hours of study per day	2.81

Advanced Degrees Offered
JD 3 yrs

Combined Degrees Offered
JD/MPA 4 yrs; JD/MBA 4yrs; JD/ Criminal Justice PhD 5 yrs

Academics

Located in Grand Forks, the "underrated" University of North Dakota School of Law is home to one of the smallest law student populations. The resulting small class sizes make for "a better learning experience" than some larger schools, as "you get to hear opinions from all of the students" rather than just a few. Those who attend UND relish the intimacy this affords. "The first year class starts at eighty-five students, and that is as high as it will go," says a student. "Anything beyond that would be too big." UND School of Law "will prepare you to be a real legal practitioner." "You will be confident in your ability to handle your clients when you graduate," says a 1L.

The professors here "are the school's greatest resource." These "wonderful" and "accessible" teachers "are very willing to just meet with students to chat," and the faculty offices are in a location that is "very inviting" to students. "They all know my name and are eager to meet whenever possible. This proved very helpful as a nervous 1L," says a student. Most have plenty of legal experience and are able to bring those experiences into the classroom in order to "help contextualize the complicated content in a way that allows the students to make sense of it." The deans are "very nice and personable," and the Dean has a "commanding presence;" she "is cleaning house of mediocre professor[s]," meaning that "newly hired professors are proving to be definitely outstanding and fresh." "The administration is similarly receptive, and "students are very involved in the process" of running the law school. Students are kept well-informed about administration through "Dean's forums, email, and word-of-mouth."

One of the greatest strengths of UND is "how well connected it is in the state of North Dakota." The federal externship program offers UND students opportunities that can be scarce at other law schools, and though students admit that the school's reputation has not exactly spread nationwide among employers, "North Dakotans take care of their own." The legal job market in the state is strong and "embraces us exclusively:" "UND grads hire UND grads." The state legislature is also very supportive, especially through its legislative internship semester program; however, as strong as in-state job prospects are, quite a few students feel that Career Services Office could do more for those students seeking to go further. "Individual work needs to be done by students who are looking to be employed outside of the state," says a student. "Most of the help this office provides is generic information regarding résumés, cover letters, etc." though the Director of Career Services does meet individually with each 1L student to discuss career goals and objectives.

The size allows for courses to be "conducted with the students needs as the focus," but it also implies that "specializ[ing] is very hard to do at this particular school." There are two certificate options through the school (in Native American law and another in Aviation law), but outside of those two areas, a student is hard pressed to focus on the curriculum unless he or she forms a project with a professor, "which does not happen often." For students who want to branch out, UND Law also supports student participation in study abroad programs sponsored by other ABA-accredited law schools.

The building classrooms are definitely "outdated," but "the school is making improvements." The School of Law plans to begin the 2015-2016 academic year in its newly renovated space, which will add classroom and meeting space, a modern teaching courtroom, and a new case study classroom, as well as a completely renovated suite for its Clinical Legal Education program. The library is an excellent resource—"far better than using the online tools. The library staff goes above and beyond to help the students find what they need."

BEN HOFFMAN, DIRECTOR OF ADMISSIONS & RECORDS
CENTENNIAL DRIVE, P.O. BOX 9003, GRAND FORKS, ND 58202
TEL: 701-777-2260 • FAX: 701-777-2217
E-MAIL: HOFFMAN@LAW.UND.EDU • WEBSITE: WWW.LAW.UND.EDU

Life

The combination of "low tuition for residents, low cost of living in North Dakota, [and a] booming economy in North Dakota" make UND Law a wise decision for in-state students and allows for a comfortable three years. The student body may "lack diversity" culturally, but there is "quite an age range," and though "everyone gets along great... there is a slight social divide." The younger students "have more time and freedom from familial obligations to go downtown on the weekends," but fun events also exist, which include: "the malpractice bowl, annual golf scramble, Halloween party. . . and numerous other student organization led gatherings that most, if not all, students attend." There is also an annual Art Auction in which the graduating class raises money for their graduation party and class gift to school. At this auction, students bid "on such things as gourmet dinner parties prepared by professors and held at their homes, ice climbing with a professor, bowling with a professor, or the dean's parking spot for a week."

Grand Forks itself "is a small town with few activities to speak of." The weather can really be "a downer," though students claim it helps motivate them to study. The overall small law school size "allows the student[s] to get to know everyone quite well if they choose to," which can create excellent friendships among "future colleagues," not to mention "a friendly, understanding, and cooperative atmosphere." "Personally, these relationships have been vitally important for my overall well-being and experience," says a first year student.

Getting In

The admissions committee considers the following when considering candidates for admission: LSAT scores, undergraduate GPAs, personal essays, and letters of recommendation. It also considers oral and written communication skills. For a recent entering class, the average undergraduate grade point average was 3.26 and the median LSAT score was 148.

Clinical program required	No
Legal writing course requirement	Yes
Legal methods course requirement	Yes
Legal research course requirement	Yes
Moot court requirement	No
Public interest law requirement	No

ADMISSIONS

Selectivity Rating	78
# applications received	323
% applicants accepted	56
% acceptees attending	40
Average LSAT	148
Median LSAT	148
LSAT Range (25th to 75th percentile)	143–152
Average undergrad GPA	3.26
Median undergrad GPA	3.25
Application fee	$35
Regular application deadline	4/1
Transfer students accepted	Yes
Evening division offered	No
Part-time accepted	No
CAS accepted	Yes

FINANCIAL FACTS

Annual tuition (in-state/out-of-state)	$7,715/$20,601
Books and supplies	$1,533
Fees	$2,953
Room & Board	$8,520
% first-year students receiving some sort of aid	63
% all students receiving some sort of aid	77
% of aid that is merit based	20
% receiving scholarships	43
Average grant	$4,433
Average loan	$23,690
Average total aid package	$21,883
Average debt	$64,552

EMPLOYMENT INFORMATION

Career Rating	83	
Total 2014 JD Grads	76	
% for whom you have useable information	95	
% grads employed ten months out	86	
# employed full-time	58	
# employed part-time	3	
# employed bar required	47	
# employed JD preferred	5	
# employed professional/other	4	
# employed non-professional	4	
# pursuing advanced degree	1	
# unemployed and seeking employment	6	
# not seeking employment	4	
State for bar exam	ND, MN, AZ, WA, IN	
Pass rate for first-time bar	74.0	

Prominent Alumni
Hon. Kermit Bye, U.S. Circuit Judge, 8th Circuit Court of Appeals; Mark Chipman, Executive Chairman, True North Sports & Entertainment/Governor, Winnipeg Jets; Peter Pantaleo, Managing Partner, DLA Piper (New York); Rosanna Malouf Peterson, Chief Judge, U.S. District Court (E.D. Wa.); Hon. Gerald W. VandeWalle, Chief Justice, North Dakota Supreme Court

Grads Employed by Field (%)
Academic (2)
Business/Industry (21)
Government (8)
Judicial Clerkship (24)
Private Practice (42)

UNIVERSITY OF NOTRE DAME
LAW SCHOOL

INSTITUTIONAL INFORMATION

Public/private	Private
Affiliation	Roman Catholic
% faculty part-time	52
% faculty female	37
% faculty underrepresented minority	9
Total faculty	116

SURVEY SAYS...
Conservative students, Strong sense of community

STUDENTS

Enrollment of law school	549
% male/female	58/42
% from out-of-state	93
% part-time	0
% underrepresented minority	24
% international	2
# of countries represented	7
Average age of entering class	23

ACADEMICS

Academic Experience Rating	**93**
Profs interesting rating	95
Profs accessible rating	89
Hours of study per day	4.16

Academic Specialties
Constitutional, Corporation Securities, Criminal, Environmental, Human Rights, International, Legal Philosophy, Intellectual Property

Advanced Degrees Offered
LLM International Human Rights, 1 yr; JSD International Human Rights, 3 5 yrs including 2 yrs of residency; LLM International and Comparative Law, London campus only, 1 yr; LLM in U.S. Law, 1 yr

Combined Degrees Offered
JD/MBA, 4 yr and 3 yr-plus summer programs; JD/ME, 3 yrs; JD/MA in English, 3–4 yrs; JD/MS, 3–4 yrs; JD/PhD, varies.

Academics

Notre Dame, named for the Virgin Mary of the school's Catholic faith, provides a "great education," a "strong" brand, and "academic freedom" all tinged with a "Catholic character." The Catholic roots provide a "strong moral compass" and helps Notre Dame have "an intangible that you just can't put your finger on. It feels special." Notre Dame's great brand name comes complete with a "close-knit" and "nationwide" alumni base. This is "tremendously useful to young lawyers due to its active and engaged membership base" and "leads to stronger networking/ job opportunities." "The experience here has been second to none," a happy 1L says. Notre Dame "respects and encourages public service." One 3L says that "of all the law schools I contemplated attending, none respected and encouraged public service like Notre Dame."

Students rave about the school's facilities, dubbing them "state of the art," "top notch," "outstanding," and "of the highest caliber." "I don't think there is a better place to study law," one student says of the building. "The law school is still brand new" and the "beautiful" library is "conveniently located on campus." "The technology is top of the line" in this "spacious" "new" building, including "strong WiFi throughout and monitors/ projectors to assist in classroom presentation." "It's modern and yet has the rich feel of an old and prestigious school. It's like Hogwarts, especially during the winter," a 3L says while invoking *Harry Potter*.

The academic environment is one "where the faculty and administration truly care about the success and growth of their students." "While many law schools may be very cutthroat and competitive," a 3L explains, "Notre Dame emphasizes a more collaborative, cohesive atmosphere." Career services "is diligent and genuinely cares," while the administration is labeled by many as "superb." However, several students note that the "inaccessible" dean "has a very poor reputation amongst the students." The "outstanding faculty" gets high marks, "particularly the younger faculty." These "fantastic" professors are each "a distinguished scholar in the subject that they teach." The faculty garners "a great deal of respect" from the students, especially for how they are "willing to speak to students and help the students out in any way they can." "Sure, their résumés are astounding, but they also are dedicated to teaching," a 3L explains. If there is a downside, it is that the faculty have "a strong conservative and/or religious presence" and some students wish they would have a more balanced faculty and bring in "more professors with liberal perspectives." Most students label "the overall academic experience" as "very rewarding." As a 1L puts it: "Notre Dame Law has been around a long time—they know what they're doing."

JACOB BASKA, DIRECTOR OF ADMISSIONS AND FINANCIAL AID
NOTRE DAME LAW SCHOOL, P.O. BOX 780, NOTRE DAME, IN 46556
TEL: 574-631-6626 • FAX: 574-631-5474
E-MAIL: LAWADMIT@ND.EDU • WEBSITE: LAW.ND.EDU

Life

"The best part" of life at Notre Dame "is the community, which includes the students, faculty, and alumni. Everyone takes pride in being part of Notre Dame." "The student body is fairly relaxed" although the law school "needs to improve [its student body] diversity." "Everyone in the school seems to have the same socioeconomic background," a 3L says. In addition, students think it is time that the program stopped: The school's first LGBT group was established in the fall of 2013. Students love "the atmosphere" at Notre Dame. "Unlike other programs that are cut throat and uber-competitive, the class at Notre Dame bonds together in a very unique way" and consequentially "there is a high level of trust, honesty, and appreciation for one another" that is not present at all law schools. You cannot think about Notre Dame without thinking football, and students here love to go to games and shout "Go Irish."

Getting In

Notre Dame's strong brand is built on accepting only the strongest applicants. For a recent entering class, the range (25th to 75th percentile) in GPA and LSAT were 3.43 to 3.8 and 160 to 165 respectively. The school takes great pride in its mission as a Catholic Law School, and looks for students that will respect the traditions and goals that entails.

Clinical program required	No
Legal writing course requirement	Yes
Legal methods course requirement	No
Legal research course requirement	Yes
Moot court requirement	Yes
Public interest law requirement	No

ADMISSIONS

Selectivity Rating	92
# applications received	2,416
% applicants accepted	37
% acceptees attending	22
Median LSAT	163
LSAT Range (25th to 75th percentile)	160–165
Median undergrad GPA	3.64
Application fee	$75
Regular application deadline	3/15
Transfer students accepted	Yes
Evening division offered	No
Part-time accepted	No
CAS accepted	Yes

International Students

TOEFL required of international students.	Yes

FINANCIAL FACTS

Annual tuition	$50,040
Books and supplies	$9,960
Fees	$480
Room & Board (on/off campus)	$9,450/$9,450
Financial aid application deadline	2/28
Average debt	$111,310

EMPLOYMENT INFORMATION

Career Rating	96	
Total 2014 JD Grads	179	
% for whom you have useable information	100	
% grads employed ten months out	92	
Median starting salary	$79,500	
# employed full-time	163	
# employed part-time	1	
# employed bar required	147	
# employed JD preferred	14	
# employed professional/other	3	
# pursuing advanced degree	8	
# unemployed and seeking employment	7	
% grads employed by school	15	
State for bar exam	IL, NY, CA, IN, FL	
Pass rate for first-time bar	88.1	

Grads Employed by Field (%)

Academic (1)
Business/Industry (8)
Government (17)
Judicial Clerkship (12)
Federal: (8)
State or local: (4)
Private Practice (48)
2-10: (6)
11-25: (5)
26-50: (4)
51-100: (3)
101-250: (9)
251-500: (6)
501+: (15)
Public Interest (7)

UNIVERSITY OF OKLAHOMA
COLLEGE OF LAW

Academics

Students enjoy a "familial environment at [the University of Oklahoma College of Law] that isn't found elsewhere." A "a competitive program" in Norman, Oklahoma, OU Law is "affordable and practical" and "without the anxiety accompanied by many other similar programs." It boasts great regional prestige, an "expansive course selection covering a broad range of practice areas," as well as specialties like "the oil and gas programs and offerings [which] are some of the best in the country." The facilities are "absolutely breathtaking," including "a huge, beautiful courtroom that has been used by the Tenth Circuit to hold oral arguments." Students feel like they are part of a tightly knit community: "Each and every student is competitive, but with themselves—not each other" and "the deans know students by name, teach courses, and are active at almost all school activities, including competitions, guest speakers, awards luncheons."

Students claim to "have never had a 'bad' professor" and universally praise "the administration and support staff" as "phenomenal." Faculty and administrators are responsive to student needs and Dean Harroz "has made amazing changes and improvements at OU Law in just his fourth year as dean." Students agree that through these improvements the "administration has responded to the changing job market with moderated adjustments instead of overreaction or denial." One such improvement is the school's "Digital Initiative, which began in the fall of 2014" and "gave every student an iPad and access to several legal apps, as well as Microsoft Office." Students also enjoy "weekly training sessions on different [legal] apps" that help students understand how "to integrate technology into our future practice" and "to better associate ourselves with [the] technology and apps we will likely use at firms."

In the first year students take a core curriculum and "1Ls are split into four, thirty to forty person sections for [these] required courses." They agree that these sections "[allow] for greater visibility with faculty and "the benefit of the small section size can't be overstated." After that students can pursue a specialization and "certifications in various niche practice areas." In addition to the world-class programs in natural resources, students are drawn to "OU's amazing Native American Law program . . . and international human rights clinic." In addition, students say that the school has been developing other specialties: "OU's environmental law area has gotten pretty strong" and "the administration is encouraging about new courses, and is constantly working to offer additional joint programs, certificates in specialized areas, and practical experience opportunities." Indeed, students say that externship and clerkship opportunities are one of the school's greatest strengths, and "the opportunities to gain practical experience, are some of the best in the country." While students say "the Oklahoma Bar passage rate for OU students is high," they think the school "[needs] to provide more attention to out of state students that are trying to return to their home state." "Career services is good but not great," and students would like to see "more pairing with industry for internships and more pairing with firms for internships for those students not in the top 25 percent but who are fully capable of high quality work." But students also report getting summer internships through Career Services and the "administration brings in employers multiple times a week." Through the "Lunch and [Learn]" program students "get free food and listen to practicing attorneys as they discuss their field and potential internships."

Life

Students "couldn't ask for a better experience" than the "comfortable, relaxed pace that makes you feel at home and able to study or just hang out with friends between classes."

Everyone enjoys "[studying] together" and "[spending] time together outside of class." "We don't have a toxic atmosphere that some other law schools have," one current student explained. Instead of emphasizing "cut-throat" competition, the administration encourages students to "focus on building one another up," and students say this collegial atmosphere "contributes greatly to the school's and students' successes." In the weeks before classes start, "OU kind of beats the competitiveness out of the students" with "older mentors that speak with the sections" and emphasize the "how important it is" to cultivate "a reputation as a good person on top of being a hard worker."

While "the LLM programs bring in students from all across the county and the world to our campus," students still feel that "one of the downfalls is the lack of much racial/religious diversity." But the friendly atmosphere and "social life enables students to work hard at studying but also enjoy Norman's famous Campus Corner." The OU Law campus is "close enough to main campus that it has the university vibe, but far enough away that we are sheltered from all those undergrads." Ample parking makes it "easy to access," and "great amenities and resources like twenty-four-hour printing and the Amicus Cafe" keep students keep students productive. Administrators make it easy for students to organize study or group activities. "Any organization or group of students can reserve any classroom, study room, conference room, or even court room with ease." Local distractions like the "Norman Music Festival, the Huge Renaissance Fair, and local music and art scenes in Oklahoma City and the surrounding areas ensure there is never a shortage of various study breaks."

Getting In

Admission to the program is fairly selective. The average LSAT score for incoming students is 155-158, and the median GPA of the 2014 1L class was 3.52. The admissions committee does not average LSAT scores and only considers one's highest score. Students are admitted once a year for a fall start-date.

Clinical program required	No
Legal writing course requirement	Yes
Legal methods course requirement	No
Legal research course requirement	Yes
Moot court requirement	Yes
Public interest law requirement	No

ADMISSIONS

Selectivity Rating	88
# applications received	961
% applicants accepted	43
% acceptees attending	38
Median LSAT	157
LSAT Range (25th to 75th percentile)	155–158
Median undergrad GPA	3.52
Application fee	$50
Regular application deadline	3/15
Early application deadline	3/15
Transfer students accepted	Yes
Evening division offered	No
Part-time accepted	No
CAS accepted	Yes

International Students

TOEFL recommended of international students.	Yes

FINANCIAL FACTS

Annual tuition (in-state/out-of-state)	$14,190/$24,615
Books and supplies	$1,140
Fees	$5,783
Room & Board	$18,722
Financial aid application deadline	3/1
% first-year students receiving some sort of aid	82
% all students receiving some sort of aid	82
% of aid that is merit based	62
% receiving scholarships	75
Average grant	$5,650
Average loan	$27,338
Average total aid package	$29,220
Average debt	$81,789

EMPLOYMENT INFORMATION

Career Rating	92	
Total 2014 JD Grads	143	
% for whom you have useable information	100	
% grads employed ten months out	91	
Median starting salary	$56,000	
% job accepting grads providing useable salary information	92	
# employed full-time	124	
# employed part-time	6	
# employed bar required	107	
# employed JD preferred	15	
# employed professional/other	8	
# pursuing advanced degree	2	
# unemployed and seeking employment	10	
# not seeking employment	1	
% grads employed by school	1	
State for bar exam	OK, TX, MO, CA, CO	
Pass rate for first-time bar	89.1	

Prominent Alumni
David L. Boren, Pres. of OU (Former U.S. Senator); Frank Keating, Former Governor of Oklahoma

Grads Employed by Field (%)
Academic (2)
Business/Industry (14)
Government (14)
Judicial Clerkship (3)
Federal: (2)
State or local: (1)
Private Practice (56)
Public Interest (2)

UNIVERSITY OF OREGON
SCHOOL OF LAW

INSTITUTIONAL INFORMATION

Public/private	Public
% faculty part-time	50
% faculty female	41
% faculty underrepresented minority	12
Total faculty	58

SURVEY SAYS...
Liberal students, Strong sense of community, Good social life

STUDENTS

Enrollment of law school	372
% male/female	59/41
% from out-of-state	66
% part-time	0
% underrepresented minority	20
% international	1
# of countries represented	2
Average age of entering class	26

ACADEMICS

Academic Experience Rating	**82**
Profs interesting rating	73
Profs accessible rating	78
Hours of study per day	4.48

Academic Specialties
Civil Procedure, Commercial, Constitutional, Corporation Securities, Criminal, Environmental, Government Services, Human Rights, International, Property, Taxation, Intellectual Property

Advanced Degrees Offered
JD, LLM, Master's in Conflict and Dispute Resolution

Combined Degrees Offered
JD/MBA; JD/MCRP Community and Regional Planning; JD/MA or MS Conflict & Dispute Resolution; JD/MA or MS Environmental Studies; JD/MA International Studies; JD/MA or MS in Journalism; JD/MNM Nonprofit Management; JD/MPA; JD/MS Water Sciences w/ Oregon State University. All approx. 4 yrs.

Academics

As the state's only public law, the University of Oregon's School of Law provides numerous opportunities for interdisciplinary learning that go beyond the traditional curriculum (such as intersections with journalism, conflict resolution, and environmental studies), and a robust commitment to public service and public interest law. The school's clinics and externship opportunities and "amazing" legal writing and research program round out the affordable and respected degree on offer here.

Every faculty and staff member at Oregon is "extremely focused on the student experience." "You can always get ahold of your professor, and the Dean even holds office hours, allowing you to go and discuss whatever you'd like with him," says a student. For common occurrences like clinics, externships and registration, the "amazingly helpful" administration "has made everything flow very easily." Conversely, if you have a special situation, "administrators are always available to meet and discuss solutions with you." "The school is small enough that you really get to know the faculty and administration, and they will help you in any way they can to network and get jobs," says a 2L (though some admit that the school "could use more career services related to jobs out of state"). The school's major focus is on public interest law, but it has "a high number of specialized programs and great faculty that allow for students to get a great education in their area of interest," and "is very supportive of students who want to pursue non-Big Law careers."

The classroom experience is "very collaborative," and members of the "empowered student body" are supportive of one another all hours of the day. Students do worry that the University of Oregon (and law schools in general) are "not concerned enough about practical lawyering skills," and wish that the administration could hurry along the process for creating even more clinics. "In order for the legal job market to weather this ongoing crisis, law schools must take swift measures to make law schools more affordable, practical, and efficient," says one. Top programs and centers such as the Appropriate Dispute Resolution Center, the Wayne Morse Center for Law and Politics, and the Center for Law and Entrepreneurship's Small Business Clinic (which assists small and microbusinesses) help to offset this need and add to the school's reputation.

The law school has addressed these issues through offering nine different clinical opportunities each year wither between 110 and 180 seats. There is also a robust externship program. Top programs and centers such as the Appropriate Dispute Resolution Center, the Wayne Morse Center for Law and Politics, and the Center for Law and Entrepreneurship's Small Business Clinic (which assists small and microbusinesses) help to offset most other experiential complaints and add to the school's reputation.

LAWRENCE SENO, JR., ASSISTANT DEAN OF ADMISSIONS
1221 UNIVERSITY OF OREGON, EUGENE, OR 97403-1221
TEL: 541-346-3846 • FAX: 541-346-3984
E-MAIL: ADMISSIONS@LAW.UOREGON.EDU • WEBSITE: WWW.LAW.UOREGON.EDU

Life

Oregon is "a pretty white state," so "while the administration does a lot of outreach to attract minority students, the overall population is really white." The school and students may tend towards younger and liberal, but "there is a healthy dose of differing opinions and political backgrounds." The "tech-savvy" school "makes most students feel welcome in what is a very stressful environment:" "Everyone is very friendly," the law school "has a great vibe," the building is "amazing," and the library is "great." The city of Eugene itself is "generally a pretty great place to live," and students also get "free tickets to Ducks football," which helps relax the soul and bolster school spirit.

"Student groups are very active on campus," and this social bunch take advantage whenever they can find the time. The "geographically breathtaking location" provides "biking trails, hills to climb, [and]outdoor activities galore," which is par for the course of any Oregonian (less than half of the student body is an Oregon resident when they enroll).

Getting In

When applying to a strong law program located in a gorgeous setting, expect some competition. Oregon's admitted students at the 25th percentile have LSAT scores of 154 and GPAs of 3.09. Admitted students at the 75th percentile have LSAT scores of 159 and GPAs of 3.63.

Clinical program required	No
Legal writing course requirement	Yes
Legal methods course requirement	No
Legal research course requirement	Yes
Moot court requirement	No
Public interest law requirement	No

ADMISSIONS

Selectivity Rating	84
# applications received	1,140
% applicants accepted	54
% acceptees attending	19
Average LSAT	157
Median LSAT	157
LSAT Range (25th to 75th percentile)	154–159
Average undergrad GPA	3.26
Median undergrad GPA	3.33
Application fee	$50
Regular application deadline	3/1
Early application deadline	3/1
Transfer students accepted	Yes
Evening division offered	No
Part-time accepted	No
CAS accepted	Yes

International Students
TOEFL required of international students.	Yes

FINANCIAL FACTS

Annual tuition (in-state/out-of-state)	$30,586/$38,056
Books and supplies	$1,050
Fees	$1,732
Room & Board	$10,932
Financial aid application deadline	3/1
% first-year students receiving some sort of aid	96
% all students receiving some sort of aid	93
% of aid that is merit based	42
% receiving scholarships	81
Average grant	$16,637
Average loan	$30,069
Average total aid package	$34,912
Average debt	$105,777

EMPLOYMENT INFORMATION

Career Rating	80
Total 2014 JD Grads	184
% for whom you have useable information	97
% grads employed ten months out	80
Median starting salary	$51,000
# employed full-time	120
# employed part-time	28
# employed bar required	96
# employed JD preferred	45
# employed professional/other	4
# employed non-professional	3
# pursuing advanced degree	5
# unemployed and seeking employment	24
% grads employed by school	12
State for bar exam	OR, CA, WA, UT, AK
Pass rate for first-time bar	80.7

Prominent Alumni
Ron Wyden, U.S. Senator; Hon. John V. Acosta, United States Magistrate Judge; Jim Carter, VP & General Counsel, Nike; Ellen Rosenblum, Attorney General of the State of Oregon; Suzanne Bonamici, U.S. Representative

Grads Employed by Field (%)
Business/Industry (10)
Government (11)
Judicial Clerkship (15)
Federal: (1)
State or local: (14)
Other: (0)
Private Practice (26)
Solo: (3)
2-10: (11)
11-25: (4)
26-50: (2)
51-100: (2)
101-250: (2)
251-500: (1)
501+: (2)
Size Unknown: (1)
Public Interest (10)

UNIVERSITY OF THE PACIFIC
McGEORGE SCHOOL OF LAW

INSTITUTIONAL INFORMATION

Public/private	Private
Affiliation	No Affiliation
Student-faculty ratio	14:1
% faculty part-time	42
% faculty female	33
% faculty underrepresented minority	14
Total faculty	76

SURVEY SAYS...
Diverse opinions accepted in classrooms

STUDENTS

Enrollment of law school	152
% male/female	42/58
% from out-of-state	11
% part-time	22
% underrepresented minority	47
% international	2
# of countries represented	3
Average age of entering class	26

ACADEMICS

Academic Experience Rating	**76**
Profs interesting rating	83
Profs accessible rating	87
Hours of study per day	3.92

Academic Specialties
Appellate Advocacy, Business, Capital Lawyering, Environmental, Health, International, Taxation, Trial, Intellectual Property

Advanced Degrees Offered
JD, 3 yrs. JD, 4 yrs. JSD International Water Law 2–4 yrs. LLM Transnational Business Practice 1–2 yrs. MSL 1–2 yrs. LLM International Law 1–2 yrs. LLLM International Law 1 yr. LLM Public Law & Policy 1 yr. LLM Experiential Law Teaching 1 yr. LM in Water Resources, 1–2 yrs.

Combined Degrees Offered
JD/MBA, JD/MPPA, JD/MA or MS upon approval. All approx. 4 yrs.

Academics

Located in Sacramento, the state capital of California, Pacific McGeorge School of Law's proximity to the courts understandably leads to an emphasis on lawyering skills and the reality of legal practice. The unique locale also offers "amazing access to California state government opportunities," and its status as the "largest law school campus in the world" (resting on thirteen acres) is made even more resounding by the fact that the campus is solely a graduate campus. "No MBA students, undergrad, or the like—everyone here is either going through what you are or can help in some way," says a 1L.

Most here say that McGeorge's great strength is its "awesome professors." "Very few of them are the dry, stuffy professors you expect to have in law school"; instead, they're "witty, friendly, very accessible, and sociable." "It's refreshing to see that they don't take themselves too seriously. Law school is just that much more fun when a professor is willing to show up to class wearing a twisted-balloon bow tie," says a student. They "are always willing to meet and talk with a student" and also "great about not only attending school sponsored events but also show up to unofficial events." For the most part, the "strong trial advocacy programs" and comprehensive curriculum "is well tailored to the student body," and professors "want more than anything for us students to become that knowledgeable and quick."

Another strength is the faculty scholarship. "I am constantly recommending to friends at other law schools supplements that were authored by Pacific McGeorge faculty simply because they are the best supplements," says a second year. Administration is as accessible as the faculty, and even the Dean has held "a résumé review session to give individuals advice on their résumés." The writing program could use some work to become more flexible, according to some, because "although the program sounds good on paper, it fails to achieve its goals because of the way it is implemented." The global lawyering skills (GLS) program "emphasizes legal writing and oral argument, which is essential for becoming a skilled lawyer"; while it is not without its merits, many agree that it "takes up too many credit hours," and "the idea that it is known in the region is not, in all likelihood, a function of its success."

Classrooms are "nice and clean," and a renovation of the library has been completed: it is "large, aesthetic," and "gorgeous," making it "a good place to study." The library staff goes "above and beyond the call of duty in locating difficult-to-find sources." Job placements "could be much better," however, and students agree that a better reputation would help out greatly. "Your degree is only worth what job it gets you," says one. Luckily, for those remaining in the area, "the school faces little competition from other schools," and alumni "are always anxious to help out students." Some wish the bar passage rates would go up, and agree that "it would be helpful if we were specifically told which electives we should take that would increase our chances of passing the bar."

TRACY L. SIMMONS, ASSISTANT DEAN OF ADMISSIONS, DIVERSITY INITIATIVES ABD
3200 FIFTH AVENUE, SACRAMENTO, CA 95817
TEL: 916-739-7198 • FAX: 916-739-7301
E-MAIL: ADMISSIONSMCGEORGE@PACIFIC.EDU • WEBSITE: WWW.MCGEORGE.EDU

Life

The students in the "very welcoming community" of McGeorge are "great," and "experiences here are memorable," according to one. Students are "much less competitive than at the majority of other law schools;" there is "a much stronger sense of community, unlike the cutthroat atmosphere" at some other law schools. "I came to McGeorge for the atmosphere, and it hasn't disappointed. My 1L section was like family," says a second year student.

While the neighborhood around the school is "less than ideal," the campus "is constantly working to ensure the students feel safe," and public safety is "always available and easily accessible." There is a "lack of on-campus housing," so most students commute to school every day. The campus itself is lovely, with brick buildings, "massive trees," and a gorgeous quad with a gazebo. "The campus is extremely beautiful and it has all the resources one could wish for a law school to have," says a student. McGeorge also cares about the environment: there's an on-campus community garden and a student-run sustainability committee which works with the administration to make the school more sustainable.

Getting In

The most important factors in admissions' decisions are a student's previous academic record, LSAT scores, graduate school or post-college career experience, and community service or extracurricular activities. For last year's entering day class, LSAT scores at the 25th percentile were 148, and GPAs were 3.09; for the 75th percentile, LSATs were 155, and GPAs were 3.57. Although the admissions office has access to all LSAT scores (for applicants who take the test multiple times), the highest score is used for purposes of admission.

Clinical program required	Yes
Legal writing course requirement	Yes
Legal methods course requirement	Yes
Legal research course requirement	Yes
Moot court requirement	Yes
Public interest law requirement	No

ADMISSIONS

Selectivity Rating	74
# applications received	1,144
% applicants accepted	72
% acceptees attending	19
Average LSAT	152
Median LSAT	151
LSAT Range (25th to 75th percentile)	148–155
Average undergrad GPA	3.13
Median undergrad GPA	3.14
Application fee	$65
Regular application deadline	4/1
Early application deadline	2/1
Early application notification	4/1
Transfer students accepted	Yes
Evening division offered	Yes
Part-time accepted	Yes
CAS accepted	Yes

International Students
TOEFL required of international students.	Yes

FINANCIAL FACTS

Annual tuition	$46,462
Books and supplies	$2,075
Room & Board	$9,738
Financial aid application deadline	3/1
% first-year students receiving some sort of aid	100
% all students receiving some sort of aid	99
% of aid that is merit based	18
% receiving scholarships	78
Average grant	$18,281
Average loan	$46,083
Average total aid package	$69,163
Average debt	$140,517

EMPLOYMENT INFORMATION

Career Rating	78	**Prominent Alumni**
Total 2014 JD Grads	187	Scott Boras, Sports Agent/Baseball; Bill
% for whom you have useable information	97	Lockyer, Attorney General/CA Gvt; Steve Martini, Novelist
% grads employed ten months out	75	**Grads Employed by Field (%)**
Median starting salary	$57,492	Academic (3)
# employed full-time	126	Business/Industry (12)
# employed part-time	15	Government (17)
# employed bar required	89	Judicial Clerkship (2)
# employed JD preferred	41	Federal: (1)
# employed professional/other	9	Private Practice (36)
# employed non-professional	2	Solo: (3)
# pursuing advanced degree	1	2-10: (17)
# unemployed and seeking employment	35	11-25: (10)
# not seeking employment	2	26-50: (2)
% grads employed by school	2	51-100: (2)
State for bar exam	CA, NV, NY, MD, GA	101-250: (2)
Pass rate for first-time bar	73.0	501+: (1)
		Size Unknown: (1)
		Public Interest (5)

UNIVERSITY OF PENNSYLVANIA
LAW SCHOOL

INSTITUTIONAL INFORMATION

Public/private	Private
Affiliation	No Affiliation
% faculty part-time	49
% faculty female	30
% faculty underrepresented minority	14
Total faculty	146

SURVEY SAYS...

Great research resources, Abundant externship/internship/clerkship opportunities, Law school well run

STUDENTS

Enrollment of law school	756
% male/female	55/45
% part-time	0
% underrepresented minority	28
% international	3
Average age of entering class	24

ACADEMICS

Academic Experience Rating	**98**
Profs interesting rating	90
Profs accessible rating	86
Hours of study per day	3.99

Academic Specialties

Civil Procedure, Commercial, Constitutional, Corporation Securities, Criminal, Environmental, Government Services, Human Rights, International, Labor, Legal History, Legal Philosophy, Property, Taxation, Intellectual Property

Advanced Degrees Offered

JD; LLM; LL.C.M, SJD

Combined Degrees Offered

3 Year Programs: JD/MBA; JD/MA or MS Crim., JD/MSEd Ed. Policy; JD/MSEd Higher Ed.; JD/MES Environmental Studies; JD/MPA Government; JD/MA Int'l. Studies; JD/MBE Bioethics, JD/MSSP Social Policy; JD/MA Econ. Law w. Specialization in Global Governance; JD/MSW w/ a BSW; JD/LLM Hong Kong. OTHER: JD/MCIT Computing and Info. Tech.; JD/MCP City &

Academics

Founded in 1850, Penn Law is one of the country's most outstanding law schools, boasting a "stellar" academic reputation and a cross-disciplinary program nearly unrivalled by other schools. The school "has a lot of resources and ensures that it remains a place of cutting edge legal thinking and teaching," and the environment is one that fosters "academic success and personal friendships at the same time." Overall, the school is "the perfect mix of academic rigor, opportunity, and collegial environment," according to a 2L.

The professors are "incredible," comprising a faculty of "nothing but pure geniuses." They "genuinely care about the students and take the time to mentor them," and many seem "to genuinely enjoy working through legal issues or discussing legal scholarship with their students." Faculty members are "interesting people who've had extraordinary careers," and most feel that "it's an honor to learn from them." Students are also able to take classes outside of the law school in their second and third years in order to broaden their horizons. Beginning in Fall 2013 the legal practice skills program renamed and expanded the 1L legal writing curriculum. The appellate advocacy courses and moot court opportunities "are strong and can accommodate most if not all students who wish to participate." Clinics are "great...if you can get into one," as they tend to be small, meaning many students ultimately may not be able to capitalize on the school's strong clinical programming.

The "extremely visible" administration garners similar enthusiasm, delivering "excellence with a smile." They "consistently put in extra effort to improve your learning experience, to bring a speaker to the law school, or to implement a concern or suggestion you have to improve the law school." As examples, a student cites the staff member in the registrar's office who "emailed me a syllabus for a course I hoped to register for, so I could be current on the readings," and the times that "the library researchers will hold an impromptu meeting to help find a tricky resource." "It would be easy for Student Affairs to hear out student complaints or suggestions and never act on them. Our administrators, however, really seem invested in making this a positive experience for the students and respond with action a majority of the time."

There are "lots of pro bono opportunities" that provide practical experience, but a few students do wish that more practical opportunities were available, "particularly ones geared toward transactional, legal practice." Fortunately, professors are "very willing to help with clerkships, externships, and outside research." The lack of practical opportunities is the only resource complaint that Penn students have, yet many agree that the professors "make sure we have what we need and that we know how to use this stuff." Registering for classes can be "a hassle" though, and students gripe about the "archaic process" of having to go to the office and write your name on a waitlist, which is a slightly tedious process.

Penn alumni are very involved, returning to Penn Law to teach elective courses and to offer their support in the recruiting process; it is because of the alumni's solid reputation that "employers look at a résumé that has 'Penn Law' on it."

RENEE POST, ASSOCIATE DEAN, ADMISSIONS AND FINANCIAL AID
3501 SANSOM STREET, PHILADELPHIA, PA 19104-6204
TEL: 215-898-7400 • FAX: 215-898-9606
E-MAIL: CONTACTADMISSIONS@LAW.UPENN.EDU • WEBSITE: WWW.LAW.UPENN.EDU

Life

"I love being at Penn," says a happy student. "The size of the student body is large enough that I am still meeting people, but small enough that it feels like a real community." Penn is composed of "superbly accomplished individuals who are relatively humble about their achievements," which makes for a "superior learning environment, where everyone works to their highest capacity, but everyone is still kind and generous to others." This general feeling of being the best of the best takes a load off of the tension that can be found in many graduate programs: "Everyone is very confident that they will get a great job when they graduate, so there is no sense of competition that I hear about from my friends at comparable schools." Students "share notes and outlines at the drop of a hat, and there's a genuine feeling that we're all in it together." The school is also very LGBTQ friendly and supportive.

The facilities at Penn are "visually pleasing and practical," and classroom facilities are "mostly very high-tech and new, especially with the addition of our new building." There are always "good places to study, socialize, eat, hold events, and whatever else you want to do." The school is small, and the way it is laid out "really makes it feel friendly and like a community. You run into everyone all the time, professors and students." "Penn is as good as everyone says, and better," says a pleased student. "Law school's a tough three years. Given a choice to do it all over again, I can't imagine wanting to go anywhere else."

Getting In

Last year, the University of Pennsylvania received more than 5,000 applications for an entering class of around 251 students. The entering class had an LSAT score of 170 in the 75th percentile (and a GPA of 3.95), and a 164 in the 25th percentile (GPA of 3.52). Penn evaluates an applicant's entire academic history, including grade trends and rigor of undergraduate course work. The admissions committee also evaluates a candidate's writing ability, as well as leadership experience, personal background, and achievements.

EMPLOYMENT INFORMATION

Career Rating	99
Total 2014 JD Grads	278
% for whom you have useable information	100
% grads employed ten months out	99
Median starting salary	$160,000
% job accepting grads providing useable salary information	98
# employed full-time	273
# employed part-time	1
# employed bar required	264
# employed JD preferred	10
# employed professional/other	0
# employed non-professional	0
# pursuing advanced degree	3
% grads employed by school	3
State for bar exam	NY, PA
Pass rate for first-time bar	95.6

Prominent Alumni
Michael Richter, Chief Privacy Officer, Facebook; Libby Liu, President, Radio Free Asia

Grads Employed by Field (%)
Academic (1)
Business/Industry (4)
Government (3)
Judicial Clerkship (12)
Federal: (8)
State or local: (4)
Private Practice (76)
2-10: (1)
11-25: (2)
26-50: (1)
101-250: (5)
251-500: (9)
501+: (57)
Public Interest (4)

Regional Planning; JD/MSE Engineering; JD/MPH; JD/AM Islamic Studies; JD/MSW; JD/MBA; JD/DMD Dental Medicine; JD/MS Historic Preservation; JD/PhD Amer. Legal History; Philosophy; Psychology; Communications; JD/EdD; JD/MD; JD/BA; JD/BS

Clinical program required	No
Legal writing course requirement	Yes
Legal methods course requirement	Yes
Legal research course requirement	Yes
Moot court requirement	No
Public interest law requirement	Yes

ADMISSIONS

Selectivity Rating	98
# applications received	5,828
% applicants accepted	16
% acceptees attending	26
Median LSAT	169
LSAT Range (25th to 75th percentile)	164–170
Median undergrad GPA	3.89
Application fee	$80
Regular application deadline	3/1
Early application deadlines	11/15; 1/15
Early application notifications	12/31; 1/31
Transfer students accepted	Yes
Evening division offered	No
Part-time accepted	No
CAS accepted	Yes

FINANCIAL FACTS

Annual tuition	$53,430
Books and supplies	$8,494
Fees	$3,486
Room & Board	$14,350
Financial aid application deadline	3/1
% first-year students receiving some sort of aid	75
% all students receiving some sort of aid	74
% of aid that is merit based	63
% receiving scholarships	51
Average grant	$20,935
Average loan	$50,675
Average total aid package	$71,610
Average debt	$130,002

UNIVERSITY OF PITTSBURGH
SCHOOL OF LAW

INSTITUTIONAL INFORMATION

Public/private	Public
Student-faculty ratio	13:1
% faculty part-time	75
% faculty female	31
% faculty underrepresented minority	7
Total faculty	161

SURVEY SAYS...
Diverse opinions accepted in classrooms

STUDENTS

Enrollment of law school	560
% male-female	56/44
% from out-of-state	41
% part-time	1
% underepresented minority	8
% international	1
# of countries represented	2
Average age of entering class	23

ACADEMICS

Academic Experience Rating	**86**
Profs interesting rating	80
Profs accessible rating	85
Hours of study per day	3.44

Academic Specialties
Civil Procedure, Environmental, International, Property, Taxation, Intellectual Property

Advanced Degrees Offered
LLM, JD, MSL

Combined Degrees Offered
JD/MPA, 4 yrs; JD/MPIA International Affairs, 4 yrs; JD/MBA, 3.5 yrs; JD/MPH, 3.5 yrs; JD/MA Medical Ethics, 3.5 yrs; JD/MS Public Management, 4 yrs (w/ Carnegie Mellon University); JD/MBA (w/ Tepper School Carnegie Mellon University; JD/MSW w/ School of Social Work, 4 yrs

Academics

The University of Pittsburgh School of Law's long history of turning out educated, practical attorneys dates back more than 110 years, and the school (located in the lively Oakland neighborhood of Pittsburgh) continues to uphold the standards of excellence set into place way back when. Those who want to focus or broaden their expertise can enroll in one of seven joint degree programs (including two partnerships with Carnegie Mellon University) or five certificate programs, which come with possibilities for international externships, skills instruction by teams of practicing litigators, or membership on an intellectual property moot court team.

Pitt Law often flies under the radar, but boasts "a surprisingly impressive faculty and staff" and an "incredible and very accessible" dean. "I often joke that I accidentally went to the best school I applied to without knowing it," says a 1L. The "extremely high quality" professors are "fantastic," "universally reasonable, engaged, and knowledgeable," and are "accessible without any reservation." Some "will even give personal phone numbers to contact in case of emergency or to arrange a meeting outside the law school." "I've been impressed at how passionate a lot of the professors are about their subjects. If you go talk to them, you may pick up a bit of that passion, too," says another.

The "breadth of available academic concentrations and hands-on skills courses" afforded to students are what really drive home the value of a Pitt Law degree; the health law and international law programs are "of a very high caliber" and offer "diverse opportunities and successful job placement," and Pitt Law students can also serve as editors at JURIST, the world's only web-based, student-powered legal news source, which is based at the law school. Students can also take advantage of "the help and resources of Pitt Law's internal organizations" such as the Center for International Legal Education, which helps to organize international internships and other opportunities, and the Innovation Practice Institute, which connects law students with local start-ups.

The financial aid and admissions offices "are run more smoothly than any other school of which I know," according to a student. Career services "has often seemed meandering in focus," but "the new head of the career services office is more aggressive in pursuing opportunities for students." She is "incredibly well networked and goes above and beyond to assist students in finding and landing internships and jobs." The alumni network is also quite expansive, and most former students "seem to hold a special place in their hearts for their alma mater and a strong willingness to help current students achieve their goals."

CHARMAINE C. MCCALL, ASSISTANT DEAN FOR ADMISSIONS AND FINANCIAL AID
3900 FORBES AVENUE, PITTSBURGH, PA 15260
TEL: 412-648-1413 • FAX: 412-648-1318
E-MAIL: ADMITLAW@PITT.EDU • WEBSITE: WWW.LAW.PITT.EDU

Life

Pittsburgh "is pretty much the perfect city for law school" ("the city as a whole is united around the sports teams"), and the school's location is in a neighborhood known for being the city's bustling academic and cultural center. Regrettably, the law school building is "a 1970s concrete monstrosity" ("The architecture of this place kills me every time," says a student); the facilities inside are "well-equipped [and] sufficient for learning," but "you will never have a classroom lit with natural light." Pitt Law is in the middle of a remodeling project to address these aesthetic issues. The library is "outstanding," though. The school goes out of its way to "ensure that we have access to a wide breath of electronic resources." Also, "professional research librarians are always on duty to help whenever the library is open."

One of the greatest boons to Pitt Law life is the "strength of the community," in which one's peers "can routinely be described as collaborative." "The goal is to learn the material, not to beat each other," says a 2L. This "hard-working yet friendly student body" creates "a community atmosphere where classmates drive each other to succeed." Everyone "cheers each other on and shares in motivating each student to achieve everything they wish to pursue."

Getting In

Admitted students at the 25th percentile have LSAT scores of roughly 152 and GPAs of 3.09. Admitted students at the 75th percentile have LSAT scores of about 160 and GPAs of just over 3.6. Pitt's administration says that it will consider your highest score if you take the LSAT multiple times. Decisions are based on many factors (it is strongly recommended that you submit a résumé), and the admissions committee requires online applications through LSAC starting September 1 through April 1. Applications are considered for only the current year for the full semester.

Clinical program required	No
Legal writing course requirement	Yes
Legal methods course requirement	No
Legal research course requirement	Yes
Moot court requirement	No
Public interest law requirement	No

ADMISSIONS

Selectivity Rating	86
# applications received	1,172
% applicants accepted	44
% acceptees attending	30
Average LSAT	156
Median LSAT	157
LSAT Range (25th to 75th percentile)	152–160
Average undergrad GPA	3.39
Median undergrad GPA	3.46
Application fee	$65
Regular application deadline	4/1
Early application deadline	4/1
Transfer students accepted	Yes
Evening division offered	No
Part-time accepted	No
CAS accepted	Yes

International Students

TOEFL required of international students. Yes

FINANCIAL FACTS

Annual tuition (in-state/out-of-state)	$30,816/$38,300
Books and supplies	$1,610
Fees	$1,014
Room & Board	$16,568
Financial aid application deadline	3/1
% first-year students receiving some sort of aid	91
% all students receiving some sort of aid	95
% of aid that is merit based	56
% receiving scholarships	61
Average grant	$23,318
Average loan	$34,610
Average total aid package	$42,462
Average debt	$103,461

EMPLOYMENT INFORMATION

Career Rating	83
Total 2014 JD Grads	221
% grads employed ten months out	85
Median starting salary	$60,000
# employed full-time	176
# employed part-time	11
# employed bar required	124
# employed JD preferred	53
# employed professional/other	6
# employed non-professional	4
# pursuing advanced degree	2
# unemployed and seeking employment	22
# not seeking employment	2
State for bar exam	PA, VA, MA, NY, OH
Pass rate for first-time bar	85.4

Prominent Alumni
Richard Thornburgh, Former U.S. Attorney General; Orrin Hatch, Senator, Utah; Joseph Weis, Former Senior Judge for the Third Circut

Grads Employed by Field (%)
Business/Industry (30)
Government (6)
Judicial Clerkship (6)
Federal: (2)
State or local: (4)
Private Practice (40)
Solo: (2)
2-10: (18)
11-25: (4)
26-50: (5)
51-100: (1)
101-250: (4)
251-500: (1)
501+: (5)
Public Interest (3)

UNIVERSITY OF RICHMOND
SCHOOL OF LAW

INSTITUTIONAL INFORMATION

Public/private	Private
Affiliation	No Affiliation
Student-faculty ratio	10:1
% faculty part-time	42
% faculty female	39
% faculty underrepresented minority	8
Total faculty	88

SURVEY SAYS...

Students love Richmond, VA, Diverse opinions accepted in classrooms, Great research resources, Abundant externship/internship/clerkship opportunities, Law school well run

STUDENTS

Enrollment of law school	458
% male/female	54/47
% from out-of-state	42
% part-time	1
% underrepresented minority	12
% international	2
# of countries represented	4
Average age of entering class	24

ACADEMICS

Academic Experience Rating	93
Profs interesting rating	87
Profs accessible rating	93
Hours of study per day	4.05

Academic Specialties

Civil Procedure, Commercial, Constitutional, Corporation Securities, Criminal, Environmental, International, Labor, Legal History, Property, Taxation, Intellectual Property

Advanced Degrees Offered

JD 3 yrs; JD 2-year degree for international attorneys; LLM for international attorneys

Combined Degrees Offered

JD/MBA; JD/MURP; JD/MHA; JD/MSW; JD/ MPA; each 4 yrs

Academics

University of Richmond School of Law "offers an excellent legal education in a picturesque setting." "Few people realize how amazing this city and school are," especially given how "the tuition and cost of living are also as low as you will find for a private institution." Students love the "gorgeous" 350-acre campus that "looks like Hogwarts!" The "collegial atmosphere" "is supportive and friendly, but still academic and intellectual." Students here feel "an overwhelming sense of community" and proudly call themselves "Gunners." "The cutthroat dynamic between students you see at other universities simply isn't at play here," one student explains. "Students at U of R Law cheer each other on and support one another: we rejoice in each other's victories and mourn each other's losses."

Professors at Richmond "are always friendly and approachable" and "stick" to the "school-wide open door policy." The "top notch" faculty "know your name if you make any effort at all to connect." "Quite a few of them are actually at the forefront of their field of research," although professors are "chosen not only based on their résumé, but on their ability to engage students." Classes may be hard, but professors are both tough and loving. As one student explains, "the same professor whose midterm left you wracked by fear and more suited to tearful televangelism has a box of tissues at the ready while she guides you back to the light." One student suggests that there are too many "right wing professors who have no problem trying to indoctrinate students into their originalist/textualist" ideology. "There is a wide range of legal topics covered at University of Richmond" and a "strong emphasis on acquiring practical skills that will be translatable when students enter the job force." "The library staff is VERY helpful" and students get "a carrel/desk in the library of your own for the full three years."

The "well maintained, clean, quiet, and modern" facilities are "very up to date" thanks to "the school's enormous endowment." The school of law has "excellent classroom tools" that help professors to teach and students to learn. "The staff in general is amazing" and "the school runs smoothly and effectively by the current administration." "I have nothing but good things to say about the schools administration, classroom, law library, and professors," one satisfied 2L states. The entire staff "from the deans, [to] the professors, [to] the admissions office" is willing to "go to the ends of the Earth to help students out with anything they're faced with." "Despite being a smaller school, Richmond has excellent access to the legal community" in the surrounding area "as well as opportunity for experience farther afield (for example, its summer program and clinical placement with an international law focus in Cambridge)." A happy 2L says, "If I had a choice to attend any law school in the nation, I would probably choose Richmond based on its mixture of theoretical and practical academics, its location, and its faculty."

MICHELLE RAHMAN, ASSOCIATE DEAN FOR ADMISSIONS
LAW SCHOOL ADMISSIONS OFFICE, 28 WESTHAMPTON WAY, UNIVERSITY OF RICHMOND, VA 23173
TEL: 804-289-8189 • FAX: 804-287-6516
E-MAIL: LAWADMISSIONS@RICHMOND.EDU • WEBSITE: LAW.RICHMOND.EDU

Life

"Likely the biggest draw" of Richmond is the student body. "Students are not competitive despite the curve" and "everyone is still very friendly." "I have never once encountered another student actively looking for ways to undermine classmates to get their own 'leg-up,'" one student says. "There is a liberal presence on campus, but it still leans conservative," and there is a real "lack of diversity" in terms of "race and socioeconomic status." The student body is mostly "rich, white," and "a little cliquey." The school is "working on" getting a more diverse student body, but one student says "if minority enrollment has improved significantly I hate to think about what it was like before." "Luckily, Richmond is a great city with a diverse population, so it's possible to have friends outside the law school!"

"Social life is sort of non-existent," in part because "bars are too far to walk to" and "parking downtown is not easy." However, if you do manage to get off campus "there's so much to do in the city" and students say the city of Richmond is "very underappreciated." Plus, if you can't find what you are looking for in Richmond, the school has "D.C., Williamsburg, the Blue Ridge mountains, and VA beach, each a two-hour or less drive from the city."

Getting In

Richmond takes a holistic approach to applications, meaning they consider more than just GPA and LSAT scores. Your narrative statement, work history, and community service can count for a lot here. Recent students have had median LSAT and GPA scores of 160 and 3.50 respectively.

Clinical program required	No
Legal writing course requirement	Yes
Legal methods course requirement	Yes
Legal research course requirement	Yes
Moot court requirement	No
Public interest law requirement	No

ADMISSIONS

Selectivity Rating	90
# applications received	1,867
% applicants accepted	34
% acceptees attending	21
Median LSAT	160
LSAT Range (25th to 75th percentile)	155–162
Median undergrad GPA	3.50
Application fee	$50
Regular application deadline	3/1
Regular notification	3/31
Early application deadline	12/15
Early application notification	12/24
Transfer students accepted	Yes
Evening division offered	No
Part-time accepted	No
CAS accepted	Yes

International Students

TOEFL recommended of international students.	Yes

FINANCIAL FACTS

Annual tuition	$39,200
Books and supplies	$1,400
Fees	$0
Room & Board (on/ off campus)	$11,430/$11,160
Financial aid application deadline	2/25
% first-year students receiving some sort of aid	76
% all students receiving some sort of aid	90
% of aid that is merit based	92
% receiving scholarships	60
Average grant	$21,775
Average loan	$37,265
Average total aid package	$45,790
Average debt	$109,960

EMPLOYMENT INFORMATION

Career Rating	85	
Total 2014 JD Grads	149	
% for whom you have useable information	100	
% grads employed ten months out	93	
Median starting salary	$52,000	
% job accepting grads providing useable salary information	75	
# employed full-time	129	
# employed part-time	9	
# employed bar required	93	
# employed JD preferred	38	
# employed professional/other	7	
# employed non-professional	0	
# pursuing advanced degree	0	
# unemployed and seeking employment	11	
% grads employed by school	1	
State for bar exam	VA, NY, MD	
Pass rate for first-time bar	87.0	

Prominent Alumni

Lawrence L. Koontz, Justice, VA Supreme Court; Harvey E. Schlesinger, U.S. District Court Judge, Middle Dist. of FL; Frederick P. Stamp, Jr., U.S. District Court Judge, Northern District of WV; Walter S. Felton, Jr., Chief Judge, Court of Appeals of Virginia; Richard Cullen, Chairman, McGuireWoods

Grads Employed by Field (%)

Academic (2)
Business/Industry (27)
Government (15)
Judicial Clerkship (18)
Private Practice (30)
Public Interest (1)

UNIVERSITY OF SAN DIEGO
SCHOOL OF LAW

INSTITUTIONAL INFORMATION

Public/private	Private
Affiliation	Roman Catholic
% faculty part-time	50
% faculty female	31
% faculty underrepresented minority	10
Total faculty	113

SURVEY SAYS...

Students love San Diego, CA, Diverse opinions accepted in classrooms, Good social life

STUDENTS

Enrollment of law school	740
% male/female	50/50
% part-time	15
% underrepresented minority	30
% international	3
Average age of entering class	24

ACADEMICS

Academic Experience Rating	**88**
Profs interesting rating	88
Profs accessible rating	81
Hours of study per day	3.35

Academic Specialties
Commercial, Constitutional, Criminal, Environmental, International, Taxation, Intellectual Property

Advanced Degrees Offered
JDate, 3 yrs day, 4 yrs evening. Master of Law, General, Taxation, Business and Corporate, International, Comparative Law for Foreign Attorneys, approx. 1 year; Master's in Legal Studies, approx. 1 year.

Combined Degrees Offered
JD/MBA, JD/MA International Relations, JD/IMBA (International MBA); 4–4.5 yrs

Academics

The University of San Diego School of Law boasts a lengthy sixty-year history, an ideal location, and an alumni roster of sixty judges, senior partners at major law firms, as well as city attorneys in cities like San Diego and Denver. The well-reputed national mock trial team and appellate moot court program all make for a "wonderful experience" and a "grand" academic life. At USD, "the opportunities are endless, it doesn't matter what field you want to enter."

The "great" faculty members here "genuinely like teaching" and "make an effort beyond the classroom to reach out to students." There is "supportive academic advising in every aspect of learning," and "professors are very interested in helping their students excel." Research opportunities are also readily available. Many of the first year professors use the Socratic method, but this becomes less and less frequent as a student advances, and the legal writing course was recently changed to being graded instead of pass/fail, which means that "if you let it, it will consume much more of your time." Some of the more popular classes "are really hard to get into, especially if a particular professor is good." Several professors are practitioners in the San Diego legal community, and offer "current, pertinent information necessary to 'survive' in the legal world today." The Legal Research and Writing Department is a standout here among students, as it "teaches us legal research and writing during our 1L year, and is a great program." Students also appreciate the legal clinics on campus that service low-income families in a variety of legal areas. A few students do wish that there was a "bar course integrated into the education," as the post-graduate bar prep courses can be pricey.

The administration is "flexible and willing to change with the times and adapt to unsuccessful programming, classes, or past precedent." A staff that "knows you by name" proves to be "highly desirable as a law student," as many here are paying a great deal of money and "don't want to just be another number."

The "service-oriented" administration at USD may be "great," but the office of career services is a mixed bag. Some say it is "very helpful" and "run very well," while others wish it could do more. "I go there every few weeks but never really get much out of them," says one student. It definitely helps that the "small market of San Diego yields constant opportunity to network and build your personal brand." "My school is well-ranked within the city, which allowed me to work at the ACLU and the IRS. If I went to a school of a similar ranking in LA, I doubt I would have had the same opportunities. Or if I went to Iowa, neither of those organizations have offices there," says a student.

Jorge Garcia, Assistant Dean of Admissions, Diversity Initiatives, and Financial Aid
5998 Alcala Park, San Diego, CA 92110
Tel: 619-260-4528 • Fax: 619-260-2218
E-Mail: jdinfo@SanDiego.edu • Website: www.law.sandiego.edu

Life

As one student puts it, "Law school is challenging enough, you do not need your school making it harder than it needs to be. USD makes the transition into law school life so smooth and effortless." This "quaint" school truly has a "student body that is willing to help each other succeed." It "feels small and it feels like you know everyone." The pleasant mood of students here flows easily, since the school is located five minutes from the beach "in a beautiful setting" and is laid out "very conveniently in regards to the classrooms and research center." "The San Diego area is wonderful, but also the campus culture is laid back and cooperative rather than combative," says one student.

The school also has a good understanding of the need for creature comforts and stress-relieving practices: it "provides coffee and snacks during finals," "there is candy in every office, [and] the Dean's mixers are well attended and delicious."

Getting In

While there are no pre-legal courses required for entry to the USD law program, all applicants must have a bachelor's degree from an accredited college. LSAT scores and GPA are important to an admissions decision, as are the personal qualities and skills demonstrated by your personal statement and letters of recommendation. The 2013–2014 entering class had a median LSAT score of 159 and a median GPA of 3.50.

Clinical program required	No
Legal writing course requirement	Yes
Legal methods course requirement	Yes
Legal research course requirement	Yes
Moot court requirement	Yes
Public interest law requirement	No

ADMISSIONS

Selectivity Rating	87
# applications received	2,738
% applicants accepted	47
% acceptees attending	18
Average LSAT	159
Median LSAT	159
LSAT Range (25th to 75th percentile)	155–161
Average undergrad GPA	3.39
Median undergrad GPA	3.50
Early application deadline	2/1
Transfer students accepted	Yes
Evening division offered	Yes
Part-time accepted	Yes
CAS accepted	Yes

International Students

TOEFL required of international students.	Yes

FINANCIAL FACTS

Annual tuition	$48,480
Books and supplies	$1,516
Room & Board	$12,885
Financial aid application deadline	3/1
% first-year students receiving some sort of aid	97
% all students receiving some sort of aid	90
% of aid that is merit based	61
% receiving scholarships	61
Average grant	$22,933
Average loan	$38,703
Average total aid package	$53,232
Average debt	$129,064

EMPLOYMENT INFORMATION

Career Rating	89	
Total 2014 JD Grads	268	
% for whom you have useable information	100	
% grads employed ten months out	80	
Median starting salary	$80,000	
# employed full-time	174	
# employed part-time	41	
# employed bar required	168	
# employed JD preferred	31	
# employed professional/other	7	
# employed non-professional	8	
# pursuing advanced degree	3	
# unemployed and seeking employment	38	
# not seeking employment	5	
% grads employed by school	3	
State for bar exam	CA, NY, AZ, CO, MA	
Pass rate for first-time bar	73.4	

Prominent Alumni
Beth Baier, Principal Counsel, Media Distributions, Disney Co.; Theodore Epstein, President of Baseball Operations, Chicago Cubs; Hon. Thomas Whelan, U.S. District Court, So. California; Derek Aberle, President, Qualcomm; Karen Hewitt, Partner-in-Charge, Jones Day, San Diego

Grads Employed by Field (%)
Academic (1)
Business/Industry (18)
Government (10)
Judicial Clerkship (2)
Federal: (1)
Private Practice (44)
Solo: (2)
2-10: (19)
11-25: (4)
26-50: (3)
51-100: (5)
101-250: (3)
251-500: (0)
501+: (7)
Size Unknown: (0)
Public Interest (5)

UNIVERSITY OF SAN FRANCISCO
SCHOOL OF LAW

INSTITUTIONAL INFORMATION

Public/private	Private
Affiliation	Roman Catholic
% faculty part-time	57
% faculty female	37
% faculty underrepresented minority	28
Total faculty	144

SURVEY SAYS...

Students love San Francisco, CA, Diverse opinions accepted in classrooms, Great research resourcesLiberal students, Strong sense of community, Good social life

STUDENTS

Enrollment of law school	561
% male/female	45/55
% part-time	18
% underrepresented minority	45
% international	1
# of countries represented	38
Average age of entering class	27

ACADEMICS

Academic Experience Rating	**80**
Profs interesting rating	89
Profs accessible rating	86
Hours of study per day	3.72

Academic Specialties

Commercial, International, Labor, Taxation, Intellectual Property

Advanced Degrees Offered

LLM International Transactions and Comparative Law, 1 yr. LLM Intellectual Property & Technology Law, 1 yr. LLM Taxation, 1 yr. Master of Legal Studies in Taxation (MLST) for non-JDs, 1 yr.

Combined Degrees Offered

JD/MBA, 4 yrs; JD/Masters of Urban Affairs, 4 yrs; JD, 4 yrs

Academics

Although the University of San Francisco itself is a Jesuit institution, the law school "is not in any apparent way Jesuit affiliated," with one student going so far as to note that "the only sign of religion I have experienced at school are holiday decorations around Christmas." Meanwhile, "a majority of the staff in the Office of Career Planning has changed. They are extremely dedicated to professional development and career placement. They are very, nice, outgoing, and well connected." "It's up to each student to work hard and seal [the] deal within the job market but the office of career planning does a great job of putting students in positions to succeed within the job market."

With a "highly supportive administration and faculty, who are always willing to work with students to help them excel and provide support/flexibility for part-time students who work full-time," USF students say that "faculty are more than accessible—they respect students as lawyers in training rather than underlings." Some feel the 1L curve "is a little bit too strict for our academic reputation and lends to professors grading more harshly than necessary," but they note that the overall academic experience can be described as "intellectually stimulating."

Students do wish that the administration would focus a bit more on "being open and transparent about how the tuition money of students is spent and managing costs, so students are not burdened with heavy debt," and several students call for a more practical approach to law that deals less with the "Socratic method of teaching, exam taking, and grading curve," wishing that USF would focus more on "preparing students from the very beginning on taking and passing the CA and other Bar Exams successfully" and "preparing students for actual practice of law such as research, procedure, writing skills, client skills, business skills, etc."

Some students note that "the school recently got rid of the Child Advocacy Clinic, led by the amazing and well-respected Professor Fitzsimmons." But the school replaced it with the course/externship hybrid focused on child and family law, and the school also recently added a new Immigration and Deportation Defense Law Clinic. In addition, "Public Interest Law is really big and the school does a lot in helping the surrounding communities. Also the teachers here are great. Most of them are amazing with very diverse backgrounds. Every teacher I have had really wants you to do well and understand the subject and they go out of their way to be there when you need them to." Another student adds, "Many of my peers are successfully pursuing business law careers," which is no doubt helped by the fact that "USF Law is located near the tech capital of the world, with currently the strongest economy in the country."

ALAN GUERRERO, DIRECTOR OF ADMISSIONS
2130 FULTON STREET, SAN FRANCISCO, CA 94117
TEL: 415-422-6586 • FAX: 415-422-5442
E-MAIL: LAWADMISSIONS@USFCA.EDU • WEBSITE: WWW.USFCA.EDU/LAW

Life

Students love the location in San Francisco, the intense amount of diversity (with one student going so far as to say, "USF is one of the most diverse schools in the nation however that diversity is not just color based but on sexual orientation and cultural and sexual identity"). As for the sense of community, USF is "a very inclusive campus and everyone from professors, faculty and the students are very supportive." From a purely cosmetic standpoint, "the classrooms and library are really new and nice with amazing views of SF and the USF campus. Resources are widely available and updated, including study rooms with projectors and a state of the art moot court room." Furthermore, "the food in the cafeteria is literally the worst thing [we] have to complain about." A typical student comment is, "I could not be happier to be at this school. The quality of life is excellent and everyone from faculty to students are really invested in your success."

Getting In

Admitted students at the 25th percentile have LSAT scores of approximately 151, and undergraduate GPAs just higher than 3.0. At the 75th percentile, LSAT scores are a little higher than 156, and GPAs are about 3.6.

Clinical program required	No
Legal writing course requirement	Yes
Legal methods course requirement	No
Legal research course requirement	Yes
Moot court requirement	Yes
Public interest law requirement	No

ADMISSIONS

Selectivity Rating	77
# applications received	2,329
% applicants accepted	61
% acceptees attending	12
Median LSAT	153
LSAT Range (25th to 75th percentile)	151–156
Median undergrad GPA	3.19
Application fee	$60
Regular application deadline	2/1
Transfer students accepted	Yes
Evening division offered	Yes
Part-time accepted	Yes
CAS accepted	Yes

International Students

TOEFL required of international students.	Yes

FINANCIAL FACTS

Annual tuition	$46,780
Books and supplies	$1,600
Fees	$80
Room & Board	$18,000
Financial aid application deadline	2/15
% first-year students receiving some sort of aid	90
% all students receiving some sort of aid	84
% receiving scholarships	30
Average grant	$20,000
Average loan	$53,581
Average total aid package	$73,581
Average debt	$154,990

EMPLOYMENT INFORMATION

Career Rating	**75**	
Total 2014 JD Grads	197	
% for whom you have useable information	97	
% grads employed ten months out	63	
Median starting salary	$70,000	
# employed full-time	108	
# employed part-time	16	
# employed bar required	73	
# employed JD preferred	41	
# employed professional/other	7	
# employed non-professional	3	
# pursuing advanced degree	4	
# unemployed and seeking employment	48	
# not seeking employment	7	
% grads employed by school	1	
State for bar exam	CA, WA, NY, FL, TX	
Pass rate for first-time bar	61.8	

Prominent Alumni
Justice Ming Chin, CA Supreme Court; Judge Martin Jenkins, California Court of Appeal for the First District; Judge Saundra B. Armstrong, U.S. District Court Northern California; Brendon Woods, Public Defender of Alameda County

Grads Employed by Field (%)
Academic (2)
Business/Industry (23)
Government (10)
Judicial Clerkship (1)
State or local: (1)
Private Practice (56)
Solo: (2)
2-10: (27)
11-25: (10)
26-50: (5)
51-100: (2)
101-250: (2)
501+: (8)
Public Interest (9)

UNIVERSITY OF SOUTH CAROLINA
SCHOOL OF LAW

Academics

Conveniently located on the campus of the state's flagship university, the University of South Carolina School of Law is in the state capital, which also doubles as the state's largest city. With many of the state's courts in such close proximity of school grounds, opportunities for finding internships and making pertinent connections are right outside students' doors.

On the internal side, law students at the University of South Carolina have the option of participating in a variety of extracurricular activities and joint-degree programs to help them succeed. The pro bono program is celebrated as well as the five clinics covering nonprofit organizations, criminal practice, consumer bankruptcy, child protection advocacy, and federal litigation. "This university places a special emphasis on developing students into professionals that will promote society and the common good, regardless of the chosen field. Pro bono efforts are praised and encouraged," says a 1L.

Law students that have an interest in working in the realm of family court, juvenile cases, or child welfare have an opportunity to gain experience by representing litigants in family court with the school's Children's law externships. Partnerships with schools and firms in London make it possible for students interested in foreign practice to work or study abroad for three weeks.

However, the most popular amenity at USC is the school's faculty, according to gushing students. "The school's administration is top notch, and ready to serve the student body. They are accessible, informed, and frank with their advice. The faculty treats you like the adult that you are and expect a lot out of you in return." The students aren't the only ones that think so either: "The school administration and professors are well respected in the legal community," one student reveals.

"The school administration is on the up-and-up. The new Dean is doing an excellent job fixing any problems that may have existed with the school in the past. There is a real new energy in the building. This is reflected in a new curriculum and the addition of new externships and clinical courses, and the continued expansion of offerings for upper-level courses that cover both substantive law, theory of laws, and practical skills," says an excited 3L.

The support, coupled with the top-notch resources, makes USC a fertile ground for producing lawyers ready to become contenders in the law arena upon graduation. The law library is among the largest in the southeast. "The librarians are super helpful and great resources." "The University of South Carolina School of Law gives students challenging and rigorous curriculum lead by phenomenal faculty for a reasonable price," says a 3L.

Alumni ties to USC are strong in South Carolina so if you plan to practice at any firm, large or small, in this state, this is the school for you. That being said, it's important to note that the curriculum and programs are geared toward working locally. If your goal is to practice out of state you may be at a disadvantage. "Someone once told me that if you want to practice law in South Carolina, you better have a darn good excuse if you didn't go to USC. That is really the truth," counsels a 3L. Jobs in the private sector make up two-thirds of the positions taken upon graduation, including a significant amount of students opting for the judicial clerkship route.

INSTITUTIONAL INFORMATION

Public/private	Public
Affiliation	No Affiliation
Student-faculty ratio	15:1
% faculty part-time	35
% faculty female	35
% faculty underrepresented minority	10

Total faculty
63 SURVEY SAYS...
Diverse opinions accepted in classrooms, Good social life

STUDENTS

Enrollment of law school	619
% male/female	56/44
% part-time	0
% underrepresented minority	18
% international	1
Average age of entering class	24

ACADEMICS

Academic Experience Rating	**81**
Profs interesting rating	80
Profs accessible rating	83
Hours of study per day	3.75

Advanced Degrees Offered
JD, 3 yrs

Combined Degrees Offered
MAcc, Master of Criminology and Criminal Justice (MCJ), Master of Earth and Environmental Resource Management (MEERM), Master of Economics, Master of Studies in Environmental Law and Policy (with Vermont Law School) (MELP), Master of Health Services Policy & Management (MHA), Master of Human Resources (MHR), International MBA (IMBA), Master of Mass Communication (MMC), MPA, MSW. All programs 4 yrs.

LEWIS L. HUTCHISON, JR., ASSISTANT DEAN FOR ADMISSIONS
701 SOUTH MAIN STREET, COLUMBIA, SC 29208
TEL: 803-777-6605 • FAX: 803-777-7751
E-MAIL: USCLAW@LAW.SC.EDU • WEBSITE: WWW.LAW.SC.EDU

Life

The majority of the students at USC come from South Carolina or the surrounding states; however, those who choose to study here have many things in common. They "work hard, play harder, make connections, root for each other, [and] build each other." While you'll find that the majority of the student body is rather conservative, there is enough diversity of political beliefs and backgrounds for almost anyone to find their niche," promises a 1L. "There are lots of liberals in the student body" and Columbia is, "almost without question, the most liberal place in South Carolina (for whatever that's worth)." Ethnic minorities make up about 12 percent of the population.

On campus students find it easy to get along and to fit in. "The students treat each other with kindness and respect no matter where they stand on the law school hierarchy." "We all help each other out and share notes," adds a 1L. "The professors and fellow law students have a strong interest in maintaining balance between school and person life." When time is not spent studying, students often find plenty to do around the city of Columbia. "We go out on the weekends, go to sporting events, [and] study together." The cost of living and playing here is very affordable in this college town. The "big university feel" is unmistakable, providing a wealth of entertainment, including "a number of bars."

Getting In

Getting into USC Law isn't easy. Admitted students at the 25th percentile have LSAT scores around 152 and undergraduate grade point averages a little over 3.0. At the 75th percentile, LSAT scores are right at 157 and GPAs are approximately 3.6.

Clinical program required	No
Legal writing course requirement	Yes
Legal methods course requirement	No
Legal research course requirement	Yes
Moot court requirement	No
Public interest law requirement	No

ADMISSIONS

Selectivity Rating	81
# applications received	1,245
% applicants accepted	57
% acceptees attending	30
Median LSAT	155
LSAT Range (25th to 75th percentile)	152–157
Median undergrad GPA	3.23
Application fee	$60
Regular application deadline	3/1
Transfer students accepted	Yes
Evening division offered	No
Part-time accepted	No
CAS accepted	Yes

International Students

TOEFL recommended of international students.	Yes

FINANCIAL FACTS

Annual tuition (in-state/out-of-state)	$23,074/$46,180
Books and supplies	$1,000
Fees	$400
Room & Board	$12,802
Financial aid application deadline	4/1
% receiving scholarships	61
Average grant	$20,564
Average debt	$75,718

EMPLOYMENT INFORMATION

Career Rating	88
Total 2014 JD Grads	217
% for whom you have useable information	98
Median starting salary	$54,500
% job accepting grads providing useable salary information 57 # employed	
full-time	176
# employed part-time	10
# employed bar required	156
# employed JD preferred	22
# employed professional/other	6
# employed non-professional	2
# pursuing advanced degree	4
# unemployed and seeking employment	17
# not seeking employment	5
State for bar exam	SC, NC, GA, FL
Pass rate for first-time bar	84.7

Prominent Alumni

Richard W. Riley, Former U.S. Secretary of Education; Lindsey Graham, US Senate; Karen J. Williams, 4th Circuit Court of Appeals; Joe Wilson, US Congress

Grads Employed by Field (%)

Academic (1)
Business/Industry (13)
Government (13)
Judicial Clerkship (18)
Federal: (3)
State or local: (15)
Private Practice (340)
 Solo: (1)
 2-10: (19)
 11-25: (6)
 26-50: (2)
 51-100: (3)
 101-250: (1)
 251-500: (5)
 501+: (2)
Public Interest (1)

THE UNIVERSITY OF SOUTH DAKOTA
SCHOOL OF LAW

INSTITUTIONAL INFORMATION

Public/private	Public
Student-faculty ratio	13:1
% faculty part-time	11
% faculty female	25
Total faculty	16

SURVEY SAYS...

Diverse opinions accepted in classrooms

STUDENTS

Enrollment of law school	198
% male/female	60/40
% from out-of-state	16
% part-time	2
% underrepresented minority	4
% international	1
# of countries represented	1
Average age of entering class	29

ACADEMICS

Academic Experience Rating	**71**
Profs interesting rating	74
Profs accessible rating	87
Hours of study per day	3.84

Academic Specialties

Civil Procedure, Commercial, Constitutional, Criminal, Environmental, Property, Taxation

Advanced Degrees Offered

None

Combined Degrees Offered

JD/MBA, JD/MPA Professional Accountancy, JD/MA Educational Administration, JD/MA English-Literature, JD/MA History, JD/MA Political Science, JD/MPA Public Administration, JD/MA Psychology, JD/MS Administrative Studies. All 3 yrs.

Academics

Despite being the only law school in the entire state, the School of Law at The University of South Dakota attract students from across the region, with nearly half of all those enrolled coming from out of state. Many students find their education "perfect for practice in rural America," and others go on to larger urban practices, yet the cost of tuition is "fairly inexpensive." "Having gone to a New York private school for undergrad and paying the private New York school price, when I got my first bill from USD I thought maybe they had left something major off," says one student.

The "mostly excellent" professors provide students with practical applications for the workplace and "focus on the real world more than just understanding case law and the bar exam materials." There are very few professors who "don't care about actually teaching you in class, they just get through the material," but for the most part, "all of the professors really care about your education at USD and are willing to meet outside of class to discuss exams or just to chat." This "diverse, non-judgmental, reputable, and highly knowledgeable" faculty aptly maintains "a youthful and inexperienced cognizant approach when proffering to that particular audience," and "more than make up for any of the limitations with resources."

There are no formal law specialization options at USD; students say that "specialization" here means taking a few "mostly overview courses" in Native American or environmental law, for which "there is no indication on your degree that you specialized in a particular field." The administration helps by "supplanting our academic needs with a broad range of extern and internships, and facilitate our transition from layman to lawyer."

However, this same administration can often be unresponsive and "disorganized," but hopefully the arrival of a new dean will help set it right. As a smaller school, "it's hard NOT to get to know your professors." The professor that teaches criminal procedure and evidence trains police officers and "is one of the best teachers I have ever had," according to one student. The civil procedure and insurance law professor is "nationally renowned in the area of ERISA," and the Native American Law professor is on the Rosebud Supreme Court. "Not only that, but you can watch him read poetry on YouTube."

Understandably, the school has an excellent relationship with the state bar association, the Circuit Court, and the State Supreme Court, which convenes here every year. Unfortunately, Career Services and on-campus recruitment does not fare as well in the students' opinions. There is "a constant anxiety over getting jobs because according to one student. Luckily, "there is a strong alumni" group that is willing to help students out when and where they can. "I think the school does the best with what it has," says a 2L transfer student.

Life

Vermillion, though small, has "a lot of cultural and entertainment opportunities—you just have to look." The law school itself has plenty of opportunities to socialize, students "just have to be open to them." Having Sioux Falls and Sioux City so close "makes it an ideal environment for law school," as "there are few distractions within the city but plenty of distractions within forty-five minutes when you need one."

LEE BENTON, ADMISSION OFFICER/REGISTRAR
414 EAST CLARK STREET, VERMILLION, SD 57069-2390
TEL: 605-677-5444 • FAX: 605-677-5417
E-MAIL: LAW.@USD.EDU • WEBSITE: WWW.USD.EDU/LAW

With such a small student body, everyone does know everyone, which "can be annoying during stressful times of the year, but by graduation time, I have a feeling we will all love each other like a family." "During my first semester there was a death in my family and the whole law-school staff, professors, and students were very supportive. Accommodations and help was readily available from everyone," says one student. There is still competition among the students, but "it is a fair competition that is to be expected in coming to law school—not cutthroat and downright mean."

Facilities are universally disliked. They are "outdated but functional" because of certain particular drawbacks in some of the buildings. There "are no windows in two of the four classrooms," and the walls are "gray cinderblock, [so] when you sit in class, it feels like you're sitting in a prison." The library is transitioning towards "offering more services and relying more on electronic research for non-South Dakota state codes," but the computer lab is "small and ancient." Students do like that they each have their own carrel in which they can study in between classes. One student explains that "[you're] able to trust leaving your stuff there when [you're] not studying."

Getting In

Admission to USD is moderately competitive, with more than half of all applicants getting in. The grades of incoming students are evaluated more closely than their LSAT scores. Admitted students have an average LSAT score of 148 and an average undergraduate GPA of 3.07. The Law Screening Program offers applicants who are not regularly admitted to the School of Law an opportunity to prove themselves.

Clinical program required	No
Legal writing course requirement	Yes
Legal methods course requirement	Yes
Legal research course requirement	Yes
Moot court requirement	No
Public interest law requirement	No

ADMISSIONS

Selectivity Rating	71
# applications received	297
% applicants accepted	82
% acceptees attending	30
Average LSAT	148
Median LSAT	148
Average undergrad GPA	3.07
Median undergrad GPA	3.10
Application fee	$35
Early application deadline	3/1
Transfer students accepted	Yes
Evening division offered	No
Part-time accepted	Yes
CAS accepted	Yes

International Students

TOEFL required of international students.	Yes

FINANCIAL FACTS

Annual tuition (in-state/ out-of-state)	$7,654/$23,268
Books and supplies	$1,400
Fees	$6,121
Room & Board (on/ off campus)	$7,032/$8,409
% first-year students receiving some sort of aid	90
% all students receiving some sort of aid	92
% of aid that is merit based	90
% receiving scholarships	34
Average grant	$3,625
Average loan	$26,369
Average total aid package	$26,237
Average debt	$79,108

EMPLOYMENT INFORMATION

Career Rating	75	
Total 2014 JD Grads	100	
% for whom you have useable information	71	
% grads employed ten months out	87	
Median starting salary	$46,000	
% job accepting grads providing useable salary information	34	
# employed full-time	61	
# employed part-time	1	
# employed bar required	46	
# employed JD preferred	15	
# employed professional/other	1	
# employed non-professional	0	
# pursuing advanced degree	2	
# unemployed and seeking employment	7	
% grads employed by school	4	
State for bar exam	SD, IA, MN, CO	
Pass rate for first-time bar	80.0	

Prominent Alumni

Tim Johnson, U.S. Senator; David Gilbertson, Chief Justice, SD Supreme Court; Lori S. Wilbur, Justice, SD Supreme Court; Thomas J. Erickson, Past Commissioner, US Commodity Futures Trading Commis; Roger Wollman, US Court of Appeals for the 8th Circuit

Grads Employed by Field (%)

Academic (4)
Business/Industry (17)
Government (8)
Judicial Clerkship (19)
Private Practice (36)
Public Interest (1)

UNIVERSITY OF SOUTHERN CALIFORNIA
GOULD SCHOOL OF LAW

INSTITUTIONAL INFORMATION

Public/private	Private
% faculty part-time	15
% faculty female	46
% faculty underrepresented minority	19
Total faculty	125

SURVEY SAYS...
Good social life

STUDENTS

Enrollment of law school	602
% male/female	52/48
% from out-of-state	32
% part-time	0
% underrepresented minority	40
% international	2
Average age of entering class	24

ACADEMICS

Academic Experience Rating	94
Profs interesting rating	83
Profs accessible rating	80
Hours of study per day	2.91

Academic Specialties
Commercial, Corporation Securities, Taxation, Intellectual Property

Advanced Degrees Offered
JD, 3 yrs; LLM, 1 yr; MCL, 1 yr; Online LLM, 1 yr

Combined Degrees Offered
JD/MBA, 3.5–4 yrs; JD/MPA, 4 yrs; JD/PhD in Economics, 5 yrs; JD/MA in Economics, 4 yrs; JD/MA in International Relations, 4 yrs; JD/MA in Communications Management, 4 yrs; JD/MA in Philosophy, 4 yrs; JD/MSW, 4 yrs; JD/Master of Real Estate Development, 3.5–4 yrs; JD/Masters of Business Taxation, 3.5–4 yrs; JD/MS in Gerontology, 4 yrs; JD/MPP, 4 yrs; JD/PhD in Social Science with California Institute of Technology, 5 yrs

Academics

Students at the University of Southern California's Gould School of Law enjoy sunny weather, "wonderful faculty" and "small class sizes" that help the school cultivate a "personal and friendly environment." USC's "reputation opens up so many doors," and students generally praise the administration's personal touch. "Many members of administration know me by name," one student tells us. However, some feel that "rigid" and "arbitrary rules" mean staff members "sometimes treat students like they're children." Students advise that "the best way to get anything done is to go over the heads of the staff and appeal to a dean or a professor directly" because "the administration is looking for way to say 'yes,' even when faced with irregular requests."

Students agree that USC "professors are generally all very knowledgeable and approachable" and that "the school makes a pretty deliberate effort to provide students with broader perspectives" on legal theory. Students benefit from "multiple research classrooms, and full time research professors that are almost always available," and "the clinics at USC . . . provide real, hands-on experience with attorneys who care and are amazing at their jobs." Everyone agrees that the school's rigorous "legal writing courses are comprehensive and teach you to be an exceptional writer," noting that "the fact that it is for a grade forces you to take seriously a skill that will be very necessary in a legal career." And while students "feel very confident that [they will] leave USC with exceptional legal writing skills," some criticize the "top-down approach to the legal writing program." The school's popular clinics "provide real, hands-on experience with attorneys who care and are amazing at their jobs" and provide students with skills they "could not have received anywhere else."

While opinions are mixed on the effectiveness of Career Services, most agree "if you want to work for a firm, this is the place to go." And while "Career Services is very helpful for students who want big firm jobs or who are applying for clerkships," they may not be as helpful "about other types of work." But one student noted that "Career Services Office has improved a lot over the last few years," and everyone seems to agree that the career benefits from the extensive alumni network are unparalleled. USC's "network is incredible," and its alumni are "incredibly eager and helpful" with "potential employment opportunities and collaboration opportunities" during and after school. This means that "students are optimistic about careers." One student told us that "it seems more than half of the 3Ls have private firm positions lined up before graduation" and those pursuing "public interest don't get positions until after they take the bar."

Students complain that the law building is "probably the least attractive building on campus," and "facilities are a little outdated." While the law school building "is basically a soviet bomb shelter," the school's research facilities are "outstanding." Students say they are "much better than any law library I have been to." The personnel and "law librarians are exceptional," and students say, "I would turn to them well before asking for help from their counterparts at Westlaw or Lexis. I've always found the research I've wanted." And because "USC is a large multi-disciplinary university," students "have unparalleled access to other academic disciplines research as well."

CHLOE REID, ASSOCIATE DEAN
USC LAW SCHOOL, LOS ANGELES, CA 90089-0074
TEL: 213-740-2523 • FAX: 213-740-4570
E-MAIL: ADMISSIONS@LAW.USC.EDU • WEBSITE: WWW.LAW.USC.EDU

Life

Everyone at USC is "down to earth and outgoing," and because the school "attracts relatively laid back students" "there is no overt competitiveness among" student body. "People want to succeed," one student explained, "but they also want the people around them to succeed as well." Students are willing to share notes and outlines, and "everyone works (and commiserates) together." Because of its small size, "everyone knows each other and there is a lot of communication among all three class levels." Students are eager to explore LA, especially "if someone organizes an event." Students enjoy "going to the beach to study or for hikes on weekends." The school's "large LLM program" with approximately two hundred international students contributes to a diverse atmosphere. And "a program for JD students and LLM students to get to know each other" helps students establish relationships and network, and students say "it's a great way to meet lawyers from other countries." Clubs and student organizations "have a big presence on campus," and "the Student Bar Association does a very good job allocating the funds to each organization and dealing with scheduling events on campus." Weekly bar review events are "very well attended and are split between bars and clubs." Most students don't live near campus, "which is not a great area," but find themselves in Downtown [Los Angeles], in Hollywood, or in Culver City." Additionally, "there is 1L housing near campus" which can create a "built in group of forty friends."

Getting In

Recently admitted students at USC Law have LSAT scores that average between 163 and 167, while the median GPA of the 2014 class was 3.76. Students are only accepted for the fall term.

Clinical program required	No
Legal writing course requirement	Yes
Legal methods course requirement	Yes
Legal research course requirement	Yes
Moot court requirement	Yes
Public interest law requirement	No

ADMISSIONS

Selectivity Rating	95
# applications received	4,578
% applicants accepted	28
% acceptees attending	16
Median LSAT	166
LSAT Range (25th to 75th percentile)	163–167
Median undergrad GPA	3.76
Application fee	$75
Regular application deadline	2/1
Transfer students accepted	Yes
Evening division offered	No
Part-time accepted	No
CAS accepted	Yes

International Students

TOEFL recommended of international students.	Yes

FINANCIAL FACTS

Annual tuition	$55,084
Books and supplies	$1,990
Fees	$711
Room & Board	$16,100
Financial aid application deadline	3/1
% first-year students receiving some sort of aid	99
% all students receiving some sort of aid	95
% receiving scholarships	86
Average grant	$26,215
Average loan	$46,003
Average total aid package	$55,740
Average debt	$137,163

EMPLOYMENT INFORMATION

Career Rating	97	
Total 2014 JD Grads	217	
% for whom you have useable information	100	
% grads employed ten months out	94	
Median starting salary	$120,000	
# employed full-time	196	
# employed part-time	8	
# employed bar required	180	
# employed JD preferred	17	
# employed professional/other	6	
# employed non-professional	1	
# unemployed and seeking employment	5	
# not seeking employment	4	
% grads employed by school	16	
State for bar exam	CA, NY, IL	
Pass rate for first-time bar	88.0	

Prominent Alumni
Kenneth M. Doran, Chairman & Global Managing Partner, Gibson Dunn & Crutcher; Larry Flax, Co-founder, California Pizza Kitchen; Judge Dorothy Nelson, Judge, US Ninth Circuit Court of Appeals; John M. Lino, Managing Partner (LA) & Global Co-Chair Japan Business Team, Reed Smith; Frederick J. Ryan, Publisher, Washington Post

Grads Employed by Field (%)
Academic (4)
Business/Industry (11)
Government (11)
Judicial Clerkship (3)
Federal: (3)
Private Practice (56)
2-10: (9)
11-25: (4)
26-50: (2)
51-100: (3)

UNIVERSITY OF ST. THOMAS
SCHOOL OF LAW

Academics

Founded in 1999, the University of St. Thomas School of Law is a small, practice-oriented Catholic school in downtown Minneapolis that emphasizes professional formation and the education of the whole person. Both the administration and the faculty "are dedicated to living the school's mission" and recognize that "the foundation for a good law school is empowering strong students to become great lawyers." Through this focus on service and social justice a community is forged, and each student's education is made into "a collaborative experience."

The school's youth is also one of its main assets; as legal education deals with the challenges ahead, the law school "is committed to continuing to educate students who want to become great lawyers and legal advocates." Students say that St. Thomas "is able to bring in intelligent students each year" and the quality of the classes and student body "has not been sacrificed to maintain enrollment." Although some "upper level courses are not offered every semester,"and "the more coveted classes are hard to get into," the school has substantially expanded the range of courses and added sections of popular classes.

The professors here are all "outstanding," "welcoming," and "available," with "incredibly impressive résumés" and a love of teaching. They "go above and beyond what is required in order to help students succeed," and "it creates a very stimulating environment." "They want to be there and they care about our futures and our ability to grasp the information." "St. Thomas puts time and effort into recruiting some of the best legal minds in the nation and it is shown by my own understanding of the material," says a satisfied 2L.

There are numerous ways students can get their legal feet wet while at the school: "There are at least four externship programs, ten or so clinics, numerous classes with hands-on components, and a wealth of legal volunteering opportunities so that every student that wants practical legal experience can get it." "My overall academic experience was excellent—I got a solid foundation in legal basics, and I had multiple hands-on experiences," says a 3L. Students similarly want to help one another and "don't foster a cutthroat competition that may be present at other schools."

The administration is "generally quite good" and everything at UST runs relatively smoothly. Proximity to downtown Minneapolis is also a huge boon to the student body's professional development, and the school has steadily gained a reputation in the Twin Cities legal community for producing "great ethical lawyers." Not only are the students prepared to do the right thing, but through the experiential learning and practical experiences available, "UST graduates already have the work experience to save employers time and money training them."

CARI HAALAND, ASSISTANT DEAN FOR ADMISSIONS
1000 LASALLE AV, MSL 124, MINNEAPOLIS, MN 55403
TEL: (651) 962-4895 • FAX: (651) 962-4876
E-MAIL: LAWSCHOOL@STTHOMAS.EDU • WEBSITE: WWW.STTHOMAS.EDU/LAW

Life

The new facility (including the library) is "beautiful and well-maintained," with "very modern technology;" it was designed "to serve the changing needs of legal education for years to come." The layout of the building is "excellent" as "it allows students and faculty to meet and mingle throughout the day," and the downtown location provides "excellent access to events, seminars, [and] internships." "If we could get rid of the polar vortex winter conditions, we'd all be grateful," a student adds. The underlying Catholic values of the school really do help to foster a community atmosphere, and students are adamant about the law school being "a truly friendly environment." However, for those who are not Catholic, know that "it is not pressed upon the students, and is not included in the classroom on topics where religion is not a central factor." "Everyone here—not just the deans, professors, and admissions and registrar staff, but even the custodians, cafeteria employees, and the security personnel—strives to create a community in which everyone is treated with respect and dignity," says a student.

Getting In

Admitted students at the 25th percentile have an LSAT scores of 150 and undergraduate GPAs close to 3.0. At the 75th percentile, LSAT scores are at 158, and GPAs are about 3.66.

EMPLOYMENT INFORMATION

Career Rating	80
Total 2014 JD Grads	143
% for whom you have useable information	100
% grads employed ten months out	91
Median starting salary	$49,000
% job accepting grads providing useable salary information	65.4
# employed full-time	116
# employed part-time	14
# employed bar required	75
# employed JD preferred	51
# employed professional/other	4
# employed non-professional	0
# pursuing advanced degree	1
# unemployed and seeking employment	12
% grads employed by school	1
State for bar exam	MN, WI, IL, NY, CA
Pass rate for first-time bar	80.3

Prominent Alumni
Jake Schunk, Trial Attorney, United States Department of Justice; Jennifer Lohse, General Counsel, Hazelden Foundation; Jessica Slattery, Foreign Affairs Officer, U.S. State Department; Bree Peterson, Associate, White & Case (London)

Grads Employed by Field (%)
Academic (3)
Business/Industry (27)
Government (12)
Judicial Clerkship (19)
Federal: (1)
State or local: (18)
Other: (1)
Private Practice (27)
Solo: (1)
2-10: (13)
11-25: (1)
26-50: (1)
51-100: (2)
101-250: (5)
501+: (1)
Size Unknown: (1)
Public Interest (4)

Organizational Ethics and Compliance; 3.5 yrs.

Clinical program required	No
Legal writing course requirement	Yes
Legal methods course requirement	No
Legal research course requirement	Yes
Moot court requirement	No
Public interest law requirement	Yes

ADMISSIONS

Selectivity Rating	79
# applications received	516
% applicants accepted	73
% acceptees attending	33
Average LSAT	154
Median LSAT	154
LSAT Range (25th to 75th percentile)	150–158
Average undergrad GPA	3.35
Median undergrad GPA	3.41
Application fee	$0
Regular application deadline	7/1
Transfer students accepted	Yes
Evening division offered	No
Part-time accepted	Yes
CAS accepted	Yes

International Students

TOEFL recommended of international students.	Yes

FINANCIAL FACTS

Annual tuition	$36,844
Books and supplies	$1,600
Fees	$341
Room & Board (off campus)	$18,363
Financial aid application deadline	7/1
% first-year students receiving some sort of aid	99
% all students receiving some sort of aid	98
% of aid that is merit based	100
% receiving scholarships	96
Average grant	$21,354
Average loan	$29,648
Average total aid package	$43,159
Average debt	$98,222

THE UNIVERSITY OF TENNESSEE
COLLEGE OF LAW

INSTITUTIONAL INFORMATION

Public/private	Public
Affiliation	No Affiliation
% faculty part-time	47
% faculty female	41
% faculty underrepresented minority	8
Total faculty	94

SURVEY SAYS...
Great research resources, Good social life

STUDENTS

Enrollment of law school	442
% male/female	58/42
% from out-of-state	11
% part-time	0
% underrepresented minority	21
% international	0
# of countries represented	2
Average age of entering class	24

ACADEMICS

Academic Experience Rating	**80**
Profs interesting rating	76
Profs accessible rating	87
Hours of study per day	4.74

Advanced Degrees Offered
JD, 3 yrs/6 semesters

Combined Degrees Offered
JD/MBA, 4 yrs; JD/MPPA, 4 yrs; JD/MPH, 4 yrs; JD/MA in Philosophy, 4 yrs

Academics

Located in beautiful Knoxville, the University of Tennessee College of Law offers a great education at an affordable price. Students find the program "mentally stimulating" and leave confident in their "abilities to practice law after graduation." The university boasts "small class sizes," which make "learning more personable and focused." Students benefit not only from small class sizes, but big-name lecturers: The university has hosted lectures by three U.S. Supreme Court justices in the past five years. Students roundly praise the "practical skills classes that allow" them to "practice what they learn in theory." The clinic program—which is longest running clinical program in the country—"allows for real-world experience," and may be "one of the greatest things about UT." The university also offers a wealth of additional practical experience including externship opportunities, moot court, mock trial and Tennessee Law Review, which are "invaluable."

UT is known for its "great community" and "supportive and kind atmosphere," which offer a wealth of opportunities for students. Students say faculty and staff are "top notch." Professors "come from all over the country" and "have diverse experiences and teaching styles." However, students note that the university "could work on finding more ethnically diverse professors." That said, the "professors are all extremely qualified and have practical experience in the courses they teach." They are "dedicated educators first and foremost." There is an emphasis on "classroom dialogue, debate, and interaction" that "leads to a better learning experience." Students find their professors to be "accessible at most hours and are prompt in getting back to you." As one student notes: "Professors regularly volunteered to listen to oral arguments for moot court teams and offer their critiques, generally had an open-door policy for questions after class, and were happy to just stop and chat in the halls." The "staff, faculty, and students all provide a collegial atmosphere which facilitates outstanding legal scholarship," and the school encourages its students to give back, emphasizing "the importance of pro bono" work.

The administration is also "very accessible and open," and they "are willing to help in any way they can." Considerate of its students' financial needs, the financial aid office emails students regularly about "scholarship opportunities" as well as "graduate assistant positions" that may cover a student's "entire tuition." Students find the Career Center "very helpful." The "Career Center actually helps you find a job (unlike many schools' career centers)," notes one student.

The university also "does a great job with the type of student it admits." "There has never been a time that I have felt like I could not ask a classmate for help or an outline," says a current student. The culture at the university is "supportive, friendly, helpful, and not competitive and cruel." As one student notes, "the school did a wonderful job of preparing me for practice, and they were invaluable in the job search process." In today's tight job market, an engaged and active career center and alumni network is essential. As one student notes, many of her "colleagues opened their own practices during the tough job market," and getting the first-hand, practical experience UT offers "allows one to do that."

DR. KAREN R. BRITTON, DIRECTOR OF ADMISSIONS AND FINANCIAL AID
DIRECTOR, THE BETTY B. LEWIS CAREER CENTER
1505 WEST CUMBERLAND AVENUE, SUITE 161, KNOXVILLE, TN 37996-1810
TEL: 865-974-4131 • FAX: 865-974-1572
E-MAIL: LAWADMIT@UTK.EDU • WEBSITE: WWW.LAW.UTK.EDU

Life

Known for its great sense of community, students say school friends at UT are essentially a "second family." They also note the "incredible" " school/life balance." "UT is the place where you can get a top-notch quality education," notes one student, "but still have a life and actually enjoy your time." Another student says that she is "constantly reminded to be thankful" when she hears what it is like for "law students at other schools." The university also boasts "superb facilities" with "modern technology incorporated throughout," and students call it an "ideal place to learn."

Getting In

The University of Tennessee admits approximately 44 percent of applicants, with a median LSAT score of 157 and a GPA of 3.54. At the 25th percentile, students recently admitted to UT Law have LSAT scores of 160 and GPAs of 3.46, while admitted students at the 75th percentile have LSAT scores of 160 and GPAs of roughly 3.87.

Clinical program required	No
Legal writing course requirement	Yes
Legal methods course requirement	Yes
Legal research course requirement	Yes
Moot court requirement	No
Public interest law requirement	No

ADMISSIONS

Selectivity Rating	86
# applications received	806
% applicants accepted	51
% acceptees attending	38
Average LSAT	156
Median LSAT	157
LSAT Range (25th to 75th percentile)	153–160
Average undergrad GPA	3.48
Median undergrad GPA	3.54
Application fee	$15
Regular application deadline	2/1
Transfer students accepted	Yes
Evening division offered	No
Part-time accepted	No
CAS accepted	Yes

International Students

TOEFL required of international students.	Yes

FINANCIAL FACTS

Annual tuition (in-state/ out-of-state)	$16,078/$34,522
Books and supplies	$1,960
Fees	$3,184
Room & Board	$12,008
Financial aid application deadline	3/1
Average grant	$8,360
Average loan	$26,181
Average total aid package	$26,825
Average debt	$72,887

EMPLOYMENT INFORMATION

Career Rating	92
Total 2014 JD Grads	167
% for whom you have useable information	59
% grads employed ten months out	92
Median starting salary	$60,000
% job accepting grads providing useable salary information	60
# employed full-time	139
# employed part-time	11
# employed bar required	122
# employed JD preferred	23
# employed professional/other	4
# employed non-professional	1
# pursuing advanced degree	2
# unemployed and seeking employment	8
# not seeking employment	3
State for bar exam	TN
Pass rate for first-time bar	90.0

Prominent Alumni

Howard H. Baker, Jr., Govenment/Public Service; Joel A. Katz, Entertainment Lawyer; Dan Adomitis, President, Firestone Natural Rubber Company; Robert Link, Managing Partner, Cadwalader, Wickersham & Taft; Penny White, Former TN Supreme Court Justice

Grads Employed by Field (%)

Academic (1)
Business/Industry (16)
Government (12)
Judicial Clerkship (7)
Private Practice (60)
Public Interest (3)

THE UNIVERSITY OF TEXAS AT AUSTIN
SCHOOL OF LAW

INSTITUTIONAL INFORMATION

Public/private	Public
Affiliation	No Affiliation
Student-faculty ratio	10:1
% faculty part-time	48
% faculty female	33
% faculty underrepresented minority	12
Total faculty	215

SURVEY SAYS...
Students love Austin, TX, Abundant externship/internship/clerkship opportunities, Good social life

STUDENTS

Enrollment of law school	1,031
% male/female	56/44
% from out-of-state	25
% underrepresented minority	32
% international	1
# of countries represented	19
Average age of entering class	24

ACADEMICS

Academic Experience Rating	95
Profs interesting rating	87
Profs accessible rating	73
Hours of study per day	2.84

Academic Specialties
Civil Procedure, Commercial, Constitutional, Corporation Securities, Criminal, Environmental, Human Rights, International, Labor, Legal Philosophy, Property, Taxation, Intellectual Property

Advanced Degrees Offered
LLM; LLM Global Energy, International Arbitration and Environmental Law; LLM Latin American and International Law

Combined Degrees Offered
JD/MBA; JD/MPA; JD/MA Latin American Studies; JD/MS Community and Regional Planning; JD/MA Russian, East European & European studies; JD/MA Middle Eastern Studies; JD/MSW; JD/ Master of Global Policy Studies; JD/

Academics

At the University of Texas, bigger is better. "The large size of the school provides opportunities to specialize in or explore almost any area of law" through diverse course work, clinics, student organizations, journals, and other top-notch programs for future lawyers. The three-year JD program kicks off with a series of core courses in civil procedure, property, and other fundamental areas. These courses are often "fantastic," as "the school is very good about getting its top faculty members to teach 1L classes, exposing us to the best professors early rather than making us wait three years," says one student. Another student comments on the strength of the JD and states, "The legal writing program has recently been overhauled and is now a huge point of emphasis for first year students—which is a big strength, I think, given that every practicing attorney I've ever talked to has stressed the importance of effective legal writing." A team of attorneys with "stellar credentials,"…"the faculty at Texas has the right balance of prestige and accessibility." As at most schools, "some are better teachers than others," and not all of them are focused on students. "Some professors go out of there way to keep up with student progress," while others prefer to concentrate on their own careers or research. Fortunately, "most legitimately care about educating and some will go out of their way to make students understand and feel capable." In fact, "several professors even throw parties for students, raffle off brunch to the class and offer a variety of other ways to get to know them better in a far less formal setting."

UT's size does come with some downfalls. Specifically, students battle with the reams of red tape typical to large public institutions. "Since the law school is only one small part of the huge bureaucratic entity that is the University of Texas, things can sometimes get confusing—paying tuition, for instance, is done through one entity (not the law school), obtaining a student ID is done through another, financial aid through another, residency through another, etc." Students also note that there have been recent upheavals in the administration, and "a lot of faculty drama that happens behind the scenes." At the same time, the school works to mitigate the class size by dividing students into smaller study groups through a program known as the society system, to good effect: "The society system, which makes the large class size manageable and gives each student a smaller social group to interact with on a regular basis, helps greatly in personalizing the school and allaying feelings of being overwhelmed and alone in the school environment." Overall, students at UT Austin agree that, "the experience is comparable to an elite private school," but without the hefty price tag. With its low in-state tuition costs, "UT is probably the best value law school in the country for in-state students," while qualified "out-of-staters can either acquire residency (and get in state tuition) after a year at UT, or else can negotiate an in-state rate as a kind of scholarship offer."

Real-world preparation is taken seriously at UT Law. In addition to substantive courses in the curriculum, "students can and should participate in novice mock trial and moot court if they want more 'hands on' courtroom experience, even as 1Ls." "Being located in the state capital provides many government-related opportunities not available elsewhere," and the school offers "a lot of clinics and internship programs that allow students to get tons of real-world practice in law." Widely considered the "best in Texas," UT's "greatest strength is its regional ties. It is well-placed among two very large legal markets (Dallas and Houston), which boast salaries on par with New York, D.C., and LA along with a much lower cost of living." For better or for worse, one would be hard pressed to find a particular angle in recruiting either. "The school seems to place well enough in firms, nonprofits, and government, but does not excel in any one of those."

Monica Ingram, Assistant Dean for Admissions and Financial Aid
727 East Dean Keeton Street, Austin, TX 78705-3299
Tel: 512-232-1200 • Fax: 512-471-2765
E-Mail: admissions@law.utexas.edu • Website: www.utexas.edu/law

Life

The law school campus at UT may not win awards for beauty, but it is not a bad place to spend three years. Within the law school, "most of the classrooms don't have windows, which can get very depressing at times," and "the facilities are mediocre" at best. While not entirely ideal, students reason that "this is to be expected with the insanely low cost of attendance." On the upside, "the library is huge, and there is not the problem of undergrad kids trying to use our facilities like at other law schools."

. On the whole, the law school maintains a very "laid-back environment," populated by students who are "accomplished, mature, and professional." When it comes to making friends and networking, UT's size is again a benefit. "The school is big enough that you can find any crowd you want to hang out with, and study anything you want with an expert in the field." Competitiveness is generally kept under wraps, and most people "seem to have a good sense of humor about our experience which does wonders for our morale." Off campus, opportunities for nightlife and recreation abound. A nationally famous, fun, and funky metropolis, "Austin is a terrific city and everyone wants to stay once they come to school here."

Getting In

Admission to UT Law is competitive, especially for out-of-state students. By state law, only 35 percent of the student body can come from outside Texas, so these spots are highly coveted. To be considered for admission, students must have a minimum undergraduate GPA of 2.2. Other than that, UT has no set standards for successful applicants; each prospective student is evaluated individually. For recent entering classes, the LSAT range for the 25th to 75th percentile was 163–168.

Master of Information Studies ; JD/
PhD Philosophy

Clinical program required	No
Legal writing course requirement	Yes
Legal methods course requirement	No
Legal research course requirement	Yes
Moot court requirement	Yes
Public interest law requirement	No

ADMISSIONS

Selectivity Rating	96
# applications received	4,387
% applicants accepted	24
% acceptees attending	28
Average LSAT	167
LSAT Range (25th to 75th percentile)	163–168
Average undergrad GPA	3.68
Application fee	$70
Regular application deadline	3/1
Regular notification	4/1
Early application deadline	11/1
Early application notification	1/31
Transfer students accepted	Yes
Evening division offered	No
Part-time accepted	No
CAS accepted	Yes

FINANCIAL FACTS

Annual tuition (in-state/ out-of-state)	$33,162/$49,244
Books and supplies	$7,916
Fees	$0
Room & Board	$12,620
Financial aid application deadline	3/1
% first-year students receiving some sort of aid	92
% all students receiving some sort of aid	85
% of aid that is merit based	30
% receiving scholarships	77
Average grant	$13,577
Average loan	$36,737
Average total aid package	$50,314
Average debt	$100,868

EMPLOYMENT INFORMATION

Career Rating	97	
Total 2014 JD Grads	351	
% for whom you have useable information	100	
% grads employed ten months out	91	
Median starting salary	$105,000	
% job accepting grads providing useable salary information	86	
# employed full-time	314	
# employed part-time	5	
# employed bar required	278	
# employed JD preferred	34	
# employed professional/other	6	
# employed non-professional	1	
# pursuing advanced degree	7	
# unemployed and seeking employment	18	
# not seeking employment	4	
% grads employed by school	7	
State for bar exam	TX, CA, NY	
Pass rate for first-time bar	96.0	

Prominent Alumni
Joseph D. Jamail, Jr., Jamail & Kolius Law Firm; Kay Bailey Hutchison, United States Senator

Grads Employed by Field (%)
Academic (1) Business/Industry (8)
Government (14)
Judicial Clerkship (13)
Federal: (11)
State or local: (2)
Private Practice (50)
  Solo: (<1)
  2-10: (6)
  11-25: (3)
  26-50: (3)
  51-100: (2)
  101-250: (2)
  251-500: (7)
  501+: (26)
Public Interest (5)

UNIVERSITY OF TOLEDO
COLLEGE OF LAW

INSTITUTIONAL INFORMATION

Public/private	Public
Affiliation	No Affiliation
Student-faculty ratio	10:1
% faculty part-time	33
% faculty female	44
% faculty underrepresented minority	7
Total faculty	43

SURVEY SAYS...
Diverse opinions accepted in classrooms

STUDENTS

Enrollment of law school	299
% male/female	57/43
% from out-of-state	32
% part-time	21
% underrepresented minority	14
% international	2
# of countries represented	4
Average age of entering class	25

ACADEMICS

Academic Experience Rating	81
Profs interesting rating	76
Profs accessible rating	92
Hours of study per day	3.67

Academic Specialties
Criminal, Environmental, International, Labor, Intellectual Property

Advanced Degrees Offered
Masters of Studies in Law; two semesters if full-time.

Combined Degrees Offered
JD/MBA, 3.5–4 yrs; JD/MSE, 3.5–4; JD/Masters in Criminal Justice, 3.5–4; JD/MD 6 yrs.

Academics

The University of Toledo College of Law offers an affordable and welcoming, yet structured atmosphere designed to "accommodate, relax, and train students." The school has climbed in stature last year, yet retains its rather "humble, calm nature," partially due to its "intelligent, caring, involved, and self-regulating" students and decidedly non-arrogant professors who "are truly incredible individuals." "Every aspect of the school strikes the perfect balance between professionalism and personal attention," says a 2L. Students speak overwhelmingly of the school's obvious care and concern for their future, and the faculty's "willingness to sit and chat with students about class at any time, while connecting what we learn to real-life use." Thanks to the smaller number of students, "everyone is able to develop personal relationships with faculty and staff." In an effort to keep anxiety levels down, a lot of the professors stay away from the old version of the Socratic Method, which too often "puts you on edge." If you do want to discuss flagging grades or class issues, all professors "go out of their way to make themselves available to students." "It is not uncommon for professors to 'hang out' in the forum chatting with students," says one. "I feel I can approach them with everything: my fears, thoughts, and course questions," says another. The "relatively new" administration "takes a personal and vested interest in seeing us succeed," and "everything and everyone is very easily and readily accessible." Students do wish for a "more formalized joint degree program" and a "broader variety of courses," as well as a less rigid attendance policy.

The research and writing program is "very thorough and puts an emphasis on real-world concerns," and the school furthers each student's practical background through almost-weekly opportunities to attend speeches or lectures, like one given by U.S. Supreme Court Justice Antonin Scalia. Law Career Services "has put a great deal of effort" into the school's Public Service Externship programs to ensure that students have the opportunity to network while still in school. There's a "very big involvement of [the] Toledo Bar Association and Federal Bar Association in the school's life." The office "[does] it's best to help us in this tough economy," although the employment rate after graduation leaves something to be desired. However, students complain that much of this is due to the "oversaturated" Toledo and Midwest market, and the school's lack of national name recognition means that more help is needed in other regions.

Aside from the somewhat archaic building and library, which are "more appropriate to an era of bellbottoms and platform shoes," the law school's facilities are up-to-date (though definitely "not glamorous"), with wireless Internet access available in "every corner of the building" and Smart Boards in every classroom.

Life

Racial diversity isn't exactly at United Colors of Benetton levels here, but it "is quite good for this area of the country," and the faculty is very sensitive to both racial and gender issues. The political views also "follow a Midwestern range," ranging from liberal to conservative. The student body remains uncompetitive and "gets along great," even though many students (especially 1Ls) have GPA-based scholarships, and there's a great camaraderie among classes. The student mentor program receives raves, and to further this sense of interconnectedness, intramural sports are big. "There are many organizations to get involved with," and the Student Bar Association does "a very good job at bringing students together through social events (including weekly bar reviews) and volunteer opportunities."

"Toledo isn't exactly a party town," and it's "not the most enjoyable place to be," so there aren't too many distractions from school, but for those looking to blow off steam, "There are amazing metro parks, art, music, a zoo, and baseball and hockey games to attend." As one might expect of a small school in a small city, "the sense of community that Toledo strives for is amazing and then stems into the larger Toledo legal community." UT Law is also located within an hour of Detroit and Sandusky, within two hours of Dayton and Cleveland, and within four hours of Chicago, Indianapolis, Columbus, and Cincinnati. Still, when students are on campus, "it's difficult to get any kind of food after 11:00 P.M.," and the law school doesn't have any food options that can accommodate for the late hours students normally spend here.

Getting In

The college enrolls about 110 full-time students in each entering class, for which the college receives approximately 1,000 applications (including two required letters of recommendation) annually. The part-time program has slightly less competitive admissions requirements. Currently, the LSAT range (25th to 75th percentile) of the 1L class is 148–154, while the median LSAT score is 151 and the median undergraduate GPA is 3.33.

Clinical program required	Yes
Legal writing course requirement	Yes
Legal methods course requirement	No
Legal research course requirement	Yes
Moot court requirement	No
Public interest law requirement	No

ADMISSIONS

Selectivity Rating	78
# applications received	421
% applicants accepted	62
% acceptees attending	23
Average LSAT	151
Median LSAT	151
LSAT Range (25th to 75th percentile)	148–154
Average undergrad GPA	3.26
Median undergrad GPA	3.33
Application fee	$0
Regular application deadline	8/1
Regular notification	Rolling
Early application deadline	NA
Early application notification	NA
Transfer students accepted	Yes
Evening division offered	Yes
Part-time accepted	Yes
CAS accepted	Yes

International Students

TOEFL recommended of international students.	Yes

FINANCIAL FACTS

Annual tuition (in-state/ out-of-state)	$17,900/$29,448
Books and supplies	$4,584
Fees	$1,190
Room & Board (on/ off campus)	$10,094/$12,250
Financial aid application deadline	8/1
% first-year students receiving some sort of aid	100
% all students receiving some sort of aid	97
% of aid that is merit based	26
% receiving scholarships	69
Average grant	$10,078
Average loan	$30,248
Average total aid package	$37,278
Average debt	$96,924

EMPLOYMENT INFORMATION

Career Rating	81
Total 2014 JD Grads	123
% for whom you have useable information	98
% grads employed ten months out	77
Median starting salary	$52,000
# employed full-time	79
# employed part-time	16
# employed bar required	64
# employed JD preferred	23
# employed professional/other	3
# employed non-professional	5
# pursuing advanced degree	3
# unemployed and seeking employment	17
# not seeking employment	4
State for bar exam	OH, MI, IL, PA
Pass rate for first-time bar	85.0

Prominent Alumni
Honorable Judith Lanzinger, Justice, Ohio Supreme Court; Robert E. Latta, Ohio Fifth Congressional District; Chief Justice C. Ray Mullins, U.S. Bankruptcy Ct, Northern District of Georgia; Paul F. Hancock, Partner, K & L Gates LLP; Daniel G. Bogden, US Attorney, District of Nevada

Grads Employed by Field (%)
Academic (2)
Business/Industry (14)
Government (15)
Judicial Clerkship (7)
  Federal: (2)
  State or local: (5)
Private Practice (34)
  Solo: (7)
  2-10: (17)
  11-25: (5)
  26-50: (2)
  51-100: (0)
  101-250: (2)
  251-500: (1)
  501+: (0)
  Size Unknown: (0)
Public Interest (5)

THE UNIVERSITY OF TULSA
COLLEGE OF LAW

INSTITUTIONAL INFORMATION

Public/private	Private
Affiliation	Presbyterian
Student-faculty ratio	10:1
% faculty part-time	22
% faculty female	49
% faculty underrepresented minority	8
Total faculty	37

SURVEY SAYS...
Diverse opinions accepted in classrooms, Great research resources, Abundant externship/internship/clerkship opportunities, Good social life

STUDENTS

Enrollment of law school	266
% male/female	51/49
% from out-of-state	50
% part-time	8
% underrepresented minority	21
% international	2
# of countries represented	10
Average age of entering class	26

ACADEMICS

Academic Experience Rating	89
Profs interesting rating	88
Profs accessible rating	91
Hours of study per day	3.18

Academic Specialties
Energy, Environmental, Indian Law, International

Advanced Degrees Offered
LLM Energy & Natural Resources Law, 24 credits. LLM American Indian and Indigenous Law, 24 credits, 1–3 yrs. LLM American Law for Foreign Graduates, 24 credits, 1–2 yrs.

Combined Degrees Offered
JD/MA in Anthropology, Clinical Psychology, Computer Science, English, History, or Industrial Organization Psychology; JD/MS Biological Sciences, Finance or Geosciences; JD/MBA. All approx. 4 yrs.

Academics

Students at the University of Tulsa College of Law call their law school "amazing." "If you want a practical legal education in a happy environment," advises a 2L, "TU is certainly your best option." "Some essential courses are not offered every semester," but you'll find "a broad range of opportunities to engage in practical, professional development activities" here. There are quite a few joint-degree programs available. "Both journals are excellent." Areas of concentration include a "highly regarded energy law program" and a "strong," in-depth certificate program in Native American law. Also, the "top-notch" immigration rights clinic, which provides representation to non-citizens in immigration matters, "does great things and gives students practical experience."

Tulsa Law is on the smaller side, and "small class sizes" are the norm. Students say that "most of the professors are really good at conveying the black-letter law, policy considerations, as well as practical info." "Professors are willing to engage personally with students" as well. The faculty is "firm but fair," "dedicated to student success and achievement," and "willing to help you at the drop of the hat." "They are easy to talk with, accessible, friendly, and genuinely concerned with students' academic and professional success," declares a 2L. Reviews of management are more mixed. "The administration is dedicated first and foremost to serving the students," decrees a 3L. Some students find staffers "difficult to talk to," though. "The administration tends to spring mandatory meetings on us as well," adds a 2L.

The Professional Development Office works with students on their job searches including career opportunities outside of Oklahoma. Still, the consensus here seems to be that students with professional destinations outside of the Southwest must be prepared to sell themselves. Otherwise, though, employment prospects are respectable, and most students are satisfied. Tulsa Law has a "reputation within and throughout the state of Oklahoma" and "strong ties" locally. "The integration of the Tulsa legal community with the law school is incredible," boasts a 2L. "On a daily basis, you will see attorneys, judges, scholars, and other alumni walking around." "The Professional Development Office is also very helpful in offering mock interviews, assisting with résumés and cover letters, offering workshops in guiding students to meet their full potential, and offering a multitude of networking opportunities."

The campus at the University of Tulsa is beautiful, and the law school building, John Rogers Hall, was completely renovated in the summer of 2011, with updated classrooms and administrative facilities. "The Internet is temperamental at times," but technology is generally "state-of-the-art," and the research facilities are "wonderful." The "huge" and "exceptionally clean" library is "pretty fantastic," which "makes for a positive studying experience." The librarians are "invaluable," and "there are plenty of study areas and meeting rooms."

Life

Tulsa Law "attracts students from many states," and more than half the students hail from outside of Oklahoma. This school is highly regional, though. "Most of the students who aren't from Oklahoma are from one of the surrounding states." The academic atmosphere generally ranges from "close-knit" to "cooperative to a fault." "With the exception of a few bad apples, the students are extremely supportive of one another," says a 2L. "Competition seems to be something reserved for the mock trial teams." "There seems to be a collective understanding that the student body will cooperate and help one other,

APRIL M. FOX, ASSOCIATE DEAN OF ADMISSIONS
3120 EAST FOURTH PLACE, TULSA, OK 74104-2499
TEL: 918-631-2406 • FAX: 918-631-3630
E-MAIL: LAWADMISSIONS@UTULSA.EDU • WEBSITE: WWW.UTULSA.EDU/LAW

and we'll just leave the academic curve up to the professors," relates a 1L.

Tulsa Law's ideal size enhances life outside the classroom. "Gossip is rampant," but students tell us, "The social life at the school is fantastic." "At TU, you really get a chance to meet and grow closer to a small group of students," reflects a 3L. The Student Bar Association is very active, and "Student organizations put on many different events," such as talent shows, pub crawls, and various auctions. The law school is located on the campus of the larger university "in a mixed residential and business neighborhood" about "a five-minute drive from downtown." The surrounding city of Tulsa has devotees as well as detractors. Aficionados point out that it's a fairly large metropolis that's home to a decent number of large corporations. "Getting around Tulsa is usually easy and stress free." It's the perfect size for anyone who doesn't want to live in crowded cities, but who also doesn't want to be stuck in the middle of nowhere. Critics disagree. They say Tulsa itself is "very boring."

Getting In

Reasonable grades and test scores will do the trick in most cases here. Admitted students at the 25th percentile have LSAT scores in the lower 150s and undergraduate GPAs right about 3.0. At the 75th percentile, LSAT scores are a little lower than 160, and GPAs are a little higher than 3.6.

Clinical program required	No
Legal writing course requirement	Yes
Legal methods course requirement	Yes
Legal research course requirement	No
Moot court requirement	Yes
Public interest law requirement	No

ADMISSIONS

Selectivity Rating	87
# applications received	735
% applicants accepted	33
% acceptees attending	36
Average LSAT	155
Median LSAT	154
LSAT Range (25th to 75th percentile)	151–158
Average undergrad GPA	3.38
Median undergrad GPA	3.45
Application fee	$30
Early application deadline	2/1
Transfer students accepted	Yes
Evening division offered	No
Part-time accepted	Yes
CAS accepted	Yes

International Students

TOEFL required of international students.	Yes

FINANCIAL FACTS

Annual tuition	$34,430
Books and supplies	$1,500
Room & Board (on/off campus)	$20,328/$25,284
% first-year students receiving some sort of aid	99
% all students receiving some sort of aid	95
% of aid that is merit based	64
% receiving scholarships	82
Average grant	$20,353
Average loan	$28,447
Average total aid package	$41,638
Average debt	$99,305

EMPLOYMENT INFORMATION

Career Rating	93
Total 2014 JD Grads	98
% for whom you have useable information	100
% grads employed ten months out	94
Median starting salary	$60,000
# employed full-time	87
# employed part-time	5
# employed bar required	73
# employed JD preferred	15
# employed professional/other	3
# employed non-professional	1
# pursuing advanced degree	0
# unemployed and seeking employment	5
% grads employed by school	2
State for bar exam	OK, TX, KS, CO, MO
Pass rate for first-time bar	93.5

Prominent Alumni

Layn R. Phillips, Phillips ADR Enterprises; former U.S. District Judge, Western District of Oklahoma; Bill Carmody, Susman Godfrey, LLP; Curtis Frasier, Chairman, Shell Midstream Partners, GP; Shell Oil Co. (Americas), EVP & GC (former); Danny Williams, U.S. Attorney, Northern District of Oklahoma; Hon. John Dowdell, U.S District Judge, Northern District of Oklahoma

Grads Employed by Field (%)
Academic (1)
Business/Industry (20)
Government (8)
Judicial Clerkship (1)
Federal: (1)
Private Practice (55)
  Solo: (4)
  2-10: (35)
  11-25: (7)
  26-50: (5)
  51-100: (1)
  101-250: (2)
  251-500: (0)
  501+: (0)
  Size Unknown: (0)
Public Interest (8)

UNIVERSITY OF UTAH
S. J. QUINNEY COLLEGE OF LAW

INSTITUTIONAL INFORMATION

Public/private	Public
Student-faculty ratio	8:1
% faculty part-time	35
% faculty female	38
% faculty underrepresented minority	9
Total faculty	69

SURVEY SAYS...
Abundant externship/internship/ clerkship opportunities

STUDENTS

Enrollment of law school	351
% male/female	65/35
% from out-of-state	7
% part-time	1
% underrepresented minority	10
% international	1
# of countries represented	2
Average age of entering class	27

ACADEMICS

Academic Experience Rating	**89**
Profs interesting rating	84
Profs accessible rating	85
Hours of study per day	3.60

Academic Specialties
Constitutional, Corporation Securities, Criminal, Environmental, Government Services, International, Taxation, Intellectual Property

Advanced Degrees Offered
LLM Environmental and Resources Law, 1 yr

Combined Degrees Offered
JD/MPA 4 yrs; JD/MBA 4 yrs; JD/ MSW 4 yrs; JD/MPP 4 yrs; JD/ MRED 4 yrs

Academics

At S. J. Quinney College Of Law, expect an "excellent selection of classes" and "diverse professors" that give students an opportunity to pursue a broad array of law specializations. Though there are "many more resources devoted to environmental issues than anything else," students can pursue specializations such as "global justice/international law, and the center for law and biomedical sciences, which ranges from health policy and care systems to patent law issues." In addition to the in-classroom experience, "the school offers multiple clinical experiences to put into practice the theory that has been taught in the classroom."

This is spearheaded by a staff of educators that win major praise from students. Professors' strong credentials as published experts are important, but "the school values teaching ability just as much as academic publishing." "Marvelous, very kind and accessible," these educators "teach a wide variety of classes" that rival even some "very high-priced, private undergraduate institutions." They make themselves readily available to students, too. Indeed, this "great group of professors" are "always willing to help students understand the material or plan a career path." Basically, "if you don't develop a good relationship with them, it's because you are trying to avoid them." In fact, "some professors will even give out their personal cell phone numbers and actually expect you to call them if you have a question."

Praise for the administration, on the other hand, is mixed. Administrators make you "feel like you've inconvenienced them by being present," according to some students. But that view is far from universal, with other students saying that members of the administration are "in general more than willing to help." That same administration has constantly sought to evolve, a trait some dub "reactionary" but which others say displays a desire to improve "student experience, academic quality, and transition to real-world practice." The result is an administration that is "helpful in preparing students to succeed in law school and plan for graduation."

When it comes to the days after graduation, location plays a major role in a U of U student's success. "Practical business teaching is in short supply," and while the PDO office is good at placing people with smaller firms, they are "not very good at placement with larger firms, even when the students are fully qualified for those positions." The location, however, goes a long way towards making up for any such shortcomings. The downtown Salt Lake City campus is "minutes away from the federal and state courthouses," meaning that "getting a judicial externship is very easy." Though the current building is "older and inadequate," the class of 2014/2015 should have the privilege of being the first to graduate from a brand new facility.

Life

Though "bright and engaging," U of U students are "not the typical Type A law students" because the "top notch" students here are "willing to help each other out." Indeed, they will go the extra mile for one another. "Fellow students freely give outlines, class notes and exam advice to each other. You can walk in the day of the final exam with a question and your fellow classmates will answer your question." While there is some competition among students, it generally does not show itself "until you are actually taking your exams." Overall, "it's a small school with a small student body, an environment in which you'll know practically everyone by your second year."

Salt Lake City is a beautiful town, but it's not a particularly exciting town. The city is a conservative one, and public school or not, the Mormon influence is clear. Expect few raging parties and wild weekends. On the other hand, do expect a clean, safe environment in a part of the country filled with natural wonders. What it lacks in urban excitement, however, it makes up for in opportunities. Being near downtown Salt Lake City putting students "close to the U.S. Attorney's office, the District Attorney, the Securities and Exchange Commission, every law firm," and other opportunities.

Getting In

Students admitted recently at the 25th percentile have LSAT scores of 155 and GPAs of nearly 3.4. At the 75th percentile, recently admitted students have LSAT scores of 161 and GPAs of about 3.8. Utah will use the highest score if you take the LSAT more than once.

Clinical program required	No
Legal writing course requirement	Yes
Legal methods course requirement	Yes
Legal research course requirement	Yes
Moot court requirement	No
Public interest law requirement	No

ADMISSIONS

Selectivity Rating	88
# applications received	679
% applicants accepted	44
% acceptees attending	33
Median LSAT	158
LSAT Range (25th to 75th percentile)	155–161
Median undergrad GPA	3.58
Application fee	$60
Regular application deadline	2/15
Transfer students accepted	Yes
Evening division offered	No
Part-time accepted	No
CAS accepted	Yes

International Students

TOEFL required of international students.	Yes

FINANCIAL FACTS

Annual tuition (in-state/ out-of-state)	$23,845/$46,218
Books and supplies	$1,916
Fees	$1,072
Room & Board (on/ off campus)	$10,746/$8,802
Financial aid application deadline	3/1
% first-year students receiving some sort of aid	91
% all students receiving some sort of aid	90
% of aid that is merit based	16
% receiving scholarships	61
Average grant	$12,600
Average loan	$27,725
Average total aid package	$45,582
Average debt	$78,725

EMPLOYMENT INFORMATION

Career Rating	76
Total 2014 JD Grads	123
% for whom you have useable information	81
% grads employed ten months out	91
Median starting salary	$60,000
% job accepting grads providing useable salary information	73
# employed full-time	101
# employed part-time	11
# employed bar required	90
# employed JD preferred	16
# employed professional/other	5
# employed non-professional	1
# pursuing advanced degree	1
# unemployed and seeking employment	8
State for bar exam	UT, CO, ID, MT, WA

Prominent Alumni
David Schwediman, Chief Prosecutor for the European Union Special Investigative Task Force (SITF); Roberta Achtenberg, Commissioner of the US Commission on Civil Rights; Larry Echo Hawk, General Authority, The Church of Jesus Christ of Latter Day Saints

Grads Employed by Field (%)
Academic (2)
Business/Industry (15)
Government (14)
Judicial Clerkship (10)
Federal: (2)
State or local: (7)
Private Practice (40)
Solo: (8)
2-10: (14)
11-25: (7)
26-50: (4)
51-100: (2)
101-250: (3)
251-500: (2)
Public Interest (10)

UNIVERSITY OF VIRGINIA
SCHOOL OF LAW

Academics

Founded by Thomas Jefferson himself, the University of Virginia School of Law is one of the oldest law schools in the country, and has educated generations of lawyers and turned out hundreds of law firm heads, law clerks, and judges. This "unique and great place" is one of the country's most selective law schools, and currently offers thirteen dual degrees, twenty clinics, eight international exchange programs, and ten student-run academic journals, including the prestigious Virginia Law Review. UVA is on "a very positive trajectory" at the moment, with student quality on the rise, improved fundraising, ongoing facilities improvements, and good job placement rates.

One of the first things students are made aware of is how "pulled together" UVA feels. "Everyone I spoke with in administration, as well as the faculty, was focused on making the law school an excellent place to learn and grow as a future lawyer," says a 2L of his first visit. There is a wide variety of classes to choose from (including a selection of short courses in January), and there are "plenty of opportunities to get practical experience through a well-developed pro bono program" and the clinics. "For example, right now I'm taking an estate planning class where I actually get to draft wills and trusts under the guidance of two leading practitioners," says a 2L.

The focus on the student experience is "apparent throughout the entire law school," and the faculty is "incredibly accessible," which gives students the "unparalleled" opportunity to rub elbows with "some of the best legal scholars in the nation." Members of the faculty have previously served in high level government positions, or are former federal prosecutors, to name a few. The school's reputation among lawyers is "phenomenal," and the Career Services department "gives fantastic advice, works hard to help students make connections to markets all across the U.S., and are incredibly friendly and accessible." The staff "walk us through every step of finding and getting jobs that we are excited about." There is a ton of engagement with the institution at UVA, "precisely because students don't vanish into the ether once class ends for the day." Students also have many opportunities to have "a significant influence" on the law school's governance and policies through the Student Bar Association. The school is generally receptive of student influence in the improvement and alteration of academic policies, "which is quite empowering for students."

Life

Everyone is "friendly and helpful, from the Dean to the librarians to the people who work in the coffee shop." The UVA peer advisory system, in which each 1L section is assigned six upper-class mentors to welcome them to school, helps ease new students into life at this "friendly, welcoming, and well-organized environment," and provides guidance on "everything from learning how to brief cases to applying for jobs to navigating the social scene." This type of mentorship "is invaluable" and "fosters UVA's famous sense of collegiality from year to year."

CORDEL FAULK, INTERIM ASSISTANT DEAN
580 MASSIE ROAD, CHARLOTTESVILLE, VA 22903-1738
TEL: 434-924-7351 • FAX: 434-982-2128
E-MAIL: LAWADMIT@VIRGINIA.EDU • WEBSITE: WWW.LAW.VIRGINIA.EDU

Classrooms are well-equipped with the latest technology, and there are "plenty of comfortable and well-lit places to study throughout the law school." The student services wing of the law school building was "beautifully renovated" over the summer to expand the admissions, career services, and clinic offices, and the city of Charlottesville is "amazing." There's "a lot to do around here for such a relatively small place," including "great food, great music, UVA sports... [and] good hiking nearby," and D.C. is just a couple of hours away. "I think that it is telling that 3Ls dislike talking about having to leave the law school at the end of the year, wishing that their law school careers could last longer," says a happy student.

Getting In

Admitted students at the 25th percentile have LSAT scores of roughly 166 and GPAs of about 3.5. Admitted students at the 75th percentile have LSAT scores of about 170 and GPAs of just over 3.9. In the case of multiple LSAT scores, UVA gives the most weight to the highest submitted LSAT score; however, the school evaluates all information submitted as part of the application for admission, and encourages applicants with a significant difference in LSAT scores to include with their application any information that may be relevant to the interpretation of test results, such as illness or testing conditions. Keep in mind that this is a holistic approach, and at no point in admissions deliberations are numbers employed in a way that would trigger an automatic decision to offer or deny admission.

JD/MPP, 4 yrs; JD/MPA, 4 yrs; JD/MA Law and Diplomacy, 4 yrs; JD/MA International Relations, 4 yrs; JD/Masters in Economic Law, 3 yrs; JD/MD, 6 yrs.

Clinical program required	No
Legal writing course requirement	Yes
Legal methods course requirement	Yes
Legal research course requirement	Yes
Moot court requirement	No
Public interest law requirement	No

ADMISSIONS

Selectivity Rating	98
# applications received	5,233
% applicants accepted	18
% acceptees attending	32
Median LSAT	169
LSAT Range (25th to 75th percentile)	166–170
Median undergrad GPA	3.85
Application fee	$80
Regular application deadline	3/1
Regular notification	4/15
Transfer students accepted	Yes
Evening division offered	No
Part-time accepted	No
CAS accepted	Yes

FINANCIAL FACTS

Annual tuition (in-state/out-of-state)	$49,246/$51,564
Books and supplies	$4,463
Fees	$3,236
Room & Board	$16,560
Financial aid application deadline	2/19
% first-year students receiving some sort of aid	75
% all students receiving some sort of aid	78
% receiving scholarships	43
Average grant	$27,560
Average loan	$53,876
Average total aid package	$57,602
Average debt	$103,018

EMPLOYMENT INFORMATION

Career Rating	98	Grads Employed by Field (%)	
Total 2014 JD Grads	349	Business/Industry (4)	
% for whom you have useable information	100	Government (10)	
% grads employed ten months out	97	Judicial Clerkship (19)	
Median starting salary	$135,000	Federal: (15)	
# employed full-time	338	State or local: (4)	
# employed part-time	1	Private Practice (59)	
# employed bar required	331	Solo: (0)	
# employed JD preferred	8	2-10: (2)	
# pursuing advanced degree	1	11-25: (1)	
# unemployed and seeking employment	3	26-50: (1)	
# not seeking employment	3	51-100: (2)	
% grads employed by school	10	101-250: (4)	
State for bar exam	VA, NY, CA, TX, GA	251-500: (8)	
Pass rate for first-time bar	93.0	501+: (40)	
		Size Unknown: (0)	
		Public Interest (5)	

UNIVERSITY OF WASHINGTON
SCHOOL OF LAW

INSTITUTIONAL INFORMATION

Public/private	Public
Affiliation	No Affiliation
Student-faculty ratio	9:1
% faculty part-time	61
% faculty female	37
% faculty underrepresented minority	13
Total faculty	264

SURVEY SAYS...

Students love Seattle, WA, Great research resources, Liberal students

STUDENTS

Enrollment of law school	516
% male/female	52/48
% from out-of-state	29
% underrepresented minority	27
% international	2
# of countries represented	11
Average age of entering class	25

ACADEMICS

Academic Experience Rating	**87**
Profs interesting rating	72
Profs accessible rating	75
Hours of study per day	4.52

Academic Specialties

Asian Law, Civil Procedure, Commercial, Constitutional, Corporation Securities, Criminal, Disupute Resolution, Environmental, Government Services, Health Law, Human Rights, International, Labor, Legal History, Legal Philosophy, Property, Taxation, Intellectual Property

Advanced Degrees Offered

LLM in Asian & Comparative Law, Global Business Law, Sustainable International Development Law, Health Law, Intellectual Property Law & Policy, and Taxation.

Combined Degrees Offered

Can set up with over 90 graduate programs at the University of Washington.

Academics

Situated in the hip, relaxed seaside city of Seattle, the University of Washington School of Law is arguably the top law college in the Pacific Northwest. Deemed a "veritable paradise" by one student, the "regional powerhouse" has "huge respect" and its "reputation helps [students] . . . [compete] with [students from] other schools for internships and jobs." With a 115-year legacy, "left-leaning" UW prides itself on its "strong focus on social justice and minority issues" and the students in general "care a lot about doing good" via forty-five-plus student-run organizations and a required sixty hours of public service legal work. Still, attendees find that the administration is "geared at getting students . . . high-paying jobs at big firms" and ultimately encourages students to "[pursue] . . . [careers] in big law." Career services, however, "are not the strongest part of UW Law," with several students lamenting that it's difficult to find jobs outside of the Seattle area with a UW Law degree.

The school is one of only a handful in the country on the quarter system, which some believe makes for "tighter . . . schedules." UW Law offers eight concentration tracks: Asian law, business law, dispute resolution, environmental law, health law, intellectual property, international and comparative law, and public service law. Curriculum highlights include a "range of course offerings . . . that give ample room for exploring different interests" and a "well-developed legal writing program." Students happily share that the "1L experience is well-tailored to helping students transition into a new environment," as "the school . . . sets up 1Ls with a professional mentor from the Seattle community and a faculty member." But classes are certain to be vigorous—the curve is apparently "absurd"—and some students wished that the school "[helped] guide students in their practice area selection." But there are "tons of opportunities for involvement in the community" (such as internships and externships) and more than 60 percent of UW Law students participate in at least one out of thirteen clinics.

"Rigorous, prestigious, and [known for bringing] immense intellectual insight to the classroom," the faculty includes "top-notch professors who are accessible and supportive" and who know how to make "even boring topics more approachable and enjoyable, thanks to their enthusiasm." Plus, "most . . . have been or still are highly successful practitioners," "many have Supreme Court experience," and "almost all instructors publish." And they're primarily there to teach: "Despite [their] amazing credentials, the professors have an astounding ability to break down the subject matter and help the students to understand and excel academically." The student-faculty ratio is also an awesome 9:1, so students "get individualized attention when [they] need it."

Housed in the new, modern William H. Gates Hall (which is named after Bill Gates' father), UW's facilities are reportedly breathtaking. "Beautiful and full of light," the "world-class" Gallagher Law Library boasts "tons of materials" (technically, 650,000-plus volumes, making it one of the largest law libraries west of the Mississippi) and is an envy-inducing "gem in every other law school's eye," staffed by "friendly research librarians." The "classrooms are well-maintained" (with "fairly ergonomic chairs," no less) and "offer state-of-the-art technology for pedagogical use."

Mathiew Le, Assistant Dean of Admissions & Financial Aid
William H. Gates Hall, Box 353020, Seattle, WA 98195-3020
Tel: 206-543-4078 • Fax: 206-685-4201
E-Mail: lawadm@uw.edu • Website: www.law.washington.edu

Life

What's the one thing pretty much all UW Law students have on their wish list of school improvements? Diversity. While "just about everyone can find a group of people to call their friends," attendees remark that there sure are "a lot of white, privileged individuals at the school" (though some students noted that it's a problem endemic to law school in general, not just UW).

Otherwise, the scene "is much less competitive and more supportive than most law schools" and the "friendly and good-natured" students "do a pretty good job of looking out for each other"—all without too many "overt personality clashes." As for the social calendar, "parties or pot lucks happen almost every weekend as a nice break from the day to day stresses" and "student organizations sponsor happy hours and mixers." With its coffee house culture and exposure to art and music, the city of Seattle also provides plenty of opportunities to blow off steam.

Getting In

As the premier law school in its region, UW Law is very selective: Out of 2,946 applicants, only 776 were admitted in 2014. The median LSAT score is 164 and GPA is 3.67, but the school favors a holistic approach and looks for strong personal statements, excellent recommendation letters, and job history that shows a passion for legal work.

Clinical program required	No
Legal writing course requirement	Yes
Legal methods course requirement	Yes
Legal research course requirement	Yes
Moot court requirement	No
Public interest law requirement	Yes

ADMISSIONS

Selectivity Rating	93
# applications received	2,946
% applicants accepted	26
% acceptees attending	21
Average LSAT	163
Median LSAT	164
LSAT Range (25th to 75th percentile)	160–166
Average undergrad GPA	3.62
Median undergrad GPA	3.67
Application fee	$60
Regular application deadline	3/15
Regular notification	4/1
Early application deadline	11/15
Transfer students accepted	Yes
Evening division offered	No
Part-time accepted	No
CAS accepted	Yes

FINANCIAL FACTS

Annual tuition (in-state/out-of-state)	$30,891/$43,932
Books and supplies	$1,206
Fees	$1,089
Room & Board	$14,076
Financial aid application deadline	2/28
% of aid that is merit based	17
% receiving scholarships	53
Average grant	$8,000
Average loan	$57,769

EMPLOYMENT INFORMATION

Career Rating	88	
Total 2014 JD Grads	200	
% for whom you have useable information	100	
% grads employed ten months out	87	
Median starting salary	$65,000	
% job accepting grads providing useable salary information	67	
# employed full-time	156	
# employed part-time	9	
# employed bar required	133	
# employed JD preferred	26	
# employed non-professional	4	
# pursuing advanced degree	6	
# unemployed and seeking employment	21	
# not seeking employment	4	
% grads employed by school	1	
State for bar exam	WA, CA	
Pass rate for first-time bar	85.0	

Prominent Alumni

Tom Foley, Former Speaker, U.S. House of Representatives; Gerry Alexander, Chief Justice, Washington Supreme Court; Betty Fletcher, Judge, U.S. Court of Appeals (9th Circuit)

Grads Employed by Field (%)
Academic (2)
Business/Industry (12)
Government (13)
Judicial Clerkship (11)
  Federal: (5)
  State or local: (6)
Private Practice (38)
  Solo: (3)
  2-10: (14)
  11-25: (3)
  26-50: (4)
  51-100: (2)
  101-250: (1)
  251-500: (3)
  501+: (8)
  Size Unknown: (2)
Public Interest (8)

UNIVERSITY OF WISCONSIN—MADISON
LAW SCHOOL

INSTITUTIONAL INFORMATION

Public/private	Public
Affiliation	No Affiliation
Faculty-student ratio	8:1
% faculty part-time	42
% faculty female	50
% faculty underrepresented minority	14
Total faculty	117

SURVEY SAYS...

Students love Madison, WI, Great research resources, Abundant externship/internship/clerkship opportunities, Good social life

STUDENTS

Enrollment of law school	573
% male/female	57/43
% from out-of-state	38
% part-time	8
% underrepresented minority	17
% international	4
# of countries represented	8
Average age of entering class	25

ACADEMICS

Academic Experience Rating	**87**
Profs interesting rating	83
Profs accessible rating	79
Hours of study per day	3.69

Academic Specialties

Criminal, Environmental, International, Labor, Property, Intellectual Property

Advanced Degrees Offered

JD, 3 yrs; LLM, 1–2 yrs; SJD, 4–5 yrs.

Combined Degrees Offered

4 yrs: business, environmental studies, Latin American studies, library and information studies, public affairs, public health, philosophy, political science and sociology.

Academics

As the flagship law school in the state of Wisconsin, the University of Wisconsin Law School "excels at practical experience to get you prepared for real-world experiences." Strong programs in public interest and criminal law, "outstanding" clinic programs, and "an unusually high amount of student choice in curriculum selection" are just a few of the benefits of a Wisconsin education. The Academic Enhancement Program (for student academic support) is "second to none," offering "extensive resources to navigate your 1L year and beyond" (such as weekly skills lectures and tutorials), and there are also many clinics open to first-years, which allow students to advocate for various people right away.

The writing program has always been the school's centerpiece, and "they pride themselves at ripping your writing apart, only to build it back up."; the program has recently been overhauled and some kinks are still being worked out, but under the new, stronger program "emphasis is placed on writing from day one." "At the end of the first semester everyone has a writing sample and the professors went out of their way to offer assistance, making sure we knew they were available via email over break," says a 1L.

Professors "take a personal interest in students by providing mentorship and networking opportunities." "There are some absolutely superb teachers who truly care about your success in and out of law school," says a student. "They were patient in answering my questions, and when they noticed I might have trouble understanding the materials, they were willing to set up extra appointments to explain the question to me," says another. Recently, there have been a series of new hires, and the addition of younger adjuncts with real-world experience has students raving.

Career Services has seen a marked improvement in recent years, and is "very accessible and knowledgeable." Job placement numbers are strong, and the school has excellent integration into the state's legal community, providing opportunities for students to network. The administration is equally accessible, and the Dean "even holds weekly office hours." Clinical opportunities cover a wide variety of subjects, and give students the opportunity to "put the school's teaching method of 'law in action' to the test." "The clinical program has allowed me to represents my own clients in my 2L year, file countless briefs and motions, and gain beneficial attorney oversight," says a student. One caveat for working students: you are allowed to go to Wisconsin Law part-time, but there isn't an actual program so it can be "hard to find classes that are offered in the evening."

REBECCA L. SCHELLER, ASSISTANT DEAN FOR ADMISSIONS AND FINANCIAL AID
975 BASCOM MALL, MADISON, WI 53706
TEL: 608-262-5914 • FAX: 608-263-3190
E-MAIL: ADMISSIONS@LAW.WISC.EDU • WEBSITE: LAW.WISC.EDU

Life

The students at Wisconsin are "friendly, smart, driven, and know how to have a good time," and the school feels "more like a community than a high stress competition." Madison ("a great town") is definitely "a college community" and older students (or those coming from larger cities) "may find it difficult to quickly find enjoyable night life activities." However, "once one becomes more familiar with the city, it is easier to locate enjoyable activities away from campus." Capitol Square provides "countless" dining and entertainment options geared toward a young adult crowd. "It turns out that Madison has a terrific culture, and there are a ton of opportunities in the area--both professional and personal."

There is an "overall synchronization" with the University as a whole, which is seen as a huge benefit. "I really did enjoy being at a law school on campus at one of the largest research universities and had cross discipline experiences that I would not have been a part of at other law schools I was looking at," says a student. The law building itself "is a nice place to stay for ten hours out of the day," with good classroom technology, fast WiFi, and a "gorgeous" reading room in the library.

Getting In

Recently admitted students at UW Law at the 25th percentile have LSAT scores of 157 and GPAs in the 3.21 range. Admitted students at the 75th percentile have LSAT scores of 163 and GPAs of roughly 3.70.

Clinical program required	No
Legal writing	
course requirement	Yes
Legal methods	
course requirement	Yes
Legal research	
course requirement	Yes
Moot court requirement	No
Public interest	
law requirement	No

ADMISSIONS

Selectivity Rating	88
# applications received	1,385
% applicants accepted	49
% acceptees attending	23
Average LSAT	160
Median LSAT	161
LSAT Range (25th to	
75th percentile)	157–163
Average undergrad GPA	3.50
Median undergrad GPA	3.62
Application fee	$56
Regular application deadline	4/1
Early application deadline	11/15
Early application notification	12/15
Transfer students accepted	Yes
Evening division offered	No
Part-time accepted	Yes
CAS accepted	Yes

International Students

TOEFL required of international students.	Yes

FINANCIAL FACTS

Annual tuition (in-state/ out-of-state)	$21,372/$40,068
Books and supplies	$2,450
Room & Board	$9,400
Financial aid application deadline	4/1
% receiving scholarships	58
Average grant	$13,155
Average debt	$79,373

EMPLOYMENT INFORMATION

Career Rating	96
Total 2014 JD Grads	236
% for whom you have useable information	42
% grads employed ten months out	91
Median starting salary	$80,000
# employed full-time	206
# employed part-time	9
# employed bar required	172
# employed JD preferred	35
# employed professional/other	5
# employed non-professional	3
# pursuing advanced degree	3
# unemployed and seeking employment	17
State for bar exam	WI
Pass rate for first-time bar	100.0

Prominent Alumni
Tommy Thompson '66, Former U.S secretary of health and human services, former governor of Wisconsin.; Tammy Baldwin '89, U.S. senator, former U.S. congresswoman.

Grads Employed by Field (%)
Academic (1)
Business/Industry (19)
Government (13)
Judicial Clerkship (5)
Federal: (1)
State or local: (4)
Private Practice (48)
Solo: (3)
2-10: (20)
11-25: (6)
26-50: (1)
51-100: (2)
101-250: (7)
251-500: (3)
501+: (6)
Size Unknown: (1)
Public Interest (5)

UNIVERSITY OF WYOMING
COLLEGE OF LAW

INSTITUTIONAL INFORMATION

Public/private	Public
Student-faculty ratio	10:1
% faculty part-time	31
% faculty female	47
% faculty underrepresented minority	11
Total faculty	36

SURVEY SAYS...
Abundant externship/internship/ clerkship opportunities, Strong sense of community

STUDENTS

Enrollment of law school	228
% male/female	56/44
% from out-of-state	40
% part-time	0
% underrepresented minority	14
% international	3
# of countries represented	3
Average age of entering class	28

ACADEMICS

Academic Experience Rating	**77**
Profs interesting rating	69
Profs accessible rating	86
Hours of study per day	3.80

Advanced Degrees Offered
JD, 3 yrs

Combined Degrees Offered
JD/MPA, 3.5–4 yrs; JD/MBA, 3.5–4 yrs; JD/MA Environment & Natural Resources, 3.5–4yrs

Academics

"Small but mighty," University of Wyoming's College of Law is the state's premiere law school. Its intimate size guarantees that "you are a name and a face, not a number," and its students are privy to "individualized attention and amazing opportunities." The school offers some phenomenal programs including "excellent environmental and natural resources law" and many "practical experiences...through the legal clinics...and the summer trial institute." The "legal clinics [allow] students [to] get actual lawyering experience help[ing] low-income individuals in many different areas of law, and several students have even had the opportunity to argue in front of the state supreme court." Even more impressive, "the WY Supreme Court and the Tenth Circuit Court of Appeals come here and hear oral arguments at least once a year in our state of the art moot court room." The school is also "very affordable, even for out of state students." It is also "one of the few to still give merit-based scholarships 2L and 3L year for substantial amounts." And many laud the fact that the university "is not a school that tries to be a lawyer factory. They focus on quality, not quantity."

Students at Wyoming also speak glowingly of their professors. To begin with, the faculty "is more than happy to address specific legal questions, issues about students' future practice of law, or to just chat." They've even been known "to share a beer on [a] Friday." And a 1L shares, "the professors are not guarded in ivory towers but [are] always available (they usually supply their cell numbers) for supplemental questions as well as mentoring relationships." This openness also extends to the administration which most find to be "very accessible and strongly committed to ensuring a successful education for the students enrolled here." They "do a great job of advocating on our behalf and are wonderful overall advocates of the school and University in general."

Importantly, students find career services to be "a great resource." They help to "facilitate job opportunities...by hosting weekly panels from regional professionals/ alumni, workshops on interviewing and résumé writing, as well as developing externship programs throughout the region for Wyoming students." One pleasantly surprised 2L interjects, "The director will look over your résumé at a moment's notice. The faculty here [has] an open door policy so you don't need to make appointments—you can stop by their offices at any time and they will take the time to meet with you." Certainly, attending law school "in a state with only one law school provides students the best opportunity for judicial clerkships, clinic placements, and internships." Also of note, "For students that wish to stay in the Rocky Mountain inter-west region, the job opportunities are plentiful—especially for energy related legal careers."

Life

Though most students are recent graduates and in their mid-twenties, the school nets a number of older students as well. And while Wyoming encourages its students to invite their "spouses, kids, dogs and friends to school functions," many feel these efforts often fall short. As an insightful 1L shares, "I would agree that the administration could do more to embrace the needs of individual students sometimes. There are a lot of married/parent students and sometimes the schedule of events is hard for those students." One 3L feels "successful completion of competitions is highly regarded, yet competitions are held at times when one is required to hire a baby sitter." Fortunately, the small classes really help to foster relationships and many students find "lifelong friends." Furthermore, many find their peers "very friendly" and insist "the competition is not

COORDINATOR OF ADMISSIONS
DEPT. 3035, 1000 E. UNIVERSITY AVE., LARAMIE, WY 82071
TEL: 307-766-6416 • FAX: 307-766-6417
E-MAIL: LAWADMIS@UWYO.EDU • WEBSITE: LAWADMIS@UWYO.EDU

cutthroat," and that there is "a great sense of community pride" and "more of a cooperative environment." "We cheer for high achievers and encourage those who aren't." Indeed, this student body "takes care of one another and [is] quick to help each other in tough times."

Hometown Laramie is a "quaint community" and while "winters may be harsh, the summers are beautiful and the people are friendly." In addition, "there is most always a sports event or cultural event to attend and hiking, skiing, and snowshoeing are close, as is Cheyenne to get in some bigger shopping or attend an oral argument." The university is a "very short drive to big cities like Denver;" however, "if you are a fan of the outdoors...this is a perfect place for you." And the best part is that "because it's a small town, it is easy to find classmates and law students out in the community almost all the time."

Getting In

Admission requirements at University of Wyoming College of Law are pretty standard. Accepted students in the 25th percentile earned around a 145 on the LSAT and an undergraduate GPA of 3.13. Accepted students in the 75th percentile earned around a 156 on the LSAT and an undergraduate GPA of 3.60.

Clinical program required	No
Legal writing course requirement	Yes
Legal methods course requirement	Yes
Legal research course requirement	Yes
Moot court requirement	Yes
Public interest law requirement	No

ADMISSIONS

Selectivity Rating	81
# applications received	538
% applicants accepted	54
% acceptees attending	29
Average LSAT	153
Median LSAT	153
LSAT Range (25th to 75th percentile)	145–156
Average undergrad GPA	3.35
Median undergrad GPA	3.36
Application fee	$50
Regular application deadline	3/1
Regular notification	4/1
Early application deadline	12/1
Early application notification	1/15
Transfer students accepted	Yes
Evening division offered	No
Part-time accepted	No
CAS accepted	Yes

International Students

TOEFL required of international students.	Yes

FINANCIAL FACTS

Annual tuition (in-state/ out-of-state)	$14,918/$30,241
Books and supplies	$1,200
Fees	$1,256
Room & Board	$12,542
Financial aid application deadline	3/1
% first-year students receiving some sort of aid	93
% all students receiving some sort of aid	95
% of aid that is merit based	75
% receiving scholarships	52
Average grant	$8,045
Average loan	$26,666
Average total aid package	$27,606
Average debt	$50,799

EMPLOYMENT INFORMATION

Career Rating	80
Total 2014 JD Grads	71
% for whom you have useable information	100
% grads employed ten months out	73
Median starting salary	$55,000
# employed full-time	46
# employed part-time	6
# employed bar required	36
# employed JD preferred	13
# employed professional/other	3
# pursuing advanced degree	2
# unemployed and seeking employment	13
# not seeking employment	. 1
% grads employed by school	3
State for bar exam	WY, CO, MT, CA, NV
Pass rate for first-time bar	77.0

Prominent Alumni
Mike Sullivan, Former Ambassador to Ireland & Governor-Wyoming; Gerry Spence, Trial Lawyer, Author, TV personality; Alan K. Simpson, Former US Senator-Wyoming, Political Commentator; Nancy Freudenthal, Federal Judge; Marilyn Kite, Wyoming Supreme Court Justice

Grads Employed by Field (%)
Academic (3)
Business/Industry (14)
Government (18)
Judicial Clerkship (11)
Federal: (4)
State or local: (7)
Other: (1)
Private Practice (35)
  2-10: (30)
  11-25: (3)
  26-50: (0)
  51-100: (1)
  101-250: (1)
  251-500: (0)
  501+: (0)
  Size Unknown: (0)
Public Interest (1)

VANDERBILT UNIVERSITY
LAW SCHOOL

INSTITUTIONAL INFORMATION

Public/private	Private
Affiliation	No Affiliation
Student-faculty ratio	12:1
% faculty part-time	51
% faculty female	38
% faculty underrepresented minority	15
Total faculty	132

SURVEY SAYS...

Students love Nashville, TN, Diverse opinions accepted in classrooms, Great research resources, Abundant externship/internship/clerkship opportunities, Law school well run, Strong sense of community, Good social life

STUDENTS

Enrollment of law school	525
% male/female	54/46
% part-time	0
% underrepresented minority	21
% international	4
# of countries represented	7
Average age of entering class	23

ACADEMICS

Academic Experience Rating	96
Profs interesting rating	96
Profs accessible rating	89
Hours of study per day	3.29

Academic Specialties

Civil Procedure, Commercial, Constitutional, Corporation Securities, Criminal, Environmental, Government Services, Human Rights, International, Labor, Legal History, Legal Philosophy, Property, Taxation, Intellectual Property

Advanced Degrees Offered

LLM, 1 yr; PhD Law and Economics, 5–6 yrs

Combined Degrees Offered

JD/MSF. JD/MBA, 4 yrs. JD/MA, 4 yrs. JD/PhD, 7 yrs. JD/MDiv, 4 yrs. JD/MTS, 4 yrs. JD/MD 6 yrs. JD/MPP, 4 yrs. LLM/MA Latin American

Academics

Located in the heart of Nashville, Vanderbilt University Law School welcomes its students into a "friendly and welcoming atmosphere [with] very casual and approachable faculty." More students say they are "continually impressed with the quality of the professors," who are "extremely dynamic" and "some of the best teachers I have ever had at any level in any subject." Students take courses in "beautiful and modern" classrooms.

The professors are a big part of what makes Vanderbilt's Law School so successful. Students report that "most professors here love teaching," and "my professors are excellent, every class is fun and engaging." Another mentions that the "professors could not be better, incredibly intelligent and engaged, they care very much about the students and are incredibly dedicated to their students' academic progress. I could not be happier with my academic experience."

Law students are happy with the academics, but mention that they'd like the school to "place greater emphasis on practice of law and the changing landscape of the legal profession." Students still mention how supportive the entire administration is for their academics and their future careers, saying, "it's hard to emphasize enough how much the tone of collegiality starts with the administration—they treat students as colleagues, not customers."

A few students are concerned about what's next after graduation and believe "career services could use some work," while others say "our Career Services staff is committed and involved." In addition to using the traditional roadmap set out by career services, finding a strong position after graduation may mean taking advantage of "the network" of VLS alumni across the nation, and more and more students get help from their professors, "who are reliably wonderful when it comes to help with the job search."

A few students also imply everyone's a little young: "To reach the next level, Vandy will need to recruit students who have been in the workforce before law school. As it is, students may arrive without much clear direction for their careers, and they may not find it in law school." Still, the majority of entering students have a least one year of work experience prior to enrolling in law school. The school continues to make strides in diversity, and students point out that "groups for women and minorities are very active within the law school community."

G. TODD MORTON, ASSISTANT DEAN FOR ADMISSIONS
131 21ST AVENUE SOUTH, NASHVILLE, TN 37203
TEL: 615.322.6452 • FAX: 615.322.1531
E-MAIL: ADMISSIONS@LAW.VANDERBILT.EDU • WEBSITE: WWW.LAW.VANDERBILT.EDU

Life

Vanderbilt Law "does a great job of ensuring that people don't forget to be good to one another while still pursuing academic success." On the whole, students describe life in Nashville as "pretty solid." Applicants are clearly drawn to Vanderbilt and Nashville's style. Many list "quality of life" as a main reason for attending, along with "collegiality" and a "friendly student body." Students usually "gather in the on site ABP cafe or on Main Street to socialize in the mornings and lunch time."

The law school has been described as "relatively small" with a "happy, sociable student body." The compact size allows students to create "personal relationships with our professors." Every Friday, students gather with professors and staff for social events sponsored by a student group, academic program, administrative office, or legal employer, and they are "encouraged to take breaks from studying and go out and see Nashville." Other students point out that financial concerns can somehow alter their social lives, saying "as much as I love my colleagues here, most of them come from money" to the point that some students report they "often feel out of place." The social students seem to be less concerned about finding a job after graduation, and the "'book smart' students and the 'social butterflies' are rarely the same people." Still, as one graduating student told us, "The people are what make the school."

Getting In

Vanderbilt accepts a large amount of applications from students on a rolling admissions policy and usually has an extensive waitlist. The median undergraduate GPA for the new 2017 class was 3.70 with a median LSAT score of 167.

EMPLOYMENT INFORMATION

Career Rating	96
Total 2014 JD Grads	194
% for whom you have useable information	98
% grads employed ten months out	93
Median starting salary	$85,000
# employed full-time	164
# employed part-time	5
# employed bar required	164
# employed JD preferred	5
# employed professional/other	2
# employed non-professional	1
# pursuing advanced degree	9
# unemployed and seeking employment	5
% grads employed by school	12
State for bar exam	TN, NY, GA, CA, TX
Pass rate for first-time bar	92.0

Prominent Alumni
Greg Abbott, Texas Governor; Fred Thompson, Senator, Actor; Martha Craig Daughtrey, United States Court of Appeals for the Sixth Circuit

Grads Employed by Field (%)
Academic (1)
Business/Industry (4)
Government (10)
Judicial Clerkship (15)
Federal: (11)
State or local: (4)
Private Practice (47)
  2-10: (2)
  11-25: (3)
  26-50: (3)
  51-100: (2)
  101-250: (6)
  251-500: (9)
  501+: (15)

Studies, 2 yrs. JD/PhD Law and Economics 5–6 yrs.

Clinical program required	No
Legal writing course requirement	Yes
Legal methods course requirement	No
Legal research course requirement	Yes
Moot court requirement	No
Public interest law requirement	No

ADMISSIONS

Selectivity Rating	94
# applications received	3,673
% applicants accepted	35
% acceptees attending	13
Median LSAT	167
LSAT Range (25th to 75th percentile)	162–168
Median undergrad GPA	3.70
Application fee	$50
Regular application deadline	4/1
Regular notification	5/1
Transfer students accepted	Yes
Evening division offered	No
Part-time accepted	No
CAS accepted	Yes

International Students

TOEFL required of international students.	Yes

FINANCIAL FACTS

Annual tuition	$49,300
Books and supplies	$1,842
Fees	$422
Room & Board (off campus)	$13,904
Financial aid application deadline	2/15
% first-year students receiving some sort of aid	95
% all students receiving some sort of aid	90
% of aid that is merit based	77
% receiving scholarships	90
Average grant	$20,000
Average loan	$44,012
Average total aid package	$71,104
Average debt	$122,327

VERMONT LAW SCHOOL

Size Unknown: (4)
Public Interest (10)

INSTITUTIONAL INFORMATION

Public/private	Private
% faculty part-time	0
% faculty female	51
% faculty underrepresented minority	6
Total faculty	63

SURVEY SAYS... Diverse opinions accepted in classrooms, Abundant externship/internship/clerkship opportunities, Liberal students, Strong sense of community

STUDENTS

Enrollment of law school	424
% male/female	44/56
% part-time	0
% underrepresented minority	20
Average age of entering class	27

ACADEMICS

Academic Experience Rating	**78**
Profs interesting rating	84
Profs accessible rating	91
Hours of study per day	4.60

Academic Specialties

Criminal, Environmental, Government Services, Human Rights, International, Public Interest

Advanced Degrees Offered

JD, 2–4 yrs; MELP (Master of Environmental Law and Policy), 1 yr; MERL (Master of Energy Regulation and Law), 1 yr; MFALP (Master of Food and Agriculture Law and Policy), 1 yr; LLM Environmental Law, 1 yr; LLM American Legal Studies, 1 yr; LLM Energy Law, 1 yr; LLM Food and Agriculture Law, 1 yr

Combined Degrees Offered

JD/Master of Environmental Law and Policy(MELP), 3 yrs; JD/Master of Energy Regulation and Law (MERL), 3 yrs; JD/Master of Food and Agriculture Law and Policy (MFALP), 3 yrs.

Academics

At Vermont Law School, the students, faculty, and staff "are anything but 'typical.'" Students are drawn here for the school's "environmental focus, non-competitive atmosphere, great professors with a variety of legal experience, and the willingness of professors/students to help you." As one student notes, "The high moral and ethical fiber of the school's community cannot be overstated." Vermont Law provides an "educational environment [which] emphasizes community above competition and everyone is encouraged to use their legal degree to give back." In essence, "Vermont Law is the place to go if you want to feel like you're part of a community."

Many choose VLS for its "stellar reputation in environmental law;" however, others say they are "equally impressed by their international law program and their unbelievable foreign exchange and dual-degree opportunities." "At the end of my law school career, I hope to be eligible to take the bar in both France and the U.S., and to practice environmental law on an international scale," says one student. Administration and professors here "are all highly regarded in their respective fields and are completely available and willing to help students with intern/externships and employment opportunities." On the whole, instructors "are intelligent, kind, and accessible people." "It is easy to find a mentor you connect with because our faculty possess[es] a broad range of experience and specialties." Perhaps unsurprisingly, others note, "Much of the faculty is overly liberal. However, they are also extremely approachable and always willing to assist outside of class. If you are looking to study environmental law, there's no place on Earth like VLS. The number and depth of environmental classes is unbeatable." In addition, "The Academic Success Program is an excellent resource and utilizes student mentors to make asking for help a lot less frightening."

Classroom and research facilities on campus "are brand-new, state-of-the-art, and are comfortable." True to the school's sustainable roots, "even the desks and podiums in the classrooms are made by local Vermont woodworkers with local materials." In addition, "the majority of the buildings that VLS students frequent (i.e., those that house all the classrooms, the cafeteria, the student center, the library, student mailboxes, the Environmental Law Center, and IT) are all interconnected—which is ideal during cold and snowy Vermont winters!" The library "is beautiful" with "a lot of sunlight on the top floor." Whatever it may be "lacking in books in-house," it is "helpful in acquiring through interlibrary loan." The IT department, however, "is a nightmare. E-mail tends to be slow, [and] the Internet connection on campus is often slower than at home."

When it comes to post-law school placement, first-year JD students are assigned a personal career and academic counselor who works with them over the course of their time at VLS. Still, some students feel "career development and alumni relations are very, very weak and need a huge revamping." However, "the administration is awesome. They always have their doors open to all students no matter what our issues may be. Especially Dean J., she's an amazing woman that inspires me to be a better person and motivates me to change the world around me."

Life

Attending Vermont Law School "is a lot like summer camp." Located in the Green Mountains with the White River running through campus "(complete with a nearby rope swing and kayak/tubing drop-in point)," the school's facilities "even offer composting toilets, which give it an outhouse sort of feeling (don't worry, we have real toilets, too)."

JOHN D. MILLER JR., ASSOCIATE DEAN FOR ENROLLMENT AND MARKETIING
CHELSEA STREET, SOUTH ROYALTON, VT 05068-0096
TEL: 888-277-5985 • FAX: 802-831-1174
E-MAIL: ADMISS@VERMONTLAW.EDU • WEBSITE: WWW.VERMONTLAW.EDU

The campus itself "is beautiful; it's in rural Vermont which affords wonderful opportunities to do activities outdoors: skiing, hiking, floating down the river, etc." Amenities-wise, an energy-efficient fitness center is equipped with rowing machines and spinning bikes, weight-training equipment, stair-steppers, free weights and more.

Some say hometown South Royalton "is a perfect example of a small, New England village." "You're about thirty minutes from the nearest 'city.'" Others say, the "town is quaint but in the middle of nowhere and has no facilities. I mean none. One bar, [one] small grocery, one restaurant. [You] have to drive over twenty minutes for anything more." Basically, "if you love doing outdoor activities every day, this place is for you. If you have any ambivalence about your feelings toward outdoor sports, seriously evaluate how happy you would be here." Students are quick to add, "What we lack in access to shopping or amenities, we make up for in community." "Most of the events on campus (I'd estimate 90 percent or more) are student-organized and student-run. This includes educational dinners, speaking events, talent shows, costume contests, movie nights, outdoor adventures, competitions, festivals, and blood drives." The "summer camp feel" also translates "into a high level of camaraderie." "Everybody is always willing to lend a hand, a book, a ride, or a shovel." And shovel they do! "We are in the middle of nowhere and it is very cold and snowy during the winter. However, I like that everyone socializes together on the weekends. We go to parties hosted by our friends or the one pub in town. We are inspired to create our own social events."

Getting In

Undergraduate GPA for the most recent entering class ranged from 2.9 (25th percentile) to 3.52 (75th percentile). LSAT scores in the same range were 146 (25th percentile) to 156 (75th percentile).

Clinical program required	No
Legal writing course requirement	Yes
Legal methods course requirement	Yes
Legal research course requirement	Yes
Moot court requirement	Yes
Public interest law requirement	No

ADMISSIONS

Selectivity Rating	75
# applications received	686
% applicants accepted	74
% acceptees attending	28
Median LSAT	152
LSAT Range (25th to 75th percentile)	146–156
Median undergrad GPA	3.19
Application fee	$60
Regular application deadline	3/1
Regular notification	4/1
Early application deadline	3/1
Early application notification	12/15
Transfer students accepted	Yes
Evening division offered	No
Part-time accepted	No
CAS accepted	Yes

International Students

TOEFL required of international students.	Yes

FINANCIAL FACTS

Annual tuition	$47,135
Books and supplies	$1,500
Room & Board	$12,234
Financial aid application deadline	3/15
% first-year students receiving some sort of aid	90
% all students receiving some sort of aid	96
% of aid that is merit based	85
% receiving scholarships	84
Average grant	$18,663
Average loan	$55,110
Average total aid package	$64,160
Average debt	$132,000

EMPLOYMENT INFORMATION

Career Rating	82	
Total 2014 JD Grads	200	
% for whom you have useable information	49	
% grads employed ten months out	79	
Median starting salary	$50,000	
# employed full-time	146	
# employed part-time	12	
# employed bar required	118	
# employed JD preferred	27	
# employed professional/other	3	
# employed non-professional	10	
# pursuing advanced degree	9	
# unemployed and seeking employment	23	
# not seeking employment	6	
% grads employed by school	1	
State for bar exam	NY, VT, MA, CO, VA	
Pass rate for first-time bar	75.5	

Prominent Alumni
Glenn Berger, Partner, Skadden Arps; Charles diLeva, Lead Environmental Counsel World Bank; Linda Smiddy, Professor of Law, Vermont Law School; Cindy Burns, Sr Representative High UN Commission on Refugees; Brian Marshall, Staff Attorney, Earth Justice in Florida-Earthjustice

Grads Employed by Field (%)
Academic (1)
Business/Industry (20)
Government (15)
Judicial Clerkship (15)
Private Practice (24)
Public Interest (24)

VILLANOVA UNIVERSITY
SCHOOL OF LAW

INSTITUTIONAL INFORMATION

Public/private	Private
Affiliation	Roman Catholic
% faculty part-time	53
% faculty female	40
% faculty underrepresented minority	11
Total faculty	112

SURVEY SAYS...

Diverse opinions accepted in classrooms, Great research resources, Abundant externship/internship/clerkship opportunities

STUDENTS

Enrollment of law school	594
% male/female	51/49
% from out-of-state	44
% part-time	0
% underrepresented minority	15
% international	0
# of countries represented	2
Average age of entering class	24

ACADEMICS

Academic Experience Rating	**85**
Profs interesting rating	73
Profs accessible rating	84
Hours of study per day	3.99

Advanced Degrees Offered
JD, 3 yrs; LLM Taxation, 25 credits

Combined Degrees Offered
JD/MBA, 3–4 yrs; JD/LLM-Taxation, 3.5 yrs; JD/LLM in International Studies (third year abroad) 3 yrs

Academics

At Villanova University School of Law, students find "a good balance in an interactive and educational atmosphere" through a blend of lecture, discussion, and serious hands-on experience. Students say the "absolutely wonderful" professors are the heart and soul of the program. "Instructors are all extremely intelligent and have a wealth of real-world experience, yet remain in touch with students," says a 1L. In fact, he tells us, "My law school professors are much more helpful and approachable than my undergrad professors were." Another student agrees that the "professors' knowledge and experience is fundamental to the Villanova experience." Many here happily report a lack of the "heavy competitive atmosphere that you hear about at other schools," noting, "We all encourage each other to do well."

Villanova takes a fairly traditional approach to introductory course work, and students say, "There is still a heavy reliance on the Socratic Method and many classes use a lecture format (especially in the first year)." In the next two years, students continue studying the basic principals of law, while adding elective courses to their schedule. Experiential learning is emphasized throughout the curriculum, and students dole out praise for the school's strong legal writing and research courses, simulation programs, clinics, and externships. The school has a "clear emphasis" on "solidifying students' legal writing skills." In addition, students take on real legal work thanks to the school's "strong commitment to community service and pro bono work."

For a Catholic institution, it should come as no surprise that a "Catholic identity" reigns supreme. However, some students wish opportunities for service were not restricted by the administration's commitment to Catholic values. ("No 'regular hours' in the forty-hour work week can be spent helping efforts to litigate for women's reproductive freedom, and the participating organization must be aware of the policy.") Ultimately, many wonder "how the administration will balance the school's Catholic mission with its mission as a legal institution."

Villanova's eagerly anticipated, state-of-the-art law school facility opened in August 2009 on a site adjacent to the university's suburban Philadelphia campus. Law students no longer have cause to bemoan the "severe lack of classrooms, computers, parking spots, hallways, lockers, and space in general" that they complained about in years prior as the new facility offers twice as much space as the old building and a new 500-car parking garage, to boot. While they may complain that the campus has a "high school atmosphere," students also say they leave Villanova well-prepared for their professional career in the adult world. Students insist that "opportunities for practical experience are abundant," and the "Career Services Department works really hard to help students find jobs in the private and public sectors." They note that the school has "strong professional contacts in Pennsylvania, New Jersey, and Delaware" and that "major firms routinely interview on campus and hire many Villanova graduates."

BAYREX MARTI, EXECUTIVE DIRECTOR, ADMISSIONS AND FINANCIAL AID
299 NORTH SPRING MILL ROAD, VILLANOVA, PA 19085
TEL: 610-519-7010 • FAX: 610-519-6291
E-MAIL: ADMISSIONS@LAW.VILLANOVA.EDU • WEBSITE: WWW.LAW.VILLANOVA.EDU

Life

When they are not hitting the books, Villanova students live the high life at the many bars, clubs, and restaurants in Philadelphia, as well as at campus events. A student assures us, "The Student Bar Association spends a lot of time planning activities to students. There are many active students groups as well." According to another, "Students get along well and the ones that choose to socialize together have a great time."

Still, many students choose to maintain a life outside of school, living off-campus with their friends or spouses. Getting to campus is easy since "the train runs literally out the front door of the law school." One student advises, "there is a bar that students usually hang out at which can be fun, but sometimes after seeing these people all day and every day, it's good to do something away from the law school crowd." Luckily, that is easy to accomplish at Villanova thanks to the school's "amazing" location. One student enthuses, "It is twenty-five minutes from Philadelphia, as well as a short drive to New York City, Washington, D.C., Baltimore, the beaches, and skiing!"

Most students say that they get along with their classmates, though some say the student body is pretty "homogenous" and "not exactly diverse." However, "Villanova has openly stated that they feel that diversity is a compelling interest at the institution" and many believe that "in time, Villanova will be one of the more diverse legal institutions."

Getting In

For the admitted class, students in the 25th percentile had an LSAT score of 153 and a 3.24 GPA. Admitted students in the 75th percentile had an LSAT score of 160 and a 3.74 GPA. However, Villanova may consider students with a lower GPA if they offer other important qualities, such as commitment to service, volunteer work, or unique professional experience. The majority of students who enter do so within a year or two of college, and the average age of a Villanova student in their first year is twenty-four.

Clinical program required	No
Legal writing course requirement	Yes
Legal methods course requirement	No
Legal research course requirement	Yes
Moot court requirement	Yes
Public interest law requirement	No

ADMISSIONS

Selectivity Rating	**85**
# applications received	1,472
% applicants accepted	55
% acceptees attending	19
Median LSAT	157
LSAT Range (25th to 75th percentile)	153–160
Median undergrad GPA	3.56
Application fee	$75
Regular application deadline	4/1
Transfer students accepted	Yes
Evening division offered	No
Part-time accepted	No
CAS accepted	Yes

FINANCIAL FACTS

Annual tuition	$39,660
Books and supplies	$5,008
Room & Board	$16,605
Financial aid application deadline	4/1
% first-year students receiving some sort of aid	86
% all students receiving some sort of aid	87
% of aid that is merit based	38
% receiving scholarships	65
Average grant	$25,134
Average loan	$38,991
Average total aid package	$42,791
Average debt	$114,796

EMPLOYMENT INFORMATION

Career Rating	71
Total 2014 JD Grads	240
% grads employed ten months out	73
# employed full-time	161
# employed part-time	14
# employed bar required	139
# employed JD preferred	30
# employed professional/other	3
# employed non-professional	3
# pursuing advanced degree	4
# unemployed and seeking employment	51
# not seeking employment	1
State for bar exam	PA, NJ, NY, DE

Prominent Alumni
Hon. Edward G. Rendell, Former Governor, Commonwealth of Pennsylvania; Doug Gaston, Senior Vice President and General Counsel, Comcast Cable; Jeffrey A. Pott, General Counsel, AstraZeneca; Kelly A. Ayotte, US Senator, New Hampshire; Jami Wintz McKeon, Chair, Morgan, Lewis & Bockius LLP

Grads Employed by Field (%)
Academic (1)
Business/Industry (14)
Government (6)
Judicial Clerkship (12)
Private Practice (36)
Public Interest (3)

WAKE FOREST UNIVERSITY
SCHOOL OF LAW

INSTITUTIONAL INFORMATION

Public/private	Private
Student-faculty ratio	10:1
Total faculty	38

SURVEY SAYS...
Diverse opinions accepted in classrooms

STUDENTS

Enrollment of law school	500
% male/female	53/47
% from out-of-state	64
% part-time	0
% underrepresented minority	21
% international	2
# of countries represented	8
Average age of entering class	24

ACADEMICS

Academic Experience Rating	**89**
Profs interesting rating	89
Profs accessible rating	95
Hours of study per day	4.00

Academic Specialties
Civil Procedure, Commercial, Constitutional, Corporation Securities, Criminal, Environmental, Human Rights, International, Labor, Property, Taxation, Intellectual Property

Advanced Degrees Offered
LLM in American Law, 1 yr; SJD; JD for International Lawyers, 2 yrs.

Combined Degrees Offered
JD/MBA, 4 yrs; JD/MA Bioethics, 3.5 yrs; JD/MA Religion, 4 yrs; JD/MDiv, 5 yrs; JD/MA Sustainability, 3 yrs

Academics

Wake Forest provides a top-notch legal education to aspiring lawyers who are prepared to work extremely hard. Classes "are incredibly difficult" and "the curriculum [has a greater number of requirements] than your average law school." While that might cause a few students to complain, most readily acknowledge that this "makes you much more prepared for the bar and practice." Additionally, Wake's relatively small size certainly comes with some advantages and disadvantages. As a knowledgeable third-year explains, "Class selection can be somewhat limited. Some classes are only offered every other year, and so a 2L will need to plan ahead for two years, in some instances, in order to ensure he gets a specific course. On the other hand, the small size contributes to a familial setting that I have always found to be one of the school's strongest points."

Students at Wake also agree that professor accessibility is a boon to their education. Indeed, the faculty makes a concerted effort to "actually know your name and get to know you outside the classroom setting, which makes an exceptional academic experience." Moreover, their "doors are always open" and they frequently "welcome students...[into] their office to discuss course material or career advice." It's truly evident that professors at Wake genuinely "care about your education and want you to understand the material." A thrilled third-year eagerly adds, "All [faculty] members have a true love of teaching (as opposed to research) and their passion shows. I am not exaggerating when I say that most professors are accessible the entire week and most weekends. They will literally bend over backwards to help a student."

Perhaps not surprisingly, this openness and accessibility extends to the "very friendly and personable" administration as well. As an impressed second-year tells us, "A few of the deans know all of the students by name, which makes the school feel like a big family." Students also appreciate that they "don't dodge tough questions when it comes to policy decisions." Or, as one happy second-year simply sums up, "The administration at Wake Forest is run like a well-oiled machine."

Life

Students are generally at ease the moment they step onto Wake's campus. As a second-year shares, "I noticed from my first visit and it still holds true that the quality of people here are second to none. There will always be a spectrum, but on the whole the administrators, professors, and students really do strive for a family atmosphere. All schools pitch this, but Wake really delivers."

R. Jay Shively, Assistant Dean of Admissions and Financial Aid
Box 7206, Winston-Salem, NC 27109
Tel: 336-758-5437 • Fax: 336-758-3930
E-Mail: admissions@law.wfu.edu • Website: www.law.wfu.edu

Moreover, there's a lot of learning to be done outside of the classroom at Wake as well. For example, "respected practicing attorneys, renowned authors, and public figures often speak at on-campus events, and stick around to talk privately with smaller groups of students as well." Impressively, Wake has also managed to lure United States Supreme Court Justices to campus. Indeed, one ecstatic student brags that a justice "visited an entire day with students during my second year and another... is a regular contributor to the study abroad program in the summer." This helps to ensure that the court is not seen as" simply some mythical creature students discuss in class, but a tangible entity filled with real people."

While hometown Winston-Salem might not have the bustling night-life of other, more urban areas, it certainly has "an abundance of great restaurants" of which students are quick to take advantage. Moreover, "nearby outdoor activities make it a great place to spend three years. If you are into hiking or mountain biking you will have ample opportunities to exploit the great locations all over the area, just within a thirty minute drive."

Getting In

Securing admission to Wake Forest Law is no simple feat. The median GPA of successful applicants is 3.58 and the median LSAT score is 161. Therefore, you'll need a strong undergraduate record if you hope to be a competitive candidate.

Clinical program required	No
Legal writing course requirement	Yes
Legal methods course requirement	No
Legal research course requirement	Yes
Moot court requirement	No
Public interest law requirement	No

ADMISSIONS

Selectivity Rating	87
# applications received	2,028
% applicants accepted	53
% acceptees attending	17
Average LSAT	161
Median LSAT	161
LSAT Range (25th to 75th percentile)	157–163
Average undergrad GPA	3.58
Median undergrad GPA	3.58
Application fee	$75
Regular application deadline	3/15
Regular notification	5/1
Transfer students accepted	Yes
Evening division offered	No
Part-time accepted	No
CAS accepted	Yes

International Students

TOEFL required of international students.	Yes

FINANCIAL FACTS

Annual tuition	$41,900
Books and supplies	$1,400
Room & Board	$9,900
Financial aid application deadline	3/15
% first-year students receiving some sort of aid	96
% all students receiving some sort of aid	95
% of aid that is merit based	30
% receiving scholarships	92
Average grant	$22,000
Average loan	$36,652
Average total aid package	$62,000
Average debt	$98,148

EMPLOYMENT INFORMATION

Career Rating	94	
Total 2014 JD Grads	187	
% for whom you have useable information	53	
% grads employed ten months out	91	
Median starting salary	$70,000	
# employed full-time	166	
# employed part-time	5	
# employed bar required	139	
# employed JD preferred	26	
# employed professional/other	6	
# pursuing advanced degree	3	
# unemployed and seeking employment	9	
# not seeking employment	1	
% grads employed by school	3	
State for bar exam	NC, GA, MD, NY, VA	
Pass rate for first-time bar	91.8	

Prominent Alumni
George Holding, U.S. Representative representing North Carolina; Robert L. Ehrlich, Former Maryland Governor and Congressman

Grads Employed by Field (%)
Academic (3)
Business/Industry (19)
Government (12)
Judicial Clerkship (9)
Federal: (4)
State or local: (5)
Private Practice (43)
Solo: (3)
2-10: (19)
11-25: (2)
26-50: (4)
51-100: (1)
101-250: (4)
251-500: (3)
501+: (6)
Public Interest (5)

WASHBURN UNIVERSITY
SCHOOL OF LAW

INSTITUTIONAL INFORMATION

Public/private	Public
Affiliation	No Affiliation
% faculty female	39
% faculty underrepresented minority	14
Total faculty	28

SURVEY SAYS...

Diverse opinions accepted in classrooms, Great research resources, Abundant externship/internship/clerkship opportunities

STUDENTS

Enrollment of law school	322
% male/female	65/35
% from out-of-state	38
% part-time	0
% underrepresented minority	16
% international	1
# of countries represented	5
Average age of entering class	27

ACADEMICS

Academic Experience Rating	**82**
Profs interesting rating	86
Profs accessible rating	95
Hours of study per day	3.83

Academic Specialties

Corporation Securities, Environmental, Government Services, International, Taxation, Intellectual Property

Advanced Degrees Offered

JD (JD) degree, 90 credit hrs, 3 yrs; LLM in Global Legal Studies, 24–30 credit hrs, 1 yr; MSL, 30 credit hrs, 1+ yrs.

Combined Degrees Offered

JD/MBA; JD/MSW; JD/MAcc

Academics

Washburn University is a school with a "hometown" feel and "great community spirit" that offers terrific "bang for the buck." Students describe their academic experience as "simply fantastic," and the school as "familial, warm, and comfortable!" If there is a downside to Washburn, it is its location in Topeka, Kansas. "'The law school is great, Topeka is really terrible' is a thought that goes through my mind regularly," a 1L says. However, Topeka, the capital of Kansas, does help the school offer "wonderful networking opportunities," and "the local alumni... are very involved with the school and student events." Topeka also "has the benefit of being the center of politics in Kansas," a 1L notes before adding "but that is about it." Some highlights of Washburn's School of Law are "the Centers for Excellence and Certificate Programs" which "are highly practical and well respected in the industry."

Students say "the administration and professors are great" at Washburn, and everyone is "very approachable, friendly, and willing to help." "The deans treat us as colleagues and not as mere students,'" a happy 1L says. "They solicit and welcome our views and input on everything we can be part of." The "highly intellectual, experienced, [and] energetic" professors "are very easy to talk to both in and out of class" and "have an open-door policy." A few students do grumble about the "grading policies," wondering "could we get rid of the curve?!" Still, "class sizes are wonderful" and the faculty and staff "are willing to do whatever it takes for their students to succeed." "Every professor has practical experience from all over the country and many of which are still highly regarded in their respected fields," one 3L says. Another student states: "I love that the curriculum is taught in a way that you can see the application of the material to real life work experience."

The law school's facility "was constructed in the 1960s" and is in desperate need of "a cosmetic makeover." Luckily, the school is "building a new law school soon" after getting "approval of funding for a brand new, $40 million law school." The current building still houses the "largest research library in the region" and "electronic resources and IT department [that] are second to none." "The library and study areas are very good," "the classrooms are all of great size," and "the resources available are more than adequate." Classes contain "ample room for books, laptop, and legal pad." However, students have nothing kind to say about the "terrible" and "nonexistent" parking situation. "If you aren't there at eight, expect to be parking half a mile away," a 3L explains. Still, the "excitement is very high with the announcement of a new building" and students are high on Washburn. "Washburn approaches learning from a community perspective," a 1L says, explaining what makes Washburn unique. "If we support one another they whole community will flourish, rather than making it a race to the top."

PRESTON NICHOLSON, DIRECTOR OF ADMISSIONS
1700 COLLEGE AVENUE, TOPEKA, KS 66621-1140
TEL: 785-670-1185 • FAX: 785-670-1120
E-MAIL: ADMISSIONS@WASHBURNLAW.EDU • WEBSITE: WASHBURNLAW.EDU

Life

The environment at Washburn is "very collaborative," and the students "all more or less tend to get along and look out for each other." The school lacks "cutthroat competition" found at some law schools. Instead, "everyone is so friendly and genuinely wants you to succeed!" "From the academic atmosphere to the social atmosphere every facet of the school has been welcoming and accommodating," a 1L says of their first semester. Other students contend, "Topeka is not really terrible." There are "a lot of wonderful attributes such as the low cost of living" and many "family friendly activities." The city is "located very close to Lawrence (twenty miles) and Kansas City (forty-five miles) both of which offer anything you could think of needing." As one student sums it up, "it's not a pleasant place to live, but definitely a pleasant place to study the law!"

Getting In

The average GPA and LSAT scores for the 2014 class were 3.25 and 152 respectively. In addition to these scores, letters of recommendation, and personal statement, Washburn looks at factors such as work experience and a history of community service when judging applicants. The admissions committee also recognizes the benefits of a diverse student body.

Clinical program required	No
Legal writing course requirement	Yes
Legal methods course requirement	Yes
Legal research course requirement	Yes
Moot court requirement	No
Public interest law requirement	No

ADMISSIONS

Selectivity Rating	78
# applications received	519
% applicants accepted	64
% acceptees attending	34
Average LSAT	152
Median LSAT	151
LSAT Range (25th to 75th percentile)	148–156
Average undergrad GPA	3.25
Median undergrad GPA	3.28
Application fee	$40
Regular application deadline	4/1
Early application deadline	4/1
Transfer students accepted	Yes
Evening division offered	No
Part-time accepted	No
CAS accepted	Yes

International Students

TOEFL recommended of international students.	Yes

FINANCIAL FACTS

Annual tuition (in-state/out-of-state)	$19,024/$29,696
Books and supplies	$1,800
Fees	$70
Room & Board	$9,261
Financial aid application deadline	7/1
% first-year students receiving some sort of aid	91
% all students receiving some sort of aid	90
% of aid that is merit based	29
% receiving scholarships	54
Average grant	$23,246
Average loan	$18,187
Average total aid package	$25,489
Average debt	$76,236

EMPLOYMENT INFORMATION

Career Rating	87
Total 2014 JD Grads	112
% for whom you have useable information	97
% grads employed ten months out	88
Median starting salary	$50,291
# employed full-time	91
# employed part-time	6
# employed bar required	82
# employed JD preferred	13
# employed professional/other	1
# employed non-professional	2
# pursuing advanced degree	1
# unemployed and seeking employment	7
# not seeking employment	2
State for bar exam	KS, MO
Pass rate for first-time bar	85.3

Prominent Alumni
Lillian A. Apodaca, Past President Hispanic Bar Association; Robert J. Dole, Former U.S. Senator; Bill Kurtis, Journalist/American Justice; Delano E. Lewis, Former Ambassador to South Africa

Grads Employed by Field (%)
Academic (2)
Business/Industry (12)
Government (19)
Judicial Clerkship (3)
State or local: (3)
Private Practice (51)
Solo: (9)
2-10: (29)
11-25: (4)
26-50: (6)
51-100: (6)
101-250: (0)
251-500: (0)
Size Unknown: (1)
Public Interest (2)

WASHINGTON AND LEE UNIVERSITY
SCHOOL OF LAW

INSTITUTIONAL INFORMATION

Public/private	Private
% faculty part-time	51
% faculty female	32
% faculty underrepresented minority	15
Total faculty	80

SURVEY SAYS...

Diverse opinions accepted in classrooms, Abundant externship/internship/clerkship opportunities, Law school well run, Strong sense of community

STUDENTS

Enrollment of law school	419
% male/female	52/48
% from out-of-state	80
% part-time	0
% underrepresented minority	17
% international	4
# of countries represented	13
Average age of entering class	24

ACADEMICS

Academic Experience Rating	95
Profs interesting rating	97
Profs accessible rating	99
Hours of study per day	4.72

Advanced Degrees Offered
LLM

Combined Degrees Offered
JD/MHA, 4.5 yrs

Academics

Washington and Lee may be "small in size, but [it] has the resources of a large tier-one law school." W&L small size means "tiny class sizes" with great "faculty to student ratio[s]." It also fosters a friendly atmosphere where everyone "genuinely care[s] about you and your success." Other benefits include a "strong alumni presence," "challenging, but fulfilling" academics, and "the slow atmosphere of Lexington, VA" that "leaves fewer distractions from school." By far the most raved about aspect of W&L's School of Law is that it has the "best 3L program in the country" that "has revolutionized legal teaching." The third year program "focuses heavily on practice preparation and client interaction" and students are "put through an 'immersion' course at the beginning of each semester, which is an intense practice-based scenario in litigation (fall semester) and transaction work (spring semester)." This is a great improvement "over the traditional law school curriculum where 3L is basically just a year of spending money and killing time."

"The facilities themselves are good, especially for such a small school," and "classrooms are equipped with up-to-date technology." While it's not in the most attractive or state of the art building...the campus as a whole is quite beautiful and homey," one student observes. Another says "Sydney Lewis Hall is a 1970s monstrosity," but "the administration is making a concerted effort to renovate the building." One benefit of Washington and Lee's facilities is that every student has "their own study carrel" in the "amazing" library. Like the building itself, these carrels may be "a bit old (and cold)," but are still a luxury that not every law school affords. As a 1L explains, "Law school is not a walk in the park but W&L makes it as nice as it can be, in a lot of ways."

Students give high ratings to the staff, saying "everyone from the cafeteria employees to the dean of the school is phenomenal." "The administration is extremely caring and helpful," but "the faculty are head and shoulders above the administration." Students say the biggest strength of the school is the "teachers, teachers, and teachers." The "brilliant" professors at W&L are "extremely accessible" with a "strict open-door policy that gives the entire school a community feel." There could be more "diversity among professors" though, and the administration "[sells] more parking passes than there are parking spots." On the downside, "The Office of Career Planning is widely regarded as an unhelpful place." Professors use "the Socratic method, and classes have always been an environment of tolerance." "If you want to stay anywhere near sane during law school, this is the place to go," a 1L concludes.

SHAWN McSHAY, ASSISTANT DEAN FOR ADMISSIONS
OFFICE OF ADMISSIONS, SYDNEY LEWIS HALL, ROOM 490, LEXINGTON, VA 24450-0303
TEL: 540-458-8503 • FAX: 540-458-8586
E-MAIL: LAWADM@WLU.EDU • WEBSITE: LAW.WLU.EDU

Life

Washington and Lee's School of Law has something of a party reputation, and "law school sports and cocktail parties are frequent." The school itself actually "fund[s] weekend parties throughout the month of February that we host at our homes (but don't pay for alcohol or cleanup the next day.)" Because of the school's small size, "the students all get to know each other very well, and the professors/administrators also get to know each of us on an individual basis." The student body is not very diverse, but "the administration is consciously making an effort to bring in students from all backgrounds." The city of Lexington is "a very slow moving place with not a lot to do other than study," although "it's close enough to Roanoke and Richmond" if students desire something only a "real city" can provide. "The Indian food in Roanoke (less than an hour away) is great," one student reports. The area is "very rural," but some students like the "natural" surroundings which allow for "tubing down the Maury River, hiking House Mountain," and many other outdoor activities.

Getting In

For a recent entering class, the range (25th to 75th percentiles) for GPA and LSAT scores were 3.36 to 3.66 and 160 to 165, respectively. In addition to these scores, Washington and Lee requires letters of recommendation and a personal statement. Interviews and work experience are optional, but are considered important factors by the admissions committee.

Clinical program required	No
Legal writing course requirement	Yes
Legal methods course requirement	No
Legal research course requirement	Yes
Moot court requirement	No
Public interest law requirement	No

ADMISSIONS

Selectivity Rating	91
# applications received	2,409
% applicants accepted	38
% acceptees attending	12
Average LSAT	162
Median LSAT	164
LSAT Range (25th to 75th percentile)	160–165
Average undergrad GPA	3.49
Median undergrad GPA	3.51
Application fee	$0
Regular application deadline	3/1
Regular notification	3/31
Transfer students accepted	Yes
Evening division offered	No
Part-time accepted	No
CAS accepted	Yes

International Students

TOEFL required of international students.	Yes

FINANCIAL FACTS

Annual tuition	$44,440
Books and supplies	$2,500
Room & Board	$16,123
Financial aid application deadline	2/15
% first-year students receiving some sort of aid	98
% all students receiving some sort of aid	94
% of aid that is merit based	98
% receiving scholarships	79
Average grant	$24,070
Average loan	$38,266
Average total aid package	$50,802
Average debt	$109,422

EMPLOYMENT INFORMATION

Career Rating	92	
Total 2014 JD Grads	143	
% for whom you have useable information	70	
% grads employed ten months out	83	
Median starting salary	$69,500	
# employed full-time	102	
# employed part-time	16	
# employed bar required	102	
# employed JD preferred	15	
# employed non-professional	1	
# pursuing advanced degree	3	
# unemployed and seeking employment	21	
# not seeking employment	1	
State for bar exam	VA, NY, CA, TX, PA	
Pass rate for first-time bar	80.4	

Prominent Alumni
Bob Goodlatte, Congressman and Chair of the House Judiciary Committee; Robert Grey, ABA President; Lewis Powell, U.S. Supreme Court Justice; Chris Wolf, Cyber Security/ Privacy Expert; Lizanne Thomas, Managing Partner, Jones Day

Grads Employed by Field (%)
Academic (1)
Business/Industry (11)
Government (13)
Judicial Clerkship (10)
Private Practice (42)
Public Interest (5)

WASHINGTON UNIVERSITY
SCHOOL OF LAW

INSTITUTIONAL INFORMATION

Public/private	Private
Affiliation	No Affiliation
% faculty part-time	52
% faculty female	43
% faculty underrepresented minority	14
Total faculty	159

SURVEY SAYS...
Diverse opinions accepted in classrooms, Great research resources, Abundant externship/internship/clerkship opportunities

STUDENTS

Enrollment of law school	753
% male/female	56/46
% part-time	<1
% underrepresented minority	22
% international	5
# of countries represented	16
Average age of entering class	23

ACADEMICS

Academic Experience Rating	**89**
Profs interesting rating	88
Profs accessible rating	87
Hours of study per day	3.59

Academic Specialties
Bankruptcy, Commercial, Consumer, Corporate & Business, Criminal, Employment & Labor, Environmental, Government Services, Human Rights, Intellectual Property, International & Comparative, Legal Practice & Legal Research, Negotiation & Dispute Resolution, Property, Public Interest, Taxation, Trial & Advocacy

Advanced Degrees Offered
JD; JSD; LLM for Foreign Lawyers; LLM in Taxation; LLM in Intellectual Property and Technology Law; LLM with Concentration in Negotiation and Dispute Resolution; MLS

Combined Degrees Offered
JD/MA Biology, East Asian Studies, International Affairs, Islamic and

Academics

The once hidden gem of Washington University School of Law has now become one of the most well-respected law communities in the nation. The excellent academics, "generous" scholarships, and "great course selections" have made this a law school on the rise, and as firms in national metropolitan centers recognize this, WashU Law's reputation only grows. This excellent reputation "has been priceless in the current job market" for recent graduates, and together, "the student body and administration create a fantastic environment which helps to lessen the inevitable stress of law school."

The "expert" professors are "as accessible as you can possibly find," and they "are very good at what they do, especially the adjuncts," keeping the material "interesting" while "really challenging you to critically think." They also "care a whole lot about your career after school is over if you take time to reach out." Experience is not difficult to come by here, as WashULaw guarantees every interested JD student at least one clinical experience during their time in law school.

One student in particular agrees: "Washington University has provided me the opportunity to gain practical experience while obtaining my JD. Since I've started last year, I've had internships with the New Jersey Attorney General, Federal Public Defender's Office, and the New York Attorney General." These individuals are "not short on theoretical understanding, either."

The Career Services Office is "top notch" and serves as a huge draw to students in choosing WashULaw as their law school; it is "extremely engaged" and "goes out of their way to connect you with employers, alumni, and other resources to aid you in your job search." "The CSO here is absolutely incredible and I wouldn't be at a different school for anything right now," says one student. If you want to take an extra semester to do an internship, the office "will work with you to make sure you are getting the educational experience you want, while still completing the requirements for graduation." Many students spend a semester in New York City working full time doing securities regulation while obtaining a full semester's worth of credits. Another claims, "When I was accepted to the school, they asked what city I wanted to work in when I graduated and what practice areas I was interested in. Soon after I provided this information, they began connecting me with countless attorneys doing exactly what I hope[d] to do in the same city that I want[ed] to do it."

While WashU guarantees funding for 1L students working in the public interest and the school has a dedicated career advisor for public service, many students agree that there is "not enough support for public interest careers" (particularly after your 1L summer). Still, it is clear to anyone who attends WashU Law that the school truly "looks out for its students," and administrators "are SUPER helpful and bend over backwards to accommodate individual situations." The schools also host "a medley of workshops every day in order to foster students' employment prospects in what is a very bad legal market." Hard work sees a direct result here. At WashULaw, students are not "guaranteed" interviews during on and off campus interview programs—they earn them on their own merit. Students are selected by employers based upon their unique qualifications.

Life

Students at WashU Law are "very friendly and social," as well as "relatively laid-back." People are "competitive, but friendly;" if you miss class, "your friends will be more than happy to give you their notes." The school does an excellent job of maintaining a culture

KATHERINE SCANNELL, ASSOCIATE DEAN FOR ADMISSIONS
1 BROOKINGS DRIVE, CAMPUS BOX 1120, ST. LOUIS, MO 63130-4899
TEL: 314-935-4525 • FAX: 314-935-8778
E-MAIL: APPLYLAW@WUSTL.EDU • WEBSITE: APPLY.LAW.WUSTL.EDU

of hard work and general sociability. "My classmates are extremely bright and I know they will be excellent connections to have throughout my career," says a student. Student life is "amazing," and everyone is "very happy…well-adjusted," and "have a lot going on outside of the classroom, including good groups of friends." "We are a very social school, I go out with my classmates frequently," says one student.

The law school building is "beautiful," particularly the twenty-four-hour library reading room ("like something out of *Harry Potter*") and the central courtyard where "students gather during the day and at weekly Happy Hour each Friday." "I feel like just being in the building makes me smarter," says one student. Aside from the Friday Happy Hour, the SBA organizes a "well-attended" bar review every Thursday, which features drink specials and more socializing. St. Louis is "a great place to spend three years," as "there's plenty of things to do, the housing is cheap, and the city has lots of personality," according to one student. The student body is a mix of recent grads and older students, and though the older students with spouses and families are "less involved in the traditional social scene," they do not feel "lost and alone amongst the twenty-two-year-olds." Most people here are more liberal-minded, and there is a consensus that this "type of homogeny could use a little breaking up," if only for the sake of discourse.

Getting In

Washington University's reputation for quality is quite well known, and the school receives over 4,500 applications for approximately 200 spots in the entering class, so admission is highly competitive. Washington University has a holistic approach to admission decisions, considering many qualities candidates offer. Some applicants are asked to provide additional information or documentation to support their application based on an expanded set of criteria. The interview process is a critical part of this holistic approach to the admissions process. A two to three page personal statement is also recommended, and two letters of recommendation are strongly encouraged. The median LSAT score for the entering class of 2014 was 166, and the median GPA was 3.62.

Near Eastern Studies, or Jewish Studies; JD/MBA; JD/MSW; JD/MPH; JD/LLM in Taxation; JD/LLM with Concentration in Negotiation and Dispute Resolution; JD/LLM in Intellectual Property and Technology Law; Flexibility for individualized degree programs.

Clinical program required	No
Legal writing course requirement	Yes
Legal methods course requirement	Yes
Legal research course requirement	Yes
Moot court requirement	No
Public interest law requirement	No

ADMISSIONS

Selectivity Rating	95
# applications received	4,649
% applicants accepted	30
% acceptees attending	19.3
Median LSAT	166
LSAT Range (25th to 75th percentile)	162–167
Median undergrad GPA	3.62
Application fee	$70
Regular application deadline	6/1
Early application deadline	12/1
Transfer students accepted	Yes
Evening division offered	No
Part-time accepted	No
CAS accepted	Yes

International Students

TOEFL recommended of international students.	Yes

FINANCIAL FACTS

Annual tuition	$51,216
Books and supplies	$2,000
Fees	$1,802
Room & Board (off campus)	$14,400
Financial aid application deadline	7/1
% of aid that is merit based	100
% receiving scholarships	76
Average grant	$26,000
Average loan	$40,327
Average total aid package	$71,000
Average debt	$109,232

EMPLOYMENT INFORMATION

Career Rating	71	Grads Employed by Field (%)	
Total 2014 JD Grads	258	Academic (3)	
% grads employed ten months out	95	Business/Industry (19)	
# employed full-time	240	Government (15)	
# employed part-time	5	Judicial Clerkship (8)	
# employed bar required	207	Private Practice (47)	
# employed JD preferred	35	Public Interest (2)	
# employed professional/other	2		
# employed non-professional	1		
# pursuing advanced degree	10		
# unemployed and seeking employment	1		
# not seeking employment	2		
% grads employed by school	6		
State for bar exam	MO, NY, IL, CA		

WAYNE STATE UNIVERSITY
LAW SCHOOL

INSTITUTIONAL INFORMATION

Public/private	Public
Affiliation	No Affiliation
Student-faculty ratio	10:1
% faculty part-time	38
% faculty female	41
% faculty underrepresented minority	14
Total faculty	56

SURVEY SAYS...
Diverse opinions accepted in classrooms

STUDENTS

Enrollment of law school	413
% male/female	57/43
% from out-of-state	3
% part-time	29
% underrepresented minority	12
% international	2
# of countries represented	2
Average age of entering class	26

ACADEMICS

Academic Experience Rating	**85**
Profs interesting rating	80
Profs accessible rating	80
Hours of study per day	3.10

Advanced Degrees Offered
JD, 3 yrs full-time. LLM, 1 year full-time.

Combined Degrees Offered
JD/MBA; JD/MA in Economics, History, Political Science, and Dispute Resolution; JD/MS in Criminal Justice. 4 yrs for each.

Academics

A proudly local institution, Wayne State University Law School maintains deep ties in the city of Detroit and with an active alumni network throughout Michigan. "Being in right in Detroit is great [because] this is the heart of the legal community in Michigan." Students get the chance to explore the multiple legal opportunities the city has to offer while still in school, and "Wayne State has a strong public interest focus, encouraging activity in Detroit and the metropolitan area." Students say that the school's clinic programs and practical work experience "[are] diverse and [have] a high level of participation. The access to community resources for placements is superior. Many students have clerk or intern positions during 2L and 3L years." In terms of co-curricular activities, "Wayne State has one of the nation's top Jessup International Moot Court teams," and this often leads to post-law school job opportunities thanks to Wayne State's "robust alumni network." "Coupled with a strong moot court and tough curriculum, attorneys from Michigan, and even Chicago, are open to hiring Wayne State students for summer associate positions and post-graduate opportunities." Students point to the Keith Center for Civil Rights as one of the school's academic draws.

Wayne State further demonstrates its commitment to producing the next generation of Detroit lawyers through its traditional full-time JD program, as well as a combined day-evening program, and an evening program. "Wayne State Law has an excellent evening program, due in large part to the fantastic professors," though "the [evening] course offerings are much less diverse—making it difficult to take courses in certain areas." For all students, the JD curriculum begins with a set of core courses in contracts, civil procedure, torts, and other key areas like legal writing and research. After completing these required courses, the upper-level courses include an extensive list of elective courses and seminars, many of them interdisciplinary in nature, covering a broad range of subjects; recent elective options have included Advanced Bankruptcy, Animal Law, European Union Law, and Taxation of Corporations. One student points out, "As with any school, a course's strength is determined by the professor" but on the whole, Wayne State students seemed pleased with the school's offerings.

The professors at Wayne State are "knowledgeable, helpful, available, and interesting"— "not only do they know their trade, they know how to effectively communicate that skill to the student." Students describe their professors as "approachable, knowledgeable, and obviously passionate about the law," though one student laments that "some are more accessible than others." The fact that "the faculty truly supports the students in their career goals" and takes "extra time to provide advice and connect students to resources" is of particular importance to law students. Unlike students at many other law schools, Wayne State students single out the Career Services department. "The Career Services Department connects students with employers and provides programs so that students can access programs" and "really works hard to connect you to the opportunities you are interested in—even if it's not the conventional route." The administration, however, does not always pass muster: It is "not very transparent and is apt to change rules and/or guidelines without much notice" and "good once you know them, but [administrators] do not make themselves accessible enough to new students." When it comes to the nuts and bolts of buildings and classrooms, students note that there are "older facilities that are in serious need of updating" and "[Basic] maintenance issues . . . persist [with] significant flooding every year rendering certain rooms unusable or undesirable for days/weeks at a time." Others counter that "the facilities, while somewhat outdated, have started to improve. The new classrooms and wings of the law school are wonderful and remind me of a well-funded law practice."

ERICKA M. JACKSON, ASSISTANT DEAN OF ADMISSIONS
471 W. PALMER, DETROIT, MI 48202
TEL: 313-577-3937 • FAX: 313-993-8129
E-MAIL: LAWINQUIRE@WAYNE.EDU • WEBSITE: WWW.LAW.WAYNE.EDU

Student Life

The law school is located on Wayne State's urban campus in midtown Detroit. Many Wayne students live in the suburbs and commute to the city for classes but say that "the area immediately around the campus is cool and well traveled." Student organizations are "pretty prominent and provide many ways to get involved if you wish to do so" and the general feeling on campus is one of a "small, tight-knit community." While some students say, "Racial diversity in the law school is not what it should be given our location in the heart of Detroit," others counter that diversity is one of the school's strengths and "there is an emphasis on diversity, which is great."

Getting In

Wayne State's admissions numbers fluctuates but on average it accepts roughly 48 percent of the students who apply. Enrolled students in the 25th percentile have an approximate GPA of 2.99 and an LSAT score of 152, while enrolled students in the 75th percentile have a GPA around 3.56 and an LSAT score around 160.

Clinical program required	Yes
Legal writing course requirement	Yes
Legal methods course requirement	No
Legal research course requirement	Yes
Moot court requirement	No
Public interest law requirement	No

ADMISSIONS

Selectivity Rating	84
# applications received	701
% applicants accepted	48
% acceptees attending	35
Average LSAT	156
Median LSAT	156
LSAT Range (25th to 75th percentile)	152–160
Average undergrad GPA	3.39
Median undergrad GPA	3.29
Application fee	$0
Regular application deadline	6/30
Transfer students accepted	Yes
Evening division offered	Yes
Part-time accepted	Yes
CAS accepted	Yes

FINANCIAL FACTS

Annual tuition (in-state/ out-of-state)	$27,266/$29,963
Books and supplies	$1,665
Fees	$1,801
Room & Board (on/ off campus)	$9,269/$12,696
Financial aid application deadline	6/30
% first-year students receiving some sort of aid	97
% all students receiving some sort of aid	50
% of aid that is merit based	36
% receiving scholarships	65
Average grant	$17,390
Average loan	$25,932
Average total aid package	$31,695
Average debt	$85,925

EMPLOYMENT INFORMATION

Career Rating	87	
Total 2014 JD Grads	169	
% for whom you have useable information	99	
% grads employed ten months out	86	
Median starting salary	$70,000	
# employed full-time	123	
# employed part-time	22	
# employed bar required	98	
# employed JD preferred	29	
# employed professional/other	17	
# employed non-professional	1	
# pursuing advanced degree	4	
# unemployed and seeking employment	19	
% grads employed by school	3	
State for bar exam	MI	
Pass rate for first-time bar	83.2	

Prominent Alumni
Eugene Driker, Business Law; Hon. Nancy G. Edmunds, Judge, U.S. District Court; Tyrone C. Fahner, Antitrust; Hon. Damon J. Keith, Civil rights; Judge, U.S. Court of Appeals for the Sixth Circuit; Jessica Cooper, Oakland County Prosecutor

Grads Employed by Field (%)
Academic (1)
Business/Industry (18)
Government (8)
Judicial Clerkship (1)
Private Practice (72)
  Solo: (4)
  2-10: (25)
  11-25: (5)
  51-100: (5)
  101-250: (9)
  251-500: (5)
  501+: (0)
  Size Unknown: (0)
Public Interest (4)

WEST VIRGINIA UNIVERSITY
COLLEGE OF LAW

INSTITUTIONAL INFORMATION

Public/private	Public
Affiliation	No Affiliation
Student-faculty ratio	10:1
% faculty part-time	34
% faculty female	40
% faculty underrepresented minority	7
Total faculty	69

SURVEY SAYS...
Great research resources

STUDENTS

Enrollment of law school	347
% male/female	61/40
% from out-of-state	25
% part-time	1
% underrepresented minority	9
% international	0
# of countries represented	2
Average age of entering class	25

ACADEMICS

Academic Experience Rating	83
Profs interesting rating	72
Profs accessible rating	81
Hours of study per day	3.64

Academic Specialties
Constitutional, Criminal, Business, Energy and Sustainable Development, Family, Healthcare, Intellectual Property, International, Labor and Employment, Public Interest, Tax

Advanced Degrees Offered
JD, 3 yrs. LLM Energy & Sustainable Development,1 yr; LLM Forensic Justice, 1 yr

Combined Degrees Offered
JD/MPA 4 yrs; JD/EMBA 3 yrs (Executive MBA)

Academics

West Virginia University's College of Law provides students with a "personal, yet professional, atmosphere," where the "emphasis [is] on being a functional lawyer." The dirt-cheap tuition (for in-state residents, who comprise the overwhelming majority of students here) and "passionate, intelligent, and helpful" people that make up the faculty, staff, and student body, all converge to offer a "great value" to the happy students that go here.

As one might expect from the only law school in the state, the school has "a great relationship with the state and state bar." This you-rub-my-back-and-I'll-rub yours relationship leads one second-year student to comment, "If you plan to practice law in West Virginia, the College of Law is a brilliant choice—who better to learn from than the justices and lobbyists who wrote the law?" Some of the greatest strengths of WVU Law are the clinical programs. "The school offers [nine] clinics ranging from general, family, tax, energy, and entrepreneurship. Clinics are offered to all 3L students; some clinics are open to 2Ls." Most students do choose to practice within the state after graduation, which helps the school focus both its curriculum and its alumni network with stellar results. But there are "diverse courses in a variety of practice areas, and many students leave the state and successfully practice law in other states." Career Services is "particularly strong" in placing students in jobs throughout West Virginia, attributable in part to "an active on-campus interview program and in part to WVU's intimate connection with the West Virginia legal community."

The College of Law enjoys faculty members who are a combination of "inspirational, well-published, and leading state authorities in their subjects." Professors "care about students as individuals" and "encourage...and help them to achieve whatever types of goals that individual has." All teachers "know material well and convey the information in an easy-to-understand way." People are torn as to the efficacy of the Legal Research and Writing Program, which has undergone a recent revamping, but the Academic Excellence Center is available to "provide an essential foundation for struggling students."

The administration at West Virginia University's College of Law is "very laid-back" and follows the same open-door policy as the faculty. Although there are around 400 students, the administration "seemingly knows everyone's names," and it's not unusual to see "both faculty and administrators lounging with students during lunch hours." Students share some grievances regarding the rather clunky and inflexible registration system, saying "you get the classes at the times they pick, no exceptions." Fortunately, the diversity of classes expands in the second year of law school. While students have said in the past that the online course registration process can feel like a "gladiatorial battle to get into the classes you like," there have been recent improvements to the WVU online registration process

The law school was "renovated [in 2014], receiving a $26 million dollar addition." The classrooms within are "fantastic," which is also how students describe WVU Law's staff—particularly the "very friendly and helpful" library staff, which includes "a librarian that will literally help you at any hour of the night (she'll even be your Facebook friend)."

TINA M. JERNIGAN, DIRECTOR OF ADMISSIONS
P.O. BOX 6130, MORGANTOWN, WV 26506-6130
TEL: 304-293-5304 • FAX: 304-293-6891
E-MAIL: WVULAW.ADMISSIONS@MAIL.WVU.EDU • WEBSITE: WWW.LAW.WVU.EDU

Life

The camaraderie among WVU Law students lends to an atmosphere that is "like one big family." "West Virginia has a small bar and we will all be practicing together after graduation, so everyone treats each other with respect," says a 2L. Students "form study groups, help each other out, and much more." "We do not see one another as competition, but as colleagues," says a student. The student body (and the faculty) is "not very racially diverse," "not too competitive," and there are "excellent relations amongst students."

The school provides a good deal of social events for students to take part in. And take part they do: Students "work during the week, and cut loose on the weekends." WVU football is the fulcrum of many social activities, and there is a fair amount of alcohol involved in the ample tailgating and extracurricular activities on offer here. Luckily, Morgantown is a "social city," providing "ample opportunities to explore your social life to any extent to which you desire," though students note it does help to have a car.

Getting In

For a recently admitted class, accepted students at the 25th percentile had an average LSAT score of 152 and an average GPA of 3.41. Applicants are required to submit two letters of recommendation from people who have personal knowledge of their character, skills, and aptitude for law study and practice. At least one recommendation must be from a former professor.

Clinical program required	No
Legal writing course requirement	Yes
Legal methods course requirement	No
Legal research course requirement	Yes
Moot court requirement	No
Public interest law requirement	No

ADMISSIONS

Selectivity Rating	**83**
# applications received	607
% applicants accepted	54
% acceptees attending	32
Average LSAT	154
Median LSAT	154
LSAT Range (25th to 75th percentile)	152–156
Average undergrad GPA	3.37
Median undergrad GPA	3.43
Application fee	$50
Regular application deadline	3/1
Transfer students accepted	Yes
Evening division offered	No
Part-time accepted	Yes
CAS accepted	Yes

International Students

TOEFL required of international students.	Yes

FINANCIAL FACTS

Annual tuition (in-state/ out-of-state)	$19,008/$35,568
Books and supplies	$3,000
Fees	$1,242
Room & Board (off campus)	$11,400
Financial aid application deadline	3/1
% first-year students receiving some sort of aid	94
% all students receiving some sort of aid	92
% of aid that is merit based	54
% receiving scholarships	54
Average grant	$11,084
Average loan	$29,956
Average total aid package	$32,056
Average debt	$84,727

EMPLOYMENT INFORMATION

Career Rating	**82**	
Total 2014 JD Grads	129	
% for whom you have useable information	98	
% grads employed ten months out	88	
Median starting salary	$55,000	
% job accepting grads providing useable salary information	68	
# employed full-time	106	
# employed part-time	8	
# employed bar required	78	
# employed JD preferred	26	
# employed professional/other	3	
# employed non-professional	5	
# pursuing advanced degree	2	
# unemployed and seeking employment	10	
# not seeking employment	1	
% grads employed by school	2	
State for bar exam	WV, PA, VA, SC, MD	
Pass rate for first-time bar	75.0	

Prominent Alumni
Robert King, Judge, U.S. Court of Appeals for the Fourth Circuit; Stephanie Thacker, Judge, U.S. Court of Appeals for the Fourth Circuit

Grads Employed by Field (%)
Academic (3)
Business/Industry (12)
Government (10)
Judicial Clerkship (14)
Federal: (4)
State or local: (10)
Other: (1)
Private Practice (46)
Solo: (2)
2-10: (17)
11-25: (9)
26-50: (3)
51-100: (1)
101-250: (5)
251-500: (4)
501+: (5)
Size Unknown: (0)
Public Interest (3)

WHITTIER COLLEGE
LAW SCHOOL

Academics

Classes are small at Whittier Law School. "This is important because it personalizes the classroom experience," explains a 2L. "The quality of teaching is extremely high" as well. The "amazing" professors at Whittier are "dedicated, smart, funny," and they are "there to teach you the law, not to hide the ball or play games." Faculty members are accessible, too, even though many adjuncts practice as real attorneys at least part time. "They are always available and attend many of our student events," beams a 2L. Students are split in their views concerning the administration. Enthusiasts note that "everyone who counts knows your name and says hello." They say that the "very responsive" top brass tries to accommodate all types of students. Critics charge that the indifferent management is "a dysfunctional nightmare." "They might find it good to start caring about their students," suggests a disgruntled 3L.

Academic bells and whistles here include a "ridiculously comprehensive legal writing program." There's a specialized certificate in Children's Rights, Environmental Law, Intellectual Property, International and Comparative Law, Trial and Appellate Practice and additional concentrations in business law and criminal law. There are four clinics and summer study abroad opportunities in China, Israel, and Spain. Whittier is also "a school that is serious about helping with bar prep." "The grading system is particularly harsh," though. The "vicious" curve allows "A" grades for no more than 10 percent of the students in any first-year course. Some 20 percent of all the students in every 1L course will get a "D" or an "F." Students at the bottom of the heap end up getting kicked out after the first year.

Career Development Office offers a Career Law Day, as well as private externship placements, and Whittier also has more than 5,000 alumni. The immediate region is pretty rich with law firms. It also happens to be the tenth largest economy on the planet. The school recently restructured their career services office, hiring three new staff members to help provide more extensive career counseling and on-campus networking opportunities.

Whittier Law School is located in "a very office building-heavy section" in the heart of suburban Orange County, "ten minutes from the Orange County and U.S. district courthouses." The library and research facilities are reportedly "excellent," but "The classrooms have no windows," observes a 2L. "There's nothing aesthetically pleasing about it at all."

Life

The student population at Whittier is pretty diverse. "Many ethnic groups and nationalities" are represented. "There also seems to be socioeconomic diversity," notes a 1L. "There are many stereotypical Orange Countians filling the parking lot with cars that cost more than houses. However, there are also many students getting by on loans and part-time jobs." Students describe themselves as "extremely intelligent." Politics vary widely. "There's a decidedly conservative bent among students who've been out in the world," though, and, on the whole, it's probably safe to say that "the students are more conservative than the teachers."

THOMAS McCOLL, ASSOCIATE DEAN FOR ENROLLMENT
3333 HARBOR BOULEVARD, COSTA MESA, CA 92626
TEL: 714-444-4141 • FAX: 714-444-3458
E-MAIL: INFO@LAW.WHITTIER.EDU • WEBSITE: WWW.LAW.WHITTIER.EDU

Some students warn that the academic environment is really intense. "Sabotage" does happen, they claim. First-year students are "crazy competitive and not always nice to each other." Others tell us that a "friendly, familial atmosphere" and a "great sense of camaraderie" pervade the campus. "We are silently competitive against each other academically. In general, we are like a big law school family," says a 3L. "Most students are very friendly and helpful." Either way, there seems to be some consensus that full-time day students are "more competitive" while the "older, working" nontraditional students who attend at night "are more willing to help each other."

The quality of life outside the classroom is pretty high, with a friendly atmosphere across campus and plenty of open green spaces for studying and socializing. The cost of living is "reasonable," at least compared to the much higher rents and costs in nearby Los Angeles. Sunshine is constant, and the weather is nice pretty much all the time. Students enjoy "close proximity to Southern California beaches such as Huntington, Newport, and Laguna." "There is an active organization on campus for just about anything a student could think of." "Students who live near the campus are exceedingly social." "There are some cliques and an in crowd." "There are many groups of people who strike me as being very tight," observes a 2L.

Getting In

Whittier has a perennially generous acceptance rate. At the same time, the raw numbers for admitted applicants are pretty high. Admitted students at the 25th percentile have LSAT scores around 143 and GPAs in the B−/C+ range. Admitted students at the 75th percentile have LSAT scores of 150 or so, and their undergraduate GPA is a tad over 3.3.

Clinical program required	No
Legal writing course requirement	Yes
Legal methods course requirement	Yes
Legal research course requirement	Yes
Moot court requirement	Yes
Public interest law requirement	No

ADMISSIONS

Selectivity Rating	70
# applications received	1,352
% applicants accepted	74
% acceptees attending	24
Average LSAT	145
Median LSAT	146
LSAT Range (25th to 75th percentile)	143–150
Average undergrad GPA	2.89
Median undergrad GPA	2.90
Application fee	$65
Early application deadline	3/15
Transfer students accepted	Yes
Evening division offered	No
Part-time accepted	Yes
CAS accepted	Yes

International Students

TOEFL required of international students.	Yes

FINANCIAL FACTS

Annual tuition	$42,300
Books and supplies	$1,750
Fees	$100
Room & Board	$16,700
Financial aid application deadline	5/1
% first-year students receiving some sort of aid	96
% all students receiving some sort of aid	91
% of aid that is merit based	16
% receiving scholarships	41
Average grant	$17,164
Average loan	$53,727
Average total aid package	$66,322
Average debt	$151,000

EMPLOYMENT INFORMATION

Career Rating	68	
Total 2014 JD Grads	194	
% for whom you have useable information	96	
% grads employed ten months out	71	
Median starting salary	$60,000	
# employed full-time	97	
# employed part-time	40	
# employed bar required	63	
# employed JD preferred	58	
# employed professional/other	10	
# employed non-professional	6	
# pursuing advanced degree	3	
# unemployed and seeking employment	39	
# not seeking employment	5	
% grads employed by school	8	
State for bar exam	CA, NV, NY, CO, TX	
Pass rate for first-time bar	46.2	

Prominent Alumni
Paul Kiesel, Kiesel Law LLP; Daniel Grigsby, General Counsel, L.A. Lakers; Steven Manning, Mgn. Partner, Manning & Kass, Ellrod, Ramirez, Trester; Christine Jones, Former Arizona Gubenatorial Candidate and Former General Counsel of Go Daddy

Grads Employed by Field (%)
Academic (8)
Business/Industry (19)
Government (2)
Private Practice (40)
  Solo: (2)
  2-10: (28)
  11-25: (5)
  26-50: (2)
  101-250: (2)
  501+: (1)
  Size Unknown: (0)
Public Interest (3)

WIDENER UNIVERSITY
DELAWARE LAW SCHOOL

INSTITUTIONAL INFORMATION

Public/private	Private
Affiliation	No Affiliation
Student-faculty ratio	13:1
% faculty part-time	54
% faculty female	48
% faculty underrepresented minority	12
Total faculty	84

SURVEY SAYS...
Diverse opinions accepted in classrooms

STUDENTS

Enrollment of law school	512
% male/female	56/44
% from out-of-state	78
% part-time	36
% underrepresented minority	25
% international	0
# of countries represented	5
Average age of entering class	23

ACADEMICS

Academic Experience Rating	**73**
Profs interesting rating	76
Profs accessible rating	80
Hours of study per day	4.04

Academic Specialties
Civil Procedure, Commercial, Constitutional, Corporation Securities, Criminal, Environmental, International

Advanced Degrees Offered
LLM in American Legal Systems, Health Law, Criminal Law, Environmental Law, Corporate and Business Law, 24 credits; MJ, 30 credits; Doctor of Laws in Health Law, 8 credits

Combined Degrees Offered
JD/MBA, 4 yrs; JD/MMP, JD/MPH: 4 yrs

Academics

Widener University Delaware Law School is "the only law school in Delaware," and in this privileged position, offers unique "access to the Delaware legal community" and opportunities "to network with the corporate capital of the United States" or, some argue, "the world." Delaware Law School builds its curricula in order to prepare students to maximize business law opportunities: "The greatest strengths this school offers are its encouragement of practical skills courses, such as judicial and clinical externships, its emphasis on legal research and writing, and its focus on business contracts drafting."

In fact, the university's location in Wilmington, Delaware Law School offers portals to extracurriculars, internships, and jobs in "the Philadelphia, Delaware, New Jersey region" as well. Many nontraditional students are attracted by Delaware Law School's "availability of an evening program" and "relatively humane tuition," in addition to the fact that "most of the professors aren't the 'Ivory Tower' type and try to keep things interesting." Student opinions of the faculty, while mostly positive, are somewhat mixed overall: "It mostly has wonderful professors that are interesting and engaging," but "the faculty varies from wildly overqualified to merely a heartbeat in the front of the room." Despite the critics, many report that "Professors are willing to help and do anything they can to help you succeed," and one student argues, "I have a graduate degree from an Ivy League university and the quality of my professors at Widener Law meet or exceed those at my prior institution."

As for how the school is run, students say the "administration of the school overall needs to improve, and to improve our school's reputation especially." "This place is a nightmare. Nothing is organized in an efficient way." As of July 2015, Delaware Law School officially separated from Widener University's other law campus in Harrisburg, Pennsylvania. By separating from the Harrisburg campus, Delaware Law School will have an administration dedicated entirely to the needs of the students in Delaware, with all student services based in Delaware. Aspiring lawyers looking to compete are eager for Widener to improve job placement—"the career development office sucks"—by doing more to raise its national ranking. "It's pretty damaging in interviews to say you go to Widener when they're also interviewing grads from Penn, Villanova, etc." Students name "availability [of] internships and externships" as a strength of the university, and tout the strong reputation of the school in the local area along with the convenient nearby corporate centers that provide a wider breadth of experiences. Facilities are very unpopular, with students calling them "terrible" and "subpar for the amount of tuition we pay," though "all classrooms are equipped with a smartboard, computer, etc." Though student feedback about some facets is mixed, many students express the belief that, "Our administration really works with the students in order to promote a healthy educational environment."

BARBARA AYARS, ASSISTANT DEAN FOR ADMISSIONS
P.O. BOX 7474, 4601 CONCORD PIKE, WILMINGTON, DE 19803-0474
TEL: 302-477-2703 • FAX: 302-477-2224
E-MAIL: LAWADMISSIONS@WIDENER.EDU • WEBSITE: LAW.WIDENER.EDU

Life

Delaware Law School's social culture, while present, is diminished by the prevalence of commuting and/or evening students. The Student Bar Association hosts some "social events." "The administration is hit and miss, the Office of Student Affairs has a wonderful staff. They work hard for the students, are easily accessible, and helpful 100 percent of the way." Many students contend that the university should retool the library to be "open 24/7 while classes are in session."

Getting In

The admissions committee at Widener gives the most weight to undergraduate GPA and LSAT scores, but they do consider other factors as well, including work experience, other graduate study, extracurricular activities and community involvement. Personal statements are required and letters of recommendation are highly encouraged as Widener takes a holistic approach to file review and looks beyond numerical indicators. Candidates are encouraged to apply early; however, applications are accepted on a rolling basis.

Clinical program required	No
Legal writing course requirement	Yes
Legal methods course requirement	Yes
Legal research course requirement	Yes
Moot court requirement	No
Public interest law requirement	No

ADMISSIONS

Selectivity Rating	**74**
# applications received	808
% applicants accepted	65
% acceptees attending	18
Average LSAT	150
Median LSAT	150
LSAT Range (25th to 75th percentile)	148–151
Average undergrad GPA	3.06
Median undergrad GPA	3.09
Application fee	$60
Regular application deadline	5/15
Transfer students accepted	Yes
Evening division offered	Yes
Part-time accepted	Yes
CAS accepted	Yes

International Students

TOEFL required of international students.	Yes

FINANCIAL FACTS

Annual tuition	$40,620
Books and supplies	$1,550
Room & Board	$11,034
Financial aid application deadline	4/1
% first-year students receiving some sort of aid	99
% all students receiving some sort of aid	96
% of aid that is merit based	19
% receiving scholarships	52
Average grant	$12,349
Average loan	$40,965
Average total aid package	$55,102
Average debt	$133,568

EMPLOYMENT INFORMATION

Career Rating	**76**	
Total 2014 JD Grads	236	
% for whom you have useable information	92	
% grads employed ten months out	84	
Median starting salary	$50,121	
% job accepting grads providing useable salary information	46	
# employed full-time	172	
# employed part-time	26	
# employed bar required	119	
# employed JD preferred	35	
# employed professional/other	33	
# employed non-professional	11	
# pursuing advanced degree	0	
# unemployed and seeking employment	16	
# not seeking employment	3	
State for bar exam	PA, NJ, DE	
Pass rate for first-time bar	68.0	

Prominent Alumni
Carl W. Battle, Class of '82, Senior Vice President and Chief Patent Counsel Glaxo Smith Kline; Cynthia Rhoades Ryan, Class of '79, Chief Counsel, Natl Geospatial Intell Agency; Honorable Lee. A. Solomon, Class of 78, Justice, New Jersey Supreme Court; Vivian L. Medinilla, Class of '93, Delaware Superior Court Judge

Grads Employed by Field (%)
Academic (1)
Business/Industry (20)
Government (11)
Judicial Clerkship (19)
State or local: (19)
Private Practice (33)
Solo: (1)
2-10: (21)
11-25: (6)
26-50: (2)
51-100: (1)
101-250: (1)
251-500: (0)
501+: (1)
Public Interest (0)

WIDENER UNIVERSITY
SCHOOL OF LAW—HARRISBURG CAMPUS

INSTITUTIONAL INFORMATION

Public/private	Private
Affiliation	No Affiliation
% faculty part-time	36
% faculty female	44
% faculty underrepresented minority	8
Total faculty	39

SURVEY SAYS...

Diverse opinions accepted in classrooms

STUDENTS

Enrollment of law school	245
% male/female	56/44
% from out-of-state	13
% part-time	29
% underrepresented minority	18
% international	0
# of countries represented	0
Average age of entering class	23

ACADEMICS

Academic Experience Rating	**75**
Profs interesting rating	84
Profs accessible rating	88
Hours of study per day	4.39

Academic Specialties

Constitutional, Environmental, Government Services

Combined Degrees Offered

JD/MSLS (Library Sciences) (w/ Clarion University of PA), 4 yrs

Academics

Some two hours away from the nearest major urban center, Widener may feel far removed from the region's major centers of education, but you'd never know it from the curriculum. Course work can be challenging but rewarding, such as the "aggressive legal methods curriculum," which is "designed to work in tandem with the core classes to help set the theory in a practical context." When it comes to grading, "the curve at Widener is unusually strict and is a major cause for concern among new students," even if "the material itself is entirely fair." However, if the "numerous tools and resources" provided to students and the "extremely knowledgeable and very accessible" professors don't help them overcome these obstacles, mentoring programs with upper level students and "practicing attorneys who have graduated from this school" will.

In addition, the faculty here "seems to genuinely care about the welfare of the students," led by professors who "truly make sure that students have every opportunity to excel." Indeed, the "passionate" professors at Widener are "the school's greatest asset," a group who "strive to ensure that the students succeed both academically and professionally." This is helped out by the tools provided to students. Technology is embraced on campus. "Every classroom is equipped with smart boards, dry erase boards, and chalkboards, as well as overhead flat screen televisions to enable easier viewing for those sitting in the rear of the room." The "exceptional" resources that are at your fingertips are a sign that "every avenue is used as a learning tool at Widener."

Students feel they have a voice in their education because the "very accessible and helpful" administration "welcomes new ideas" and "works hard to ensure that the ideas are heard," making it "eminently clear how much the administration cares about the academic and professional success of their students." If there is a gripe, it is that the administration "seems to be oblivious to the state of the job market." While educators do a good job of preparing students for job opportunities, "career services is not very helpful or good with informing students of opportunities for internships or for on campus groups." "With such huge emphasis placed on trying to find internships and legal experience," one student complains, "I feel as though the Career Development Office could use some work." That said, "a lot of the frustration stems from a practicality beyond the CDO's control; there are many law students and not very many openings for them."

Life

The "small feel" of Widener makes it a place "where everyone knows each other." Students can display "high competition," but because it's not cutthroat competition it "raises everyone's drive to achieve." A few feel there is too much closeness among students, with "people knowing too much of each other's business" and suggesting that perhaps "there's not much that can be done about this at such a small school." Still, though the small campus results in an intimacy not found in larger schools, "you can stay out of other people's business fairly easily."

BARBARA AYARS, ASSISTANT DEAN OF ADMISSIONS
3800 VARTAN WAY, P.O. BOX 69380, HARRISBURG, PA 17106-9380
TEL: 717-541-3903 • FAX: 717-541-3999
E-MAIL: LAWADMISSIONS@WIDENER.EDU • WEBSITE: LAW.WIDENER.EDU

Harrisburg is a short hop from plenty of diversions from course work, including multiple state parks and the popular Hershey amusement park. It is also less than two hours from Philadelphia, making the city's lively culture, thriving nightlife and historic interest a popular day or weekend trip. For those seeking good times in town, however, the nature of social interaction can be one-dimensional. There are minor league baseball and hockey teams, but "if you don't like bars, don't count on having a social life, because all people like to do is drink." In addition, those juggling school with full-time work and family may find that their road is an uphill one, since students in the extended division complain it is run "just like the day division," which shows "no regard to the fact that all extended division students work and most have families."

Getting In

The admissions committee at Widener gives the most weight to undergraduate GPA and LSAT scores, but they do consider other factors as well, including work experience, other graduate study, extracurricular activities and community involvement. Personal statements are required and letters of recommendation are highly encouraged as Widener takes a holistic approach to file review and looks beyond numerical indicators. Candidates are encouraged to apply early; however, applications are accepted on a rolling basis. If candidates choose to apply to both the Harrisburg and Delaware campuses, they may waive their right to choose which campus they will attend.

Clinical program required	No
Legal writing course requirement	Yes
Legal methods course requirement	Yes
Legal research course requirement	Yes
Moot court requirement	No
Public interest law requirement	No

ADMISSIONS

Selectivity Rating	73
# applications received	484
% applicants accepted	67
% acceptees attending	21
Average LSAT	148
Median LSAT	148
LSAT Range (25th to 75th percentile)	146–152
Average undergrad GPA	3.02
Median undergrad GPA	3.10
Application fee	$60
Regular application deadline	5/15
Transfer students accepted	Yes
Evening division offered	Yes
Part-time accepted	Yes
CAS accepted	Yes

International Students

TOEFL required of international students.	Yes

FINANCIAL FACTS

Annual tuition	$40,620
Books and supplies	$1,550
Room & Board (off campus)	$11,034
Financial aid application deadline	4/1
% first-year students receiving some sort of aid	97
% all students receiving some sort of aid	100
% of aid that is merit based	14
% receiving scholarships	61
Average grant	$10,832
Average loan	$45,454
Average total aid package	$47,458
Average debt	$149,693

EMPLOYMENT INFORMATION

Career Rating	81
Total 2014 JD Grads	113
% for whom you have useable information	98
% grads employed ten months out	88
Median starting salary	$50,000
% job accepting grads providing useable salary information	38
# employed full-time	86
# employed part-time	13
# employed bar required	62
# employed JD preferred	16
# employed professional/other	9
# employed non-professional	12
# pursuing advanced degree	1
# unemployed and seeking employment	11
State for bar exam	PA, MD
Pass rate for first-time bar	83.3

Prominent Alumni
Eugene DePasquale, class of '02, Pennsylvania Auditor General; Michael J. Aiello, Class of '94, Partner, Weil, Gotshal & Manges; Megan Totino Consedine, Class of '94, Pennsylvania Ststae Senate Secretary and Parliamentarian; Douglas J. Steinhardt, Class of '94, Partner, Florio Perrucci Steinhardt & Fader, LLC; William P. Doyle, Class of 2000, Federal Maritime Commisioner

Grads Employed by Field (%)
Academic (1)
Business/Industry (18)
Government (20)
Judicial Clerkship (7)
  Federal: (1)
  State or local: (6)
Private Practice (41)
  Solo: (2)
  2-10: (31)
  11-25: (4)
  26-50: (0)
  51-100: (3)
  251-500: (1)
Public Interest (0)

WILLAMETTE UNIVERSITY
COLLEGE OF LAW

INSTITUTIONAL INFORMATION

Public/private	Private
Affiliation	Methodist
Student-faculty ratio	13:1
% faculty part-time	33
% faculty female	31
% faculty underrepresented minority	13
Total faculty	52

SURVEY SAYS...

Diverse opinions accepted in classrooms, Great research resources

STUDENTS

Enrollment of law school	390
% male/female	64/36
% from out-of-state	63
% part-time	0
% underrepresented minority	18
% international	0
# of countries represented	0
Average age of entering class	26

ACADEMICS

Academic Experience Rating	**71**
Profs interesting rating	68
Profs accessible rating	70
Hours of study per day	3.75

Academic Specialties

Government Services

Advanced Degrees Offered

LLM in Transnational Law 1 yr; LLM in Dispute Resolution 1 yr

Combined Degrees Offered

Joint degree with Willamette University Atkinson Graduate School of Management (4-year JD/MBA); BA/JD (accelerated 6-year undergraduate degree/JD program) with Willamette University; 3+3 (accelerated 6 year undergraduate degree/JD program) with Oregon State University

Academics

Willamette University College of Law is "a smaller school in the Pacific Northwest," "in the state capital city" of Salem, Oregon. Highlights here include an exemplary legal research and writing program. A JD/MBA program allows students to earn both degrees in four years. There are three journals, six specialized clinics, and a broad externship program. Certificates are available in dispute resolution, business law, international and comparative law (reportedly "wonderful"), law and government, and sustainability law. Study abroad programs in Hamburg, Germany; Quito, Ecuador; and Shanghai, China are another big hit. Students also laud their surroundings. "The facilities at Willamette are, by far, among the best," they say. The "beautiful building" is located on the peaceful and collegiate-looking campus of the larger university. Classrooms are recently renovated and modern. "You have access to the library 24/7," too, which can be an invaluable perk when finals roll around each semester.

Classes are definitely on the smaller side, and they're generally "entertaining." "The greatest strength of Willamette Law has to be the faculty," relates a 2L. "The faculty is knowledgeable, accessible, and seems to generally enjoy teaching students—an extremely valuable trifecta." The "very helpful" top brass gets a lot of love as well. "The school's administration works as effectively as possible," says a 3L. "They are very focused on getting us to pass the bar," agrees a happy 1L, "and very focused on getting us a job post-graduation."

Course scheduling is probably the biggest single source of frustration among students. After the first year, it can be hard to get into the classes you want (and occasionally need). The fairly strict grading curve comes in for some grief as well. "Grade deflation" is alive and well, and a handful of 1Ls at the bottom of the class at Willamette are inevitably asked to leave each year. On one hand, it's an intimidating situation. On the other hand, it "will really help motivate."

When the time comes to get a job as an actual attorney, there's good news and bad news for newly minted Willamette alums. On the minus side, the generally mild climate and the culture of Oregon are both professionally appealing for many people. Competition for jobs (especially in Portland) is fierce because the legal market is not huge and a lot of transplant lawyers want to work in the state. On the plus side, the law school here is "down the street from" the Capitol building and various courts. Consequently, students have "fantastic access" to state legislative bodies, state courts, and state agencies. "Great networking opportunities" and prospects for practical experience outside of school abound. Students can "cooperate with the judicial process" in ways that students at the other two law schools in the state cannot.

Life

Students tell us that ethnic diversity is "increasing" at Willamette. More than 20 percent of the population here represents some minority group. "No longer can you count the number of minority students on one hand." Diversity shows itself in other ways, too. There's a decent-sized contingent of older students who are looking to transition into another, more lucrative career, for example. Also, just more than half the students come from a state other than Oregon. Some students are "very competitive" when it comes to grades. At the same time, "Willamette is a tight-knit community." "People generally hang out with the same group of friends they made in their first year of law school, but everyone still remains friendly to others."

CAROLYN DENNIS, DIRECTOR OF ADMISSION
245 WINTER STREET SE, SALEM, OR 97301-3922
TEL: 503-370-6282 • FAX: 503-370-6087
E-MAIL: LAW-ADMISSION@WILLAMETTE.EDU • WEBSITE: WWW.WILLAMETTE.EDU/WUCL

Views about life outside the classroom vary. Some students consider the "small" surrounding burg of Salem "an inexpensive and livable town in a pleasant state." They call the immediate location "great for serious students." They point out that "Salem is less than an hour's drive from Portland and is in the heart of wine country." They also note that temperatures are mild all year, and the surrounding area is a paradise for lovers of the outdoors. Opportunities for hiking, skiing, and frolicking at the beach are all within relatively easy reach. Closer to home, students also have access to a fabulous campus recreation center.

Getting In

The acceptance rate is high, but Willamette is a small school and the candidates competing for spots tend to have solid credentials. Admitted students at the 25th percentile have LSAT scores that hover in the low 150s and GPAs around 3.0. Admitted students at the 75th percentile have LSAT scores of 156 or so; their GPAs are about 3.5.

Clinical program required	No
Legal writing course requirement	Yes
Legal methods course requirement	No
Legal research course requirement	Yes
Moot court requirement	Yes
Public interest law requirement	No

ADMISSIONS

Selectivity Rating	**80**
# applications received	1,092
% applicants accepted	49
% acceptees attending	26
Average LSAT	153
LSAT Range (25th to 75th percentile)	151–156
Average undergrad GPA	3.18
Application fee	$50
Regular application deadline	3/1
Transfer students accepted	Yes
Evening division offered	No
Part-time accepted	No
CAS accepted	Yes

International Students

TOEFL required of international students.	Yes

FINANCIAL FACTS

Annual tuition	$36,210
Books and supplies	$1,534
Room & Board (on/ off campus)	$0/$15,300
Financial aid application deadline	3/1
% first-year students receiving some sort of aid	100
% all students receiving some sort of aid	97
% of aid that is merit based	16
% receiving scholarships	69
Average grant	$11,000
Average loan	$43,515
Average total aid package	$48,081
Average debt	$119,468

EMPLOYMENT INFORMATION

Career Rating	**81**
% grads employed ten months out	86
Median starting salary	$54,500
State for bar exam	OR, WA, AK, ID, CA
Pass rate for first-time bar	73.0

Prominent Alumni
Lisa Murkowski, U.S. Senator, State of Alaska; Jay Inslee, Governor, State of Washington; Virginia Linder, Justice, State of Oregon Supreme Court; Mark Prater, Chief Tax Counsel, US Senate Committee on Finance; Amanda Marshall, US Attorney for the District of Oregon

Grads Employed by Field (%)
Academic (4)
Business/Industry (15)
Government (16)
Judicial Clerkship (2)
Private Practice (60)
Public Interest (2)

WILLIAM MITCHELL COLLEGE OF LAW

INSTITUTIONAL INFORMATION

Public/private	Private
Affiliation	No Affiliation
Student-faculty ratio	13:1
% faculty part-time	87
% faculty female	50
% faculty underrepresented minority	11
Total faculty	230

SURVEY SAYS...

Students love St. Paul, MN, Great research resources, Abundant externship/internship/clerkship opportunities

STUDENTS

Enrollment of law school	668
% male/female	45/55
% from out-of-state	28
% part-time	31
% underrepresented minority	16
% international	2
# of countries represented	21
Average age of entering class	25

ACADEMICS

Academic Experience Rating	**80**
Profs interesting rating	80
Profs accessible rating	83
Hours of study per day	3.43

Academic Specialties

Business, Child Protection, Civil Litigation, Criminal, Family, Indian Law, Intellectual Property, Public Interest

Advanced Degrees Offered

JD, 3 yrs full-time, 4 yrs part-time (on campus and hybrid) LLM, 1 yr full-time

Academics

Located in St. Paul's scenic Summit Avenue neighborhood, just minutes from the downtowns of Minneapolis and St. Paul, William Mitchell is known for "wonderful professors," "generous scholarships," and a "good balance of legal theory and practical experience." It offers a flexible program that allows students to attend full time, part time, or on campus/online. In fact, it's the first on-campus/online hybrid program at an ABA-approved law school. The hybrid program combines "intensive in-person experiential learning and online coursework that allows students to study the law from anywhere in the world." This is especially beneficial for "non-traditional" students who need to "work and go to school."

Students appreciate the "emphasis on practical education." William Mitchell's "great instructors" focus on "experiential learning," and there are "numerous opportunities to practice skills in the real world and in areas that are of greatest interest to you." The "courses focus on practical skills, while still teaching the necessary doctrine." Students praise the "focus on how the concepts will actually apply in practice." Also, all "Mitchell students take a three-credit hands-on skill-building Advocacy course that focuses on client representation, negotiation, and advocacy skills." In a lot of the classes, one student notes, "I feel like I'm doing work similar to a 'real lawyer.'" Recently, the program has been especially "innovative, responsive, and creative in reworking the curriculum," notes another. William Mitchell offers thirteen clinics—including Business Law, Child Protection, Civil Advocacy, Community Development, Criminal Appeals, Immigration Law, Indian Law, Intellectual Property Law, Law and Psychiatry, Legal Assistance to Minnesota Prisoners (LAMP), Legal Planning Clinic for Tax-Exempt Organizations and Low Income Clients Misdemeanor, and the Reentry Clinic. The Indian law program is of special interest, as the "professors are truly experts in the field." William Mitchell also offers eleven simulation courses, and seventeen externships, which are "encouraged and highly facilitated," but some students say popular classes can be hard to get into.

There are big changes afoot at William Mitchell as it combines with Hamline Law, and some students worry that they will lose the small-class environment, but others welcome the change. Either way, "everyone at William Mitchell is there to support you in excelling," says one student. William Mitchell "provides highly accessible staff and admin." Every "opportunity you could ask for awaits at your fingertip at this school," and if you "reach out to alumni, faculty or staff members, they will give their all in trying to help you succeed."

The "long tradition of the school gives the students a huge alumni base to access," and "the alumni are hungry to help current students." "Mitchell people help out other Mitchell people," says one student. "I could not believe how prevalent this sentiment was when I started." "I feel very prepared to enter the legal field upon graduation—both in knowledge and support," notes a 2L. William Mitchell has an especially "strong alumni base in the Twin Cities." For students who wish to stay in "Minnesota or the surrounding states (i.e. North Dakota, Iowa, etc.)," "finding a job after graduating from William Mitchell is very likely."

JULIE EKKERS, ASST. DEAN AND DIRECTOR OF ADMISSIONS
875 SUMMIT AVENUE, ST. PAUL, MN 55105
TEL: 651-290-6476 • FAX: 651-290-6414
E-MAIL: ADMISSIONS@WMITCHELL.EDU • WEBSITE: WWW.WMITCHELL.EDU

Life

When not in class or studying, William Mitchell students can be found "relaxing on nearby Grand Avenue," "making connections with the thousands of Mitchell alumni who live and work in the area, and enjoying the vibrant cultural, entertainment, and nightlife that the area has to offer." There are also "more than sixty student groups and organizations" from "academic and professional to athletics and recreation to religious and multicultural." Students praise the campus facilities and note that "multiple other campuses use [William Mitchell's] library because of its ambiance and resources."

Getting In

William Mitchell accepts both on-campus and hybrid students, so make sure to check out the different applications online. LSAT scores, undergraduate GPAs, a personal essay, and letters of recommendation are all considered important by the admissions committee. At the 25th percentile, students recently admitted to William Mitchell College of Law have LSAT scores of 149 and GPAs in the 2.98 range, while admitted students at the 75th percentile have LSAT scores of 156 and GPAs of roughly 3.59.

Clinical program required	No
Legal writing course requirement	Yes
Legal methods course requirement	Yes
Legal research course requirement	Yes
Moot court requirement	No
Public interest law requirement	No

ADMISSIONS

Selectivity Rating	76
# applications received	721
% applicants accepted	72
% acceptees attending	32
Average LSAT	153
Median LSAT	152
LSAT Range (25th to 75th percentile)	149–156
Average undergrad GPA	3.24
Median undergrad GPA	3.25
Application fee	$0
Regular application deadline	8/1
Transfer students accepted	Yes
Evening division offered	Yes
Part-time accepted	Yes
CAS accepted	Yes

International Students

TOEFL required of international students.	Yes

FINANCIAL FACTS

Annual tuition	$38,400
Books and supplies	$1,550
Fees	$260
Room & Board (on/ off campus)	$0/$17,900
Financial aid application deadline	4/15
% first-year students receiving some sort of aid	100
% all students receiving some sort of aid	99
% of aid that is merit based	100
% receiving scholarships	92
Average grant	$20,575
Average loan	$31,917
Average total aid package	$45,320
Average debt	$101,651

EMPLOYMENT INFORMATION

Career Rating	86	
Total 2014 JD Grads	288	
% for whom you have useable information	99	
% grads employed ten months out	93	
Median starting salary	$55,000	
# employed full-time	240	
# employed part-time	23	
# employed bar required	177	
# employed JD preferred	58	
# employed professional/other	21	
# employed non-professional	7	
# pursuing advanced degree	1	
# unemployed and seeking employment	18	
# not seeking employment	2	
State for bar exam	MN	
Pass rate for first-time bar	89.0	

Prominent Alumni
Warren E. Burger, Chief Justice, U.S. Supreme Court (1969-1986); Rosalie Wahl, Justice, Minnesota Supreme Court (retired); Susan Haigh, CEO, Twin Cities Habitat for Humanity

Grads Employed by Field (%)
Academic (2)
Business/Industry (25)
Government (23)
Judicial Clerkship (13)
State or local: (10)
Private Practice (36)
  Solo: (3)
  2-10: (16)
  11-25: (5)
  26-50: (3)
  51-100: (3)
  101-250: (2)
  251-500: (1)
  501+: (1)
  Size Unknown: (1)
Public Interest (5)

YALE UNIVERSITY
LAW SCHOOL

INSTITUTIONAL INFORMATION

Public/private	Private
Affiliation	No Affiliation
Total faculty	71

SURVEY SAYS...

Abundant externship/internship/ clerkship opportunities

STUDENTS

Enrollment of law school	607
% male/female	52/48
% underrepresented minority	30
Average age of entering class	24

ACADEMICS

Academic Experience Rating	**96**
Profs interesting rating	67
Profs accessible rating	69
Hours of study per day	2.50

Advanced Degrees Offered
JD, 3 yrs; LLM, 1 yr; MSL, 1 yr;
JSD, up to 5 yrs; PhD, 3 yrs.

Combined Degrees Offered
JD/PhD, JD/MS, JD/MBA, JD/MD,
JD/MPH and others

Academics

It's hard to beat Yale Law School, where the atmosphere is "highly intellectual" and classes are mostly "small" (first-year classes vary in size from fifteen to ninety students). One of the many uniquely cool things about Yale is that "there aren't very many required courses." All 1Ls must complete course work in constitutional law, contracts, procedure, and torts. There's also a small, seminar-style legal research and writing course, and that's pretty much it. Best of all, there are "no grades." First semester classes are graded pass/ fail. After first semester, there is some semblance of grades but, since Yale doesn't keep track of class rank, it's not a big deal.

Academically, "this is the best place in the world." "It's easy to learn about whatever you're interested in, from medieval European law to helping immigrants in the modern-day United States," says one student. Yale is home to cutting-edge centers and programs galore. Clinical opportunities are vast and available "in your first year," which is a rarity. You can represent family members in juvenile neglect cases, provide legal services for nonprofit organizations, or participate in complicated federal civil rights cases. It's also "easy" to obtain joint-degrees or simply "cross-register for other classes" at Yale. A particularly unique program allows students to get a joint-degree at the Woodrow Wilson School of Public and International Affairs at Princeton.

Student report that the administration is "generally friendly." Word on the faculty is mixed. "I love all my professors," beams a 2L. "They will help me with anything." Nearly all agree that "most professors are delighted to help you." When jobs and clerkships are on the line, it's not uncommon for professors to personally make calls on behalf of students "to high-profile firms or government officials." Other students, however, tell us the faculty isn't all it's cracked up to be. "Quality teaching is not valued enough," gripes a critic. "Professors are hired based on their scholarship rather than their ability to teach or their interest in interacting with students."

Employment prospects are simply awesome. A degree from Yale virtually guarantees "an easy time finding a good job" and a lifetime of financial security. There is "very solid career support" (including "lots of free wine" at recruiting events). But did you know that Yale prolifically produces public interest attorneys? It's true. Every one of Yale's graduates could immediately take the big firm route but, each year, hordes of them don't. Yale "encourages diverse career paths" and "nontraditional routes" ("especially in academia and public interest") and annually awards dozens of public interest fellowships to current students and newly minted grads. There's a "great" loan forgiveness program too.

Facilities are phenomenal. Yale boasts wireless Internet access throughout the Law School, wireless common areas, and perhaps the greatest law library in the history of humanity. "The research facilities are spectacular." Aesthetically, "everything is beautiful," especially if you are into "wood paneling, stained glass windows, and hand-carved moldings." "If you care about architecture and Ivy League ambiance, come to Yale."

Asha Rangappa, Associate Dean
P.O. Box 208215, New Haven, CT 06520-8215
Tel: 203-432-4995
E-Mail: ADMISSIONS.LAW@YALE.EDU • Website: WWW.LAW.YALE.EDU

Life

Though the student population "is a bit Ivy heavy," it doesn't necessarily follow that everyone is wealthy. Approximately 75 percent of the lucky souls here receive financial assistance of some kind. It does follow, however, that students are pretty conceited about their intelligence and their privileged educational status. "If egos were light, an astronaut on the moon would have to shade his eyes from the glare of New Haven," analogizes one student. "I'm not sure there's a cure for that, but it might not be wise to tell us in the first week of torts that many of us will wind up on the federal bench."

"There are parties," swears a 1L. However, for many students, the social scene at Yale is simply an extension of academic life. Lectures and cultural events of all kinds are, of course, never-ending. The surrounding city of New Haven is lively in its own way and New York City and Boston are both easily accessible by train. On campus, Yale offers an "encouraging environment" and a "wonderful community." "Because of the small size of each class and the enormous number of activities, it is incredibly easy to get involved with journals (even the *Journal*) and any other student group you might want to try." "Students are very engaged and motivated, but not generally in a way that stresses everyone else out," explains one student. "The no-grades policy for first semester completely eliminates the competition I expect exists at other schools." "People ask me what law school is like, and I can honestly say, 'I work pretty hard, but it's fun,'" says a satisfied student. "Then those people stare at me oddly, and maybe they're right that 'fun' isn't exactly the right word. But I've found it enriching and enjoyable and the people I've met here have been great."

Getting In

Let's not sugarcoat the situation: It's ridiculously hard to get into Yale Law School. The folks in admissions at Yale say that they don't use any kind of formula or index. They consider many factors including grades; LSAT scores (including multiple LSAT scores), extracurricular activities, ethnic and socioeconomic diversity, and letters of recommendation.

EMPLOYMENT INFORMATION		
Career Rating	91	
Total 2014 JD Grads	230	**Grads Employed by Field (%)**
% for whom you have useable		Academic (4)
information	100	Business/Industry (7)
% grads employed ten months out	91	Government (6)
Median starting salary	$65,704	Judicial Clerkship (31)
# employed full-time	207	Federal: (28)
# employed part-time	3	State or local: (2)
# employed bar required	169	Other: (1)
# employed JD preferred	34	Private Practice (40)
# employed professional/other	7	2-10: (1)
# pursuing advanced degree	10	11-25: (1)
# unemployed and seeking		26-50: (1)
employment	2	51-100: (1)
# not seeking employment	3	101-250: (3)
% grads employed by school	10	251-500: (3)
State for bar exam	NY, CA	501+: (32)
Pass rate for first-time bar	96.2	Public Interest (12)

Clinical program required	No
Legal writing course requirement	
Legal methods course requirement	
Legal research course requirement	No
Moot court requirement	No
Public interest law requirement	No

ADMISSIONS

Selectivity Rating	99
# applications received	2,859
% applicants accepted	9
% acceptees attending	78
Average LSAT	173
Median LSAT	173
LSAT Range (25th to 75th percentile)	170–176
Average undergrad GPA	3.89
Median undergrad GPA	3.91
Application fee	$60
Regular application deadline	2/28
Transfer students accepted	Yes
Evening division offered	No
Part-time accepted	No
CAS accepted	Yes

FINANCIAL FACTS

Annual tuition	$55,800
Books and supplies	$1,100
Room & Board	$17,000/
Financial aid application deadline	3/15
% first-year students receiving some sort of aid	71
% all students receiving some sort of aid	73
% of aid that is merit based	0
% receiving scholarships	59
Average grant	$22,709
Average loan	$44,537
Average total aid package	$59,628
Average debt	$117,093

LAW SCHOOL DATA LISTINGS

In this section you will find data listings of the ABA-approved schools not appearing in the "Law School Descriptive Profiles" section of the book. Here you will also find listings of the California Bar Accredited, but not ABA-approved law schools, as well as listings of Canadian law schools. Explanations of what each field of data signifies in the listings may be found in the "How to Use This Book" section.

ATLANTA'S JOHN MARSHALL LAW SCHOOL

Atlanta's John Marshall Law School

Rebecca Stafford, Director of Admissions
1422 W. Peachtree St. NW, Atlanta, GA 30309
Tel: 404-872-3593 • **Fax:** 404-873-3802
Email: admissions@johnmarshall.edu • **Website:** www.johnmarshall.edu

INSTITUTIONAL INFORMATION
Public/Private: Private
Affiliation: No Affiliation
% faculty part-time: 18
% faculty female: 48
% faculty underrepresented minority: 29
Total faculty: 82

STUDENTS
Enrollment of law school: 235
% male/female: 46/54
% from out-of-state: 38
% part-time: 31
% underrepresented minority: 38
% international: 1
# of countries represented: 3
Average age of entering class: 30

ACADEMICS
Academic Specialties:
Criminal
Advanced Degrees Offered:
The Law School's academic year consists of two semesters of fourteen weeks of instruction, each followed by a two-week examination period. Juris Doctor(JD)– 88 Credit Hour Program; Full-time, 4 years; Part-time, 3 years JD Honors Program in Criminal Justice(JD HPCJ)– 88 Credit Hour Program Master of Laws(LLM) degree in American Legal Studies– Residential– 24 Credit Hour Program LLM in American Legal Studies– Online– 24 Credit Hour Program LLM in Employment Law– Online– 24 Credit Hour Program
Clinical program required: No
Legal writing course requirement: Yes
Legal methods course requirement: No
Legal research course requirement: Yes
Moot court requirement: Yes
Public interest law requirement: No

ADMISSIONS
Selectivity Rating: 75
 # applications received: 1,109
% applicants accepted: 54
% acceptees attending: 27
Average LSAT: 149
Median LSAT: 149
LSAT Range (25th to 75th percentile): 146—152
Average undergrad GPA: 2.98
Median undergrad GPA: 2.99
Application fee: $0

Early application deadline: 11/15
Early application notification: 2/1
Transfer students accepted: Yes
Evening division offered: Yes
Part-time accepted: Yes
CAS accepted: Yes
International Students:
TOEFL required of International Students

FINANCIAL FACTS
Annual tuition (in-state): $37,350
Books and supplies: $2,756
Room & Board (off-campus): $24,176
Financial aid application deadline: 6/1
% of aid that is merit based: 3

EMPLOYMENT INFORMATION
Total 2014 JD Grads: 234
% for whom you have useable information: 43
% grads employed ten months out: 86
Median starting salary: $50,000
% grads employed by school: 4
State for bar exam: GA, TN, FL, VA, NY
Pass rate for first-time bar: 69.1
Prominent Alumni:
Honorable Alan Blackburn, Former Judge, Court of Appeals / Balch & Bingham; Honorable Alvin T. Wong, Judge, State Court of DeKalb County; Honorable James Bodiford, Chief Judge, Cobb Superior Court; Honorable Albert Rahn III, Senior Judge, Superior Court; Adam Malone, Attorney, Malone Law Office
Grads Employed by Field (%):
Academic (2)
Business/Industry (25)
Government (13)
Judicial Clerkship (1)
Private Practice (55)
Public Interest (5)

BARRY UNIVERSITY

Barry University School of Law

Roxanna P. Cruz, Assistant Dean of Admissions
6441 E. Colonial Drive, Orlando, FL 32807
Tel: 321-206-5600 • **Fax:** 321-206-5738
Email: rpcruz@barry.edu • **Website:** www.barry.edu/law

INSTITUTIONAL INFORMATION
Public/Private: Private
Affiliation: Roman Catholic
% faculty part-time: 41
% faculty female: 35
% faculty underrepresented minority: 24
Total faculty: 67

STUDENTS

Enrollment of law school: 251
% male/female: 42/58
% from out-of-state: 32
% part-time: 21
% underrepresented minority: 41
% international: 1
# of countries represented: 7
Average age of entering class: 27

ACADEMICS

Academic Specialties:
Environmental
Clinical program required: No
Legal writing course requirement: Yes
Legal methods course requirement: No
Legal research course requirement: Yes
Moot court requirement: No
Public interest law requirement: Yes

ADMISSIONS

Selectivity Rating: 70
applications received: 1,929
% applicants accepted: 76
% acceptees attending: 20
Average LSAT: 148
Median LSAT: 147
LSAT Range (25th to 75th percentile): 145—151
Average undergrad GPA: 2.92
Median undergrad GPA: 2.92
Application fee: $0
Regular application deadline: 5/1
Transfer students accepted: Yes
Evening division offered: Yes
Part-time accepted: Yes
CAS accepted: Yes
International Students:
TOEFL required of International Students

FINANCIAL FACTS

Annual tuition (in-state/out-of-state) $34,300/$34,300
Books and supplies: $2,400
Fees: $0
Room & Board (on/off campus): $0/$14,850
Financial aid application deadline: 6/30
% first-year students receiving some sort of aid: 100
Average grant: $8,213
Average loan: $47,799
Average debt: $148,372

EMPLOYMENT INFORMATION

Total 2014 JD Grads: 201
% grads employed ten months out: 60
Median starting salary: $43,500
employed full-time: 109
employed part-time: 11
employed bar required: 83
employed JD preferred: 23
employed professional/other: 12
employed non-professional: 0
pursuing advanced degree: 6
unemployed and seeking employment: 29
not seeking employment: 2
% grads employed by school: 1
State for bar exam: FL

Pass rate for first-time bar: 79.3
Grads Employed by Field (%):
Academic (3)
Business/Industry (8)
Government (11)
Judicial Clerkship (1)
Private Practice (33)
Public Interest (3)

CALIFORNIA WESTERN

California Western School of Law

Traci Howard, Assistant Dean for Admissions
225 Cedar Street, San Diego, CA 92101
Tel: 619-525-1401 • Fax: 619-615-1401
Email: admissions@cwsl.edu • Website: www.californiawestern.edu

INSTITUTIONAL INFORMATION

Public/Private: Private
Affiliation: No Affiliation
Student-faculty ratio: 17:1
% faculty part-time: 22
% faculty female: 35
% faculty underrepresented minority: 11
Total faculty: 118

STUDENTS

Enrollment of law school: 905
% male/female: 47/53
% from out-of-state: 45
% part-time: 10
% underrepresented minority: 34
% international: 1
# of countries represented: 15
Average age of entering class: 25

ACADEMICS

Academic Specialties:
Constitutional, Criminal, Human Rights, International, Labor, Taxation, Intellectual Property
Advanced Degrees Offered:
JD—2 to 3 Years. MCL/LLM (Master of Comparative Law, Master of Laws on Comparative Law)—9 months. LLM-Trial Advocacy—1 Year.
Combined Degrees Offered:
JD/MSW Juris Doctor/Master of Social Work—4 years. JD/MBA Juris Doctor/Master of Business Administration—4 years. JD/PhD Juris Doctor/Doctor of Philosophy in Political Science or History—5 years. Master's in Health Law
Clinical program required: No
Legal writing course requirement: Yes
Legal methods course requirement: Yes
Legal research course requirement: Yes
Moot court requirement: No
Public interest law requirement: No

ADMISSIONS

Selectivity Rating: 80
applications received: 2,433
% applicants accepted: 54

% acceptees attending: 26
Average LSAT: 153
LSAT Range (25th to 75th percentile): 150—155
Average undergrad GPA: 3.25
Application fee: $55
Regular application deadline: 4/1
Transfer students accepted: Yes
Evening division offered: No
Part-time accepted: Yes
CAS accepted: Yes
International Students:
TOEFL required of International Students

FINANCIAL FACTS
Annual tuition (in-state): $38,400
Books and supplies: $1,300
Room & Board (off-campus): $11,600
Financial aid application deadline: 4/1
% first-year students receiving some sort of aid: 87
% all students receiving some sort of aid: 87
% receiving scholarships: 29
Average grant: $20,918
Average loan: $51,750
Average total aid package: $59,612
Average debt: $96,502

EMPLOYMENT INFORMATION
% grads employed ten months out: 86
Median starting salary: $73,999
State for bar exam: CA, NV, AZ, NY
Pass rate for first-time bar: 86.0
Prominent Alumni:
Lisa Haile, Partner at DLA Piper, Rudnick, Gray, Cary; Garland Burrell, US District Court Judge; Duane Layton, Partner at Mayer, Brown, Rowe and Maw; David Roger, D.A., Clark County, Nevada; James Lorenz, US District Court Judge
Grads Employed by Field (%):
Academic (1)
Business/Industry (13)
Government (12)
Judicial Clerkship (5)
Private Practice (60)
Public Interest (7)

DUQUESNE UNIVERSITY
School of Law

Sarah Arimoto-Mercer, Assistant Dean
900 Locust Street, Pittsburgh, PA 15282
Tel: 412-396-6296 • Fax: 412-396-1073
Email: lawadmissions@duq.edu • Website: www.law.duq.edu

INSTITUTIONAL INFORMATION
Public/Private: Private
Student-faculty ratio: 23:1
% faculty female: 21
% faculty underrepresented minority: 16
Total faculty: 26

STUDENTS
Enrollment of law school: 630
% male/female: 50/50
% from out-of-state: 38
% part-time: 35
% underrepresented minority: 7
% international: 0
Average age of entering class: 23

ACADEMICS
Combined Degrees Offered:
JD/MBA, 4 years; JD/M.Div., 5 years; JD/M Environmental Science and Management, 4 years. JD/MS Taxation, 4 years.
Clinical program required: No
Legal writing course requirement: Yes
Legal methods course requirement: Yes
Legal research course requirement: Yes
Moot court requirement: No
Public interest law requirement: No

ADMISSIONS
Selectivity Rating: 60
applications received: 0
Average LSAT: 154
Average undergrad GPA: 3.40
Application fee: $60
Regular application deadline: 3/1
Regular notification: 4/1
Early application deadline: 12/1
Early application notification: 12/31
Transfer students accepted: Yes
Evening division offered: Yes
Part-time accepted: Yes
CAS accepted: Yes
International Students:
TOEFL required of International Students

FINANCIAL FACTS
Annual tuition: $34,634
Books and supplies: $1,500
Room & Board (off-campus): $10,930
Financial aid application deadline: 5/1

EMPLOYMENT INFORMATION
Median starting salary: $59,693
State for bar exam: PA
Pass rate for first-time bar: 71.0
Grads Employed by Field (%):
Academic (1)
Business/Industry (25)
Government (4)
Judicial Clerkship (6)
Private Practice (61)
Public Interest (3)

FLORIDA COASTAL SCHOOL OF LAW

Florida Coastal School of Law

Anthony Cardenas, Dean of Admissions
8787 Baypine Road, Jacksonville, FL 32256
Tel: 904-680-7710 • Fax: 904-680-7692
Email: admissions@fcsl.edu • Website: www.fcsl.edu

INSTITUTIONAL INFORMATION
Public/Private: Private
Affiliation: No Affiliation

STUDENTS
Enrollment of law school: 1,030
% male/female: 46/54
% part-time: 6
% underrepresented minority: 56
% international: 2
Average age of entering class: 27

ACADEMICS
Academic Specialties:
Commercial, Corporation Securities, Criminal, Environmental, International, Property, Taxation, Intellectual Property
Advanced Degrees Offered:
JD, JD/MBA, JD/M.P.P, LLM
Combined Degrees Offered:
JD/MBA The Davis College of Business at Jacksonville University (JU) and Florida Coastal School of Law (Coastal Law) created a joint degree program through which qualified individuals may enroll in the Coastal Law JD and the Davis MBA programs simultaneously. By allowing a number of courses to satisfy requirements in both programs at the same time, the time required to earn both degrees is shortened. Students in the dual degree program may obtain both degrees in as little as 3 years. Part-time students typically can complete both degrees in five years. JD/M.P.P. The Jacksonville University Public Policy Institute-Florida Coastal School of Law JD/MPP joint degree program is a 4 year program.
Clinical program required: Yes
Legal writing course requirement: Yes
Legal methods course requirement: Yes
Legal research course requirement: Yes
Moot court requirement: No
Public interest law requirement: No

ADMISSIONS
Selectivity Rating: 69
 # applications received: 2,388
% applicants accepted: 76
% acceptees attending: 18
Average LSAT: 143
Median LSAT: 143
LSAT Range (25th to 75th percentile): 141—147
Average undergrad GPA: 2.91
Median undergrad GPA: 2.96
Application fee: $0
Transfer students accepted: Yes
Evening division offered: Yes
Part-time accepted: Yes

CAS accepted: Yes
International Students:
TOEFL required of International Students

FINANCIAL FACTS
Annual tuition (in-state/out-of-state) $40,664/$40,664
Books and supplies: $1,450
Fees: $2,337
Room & Board (on/off campus): NA/$20,402
Financial aid application deadline: 8/1
% first-year students receiving some sort of aid: 99
% all students receiving some sort of aid: 88
% of aid that is merit based: 10
% receiving scholarships: 28
Average grant: $16,500
Average loan: $53,000
Average total aid package: $64,500
Average debt: $147,900

EMPLOYMENT INFORMATION
Total 2014 JD Grads: 484
% for whom you have useable information: 100
% grads employed ten months out: 71
 # employed full-time: 310
 # employed part-time: 31
 # employed bar required: 191
 # employed JD preferred: 91
 # employed professionai/other: 50
 # employed non-professional: 9
 # pursuing advanced degree: 13
 # unemployed and seeking employment: 95
 # not seeking employment: 35
% grads employed by school: 7
State for bar exam: FL, GA, NY, TX
Pass rate for first-time bar: 68.4
Grads Employed by Field (%):
Academic (2)
Business/Industry (16)
Government (9)
Judicial Clerkship (2)
  Federal (0)
  State or local (2)
Other (0)
Private Practice (37)
  Solo (1)
  2-10 (28)
  11-25 (4)
  26-50 (2)
  51-100 (1)
  101-250 (0)
  251-500 (0)
  501+ (0)
  Size Unknown (0)
Public Interest (4)

GOLDEN GATE UNIVERSITY

Golden Gate University School of Law

Angela Dalfen, Associate Dean for Admissions
Law Admissions Office, 536 Mission Street, San Francisco, CA 94105
Tel: 415-442-6630 • *Fax:* 415-442-6631
Email: lawadmit@ggu.edu • *Website:* www.law.ggu.edu

INSTITUTIONAL INFORMATION
Public/Private: Private
Affiliation: No Affiliation
Student-faculty ratio: 14:1
% faculty part-time: 68
% faculty female: 47
% faculty underrepresented minority: 14
Total faculty: 140

STUDENTS
Enrollment of law school: 150
% male/female: 37/63
% from out-of-state: 16
% part-time: 23
% underrepresented minority: 55
% international: 3
# of countries represented: 20
Average age of entering class: 27

ACADEMICS
Academic Specialties:
Criminal, Environmental, International, Labor, Property, Taxation, Intellectual Property
Advanced Degrees Offered:
JD full-time (3 years), JD part-time evening (4 years), LLM (1 year), SJD (1 year), accelerated JD/LLM in Taxation (3.5 years)
Combined Degrees Offered:
JD/MBA—3.5 to 4 years
Clinical program required: No
Legal writing course requirement: Yes
Legal methods course requirement: No
Legal research course requirement: Yes
Moot court requirement: Yes
Public interest law requirement: No

ADMISSIONS
Selectivity Rating: 75
applications received: 1,575
% applicants accepted: 63
% acceptees attending: 15
Average LSAT: 149
Median LSAT: 150
LSAT Range (25th to 75th percentile): 147—153
Average undergrad GPA: 3.05
Median undergrad GPA: 3.11
Application fee: $60
Regular application deadline: 4/1
Early application deadline: 12/31
Early application notification: 2/15
Transfer students accepted: Yes
Evening division offered: Yes
Part-time accepted: Yes
CAS accepted: Yes

International Students:
TOEFL required of International Students

FINANCIAL FACTS
Annual tuition (in-state): $43,350
Books and supplies: $1,400
Room & Board (off-campus): $14,850
% first-year students receiving some sort of aid: 96
% all students receiving some sort of aid: 89
% of aid that is merit based: 90
% receiving scholarships: 50
Average grant: $12,020
Average loan: $30,000
Average total aid package: $70,000
Average debt: $138,000

EMPLOYMENT INFORMATION
Total 2014 JD Grads: 228
% for whom you have useable information: 42
% grads employed ten months out: 57
# employed full-time: 97
# employed part-time: 34
# employed bar required: 87
# employed JD preferred: 25
# employed professional/other: 14
# employed non-professional: 5
# pursuing advanced degree: 4
# unemployed and seeking employment: 66
# not seeking employment: 2
% grads employed by school: 13
State for bar exam: CA
Pass rate for first-time bar: 56.0
Prominent Alumni:
Justice Jesse Carter (deceased), California Supreme Court Justice; Morgan Christen, Circuit Judge of the United States Court of Appeals for the Ninth Circuit; Karen Hawkins, Director of Professional Responsibility, IRS; Mark S. Anderson, Vice President and General Counsel, Dolby Labs.; Marjorie Randolph, Senior VP for HR and Admin., Walt Disney Studios
Grads Employed by Field (%):
Academic (5)
Business/Industry (24)
Government (13)
Judicial Clerkship (5)
Private Practice (35)
Public Interest (18)

HOWARD UNIVERSITY

Howard University School of Law

Reginald McGahee, JD, Assistant Dean of Admission/Director of Admissions
2900 Van Ness Street, NW, Suite 219, Washington, DC 20008
Tel: 202-806-8008 • *Fax:* 202-806-8162
Email: admissions@law.howard.edu • *Website:* www.law.howard.edu

INSTITUTIONAL INFORMATION
Public/Private: Private
Student-faculty ratio: 13:1
% faculty part-time: 45

% faculty female: 40
% faculty underrepresented minority: 78
Total faculty: 67

STUDENTS
Enrollment of law school: 402
% male/female: 40/60
% underrepresented minority: 94

ACADEMICS
Academic Specialties:
Commercial, Constitutional, Corporation Securities, Criminal, Environmental, Human Rights, International, Labor, Property, Taxation, Intellectual Property
Advanced Degrees Offered:
LLM (foreign lawyers only) 1 to 2 years
Combined Degrees Offered:
JD/MBA—4 years
Clinical program required: No
Legal writing course requirement: Yes
Legal methods course requirement: Yes
Legal research course requirement: No
Moot court requirement: No
Public interest law requirement: No

ADMISSIONS
Selectivity Rating: 86
applications received: 2,550
% applicants accepted: 17
% acceptees attending: 37
Average LSAT: 153
LSAT Range (25th to 75th percentile): 148—158
Average undergrad GPA: 25.00
Application fee: $60
Regular application deadline: 3/31
Transfer students accepted: Yes
Evening division offered: No
Part-time accepted: No
CAS accepted: Yes
International Students:
TOEFL required of International Students

FINANCIAL FACTS
Annual tuition (in-state): $15,990
Books and supplies: $1,103
Room & Board (on/off campus): $98,698/$10,169
Financial aid application deadline: 3/1
% first-year students receiving some sort of aid: 90
% all students receiving some sort of aid: 95
% of aid that is merit based: 58
Average grant: $13,000
Average loan: $18,500
Average total aid package: $29,000
Average debt: $60,000

EMPLOYMENT INFORMATION
% grads employed ten months out: 96
Median starting salary: $72,465
Grads Employed by Field (%):
Academic (3)
Business/Industry (13)
Government (18)
Judicial Clerkship (15)
Private Practice (43)
Public Interest (7)

LIBERTY UNIVERSITY
Liberty University School of Law

Annette Pettyjohn, Director of Admissions
1971 University Boulevard, Lynchburg, VA 24515
Tel: 434-592-5300 • Fax: 434-592-5800
Email: LawAdmissions@liberty.edu • Website: law.liberty.edu

INSTITUTIONAL INFORMATION
Public/Private: Private
Affiliation: Christian
% faculty part-time: 16
% faculty female: 27
% faculty underrepresented minority: 27
Total faculty: 37

STUDENTS
Enrollment of law school: 207
% male/female: 61/39
% from out-of-state: 37
% part-time: 0
% underrepresented minority: 17
% international: 2
# of countries represented: 2
Average age of entering class: 26

ACADEMICS
Academic Specialties:
Commercial, Constitutional, Corporation Securities, Criminal, International, Property, Taxation
Advanced Degrees Offered:
JD—3 years Other degrees are in development
Combined Degrees Offered:
JD/MBA; JD/MEd; JD/EdS; JD/EdD; JD/MAR; JD/MDiv; JD/MA History; JD/MA Public Policy; JD/MA Human Services; JD/MA Public Health
Clinical program required: No
Legal writing course requirement: Yes
Legal methods course requirement: Yes
Legal research course requirement: Yes
Moot court requirement: Yes
Public interest law requirement: No

ADMISSIONS
Selectivity Rating: 78
applications received: 297
% applicants accepted: 65
% acceptees attending: 44
Median LSAT: 151
LSAT Range (25th to 75th percentile): 148—155
Median undergrad GPA: 3.24
Application fee: $50
Regular application deadline: 6/1
Transfer students accepted: Yes
Evening division offered: No
Part-time accepted: No
CAS accepted: Yes
International Students:
TOEFL required of International Students

FINANCIAL FACTS
Annual tuition (in-state/out-of-state) $30,396/$30,396
Books and supplies: $3,668

Fees: $1,482
Room & Board (off-campus): $10,955
Financial aid application deadline: 6/2
% first-year students receiving some sort of aid: 100
% all students receiving some sort of aid: 100
% of aid that is merit based: 99
% receiving scholarships: 99
Average grant: $18,601
Average loan: $24,033
Average total aid package: $37,210
Average debt: $72,236

EMPLOYMENT INFORMATION
Total 2014 JD Grads: 93
% grads employed ten months out: 67
Median starting salary: $45,500
% job accepting grads providing useable salary information: 43
# employed full-time: 50
# employed part-time: 12
# employed bar required: 42
# employed JD preferred: 12
# employed professional/other: 5
# employed non-professional: 3
# pursuing advanced degree: 1
# unemployed and seeking employment: 12
# not seeking employment: 7
% grads employed by school: 3
State for bar exam: VA, NC, FL, MD, CA
Pass rate for first-time bar: 71.0
Prominent Alumni:
Matthew Krause, Texas State House Representative, Texas State House; Sarah Seitz, Legislative Director and Counsel, The United States House of Representatives; Benjamin Boyd, Alabama Supreme Court; Benjamin Walton, Sixth Circuit Court of Appeals; Melanie Good, Texas Securities Exchange Commission
Grads Employed by Field (%):
Academic (4)
Business/Industry (12)
Government (14)
Judicial Clerkship (4)
 Federal (1)
 State or local (1)
Private Practice (28)
 Solo (7)
 2-10 (29)
Public Interest (4)

NORTHERN KENTUCKY UNIVERSITY

Northern Kentucky University—Salmon P. Chase College of Law

Ashley Gray, Director of Admissions
Nunn Hall, Room 101, Highland Heights, KY 41099
Tel: 859-572-5490 • Fax: 859-572-6081
Email: chaselaw.nku.edu/admissions • Website: chaselaw.nku.edu

INSTITUTIONAL INFORMATION
Public/Private: Public
Affiliation: No Affiliation
% faculty part-time: 35
% faculty female: 37
% faculty underrepresented minority: 10
Total faculty: 49

STUDENTS
Enrollment of law school: 460
% male/female: 72/28
% from out-of-state: 22
% part-time: 30
% underrepresented minority: 7
% international: 0
# of countries represented: 0
Average age of entering class: 27

ACADEMICS
Academic Specialties:
Labor, Taxation
Combined Degrees Offered:
JD/MBA: 3.5—4 years full-time; JD/MBI: 3.5—4 years full-time; JD/MHI: 3.5—4 years full-time
Clinical program required: No
Legal writing course requirement: Yes
Legal methods course requirement: Yes
Legal research course requirement: Yes
Moot court requirement: No
Public interest law requirement: Yes

ADMISSIONS
Selectivity Rating: 74
applications received: 514
% applicants accepted: 72
% acceptees attending: 32
Average LSAT: 150
Median LSAT: 150
LSAT Range (25th to 75th percentile): 146—154
Average undergrad GPA: 3.09
Median undergrad GPA: 3.09
Application fee: $40
Regular application deadline: 4/1
Early application deadline: 2/1
Transfer students accepted: Yes
Evening division offered: Yes
Part-time accepted: Yes
CAS accepted: Yes

International Students:
TOEFL recommended of International Students

FINANCIAL FACTS
Annual tuition (in-state/out-of-state) $17,056/$27,586
Books and supplies: $1,200
Fees: $358
Room & Board (on/off campus): $7,750/$8,726
Financial aid application deadline: 2/1
% first-year students receiving some sort of aid: 92
% all students receiving some sort of aid: 91
% of aid that is merit based: 24
% receiving scholarships: 50
Average grant: $14,126
Average loan: $25,719
Average total aid package: $30,318
Average debt: $81,912

EMPLOYMENT INFORMATION
Total 2014 JD Grads: 156
% for whom you have useable information: 97
% grads employed ten months out: 87
Median starting salary: $50,000
% job accepting grads providing useable salary information: 64
# employed full-time: 124
# employed part-time: 11
# employed bar required: 77
# employed JD preferred: 42
# employed professional/other: 15
# employed non-professional: 1
# pursuing advanced degree: 1
# unemployed and seeking employment: 12
# not seeking employment: 1
% grads employed by school: 0
State for bar exam: KY, OH
Pass rate for first-time bar: 72.0
Prominent Alumni:
Steve J. Chabot, United States Congressman; Patricia L. Herbold, Former United States Ambassador to Singapore; Michelle M. Keller, Kentucky Supreme Court Justice; W. Bruce Lunsford, Chair & CEO, Lunsford Capital, LLC; Dustin E. McCoy, Chair & CEO, Brunswick Corporation
Grads Employed by Field (%):
Academic (2)
Business/Industry (26)
Government (15)
Judicial Clerkship (6)
Private Practice (40)
Public Interest (4)

THE PENNSYLVANIA STATE UNIVERSITY
The Dickinson School of Law

R. Jay Shively, Assistant Dean, Admissions & Financial Aid
Lewis Katz Building, University Park, PA 16802
Tel: 814-867-1251 • Fax: 814-863-7274
Email: admissions@law.psu.edu • Website: www.law.psu.edu

INSTITUTIONAL INFORMATION
Public/Private: Public
Affiliation: No Affiliation
% faculty part-time: 21
% faculty female: 43
% faculty underrepresented minority: 13
Total faculty: 89

STUDENTS
Enrollment of law school: 617
% male/female: 58/42
% underrepresented minority: 14
% international: 2
Average age of entering class: 24

ACADEMICS
Academic Specialties:
Civil Procedure, Commercial, Constitutional, Corporation Securities, Criminal, Environmental, Government Services, Human Rights, International, Labor, Legal History, Legal Philosophy, Property, Taxation, Intellectual Property
Advanced Degrees Offered:
JD 3 years, LLM in Comparative Law 1 year
Combined Degrees Offered:
JD/Master of International Affairs; JD/Masters of Business Administration; JD/Master of Public Administration; JD/Masters of Environmental Pollution Control; JD/Master of Science in Information Systems; JD/MS or PhD—Forest Resources; JD/ MA or PhD—Educational Theory & Policy; JD/ MEd or MS or D.Ed or Ph.D—Educational Leadership; JD/ MEd or D.Ed. or PhD—Higher Education; JD/Master of Science in Human Resources & Employment Relations.
Clinical program required: No
Legal writing course requirement: Yes
Legal methods course requirement: Yes
Legal research course requirement: Yes
Moot court requirement: No
Public interest law requirement: No

ADMISSIONS
Selectivity Rating: 90
applications received: 5,326
% applicants accepted: 29
% acceptees attending: 15
Median LSAT: 159
LSAT Range (25th to 75th percentile): 151—172
Median undergrad GPA: 3.60
Application fee: $60
Regular application deadline: 3/1
Transfer students accepted: Yes
Evening division offered: No
Part-time accepted: No
CAS accepted: Yes

International Students:
TOEFL required of International Students

FINANCIAL FACTS
Annual tuition (in-state/out-of-state) $35,928/$35,928
Books and supplies: $1,456
Fees: $888
Room & Board (on/off campus): $22,300/$22,300
Financial aid application deadline: 3/1
% first-year students receiving some sort of aid: 95
% all students receiving some sort of aid: 92
% of aid that is merit based: 83
% receiving scholarships: 60
Average grant: $12,172
Average loan: $38,987
Average total aid package: $45,672
Average debt: $117,988

EMPLOYMENT INFORMATION
% grads employed ten months out: 78
State for bar exam: PA
Pass rate for first-time bar: 89.0
Prominent Alumni:
Hon. Thomas Ridge, Secretary of Homeland Security and PA Governor; Hon. Pedro Cortes, PA Secretary of the Commonwealth; Hon. D. Brooks Smith, Third Circuit Court of Appeals; Hon. Thomas Vanaskie, Third Circuit Court of Appeals; Hon. J. Michael Eakin, PA Supreme Court
Grads Employed by Field (%):
Academic (4)
Business/Industry (23)
Government (14)
Judicial Clerkship (19)
Private Practice (31)
Public Interest (3)

TEXAS A&M UNIVERSITY
School of Law

Terence L. Cook, Director of Admissions and Scholarships
1515 Commerce Street, Office of Admissions, Fort Worth, TX 76102
Tel: 817-212-4040 • Fax: 817-212-4141
Email: law-admissions@law.tamu.edu • Website: law.tamu.edu

INSTITUTIONAL INFORMATION
Public/Private: Public
% faculty part-time: 41
% faculty female: 40
% faculty underrepresented minority: 19
Total faculty: 63

STUDENTS
Enrollment of law school: 702
% male/female: 52/48
% from out-of-state: 10
% part-time: 35
% underrepresented minority: 26
% international: 1

# of countries represented: 7
Average age of entering class: 26

ACADEMICS
Academic Specialties:
Commercial, Property, Taxation, Intellectual Property
Advanced Degrees Offered:
JD Degree: Full time—3 years to complete; Part Time—4 years to complete.
Combined Degrees Offered:
NA
Clinical program required: No
Legal writing course requirement: Yes
Legal methods course requirement: Yes
Legal research course requirement: Yes
Moot court requirement: Yes
Public interest law requirement: Yes

ADMISSIONS
Selectivity Rating: 83
applications received: 1,714
% applicants accepted: 42
% acceptees attending: 22
Average LSAT: 154
Median LSAT: 154
LSAT Range (25th to 75th percentile): 152—156
Average undergrad GPA: 3.16
Median undergrad GPA: 3.21
Application fee: $55
Regular application deadline: 3/31
Transfer students accepted: Yes
Evening division offered: Yes
Part-time accepted: Yes
CAS accepted: Yes
International Students:
TOEFL required of International Students

FINANCIAL FACTS
Annual tuition (in-state/out-of-state) $5,370/$13,794
Books and supplies: $2,050
Fees: $19,298
Room & Board (off-campus): $15,526
% first-year students receiving some sort of aid: 91
% all students receiving some sort of aid: 87
% of aid that is merit based: 0
% receiving scholarships: 37
Average grant: $15,741
Average loan: $38,724
Average total aid package: $41,344
Average debt: $103,500

EMPLOYMENT INFORMATION
Total 2014 JD Grads: 232
% for whom you have useable information: 99
% grads employed ten months out: 79
Median starting salary: $59,000
% job accepting grads providing useable salary information: 55
# employed full-time: 175
# employed part-time: 9
# employed bar required: 127
# employed JD preferred: 32
# employed professional/other: 22
# employed non-professional: 3
# pursuing advanced degree: 2
# unemployed and seeking employment: 34
# not seeking employment: 8

% grads employed by school: 1
State for bar exam: TX, PA, KY
Pass rate for first-time bar: 77.0
Grads Employed by Field (%):
Academic (3)
Business/Industry (26)
Government (6)
Judicial Clerkship (1)
  State or local (1)
Private Practice (43)
  Solo (7)
  2-10 (26)
  11-25 (4)
  26-50 (2)
  51-100 (2)
  101-250 (1)

THOMAS JEFFERSON SCHOOL OF LAW

Thomas Jefferson School of Law

Beth Kransberger, Associate Dean for Student Affairs
1155 Island Avenue, San Diego, CA 92101
Tel: 619-297-9700 • *Fax:* 619-961-1300
Email: admissions@tjsl.edu • *Website:* www.tjsl.edu

INSTITUTIONAL INFORMATION
Public/Private: Private
Student-faculty ratio: 19:1
% faculty part-time: 49
% faculty female: 37
% faculty underrepresented minority: 7
Total faculty: 84

STUDENTS
Enrollment of law school: 440
% male/female: 63/37
% from out-of-state: 31
% part-time: 23
% underrepresented minority: 25
% international: 2
# of countries represented: 1
Average age of entering class: 26

ACADEMICS
Academic Specialties:
Civil Procedure, Commercial, Constitutional, Corporation Securities, Criminal, Environmental, Government Services, Human Rights, International, Labor, Property, Taxation, Intellectual Property
Advanced Degrees Offered:
JD 3 years full-time; JD 4 years part-time
Combined Degrees Offered:
JD/MBA with San Diego State University 4 years
Clinical program required: No
Legal writing course requirement: Yes
Legal methods course requirement: No

Legal research course requirement: No
Moot court requirement: No
Public interest law requirement: No

ADMISSIONS
Selectivity Rating: 77
applications received: 2,697
% applicants accepted: 55
% acceptees attending: 30
Average LSAT: 150
Median LSAT: 151
LSAT Range (25th to 75th percentile): 139—167
Average undergrad GPA: 3.00
Median undergrad GPA: 3.00
Application fee: $50
Early application deadline: 12/1
Transfer students accepted: Yes
Evening division offered: Yes
Part-time accepted: Yes
CAS accepted: Yes
International Students:
TOEFL required of International Students

FINANCIAL FACTS
Annual tuition (in-state): $41,000
Books and supplies: $1,900
Room & Board (on/off campus): $17,280/$17,280
Financial aid application deadline: 4/15
% first-year students receiving some sort of aid: 93
% all students receiving some sort of aid: 93
% of aid that is merit based: 9
% receiving scholarships: 49
Average grant: $15,047
Average loan: $51,533
Average total aid package: $57,480
Average debt: $153,000

EMPLOYMENT INFORMATION
Total 2014 JD Grads: 236
% grads employed ten months out: 61
Median starting salary: $60,000
employed full-time: 98
employed part-time: 39
employed bar required: 96
employed JD preferred: 18
employed professional/other: 17
employed non-professional: 6
pursuing advanced degree: 6
unemployed and seeking employment: 74
not seeking employment: 10
% grads employed by school: 0
State for bar exam: CA, NY, AZ, NJ, NV
Pass rate for first-time bar: 72.9
Prominent Alumni:
Bonnie Dumanis, San Diego District Attorney; Duncan Hunter, Member of U.S. Congress; Roger Benitez, U.S. District Court, Southern District, CA; Mattias Luukkonen, DLA Piper US LLP; Dan Vrechek, Qualcomm
Grads Employed by Field (%):
Academic (1)
Business/Industry (27)
Government (9)
Judicial Clerkship (7)
Private Practice (54)
Public Interest (2)

UNIVERSITY OF BALTIMORE
School of Law

Jeffrey Zavrotny, Assitant Dean for Admissions
1420 North Charles Street, Baltimore, MD 21201
Tel: 410-837-5809 • Fax: 410-837-4188
Email: lawadmissions@ubalt.edu • Website: law.ubalt.edu

INSTITUTIONAL INFORMATION
Public/Private: Public
% faculty part-time: 60
% faculty female: 37
% faculty underrepresented minority: 11
Total faculty: 190

STUDENTS
Enrollment of law school: 864
% male/female: 50/50
% from out-of-state: 13
% part-time: 35
% underrepresented minority: 26
% international: 1
# of countries represented: 3
Average age of entering class: 25

ACADEMICS
Academic Specialties:
Criminal, Government Services, International, Property, Intellectual Property
Advanced Degrees Offered:
LL.M in Taxation LL.M in Law of the United States
Combined Degrees Offered:
JD/MBA, JD/MS in Criminal Justice, JD/MPA, JD/PhD in Policy Science in conjuction with the Univ. of Maryland @ Baltimore, JD/LLM in taxation, JD/MS in Negotiation and conflict Management. Most Combined degrees add 1 year of study.
Clinical program required: No
Legal writing course requirement: Yes
Legal methods course requirement: Yes
Legal research course requirement: Yes
Moot court requirement: No
Public interest law requirement: No

ADMISSIONS
Selectivity Rating: 79
applications received: 1,222
% applicants accepted: 59
% acceptees attending: 32
Average LSAT: 151
Median LSAT: 152
LSAT Range (25th to 75th percentile): 148—154
Average undergrad GPA: 3.13
Median undergrad GPA: 3.26
Application fee: $60
Regular application deadline: 7/30
Transfer students accepted: Yes
Evening division offered: Yes
Part-time accepted: Yes
CAS accepted: Yes
International Students:
TOEFL recommended of International Students

FINANCIAL FACTS
Annual tuition (in-state/out-of-state) $26,014/$39,174
Books and supplies: $1,600
Fees: $1,870
Room & Board (off-campus): $14,200
Financial aid application deadline: 4/1
% first-year students receiving some sort of aid: 44
% all students receiving some sort of aid: 29
% of aid that is merit based: 100
% receiving scholarships: 29
Average grant: $13,000
Average loan: $37,006
Average total aid package: $43,000
Average debt: $118,000

EMPLOYMENT INFORMATION
Total 2014 JD Grads: 311
% grads employed ten months out: 85
Median starting salary: $50,000
% job accepting grads providing useable salary information: 49
# employed full-time: 234
# employed part-time: 26
# employed bar required: 158
# employed JD preferred: 84
# employed professional/other: 14
# employed non-professional: 4
# pursuing advanced degree: 6
# unemployed and seeking employment: 37
# not seeking employment: 4
% grads employed by school: 1
State for bar exam: MD
Pass rate for first-time bar: 86.0
Prominent Alumni:
William Donald Schaefer, Former Governor of Maryland; Catherine O'Malley, Judge, First Lady of Maryland; C.A. Dutch Ruppersberger, US Congress, House of Representatives; Joseph Curran, Former Attorney General of Maryland; Peter Angelos, Owner, Baltimore Orioles
Grads Employed by Field (%):
Academic (5)
Business/Industry (12)
Government (14)
Judicial Clerkship (15)
Private Practice (33)
Public Interest (5)

University of California—Irvine

School of Law

Janice Austin, Asst Dean for Admissions & Student Financial Services
401 E. Peltason Drive, Suite 1000, Irvine, CA 92697-8000
Tel: 949-824-0066 • **Fax:** 949-824-2966
Email: admissions@law.uci.edu • **Website:** www.law.uci.edu

INSTITUTIONAL INFORMATION
Public/Private: Public
Affiliation: No Affiliation
Student-faculty ratio: 8:1
% faculty part-time: 39
% faculty female: 46
% faculty underrepresented minority: 27
Total faculty: 67

STUDENTS
Enrollment of law school: 326
% male/female: 52/48
% from out-of-state: 14
% underrepresented minority: 43
% international: 6
# of countries represented: 6
Average age of entering class: 25

ACADEMICS
Academic Specialties:
Civil Procedure, Commercial, Constitutional, Corporation Securities, Criminal, Environmental, Human Rights, International, Labor, Legal History, Property, Taxation, Intellectual Property
Advanced Degrees Offered:
JD—3 years
Combined Degrees Offered:
JD/MA, JD/MBA, JD/MS, JD/Ph.D
Clinical program required: Yes
Legal writing course requirement: Yes
Legal methods course requirement: No
Legal research course requirement: Yes
Moot court requirement: No
Public interest law requirement: No

ADMISSIONS
Selectivity Rating: 93
applications received: 1,608
% applicants accepted: 22
% acceptees attending: 25
Average LSAT: 163
Median LSAT: 164
LSAT Range (25th to 75th percentile): 162—166
Average undergrad GPA: 3.47
Median undergrad GPA: 3.53
Application fee: $0
Transfer students accepted: Yes
Evening division offered: No
Part-time accepted: No
CAS accepted: Yes

FINANCIAL FACTS
Annual tuition (in-state/out-of-state) $42,875/$49,469
Books and supplies: $6,863
Fees: $1,742
Room & Board (on/off campus): $11,920/$18,523
Financial aid application deadline: 3/2
% first-year students receiving some sort of aid: 100
% all students receiving some sort of aid: 97
% of aid that is merit based: 46
% receiving scholarships: 93
Average grant: $24,221
Average loan: $38,337
Average total aid package: $51,350
Average debt: $102,891

EMPLOYMENT INFORMATION
Total 2014 JD Grads: 93
% for whom you have useable information: 98
% grads employed ten months out: 86
Median starting salary: $65,000
% job accepting grads providing useable salary information: 80
# employed full-time: 79
# employed part-time: 1
# employed bar required: 69
# employed JD preferred: 10
# employed professional/other: 0
# employed non-professional: 1
# pursuing advanced degree: 1
# unemployed and seeking employment: 10
# not seeking employment: 0
% grads employed by school: 14
State for bar exam: CA, TX, OR, CO
Pass rate for first-time bar: 78.0
Grads Employed by Field (%):
Academic (2)
Business/Industry (11)
Government (10)
Judicial Clerkship (11)
 Federal (11)
Private Practice (39)
 Solo (1)
 2-10 (9)
 11-25 (5)
 26-50 (3)
 51-100 (3)
 101-250 (4)
 251-500 (2)
 501+ (11)
Public Interest (14)

UNIVERSITY OF DETROIT MERCY

School of Law

Kimberly Jones, Director of Admissions
651 East Jefferson Avenue, Detroit, MI 48226
Tel: 313-596-0264 • *Fax:* 313-596-0280
Email: udmlawao@udmercy.edu • *Website:* www.law.udmercy.edu

INSTITUTIONAL INFORMATION
Public/Private: Private
Affiliation: Roman Catholic
% faculty part-time: 45
% faculty female: 37
% faculty underrepresented minority: 0
Total faculty: 71

STUDENTS
Enrollment of law school: 540
% male/female: 51/49
% from out-of-state: 47
% part-time: 17
% underrepresented minority: 11
% international: 41
# of countries represented: 5
Average age of entering class: 25

ACADEMICS
Academic Specialties:
Commercial, Criminal, Human Rights, International, Labor, Taxation, Intellectual Property
Advanced Degrees Offered:
JD—three years full time; JD/MBA—four years full time Canadian & American Dual JD—three years full time
Combined Degrees Offered:
JD/MBA—four years full time Canadian & American Dual JD—three years full time JD/LED—five to six years full time Canadian & American Dual JD/LED—six years full time
Clinical program required: Yes
Legal writing course requirement: Yes
Legal methods course requirement: Yes
Legal research course requirement: Yes
Moot court requirement: Yes
Public interest law requirement: Yes

ADMISSIONS
Selectivity Rating: 79
applications received: 1,083
% applicants accepted: 51
% acceptees attending: 33
Average LSAT: 152
Median LSAT: 151
LSAT Range (25th to 75th percentile): 147—156
Average undergrad GPA: 3.12
Median undergrad GPA: 3.12
Application fee: $50
Regular application deadline: 4/15
Transfer students accepted: Yes
Evening division offered: Yes
Part-time accepted: Yes

CAS accepted: Yes
International Students:
TOEFL required of International Students

FINANCIAL FACTS
Annual tuition (in-state/out-of-state) $39,630/$39,630
Books and supplies: $11,496
Fees: $80
Room & Board (on/off campus): NA/$12,664
Financial aid application deadline: 4/1
% first-year students receiving some sort of aid: 56
% all students receiving some sort of aid: 68
% of aid that is merit based: 100
% receiving scholarships: 26
Average grant: $13,365
Average loan: $40,932
Average total aid package: $43,340
Average debt: $135,273

EMPLOYMENT INFORMATION
Total 2014 JD Grads: 211
% grads employed ten months out: 84
Median starting salary: $80,000
employed full-time: 167
employed part-time: 6
employed bar required: 117
employed JD preferred: 31
employed professional/other: 21
employed non-professional: 4
pursuing advanced degree: 4
unemployed and seeking employment: 24
not seeking employment: 5
% grads employed by school: 0
State for bar exam: MI
Pass rate for first-time bar: 64.3
Grads Employed by Field (%):
Academic (3)
Business/Industry (19)
Government (10)
Judicial Clerkship (2)
Private Practice (61)
Public Interest (6)

UNIVERSITY OF LA VERNE

College of Law

Andrew Woolsey, Director of Admissions
320 East D Street, Ontario, CA 91764
Tel: 877-858-4529 • *Fax:* 909-460-2082
Email: lawadm@laverne.edu • *Website:* law.laverne.edu

INSTITUTIONAL INFORMATION
Public/Private: Private
Student-faculty ratio: 16:1
% faculty part-time: 46
% faculty female: 39
% faculty underrepresented minority: 27
Total faculty: 41

STUDENTS

Enrollment of law school: 425
% male/female: 55/45
% part-time: 27
% underrepresented minority: 40
% international: 3
Average age of entering class: 27

ACADEMICS

Advanced Degrees Offered:
JD (Full Time—3 years, Part Time—4 years)
Combined Degrees Offered:
JD/MBA—4 years JD/MPA—4 years
Clinical program required: No
Legal writing course requirement: Yes
Legal methods course requirement: Yes
Legal research course requirement: Yes
Moot court requirement: No
Public interest law requirement: No

ADMISSIONS

Selectivity Rating: 80
applications received: 1,231
% applicants accepted: 45
% acceptees attending: 24
Average LSAT: 153
Median LSAT: 153
LSAT Range (25th to 75th percentile): 150—155
Average undergrad GPA: 3.06
Median undergrad GPA: 3.07
Application fee: $50
Transfer students accepted: Yes
Evening division offered: Yes
Part-time accepted: Yes
CAS accepted: Yes
International Students:
TOEFL recommended of International Students

FINANCIAL FACTS

Annual tuition (in-state): $39,900
Books and supplies: $1,656
Room & Board (on/off campus): $18,225/$18,225
Financial aid application deadline: 3/2

EMPLOYMENT INFORMATION

% grads employed ten months out: 60
Median starting salary: $61,002
State for bar exam: CA, TX, AZ, UT, MT
Pass rate for first-time bar: 53.0
Prominent Alumni:
Thomas M. Finn, HSC Regional Director (S.Region), Dublin, Ireland; The Honorable Dennis Aichroth, Judge, Superior Court, Los Angeles, CA; The Honorable Jean Pfeiffer Leonard, Judge, Juvenile Court, Riverside, CA; Eileen M. Teichert, City Attorney for the City of Sacramento, CA; James J. Manning, Jr., Senior Attorney, Reid & Hellyer, Riverside, CA
Grads Employed by Field (%):
Academic (3)
Business/Industry (26)
Government (7)
Judicial Clerkship (2)
Private Practice (62)
Public Interest (0)

UNIVERSITY OF LOUISVILLE

Louis D. Brandeis School of Law

Brandon L. Hamilton, Assistant Dean for Admissions
University of Louisville, Wyatt Hall—Room 108, Louisville, KY 40292
Tel: 502-852-6364 • Fax: 502-852-8971
Email: lawadmissions@louisville.edu • Website: www.law.louisville.edu

INSTITUTIONAL INFORMATION

Public/Private: Public
Student-faculty ratio: 13:1
% faculty part-time: 0
% faculty female: 40
% faculty underrepresented minority: 8
Total faculty: 35

STUDENTS

Enrollment of law school: 400
% male/female: 59/41
% from out-of-state: 21
% part-time: 7
% underrepresented minority: 5
% international: 1
# of countries represented: 2
Average age of entering class: 26

ACADEMICS

Academic Specialties:
Civil Procedure, Commercial, Constitutional, Corporation Securities, Criminal, Environmental, International, Labor, Legal Philosophy, Property, Taxation, Intellectual Property
Advanced Degrees Offered:
JD, full-time three years, part-time four or five years
Combined Degrees Offered:
Dual Degree Programs: JD/MBA, JD/MSSW, JD/M.Div., JD/MA in Humanities, JD/MA in Poli Sci, and a JD/MA in Urban Planning; JD/MA Bioethics (4 to 5 years)
Clinical program required: Yes
Legal writing course requirement: Yes
Legal methods course requirement: Yes
Legal research course requirement: Yes
Moot court requirement: Yes
Public interest law requirement: Yes

ADMISSIONS

Selectivity Rating: 87
applications received: 1,495
% applicants accepted: 31
% acceptees attending: 28
Median LSAT: 156
LSAT Range (25th to 75th percentile): 152—158
Median undergrad GPA: 3.42
Application fee: $50
Regular application deadline: 3/15
Early application deadline: 3/15
Transfer students accepted: Yes
Evening division offered: No
Part-time accepted: Yes
CAS accepted: Yes
International Students:
TOEFL recommended of International Students

FINANCIAL FACTS
Annual tuition (in-state/out-of-state) $16,536/$31,948
Books and supplies: $1,000
Room & Board (on/off campus): $8,370/$8,370
Financial aid application deadline: 3/15
% first-year students receiving some sort of aid: 85
% all students receiving some sort of aid: 85
% of aid that is merit based: 100
% receiving scholarships: 75
Average grant: $10,000
Average loan: $25,488
Average total aid package: $35,488

EMPLOYMENT INFORMATION
% grads employed ten months out: 98
Median starting salary: $63,000
State for bar exam: KY, IN, TN, OH
Pass rate for first-time bar: 89.0
Prominent Alumni:
Chris Dodd, US Senator; Ron Mazzoli, Former US Congressman; Joseph Lambert, Chief Justice of Kentucky; Stanley Chauvin, Former ABA President; Ernie Allen, Director, National Center for Missing & Exploited Children
Grads Employed by Field (%):
Academic (5)
Business/Industry (17)
Government (17)
Judicial Clerkship (7)
Private Practice (54)
Public Interest (7)

UNIVERSITY OF MONTANA
University of Montana School of Law

Lori Freeman, Director of Admissions
University of Montana School of Law, Room 181, Missoula, MT 59812
Tel: 406-243-2698 • Fax: 406-243-6601
Email: lori.freeman@umontana.edu • Website: www.umt.edu/law

INSTITUTIONAL INFORMATION
Public/Private: Public
Affiliation: No Affiliation
Student-faculty ratio: 15:1
% faculty part-time: 47
% faculty female: 50
% faculty underrepresented minority: 7
Total faculty: 30

STUDENTS
Enrollment of law school: 247
% male/female: 57/43
% from out-of-state: 20
% part-time: 0
% underrepresented minority: 11
% international: 1
# of countries represented: 1
Average age of entering class: 29

ACADEMICS
Academic Specialties:
Environmental
Advanced Degrees Offered:
JD, 3 years
Combined Degrees Offered:
JD/MPA—4 years; JD/MBA—4 years; JD/MS-EVST—4 years.
Clinical program required: Yes
Legal writing course requirement: Yes
Legal methods course requirement: Yes
Legal research course requirement: Yes
Moot court requirement: No
Public interest law requirement: Yes

ADMISSIONS
Selectivity Rating: 82
applications received: 422
% applicants accepted: 57
% acceptees attending: 34
Average LSAT: 154
Median LSAT: 154
LSAT Range (25th to 75th percentile): 151—158
Average undergrad GPA: 3.35
Median undergrad GPA: 3.38
Application fee: $60
Regular application deadline: 3/15
Early application deadline: 2/15
Transfer students accepted: Yes
Evening division offered: No
Part-time accepted: No
CAS accepted: Yes
International Students:
TOEFL required of International Students

FINANCIAL FACTS
Annual tuition (in-state/out-of-state) $9,527/$27,448
Books and supplies: $1,200
Fees: $1,880
Room & Board (on/off campus): $13,531/$13,531
Financial aid application deadline: 3/1
% first-year students receiving some sort of aid: 99
% all students receiving some sort of aid: 91
% of aid that is merit based: 77
% receiving scholarships: 43
Average grant: $3,786
Average loan: $25,915
Average total aid package: $24,956
Average debt: $81,800

EMPLOYMENT INFORMATION
Total 2014 JD Grads: 80
% for whom you have useable information: 100
% grads employed ten months out: 86
Median starting salary: $50,790
% job accepting grads providing useable salary information: 72
# employed full-time: 65
# employed part-time: 4
# employed bar required: 57
# employed JD preferred: 7
# employed professional/other: 2
# employed non-professional: 3
# pursuing advanced degree: 2
# unemployed and seeking employment: 8
# not seeking employment: 1

% grads employed by school: 0
State for bar exam: MT, AK, ND, UT, WA
Pass rate for first-time bar: 70.0
Prominent Alumni:
Hon. Justin Miller, U. S. Court of Appeals for the District of Columbia Cir; Dean USC School of Law & Duke Law School; Hon. James R. Browning, U. S. Court of Appeals for the 9th Cir.; Clerk of U. S. Supreme Court; Hon. William J. Jameson, U. S. District Court, Montana Div.; Past President of the American Bar Association; Gov. Marc F. Racicot, Governor for State of Montana; Attorney General for State of Montana; Denise Juneau, 1st Native American state-wide elected official, Montana Superintendent of Public Instruction
Grads Employed by Field (%):
Academic (3)
Business/Industry (9)
Government (9)
Judicial Clerkship (19)
  Federal (8)
  State or local (11)
Private Practice (41)
  Solo (1)
  2-10 (29)
  11-25 (4)
  26-50 (1)
  101-250 (6)
Public Interest (6)

VALPARAISO UNIVERSITY

Valparaiso University School of Law

Tony Credit, Tony Credit, JD Executive Director of Admissions
Wesemann Hall, Valparaiso, IN 46383
Tel: *888-825-7652* • ***Fax:*** *219-465-7808*
Email: *valpolaw@valpo.edu* • ***Website:*** *www.valpo.edu/law/*

INSTITUTIONAL INFORMATION
Public/Private: Private
Affiliation: Lutheran
Student-faculty ratio: 17:1
% faculty part-time: 50
% faculty female: 42
% faculty underrepresented minority: 6
Total faculty: 50

STUDENTS
Enrollment of law school: 523
% male/female: 55/45
% from out-of-state: 68
% part-time: 8
% underrepresented minority: 12
% international: 2
# of countries represented: 4
Average age of entering class: 24

ACADEMICS
Academic Specialties:
Civil Procedure, Commercial, Constitutional, Corporation Securities, Criminal, Environmental, Government Services, Human Rights, International, Labor, Legal History, Legal Philosophy, Property, Intellectual Property

Advanced Degrees Offered:
JD, three years full-time, five years part-time; LLM, one year full-time;
Combined Degrees Offered:
All Dual Degree programs take 4 years JD/MBA JD/CMHC JD/PSY JD/MA International Commerce and Policy JD/MA Sports Administration JD/MALS-Create your own program
Clinical program required: No
Legal writing course requirement: Yes
Legal methods course requirement: Yes
Legal research course requirement: Yes
Moot court requirement: No
Public interest law requirement: Yes

ADMISSIONS
Selectivity Rating: 84
 # applications received: 2,589
% applicants accepted: 30
% acceptees attending: 22
Average LSAT: 151
LSAT Range (25th to 75th percentile): 144—162
Average undergrad GPA: 3.31
Application fee: $60
Regular application deadline: 6/1
Transfer students accepted: Yes
Evening division offered: No
Part-time accepted: Yes
CAS accepted: Yes
International Students:
TOEFL required of International Students

FINANCIAL FACTS
Annual tuition: $28,250
Books and supplies: $2,000
Room & Board (on/off campus): $7,300/$7,300
Financial aid application deadline: 4/1
% first-year students receiving some sort of aid: 90
% all students receiving some sort of aid: 95
% of aid that is merit based: 35
% receiving scholarships: 34
Average grant: $15,214
Average loan: $18,500
Average total aid package: $39,850
Average debt: $56,000

EMPLOYMENT INFORMATION
Median starting salary: $56,000
State for bar exam: IN, IL, MI, WI, GA
Pass rate for first-time bar: 84.0
Prominent Alumni:
Stephan Todd, VP Law & Environment US Steel Corporation; Cornell Boggs, VP & General Counsel, Tyco Plastics & Adhesives; Honorable Nancy Vaidik, Justice, Indiana Court of Appeals; Koreen Ryan, Senior Council, South Asia McDonald's Corporation; Honorable Robert Rucker, Justice, Supreme Court of Indiana
Grads Employed by Field (%):
Academic (1)
Business/Industry (16)
Government (12)
Judicial Clerkship (4)
Private Practice (63)
Public Interest (2)

WESTERN NEW ENGLAND UNIVERSITY

Western New England University School of Law

Michael Johnson, Associate Dean for Student Affairs and Enrollment Planning
1215 Wilbraham Road, Springfield, MA 01119
Tel: 413-782-1406 • *Fax:* 413-796-2067
Email: admissions@law.wne.edu • *Website:* www.law.wne.edu

INSTITUTIONAL INFORMATION
Public/Private: Private
Student-faculty ratio: 11:1
% faculty part-time: 48
% faculty female: 54
% faculty underrepresented minority: 15
Total faculty: 64

STUDENTS
Enrollment of law school: 343
% male/female: 45/55
% from out-of-state: 64
% part-time: 33
% underrepresented minority: 29
% international: 0
# of countries represented: 2
Average age of entering class: 26

ACADEMICS
Academic Specialties:
Criminal, International
Advanced Degrees Offered:
Western New England University School of Law offers classes towards an LLM in Estate Planning and Elder Law. The program can be completed over one, two or three years. The program is offered entirely on-line.
Combined Degrees Offered:
JD/Master of Regional Planning with University of Masssachusetts-4 years total; JD/Masters of Social Work with Springfield College—4 years total; JD/Masters of Business Administration with Western New England University—as short as 3 years or as long as 4 years; JD/Masters of Accounting with Western New England University—4 years total.
Clinical program required: No
Legal writing course requirement: Yes
Legal methods course requirement: Yes
Legal research course requirement: Yes
Moot court requirement: Yes
Public interest law requirement: No

ADMISSIONS
Selectivity Rating: 70
applications received: 527
% applicants accepted: 84
% acceptees attending: 21
Average LSAT: 146
Median LSAT: 146
LSAT Range (25th to 75th percentile): 143—148
Average undergrad GPA: 3.15
Median undergrad GPA: 3.16
Application fee: $50

Transfer students accepted: Yes
Evening division offered: Yes
Part-time accepted: Yes
CAS accepted: Yes
International Students:
TOEFL recommended of International Students

FINANCIAL FACTS
Annual tuition (in-state): $39,450
Books and supplies: $1,600
Room & Board (on/off campus): $10,024/$14,562
% first-year students receiving some sort of aid: 98
% all students receiving some sort of aid: 97
% receiving scholarships: 73
Average grant: $15,729
Average loan: $41,120
Average total aid package: $53,278
Average debt: $134,725

EMPLOYMENT INFORMATION
Total 2014 JD Grads: 98
% for whom you have useable information: 94
% grads employed ten months out: 74
Median starting salary: $56,000
% job accepting grads providing useable salary information: 40
# employed full-time: 66
# employed part-time: 6
# employed bar required: 38
# employed JD preferred: 19
# employed professional/other: 14
# employed non-professional: 1
# pursuing advanced degree: 0
# unemployed and seeking employment: 20
# not seeking employment: 0
% grads employed by school: 0
State for bar exam: CT, MA
Pass rate for first-time bar: 73.1
Prominent Alumni:
Hon. Mark Mastrioanni, U.S. District Court Judge; Jonathan Blum, Senior Vice President/Yum Brands; Amy Fliegelman Olli, Executive Vice President and General Counsel/CA International; Barry Skolnick, Senior Vice President and General Counsel/Merrill Lynch; Katherine Robertson, District Court Magistrate
Grads Employed by Field (%):
Academic (5)
Business/Industry (10)
Government (15)
Judicial Clerkship (8)
 State or local (8)
Private Practice (28)
 Solo (1)
 2-10 (13)
 11-25 (4)
 26-50 (4)
 101-250 (1)
 251-500 (1)
Public Interest (2)

WESTERN STATE COLLEGE OF LAW AT ARGOSY UNIVERSITY

Western State College of Law at Argosy University

Rhonda Cohen, Assistant Director of Admission
1111 North State College Boulevard, Fullerton, CA 92831
Tel: 714-459-1101 • Fax: 714-441-1748
Email: adm@wsulaw.edu • Website: www.wsulaw.edu

INSTITUTIONAL INFORMATION
Public/Private: Private
% faculty part-time: 48
% faculty female: 46
% faculty underrepresented minority: 25
Total faculty: 48

STUDENTS
Enrollment of law school: 353
% male/female: 51/49
% part-time: 38
% underrepresented minority: 42
% international: 1
# of countries represented: 3
Average age of entering class: 27

ACADEMICS
Academic Specialties:
Criminal
Advanced Degrees Offered:
Juris Doctor, Part-time—4 years; Full-time—3 years
Clinical program required: No
Legal writing course requirement: Yes
Legal methods course requirement: Yes
Legal research course requirement: Yes
Moot court requirement: Yes
Public interest law requirement: No

ADMISSIONS
Selectivity Rating: 74
applications received: 768
% applicants accepted: 64
% acceptees attending: 19
Average LSAT: 149
Median LSAT: 149
LSAT Range (25th to 75th percentile): 146—151
Average undergrad GPA: 3.06
Median undergrad GPA: 3.09
Application fee: $60
Early application deadline: 6/1
Early application notification: 6/1
Transfer students accepted: Yes
Evening division offered: Yes
Part-time accepted: Yes
CAS accepted: Yes
International Students:
TOEFL required of International Students

FINANCIAL FACTS
Annual tuition (in-state/out-of-state) $41,612/$41,612
Books and supplies: $2,400
Fees: $490
Room & Board (off campus): $9,265
Financial aid application deadline: 4/15
Average grant: $21,737
Average loan: $38,341
Average total aid package: $48,901
Average debt: $113,384

EMPLOYMENT INFORMATION
Total 2014 JD Grads: 150
% for whom you have useable information: 89
% grads employed ten months out: 74
Median starting salary: $60,000
% job accepting grads providing useable salary information: 74
# employed full-time: 81
# employed part-time: 17
# employed bar required: 55
# employed JD preferred: 28
# employed professional/other: 12
# employed non-professional: 3
# pursuing advanced degree: 1
# unemployed and seeking employment: 30
# not seeking employment: 3
% grads employed by school: 0
State for bar exam: CA, UT, AZ, NY, TX
Pass rate for first-time bar: 77.0
Prominent Alumni:
Lucetta Dunn, CEO, Orange County Business Council; George Gascon, District Attorney of San Francisco County; Kevin Calcagnie, Partner, Robinson, Calagnie, Robinson, Shapiro & Davis; Shawn Nelson, Supervisor, County of Orange; John Montevideo, President, Consumer Attorneys of California
Grads Employed by Field (%):
Academic (2)
Business/Industry (15)
Government (5)
Private Practice (41)
  Solo (7)
  2-10 (25)
  11-2 (7)
  101-250 (1)
  251-500 (1)
Public Interest (2)

QUEEN'S UNIVERSITY

Faculty of Law, Queen's University

Aimee Burtch, Admissions and Career Services Coordinator
Macdonald Hall, Rm 200, 128 Union St., Queen's University, Kingston, ON K7L 3N6

Tel: 613-533-2220 • *Fax:* 613-533-6611

Email: jd@queensu.ca • *Website:* law.queensu.ca

INSTITUTIONAL INFORMATION
Public/Private: Public
Affiliation: No Affiliation
Student-faculty ratio: 17:1
Total faculty: 77

STUDENTS
Enrollment of law school: 165
% male/female: 50/50
% part-time: 2
Average age of entering class: 23

ACADEMICS
Clinical program required: No
Legal writing course requirement: Yes
Legal methods course requirement: Yes
Legal research course requirement: Yes
Moot court requirement: Yes
Public interest law requirement: Yes

ADMISSIONS
Selectivity Rating: 95
applications received: 2,690
% applicants accepted: 20
% acceptees attending: 30
Average LSAT: 162
Median LSAT: 162
LSAT Range (25th to 75th percentile): 160—164
Average undergrad GPA: 3.80
Application fee: $185
Regular application deadline: 11/1
Transfer students accepted: Yes
Evening division offered: No
Part-time accepted: Yes
CAS accepted: No
International Students:
TOEFL required of International Students

FINANCIAL FACTS
Annual tuition (in-state/intl) $15,357/$29,575
Books and supplies: $2,830
Fees: $1836 intl
Room & Board (on/off campus): $6,930–10,430/$6,930–10,430
Financial aid application deadline: 10/31
% all students receiving some sort of aid: 85
% of aid that is merit based: 25
% receiving scholarships: 25
Average grant: $2,828
Average loan: $12,225
Average total aid package: $11,985

EMPLOYMENT INFORMATION
% grads employed ten months out: 98
Median starting salary: $60,000
State for bar exam: NY, MA
Pass rate for first-time bar: 100.0
Prominent Alumni:
David R.Allgood (Artsci '70), Law '74, Executive Vice President & General Counsel, Royal Bank of Canada; The Honourable Annemarie Bonkalo, (Artsci '71), Law '76, Chief Justice, Ontario Court of Justice; The Honourable Thomas A. Cromwell, (Mus'73),Law '76, Justice, Supreme Court of Canada; The Right Honourable David Johnston Law '66, LLD'91, Governor General of Canada; The Honourable David Stratas, Law '84, Justice, Federal Court of Appeal
Grads Employed by Field (%):
Academic (0)
Government (10)
Judicial Clerkship (7)
Private Practice (83)
Public Interest (0)

UNIVERSITY OF BRITISH COLUMBIA

Peter A. Allard School of Law

Elaine L. Borthwick, Director, JD Admissions
1822 East Mall, Vancouver, BC V6T 1Z1

Tel: 604-822-6303 • *Fax:* 604-822-9486

Email: admissions@allard.ubc.ca • *Website:* www.allard.ubc.ca

INSTITUTIONAL INFORMATION
Public/Private: Public
Student-faculty ratio: 4:1
% faculty part-time: 71
% faculty female: 30
% faculty underrepresented minority: 12
Total faculty: 154

STUDENTS
Enrollment of law school: 611
% male/female: 52/48
% from out-of-state: 39
% part-time: 2
% international: 2
# of countries represented: 10
Average age of entering class: 25

ACADEMICS
Academic Specialties:
Corporation Securities, Criminal, Environmental, Human Rights, International, Legal History, Taxation
Advanced Degrees Offered:
The Juris Doctor (JD) Degree is a 3 year program full-time. The Master of Laws (LLM)Degree is a 12 month program. The LLM (Master of Laws) and the LLMCL.

(Master of Law in Common Law) are 1 year programs. The Doctorate (Ph.D. Degree is a 2-4 year program.

Combined Degrees Offered:
The combined JD/MBA Program is 4 years in length and is administered jointly by the Faculty of Commerce and the Faculty of Law. Students are required to complete 86 credits in law and 45 credits in the MBA program. The University of British Columbia (UBC) Faculty of Law and the University of Hawai'i (UH) at Manoa William S. Richardson School of Law Joint Legal Education Program allows students who complete the 4 year program to receive a JD degree from UBC and a JD degree from UH. The University of British Columbia (UBC) and the University of Hong Kong (HKU) Joint Legal Education Program allows students who complete the 4 year program to receive a JD degree from UBC and a Postgraduate Certificate in Laws (PCLL program) from HKU.

Clinical program required: No
Legal writing course requirement: Yes
Legal methods course requirement: No
Legal research course requirement: Yes
Moot court requirement: Yes
Public interest law requirement: No

ADMISSIONS
Selectivity Rating: 97
 # applications received: 1,822
% applicants accepted: 23
% acceptees attending: 44
Average LSAT: 166
Median LSAT: 166
LSAT Range (25th to 75th percentile): 161—168
Average undergrad GPA: 3.88
Median undergrad GPA: 3.88
Application fee: $87
Regular application deadline: 12/1
Regular notification:
Early application deadline: 9/30
Transfer students accepted: Yes
Evening division offered: No
Part-time accepted: Yes
CAS accepted: No

FINANCIAL FACTS
Annual tuition (in-state/out-of-state) $11,448/$24,862
Books and supplies: $2,293
Fees: $1,052
Room & Board (on/off campus): $9,400/$11,300
% first-year students receiving some sort of aid: 69
% all students receiving some sort of aid: 70
% of aid that is merit based: 8
% receiving scholarships: 65
Average grant: $4,957
Average loan: $10,525
Average total aid package: $13,130
Average debt: $30,015

EMPLOYMENT INFORMATION
Total 2014 JD Grads: 183
% for whom you have useable information: 94
% grads employed ten months out: 91
 # employed full-time: 148
 # pursuing advanced degree: 3
 # unemployed and seeking employment: 11
 # not seeking employment: 10
State for bar exam: BC, AB, ON, NY
Pass rate for first-time bar: 99.0

Prominent Alumni:
Frank Iacobucci, Former Justice Supreme Court of Canada; Lance Finch, Chief Justice of British Columbia; Kim Campbell, Former Prime Minister of Canada; Don Brenner, Chief Justice of British Columbia Supreme Court; Ujjal Dosanjh, Former Premier of British Columbia & Attorney Gen.

Grads Employed by Field (%):
Business/Industry (1)
Government (7)
Judicial Clerkship (9)
Private Practice (76)
Public Interest (1)

UNIVERSITY OF CALGARY
Faculty of Law

Karen Argento, Admissions/Student Services Officer
Murray Fraser Hall, 2500 University Drive NW, Calgary, AB T2N 1N4
Tel: 403-220-4155 • Fax: 403-210-9662
Email: law@ucalgary.ca • Website: www.law.ucalgary.ca/

INSTITUTIONAL INFORMATION
Public/Private: Public
Affiliation: No Affiliation
Student-faculty ratio: 12:1
% faculty female: 50
Total faculty: 21

STUDENTS
Enrollment of law school: 325
% male/female: 48/52
% from out-of-state: 53
% part-time: 0
% underrepresented minority: 0
% international: 0
# of countries represented: 2
Average age of entering class: 25

ACADEMICS
Academic Specialties:
Environmental
Advanced Degrees Offered:
JD—3 YEARS; LLM—15-18 MONTHS
Combined Degrees Offered:
JD/MBA—4 years law and masters of business administration; JD/MED—law and masters of environmental design
Clinical program required: No
Legal writing course requirement: Yes
Legal methods course requirement: Yes
Legal research course requirement: Yes
Moot court requirement: Yes

ADMISSIONS
Selectivity Rating: 94
 # applications received: 1,243
% applicants accepted: 19
% acceptees attending: 48
Average LSAT: 160
Average undergrad GPA: 3.57

Application fee: $100
Regular application deadline: 11/1
Transfer students accepted: Yes
Evening division offered: No
Part-time accepted: Yes
CAS accepted: No
International Students:
TOEFL required of International Students

FINANCIAL FACTS
Annual tuition (in-state/out-of-state) $13,000/$12,500
Books and supplies: $1,800
Fees: $581
Room & Board (on/off campus): $8,000/$12,000

EMPLOYMENT INFORMATION
State for bar exam: AB

UNIVERSITY OF MANITOBA
Robson Hall, Faculty of Law

Marie Jivan, Admissions Coordinator
306B Robson Hall, 224 Dysart Road, University of Manitoba, Winnipeg, MB R3T 2N2
Tel: 204-480-1485 • Fax: 204-474-7580
Email: lawadmissions@umanitoba.ca • Website: www.umanitoba.ca/law

INSTITUTIONAL INFORMATION
Public/Private: Public
Affiliation: No Affiliation
Student-faculty ratio: 15:1
% faculty part-time: 43
% faculty female: 30
Total faculty: 23

STUDENTS
Enrollment of law school: 106
% male/female: 59/41
% from out-of-state: 28
% part-time: 0
% international: 1
Average age of entering class: 25

ACADEMICS
Academic Specialties:
Civil Procedure, Commercial, Constitutional, Corporation Securities, Criminal, Environmental, Government Services, Human Rights, International, Labor, Legal History, Legal Philosophy, Property, Taxation, Intellectual Property
Advanced Degrees Offered:
LLM 1 year
Clinical program required: No
Legal writing course requirement: Yes
Legal methods course requirement: Yes
Legal research course requirement: Yes
Moot court requirement: Yes
Public interest law requirement: No

ADMISSIONS
Selectivity Rating: 97
applications received: 1,109
% applicants accepted: 17
% acceptees attending: 55
Average LSAT: 161
Median LSAT: 161
LSAT Range (25th to 75th percentile): 154—171
Average undergrad GPA: 3.99
Median undergrad GPA: 3.90
Application fee: $125
Regular application deadline: 11/1
Early application deadline: 11/1
Transfer students accepted: Yes
Evening division offered: No
Part-time accepted: Yes
CAS accepted: No
International Students:
TOEFL required of International Students

FINANCIAL FACTS
Annual tuition (in-state): $9,093
Books and supplies: $3,000
Room & Board (on/off campus): $10,000/$20,000
Financial aid application deadline: 10/1
% of aid that is merit based: 0
Average loan: $13,900
Average debt: $22,000

EMPLOYMENT INFORMATION
% grads employed ten months out: 97
Median starting salary: $45,000
Pass rate for first-time bar: 100.0

UNIVERSITY OF SASKATCHEWAN
College of Law

Mark Carter, Admissions Chair
College of Law University of Saskatchewan, 15 Campus Drive, Saskatoon, SK S7N 5A6
Tel: 306-966-5045 • Fax: 306-966-5900
Email: law_admissions@usask.ca • Website: www.usask.ca/law/

INSTITUTIONAL INFORMATION
Public/Private: Public
% faculty part-time: 10
% faculty female: 12
Total faculty: 31

STUDENTS
Enrollment of law school: 300
Average age of entering class: 27

ACADEMICS

Legal writing course requirement: Yes
Legal methods course requirement: No
Legal research course requirement: Yes

ADMISSIONS

Selectivity Rating: 92
applications received: 1,082
% applicants accepted: 25
% acceptees attending: 47
Average LSAT: 160
LSAT Range (25th to 75th percentile): 151—172
Average undergrad GPA: 3.32
Application fee: $125
Regular application deadline: 2/1
Transfer students accepted: Yes
Evening division offered: No
Part-time accepted: Yes
CAS accepted: No

FINANCIAL FACTS

Annual tuition (in-state/out-of-state) $8,490/$8,490
Books and supplies: $2,200
Fees: $729

UNIVERSITY OF WINDSOR

University of Windsor, Faculty of Law

Michelle Pilutti, Assistant Dean (Administration)
Faculty of Law, 401 Sunset Avenue, Windsor, ON N9B 3P4
Tel: 519-253-3000 • Fax: 519-973-7064
Email: lawadmit@uwindsor.ca • Website: www.uwindsor.ca/law

INSTITUTIONAL INFORMATION

Public/Private: Public
Student-faculty ratio: 9:1
% faculty part-time: 58
% faculty female: 50
% faculty underrepresented minority: 17
Total faculty: 77

STUDENTS

Enrollment of law school: 662
% male/female: 42/58
% part-time: 1
% international: 1
Average age of entering class: 24

ACADEMICS

Academic Specialties:
Civil Procedure, Commercial, Constitutional, Corporation Securities, Criminal, Environmental, Human Rights, International, Labor, Legal History, Legal Philosophy, Property, Taxation, Intellectual Property
Combined Degrees Offered:
Canadian & American Dual JD Program—3 yrs MSW/JD Program—3 to 4 yrs MBA/JD Program—3 yrs
Clinical program required: No
Legal writing course requirement: Yes

Legal methods course requirement: Yes
Legal research course requirement: Yes
Moot court requirement: Yes
Public interest law requirement: No

ADMISSIONS

Selectivity Rating: 60
Application fee: $200
Regular application deadline: 11/1
Transfer students accepted: Yes
Evening division offered: No
Part-time accepted: Yes
CAS accepted: No
International Students:
TOEFL recommended of International Students

FINANCIAL FACTS

Annual tuition (in-state/out-of-state) $16,610/$28,494
Books and supplies: $2,000
Fees: incl
Room & Board (on/off campus): $10,000/
% of aid that is merit based: 25
% receiving scholarships: 50
Average grant: $6,200

EMPLOYMENT INFORMATION

Total 2014 JD Grads: 210
% for whom you have useable information: 98
# unemployed and seeking employment: 15
# not seeking employment: 2
State for bar exam: ON, AB, BC, NS, NF
Grads Employed by Field (%):
Academic (1)
Government (17)
Judicial Clerkship (3)
Private Practice (60)
Public Interest (20)

YORK UNIVERSITY

Osgoode Hall Law School

Louise Resendes, Recruitment and Admissions Officer
1012 Ignat Kaneff Bldg., 4700 Keele Street, Toronto, ON M3J 1P3
Tel: 416-736-5712 • Fax: 416-736-5618
Email: admissions@osgoode.yorku.ca • Website: www.osgoode.yorku.ca

INSTITUTIONAL INFORMATION

Public/Private: Public
% faculty female: 45
Total faculty: 180

STUDENTS

Average age of entering class: 25

ACADEMICS

Advanced Degrees Offered:
JD—3 years LLM
Combined Degrees Offered:
JD/MBA—3 and 4 years; JD/MES—4 years; JD/MA (Philosophy)—4 years; JD/BCL—4 years.
Clinical program required: Yes
Legal writing course requirement: Yes
Legal methods course requirement: Yes
Legal research course requirement: Yes
Moot court requirement: No
Public interest law requirement: Yes

ADMISSIONS

Selectivity Rating: 60
 # applications received: 2,725
% applicants accepted: 21
% acceptees attending: 51
Application fee: $90
Regular application deadline: 11/1
Transfer students accepted: Yes
Evening division offered: No
Part-time accepted: Yes
CAS accepted: No
International Students:
TOEFL required of International Students

FINANCIAL FACTS

Annual tuition (in-state/out-of-state) $22,672/$23,497
Books and supplies: $1,000
Fees: $927
Room & Board (on/off campus): $10,000/$10,000
Financial aid application deadline: 11/1

SCHOOL SAYS . . .

In this section, you'll find schools with extended listings describing admissions, curriculum, internships, and much more. This is your chance to get in-depth information on programs that interest you. The Princeton Review charges each school a small fee to be listed, and the editorial responsibility is solely that of the university.

CHAPMAN UNIVERSITY
Fowler School of Law

AT A GLANCE

Chapman University Dale E. Fowler School of Law offers a collaborative, personalized, and rigorous legal education. Graduates develop the skills needed to provide ethical and professional service to their clients and to society. Fowler School of Law offers small class sizes and greater access to faculty, with an emphasis on advanced legal analysis, practice skills, and professionalism. The law school is ABA accredited and has a dedicated staff to help graduating students obtain positions of responsibility in the legal workforce.

CAMPUS AND LOCATION

The School of Law is located on the 42-acre Chapman University campus, in the heart of the historic Old Towne dining and shopping district in Orange, California. The law school is approximately 35 miles south of Los Angeles, and just a short drive to nearby beaches, legal and business hubs, courthouses, cultural centers, and major sports complexes.

For visitor information, see http://www.chapman.edu/law/about.

DEGREES OFFERED

The School of Law offers a traditional JD as well as options to pursue a joint JD/MBA or JD/MFA at Chapman University's acclaimed business or film schools. LLM programs are offered in Business and Economics, Entertainment/Media Law, International and Comparative Law, Taxation, and Trial Advocacy, as well as a new Double Masters LLM/MBA.

PROGRAMS AND CURRICULUM

JD students must complete 88 academic credits to graduate. Required first-year courses cover Contracts, Torts, Civil Procedure (with Practice Lab), Property, Criminal Law, and Legal Research & Writing (with Practice Lab). Upper-level courses are also required in Practice Foundation Transactions, Constitutional Law, Corporations or Business Associations, Evidence, Federal Income Taxation, Criminal Procedure/Police Practice, Remedies, Wills & Trusts, and Professional Responsibility. Law students may choose from a wide range of non-required electives, or may opt to earn an emphasis certificate in Advocacy/Dispute Resolution, Business Law, Entertainment Law, Environmental, Land Use/Real Estate, International Law, or Tax Law.

FACILITIES

The School of Law is housed in an architecturally striking four-story facility that includes an award-winning law library, two state-of-the-art mock courtrooms, and fully wireless classrooms. The law school provides an expansive student lounge with televisions, a game room, and comfortable couches and tables. The Chapman University campus offers a number of eateries and cafes, as well as a fitness/aquatic center, lighted tennis courts, indoor basketball courts, and an outdoor track.

EXPENSES AND FINANCIAL AID

In the 2014–2015 academic year, Chapman paid over $7.8 million in scholarships/grants to JD and LLM students. Most scholarships are merit-based (based on LSAT/GPA), with special funds also awarded. Tuition and fees for 2015–2016 full-time JD students (in-state or out-of-state) are $48,602 and estimated living expenses are $25,524. Federal Loans are available to cover costs not met with scholarships.

FACULTY

The School of Law professors include four former U.S. Supreme Court clerks, a former U.S. congressman, a Nobel laureate, and a host of distinguished scholars, visiting professors, and practitioner adjunct professors. Students have easy access to faculty members in both formal and informal settings. Faculty members are frequently cited in print and online media and have published papers in prestigious law journals.

STUDENTS

The School of Law has earned a unique reputation for its friendly, collegial and collaborative students and its ideal studying environment. Every year since 2005, the school has been ranked as a top ten law school for "Best Quality of Life" by The Princeton Review. Fowler School of Law has approximately 40 student organizations, providing valuable networking opportunities, special events, and guest speakers. Students edit law journals, coordinate major symposia, and compete on award-winning competition teams. Each spring, students attend the Barrister's Ball, a popular dinner and dance party.

ADMISSIONS

The School of Law has a rolling admissions policy, enrolling approximately 160 law students in each first year class. The school seeks to admit students passionately interested in a legal education that will challenge them to grow intellectually, ethically, and professionally.

Each application is individually reviewed and the applicant's entire file is considered in the review process. There are many factors utilized in the decision-making process. In addition to cumulative undergraduate GPA and LSAT score(s), other components are also considered in determining the applicant's potential to succeed in law school. Such indicators include nature and rigor of the undergraduate discipline, an upward trend in academic performance, types of courses completed, writing ability, work experience, graduate level courses taken and degrees earned, scholarly achievements, community and volunteer service, research projects, demonstrated leadership ability, life experiences, overcoming obstacles, and fluency in foreign languages.

First year JD applications are due April 15. June LSAT scores are accepted so long as applications are submitted by the April 15 deadline.

SPECIAL PROGRAMS

The School of Law has a thriving legal clinical program, providing pro bono services to individuals in a diverse range of legal subject areas, including tax, entertainment, elder law, family protection, immigration law, constitutional law and mediation. Each clinic is directed by a faculty member with significant clinical experience. Students conduct classroom and hands-on field work that may include client contact, research projects, document preparation, brief writing, and court appearances. The law school offers broad externship opportunities and a rigorous supplemental bar preparation program designed to provide intensive bar examination practice and preparation.

CAREER SERVICES AND PLACEMENT

The School of Law's Career Services Office offers comprehensive services to aid law students and alumni in developing career paths and achieving employment goals. Attorney counselors help match students' education, skill sets, and interests with employment opportunities. In keeping with the law school's mission of personalized education and recognizing the changing legal job market, Fowler School of Law includes a Professional Development Program, which offers regular one-on-one counseling and workshops taught by local practitioners to ensure students' successful transition from the classroom into practice. Staff members provide a wide variety of services, programs, and resources, and they meet frequently with students to help in self-assessment and goal orientation, to review resumes and cover letters, to provide job-search training, and to assist in building professional networks.

PACE UNIVERSITY LAW

AT A GLANCE

Pace Law School, founded in 1976, has over 8,400 alumni throughout the country and the world, and its environmental law program is consistently ranked among the top five in the nation. The Law School is recognized for excellence in other areas as well, including but not limited to its international, criminal justice, public interest law, and clinical training and skills programs. The Law School offers full-time and part-time day J.D. programs, as well as a January Accelerated Program that provides students the opportunity to complete law school in two and a half years instead of three. Also offered are the Master of Laws degrees in Comparative Legal Studies and Environmental Law, including the nation's first graduate-level programs in Climate Change and Land Use and Sustainable Development, and a Doctor of Laws degree in Environmental Law. The Law School is part of Pace University, a comprehensive, independent, and diversified university with campuses in New York City and Westchester County.

CAMPUS AND LOCATION

The Law School's White Plains campus houses its academic facilities, student activities center, and residence hall. Just twenty miles from Manhattan, the campus provides a suburban feel in an urban setting. With convenient access to New York City, as well as nearby Connecticut and New Jersey, White Plains is headquarters to some of the nation's largest corporations, a large legal community, and local, county, state, and federal courts. This concentration of resources enables the Law School to attract dynamic professors and speakers and to offer excellent opportunities for internships and post-graduation employment.

DEGREES OFFERED

The Law School offers: J.D., LL.M. in Comparative Legal Studies, J.D./LL.M. and S.J.D. in Environmental Law, J.D./M.B.A. and J.D./M.P.A. with Pace University, J.D./M.E.M. with Yale University School of Forestry and Environmental Studies, J.D./M.S. with Bard College, Center for Environmental Policy, J.D./M.A. with Sarah Lawrence College in Women's Studies.

PROGRAMS AND CURRICULUM

Students can explore a range of subject areas or pursue a concentrated curriculum. The academic program prepares students to practice in any jurisdiction in the United States. The Law School's accomplished faculty—comprised of dedicated scholars, researchers, and practitioners—brings extensive experience and innovative teaching techniques to the classroom. Many classes have fewer than twenty-five students, facilitating close faculty-student relationships. Beyond the rich curricular programs, students have access to many extracurricular activities, such as student-run organizations and law reviews, prominent on-campus lecture series, and research in highly regarded Centers.

FACILITIES

The library is an airy, modern facility with wireless access, two computer labs, and six public terminals. Housing over 403,000 volumes, the library also provides access through interlibrary loan to materials held in libraries throughout the United States. It is a member of several library consortia, through which students can use academic libraries located in the New York metropolitan region. The library subscribes to many online databases, including Lexis, Westlaw, HeinOnline, and BNA.

EXPENSES AND FINANCIAL AID

Tuition for the 2015–2016 academic year is $45,376 for full-time students and $34,034 for part-time students. The on-campus residence hall houses 109 full-time students and features single rooms with internet access and cable television.

A comprehensive aid program includes scholarships, need-based grants, employment loans, and a loan forgiveness program for graduates who choose a public interest career. In 2014, the average scholarship award totaled $25,000/year. Criteria for funds may include financial need, academic merit, education costs, or credit considerations.

FACULTY

The Law School includes forty full-time and ninety-five adjunct professors. Faculty scholarship covers diverse areas of law such as Civil Litigation, Civil Procedure, Constitutional Law, Contracts, Evidence, Family Law, Federalism and Separation of Powers, Federal Jurisdiction, Federal Law and Procedure, Property, Torts, Animal Law, Gender Law, Prisoner's Rights, Feminist Legal Theory, Americans with Disabilities Act, Children's Legal Representation, Sexual Orientation and Gender Identity, Environmental, International Commercial Law, Land Use, and Prosecutorial and Judicial Ethics. Many faculty members author widely circulated, influential legal publications and have drafted groundbreaking legislation.

STUDENTS

The diverse 2014 entering class represented sixteen states, several countries, and over ninety-five undergraduate schools. The average age is 24 and the age range is 20–56. The diversity population is 26 percent. The new January-entering class, now in its fifth year, enrolled thirty new students.

SPECIAL PROGRAMS

The Law School offers many clinics, simulation courses, and externships through on-campus centers, institutes, and lawyering skills programs. Students represent clients through the Pace Women's Justice Center's Family Court Externship, preserve individual liberties through the John Jay Legal Services Immigration Justice Clinic, and prosecute criminal cases with Assistant District Attorneys through a prosecution externship. Environmental students work on conservation and development through the Land Use Law Center and accelerate the transition to clean, efficient, and renewable energy alternatives through the Pace Energy and Climate Center.

The international programs allow students to spend a summer abroad at a United Nations War Crimes Tribunal, or intern abroad with law firms and corporate legal departments handling international trade matters. Through judicial externship programs, students hone legal writing skills in the chambers of a state or federal judge.

ADDITIONAL INFORMATION

Address: 78 North Broadway, White Plains, NY 10603 Admissions Phone: 914-422-4210; Admissions E-mail: admissions@law.pace.edu, Web Address: www.law.pace.edu

CAREER SERVICES AND PLACEMENT

Through a variety of outreach activities, the Law School's Center for Career and Professional Development (CCPD) and Public Interest Law Center actively work to foster and maintain relationships with the legal community. The CCPD maintains a website for job postings and recruitment programs and hosts an annual career fair. In addition, the CCPD provides direct, personal career counseling to students and arranges panels, networking events, and presentations to enable students to learn about legal fields and meet members of the bench and bar. The Public Interest Law Center (PILC) provides individual career counseling and a range of events and support for students focused on public interest careers. The PILC also sponsors a Pro Bono Justice Program, offering over ten programs through which law students gain hands-on legal skills while providing needed legal services, and facilitates funding for students working in public interest summer internships.

ST. THOMAS UNIVERSITY LAW

AT A GLANCE

St. Thomas University School of Law is a highly-regarded student-centered law school where diversity is cherished, a commitment to human rights and international law flourishes, and the Catholic heritage of social justice enhances the education of all faiths.

One of the greatest strengths of our law school is the profound sense of community shared by students, faculty, and administration. St. Thomas Law is a leader in diversity, boasting one of the most culturally diverse student bodies in the country. This global diversity, within such a close-knit community, facilitates a cosmopolitan learning environment where intellectual discovery thrives.

A hallmark of St. Thomas Law is our emphasis on practical training, student engagement, social justice, and ethical behavior. Our students and alumni have a deep sense of justice and charity, and fully utilize their education and experience to lead the way in making our legal system one that truly champions the rights of the powerless.

CAMPUS AND LOCATION

St. Thomas University School of Law's location in Miami, Florida, provides an ideal setting for the study of law. Miami is a vibrant, thriving international community. As a hub of domestic and international trade, an innovative center for fine arts and one of the world's most popular vacation spots, Miami is a dynamic place to live and study. Miami enjoys a rapidly expanding multinational legal community and is home to federal and state trial and appellate courts.

DEGREES OFFERED

St. Thomas University School of Law offers the traditional J.D. degree, several joint degrees, an LL.M. and J.S.D. degree and an LL.M in Environmental Sustainability. Our joint degree program includes:

J.D./M.B.A. or M.S. in Sports Administration;

J.D./M.B.A. in International Business;

J.D./M.B.A. in Accounting; and,

J.D./M.S. in Marriage and Family Counseling.

St. Thomas University School of Law also offers advanced degrees: the LL.M. and the J.S.D. in Intercultural Human Rights and the LL.M. in Environmental Sustainability.

J.D. students are able to enroll in the classes offered through the LL.M. programs and can earn Certificates in Human Rights and Environmental Sustainability.

SPECIAL PROGRAMS

St. Thomas University School of Law is committed to student success both in law school and beyond. Using an interactive and cooperative approach to learning, the Academic Support and Legal Research and Writing Programs emphasize the practical skills required for the successful practice of law.

Additionally, St. Thomas Law has a national reputation for its Appellate and Trial Advocacy Programs.

FACILITIES

The law school is designed to provide our students with an outstanding environment for learning the law. Computers and printers are in abundant supply throughout the law library. The law library offers Internet access to online databases and has been a leader in applying technology to legal education. Our wireless network allows students to conduct Internet-based research from anywhere on the law school's campus. Our classrooms and Moot Court Room have all been recently renovated.

EXPENSES AND FINANCIAL AID

Tuition & Fees for 2015–16: $39,178. St. Thomas Law's tuition and fees includes the student's choice of bar review program from a selected list of providers.

FACULTY

The faculty at St. Thomas is committed to teaching, research and service. Our exceptional faculty members have earned law degrees from some of the nation's most prestigious institutions, including Harvard, Yale, Columbia, Michigan, Pennsylvania, Georgetown, and New York University and many hold advance degrees. They are leaders in their fields with impressive records of publication in top law reviews and extensive practical experience.

A hallmark of the St. Thomas experience is the genuinely close relationship between faculty and students. Because of this relationship St. Thomas Law ranked 4th in the country for "Best Quality of Life" in the 2011 Princeton Reviews' Best 172 Law Schools (2011 edition).

STUDENT LIFE

St. Thomas University School of Law offers a rich student life. With more than twenty student organizations to choose from, students easily find activities that appeal to their interests. Students also enjoy the wealth of activities, cultural and sporting events, and nightlife offered in Miami and Fort Lauderdale.

ADMISSIONS

The Law School Admissions Committee evaluates each applicant's potential for excellence in the study of law. The Law School Admission Test (LSAT) score and undergraduate grade point average are factors; the committee also considers course of study, graduate degrees, work experience, community service, and so forth.

St. Thomas also offers an alternative process for admission for a select group of candidates through our Summer Conditional Admit Program. The Program targets candidates who demonstrate excellent qualitative credentials but lack certain quantitative measurements. Successful candidates are offered admission to the law school for that year's fall entering class.

CAREER SERVICES AND PLACEMENT

St. Thomas Law provides first-rate career services that result in successful and rewarding employment for our graduates, whether their goals are to enter into private law practice, government, business and industry, or public interest areas of law. St. Thomas Law graduates are partners in major national law firms.

STETSON UNIVERSITY

AT A GLANCE

Stetson University College of Law, Florida's first law school, offers full- and part-time J.D. and LL.M. programs in Tampa Bay. Stetson ranks first for advocacy and second for legal writing.

CAMPUS AND LOCATION

Stetson's main law campus is located in Gulfport, a suburb of St. Petersburg. A satellite campus near downtown Tampa hosts evening classes, conferences, and the Tampa branch of Florida's Second District Court of Appeal. Tampa Bay is the second-largest metro region in Florida with magnificent beaches, pro sports teams, a vibrant cultural scene, and numerous options for recreation and entertainment.

DEGREES OFFERED

In addition to the juris doctor degree, Stetson offers joint and dual-degree programs for the J.D./LL.M. in Advocacy, J.D./M.B.A., J.D./M.P.H., J.D./M.I.E.L. in International Economic Law in France, and J.D./M.E.B.L in European Business Law in Spain. Stetson also offers an on-campus LL.M. in International Law and online LL.M. programs in Advocacy and Elder Law.

PROGRAMS AND CURRICULUM

Stetson's curriculum combines a strong foundation of legal doctrine and theory with a nationally ranked program in the practical advocacy, legal research and writing skills required to become a successful attorney.

Stetson allows students the opportunity to specialize their legal education through a variety of programs. J.D. students may earn certificates of concentration in advocacy, elder law, environmental law, international law and social justice advocacy. High-achieving students may be invited to participate in Stetson's Honors Program based on several factors including excellent performance in the required curriculum. Each year, a limited number of students interested in intellectual property may participate in Stetson's semester exchange program with the University of New Hampshire School of Law.

Stetson's extensive international offerings include a semester in London, exchange programs with law schools in Australia, France, Spain, Ireland, and the U.K. Stetson Law summer study abroad programs are in the Netherlands, Oxford, England and Granada, Spain as well as a winter break course in the Cayman Islands and a spring break course in Cuba.

Stetson also has centers for excellence and institutes in the fields of advocacy, biodiversity law, Caribbean law, elder law, higher education law, international law, legal communication and veterans law. Stetson is home to the Stetson Law Review, the Journal for International Aging Law and Policy, the Journal for International Wildlife Law and Policy, and the new Stetson Journal of Advocacy and the Law.

FACILITIES

Stetson's main law campus features technologically advanced classrooms, five courtrooms, recreational facilities and the Dolly and Homer Hand Law Library, culminating in an idyllic environment for legal study. The Tampa Law Center includes two courtrooms, fully equipped classrooms and seminar rooms, study rooms, and a satellite law library. The law libraries contain more than 419,000 volumes, 750,000 titles and 50 group study rooms. There is a laptop requirement for all students, and high-speed wireless access is available throughout both campuses.

EXPENSES AND FINANCIAL AID

2014–2015 full-time tuition (fall/spring): $38,584

2014–2015 part-time tuition (fall/spring/summer): $33,370

Scholarships are offered on a competitive basis, and need and merit scholarships are offered for continuing students. There is no financial aid deadline, and a completed FAFSA is the only required form.

FACULTY

Stetson's full-time regular faculty of 52 professors engage in projects of regional, national, and international prominence, and they make teaching and working with students their top priority. More than 50 practicing attorneys and judges serve as adjunct professors.

STUDENTS

Stetson offers cultural programs, experiential education trips, community service opportunities, leadership workshops, and around 45 active student organizations. The ABA Law Student Division has recognized Stetson with numerous regional and national awards, and Stetson's Student Leadership Development Program was awarded the ABA's prestigious E. Smythe Gambrell Award for excellence in professionalism. Stetson students donate more than 30,000 hours of pro bono service annually to more than 150 organizations.

ADMISSIONS

Stetson University College of Law admits full-time and part-time students each fall. As a prerequisite to enrollment, applicants are required to have earned a baccalaureate degree from a college or university that is accredited by an accrediting agency recognized by the U.S. Department of Education. A final, official transcript evidencing the conferral of the degree must be submitted before enrollment. All applicants are required to take the LSAT and register with the JDCAS. One letter of recommendation is required, and a maximum of three letters will be accepted. The personal statement is also required. More details are available at www.law. stetson.edu/admissions. An equal opportunity educational institution, Stetson is fully accredited by the American Bar Association and has been an Association of American Law Schools member since 1931.

SPECIAL PROGRAMS

Recognized by U.S. News as No. 1 for advocacy and No. 2 for legal writing, Stetson routinely wins international, national, regional and state competitions for alternative dispute resolution, mock trial and moot court.

Stetson offers upper-level students a wide variety of opportunities to work closely with attorneys and judges, and, in some cases, actually represent clients and try cases. Hundreds of students are placed annually into 36 different clinical, internship and externship programs, including competitive opportunities to intern with the Florida and Georgia Supreme Courts, the U.S. Court of Appeals for Veterans Claims, and organizations in Washington, D.C.

Stetson University College of Law has been named a Military Friendly® School. The Military Friendly® Schools designation, now in its sixth year, is awarded to 16 percent of colleges, universities and trade schools in the country that are doing the most to help military students to succeed in the classroom and after graduation.

CAREER SERVICES AND PLACEMENT

Stetson's commitment to helping students achieve their goals is reflected in its strong career development program. An accessible career development staff supports students' professional choices through individual coaching sessions and group workshops on subjects ranging from interviewing techniques to résumé writing. Stetson also offers a comprehensive program of bar preparation services, including custom study plans, individual counseling, bar-prep seminars, and sample exam grading by a former bar exam grader. Stetson Law alumni reside in 48 states and 22 countries, and most recent graduates practice in Florida.

TOURO LAW CENTER

AT A GLANCE

Touro Law Center, located in Central Islip, NY, is the only law school located adjacent to both federal and state courthouses and the only law school to house offices for non-profit organizations in our Public Advocacy Center; as a result, students have the immediate opportunities to work with groups and leaders making a difference in our local, state, and national communities. Touro Law is also one of a handful of law schools that guarantees clinical experience to its students and is a national leader in the incubator movement, teaching recent grads the skills needed to start their own social justice-oriented practice. All lawyers are educated, but Touro lawyers are prepared. Touro Law, accredited by the American Bar Association (ABA) and a member of the Association of American Law Schools (AALS), offers students full-time and part-time J.D. programs in 2, 3, 4, or 5 years as well as dual degree and LL.M. programs. In addition, Touro Law offers a January start option.

CAMPUS AND LOCATION

Touro Law occupies a 185,000 square foot state-of-the-art building in Central Islip on the south shore of Long Island, New York. Touro Law is at the center of what is arguably the nation's first integrated "law campus," comprised of a U.S. courthouse and New York State court center. More than mere physical proximity, students interact with legal professionals daily through classroom instruction, court visits, clinics, externships and other academic and social forums.

DEGREES OFFERED

Touro Law offers full-time and part-time (4 year part-time day, 4 year part-time evening and 5 year part-time evening) as well as an accelerated 2 year program. Juris Doctor programs as well as J.D./M.B.A., J.D./M.P.A. and J.D./M.S.W. dual degrees. Touro Law also offers an LL.M. degree in General Studies to graduates of U.S. law schools and an LL.M. degree in U.S. Legal Studies for foreign law graduates.

PROGRAMS AND CURRICULUM

Touro Law Center's Portals to Practice is a cutting-edge program that reconceives and restructures the law school experience. Portals to Practice expands the scope and quality of legal education by focusing on the development of legal professionals, from pre-law through post-graduation. The cornerstone of the program is experiential learning. Starting in the first year of law school, students gain hands-on legal experience and get into the courtroom. This comprehensive learning method has been designed to prepare students for the successful practice of law. Touro Law also requires all incoming students to enroll in a clinic as a graduation requirement and encourages participation in externships. Clinics currently offered include: Advanced Bankruptcy, Bankruptcy, Criminal Defense, Criminal Prosecution, Disaster Relief, Elder Law, Family Law, Federal Prosecution, Immigration Law, Mortgage Foreclosure, Small Business and Not-for-Profit Law and Veterans' and Service Members' Rights. In addition, we have four academic concentrations for students looking to study a specific field of law in depth including Aging and Longevity Law, Criminal Law, land Use and Sustainable Development Law and Solo and Small Practice Law.

FACILITIES

Touro Law Center's facility was designed to be a student-centered learning center. The building houses a clinical wing, a state-of-the-art auditorium, a public advocacy center, mock trial classrooms, computer labs, meeting spaces, cafeteria, bookstore, the Gould Law Library and more. The infrastructure is high-tech, supporting wireless access, smart classrooms and new technology.

EXPENSES AND FINANCIAL AID

Generous institutional scholarship aid is available to entering and continuing students. Awards up to full tuition include Dean's fellowships, merit scholarships, and incentive awards. Touro Law also offers stipends for Public Interest Law Fellowships, judicial clerkships, and summer federal work-study placements. Touro provides access to federal loans and work study, New York State loan and assistance programs, and need-based Touro Grants. Most students receive some form of financial aid, and 84 percent of entering students receive scholarships. Significant scholarships are awarded to continuing students during their law school career.

FACULTY

Touro Law's faculty is comprised of forty-five full-time faculty members. Every entering student is assigned a faculty advisor, matched by background or interest area, for discussions on any aspect of the law school experience including study strategy, course selection, career goals, etc. With an open-door policy and a student faculty ratio of 16:1, Touro Law students benefit from a personal and dynamic educational experience.

STUDENTS

The Law Center's students, coming from diverse backgrounds and experiences, represent over 112 undergraduate institutions and a broad mix of majors. Women comprise approximately 53 percent of the total enrollment; minorities, 38 percent.

ADMISSIONS

Touro Law Center seeks to identify applicants who show an ability to pursue the study of law successfully and to make an important contribution to the Law Center's educational program, to the legal profession and to society. While significant weight is attached to a student's undergraduate cumulative grade point average and Law School Admission Test (LSAT) score(s), the selection process is not strictly mathematical and includes an evaluation of several other factors including professional experiences and achievement, writing ability, rigor of undergraduate institution, letters of recommendation, and more.

SPECIAL PROGRAMS

Touro Law Center is home to the William Randolph Hearst Public Advocacy Center, the first of its kind in the nation. Touro Law provides furnished offices at no cost to approximately twelve non-profit legal advocacy agencies while providing hands-on working opportunities for students.

ADDITIONAL INFORMATION

Touro Law Center provides a unique program of outside-the-classroom assistance. Teaching assistants (TAs) review material covered in class and conduct small-group sessions on effective study methods and test-taking techniques. The Writing Resources Center offers workshops and tutorials to assist students in producing a professional work product. The Legal Education Access Program (LEAP) enhances the experience of students of color through a four-week summer program for new students with additional mentoring during the academic year. The Honors Program, beginning in the second year, allows outstanding opportunities for students who receive additional scholarship assistance and access to academic enrichment initiatives.

CAREER SERVICES AND PLACEMENT

The Career Services staff assists students and graduates in securing part-time, full-time and summer employment. In addition to placing students with national, regional and local law firms, there are opportunities in federal, state, and local courts and government agencies, and in the legal departments of corporations and municipalities.

THE UNIVERSITY OF THE DISTRICT OF COLUMBIA
David A. Clarke School of Law

AT A GLANCE

The University of the District of Columbia David A. Clarke School of Law (UDC-DCSL), the only public law school in the nation's capital, is unique among law schools: with a mission to recruit and enroll students from under-represented communities and the most extensive clinical requirements of any law school in the country, UDC-DCSL has one of the most diverse student bodies in the country and provides over 100,000 hours of legal service to low-income people and the public interest.

CAMPUS AND LOCATION

UDC-DCSL is located on the campus of the University of the District of Columbia, the country's only urban public land grant Historically Black University. The University and School of Law are located in the upper Northwest section of the District on Connecticut Avenue, one of the city's major thoroughfares. The Van Ness/UDC Metro station is located directly in front of the University, making the campus easily accessible. The campus, which is undergoing a major "greening" with over 100,000 square feet of green roofs and other amenities, is surrounded by a quiet tree-lined residential community, Rock Creek Park, the National Zoo, embassies and small businesses. The University sits on several acres of land on Connecticut Avenue, NW.

DEGREES OFFERED

The School of Law offers the Juris Doctor (J.D.) degree and full-time day and part-time evening divisions, and the LL.M. degree in Clinical Legal Education, Social Justice and Systems Change.

PROGRAMS AND CURRICULUM

The School of Law offers the best of both worlds for the study of law—a traditional legal education supplemented by *hands-on* clinical training. Students are required to complete 90 credits to graduate, 14 of which are earned in two semesters of clinical work. The Clinics are: Legislation, Juvenile & Special Education, Community Development, Low-Income Tax, General Practice, Immigration & International Human Rights, Housing and Consumer, Criminal Law and Whistleblower Protection (at the Government Accountability Project.) Students are also required to complete 40 hours of community service, and may participate in the Summer Public Interest Fellowship and a ten- or four-credit Externship Program elective.

FACILITIES

UDC-DCSL moved to a new spacious five-story facility, located about one block from the main University campus at 4340 Connecticut Avenue, NW.

Every seat in the Mason Law Library is wired and WIFI access is available everywhere in the library. The classrooms and lecture halls are also wired and high-tech.

EXPENSES AND FINANCIAL AID

The School of Law offers its students an affordable legal education and a comprehensive financial aid program. Tuition for District of Columbia resident full-time students is $10,886 per year (2015–16). Tuition for non-DC resident full-time students is $21,772 per year (2015–16). Tuition for DC resident part-time students is $7,749 per year (2015–16), and $15,498 per year for non-DC resident part-time students. Non-DC resident students may be eligible for resident tuition after residing in the District for one year. Students may be eligible as well for the following financial assistance: Federal loans, merit scholarships, need-based grants, work-study, Dean's Fellowships, Continuing Student Scholarships, and the full-tuition three-year *Advocate for Justice Scholarship*. For more information on the law school's financial aid program, you may visit www.law.udc.edu.

ADMISSION

The School of Law considers the entire applicant profile when rendering an admission decision. While the candidate's LSAT and grades play an important role in the admission process, other factors are also considered, e.g., the applicant's range of life experiences, the content and mechanics of the candidate's application essays, community involvement, family background, and letters of recommendations.

The Committee on Admission requests TOEFL on a case-by-case basis.

SPECIAL PROGRAMS

First and second year students are eligible for Summer Public Interest Fellowships funded by the law school for full-time placements supervised by an attorney in public interest, government or judicial settings. Approved placements include locations throughout the USA, and internationally. Upper-level students may earn academic credit for placements through the Externship Program. Students may also qualify for federal work-study positions.

The School of Law also offers the Pathways to Practice Program, which helps students build a body of knowledge, skills and experience that will prepare them for practice in a chosen field. Students will also build a network of like-minded colleagues, faculty advisors, alumni and prospective employers to help them make the transition from law school to practice.

ADDITIONAL INFORMATION

Students enjoy a 12-to-1 student-faculty ratio and individualized attention from and access to faculty and administration. The School of Law also affords students a spirited, committed and collegial setting and community in which to study law.

CAREER SERVICES AND PROFESSIONAL DEVELOPMENT

The Office for Career and Professional Development (OCPD) assists law students and alumni through individual meetings and group programs, an electronic database with internship and job announcements, and many other activities. For more information, visit the school website at www.law-udc.edu or contact Adrienne Jones at Adrienne.Jones3@udc.edu . The School of Law has more than 3,300 alumni, the majority of whom are connected to the School of Law via email. Alumni provide invaluable resources to both students and other alumni. For more information, contact Alumni Director Joe Libertelli at jfl@udc.edu

WESTERN NEW ENGLAND UNIVERSITY SCHOOL OF LAW

AT A GLANCE

2014 Entering Class:

LSAT Scores

75th Percentile 149

Median   146

25th Percentile 143

GPA median 3.12

Average age 26

Age range 21-53

States represented 16

Students of color: 36%

CAMPUS AND LOCATION

Founded in 1919, the School of Law was originally part of Northeastern University and merged with Western New England University which itself was founded in 1951. Western New England University School of Law is located in Springfield, Massachusetts. Springfield is the third largest city in the Commonwealth, with 153,000 residents, and is home to a lively cultural scene. In the heart of the Pioneer Valley, Springfield is conveniently located near Boston, New York City, and Hartford, Connecticut.

DEGREES OFFERED

Western New England University School of Law offers many ways to earn a law degree. In addition to our three-year, full-time program, the School of Law also offers four-year, part-time evening and part-time day programs. Students may earn an LLM, an advanced law degree, in Estate Planning and Elder Law. The School of Law also offers a Master of Science in Estate Planning and Elder Law. In addition, the school of law also offers several joint degree options: JD/MBA, JD/MSA, JD/MRP, JD/MSW, JD/BSME, JD/BSEE, JD/BSIE, JD/BSCE.

PROGRAMS AND CURRICULUM

To assist students in preparing for their careers, and selecting among electives, the School of Law currently offers seven areas of concentration: Business Law, Criminal Law, Estate Planning, International and Comparative Law, Public Interest Law, Real Estate, and Gender and Sexuality Studies.

Western New England University School of Law affords students the opportunity to merge theory with practice. Students take advantage of clinical course work, internships and externships, a wide variety of simulation courses, and participate in a number of moot court teams in order to hone their lawyering skills.

At Western New England University School of Law, we keep our class size small to promote a collegial learning environment in which students are challenged to actively participate in their legal education. Our 11:1 student to faculty ratio promotes greater interaction with peers and professors.

FACILITIES

The tri-level library houses classic law volumes side-by-side with a wealth of state-of-the-art electronic resources. Virtually every seat has computer-network ports. Working with remote online databases, CD-ROM services, and research software, our students hone their lawyering skills in this dynamic atmosphere. The law library also maintains a consortium relationship with Cal State, giving our students access to CSUF's 1.5 million volume collection.

EXPENSES AND FINANCIAL AID

In 2015, tuition for fulltime students is $39,450; part-time students pay $29,588 which includes their part-time credit hours during the summer. Incoming students will enjoy a tuition freeze through 2017–2018. Renewable Institutional scholarships, including full-tuition Oliver Wendell Holmes, Jr. Scholarships, are typically awarded to approximately 70% of each incoming class. Partial Scholarships may range from $8,000 to $39,000 a year.

Western New England University School of Law's support for Public Interest Lawyering includes the establishment of its Public Interest Scholars Program. Public Interest Scholars receive three-year tuition scholarships. In addition to their tuition scholarships, Public Interest Scholars are awarded a one-time public interest stipend of $3,500 for approved public interest work in the summer months after the first or second year of law school.

FACULTY

Our twenty-five full-time faculty members have been educated at the nation's most prestigious law schools. All have practiced law before joining our faculty and several hold additional graduate degrees in other disciplines. The School of Law places a strong emphasis on collaborative learning and student-professor interaction. Faculty members foster an open and collegial interaction with the students that provides a positive legal education in a comfortable atmosphere. The School of Law also has more than 30 adjunct faculty members, including practicing attorneys and judges, who bring their current legal practices into the classroom setting.

STUDENT BODY

The Student Bar Association (SBA) is the student government of the School of Law. The SBA plays a significant role in the administration of the School of Law with representation at Faculty Meetings and on the joint Faculty/Student Committees.

As of 2014:

Total JD enrollment:	343
% Female/Male:	55/45
% fulltime enrolled	70
Student/Faculty ratio	11:1

ADMISSIONS

Each year, the Admissions Committee assembles a talented, interesting, and diverse class of students. We enroll a class whose members come from various races and ethnicities, ages, academic and professional backgrounds, and geographic areas.

Each completed application is read in its entirety and carefully reviewed to determine whether the applicant possesses the academic preparation and motivation necessary to complete the demanding workload of law school. Committee members attempt to gauge each applicant's prior academic performance, expected academic performance, and writing skills. While LSAT scores and undergraduate GPA are important to the Admissions Committee, they form just one part of the picture. We recognize that the ability to succeed in law school and contribute to our law school community and the legal profession is also demonstrated through the personal statement, letters of recommendation, and supplemental essays provided by the applicant. We therefore review these materials closely.

We encourage you to submit your application early since admissions decisions are made on a rolling basis. The Admissions Committee begins admitting applicants by December and completes the majority of its work by April. It is strongly recommended that applications for full-time enrollment be completed by March 15. Applications for part-time enrollment should be submitted by June 1.

Please visit our website at www.law.wne.edu to view more details on admissions, our curriculum, and scholarship opportunities.

DEAN INTERVIEW

In this section, deans from several schools provide detailed answers to our questions about their law schools' resources, academic programs, and financial aid, as well as questions about students, graduates, and applicants. The Princeton Review charges each school a small fee to appear in this section.

UNIVERSITY OF THE DISTRICT OF COLUMBIA
DAVID A. CLARKE SCHOOL OF LAW

Dean's Interview Guide

SCHOOL OVERVIEW

PROGRAMS

The University of the District of Columbia David A. Clarke School of Law (UDC-DCSL) offers a J.D. degree that includes the core of the traditional law school curriculum in the classroom, enriched by an array of electives taught by experienced practitioners and judges. In addition to requiring basic course work, the law school offers the strongest commitment to clinical legal education in the nation. UDC-DCSL's 14-credit, required clinical program teaches substantive legal knowledge and a wide range of lawyering skills while serving those most in need of legal services. Students provide comprehensive representation on ongoing cases, appearing before the courts, legislative bodies, and regulatory agencies of the nation's capital. In addition, every first-year student participates in the Law and Justice/Community Service Program, performing *pro bono* community service under faculty supervision. This innovative curriculum provides students with an early opportunity to translate legal theories and concepts into practical work on behalf of real clients.

In addition to our full-time program, we offer a part-time evening option for those seeking a quality education and degree while continuing to work and meet other responsibilities.

UDC-DCSL also offers a two-year LL.M. program, which includes coursework in clinical pedagogy, public interest law, and systems change. LL.M. candidates work under the supervision of the Law School's experienced faculty to supervise and teach J.D. students enrolled in our clinics. Each LL.M. candidate also produces a culminating project in the form of a scholarly work of publishable quality or project designed to impact systems change.

STUDENT BODY

Students who are interested in learning legal principles and practical lawyering skills while working on actual cases, who want to use their knowledge and skills to help balance the scales of justice for disadvantaged people, and who welcome the opportunity to work jointly with individuals from varied backgrounds will find a welcome environment at UDC-DCSL. We are particularly committed to admitting students from groups, such as minorities and women, which have traditionally been, and remain, under-represented in the Bar. The school also values the wealth of knowledge and experience possessed by older students for whom the law represents a second career.

MISSION AND HISTORY

A spirit of excellence, imagination, and public service pervades UDC-DCSL. It is a diverse community dedicated to legal education that produces graduates who are competent to practice law and who are committed to living up to the highest ethical traditions and ideals for which the legal profession stands.

UDC-DCSL evolved from two predecessor schools: the Antioch School of Law and the District of Columbia School of Law. Antioch School of Law was created in 1972 by Edgar S. and Jean Camper Cahn who championed the rights of low-income people and minorities. The school was also committed to training public interest lawyers and pioneered a comprehensive clinical legal education model adopted now, in small part at least, in nearly every law school in the country.

Dean Shelley Broderick

Carrying on Antioch's traditions, the UDC-DCSL's statutory missions are to recruit and enroll students from groups underrepresented at the bar; to provide a well-rounded theoretical and practical legal education that will enable students to be effective and ethical advocates; and to represent the legal needs of low-income residents through the school's legal clinics.

ACCOLADES

The University of the District of Columbia David A. Clarke School of Law (UDC-DCSL) is ranked #2 in diversity and #7 in clinical training by *US News & World Report* in its 2016 Best Graduate School rankings.

This distinction comes on the heels of *PreLaw Magazine* giving UDC-DCSL an "A+" and ranking it the second most diverse law school in the nation for students and faculty.

In 2014, The Princeton Review ranked UDC-DCSL #1 for "Most chosen by older students," 2nd for "Most Diverse Faculty," 8th for "Best Environment for Minority Students," and 8th for "Most Liberal Students."

ADMISSIONS

TRENDS

As the national pool of law school applicants has become smaller, the School of Law has continued to offer one of the most affordable tuition rates in the country, generous student scholarship opportunities and extensive clinical and other valuable practical experiences in the Nation's Capital. Our commitment to admitting public interest-minded candidates, students of color with compelling backgrounds and non-traditional students continues to reflect our unique mission and philosophy. Like many other law schools, our class sizes are smaller, but UDC-DCSL's student body continues to be rich in experience, potential, accomplishments and diversity. The School of Law has used this contraction in legal education as another opportunity to develop new programs, re-visit its curriculum, enhance student scholarships, and discuss student affairs practices and institutional mission. Given our diversity and public service-oriented niche, we are optimistic about our future as a unique law school in the ever changing world of the academy and within the community of legal education institutions.

ADMISSIONS PROCESS

The law school candidate's undergraduate grade point average and Law School Admission Test (LSAT) score continue to be important factors in the admission process. The School of Law does not rely solely, however, on the above two factors to render its admission decisions. The Committee on Admission is interested in the whole candidate – for example, his or her record of community service and volunteer work, graduate study, range of life experience, employment experience, family background, effort expended in completing the college degree, quality of recommendations, extracurricular activities, career goals, contribution potential, etc. The School of Law believes that each applicant has a unique life journey and set of experiences. The School of Law's admission application and process encourage candidates to advocate for themselves and to provide information and bio-data that the application questions, grades and scores may not elicit.

INTERNATIONAL STUDENTS

UDC-DCSL is considered a small to mid-size law school and has a relatively small international student population. It has enrolled as many as ten to as few as five international students in any given year. Some of the countries represented in the student body have been Canada, India, Israel, Egypt, and Jamaica. Generally, the Admission Committee uses the same admission criteria when considering U.S. candidates' applications as it does for international applicants for admission. When reviewing applications from International students, it is mindful of possible language interference and cultural differences and of how it interprets the academic transcript from non-US institutions. The international student population further enriches our diverse student body, some members of whom were born in other countries but are now US citizens.

APPLICATION ROUNDS

There is one application round. The School of Law considers applicants for admission for the Fall of each year. We encourage applicants to apply as early in the admission cycle as possible, usually in early fall. *The Early Bird Admission Program*, in which candidates with completed applications receive early decisions and an *Early Bird Admission* grant, runs from early October to mid-December. The application deadline is March 16.

FACULTY AND ACADEMICS

FACULTY

UDC-DCSL is fortunate to have a committed group of teacher-scholar-practitioners who provide role models for the students the School of Law hopes to attract. And the diversity of the faculty reflects the School's mission to bring those under-represented at the bar into the practice of law, particularly public interest law.

Our faculty members are known for their scholarship on issues of social justice, including AIDS/HIV legal issues; prisoner rights; the rights of people with disabilities; juvenile justice and redefining the problem of delinquency education; and challenges to the foster care system.

Over the past six years, we have added ten diverse new faculty members who are already making an impact in the areas of juries and big data scholarship; immigration law issues; children's rights; critical race theory; and the constitutional aspects of decolonization.

We pride ourselves on the "family" atmosphere of our law school. Most faculty members have an open-door policy and generous office hours, where they provide both formal and informal advice and mentoring to students.

SPECIALIZATIONS

In 2014, the faculty adopted Pathways to Practice in eight broad practice areas: Civil Rights and Equality; Criminal Law; Family and Juvenile Law; General Transactional Law Practice; Housing and Community Development Law; Immigration Law and Human Rights; Public Service/Public Policy; and Solo and Law Firm Practice.

The Pathways are designed to help students choose core courses, electives, clinics and other experiential learning opportunities that connect with specific areas of study and career paths. They build upon the School of Law's clinical offerings, as well as areas of law that offer viable employment opportunities for our graduates.

Students may choose a pathway at any point in their legal education. Some select a pathway when they are admitted, and design their community service, clinics and externship opportunities to develop a body of skills and knowledge in their chosen field. Others elect to follow a general curriculum to gain exposure to several areas of law that may be of interest.

CAREER / INTERNSHIP PLACEMENT

Preparing a bench memo for a judge, conducting intake at a legal aid clinic, and visiting detainees with an immigrant advocacy office are typical internship sites for our students. Every summer, dozens of students work full-time funded by a law school stipend, honing their legal skills and building their professional networks at public interest organizations, at local and federal government agencies and with members of the judiciary. They work in the District of Columbia, around the metro area, and across the country; we even have a few international placements. For example, last summer, one of our rising 3Ls worked for The Hague. Other recent and representative internship placements include DC Superior Court judges, the DC and Maryland Public Defenders, the DC Office of the Attorney General, the US Environmental Protection Agency and the Leadership Conference on Civil Rights. Through generous funding from Equal Justice America and most recently Freddie Mac, our students are continuing their work in UDC-DCSL clinics under the close supervision of our outstanding clinicians.

During the summer and spring semester, students may earn academic credit through our externship class for similar placements. The externship class is co-taught by one of our senior faculty members and our director of career and professional development. Our networks are strong in the DC community in particular, with many eager to recruit our students for internships and to consider them for post-graduate employment.

Post-graduation, we are seeing more graduates taking jobs with small law firms, where they represent individuals, families and local businesses, on a wide variety of issues such as criminal defense and immigration matters. We have also seen growth in the business sector, with graduates taking compliance positions, for example. Graduates continue to work at various levels of government, and every year we've had graduates in judicial clerkships with local and state judges. A few graduates every year elect to continue their legal education by pursuing an LL.M. degree. Most of our graduates begin their careers in the metropolitan area, but we have recent alumni in California, Texas, Colorado, New York and Georgia, among other locations.

In 2014, the median salary for that class (with about 1/3 reporting) was $63,000. That has not changed significantly in recent years; however, many graduates do not report their salaries.

FINANCIAL AID AND SCHOLARSHIPS

At UDC-DCSL, approximately 90 percent of our students receive financial aid and scholarships. In addition to the Title IV federal aid, we offer need-based and merit-based scholarships. The need-based scholarship offered at UDC-DCSL is available to students who have demonstrated a financial need based on the assets and income disclosed by the student on the scholarship application. In addition to the scholarship application, applicants are given the opportunity to submit supplemental documents that may indicate a change in their financial status (loss of income) or expenses that are not accounted for in the cost of attendance, such as dependent care.

The institution offers various merit-based scholarships for our incoming and continuing students. Our incoming students can apply for the Advocate for Justice Scholarship, which is awarded to students with outstanding academic credentials paired with a demonstrated commitment to social justice. The applicants who are accepted into UDC-DCSL may also be offered our Incoming Merit Scholarship based on the information submitted in their application package. For our continuing students, there is the opportunity to apply for the Continuing Merit Scholarship or being selected for the Dean's Fellowship. The Continuing Merit Scholarship is awarded based on academic performance, contribution in the classroom, contribution to the community and/or clinical program, and personal adversaries. The Dean's Fellowship is awarded to 1L students who have earned a GPA of 3.0 or better. This determination is made after the first semester for our full-time students and at the end of the second semester for our part-time students. UDC-DCSL is committed to providing financial support to our students as they persevere to promote and contribute to social justice.

ALUMNI

The School of law has more than 3,000 alumni spread all across the nation, some of whom began the practice of law in 1975 when Antioch School of Law graduated its first class.

While several dozen alumni are state and local trial court and administrative law judges, certainly state supreme court justices Thomas Kilbride (IL) and Michael Wilson (HI), as well as Florida Federal District Judge Joan Lenard, deserve special mention. Other notables include Penny Wilrich, the first African American female judge in Arizona. Anil Singh was the first East Indian American state Supreme Court judge in New York State.

Until this year, energy lawyer Jon Wellinghoff was the Chair of the Federal Energy Regulatory Commission. Julie Williams is a former Treasurer of the United States. Tim Rieser, longtime staffer for Senator Pat Leahy (D-VT) is known as one of the Hill's most effective staffers and has been credited with brokering the recent rapprochement with Cuba.

Numerous graduates have served in state and local elected offices; William Stanley (R-VA) and W. Curtis Thomas (D-PA) are current state legislators. Kieffer Mitchell is a Baltimore Councilmember and LaRuby May just won the Democratic primary to replace the late Marion Barry on the DC Council.

Melinda Douglass is the founder and long-time director of the Alexandria, Virginia, Public Defender Service. Criminal defender Bernie Grimm is a regular commentator on Greta Van Susteren's FOX News show. Other top criminal defense and death penalty lawyers include Andrea Lyon, George Kendall, Marshall Dayan, Joe Teefey, Rene Sandler and Ellen Barry.

Tom Devine was the founding Legal Director of the Government Accountability Project and a pioneer in the development of whistleblower protection law. Alums Michael Kohn and David Colapinto are also top whistleblower attorneys with the National Whistleblower Center and their firm, Kohn, Kohn and Colapinto. Darrin Sobin heads the District's Board of Ethics and Government Accountability.

Jan May has served as the Legal Director of Legal Counsel for the AARP Elderly for several decades. Tony Oppegard is a legendary Appalachian coal miner's lawyer. Sandra Mattavous Frye is the People's Counsel for the District of Columbia and Paula Carmody is People's Counsel for the State of Maryland. Sara Patton directs the NW Energy Alliance and Mike Ewall directs the Energy Justice Network.

Joyce McConnell was dean of West Virginia University School of Law and is now the University's provost. Renown death penalty lawyer Andrea Lyon is now dean of Valparaiso School of Law. UDC Law Dean I, Shelley Broderick, earned an MAT degree from our predecessor law school. We have numerous other law school faculty at George Washington, CUNY, Denver's Sturm College of Law, Brooklyn, University of Wisconsin and other law schools. Jonathan Smith, until recently the head of special investigations for the US Department of Justice's Civil Rights Division, is now an Associate Dean for Clinics and Experiential Learning at UDC Law. Bonnie Reiss served as California Secretary of Education, and is currently on the University of California Board of Regents. Gwynn Swinson, a former Dean of Admission at Duke Law, was also a Vice President for Duke University and now co-chairs the NC Governor's Commission on Women.

KEY ADVANTAGES OF ATTENDING UDC-DCSL

UDC-DCSL is committed to the public interest, using the law to help those in need and to reshape our community. Each year, our faculty and students provide more than 100,000 hours of essential legal services to DC residents.

We are focused on extensive practical training, with the largest clinical requirement of any U.S. law school. Each student provides more than 700 hours of pro bono legal service, gaining direct, hands-on work experience and acquiring the skills needed to solve real problems.

Our tuition is a fraction of the cost of other law schools and 75 percent of our students receive scholarships and financial support. Graduating with less debt means you will have more flexibility to choose public interest or other employment options after graduation.

In addition to our full-time program, we offer a part-time evening option for those seeking a quality education and degree while continuing to work and meet other responsibilities.

Our faculty includes attorney-professors who work side-by-side with students to pursue practical advocacy in the courtroom in legislative or regulatory processes, and in other arenas for citizen activism.

UDC-DCSL is recognized as one of the nation's most diverse law schools both for our faculty and students, making us a welcoming place where students of all backgrounds feel at home.

We are located in our nation's capital, offering many opportunities to meet leaders in law and policy and participate in creating litigation, and legislative, regulatory and organizing strategies focused on solving society's toughest problems.

Our school's small size means that you will not be lost in the crowd, competing for attention, but will personally know our faculty and administrators. Our students become true colleagues, and our spirit of support and collaboration runs deep.

STRATEGIC GOALS

Over the next three years, we will continue to enhance our experiential and clinical programs by adding capacity in areas such as veterans' benefits, civil rights legislative reform, equal housing, and other areas of critical need in the District of Columbia.

INDEX

ALPHABETICAL INDEX

INDEX BY LOCATION

INDEX BY COST